HIGHER PSYCHOLOGY

SECOND EDITION

Gerard Keegan

HODDER
GIBSON
AN HACHETTE UK COMPANY

Dedication

This book is dedicated to my dear mum Anna Keegan O. B. E. who 'was born in a single end in the Gallowgate in 1926, the year of the General Strike'. You made me live for greater things the minute you brought me into the world and have nurtured that spirit ever since. Socialism is not bread alone.

Had I the heavens' embroidered cloths,
Enwrought with golden and silver light,
The blue and the dim and the dark cloths
Of night and light and the half-light,
I would spread the cloths under your feet.

W. B. Yeats

He Wishes for the Cloths of Heaven

The Publishers would like to thank the following for permission to reproduce copyright material:

Photo credits

Page 3 © Sheila Terry/Science Photo Library; page 4 © AKG Images; page 5 (left) © The Granger Collection, NYC/TopFoto, (right) © Bettmann/Corbis; page 19 © DK Limited/Corbis; page 30 © Bettmann/Corbis; page 56 © AP/Press Association Images; page 58 © Bob Thomas/Getty Images; page 59 © Bettmann/Corbis; page 65 © The Granger Collection, NYC/TopFoto; page 95 © Nina Leen/Time Life Pictures/ Getty Images; page 96 © Nina Leen/Time Life Pictures/Getty Images; page 98 © Jose Luis Pelaez, Inc./Corbis; page 122 © Bettmann/Corbis; page 124 © Christopher Furlong/Getty Images; page 126 © Hybrid Medical Animation/Science Photo Library; page 209 © Bubbles - Lucy Tizard; page 211 (top) © Juniors Bildarchiv/Alamy, (middle) © Danilo Ascione - Fotolia.com, (bottom) © Arco Images GmbH/Alamy; page 219 Courtesy of Alfred Bandura; page 230 © Nick Kennedy/ Alamy; page 250 © Rex Features; page 251 © Richard T. Nowitz/Corbis; page 275 (left) © 2004 Fortean/TopFoto, (right) © PA Archive/Press Association Images; page 277 © Martyn Chillmaid; page 316 © 1965 by Stanley Milgram from the film Obedience, with kind permission by Alexandra Milgram; page 323 © With kind permission of Philip Zimbardo, Inc.; page 325 © Courtesy of NO2ID (www.no2id.net); page 326 © 2000 Topham Picturepoint/TopFoto; page 336 © TravelOK.com; page 344 © Courtesy of Show Racism The Red Card; page 347 © AP/Press Association Images; page 348 © David Turnley/Corbis; page 356 © David Gifford/Science Photo Library; page 358 © Bettmann/Corbis; page 360 © 2009 photolibrary.com; page 366 © Frank May/epa/ Corbis; page 369 © Alfred Pasieka/ Science Photo Library; page 371 © 1999 Topham Picturepoint/TopFoto; page 377 © Bettmann/Corbis; page 378 © Bettmann/ Corbis; page 379 © Ted Streshinsky/Corbis: page 387 © Bettmann/ Corbis; page 397 © Anthea Simms/Camera Press; page 400 © AP/Press Association Images

Acknowledgements

Extract from *He Wishes for the Cloths of Heaven* reproduced by permission of A P Watt Ltd on behalf of Gráinne Yeats

Every effort has been made to trace all copyright holders, but if any have been inadvertently overlooked the Publishers will be pleased to make the necessary arrangements at the first opportunity.

Although every effort has been made to ensure that website addresses are correct at time of going to press, Hodder Gibson cannot be held responsible for the content of any website mentioned in this book. It is sometimes possible to find a relocated web page by typing in the address of the home page for a website in the URL window of your browser.

Hachette's policy is to use papers that are natural, renewable and recyclable products and made from wood grown in sustainable forests. The logging and manufacturing processes are expected to conform to the environmental regulations of the country of origin.

Orders: please contact Bookpoint Ltd, 130 Milton Park, Abingdon, Oxon OX14 4SB. Telephone: (44) 01235 827720. Fax: (44) 01235 400454. Lines are open 9.00 – 5.00, Monday to Saturday, with a 24-hour message answering service. Visit our website at www.hoddereducation.co.uk. Hodder Gibson can be contacted direct on: Tel: 0141 848 1609; Fax: 0141 889 6315; email: hoddergibson@hodder.co.uk

© Gerry Keegan 2009
First published in 2009 by
Hodder Gibson, an imprint of Hodder Education,
An Hachette UK Company,
2a Christie Street
Paisley PA1 1NB

Impression number   5 4 3 2 1
Year   2013 2012 2011 2010 2009

Cover photo © Chris Alan Wilton/Stone/Getty images
Illustrations by Tony Wilkins Design, Richard Duszczak Cartoon Studio, Clive Spong (Linden Artists), Barking Dog Art and GreenGate Publishing Services
Typeset in ITC Century Light 10.5 pt by GreenGate Publishing Services, Tonbridge, Kent
Printed in Italy

A catalogue record for this title is available from the British Library

ISBN-13: 978 0340 914 755

CONTENTS

PREFACE

The second edition of *Higher Psychology* has taken four years to write, primarily due to changes in the syllabus coupled with the trials and tribulations of life. Both influence the context and content of this book. An appreciation of psychology is so important that it is right we continually review its teaching and learning to gain an insight into some of the very real psychological issues that impinge upon on us all. Such psychological understanding should contribute to a more mentally healthy Scotland. I am privileged to be a conduit.

Gerry Keegan

Hurlford
August 2009

www.gerardkeegan.co.uk
E-mail: psychology@gerarkeegan.co.uk

AUTHOR'S ACKNOWLEDGMENTS

Thank you to everyone at Hodder Gibson involved in the production of this book, especially Katherine Bennett, my editor, and John Mitchell, my Managing Director. Your patience and encouragement has been much appreciated.

Thanks must also go to the late Tim Gregson-Williams who first gave me the opportunity to write for Hodder and Stoughton. I think good things of you every time I touch my keyboard.

Thank you to my marvellous readers: Helen Cosgrove, Cheryl Graham, Anne-Marie Roy and Linda Skinner. A massive thanks is also extended to my Web Designer and mate Graeme Houston. Your talents are amazing.

As well as those friends above, I would like to thank Polly Barnes, Martha Birch, Lee Bisset, Isabella Boyd, Jason Bryce, Anna Cathcart, Alison Clark, Una Connell, Mark Diamond, Elaine Edwards, Yasemin Erdil, Nicol Fergusson, Jeane Freeman, Liz Gilmour, Tony and Liz Halligan, Antonia Hayes, Tony Hendry, Alan Lafferty, Iris Law, Len Keating, Kath Mair, Ally Mathieson, Tony McDonald, Margo McMillan, Paigham Mustafa, Danny Parkinson, Tom Provan, Alison and Athol Rice, Claire Runcie, Lynn Smith, Ian Stevenson, Lesley Todd, Linda and Faans Van Heerden, Jenni Vater, Barry Wallace, Dave Wilcock, Mandy Wilmott and all at Celtic Football Club.

I am also grateful to my fellow Redistributionists: Hughie Ferguson, Peter Murray, Jamie McGhee, Eileen and Ann Marie O'Donnell, Titch Orr, Colin Rutherford and Annie Siszer. Our Mogadon v Valium debate will become the stuff of legend! Our day will come.

My appreciation is also extended to those who are no longer with us. Their presence is sorely missed: Willie Boyle, Ricky Hall, Jack Harkness, Elaine Herrera and Maria 'Mina' Hughes-Schulpen.

These wonderful people, individually and collectively, have helped me through the bad times of the last few years. I am eternally grateful for you being there for me.

Finally to Kathleen Rooney, my fantastic partner - Is tú mo ghrá. Tá mo chroí istigh ionat.

With all this now said let's get some work done! And the first thing you are probably doing is using an Internet search engine to find a translation of the above. This is as it should be!

CHAPTER ONE

What *is* Psychology, then?

What is the book all about?

Higher Psychology is a resource intended to support students studying the 2009 revised Higher Psychology course awarded by the Scottish Qualifications Authority. It is also appropriate for those doing HNC and HND psychology, and anyone new to the subject at university level.

The aim of the book is to stimulate interest in psychology. It will do this by providing a broad overview of the discipline, and an opportunity to study a variety of topics in some depth. The reader will develop an understanding of psychological theories, concepts, research studies, research methods, terminology and applications. This will be done within a historical context, illustrating the importance to psychology of both classic and contemporary research and theory.

The science of psychology emphasises a critical approach to its work. *Higher Psychology* will thus emphasise empirical research methods, and evidence-based theory and applications. Central to this will be a consideration of ethics.

New technology will also provide us with a continuing opportunity to update our knowledge of psychology in the light of the content of the book.

The rationale of *Higher Psychology* is largely dictated by the knowledge, skills and understanding required by the 2009 revised Higher Psychology internal assessments and external exam. By the end of the book you want to be able to:

- Demonstrate knowledge and understanding of two topics from developmental, cognitive, and physiological psychology.

- Analyse and evaluate two topics from developmental, cognitive, and physiological psychology.

- Demonstrate knowledge and understanding of psychological research methods.

- Analyse and evaluate psychological research methods.

- Demonstrate practical research skills, and carry out a psychological research investigation.

- Demonstrate knowledge and understanding of two topics from social psychology, and the psychology of individual differences.

- Analyse and evaluate two topics from social psychology, and the psychology of individual differences.

What is psychology?

The word psychology comes from the Greek words, *psyche* (mind) and *logos* (study). When the subject of psychology emerged in the late nineteenth century, it was interested solely in the study of the mind. However, this early study of our mind, and its mental processes such as perception, attention, language, memory and thinking was heavily criticised. The reason for this is that our mind and its elements are hypothetical constructs. A **hypothetical construct** is something that does not exist in reality. Something that does not exist in reality is very hard to support scientifically. The methods psychology used to study the mind at this time did not give rise to the production of such scientific evidence. This was problematic because a science, or any subject claiming to be a science, needs objective (factual) data to support what it discovers. An ability to generate this empirical data was seen as vital to the new subject of psychology, which clearly wished to be a *science* like physics and chemistry. Empirical data is data about our experiences obtained by us through our senses.

Psychology, as exclusively the study of the mind thus declined in popularity for a while.

From the 1910s to the 1960s, psychology alternatively emphasised the study of observable behaviour. This was because behaviour exists. As behaviour is real, behaviour can be controlled, observed and measured. This is important because the control, observation, and measurement of phenomena, the hallmarks of a *science*, allow for the generation of essential empirical data. Observed behaviours were studied extensively by psychology in the first half of the twentieth century, especially in the USA. The study of the mind did, however, make a comeback in the 1960s when the methodological difficulty in producing objective, factual, empirical data about our mental processes was overcome.

The scientific study of behaviour and mental processes

It is then generally agreed nowadays that psychology is the study of both behaviour and mental processes. Psychology can also be further defined as the scientific study of behaviour and mental processes in humans and animals. This reflects the importance psychology gives to the *scientific* study of mind and behaviour in order to generate scientific support, or otherwise, for its many rich and diverse theories regarding why we think, feel and behave as we do.

Why study psychology?

A simple answer is because psychology is one of the most popular subjects in schools, colleges and universities in the UK!

But by the time you finish this book you might agree with the author that an understanding of psychology will positively influence those exposed to its message. Its study allows us to understand why we are as we are, and how and why we become what we become. It helps explain why other people are as they are, and how and why they become what they become. Psychology's big attraction lies in the insight it gives us into how and why we *all* think, feel and behave as we do.

A brief history of psychology
Psychology emerged from philosophy

As far back as Plato (427–347 BC) and Aristotle (384–322 BC), the earliest psychologists were often philosophers. Philosophers spent, and spend, a great deal of time analysing their own feelings and mental experiences. This is in order to develop ideas about what it means to be human. This pure *self*-analysis of our own feelings and mental experiences is called **introspection**, or 'looking within'. Philosophy, the parent of psychology, has used introspection ever it began enquiring into questions like, 'Who am I?' 'Where have I come from?' 'What will I become?'

Descartes

It was the French mathematician and philosopher René Descartes (1596–1650) who first questioned the belief that we were *unexplainable* creatures of God's will. He tried to be analytical and set about exploring answers to the questions posed above, and developed the notion of *ex machina* – that humankind can be studied and understood like a machine. Humans, understood as machines, are made up of two parts, our mind (our knowledge, awareness, consciousness and free will) and body (our physiology: arms, legs, heart, lungs and so on). In his theory of **interactive dualism**, Descartes suggested that our mind and body interact in the pineal gland in the brain. This still mysterious structure is nowadays thought to have something to do with sleep and hormonal activity controlling the body's internal environment, and our motivation to eat, drink, and sexually reproduce.

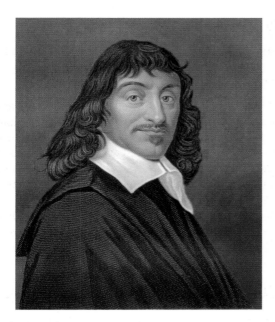

Figure 1.1 René Descartes

Empiricists and *tabula rasa*

Britain also played its part in the early formation of psychology. In the seventeenth century, philosophers John Locke (1632–1704) and Thomas Hobbes (1588–1679) founded the **empiricist** movement. Empiricism tries to understand the human mind in a systematic, factual and objective way. As already stated, information or *data* collected in a systematic, factual and objective way is called 'empirical data'. The empiricists thought the content of the human mind came about as a result of our interaction in, and thus sensory information of, our world. This is reflected in Locke's important idea that when we are born our mind is **tabula rasa**. The mind is but a 'blank slate' upon which experience writes. For empiricists, our human awareness or consciousness is *subsequently* made up of all the sensory experiences we get of objects, events and people as we journey through life.

Nativists and innate abilities

The empiricist idea of *tabula rasa*, or born with a mind like a blank slate, is in sharp contrast to Descartes who thought *some* human abilities were present in us from birth. Any ability we possess when born is called an **innate ability**. Innate abilities are abilities that are *universal* to a species. All of that species have it. An example of a universal innate ability in a species would be a sparrow's ability to fly. Any innate ability particular to a species usually has a high survival value for it. In our example a sparrow with an innate ability to fly can

avoid danger better and escape to warmer climates when the weather gets colder. An innate ability like flight is a huge asset to a species in its individual, and general, struggle for survival.

Those in psychology who follow in the tradition of Descartes and believe that we naturally possess innate abilities at birth are called **nativists**. Those, like Locke and Hobbes, who believe we become what we become as a result of experiences in our environment, are, as we now know, called empiricists. The degree to which nature (innate abilities) or nurture (experiences in our environment) explain why we think, feel and behave as we do is known in psychology as the **nature–nurture** debate. Also known as the heredity–environment, or **nativist–empiricist** debate, the influence of heredity, environment, and their interface are studied in many areas of psychology. We shall return to nature–nurture later, when we consider such issues as atypical, or abnormal, behaviour.

The advent of scientific psychology

In the early part of the nineteenth century, German physiologists, Weber, Helmholz and Fechner made further important contributions to the emerging subject of psychology.

> A physiologist is a scientist interested in the study of bodily processes and functions.

Weber offered to early psychology his theory of touch and tactile perception. He discovered, for instance, that we have the ability, by using touch alone, to perceive differences in weight between two similar objects. Helmholz provided us with his theories on nerves, nerve fibres, nerve impulses, colour vision, hearing and resonance. Fechner gave to psychology information about our senses and perception, and emphasised the use of the **experimental method** in psychological investigation. The experimental method, as we will read later, emphasises the observation and measurement of phenomena under controlled conditions.

Wilhelm Wundt 1879

Germany is currently credited with founding psychology as a scientific discipline. In 1879, Wilhelm Wundt (1832–1920) opened up the world's first psychology laboratory at the University of

Leipzig. An introspectionist, he began in controlled laboratory conditions to measure and record people's reactions to a stimulus.

A stimulus (plural: stimuli) is an object, event or person that makes or motivates us to think, feel and behave as we do.

Figure 1.2 Wilhelm Wundt

It was Wilhelm Wundt's emphasis on the observation, measurement and control of experiences that began to set psychology apart from philosophy. Indeed, the controlled observation and measurement of our behaviours and mental processes is the hallmark of modern-day psychology.

Nineteenth-century schools of psychology

Structuralism

Wundt established a particular school of thought in nineteenth-century psychology called structuralism. Structuralists tried to discover the processes and elements that make up human sensory experience. Searching for the elements of our conscious experience, structuralism investigated some of its component parts, such as sight, sound, taste, smell and touch. Wundt would ask his subjects to self-report those elements they thought made particular visual experiences for them. One such experience is *apparent movement*. An example of apparent movement is the experience you might have had of sitting on a train in Central Station, Glasgow, when

the train alongside pulls out. For a few seconds you think it is *your* train that is moving. Wundt would ask his participants to try an isolate the mental processes of that movement. He would ask them to identify the sensations and feelings that accompanied such visual experiences.

Structuralists analysed other human experiences, such as taste perception, thinking that taste perception was based purely on those structures responsible for our ability to sense information from our outside world. An example of this is their work investigating the salty, sour, bitter and sweet-detecting regions on the tongue. Structuralists ultimately saw human consciousness and its elements, such as our ability to be aware of such things as taste, as comprising many independent sensations, feelings and images drawn together in our mind.

Remarkably, Wundt taught three other major figures in the history of psychology: Edward Titchener (1867–1927), the British-born founder of the first psychology laboratory in the USA in 1892; James McKeen Cattell (1860–1944), who played a leading role as founder of the American Psychological Association; and Charles Spearman (1863–1945), who is still very influential today in the areas of intelligence, intelligence testing and statistics.

Structuralists did however experience difficulties in finding agreement on the common elements of those mental experiences that we share. Confirmation of results was exacerbated by their use of the non-scientific method of introspection. Introspection is subjective, and so can be accused of personal bias, which is of no use in a scientific enquiry.

Science and subjects like psychology, which claim a scientific identity, need more than mere opinion upon which to base their theories. Structuralism eventually declined as an area of study because of its use of introspectionism, the consequent inability to confirm its findings, and the advent of more attractive schools like functionalism, psychoanalysis, and behaviourism.

It is now fair to say that structuralism is only of historical importance to psychology today.

Functionalism

Functionalism, another early school in psychology, was also established by the late nineteenth century. Functionalism was heavily influenced by biology, and became concerned with the function of human mental activity. Functionalism investigated what the mind does and why. Its historical influence can be seen in present-day psychology, because nowadays, as you will see, psychology looks to the *purpose* behind why we think, feel and behave as we do.

William James

Figure 1.3 William James

Influential functionalists include William James (1842–1910) and Charles Darwin (1809–1882). James was a brilliant American who believed that the function of consciousness was to enable us to survive. His book *Principles of Psychology* (1890) is perhaps the most influential text in the history of psychology.

James had been impressed with Charles Darwin's book *On The Origin of Species By Means of Natural Selection* published in 1859, and agreed with Darwin that any evolutionary characteristic a species has must serve some purpose or function for it. James thought consciousness had an important function for humans. Essentially, he believed that our *consciousness*, and aspects of it such as our emotions, had evolved over time.

For James and his fellow functionalists the purpose of human consciousness was, and is, to give us a better chance of survival in our environment.

James's work prompted others such as James McKeen Cattell and John Dewey (1859–1952) to begin to explore other avenues of psychological interest such as intelligence testing and child psychology. Intelligence and intelligence testing can

be studied in a **domain** we will explore later called the psychology of individual differences. Child psychology has become developmental psychology, which is also a feature of this book.

Figure 1.4 John Dewey

Developmental psychology examines physical, cognitive (mental), social and emotional changes as they affect our psychological development.

Psychology's competing early influences of structuralism and functionalism were to contribute towards an unsettled definition of the subject for a hundred years. In the study of our various domains and topics we shall see that famous early psychologists, like Freud, investigated the mind. Others, like Pavlov and Skinner, investigated observable behaviour in response to an environmental stimulus. And yet others like Tolman and Piaget looked at the interaction, and relationship between mind and environment.

All heavily influence our idea of what psychology is today: the scientific study of behaviour and mental processes.

Approaches in psychology

What do we mean by an approach in psychology?

An approach is a perspective or school of thought. In psychology an approach is one particular view as to the origin, and development of behaviours and mental processes. Psychology has during its history developed five approaches, and each has a different outlook on why we think, feel and behave as we do. Each offers different solutions as to how to help people. This is because each approach favours a particular course of treatment, or **psychotherapy**, based on what is believed to be the root cause of a particular behavioural or mental difficulty. Each approach thus puts forward its own psychotherapeutic techniques determined by what each believes to be the cause of a psychological problem or *dysfunction*.

The five approaches in psychology are:

➤ the psychoanalytic approach.

➤ the behaviourist approach.

➤ the cognitive approach.

➤ the biological approach.

➤ the humanistic approach.

Overview of the five approaches

The **psychoanalytic approach** states that thoughts, feelings and behaviours are the result of unconscious mental processes formed by early childhood experiences.

The **behaviourist approach** states that our thoughts, feelings and behaviours are the result of learning in the environment.

The **cognitive approach** states that our thoughts, feelings and behaviours are the result of thinking or problem-solving. Thinking and problem-solving are also referred to as information processing.

The **biological approach** states that our thoughts feelings and behaviours are the result of genetics and physiology.

The **humanistic approach** states that our thoughts, feelings and behaviours are the result of a psychologically healthy or unhealthy self, or self-image.

As you will discover, each of the above approaches has significance for the psychological topics we will discuss in this book. At this point it is useful to pose the following question.

Is any one approach *better* than another?

 Most psychologists are not adherents to schools but are theoretical eclectics who use different concepts for different phenomena".

Brown and Hernstein (1975)

In the study of any topic in psychology no single approach to it is viewed as necessarily better than another. Psychology is a *holistic* subject. Holistic means having a place for all approaches, which allows for a more comprehensive and rounded psychological understanding of phenomena.

In the case of an individual who seeks treatment, one particular approach *may* be more appropriate than another. This is because the application of an approach, in the form of a treatment, should be driven by what is best for that person. When you apply the most appropriate approach in psychology to a person, object, event, situation or topic you are taking an *eclectic* view.

It should also be noted that each approach should be seen as *complementary* to another. This is reflected in the world of clinical application, or treatment, where very often a variety of different psychotherapies from different approaches are used *together* to help an individual in psychological distress.

We will come across all the above approaches in psychology throughout this book as we investigate our various topics set within their particular psychological domains.

Domains in psychology

The 2009 revised Higher psychology course consists of three Units entitled:

● Understanding the Individual

● Investigating Behaviour

● The Individual in the Social Context

Higher students study all three Units, each of which emphasises domains in psychology. A **domain** refers to an area of learning, or study.

Thus in **Understanding the Individual** we will look at *three* domains, and mostly study one topic from each of them. The domain of **cognitive psychology** will see us investigate memory. The domain of **developmental psychology** will see us investigate early socialisation, and the domain of **physiological psychology** will see us investigate stress.

In **Investigating Behaviour** we will look at *one* domain, **research methods**, and in so doing develop *practical research skills* in psychology.

In **The Individual in the Social Context** we will look at *two* domains. The domain of **social psychology** will see us investigate *conformity and obedience* followed by *prejudice*. The domain the **psychology of individual differences** will see us investigate *atypical behaviour*.

What do our various domains mean?

As can be seen, Higher psychology has us explore a number of topics within six domains, or general areas of psychological enquiry.

It is useful at this stage to determine in a psychological sense what each domain means. This is because if we set the psychological context within which each of our topics lie, it helps in their ultimate understanding.

Cognitive psychology

Cognitive psychology involves the study of the human mind in terms of **information processes**, and how these influence our individual thoughts, feelings, and behaviours. Our information processes help us *obtain, organise and use information from our world, to operate successfully within it.*

Sometimes also known as mediational processes, our information processes consist of perception, attention, language, memory, and thinking.

We will study **memory** within the domain of cognitive psychology in Chapter Two.

Developmental psychology

Developmental psychology concerns the study of *physical, cognitive, social, and emotional change* during our lifetime. It is an area in psychology that takes a **lifespan approach** in its work. What this means is that developmental psychology looks at each area of change mentioned above, and examines associated developments that occur during *infancy, childhood, adolescence* and *adulthood*. This allows developmental psychology to chart the course of psychological development, both within, and across our human lifespan.

We will study **early socialisation** within the domain of developmental psychology in Chapter Three.

Physiological psychology

Physiological psychology explains our individual thoughts, feelings and behaviours with reference to our brain, bodily structures and functions, or our **physiology**. It is the area in psychology where biology is of some importance. Physiological psychology studies dreams, dream states, emotion, and motivation.

We will study **stress** within the domain of physiological psychology in Chapter Four.

Research Methods

Research methods are of major importance to psychology. It is a domain of enquiry that is rightly given great weight in Higher psychology.

Our **research methodology**, or how we go about doing research, is what makes psychology different from other social sciences such as history, philosophy, politics, sociology etc. They do not claim to be sciences in the same sense as psychology, and therefore don't need to adopt a rigorous scientific approach. The main method of research used in psychology is, as you will discover, the experimental method. Other non-experimental methods are also used to generate evidence to support our findings and related theories.

We will study **research methods** and the research process extensively in Chapters Five to Seven.

Social psychology

Social psychology is a branch of psychology that studies individuals in the **social context**. Social psychology examines how our thoughts, feelings and behaviours are influenced by *the actual, imagined, or implied presence of others* in our world. To this end, social psychology is particularly interested in such topics as attitudes, aggression etc.

We will study **conformity and obedience**, and **prejudice** within the domain of social psychology in Chapter Eight.

The psychology of individual differences

The psychology of individual differences looks at those areas *where we differ from each other*, and why this might be the case. As you will discover the psychology of individual differences emphasises the importance of our genetics, our environment, and the interaction of each as they affect such things as our personality etc. The nature–nurture debate, which was introduced earlier, is thus of some significance to the psychology of individual differences, as we will see.

We will study the topic of **atypical behaviour** within the domain of the psychology of individual differences in Chapter Nine.

But before we turn to this, let us answer a couple of questions that are often asked by students embarking on a psychology course for the first time.

What is, and how do you become, a psychologist?

In order to decide if you want to become a psychologist, here is an idea of what they do.

- Psychologists conduct research.
- Psychologists work in the community.
- Psychologists help people learn.
- Psychologists promote good mental and physical health.
- Psychologists study, and contribute to the world of work.

To become a psychologist you would first have to go to university and get an *accredited* degree in psychology. An accredited psychology degree is one that allows Graduate Basis for Registration (GBR) with the British Psychological Society (BPS).

The British Psychological Society

Founded in 1901, the BPS with over 36,000 members in the UK, is the representative body for psychologists and psychology in Britain. Its Royal Charter entrusts the BPS with the responsibility to guide psychology for the public good and to be concerned with ethical issues.

The BPS (www.bps.org.uk) has divisions for particular specialist areas. On the basis of your GBR you *could* pursue a career in psychology such as:

- ➤ **Clinical psychologist:** helps people with mental health problems.
- ➤ **Educational psychologist:** provides learning support for children, parents, and teachers within the school system.
- ➤ **Counselling psychologist:** helps people with personal and relationship problems.
- ➤ **Health psychologist:** promotes mental health, and helps people adjust to, or recover from, physical illness. Health psychologists also foster

an understanding of the relationship between our mind, our body, and our environment.

- ➤ **Forensic psychologist:** helps to understand and change criminal behaviour and often works alongside the police.
- ➤ **Research psychologist**: conducts research in academic, industrial or other settings.
- ➤ **Consumer psychologist**: works with businesses and other organisations to understand consumer behaviour.
- ➤ **Sports psychologist**: helps enhance individual performance and works with organisations, teams, and sports clubs. Sports psychologists work alongside coaches, and also teach.
- ➤ **Occupational psychologist**: helps to enhance training and work-related performance of people in employment.

It should also be said that psychology graduates are employed in many other areas, such as health, social work, industrial, commercial, and retail management, teaching psychology in schools and further education colleges, finance, information technology, marketing, public relations, advertising, journalism and the media.

If you intend studying psychology at university it is imperative that you check precisely what qualifications your intended university requires. If in doubt – ask. All should be happy to hear from you. Applications should be made to UCAS (University and College Admissions Service). Details of UCAS procedures can be obtained from your school, college, or local careers office and from UCAS itself at www.ucas.ac.uk.

Entry to HE courses is now based on a points system. All pre-university qualifications have point weightings. Called the UCAS Tariff system, an A in a Higher is worth 72 points, a B 60, and a C 48. An A at Intermediate 2 is worth 42 points. Total points need to study psychology will vary from institution to institution. To embark *somewhere* on a Scottish university Bachelor of Science (BSc), Batchelor of Arts (BA) or Master of Arts (MA) undergraduate degree course with psychology, in whole or in part, you should investigate what entry requirements are needed. A number of psychology departments in Scotland emphasise that progression into second and subsequent years of psychology depends entirely on your performance in university examinations and assessments.

To help you decide where to study psychology you might like to search for the Learning and Teaching Support Network for psychology on the internet.

LTSN is a UK network of 24 UK University psychology departments, whose aim is to promote the high quality learning and teaching of psychology in our universities. Like the BPS, the LTSN site is well worth the visit.

ONLINE INTERACTIVES

1   Go to the Higher Psychology Learning Suite at **www.gerardkeegan.co.uk/index.htm**. Click Chapter 1 'What then is psychology?' to access direct links to all websites mentioned in this chapter.

2   Go to the Higher Psychology Learning Suite at **www.gerardkeegan.co.uk/index.htm**. Click Chapter 1 'What then is psychology?' and do the online interactive crossword. But don't cheat!

3   Go to the Higher Psychology Learning Suite at **www.gerardkeegan.co.uk/index.htm**. Click Chapter 1 'What then is psychology?' and do the online interactive hangman game. Try and beat the executioner!

4   Go to the Higher Psychology Learning Suite at **www.gerardkeegan.co.uk/index.htm**. Click Chapter 1 'What then is psychology?' and print off the hard copy crossword. When finished you might like to hand it into your teacher as homework.

5   Go to the Higher Psychology Learning Suite at **www.gerardkeegan.co.uk/index.htm**. Click Chapter 1 'What then is psychology?' and do the online interactive quiz. Try and win the prize!

GLOSSARY

Atypical behaviour: A behaviour that is deemed abnormal, e.g. schizophrenia. How 'abnormal' is itself defined is controversial in psychology. As we will see when we turn to the psychology of individual differences and the topic of atypical behaviour in Chapter Nine, (ab)normal behaviour can be identified in terms of its statistical frequency, how much the behaviour deviates from social norms, or how mentally unwell an individual appears to be etc.

Cognitive psychology: An area, or domain, in psychology that investigates the human mind and its processes of perception, attention, language, memory, thinking or problem-solving, and how these influence our thoughts, feelings and behaviours.

Developmental psychology: Developmental psychology is a domain, branch, or area in psychology that studies physical, cognitive, social and emotional changes and developments across the human lifespan.

Domain: A domain is an educational term that refers to an area of study.

Early socialisation: Early socialisation is the study during infancy of sociability and attachment, and occurs within the domain of developmental psychology. Important to our social and emotional development, attachment, an aspect of early socialisation is examined in greater detail in Chapter Three.

Empiricist: An empiricist is someone who follows in the tradition of John Locke or his fellow English philosopher Thomas Hobbes. If you are an empiricist you believe that at birth the human mind is *tabula rasa*.

Experimental method: The experimental method is a scientific method of enquiry that emphasises the control, observation, and measurement of variables in research. A variable is a name given to something that can change, such as our thoughts, feelings, and behaviours, the subject matter of psychology.

Hypothetical construct: A hypothetical construct is a term used to describe things in psychology that don't exist in reality.

Information processes: Collective term used in cognitive psychology for perception, attention, language, memory, thinking or problem solving. Information processes are also referred to as cognitive processes, mediational processes, or cognitions.

Innate ability: In contrast to the empiricist view of *tabula rasa*, other important philosophers like Frenchman René Descartes suggest humans do possess some abilities when born. An innate ability is thus any inborn ability we have at birth. An innate ability is *universal*, or common to all that possess it.

Introspection: Introspection, or introspectionism, is a research method popularised in philosophy. Introspection is where an individual self-reflects on an experience they have had, and then self-reports their thoughts about it.

Interactive dualism: Theory advocated by Descartes suggesting our mind and body, while separate, combine and work together in the pineal gland in our brain.

Lifespan approach: The lifespan approach is important to developmental psychology. By taking a lifespan approach developmental psychologists examine physical, cognitive, social and emotional changes at different *stages* in our lifetime. These stages are infancy, childhood, adolescence, adulthood and old age.

Memory: Memory is an important information process studied in cognitive psychology. Memory is the cognitive process that allows us organise, store, retrieve, and recognise information about our world. The fascinating cognition of memory is examined in greater depth in Chapter Two.

Nativist–empiricist: A *nativist* is someone like Descartes who thinks we have some innate or inborn abilities when born. These are understood nowadays as a result of our genetics. An *empiricist* like Locke and Hobbes alternatively think that any abilities we have come about as a result of experiences in our environment. In psychology, the nativist–empiricist debate concerns the degree of influence our genetics and/or our experience in environment have in regards to a wide range of issues, including our personality, intelligence and whether or not we will be prone to any atypical, or abnormal behaviours.

Nature–nurture: Nature–nurture is another term for the nativist–empiricist debate. As indicated above it concerns the argument over the degree to which our nature (genetic endowment) or nurture (environmental experiences) shape what we become. This dispute is also called the heredity–environment debate.

Physiological psychology: An area, or domain, in psychology that investigates the relationship between our bodily processes and functions, and related thoughts, feelings, and behaviours. Our bodily processes and functions are our brain, spinal cord, heart, arms, legs etc. Of particular interest to physiological psychology is the study of dreams, dream states, emotion, and motivation.

Physiology: Our physiology is the name given to our bodily structures and functions, such as our brain, spinal cord, heart etc.

Prejudice: Prejudice is '*an attitude that predisposes a person to feel, perceive and act in favourable or unfavourable ways towards a group or its individual members*' (Secord and Backman, 1974). We will explore the psychology of prejudice in greater depth in Chapter Eight.

Psychology of individual differences: The psychology of individual differences is an area of study, or domain, in psychology that has us look at such topics as personality, intelligence and atypical behaviour. Individual differences are thus those things we share, but differ around. Individual differences are thought influenced by our genetic inheritance. Or put another way, personality, intelligence and atypical behaviour are to some degree a consequence of our biology.

Psychotherapy: A psychotherapy is the application of a psychological theory in clinical practice.

Research methodology: Research methodology is the name given to the research strategy we use in psychological research. We will examine the importance of research methodology further in Chapters Five to Seven.

Research methods: The particular research strategies we use to generate sound evidence in psychological research. Research methods fall into two categories, the experimental and non-experimental methods. We will explore both categories in Chapters Six to Seven.

Social context: The social context, important to social psychology, is our social world.

Social psychology: Social psychology is an area, domain or branch of psychology that examines the psychological influence of the social world on an individual's thoughts, feelings and behaviours.

Stimulus: A stimulus is the general name given to an object, event, or person in psychology. The plural of stimulus is stimuli.

Stress: Stress is a topic of interest within physiological psychology. Stress concerns the relationship between external stimuli, and associated physiological and psychological change in the individual. Stress will be examined in greater detail in Chapter Four.

Tabula rasa: The idea put forward by seventeenth-century English philosopher John Locke that at birth the (human) mind is a 'blank slate' without rules for processing data. Data is added, and rules for processing it formed, by the sensory experiences we get in our environment.

CHAPTER TWO

Cognitive Psychology: Memory

BY THE END OF THIS CHAPTER YOU SHOULD BE ABLE TO:

TOPICS

● Demonstrate a knowledge and understanding of memory
● Analyse and evaluate memory

Before embarking on our topic proper, let us first locate *memory* in its parent domain of cognitive psychology.

What is cognitive psychology?

Cognitive psychology studies our information processes of **perception**, **attention**, **language**, **memory**, and **thinking**, and how these, as found in the human mind, influence our thoughts, feelings and behaviours. It considers the contribution each makes to how we operate successfully in our world.

Cognitive psychology views us as *active* processors of information from our outside world. We are not passive learners, as the earlier approach of behaviourism would have us believe. This is emphasised in the mediational nature of our information processes as illustrated by the **computer analogy**.

Individual cognitions further explore this fact. Perception, for example, is understood from the point of view of our senses working in tandem with an innate ability called *gestalten*, and our previous past experience of stimuli in our world. It is previous past experience that makes the difference between one person's perception of a stimulus and another's. What is meaningful to us as individuals also influences another crucial information process, memory, and as a result our ability, or otherwise, to think and problem solve.

All our information processes, while studied individually, work collectively as we operate in and through our environment.

The cognitive approach has had a huge influence over the last 30 years, and continues to do so. It has been applied to the world of advertising, marketing, public relations, work, society, politics etc. However, anything the cognitive approach discovers about our cognitions, and their influence on our behaviours has to be inferred. This is because cognitions are hypothetical constructs. This has led to criticisms, such as a lack of ecological validity, being levied at the approach. It also ignores biological and social factors as further reasons behind why we think, feel, and behave as we do.

Key features of cognitive psychology

Cognitive psychology concerns the study of how we take in information from our world, and how we actively process this information to respond to our world.

An information processing approach

Cognitive psychologists study our higher-level cognitions of perception, attention, language, memory and thinking (or problem-solving). They see our mind as consisting of these five information processes, which we individually and collectively use to operate in, upon, and through our environment.

Consequently, the cognitive approach explains human behaviour and mental process from the point of view of information processing. Any dysfunction in our thoughts, feelings, and behaviours are due to faulty information processing; in other words, a problem with one or more of our five mediational processes, as identified above.

We actively process information

Cognitive psychology is about how we actively process information using such mediational processes, individually and collectively, to build up our knowledge of the world. It asks about how we make meaningful sense of stimuli in our world and our behaviours in it as a result.

Cognitive psychology argues that we are not passive receptors of information, as the earlier behaviourist approach would have us believe. Our mind *actively* processes what information it receives, and using mediational processes changes this information into new forms. New information is combined, compared, transformed, and integrated with that which is already present. On the basis of our information processes, we build up an increasingly more complex picture of our world, and all the things in it, which affect our feelings and behaviours in our environment.

The fall and rise of cognitive psychology

From its earliest beginnings psychology has tried to understand the human mind in relation to feelings and behaviours. Wilhelm Wundt in 1879 is remembered for his work into perception. Freud from 1901 is remembered for his work concerning the unconscious. But with the establishment of the behaviourist approach in 1915 the study of the mind, which was the original object of investigation in psychology, became somewhat marginalised for a good part of the twentieth century.

A series of events was to occur however, which would see cognitive psychology overcome its difficulty of generating scientific support for hypothetical constructs like perception, attention, language, memory and thinking. This saw the rebirth of the cognitive approach from about the 1970s onwards, helped in its renaissance by developments in subjects as diverse as computer engineering and cognitive psychotherapy.

Tolman and Honzik (1930)

Behaviourism emphasises that psychology should study actual observable behaviour, and that we are to be understood in terms of stimulus–response (S–R) units of learned behaviour obtained via classical and operant conditioning.

It was to be a soft behaviourist, Edward Tolman, who challenged these assumptions, when in 1930 he suggested that organisms do something with learned S–R units that make them even more efficient and effective in their environment. This was to stimulate the important cognitive idea that we are active processors of information and not passive learners as behaviourism had earlier suggested.

In their famous experiment Tolman and Honzik (1930) built a maze environment to investigate latent learning in rats.

Latent learning

Latent learning is a kind of subliminal learning, which we don't know we possess, and don't use until there is some positive reinforcement, or environmental incentive, to do so. An example of latent learning would be where you got a lift to college from a friend every day. You may learn at a latent level the way to get to college, but as a passenger have no reason to demonstrate your learning by 'proving' that you know this. You don't even think about it. However, when you friend is sick and you have to drive yourself to college for the first time, if you drive following the same route as your friend did, then you have demonstrated latent learning.

Rats in mazes

In a variety of experiments with different kinds of mazes, Tolman found that a rat when introduced to his maze initially sniffed about, and explored in an erratic fashion. If it eventually discovered food placed in a food box when it was later put back into the maze, the rat searched for the food but did not make as many errors, i.e. go down blind alleys, turn back on itself – as when first introduced to the maze.

Cognitive maps

Tolman thought that what must have happened was that his rat(s) had formed a primitive cognitive map of the maze in their heads as a result of their first exploration of the maze. Whether they used it to their advantage, as measured by going quicker and with fewer errors to the food, depended upon this earlier exploration of the maze, and whether they had been previously rewarded, or otherwise, when coming across the food box.

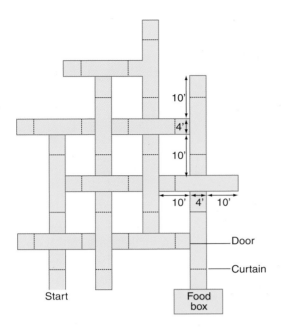

Figure 2.1 The kind of rat maze used by Tolman and Honzik

Purposive behaviourism

Tolman and Honzik concluded that cognitive maps allowed the rat to understand and react better to its maze environment. The earlier behaviourists seemed to be wrong in their assumption that organisms are passive learners. Tolman and Honzik (1930) indicated instead that rats are active processors of information about their world. Further, organisms such as rats process what they learn about their world in a very sophisticated fashion in order to obtain some mastery over it. This purposive behaviourism of non-humans, and by behaviourist definition humans, was to stimulate developments in cognitive psychology in the years to come.

Behaviourism's mechanistic and deterministic view that we passively learn in response to our environment was beginning to be questioned from within behaviourism itself.

Cognitive maps

We humans form cognitive maps of our world. Saarinen (1973) got American college students to draw maps of their campus. Students tended to enlarge those buildings that were most important to them and shrink those less important. They were often found to be completely wrong when describing campus areas that were not as familiar to them. Similarly, Briggs (1973) on asking people to judge how far they thought one landmark was from another discovered that they tended to underestimate the distance between familiar landmark objects and overestimate the distance between unfamiliar landmarks. This research helps to explain the phenomenon of the Irish mile!

A conundrum solved

Tolman and Honzik had gone some way to help solve the conundrum that had plagued cognitive research since Wundt in 1879; that is, how to investigate and generate empirical data about hypothetical constructs (which remember, don't exist in reality) in order to come to a scientific understanding of them. Tolman and Honzik externalised the construct of thinking in rats and studied it *indirectly* by obtaining empirical data in terms of times and errors made by the rats in the maze. Tolman and Honzik (1930) were then able to infer confidently on the basis of this empirical evidence that rats refine learned behaviours, and thus think in a more sophisticated fashion than earlier behaviourists had believed. They had empirical data that suggested an organism *actively* processes learned information about its environment.

Look at the study on page 14 and then answer the questions in the Interactive box below.

INTERACTIVES

1 What do you think latent learning means? Give an example in your answer.

2 What was the relationship that behaviourism suggested existed between reinforcement and learning before Tolman and Honzik's (1930) research?

3 What are the three conditions of the independent variable in Tolman and Honzik's (1930) experiment? An independent variable is the variable the experimenter manipulates or changes in an experiment.

4 What evidence did they find that reinforcement is more related to performance of a learned behaviour, rather than the learning of the behaviour itself?

Tolman, E.C. & Honzik, C.H. (1930) 'Introduction and removal of reward and maze-learning in rats', *University of California Publications in Psychology*, 4, 257–75

Aim: To investigate latent learning in rats and the relationship between reinforcement, learning and performance.

Method: Experiment and observation. Tolman and Honzik built a complex maze environment (see Figure 2.1). They had three groups of rats that underwent seventeen trials in the maze over seventeen days under three conditions. Group 1 rats were never fed in the maze, and when they reached the goal of the food box, were removed. Group 2 rats received the reinforcer of food every time they reached the food box; while on trials one to ten, Group 3 rats got no food but received reinforcement on trials eleven to seventeen.

Results: Group 1 rats always took around the same time to reach the food box and made many errors. They were observed as aimless in the maze, simply wandering around. Group 2 rats learned the intricacies of the maze quickly and over the seventeen days of trials made progressively fewer and fewer errors. From day eleven Group 3 rats showed a sudden improvement in performance time to reach the food and made as few errors as Group 2 rats by the end of the experiment.

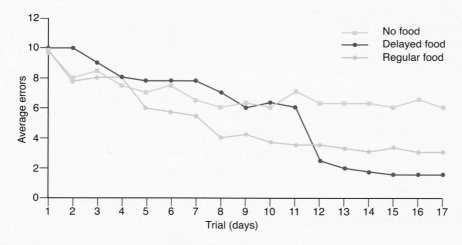

Figure 2.2 Average errors made by the three groups of rats

Conclusion: Tolman & Honzik (1930) concluded that reinforcement from the environment may not be as important to the learning process as was earlier thought. They believed reinforcement was more related to the performance of a learned behaviour. Further, this experiment helped Tolman infer that organisms such as rats and humans do something with learned units of behaviour to make them more efficient in their environment. Tolman (1946) was to say his rats had formed primitive cognitive maps of the maze environment in their heads. Whether they used this information depended upon a successful outcome to behaving in a particular way. We learn about things at a latent level that may see us behave in a particular way if there is some incentive from our environment to do so.

1956 – a very good year

It is entirely good fortune that the author's first birthday coincided with 1956 being the landmark year for the cognitive approach! It would not be inappropriate to say that 1956 precipitated the growth of cognitive psychology, as it exists today. This is because in 1956 the world famous psycholinguist Noam Chomsky presented his paper on the theory of language, Jean Piaget and Bärbel Inhelder wrote about egocentrism in *The Child's Conception of Space*, and George Miller's work on short-term memory was published. In addition, 1956 saw Bruner, Goodnow and Austin debate concept formation, or how we develop different ways of thinking about the environment around us. 1956 was also the year of the Dartmouth Conference in the USA, which saw the beginnings of the AI (artificial intelligence) movement energised by innovations in computer technology.

Of importance here is that cognitive psychology shared with the emerging computer technologies their information-processing models about human thought and problem-solving. We share a language, in that nowadays in cognitive psychology we often come across words and concepts from information technology such as input, output, storage, retrieval, parallel processing, networking, schema and filters. The approach also uses the 'computer analogy' to help explain why it believes we think, feel and behave the way we do, which is as an active processor of information about our world.

The human mind, the cognitive approach and the computer

The cognitive approach and computer engineering share the idea that the human mind/brain can be likened to a computer. What a computer tries to do is mirror how the cognitive approach suggests that human beings solve problems.

The computer analogy assists the cognitive approach in explaining the relationship between our information processes and our behaviour in our world. Models like the computer analogy are used throughout psychology to help understand hypothetical constructs, and nowhere is their use more prevalent than in the study of perception, attention and memory. Models put forward by cognitive psychologists concerning our various cognitions have greatly influenced developments in

the computing industry. The more advances that can be made in cognitive psychology, the more likely it is that the computer industry will be able to develop the ultimate in information technology – an interactive free-thinking computer that can problem-solve without direction. What the cognitive approach finds out is therefore of great interest to the likes of Bill Gates.

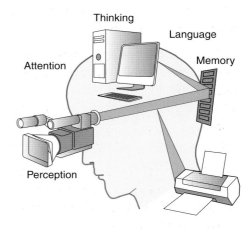

Figure 2.3 The human mind can be likened to a computer

The computer analogy

In 1997, in his book *How The Mind Works*, Steven Pinker wrote 'the behaviour of a computer comes from a complex interaction between the processor and input'. This is very much how the cognitive approach understands our behaviour as human beings.

The computer analogy is a metaphor, or story, used by the cognitive approach to understand the relationship between our thoughts, feelings, and behaviours and our environment.

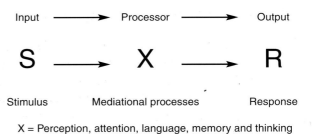

Figure 2.4 The computer analogy

Input is all the stimuli information that we encounter in our world. Input, or environmental information, about objects, people and events, comes to us via our senses in the form of light energy, sound energy, pressure – or what we see, hear and feel. All this information ultimately arrives in the brain to be interpreted, understood and acted upon. A good example of this would be the things we see in our world. What we see, or visually sense, is energy from our external environment that first strikes each eye as light waves. This information, alien to our internal biochemistry, is processed via our eyes into the only type of energy our internal body can understand: electrical energy, which ends up in our visual cortex at the back of the brain as a bundle of electrochemical impulses, or neural signals. The nature and intensity of these neural signals, we unconsciously match to what we have stored in our memory concerning the same, or a similar stimulus. Memory helps us recognise, and give meaning to, what we are visually sensing. This helps us think how best to respond, in terms of our behaviour or output, towards the stimulus object.

It is thus our information processes of perception, attention, language, memory and thinking (X) that come between the sensory inputs or stimuli (S) we receive from our world to help us understand what these sensations are, what they mean, and what might be the most appropriate way to respond (R). Mediational processes therefore intercede, or come between, external stimuli or input from our world, and our behavioural response, or output, to it. Our information processes are like the microprocessors in a computer. Microprocessors come between input in the form of keystrokes, and so on, and computer output like printouts and images.

The computer analogy helped confirm behaviourist Edward Tolman's view that we are more than just S–R units of learned behaviour. The computer analogy helps illustrate that it is our mediational processes that actively do things with the sensory information we receive, and this allows us to respond to our world in an enriched fashion.

Let us now turn to one of these mediational processes, memory, aware that the cognitive approach likens our mind to a computer – the most sophisticated evolved.

Memory

Memory is a key cognitive process closely associated with perception and attention. We perceive and attend to stimuli in our world on the basis of just how meaningful it is for us. Meaning is influenced by our memories of similar stimuli in the past (Bartlett, 1932).

> Memory is an active mediational process, which helps us organise, store, retrieve, and recognise information about our world.

Memory research: two traditions

There are two traditions of research into memory.

One tradition sees memory as the exact recording and reproducing of past experiences. This notion goes back to Plato's idea of memory as a wax tablet. In the *Theaetus* Plato writes:

And whenever we want to remember something we've seen or heard or conceived on our own, we subject the block to the perception or the idea and stamp the impression onto it, as if we were making marks with signet rings. We remember and know anything imprinted, as long as the impression remains in the block, but we forget and do not know anything, which is erased or cannot be imprinted."

The other tradition suggests that what we remember about something or someone is due to our personal interpretation of the stimulus and our reconstruction of past experiences.

Ebbinghaus

The first view of memory as an exact recording and reproducing of past experiences began with the work of German Hermann Ebbinghaus (1885, 1913).

Ebbinghaus was the first psychologist to use the experimental method to investigate memory. Using a single subject design, where only one participant takes part he himself gathered data on his own memory from 1879–80, which he replicated again from 1883–84.

Ebbinghaus not only brought the study of learning and memory into the laboratory, he also set a standard for careful scientific work in psychology that has rarely been surpassed. Indeed, since Ebbinghaus published his findings little else has been discovered about rote learning and memory retention that was not discovered by him.

Ebbinghaus, H. (1913). *Memory. A Contribution to Experimental Psychology*

Aim: To investigate the size and duration of memory.

Method: Experimental method, field experiment using a single participant design.

About 2300 syllables were mixed together and then randomly drawn to construct nonsense syllable lists of 'words' such as DAX, BUP, and LOC. Ebbinghaus made himself learn these lists to the point of being able to repeat them twice in order without error.

Ebbinghaus committed longer and longer lists of these nonsense syllables (the independent variable) to memory everyday. He then tried to recall as many as possible in exact order under a variety of conditions. This was the dependent variable.

Results: Ebbinghaus was the first to describe memory recall in terms of the shape made by a learning curve on a graph. He recorded and reported that the time required to memorise an average nonsense syllable increases sharply as the number of syllables increases.

He discovered that distributing learning trials over time is more effective in memorising nonsense syllables than massing practice into a single session; and he noted that continuing to practice material after what needs to be learned has been reached enhances retention.

INTERACTIVES

Read Ebbinghaus (1885) above.
Give three reasons why his results can be used to help you pass your Higher psychology assessments and exam.

Bartlett

Sir Frederic Bartlett established the alternative tradition to the study of memory. Rather than memory being an exact recording and reproducing of past experiences, Bartlett saw personal meaning as being crucial to what we remember about things.

For Bartlett memory is an active, dynamic cognitive process made up from what we actually remember about a stimulus, plus our previous past experience of the world.

For Bartlett our memory is *reconstructive*, as we will now see.

Schema

Bartlett was the first psychologist to investigate our use of schema, which we use to help us remember the things we come across in our world.

A schema is:

> *A mental model or representation built up through experience about a person, an object, a situation, or an event."*
>
> *(Head, 1920)*

In his book *Remembering* Bartlett (1932) reports on the influence schema have on what we remember.

The war of the ghosts

Bartlett used the Native American folk tale 'War of the Ghosts' (See the Study Box below) to study the effects our culture and social world have on the formation of schema, and thus on our memory recall.

The War of The Ghosts

STUDY

One night two young men from Egulac went down to the river to hunt seals, and while they were it became foggy and calm. Then they heard war cries and they thought; 'Maybe this is a war-party.' They escaped to the shore, and hid behind a log.

Now canoes came up, and they heard the noise of paddles and saw one canoe coming up to them. There were five men in the canoe and they said; 'What do you think? We wish to take you along. We are going up the river to make war on the people.'

One of the young men said; 'I have no arrows.'

'Arrows are in the canoe,' they said.

'I will not go along. I might be killed. My relatives do not know where I have gone. But you, 'he said turning to the other, 'May go with them.'

So one of the young men went, but the other returned home. And the warriors went on up the river to a town on the other side of Kalama. The people came down to the water and began to fight, and many were killed. But presently, one of the young men heard one of the warriors say; 'Quick let us go home. That Indian has been hit.'

Now he thought; 'Oh, they are ghosts.' He did not feel sick, but he had been shot. So the canoes went back to Egulac, and the young man went back to his house and made a fire. And he told everybody and said; 'Behold, I accompanied the ghosts, and we went to fight. Many of our fellows were killed and many of those that attacked us were killed. They said I was hit, but I did not feel sick.'

He told it all, and then he became quiet. When the sun rose, he fell down. Something black came out of his mouth. His face became contorted. The people jumped up and cried. He was dead.

He asked participants at the University of Cambridge to read the story twice, and then got them to recall and rewrite it at intervals of between fifteen minutes to three years later. The differing time intervals were the various conditions of his independent variable, while what they recalled of 'War of the Ghosts' was the dependent variable.

If you were to read the story, and then try to recall it some time later, like Bartlett's participants you would omit details, change things, and add new material.

Chandler (1995) tells us that people in the West unconsciously change and omit details of the story in the following ways:

➤ 'Something black came from his mouth' becomes 'he frothed at the mouth', 'he vomited', or 'breath escaped from his mouth'.

➤ 'Hunting seals' becomes 'fishing'.

➤ 'Canoe' becomes 'boat', and 'paddles' becomes 'oars'.

➤ The wounded Indian becomes the hero, whose wounds are then wrongly remembered as being 'bathed'.

➤ The suggestion by the Indian to the possibility of getting killed tends to be downplayed or dropped.

➤ The reference to the probable anxiety of relatives is usually given greater emphasis by Western readers, while the reference to having no arrows is often omitted.

➤ The appearance of 'the ghosts' in the story becomes changed to a 'clan called the Ghosts'; while others recall the ghosts as simply imagined by the Indian due to him being wounded.

Bartlett (1967, [1932]) himself reports that hard-to-interpret items were often omitted by his participants. Examples would be when the characters were hiding behind the log, or the link between the Indian's injury and the end of the battle.

ONLINE INTERACTIVES

Read an excellent summary of Bartlett (1932) at:

www.qeliz.ac.uk/psychology/Barlett1932.htm

Or click on the link to this article in the Chapter 2 section of the Higher Psychology Learning Suite at
www.gerardkeegan.co.uk/index.htm

The war of the ghosts, reconstructive memory and schema

According to Bartlett, recall of 'War of the Ghosts' sees British participants give a Westernised interpretation of the Native American Indian folk tale. This is because we subjectively construct and reconstruct memories of a stimulus using our own personal experience got from our own social world. We think and problem-solve using previously formed schematic representations of our world. Such schematic representations or schemata are:

> *Organised structures that capture knowledge and expectations of some aspect of the world."*
>
> *(Bartlett, 1932)*

Bartlett (1932) concludes that we use our own cultural experiences to make sense of our world.

In the case of the 'War of the Ghosts' Bartlett's Cambridge participants, changed, omitted, and transformed the story's original detail to make better sense of it from their British point of view.

For Bartlett our personal interests and experiences, which help form our schematic representations of our world, influence us when we retell stories from memory.

'Clock this!'

An excellent contemporary example concerning the influence of schemas and memory comes from French and Richards (1993).

French, C. C. and Richards, A. (1993) 'Clock this!'

Aim: To investigate the influence of schemas regarding attentional errors.

Method: Experimental method, laboratory experiment.

There were three conditions of the independent variable.

In Condition 1 participants were shown a clock with a Roman numeral face. They were asked to study it for one minute. It was then removed and all were asked to draw the clock from memory.

In Condition 2 the same initial procedure was followed but with participants being told prior to studying the clock that they would be asked to draw it from memory.

In Condition 3 the clock was left visible during the experiment with participants being asked to draw what they saw.

Figure 2.5 Roman numeral clock

Results: Normally with roman numerals the number four is represented as IV. Oddly on Roman numeral clocks the number 4 is written IIII. French and Richards found that in Condition 1 and Condition 2, where participants had to draw the clock from memory they invariably drew the number four as IV, and not IIII as they had seen it. In Condition 3, participants represented the number four exactly as it appeared – IIII.

French and Richards explain these results in terms of schema theory; a schema being a mental representation of knowledge about our world. In Condition 1 and Condition 2 when drawing the number four participants' previous schematic knowledge of the Roman numeral as 'IV' overrode what they had *actually* seen on the clock face, namely IIII

The nature of memory

Where is our memory?

Where memory occurs is a bit of a mystery! Research suggests that some aspects of memory are associated with particular areas of our brain. We store and retrieve memories of/for sounds in our temporal lobe. We remember what we see using our visual cortex. We recognise and remember patterns using our parietal lobe. We store and retrieve our memories of faces in our frontal lobe. Memory is a whole-brain information process. Memory of an event thus relies on widespread regions of the brain working together to create a gestalt or whole.

'Where is memory?'

Our perceptions first occupy an immediate, iconic memory, and then move to short-term memory, from which some will transfer to long-term memory stores. How this occurs is as a result of our brain's hippocampus. The hippocampus is situated in a fold of our temporal lobe, which is just under our temple on the left-hand side of our head. The hippocampus helps us encode new experiences, which as illustrated above are then transferred to long-term memory stores elsewhere in our brain.

INTERACTIVES

Read French and Richards (1993) and answer the following questions.

1   What is a schema?

2   An independent variable in an experiment is the thing a psychologist changes or manipulates. What are the three conditions of the independent variable in French and Richards (1993)?

3   What did French and Richards (1993) discover?

3   How can these results be explained?

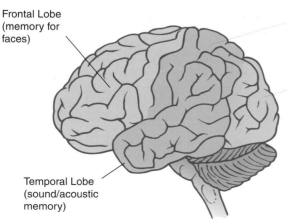

Frontal Lobe
(memory for
faces)

Parietal Lobe
(memory for
patterns)

Occipital/Visual
Lobe (visual
memory)

Temporal Lobe
(sound/acoustic
memory)

Figure 2.6 'Where is memory?'

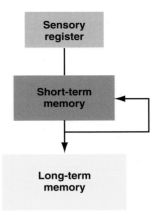

Figure 2.7 The multi-store model of memory based on Atkinson and Shiffrin (1968)

Recall of what you are sensing depends upon past perceptual experience of it.

On the basis of what Bartlett tells us above, our perception of what it is we are sensing is often coloured by the memory we have of it. This is connected to our emotions or feelings that accompanied the event.

Dull events are hard to remember, life-changing ones are easy.

Meaning is thus central to the cognitive process of memory. Memory helps us 'make sense' of our reality based upon just how meaningful that stimulus is for us. What we remember, and in what detail is very personal to us.

The structure of memory

Atkinson and Shiffrin's multi-store model of memory

While the Atkinson and Shiffrin multi-store model of memory can be criticised as being dated, it is a good starting point to our study of memory. This is because the memory stores it highlights are still appreciated today.

Atkinson and Shiffrin's **multi-store model of memory** concentrates primarily on the function of short-term memory.

They assumed the existence of sensory register rather than explore it in any great depth.

Their model thus helps us understand short- and long-term memory as two *separate* memory stores, whose capacity and duration are different.

> **Atkinson and Shiffrin (1968)**
>
> The Atkinson and Shiffrin model of memory suggests that our memory isn't that good! Our memory is selective in that we attend to some information and ignore or exclude other stimuli. Consequently we lose information.
>
> At each of the three stages of memory information is filtered, further selected, and even altered. As we read earlier this is supported by the work of Bartlett (1932) amongst others.

Encoding

The process where information gets into these two memory stores is called **encoding**.

Encoding to memory relies upon the visual, acoustic and semantic aspects of a stimulus.

Visual encoding refers to how a stimulus looks; acoustic encoding refers to how a stimulus sounds. 'Semantic' means just how meaningful a stimulus is.

The more meaningful something is for an individual, the more likely they are to remember it.

> **Encoding**
>
> Encoding is the process we use to represent knowledge in different forms in our heads.

How do we remember? Coding, storage and retrieval

Acoustic, visual, and semantic coding

As indicated above, how we put information into memory is called encoding. Encoding sees us store information about objects, events and people using the most appropriate code(s) relevant to the stimulus we come across. These codes come in three forms: acoustic code, visual code and semantic code.

Acoustic codes represent particular events stored and remembered as a sequence of sounds. This could be the tune of a song, for example.

Visual codes represent visual information stored and remembered as forms or images. This could be the words of the song as read from a CD cover.

Semantic codes see us store and remember aspects of a memory on the basis of just how *meaningful* a stimulus is. Using our example above this could be a personal memory attached to when you heard the song in the first place. It could be that the song was the one you heard when you first met your partner.

Storage

Our ability to hold a memory in our minds for any length of time is called storage. According to the Atkinson and Shiffrin model we hold or store memories in three main memory facilities, each with a far greater capacity compared to what came before.

Atkinson and Shiffrin (1968) call this sensory register, short-term memory, and long-term memory.

Sensory register or SR

Atkinson and Shiffrin (1968) say that sensory register holds information from all our senses but only momentarily. Sensory register is more a subconscious awareness of a stimulus than a storage facility as such (Sperling, 1960).

Psychology says sensory register helps us become sensitive to external information using at least two modalities called **iconic memory** and **echoic memory**.

Iconic memory allows us to become aware of visual stimuli or what we see, while echoic memory makes us aware of auditory stimuli or what we hear. Sperling (1960) discovered the duration of iconic memory to be less than one second; while echoic memory can last anything up to four seconds.

A classic example of sensory register is when you are doing something and someone is talking to you. You ask them 'What was that you said?' and in that instant remember just what it was!

Other examples of what can be held in sensory register would be our awareness of a sensation like a breath of wind or a raindrop hitting our cheek.

As can be seen from Figure 2.7 sensory memory may then subconsciously pass what it registers to short- and long-term memory for further processing at a deeper level.

Pattern recognition

When we become aware of sensory register we recognise what these sensations are by comparing them to a previously inputted knowledge structure. Kind of 'Ah ha, that's a gust of wind!' This is called **pattern recognition**.

Pattern recognition is the process where information is interpreted in sensory register, and then transferred to our short-term memory. Information not attended to in, and by, sensory register is lost to us.

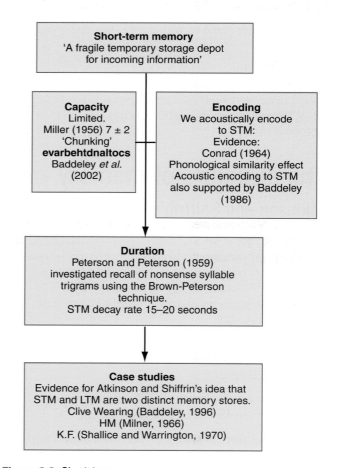

Figure 2.8 Short-term memory

Short-term memory

For Atkinson and Shiffrin (1968) short-term memory is a 'fragile temporary storage depot for incoming information' that has two functions. STM helps us to form and update a picture of our world on a minute-by-minute basis, and also helps us think and problem-solve.

The duration of short-term memory

According to Peterson and Peterson (1959) STM has a maximum duration, or decay rate, of between 15 and 20 seconds. If we do not use what we have stored in STM within this time the information is lost to us.

Think about trying to remember a one-off phone number that you haven't written down. If you don't use this information quickly, because it is stored in short-term memory when you do go to dial the number you will have forgotten it!

Rehearsal and decay rate of STM

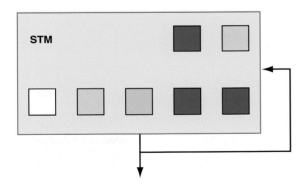

Figure 2.9 Short-term memory and rehearsal. The feedback arrow on the right of the STM diagram represents what Atkinson and Shiffrin call 'rehearsal'

The fragility of short-term memory

Sebrechts *et al.* (1989) showed lists of words made up of three common nouns. Unexpectedly they then asked them to recall what they had just been shown.

They discovered that participant recall fell to one per cent after only four seconds.

Sebrechts *et al.* (1989) indicates that unless we use maintenance rehearsal to retain information in STM it very quickly becomes lost to us.

This study reminds us of the importance of the Brown-Peterson technique. Constant acoustic rehearsal of information stored in STM is essential for later recall.

If you say over and over the information you want to commit to STM you can extend its duration to more than 15 to 20 seconds. This is called 'maintenance rehearsal'. Not only is rehearsal important to keeping information in STM, it is the main method used by us to transfer information from STM to long-term memory.

The more something is rehearsed in STM the more likely it is to end up in LTM. While engaging in maintenance rehearsal to STM we are unable to do much else (Sebrechts *et al.*, 1989).

If you are trying to remember a phone number, and the doorbell rings, you either have to answer the door, and forget the number, or use the number and not answer the door!

> **Peterson, L. R. and Peterson M. J. 'Short-term retention of individual verbal items',** *Journal of Experimental Psychology,* **58, 1959, 193–8**

Aim: To investigate the duration of Short Term Memory (STM).

Method: Experimental method, laboratory experiment.

Procedure: Participants were presented with sets of nonsense syllable trigrams e.g. BCM, presented in sets of three. They were then asked to recall them in order after 3, 6, 9, 12, 15 and 18 seconds.

The different time delays were the conditions of the independent variable.

The number of trigrams recalled was the dependent variable.

The Brown–Peterson technique was used to prevent participants rehearsing recall. This means that during the time delay before recall participants were given an interference task of counting backwards in threes from a random three-digit number.

Recall had to be 100 per cent accurate and in the correct order for it to count as being correctly recalled.

Results: Percentage recall was 80 per cent after three seconds; 50 per cent after six seconds, and less than ten per cent after eighteen seconds.

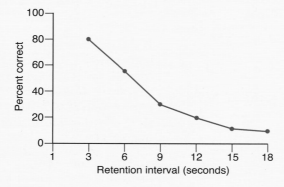

Figure 2.10 Results of Peterson and Peterson's 1959 experiment

Conclusion: Peterson and Peterson (1959) reports that short-term memory recall decreases steadily between three and eighteen seconds suggesting that the duration of our STM is not much more than eighteen seconds. Without rehearsal information held in STM is quickly lost to us.

This supports the hypothesis that the duration of STM is limited to approximately 20 seconds. The results of this study also indicate that STM is distinct from long-term memory, as LTM has a much longer duration.

Evaluation: Peterson and Peterson (1959) lacks ecological validity. Ecological validity questions whether a research procedure reflects real life situations. Here the use of trigrams does not reflect what we normally commit to everyday memory. Further, they may have got the result they did because of interference from the counting backwards task, rather then memory decay as such.

The research is useful in that it indicates a causal relationship between the independent variable of time differences, and the dependent variable of amount of information retained in STM.

ONLINE INTERACTIVES

Please read Peterson and Peterson (1959).

Click on the Chapter 2 link to this study in the Higher Psychology Learning Suite at:

www.gerardkeegan.co.uk/index.htm

or go directly to:

learningat.ke7.org.uk/socialsciences/soc-sci/psy/as/durationstm.htm

and do the interactive multiple-choice exercise.

Otherwise answer the questions below.

1   What was the aim of the research conducted by Peterson and Peterson (1959)?

2   Describe the procedure adopted by Peterson and Peterson (1959).

3   What were the conditions of the independent variable?

4   How was the dependent variable measured?

5   What do you understand by the 'Brown-Peterson technique'?

6   What were the results of the experiment?

7   What can we conclude on the basis of these results?

8   Evaluate the work of Peterson and Peterson (1959).

Some things you might not know about STM

Encoding: people from *all* cultures tend to use *acoustic* codes to encode information into STM. To remember the phone number as suggested above we often repeat, or *sound*, the number to ourselves until we use it. Visual codes decay faster than acoustic codes. In 1964 Conrad discovered that we acoustically encode to STM even when the stimulus material was initially presented to participants in a visual form, or modality.

Conrad (1964): A study of acoustic confusion

Conrad (1964) presented participants with a random sequence of sets of six letters flashed onto a screen. Each series of consonant letter strings were either acoustically similar, e.g. P, T, C, V, B, D or dissimilar, e.g. L, Z, F, X, H, W.

Participants were then asked to write down the letters in the same order as they appeared before them. Their errors were recorded.

Conrad (1964) discovered that in short-term memory serial recall, similar-sounding items are remembered less well than items that do not sound alike.

This is known as the **phonological similarity effect**. Most errors made saw participants substituting similar sounding letters for the original ones e.g. B for D, or S for X etc.

Participants reported that it was more difficult to remember those letter strings that were acoustically similar in comparison to those that were acoustically dissimilar. This was despite the fact that they were presented visually. Conrad (1964) concludes that items stored in STM are encoded acoustically rather than visually.

While acoustic encoding to STM is largely correct, Brandimonte *et al.* (1992) suggests that when acoustic encoding to STM is frustrated we may use visual encoding instead.

The size of short-term memory

Storage capacity: our *immediate memory span* is the number of items we can recall perfectly after one presentation of a stimulus. In 1956 George Miller discovered the capacity of our STM as between five and nine chunks of information long.

The power of chunking: breaking information up and trying to remember it in chunks can increase the capacity of our STM.

Bower and Springston (1970) report that the letters FBIHDTWBAIBM can be remembered if 'chunked' so as to relate to items in long-term memory, such as FBI.

The power of chunking and the capacity of STM and are illustrated below.

Without writing anything down take 25 seconds to memorise the following letter string:

evarbehtdnaltocs

After 25 seconds cover up the letter string and write it down exactly as you remember it. Don't cheat! When you have done this, check how you have done. Did you remember all the letters in sequence? At what letter (fourth, fifth, etc.) did you make your first error?

The author would be very impressed if you managed to remember all sixteen letters in sequence. This is because STM can only hold between seven plus or minus two (7±2) units, or chunks, of information at any one time (Miller, 1956). You very probably tried to chunk this into short-term memory on an individual letter-by-letter basis, i.e. e, v, a, r, b, etc. If you got the first nine letters in sequence this is excellent. After this point, however, even those with a good STM should begin to make mistakes. Sixteen chunks are just too many.

However, if you now read the sixteen-letter string backwards, you may realise how this stimulus could be stored into short-term memory using only three chunks of information!

By chunking information into larger bytes of information you can extend the capacity of your short-term memory, as you should now be able to appreciate.

More modern theories propose different ways in which STM can be represented. It is therefore a good idea to avoid suggesting 7±2 items/chunks is STM's fixed or *actual* size.

As can be seen from the study box below, British psychologist Alan Baddeley and colleagues have conducted a more recent study into the capacity of STM using immediate memory span.

An online link to the full paper can be accessed in the Chapter 2 section of the Higher Psychology Learning Suite at www.gerardkeegan.co.uk/index.htm

George Miller

In 1956 American cognitive psychologist George Miller wrote a paper in the *Psychological Review* (63, 81–97) called 'The magical number seven plus or minus two: Some limits on our capacity for processing information.' In it he examines the capacity, or size, of our short-term memory (STM).

He did this by investigating our immediate digit span. Immediate digit span is the number of digits, or numerals, we can remember serially, or in correct order, after being exposed to them once.

Miller read out a sequence of random numbers, and got participants to recall as many as they could back to him. Each sequence began with three digits and steadily got longer to a point where it became impossible for participants to repeat them in serial order.

The point at which we can recall a sequence of digits correctly 50 per cent of the time is called our immediate digit span. Also known as the *capacity* of short-term memory, George Miller identified participants immediate digit span as 7±2 bits of information long at any one time. Miller thus claims 'the magical number seven, plus or minus two' as the size of our STM.

Our ability to keep anything between five and nine units or chunks of information in STM holds good for a variety of stimuli including lists of numbers, letters, words, and larger amounts of information. As was seen in our earlier Interactive regards 'evarbehtdnaltocs'!

A useful memory strategy based on Miller's work concerns those occasions when we are presented with lots of information to remember. We stand a better chance of correctly recalling it if we recode or 'chunk' it into more manageable bits. As Miller writes

'It is a little dramatic to watch a person get 40 binary digits in a row and then repeat them back without error. However, if you think of this merely as a mnemonic trick for extending the memory span, you will miss the more important point that is implicit in nearly all such mnemonic devices. The point is that recoding is an extremely powerful weapon for increasing the amount of information that we can deal with.'

The recoding referred to is nowadays called chunking. Chunking comes from Miller (1956); and his discovery while investigating immediate digit span that the capacity of STM is 7±2 bits of information at any one time.

Questions

1   What did Miller (1956) investigate?

2   What do you understand by the term 'immediate memory span'?

3   Explain the procedure adopted by Miller to investigate immediate memory span.

4   What did Miller (1956) conclude regards the capacity of our short-term memory?

5   What practical application does knowledge of chunking have for us?

Decay and displacement

We earlier identified the duration of STM as around 20 seconds long. Maintenance rehearsal aside, if we do not use information stored in STM during this time it becomes lost to us. This is called **decay**.

According to Waugh and Norman (1965) another reason we lose information from STM is because of displacement. We now know that STM cannot accommodate lots of information because of its limited size. Consequently when we commit new information to STM we push out or *displace* any old information that may be there.

Waugh and Norman conducted an experiment using a serial probe technique.

They read sixteen numbers to participants. A random number was then repeated and the participant had to say what number came next. Participants displayed better recall if they were told numbers that came near the end of the sixteen-digit string.

Waugh and Norman (1965) concluded that the later numbers had displaced the earlier ones. This is due to the limited size of STM, and for Waugh and Norman demonstrates that forgetting in STM is due to displacement.

Waugh and Norman (1965) may be criticised as lacking in **ecological validity**. They conducted a laboratory experiment, which traditionally has problems reflecting real-life behaviour.

Another weakness in the study is their failure to account for the duration of STM. Such natural decay of information in STM after 20 seconds, rather than displacement, may have been the reason Waugh and Norman (1965) got the results that they did.

Consequently forgetting from STM can occur due to displacement *or* decay. It is often very difficult to tell which is responsible.

STUDY

Baddeley, A., Chincotta, D., Stafford, L., and Turk D. 'Is the word length effect in STM entirely attributable to output delay? Evidence from serial recognition.' *The Quarterly Journal of Experimental Psychology* **55A (2), 2002, 353–69**

Aim: To investigate the capacity of short-term memory using immediate memory span.

Method: Experimental method, laboratory experiment.

Procedure: Each participant's reading speed was assessed, and then they were quickly shown sets of five words on a screen. The sets were either one-syllable words, e. g. fit, cat, put, or polysyllable words, e.g. opportunity, university, escalator.

After the presentation participants were asked to write down the sets of five words in serial order, meaning the correct order each set of words had appeared on the screen.

The different word types (one syllable/polysyllable) were the two conditions of the independent variable.

The number and type of word recalled was the dependent variable.

Results: Participants recalled significantly more short than long words. Further, they recalled as many words as they could articulate (say) in two seconds. There also found a strong positive correlation (statistical relationship) between a participant's reading speed and their memory span. Essentially the faster our reading speed the greater our immediate memory span.

Conclusion: Baddeley *et al.* (1975) conclude that our immediate memory span can be measured in terms of the number of items, in this case short and long words, articulated, or reported by us, in around two seconds.

Evaluation: The Baddeley *et al.* (1975) experiment can be said to lack **ecological validity**. What this means is that it does not reflect real life. A laboratory experiment asking participants to recall lists of one-syllable and polysyllable words does not mirror our everyday use of short-term memory. Another criticism may be that participants found it easier to recall one-syllable words like *wit*, rather than longer words like *aluminium*, because the short words used were more familiar to them.

The study does however extend the work of Miller (1956) in that it shows that immediate memory span depends upon the *nature* of the stimulus.

It concludes that the kinds of words used, and the language in which they are spoken, influences the size of STM.

This research and its conclusions have has been supported by Schweickert and Boruff (1986) and Naveh-Benjamin and Ayers (1986).

Questions

1   What was the aim of Baddeley *et al.* (1975)?

2   What procedure did they adopt?

3   What were the results of this experiment?

4   What were the conclusions?

5   Evaluate Baddeley *et al.* (1975).

ONLINE INTERACTIVES

For an excellent presentation on short-term memory go to:

ferl.becta.org.uk/display.cfm?resid=3640and printable=1

This link can be directly accessed in the Chapter 2 section of the Higher Psychology Learning Suite at **www.gerardkeegan.co.uk/index.htm**

Long-term memory

According to the Atkinson and Shiffrin multi-store model, long-term memory (LTM) is our third memory storage facility. Long-term memory allows us to remember and retain information over a long period of time. Encoding information into LTM involves a deep level of conscious processing.

Semantic encoding and LTM

Often this will involve some form of semantic encoding, which concerns just how meaningful the event is for you. You never forget what you were doing when you hear a parent has died and events thereafter. You remember this sad time in great detail for the rest of your life. This is because most parents are very meaningful for their children.

Baddeley (1966) gave participants one of four word lists to remember. He predicted that acoustic encoding would be the preferred method of encoding to STM, while semantic encoding would be the preferred method of encoding to LTM.

Four lists of words were used: acoustically similar, acoustically dissimilar, semantically similar, and semantically dissimilar. Participants were shown one list.

When *immediately* asked to recall the lists presented his participants remembered more List B words than List A words. More of the dissimilar sounding words in List B like try pig, hut, and pen were remembered than similar sounding words in List A like man, map, can, and cap.

STUDY

Baddeley A. D. (1966), 'The influence of acoustic and semantic similarity on long-term memory for word sequences,' *Quarterly Journal of Experimental Psychology* 18, 302–309.

List A: similar sounding words like man, map, can, and cap.

List B: dissimilar sounding words like try, pig, hut, and pen.

List C: similar meaning words like great, big, huge, and wide.

List D: dissimilar meaning words like run, easy, and bright

On the immediate recall task Baddeley (1966) found little difference in word recall regards Lists C and D. His results support the idea that we acoustically encode information to our STM.

After a lapse of 20 minutes Baddeley found that his participants remembered more of the words from List D than words from List C. This indicates that we use semantic encoding to process information to our LTM.

The poor recall of *similar* sounding words and *similar* meaning words from Lists A and List C is another example of the phonological similarity effect. The phonological similarity effect appears to confuse recall from LTM *as well as* STM, as was earlier brought to our attention by Conrad (1964).

We can generally conclude from Baddeley (1966) that we use semantic encoding to LTM and acoustic encoding to STM.

The research can be criticised. Baddeley (1966) lacks **mundane realism**. In real life people rarely learn word lists, and so the recall task is not representative of everyday memory demands.

Further, acoustic and semantic encoding are not the only codes used to process information to STM and LTM. Other codes can take precedence depending on the nature of the information being encoded.

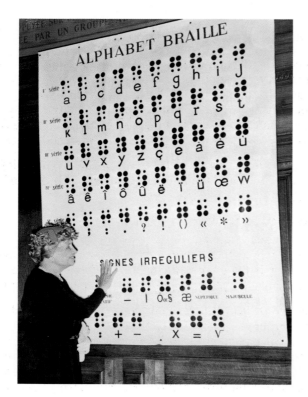

Figure 2.11 The Braille alphabet

An example would be **haptic encoding**. This is the encoding of information to memory on the basis of *touch*.

We use haptic encoding to assist sensory register. Haptic encoding is also used to process information to STM and LTM particularly by people who are visually impaired.

Visual encoding and LTM

Visual codes are also used to encode information to LTM. When you study for an exam you will commit to LTM essential information in visual code form, i.e. words, phrases, etc. from your notes and reading. Visual coding is not as effective as semantic coding to LTM. While you may do well in your examination on the basis of visual coding, you would be hard pushed a week later to remember what you actually wrote.

Craik and Tulving (1975) recommend we use both acoustic and visual codes to help us commit important things to memory. Using both is referred to as **dual coding theory**.

Here is a hard question! Why do you think this is?

You should apply your knowledge about the different ways we encode information to LTM to improve your examination technique.

Make your study of psychology more meaningful by attempting as many Interactives as possible. Do the online activities and structured questions. This is you using semantic and visual coding. As a consequence, you will remember more for much longer and in more detail.

ONLINE INTERACTIVES

Do a multiple-choice quiz on Baddeley (1966) 'Encoding to short-term and long-term memory' at:

learningat.ke7.org.uk/socialsciences/soc-sci/psy/as/encodingstm.htm

Or click on the link to this activity in the Chapter 2 section of the Higher Psychology Learning Suite at **www.gerardkeegan.co.uk/index.htm**

The duration and capacity of LTM

The duration or length of time we can remember input to LTM can be quite short. As we read earlier, Ebbinghaus (1885, 1913) was interested in the duration of LTM. He committed nonsense syllables to memory, which he tried to recall from 20 minutes to 31 days later. He found that a large amount of information in LTM was lost within an hour, but stabilised thereafter to a slower rate of loss. This is illustrated in Fig. 2.12 below.

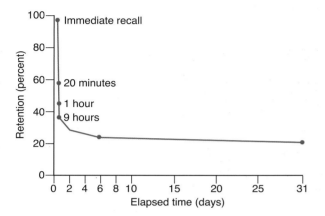

Figure 2.12 Ebbinghaus (1885, 1913)

With an eye to the **ecological validity** of the Ebbinghaus study, Linton (1982, 1986) set about trying to remember real events rather than nonsense syllables. She recorded in her diary at least two everyday events from her life every day for six years. She was later tested on what she could remember of her 5500 entries! In comparison to Ebbinghaus, Linton found a more even memory loss of around six per cent per year. She also found that pleasant memories were easier to recall than unpleasant memories. Neutral memories were the least easy.

Linton (1982, 1986) tells us that the experience we have influences what we can later remember about it.

Kind of memory	Per cent recalled
Pleasant	50 per cent
Unpleasant	30 per cent
Neutral	20 per cent

Table 2.1 From Linton (1982, 1986)

Thompson *et al.* (1982) confirm with their **self-reference effect** that pleasant events are more easily recalled. This is because pleasant things are personally more memorable for us. The self-reference effect is where we can recall events, dates etc. more accurately because they have happened to us, rather than someone else. We examine the self-reference effect later.

Capacity of LTM

As to the capacity of LTM, it is vast. Unlike STM, most theorists believe there is no limit to the amount of information that can be stored in our long-term memory.

Types of LTM and memory retrieval

We hold different types of memory in our LTM store. The type of memory influences the amount of detail we can recall about an event.

Eidetic memory

In general, memories are less clear and detailed than perceptions, but occasionally a remembered image can be recalled in every detail. This is photographic memory or eidetic memory (or eidetic imagery) found in one in 20 children (Haber, 1979). Children with a good eidetic memory can recall an entire page of writing in an unfamiliar language that they have seen for only a short time. They have no way of remembering it on the basis of meaning. It is gobbledegook to them. Unfortunately, very few possess eidetic memory in adulthood!

Procedural and declarative memory

According to the Canadian psychologist Endel Tulving, we have another two types of LTM: procedural memory and declarative memory. Declarative memory involves episodic memory and semantic memory. Each category of memory stores different types of information in an organised way.

Each is what Tulving calls **cue-dependent**, meaning they store or encode memories on the basis of one particular aspect of the stimulus.

Procedural memory
Sometimes called **implicit memory**, procedural memory is our 'knowing how to' memory. Procedural memory helps us remember how to drive a car, tie our shoelaces, play the guitar, boil an egg and so on.

Implicit or procedural memories are hard to forget. Take riding a bicycle for example! Procedural memory is resistant to brain damage. As you will read later on in this Chapter someone such as Clive Wearing who has brain damage cannot transfer new events to long-term memory. He can however learn new procedural skills such as playing table tennis.

Declarative memory

Sometimes called **explicit memory**, declarative memory involves any long-term memory that we can describe or report. A great deal of research has been done in this area particularly relating to episodic and semantic memory.

Episodic memory

Episodic memory is our autobiographical memory (Tulving, 1972) and contains our personal memories of past events, people and objects. Episodic memories have a spatio-temporal significance. This means that episodic memories are those memories we remember on the basis of when and where, or the time and place, they occurred. Episodic memory is thus our 'knowing when' memory.

A good example of episodic memory would be what you remember about your last birthday. In the author's case he vividly remembers sitting on a plane from Glasgow to Dubai beginning a marathon 30-hour journey to Cape Town in South Africa to celebrate Christmas with his cousin Len Keating, his family and friends.

Episodic memories can then be quite exact.

Lindsey and Norman (1977) asked a group of students 'What were you doing on a Monday afternoon in the 3rd week of September two years ago?' Many were able to tell them! Could you?

Semantic memory

Semantic memory is our 'knowing what' memory. It is our LTM store of general knowledge about our world including its concepts, rules and language.

Semantic memory is our 'mental thesaurus, organised knowledge about words and other verbal symbols, their meanings and referents' (Tulving, 1972).

Tulving's view of us having different and independent types of LTM store has been supported by research into different types of brain damage, and the associated difficulties patients have trying to recall different types of information – which has been encoded episodically, semantically or procedurally.

Wheeler *et al.* (1997) reported that brain-damaged patients in their study could be taught to do a puzzle (procedural memory), but had problems when asked about where and when they had learned how to do the puzzle (episodic memory).

Forgetting, or faulty retrieval of memories can thus be caused by damage, disease or accident to episodic, semantic or procedural memory stores.

INTERACTIVES

1 What do we call our 'knowing how' memory? Give three examples of this.

2 What do we call our 'knowing why' memory? Give three examples of this.

3 What do we call our 'knowing what' memory? Give three examples of this.

Interference

One reason why we lose information in LTM is **interference**. Competing information results in a LTM deficit.

Two kinds of interference are apparent in long-term memory. These are retroactive interference, and proactive interference.

Retroactive interference occurs when new information interferes with old information already stored in LTM.

Proactive interference is where old information already in LTM interferes with new information.

A classic research example of proactive interference in LTM would be Ebbinghaus (1885, 1913) whom we read about earlier. When trying to learn and remember new lists of words he found he was also recalling words from previous lists he had learnt.

Either type of interference affects both the storage and retrieval of information.

Evidence for the multi-store model of memory

	Coding	Capacity	Duration
Sensory register	Sensory, i.e. iconic, echoic, haptic etc.	Large	1/15th to 4 seconds
Short-term memory	Acoustic	7 ± 2 units/chunks	20 seconds
Long-term memory	Visual, acoustic and semantic		Limitless Forever

Table 2.2 Multi-store model of memory Atkinson and Shiffrin (1968)

According to the multi-store model we have three memory stores.

Information is registered by sensory memory and then some of this information is processed to short-term memory. We decide what is to be processed to STM as a result of pattern recognition. Maintenance rehearsal refers to how the information is kept in STM. It is then transferred to long-term memory (LTM).

Secondary evidence for the multi-store model of memory comes from research into brain damaged people such as KF, HM and Clive Wearing.

Primary evidence comes from studies Atkinson and Shiffrin and others have done using free recall tasks.

Brain damage

Case studies of brain-damaged people support the Atkinson and Shiffrin multi-store model that we have two separate and distinct memory stores called short- and long-term memory.

HM

Milner (1966) reports the case study of HM, a young man who developed severe memory impairment after having brain surgery to rectify epilepsy.

He was able to recall and talk about events from his life before surgery, but was unable to remember events thereafter.

He could not encode and store new information into his LTM due to the surgery he had unfortunately undergone.

Biologically his LTM was damaged, while his STM was not.

HM and Clive Wearing are two cases in point. Each developed anterograde amnesia as a result of brain damage to their hippocampus.

The condition is irreparable. The patient cannot transfer new factual information from STM to LTM. They become trapped in a world that lasts only as long as their short-term memory.

People with anterograde amnesia are able to remember events from long-term memory prior to their brain injury occurring. They also maintain, and can extend their procedural memory about how to do things.

Crucially however, like HM and Clive Wearing, people with anterograde amnesia cannot form new long-term declarative memories to deal with semantic or episodic information.

Korsakoff's Syndrome

Korsakoff's Syndrome comes about due to brain damage as a consequence of a thiamine deficiency. It is caused by chronic alcoholism, and affects two per cent of problem drinkers. Those suffering from Korsakoff's syndrome, amongst other things, display sound STM functioning but impaired LTM. Sufferers can neither recall events before its onset (retrograde amnesia) nor after its onset (anterograde amnesia).

Research in this area suggests we have separate and distinct memory stores. Korsakoff's syndrome is thus further support for the Atkinson and Shiffrin multi-store model of memory.

KF

Shallice and Warrington (1970) conducted a case study into KF who, following a motorcycle accident, suffered brain damage.

They discovered his STM was impaired, and LTM was intact.

This, and other studies like Milner (1966) and HM, and Baddeley (1997) and Clive Wearing support the Atkinson and Shiffrin (1968) idea that we have two separate and distinct memory stores, which we call short- and long-term memory.

The man who keeps falling in love with his wife.

In March 1985 the BBC musician Clive Wearing developed herpes simplex, a virus that normally results in cold sores. Sometimes it can attack the spinal cord or brain. Unfortunately Wearing was of these rare cases and consequently suffered brain damage to his hippocampus; the part of the brain that plays an important role regards memory. As a result he developed anterograde amnesia as a result. He cannot encode new memories, and spends spends every day 'waking up' every few minutes. He cannot remember what he has just done.

He remembers little of his life before 1985. He knows that he has children from an earlier marriage, but cannot remember their names. His love for his second wife Deborah, whom he married the year prior to his illness, is undiminished. Every time he sees her he greets her joyously as if meeting her for the first time even though she may have just left his room to get a cup of tea. When she does, and then returns, Wearing behaves towards her as if she has been away for months.

In an attempt to comprehend his problem Wearing began to keep a diary following his illness. Page after page is filled with entries such as:

~~8:31 AM: Now I am really, completely awake.~~

~~9:06 AM: Now I am perfectly, overwhelmingly awake.~~

~~9:34 AM: Now I am superlatively, actually awake.~~

His early entries of only a few minutes old are usually crossed out because he cannot remember making them and takes them to be untrue.

To find out more about this fascinating case read 'The Death of Yesterday' at **observer.guardian.co.uk/magazine/story/ 0,11913,1394684,00.html**.

A direct Link is available in Chapter 2 section of Higher Psychology Learning Suite at **www.gerardkeegan.co.uk/index.htm**

Free recall tasks

Free recall research is also used to support the multi-store model of memory.

Atkinson and Shiffrin (1968) gave participants 20 words to remember. Using free recall each was then asked to report them back *in any order*. Results were plotted onto a serial position curve. Serial position means when, where and in what order something comes.

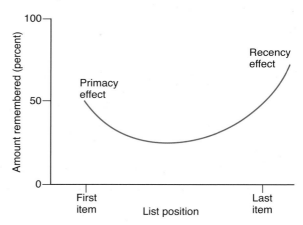

Figure 2.13 The serial position curve

The serial position curve highlights some interesting aspects to the Atkinson and Shiffrin research.

The primacy effect

The **primacy effect** demonstrates that participants recalled the first words on the list well. The reason for this was that these words had time to be rehearsed in STM. As we discovered earlier with the Brown-Peterson technique *rehearsal* in STM is important.

With Atkinson and Shiffrin (1968) these rehearsed first words were passed to LTM before the capacity of STM was reached. The primacy effect therefore involves recall from LTM.

The asymptote

The dip in the middle of a serial position curve is called an **asymptote**. This asymptote indicates that the middle items on the list were remembered less well than those at the beginning or those at the end.

This could be because as the number of words to be remembered increases STM fills up. Its capacity gets overloaded. New words displace old ones. Consequently words cannot be rehearsed and transferred to LTM. As a result participants remember fewer of them.

The recency effect

The **recency effect** in the diagram illustrates two things.

Participants recalled more of the words they heard at the end of the presentation, rather than those they heard first. They also recalled *more* of the words they heard at the end of the presentation than those from the beginning, or middle of the list.

We often demonstrate the recency effect in an exam situation. This is when we can remember more detail about the last topic we studied rather than the one we studied first!

It has been found that a slower rate of presentation can improve the primacy effect. This would be because more rehearsal time is available to us. However a slower rate of presentation does not influence the recency effect (Hill, 2001).

INTERACTIVES

1   What do you understand by the primacy effect?

2   To what does the asymptote refer in Atkinson and Shiffrin's serial position curve?

3   What do you understand by the recency effect?

4   Summarise the following case studies: HM and Clive Wearing.

5   What model of memory do these studies support? Why?

In an extension of Atkinson and Shiffrin, Glanzer and Cunitz (1966) gave participants an interference task immediately after they heard the last word on the list. They found that the recency effect disappeared, while the primacy effect remained.

STUDY

Glanzer, M., and Cunitz, A. R. (1966), 'Two storage mechanisms in free recall'. *Journal of Verbal Learning and Verbal Behaviour*, 5, 351–60

Aim: To investigate the effect interference has on the recency effect in STM (an interference task 'interferes' with the process of forming a memory).

Method: Laboratory experiment.

Procedure: Participants were asked to learn a list of words, after which they were asked to count backwards in tens.

Results: Glanzer and Cunitz (1966) found that the first few words from the list were recalled well in comparison to those recalled from the middle and end of the list that would normally indicate the primacy effect. Because of the interference task, the recency effect was eliminated, but there was no other effect on recall.

Conclusion: Words at the end of the list were not recalled very well as they were not well encoded and the interference task caused them to be forgotten. The items at the start of the list were unaffected by the interference task because they had been encoded into LTM.

Rehearsal of words at the start of the list led to more efficient encoding into LTM and better recall.

The recency effect suggests that the capacity of the STM is about two or three items. Immediate memory span, which measures how much can be stored in short-term memory at any one time alternatively suggest capacity is about seven items (Miller, 1956).

Glanzer and Cunitz (1966) conclude that interference has a detrimental effect on the quantity and quality of information we can process and recall.

Criticisms of the multi-store model of memory

The main criticism of the Atkinson and Shiffrin (1968) multi-store model of memory is that it is too simplistic. It sees memory as consisting of separate and distinct storage facilities, and plays down any interaction between them.

It disregards the influence LTM has over *why* our sensory register will make us aware of one particular stimulus rather than another.

It ignores the fact that our LTM also helps us to chunk information in short-term memory in a personally meaningful manner.

Further, maintenance rehearsal cannot solely explain the transfer of information from STM to LTM (Hill, 2001). Other factors are involved and include personal effort and memory strategies, which are often used by us when we are learning something.

Effective learning involves such **elaborative rehearsal**. Consequently elaborative rehearsal techniques allow us to store and recall more information from LTM.

This is explored shortly in the levels of processing approach put forward by Craik and Lockhart (1972).

Baddeley and Hitch (1974) are also critical of the multi-store model of memory. As we shall read later their Working Memory model suggests that STM and LTM are more complex than Atkinson and Shiffrin first believed.

It is with this in mind that we now turn to an examination of these other approaches.

The levels of processing approach

In 1972 Craik and Lockhart put forward their levels of processing approach, which is in contrast to the Atkinson and Shiffrin multi-store model of memory.

Their study of **primary memory** is interested in the *depth of processing* involved in long term memory. It is not concerned with memory as fixed memory stores, being sensory register, STM and LTM.

Craik and Lockhart look alternatively at the depth at which we process information to memory, and what we can then recall of it.

What is recalled is called a **memory trace**. Craik and Lockhart tell us that a memory trace, and just how long it lasts depends upon the level or depth to which it has been processed initially.

 It is suggested that the memory trace is better described in terms of depth of processing or degree of stimulus elaboration. Deeper analysis leads to a more persistent trace. While information may be held in PM, such maintenance will not in itself improve subsequent retention; when attention is diverted, information is lost at a rate which depends essentially on the level of analysis."

(Craik and Lockhart, 1972)

The levels of processing approach emphasises that the deeper we attend to a stimulus the more likely it is to be transferred to primary or long-term memory.

Crucially, the more personally meaningful something is for us, the more we will remember about it, and the more permanent a memory it will become.

Accordingly Craik and Lockhart identify three ways in which we process verbal information to memory. This is at the structural level, the phonetic level and the semantic level.

The structural Level

A structural level of processing occurs when we pay attention to what a word *looks* like.

The structural processing of verbal information to LTM is called **shallow analysis**. We are unlikely to transfer much verbal information to LTM using shallow analysis alone. When we merely look at something we don't remember much about it. Nor do we remember it for any length of time, or indeed at all.

The phonetic level

A phonetic level of processing occurs when we pay attention to what a word *sounds* like.

The phonetic processing of verbal information to LTM involves *some* **deep analysis**, or certainly a deeper level of processing than shallow analysis alone.

By sounding or saying a word to ourselves we are obviously paying more attention to it than just looking at it. We thus increase the likelihood of transferring the word to LTM, and should remember it for longer.

The semantic level

A semantic level of processing occurs when we pay attention to what a word *means*.

The semantic processing of verbal information to LTM involves **deep analysis**.

By making to-be-remembered information personally meaningful we will transfer that information to LTM, and remember much more about it as a consequence.

Take the eleven-digit string 01563523501. By converting it into a phone number 01563 523501 and associating it with my old workplace Kilmarnock College, I can remember it and them forever. And do!

In comparison to structural or phonetic levels of processing, semantic processing will result in a more durable and long lasting memory trace in LTM

ONLINE INTERACTIVES

See a great Flash interactive and also learn more about Craik and Lockhart's levels of processing approach. Visit:

www.psypress.co.uk/pip/resources/slp/flash/ch09-IA-06.swf

A direct Link is available in the Chapter 2 section of Higher Psychology Learning Suite at **www.gerardkeegan.co.uk/index.htm**

STUDY

Hyde T. S. and Jenkins J. J. 'Recall for Words as a Function of Semantic, Graphic and Syntactic Orienting Tasks'. *Journal of Verbal Learning and Verbal Behaviour*, 12, 1973, 471–80

Aim: To investigate under what conditions learning occurs.

Method: Experimental method, laboratory experiment.

Procedure: Hyde and Jenkins had eleven groups of participants listen to lists comprising of 24 words. The control group apart, they then had the remaining ten groups do one of the following 'orienting' tasks:

- Rate each of the words for pleasantness.

- Estimate how often each word is used in the English language.

- Identify how often the letters 'e' and 'g' occurred.

- Identify the part of speech each word represented e.g. noun, adjective.

- Decide whether the word fitted a particular sentence.

Half of the participants were told in advance that they would be expected to recall the words later. These five groups formed the *intentional* learning group. The other half were not told they had to recall the words. These five groups formed the *incidental* learning group.

Intentional learning/incidental learning were the two conditions of the independent variable.

The number of words recalled in the five orienting situations was the dependent variable.

Results: Hyde and Jenkins found minimal differences in word recall between the intentional/incidental learning groups.

Following the pleasantness orienting situation the intentional learners remembered 69 per cent of the words, while the incidental learners remembered 68 per cent. Following the 'e' and 'g' orienting situation intentional learners remembered 39 per cent of the words, while the incidental learners remembered 43 per cent, which was an insignificant difference over the piece.

Conclusion: The Hyde and Jenkins finding of no real difference in learning between the intentional and incidental learning groups was predicted by Craik and Lockhart. They said that memory retention is a by-product of processing information to memory. Intention to learn is therefore unnecessary for learning to occur. Other findings in the Hyde and Jenkins study also support levels of processing research.

Recall was significantly better for words that had been processed semantically (rated for pleasantness) than words that had been processed structurally (identifying the occurrence of 'e' and 'g').

Semantic analysis sees us process information to LTM at a deep level. It has us encode information on the basis of personal meaning and relevance. Information that has meaning for us sees us remember more about it for a longer period of time.

Questions

1 What was the aim of Hyde and Jenkins (1973)?

2 What procedure did they adopt?

3 What were the conditions of the Independent Variable?

4 What was the Dependent Variable?

5 What were the results of this experiment?

6 What were the conclusions of the Hyde and Jenkins (1973) study?

Type I elaborative rehearsal vs type II maintenance rehearsal

Craik and Lockhart also discussed the influence of rehearsal on memory recall. They say we use either maintenance or elaborative rehearsal to help us remember things.

We came across maintenance rehearsal when we looked at short-term memory.

What Craik and Lockhart call Type I maintenance rehearsal sees us repeating information to ourselves. Type II elaborative rehearsal involves a deeper, more meaningful analysis of a stimulus.

An example might be where we wanted to remember the word 'book'. Type I maintenance rehearsal would see us repeat the sound of the word 'book' over and over again. Alternatively Type II elaborative rehearsal would involve us thinking about an image of a book etc.

Craik and Lockhart (1972) believe the type of rehearsal we use strongly influences what we remember about a stimulus. In terms of memory recall Type II elaborative rehearsal has been found to be more efficient than Type I maintenance rehearsal.

Take the above example.

Using shallow maintenance rehearsal, repeating the word 'book' five times in fifteen seconds would not make it any more memorable for us.

However when using deeper elaborative rehearsal an increase in rehearsal time to fifteen seconds *would* make the word 'book' more memorable for us. We would use the time to associate the to-be-remembered concept, 'book', with more images of books.

Deep elaborative rehearsal allows us to make what we want to remember personally meaningful. Consequently we can recall much more about it for a longer period of time (Craik and Lockhart, 1972).

> ### What's a tachistoscope?
>
> A tachistoscope is a device that projects an image for a specific amount of time. It can be used to increase recognition speed, to show something too fast to be consciously recognised, or to test which elements of an image are memorable. Tachistoscopes have been used extensively in the study of memory since being invented by AW Volkmann in 1859.

Evidence for the levels of processing approach

Evidence to support the levels of processing approach comes from Craik and Tulving (1975).

In this study participants were presented with 60 words to remember. Thirty words were embedded in simple sentences, and thirty words in more complex ones.

Using a **tachistoscope** each participant was shown one of these words at random and asked a question using one of Craik and Lockhart's levels of processing strategies. Take the word 'table'.

From a structural point of view they could have been asked, 'Is the word in capital letters?'

From a phonetic point of view they could alternatively have been asked 'Does it rhyme with able?'

From a semantic point of view they could have been asked 'Does it fit in the sentence 'the man sat at the…?'

The type of level of processing question asked was their **independent variable**.

> ### Cued recall
>
> Cued recall occurs when we encounter a memory trigger in our environment that reminds us about something.
>
> An example would be on seeing salt in a supermarket. Cued recall reminds us to purchase it as we have run out of it at home.

Participants thought they were being tested on their reaction time by answering either 'yes' or 'no'.

Craik and Tulving were more interested in what participants remembered when given an unexpected recognition task that prompted **cued recall**.

Their **dependent variable** was the number of words recalled using structural, phonetic, or semantic processing.

Craik and Tulving (1975) discovered that participants remembered more words when processed at a deep semantic level rather than a structural or phonetic level.

Modifications

There have been modifications to levels of processing theory.

Research into elaboration, distinctiveness, effort and personal relevance has added to our knowledge of the deep processing of information to long-term memory.

> **The correlation**
>
> A correlation is a statistic that shows a relationship between two things.
>
> The correlation is further examined in Chapter Ten.

Elaboration

Craik and Tulving (1975) found by using a correlation that complex semantic processing resulted in better memory recall than simple semantic processing.

When shown the word 'rabbit', more participants recalled the complex sentence 'The great bird swooped down and carried off the struggling…' where they had earlier seen it, then the simpler sentence of 'She cooked the…' that they had also seen.

Because of the complexity of the first sentence they had had to use deeper elaborative rehearsal to commit it to LTM. This had made it more meaningful better remembered and easier recalled than the simpler but less memorable sentence of 'She cooked the rabbit.'

Participant	Words recalled from simple sentence condition	Words recalled from complex sentence condition
1	14	22
2	15	17
3	19	24
4	12	19
5	17	28
6	15	20

Table 2.3 From Craik and Tulving (1975)

Table 2.3 illustrates that participants remembered significantly more words from complex sentences than from simple ones.

Consequently Craik and Tulving (1975) conclude that elaborative rehearsal of complex meaningful stimuli gives rise to better recall.

Distinctiveness

Father and son psychologists Eysenck and Eysenck (1980) indicate that people are better able to recall unusual words when processed phonetically, than everyday words when processed phonetically.

Similarly Hunt and Elliot (1980) report that people recalled words better that had distinctive sequences of tall and short letters than words with less distinctive letter sequences.

Thus the more distinct something is the more likely we are to remember it, whatever level of processing strategy is used to commit it to LTM.

Effort

Tyler *et al.* (1979) found people were better able to retain words when presented as *hard-to-remember* anagrams than simpler ones. Put another way 'OCDTRO' was remembered more often by participants than 'DOCTRO'.

The more effort involved in committing information to memory, the more likely we are to remember and recall it later.

Personal relevance and the self-reference effect

In a case study of self, identity and memory Rogers *et al.* (1977) found that we remember things better when the cue or question has personal relevance for us. This is called as we now know the **self-reference effect**.

When we are asked if a particular word describes us we give much more additional detail than when merely asked what the word means. This isn't that surprising as we often deal with new information by relating it to ourselves. Take the following example.

Medical student's syndrome

You may be a student who has an interest in abnormal psychology. If so you may suffer from 'medical student's syndrome', in that you think a lot of the disorders that you come across describe yourself!

Very often at university a psychology professor will describe how a depressed person feels pessimistic about the future. Suddenly dozens of her students are wondering if their own pessimism indicates that they are clinically depressed. This is the self-reference effect.

Bower and Gilligan (1979) of Stanford University confirm this when they state that 'Trait adjectives are better remembered if they [are] judged in reference to oneself rather than judged for meaning or sound.'

We therefore remember more about a stimulus if it has personal meaning for us than if it does not.

ONLINE INTERACTIVES

An interesting variation of Craik and Lockhart (1972) and Craik and Tulving (1975) conducted by students at St. Andrews University is available at:

psy.st-andrews.ac.uk/resources/proj797.html

A direct Link is available in the Chapter 2 section of Higher Psychology Learning Suite at **www.gerardkeegan.co.uk/index.htm**

Evaluation of the levels of processing approach

The levels of processing approach proposed by Craik and Lockhart (1972) has been enormously influential in countering the more simplistic Atkinson and Shiffrin (1968) multi-store model of memory. It has made a valuable contribution to our understanding of the memory processes involved in learning.

As Craik (2002) states:

 One of the main contributions of the levels-of-processing article was to reinforce the idea of remembering as processing, as an activity of mind, as opposed to structural ideas of memory traces as entities that must be searched for."

The major point of Craik and Lockhart's work is that deeper levels of processing will produce better memory recall. This hypothesis has been widely tested.

Craik and Tulving (1975) found that people were about three times as likely to recall a word if they had originally answered questions about its meaning, than

if they had originally answered questions about its physical or structural appearance.

Similarly, Parkin (1984) discovered that people who made semantic judgements about a word's meaning performed significantly better on a surprise recall test than did people who made non-semantic judgements.

Non-semantic judgements would be structural questions about the number of vowels contained in a word, or whether a word it had been printed in capital letters etc.

Craik and Lockhart (1986) believe that deep levels of processing encourage recall because of two factors: distinctiveness and elaboration. Distinctiveness means that a stimulus is different from all other memory traces (Craik, 1979). Hunt and Elliot (1980) told us earlier that we are more likely to recall words that have distinctive sequences of short and tall letters, such as lymph, khaki, and afghan, better than words with common orthographic sequences, such as leaky, kennel, and airway.

The second factor that operates with deep levels of processing is elaboration. This as we know involves rich processing in terms of meaning.

However the levels of processing approach has been challenged because it is more *descriptive* than explanatory (Cardwell, Clark and Meldrum, 2003).

It also lacks an agreed and independent *definition* of what is meant by 'depth' of processing. It is difficult to tell the particular level of processing learners may have used as their basis for future recall (Nelson, 1977).

There is a *circularity* in the levels of processing argument. Specifically it states that if processing is deep, then retention will be better. Then it says that because retention is better, processing must have been deep. There is some evidence to suggest that this is questionable.

In the Hyde and Jenkins study the orienting task that produced the lowest level of recall was the sentence frame task. There was an assumption by Hyde and Jenkins that poor recall was because of shallow processing. Cardwell, Clark and Meldrum (2003) suggest that participants in deciding whether a word fits into a sentence frame would use *meaning*. They believe that Hyde and Jenkins participants did not use shallow analysis but semantic analysis, which as we now know is a powerful deep processing strategy. Why then was partcipants recall so poor? The levels of processing model cannot answer this inconsistency.

Another challenge comes from Challis and Brodbeck (1992). They believe that Craik and Lockhart's levels of processing model concerns *explicit memory* rather than implicit memory.

We came across explicit memory earlier when we read about declarative memory. You might remember that **declarative memory** is a category of LTM that consists of episodic memory and semantic memory. Explicit memory is information about a specific event that has occurred at a specific time and place. Explicit memory has spatio-temporal significance. We tend to associate current experiences with past experiences in the formation, storage and subsequent retrieval of explicit memories.

Implicit memory is our procedural memory. It is as we discovered earlier our 'knowing how to' memory. Implicit memory thus accounts for our ability to drive a car, tie our shoelaces, play the guitar, and boil an egg and so on.

Challis and Brodbeck (1992) found only a small levels-of-processing effect with implicit learning. A depth of processing approach cannot then apply to implicit or procedural memory. Challis and Brodbeck suggest that long-term memory depends on the *relevance* of previously stored information to the requirements of the memory task on hand.

What we input, store and can retrieve from our LTM thus depends upon what Morris *et al.* (1977) call transfer-appropriate processing.

Craik and Lockhart's notion of us having one primary memory to account for all that we know from a levels-of-processing perspective is, as with the Atkinson and Shiffrin multi-store model of memory, a little too simplistic.

INTERACTIVES

In the light of the above critically evaluate Craik and Lockhart's levels of processing approach to memory.

STM – working memory – Baddeley and Hitch

Craik and Lockhart's levels of processing approach challenged the earlier idea of memory being made up of *fixed* memory stores. One of these facilities, short-term memory, is better known nowadays as **working memory**.

Baddeley and Hitch (1974) were among the first psychologists to propose STM as working memory.

Their working memory model criticises the Atkinson and Shiffrin assumption of STM being both passive and part of larger unitary memory system.

Baddeley and Hitch think that working memory is an *active* memory system. Its function is to hold information, which we then examine and process for future use.

The working memory model

While information can be sent from working memory to LTM, and from LTM to working memory, Baddeley and Hitch (1974) see STM and LTM as consisting of separate components that make them functionally different from one another.

Baddeley and Hitch view working memory as a multi-component short-term memory store.

They say we use working memory to store and manipulate information for brief periods of time. Working memory also provides us with a mental workspace that we use to think and problem-solve.

Figure 2.14 The working memory model as proposed by Baddeley and Hitch in 1974

What they mean by this is that our working memory is multi-talented. Its various components give us the ability to multi-task in different *modalities*.

For example, working memory allows us to temporarily store and manipulate visual images. Working memory allows us to accumulate information while trying to make decisions. Working memory allows us to remember a phone number long enough to write it down and all of this at the one time if needs be!

INTERACTIVES

Baddeley and Hitch suggest you do the following to begin to understand working memory.

Work out how many windows there are in your house. When you have done this write down how you did it. What strategy did you use?

Keep this information handy, as we will return to it later.

Working memory explained

Working memory is flexible and by necessity complex! Baddeley and Hitch believe it consists of a number of components that work independently of each other. As a consequence working memory allows us to deal with more than one thing at a time.

Baddeley and Hitch call the main component of working memory the **central executive**. The central executive monitors and coordinates two 'slave' systems.

These slave systems are referred to as the **visio-spatial sketchpad**, and the **phonological loop**.

The central executive

At the heart of working memory is the central executive.

The central executive concerns itself with the 'allocation and monitoring of attentional resources to competing task demands' (Baddeley, 1996, 2001; Baddeley and Hitch, 1974).

The central executive is responsible for the encoding, storing, and retrieving of memories.

The central executive has limited capacity, and is 'modality-free'.

Modality-free means it has the ability to process information from any of our senses for a short period of time. It can deal with what we hear, see, touch, smell, taste etc.

Baddeley (1986, 1990) likens the central executive to the supervisory attentional system (SAS) as described by Norman and Shallice (1980), and Shallice (1982).

According to Shallice (1982), we use our supervisory attentional system for a variety of purposes, including:

➤ Tasks involving planning or decision-making.

➤ Trouble shooting in situations where our automatic processes appear to be having problems.

➤ Novel situations.

➤ Dangerous or technically difficult situations.

➤ Situations where strong habitual responses or temptations are involved.

Our central executive also oversees the visio-spatial sketchpad and phonological loop.

The visio-spatial sketchpad

The visio-spatial sketchpad is our *'inner eye'* that helps us to temporarily hold visual and spatial information in working memory. This is taken from either iconic input to sensory register (see earlier), or from long-term memory.

STUDY

Be amazed with your visio-spatial sketchpad!

Study the first scene above for about 20 seconds and then cover it. Use your visio-spatial sketchpad to identify what is different or missing in the second scene.

By identifying the differences you are using the visio-spatial sketchpad component of working memory. You have demonstrated that you have remembered in visual form all of the information that comprises the first scene.

The phonological loop

The phonological loop helps us temporarily store and work with a limited number of sounds. The phonological loop is made up itself of two subsystems, the articulatory control system and the phonological store.

What is the purpose of the phonological loop?

Learning to read: It has been discovered that children with impaired reading ability have smaller immediate memory spans. They have difficulties in tasks which require the manipulation of phonological information. When given the word 'stop', for example, they reply 'top'.

Language comprehension: Some people with impaired STM have difficulty in understanding the more complex sentence. They can understand 'The boys picked the apples' but have difficulty with 'The two boys picked the green apples from the tree'.

Vocabulary acquisition: There appears to be a strong correlation between non-word repetition, which strongly taxes the phonological loop, and vocabulary size (Gathercole and Baddeley, 1989).

The phonological loop: articulatory control system

The **articulatory control system** is our '*inner voice*', or verbal rehearsal system.

We use it to hold and rehearse what we want to say, until we have done so. Our articulatory control system has therefore a *time-based capacity*. The articulatory control system is unsurprisingly linked to speech production

(Baddeley 1986, 1990).

The phonological loop: the phonological store

The **phonological store** is our 'inner ear'. This is the part of the phonological loop that allows us to hold acoustically coded information for a brief period of time.

This is got from either echoic input to sensory register (see earlier), or from long-term memory. The phonological store is concerned with speech perception (Baddeley 1986, 1990).

Unless we use our articulatory control system to sub-vocally rehearse acoustically stored information, information held in our phonological store will disappear.

The duration of acoustic memory traces in the phonological store is no more than two seconds (Baddeley, 1999).

INTERACTIVES

Remember the windows exercise on page 42 that you did earlier?

Now use the Working Memory model to describe how you arrived at your final total!

Please use terms like the visio-spatial sketchpad, the phonological loop, sub-vocal rehearsal, and the central executive in your answer.

The dual task paradigm

The **dual task paradigm** has been used to investigate memory in general, and working memory in particular. The reason for this should be obvious.

This is because the dual task paradigm gets participants do two *different* things simultaneously. These could be saying a series of numbers out loud while at the same time doing a verbal reasoning task.

If one task interferes with the performance of the other then both are using the same memory component. This would support the *unitary* multi-store model of memory proposed by Atkinson and Shiffrin (1968).

If one task does not interfere with performance of the other, then each must be relying on *different* memory components. This would support the working memory model proposed by Baddeley and Hitch (1974).

If the tasks were to interfere then a single short-term memory system is being used for both; if not, then this suggests the existence of separate short-term memory systems or components.

INTERACTIVE: REFRESH YOUR WORKING MEMORY!

Use a pencil and connect the components of working memory on the left with the information they encode and store on the right:

Articulatory control system	Acoustic information
Phonological store	Visual and spatial information
Visio-spatial sketchpad	Articulation/speech information

Evidence for the working memory model

Baddeley and Hitch (1974) used a dual task paradigm to generate evidence for their working memory model.

Participants were shown a six-digit number string, which they were asked to rehearse and remember. At the same time they were given a verbal reasoning task to do. Doing each task simultaneously sounds impossible!

Remarkably participants *were* able to bring to mind the six-digit number string when later asked to recall it. Baddeley and Hitch (1974) is not compatible with Atkinson and Shiffrin (1968).

For Baddeley and Hitch STM is neither a passive part of a larger multi-store model of memory, nor is our whole memory system unitary. For Baddeley and Hitch STM is a flexible multi-component working memory store.

For supporting evidence of this let us return to the dual task study done by Baddeley and Hitch that we read about earlier.

The successful performance by participants of the two simultaneous tasks indicated that *different* components of working memory were being used.

The phonological loop and the visio-spatial sketchpad thus appear to exist and operate independently of each other. The phonological loop and the visio-spatial sketchpad allow working memory to do more than one thing at a time, especially if the two tasks involve different modalities.

Two similar tasks that simultaneously involved the phonological loop would be difficult, while two different tasks that separately involved the phonological loop and the visio-spatial sketchpad would be less problematic.

An example would be when asked to continually repeat a word while at the same time reading text from a book. Continual repetition of a word gives rise to **articulatory suppression**. Articulatory suppression would use up the phonological loop. It would interfere with our performance of another task such as trying to remember what we have just read. The articulatory suppression task denies us the advantage of rehearsing what we need to remember about the text. However if we replaced the verbal repetition task with one that involved the visio-spatial sketchpad our reading and remembering performance would be less affected.

INTERACTIVES

Use your knowledge of working memory to answer the following questions. Or better still set up the situations and find out for real!

1   Why do you think you would have difficulty recalling information from a passage in a book if simultaneously you were asked to repeat out loud 'la, la, la...'?

2   Why do you think your recall would be better be if instead of being asked to say 'la, la, la...' you were asked to put pegs of various shapes and sizes into a pegboard?

The limited nature of the phonological loop also helps us with Baddeley *et al.* (2002). As we read in the Study box on page 28 Baddeley, Chincotta, Stafford, and Turk investigated the capacity of short-term memory using immediate memory span. They discovered that more short words were recalled than long words.

If participants were asked to repeat the phrase 'la, la, la…' while trying to rehearse the groups of words they saw on the screen this word length effect disappeared. Short words were recalled no better than long words. Baddeley *et al.* (2002) believe that the 'la, la, la…' articulatory suppression task made rehearsal impossible.

Baddeley *et al.* (2002) think that the few words that were recalled by participants were as a consequence of their central executive taking over the role of the overwhelmed phonological loop.

Baddeley *et al.* (1998) and Papagno *et al.* (1991) suggest that the phonological loop may be more important in learning new words than familiar ones.

Also in 1998 Baddeley found evidence that sub-vocal rehearsal is not needed to learn vocabulary. Young children, who do not use sub-vocal rehearsal, still show a link between phonological memory and vocabulary learning.

Research evidence for the visio-spatial sketchpad has been a bit more difficult to ascertain. Baddeley *et al.* (1975) had participants do a simple tracking task where they held a pointer against a moving spot of light. They were also asked to perform an imagery task at the same time. They had to imagine that they saw a large capital 'F'. Starting from the bottom left hand corner they had then to say 'yes' if an angle was on the bottom line or top line of the letter, and 'no' if it wasn't.

Baddeley *et al.* (1975) reported that participants found it very difficult to simultaneously track the spot of light and identify the angles of the imagined letter. Doing two visio-spatial tasks concurrently

proved impossible. However participants reported no difficulty when the letter-angle task was replaced with a verbal task.

What this suggests is that the tracking task and the letter-angle task were each competing for the *same* visio-spatial resource. Essentially participants experienced 'similar information' overload. This is because, as with the phonological loop, the capacity of the visio-spatial sketchpad is limited.

When they were given the two *dissimilar* tasks, each was dealt with by a different slave component of working memory. The 'similar information' overload problem disappeared, as the information modalities were different from each other. The verbal task was dealt with by the phonological loop, and the tracking task the visio-spatial sketchpad.

Evaluation of the working memory model

The working memory model gives a more comprehensive explanation of short-term memory storage and processing than the multi-store model of STM.

The working memory model has been expanded and modified by Baddeley and others since 1974, and still continues to be developed.

Working memory can be applied to a number of immediate human abilities including reading, mental arithmetic and verbal reasoning. Its differing components better explain many STM deficits evident in brain-damaged people. There is sound research to support the phonological loop and the visio-spatial sketchpad. However, how we co-ordinate them is still a mystery.

Clarity is also needed regards what happens to information that can be encoded by both systems. An example of this would be the spatial location of a voice. How this is dealt with is still unanswered (Beaman, 2003).

The nature of the central executive remains vague. It is the most important component to working memory but the one we know least about. While the central executive is thought to govern our ability to plan and strategise in the short term, there is as yet little evidence to support this assumption (Beaman, 2003).

Baddeley *et al.* tell us it that the central executive has a limited capacity. To date its size has proved impossible to quantify, or measure scientifically.

Richardson (1984) thinks terminology like the 'central executive' is unclear. Its function is difficult to ascertain. Richardson further believes that the components of working memory can be used to explain any kind of results.

There is a circularity of argument regards the role and function of the central executive and its slave components. Why working memory sometimes cannot deal too well with information utilising one component or sub-system is often explained with reference to another.

As a model, working memory is not easy to falsify.

INTERACTIVES

Critically evaluate the working memory model as proposed by Baddeley and Hitch (1974).

Forgetting or faulty retrieval

So far we have concentrated on why and how it is we remember. Let us now turn our attention to why and how it is we forget!

 In case you have forgotten, forgetting is 'The inability to recall or recognise information."

(Eysenck, 2005)

Cognitive psychologists have studied forgetting extensively. Four general explanations of forgetting exist.

The first is that memory traces fade naturally as a result of organic processes in our brain. Related to this is that memory loss occurs because of brain damage, accident or illness.

A second explanation is that memories become systematically distorted or modified over time.

Thirdly, that new learning replaces old learning.

Fourthly, that forgetting occurs due to emotional factors.

Each can influence forgetting in short- and long-term memory.

Forgetting in STM

Short-term memory concerns the information we use to problem-solve in our immediate environment. If we do not use this information quickly, or pass it into long-term memory it disappears.

As we read previously, the earliest experiments into forgetting were conducted by Ebbinghaus in 1885.

Using himself in a single-subject design he learned a list of nonsense syllables that he tried to recall later. He found that as the retention interval increased the number of words he could correctly recall decreased.

He found also that this decrease in correctly recalled information got slower after the first hour of retention.

This is related to what Peterson and Peterson (1959) told us earlier. This is that without rehearsal 90 per cent of information in STM becomes lost to us after eighteen seconds.

Miller (1956), and other immediate memory span studies also inform us that we have problems remembering more than 7±2 units of information in STM at any one time.

Consequently cognitive psychology understands forgetting in STM in terms of trace decay and displacement theories.

Both theories are related to one another, as hopefully you will realise.

Trace decay theory

Trace decay is a theory that explains forgetting in STM on the basis of its limited *duration*. But what do we mean by 'trace decay'?

When we come across something we want to remember our brain activates a series of neurons that forms a physical memory trace of the stimulus. We can remember this **memory trace** if we rehearse or recall it regularly. Otherwise we will forget it because of **trace decay**.

Donald Hebb (1949) called a memory trace an **engram**. An engram comes about due to momentary excitation of neurons, or nerve cells in the brain. An engram is biochemical in origin and account for the persistence of memory.

Without rehearsal or active recall an engram or memory trace will fade away. However with repeated neural activity a more permanent structural change occurs. The engram transfers to long-term memory and become less prone to decay.

STM trace decay was originally thought to be anywhere between three and eighteen seconds (Peterson and Peterson, 1959).

Evaluating trace decay as a cause of forgetting in STM is problematic. This is because no new information should be presented to participants from the time they are exposed to the stimulus to be remembered, and the time they are asked to recall it.

To measure trace decay researchers have somehow to try and stop participants from rehearsing information. This is extremely difficult to control, as you might imagine.

In Peterson and Peterson (1959), participants performed a Brown-Peterson 'counting backwards' interference task before being asked to recall the trigrams.

Given that Miller (1956) tells us that the capacity of STM is 7±2 units it could be that this interference task *displaced* accumulated trigrams in STM. Was displacement a **confounding variable** in this experiment?

Was displacement in STM rather than trigram trace decay the reason why Peterson and Peterson (1959) got the results they did?

INTERACTIVES

1   What is a memory trace?

2   What were the aims, method, procedure, results and conclusions of Peterson and Peterson (1959)?

3   Evaluate Peterson and Peterson (1959).

4   What criticism of Peterson and Peterson (1959) did Reitman (1974) set out to resolve?

5   How successful was her research?

In an attempt to resolve this issue Reitman (1974) used an interesting technique. She presented her participants with a list of five words for two seconds. To try and prevent rehearsal, and the accusation of displacement as a confounding variable for her results, she got participants to listen to tones of noise via headphones for 15 seconds. This resulted in a 24 per cent decline in recall of the five words over the 15-second period. Reitman believes that deteriorating recall from STM was as a result of trace decay. While pure trace decay is a likely explanation for her results, it is impossible to ascertain if Reitman's participants did not rehearse the words they had seen while listening to the tones on their headphones!

INTERACTIVE: WHAT'S THE CAPACITY OF YOUR STM?

Slowly read out loud the digits in each single row below. At the end of each row shut your eyes and repeat the sequence in the same order back to yourself. If you make a mistake go onto the next row. The point where you cannot remember the digits in any two rows of a given length is the capacity limit of your short-term memory.

8704

2193

3172

57301

02943

73619

659420

402586

542173

6849173

7931684

3617458

27631508

81042963

07239861

578149306

293486701

721540683

5762083941

4093067215

9261835740

As regards the usefulness of Peterson and Peterson and trace decay theory Baddeley and Scott (1971) conclude that 'something like trace decay occurs in the Peterson task, but is complete within five seconds, and is certainly not sufficiently large to explain the substantial forgetting that occurs in the standard paradigm' (quoted in Baddeley, 1997).

Trace decay alone does not fully account for forgetting in STM.

Displacement theory

Displacement is another theory that explains forgetting in STM on the basis of its limited *capacity*. We have come across displacement often in this Chapter.

As we read earlier George Miller (1956) conducted research that concluded the capacity of our STM to be 7±2 units, or chunks of information long at any one time.

Consequently displacement theory believes that once STM reaches its capacity any new information that we come across will push out or *displace* old information in STM.

An alternative explanation for Peterson and Peterson (1959) may have been that the interference task of having participants count backwards *displaced* the original trigrams in STM. The limited *capacity* of STM may have been why their participants remembered fewer trigrams as the eighteen-second recall period progressed.

This is in contrast with the original Peterson and Peterson explanation. In their 1959 study forgetting was thought to occur because of trace decay due to the limited *duration* of STM.

What conclusion is the more correct?

The serial probe technique

In order to ascertain whether trace decay or displacement best explains forgetting in STM Waugh and Norman (1965) developed the serial probe technique.

Sixteen digits were shown to participants in rapid succession. The last digit given was a repeat of one that had appeared earlier. This last digit served as a cue to participants to recall the digit that came *after* it earlier in the list.

Thus with a sample list that runs 4 5 9 2 6 9, the last digit being 9 would prompt you to recall 2. This is because the number 2 occurs immediately after the first appearance of the *probe* number 9. This is the serial probe technique.

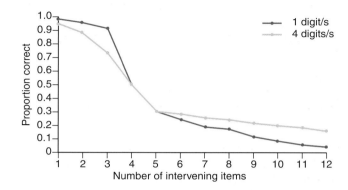

Figure 2.15 Proportion of digits got correct in free recall by participants as a function of the number of intervening items and presentation rate (Waugh and Norman, 1965)

Waugh and Norman recorded the number of digits their participants recalled correctly under two conditions.

The first condition concerned the speed at which digits were presented, being one per second and four per second. The second condition were the number of intervening digits that came between cue and target presentation of the probe digit. The amount of intervening digits varied from one to twelve.

What 'intervening' means is exemplified below where the cue and target probe digit is 9:

Example of intervening items

First example: 4 6 9 2 3 5 9   (3)

Second example: 4 9 2 3 5 6 4 3 7 9   (7)

Where the cue and target digit is 9 the number of intervening items in the first example is 3 (2, 3, 5), while in the second example it is 7 (2, 3, 5, 6, 4, 3, 7).

Waugh and Norman (1965) discovered that the nearer the end of the sixteen-digit string the probe prompt occurred, the better was participants recall of the number that came next.

Waugh and Norman (1965) supports displacement theory as digits nearer the end of the sequence had fewer following digits to displace them. These numbers were still available in participants' STM, while earlier ones were not.

Waugh and Norman (1965)

Order of sequence presented 3 7 2 9 0 4 5 6 3 1 9 0 7 8 2 6

If probe = 8 then recall of digit (2) is good (little displacement)

If probe = 4 then recall of digit (5) is poor (greater displacement)

From Hill (2001)

The number of intervening digits did have an effect on participant recall. As we can see from Figure 2.15, as the number of intervening digits increases, recall decreases. Waugh and Norman (1965) illustrates that interference from an increasing number of intervening digits has a detrimental influence on short-term memory recall.

Time and forgetting in STM

Figure 2.15 illustrates the data collected by Waugh and Norman (1965). If you look closely you will see that participants remembered nearly as many numbers in the four-digit per second presentation as in the one-digit per second presentation.

Shallice (1967) discovered the more rapid the presentation of digits in a serial probe task, the more digits from *earlier* in the sequence participants could recall.

Trace decay is responsible for *some* forgetting in STM especially when information is presented more slowly to us. In a fast sequence of events information nearer the beginning of the presentation is less prone to trace decay.

So while displacement is one reason why we forget in STM, trace decay as a result of the passage of time also still has merit.

But *is* the capacity of STM 7±2?

Displacement theory relies on George Miller's 1956 observation that the size of STM is 7±2 units or chunks of information at any one time. The capacity of STM is measured in terms of immediate memory span. Displacement theory assumes that in STM new information displaces old information once this 7±2 limit has been reached.

However thinking about the capacity of STM as a fixed value of 7±2 units or chunks may be a bit presumptuous!

Simon (1974) presented participants with a series of multi-word phrases.

These ranged in size from single word phrases to those that were ten words long. Each multi-word phrase was classified as a chunk. Participants were asked to recall each phrase immediately after being presented with it, thus measuring the capacity of their STM.

Simon discovered that when chunking went beyond a single word, participants' ability to recall more complex phrases fell. The capacity of their STM dropped.

For example, Simon found with two-word phrases the average capacity of STM was four units. With four-word phrases the average capacity of STM was three units. Simon concluded that immediate memory span is related to chunking, but the number of chunks that are remembered depends on the size of the chunks that have to be recalled.

According to Simon the capacity of STM is very much influenced by the size of the units or chunks that it has to deal with.

Related to this is the **word-length effect**, which we came across earlier.

You may remember that Baddeley *et al.* (1975) found fewer words can be retained in STM if they take longer to say! Baddeley *et al.* (1975) suggests that the capacity of STM probably depends more upon the length of time or *duration* it takes us to pronounce words, rather than the number of chunked items or words we can hold in STM at any one time.

The capacity and duration of STM as a function of pronunciation is given further impetus by Jones (2002). He reports that Chinese people have a larger immediate memory span than native Welsh speakers. When given the same lists of digits to remember a Chinese participant can remember on average 9.9 digits, while a Welsh participant 5.5.

Arabic numeral	English	Welsh	Chinese
0	Zero	Dim	Ling
1	One	Un	Yi
2	Two	Dau/dwy	Er
3	Three	Tri/tair	San
4	Four	Pedwar/pedair	Si
5	Five	Pum(p)	Wu
6	Six	Chwe(ch)	Liu
7	Seven	Saith	Qi
8	Eight	Wyth	Ba
9	Nine	Naw	Jui
10	Ten	Deg	Shi

Table 2.4 Arabic numerals in English, Welsh and Chinese.

Why each nationality appears to have a different size of STM is probably because of the length of time it takes each to pronounce the same numbers.

Chinese pronunciation of the same digits takes less time than in English. This is even more obvious when comparing Chinese to Welsh pronunciations of the same numeral (Jones, 2002).

Why don't you try it?

What a hummer!

Watkins *et al.* (1973) conducted a laboratory experiment into the effect *diversion in attention* had on STM recall. Using an independent groups design they randomly assigned their participants to one of two groups, each of which then underwent *one* condition of the independent variable.

Group 1 was asked to listen to musical notes and hum them.

Group 2 was asked to listen to the same musical notes but not hum them!

In a playback session participants then had to say whether they recognised a previously heard note or not. Correct recognition of a previously heard note was the dependent variable.

The researchers found that hummers forgot a significant number of notes, but non-hummers had perfect recall.

Watkins *et al.* (1973) believe that this provides evidence for the effect of **attentional diversion** on short-term memory recall.

This is because the hummers were asked to concentrate on two things at once; listening to notes, and then humming them. This saw them in a state of divided attention. This *attentional diversion* had a negative effect on their STM recall of musical notes.

Alternatively, the non-hummers were asked to concentrate on one thing only, which was listening to the notes. Unlike their counterparts the non-hummers used more focused attention. This more purposeful state of attention had a positive effect on their short-term memory recall.

Watkins *et al.* (1975) concludes that the more we concentrate on something the less chance we have of forgetting it.

How surprising is that!

INTERACTIVES

1. What was the aim of Watkins *et al.* (1975)?

2. What do you understand by the term 'independent groups design'?

3. How could Watkins *et al.* (1975) have randomly assigned participants to either group in their experiment?

4. What were their two conditions of the independent variable?

5. What was their dependent variable?

6. What were their results?

7. What conclusions can be drawn from Watkins *et al.* (1975)?

Brain damage and forgetting in STM

Earlier we mentioned the famous case study of HM conducted by Dr Brenda Milner in 1953. HM, or Henry M, was a young man of 27. To help cure his grand mal epileptic fits he underwent radical brain surgery. Following the surgery he seemed normal. His personality, IQ, and knowledge of the world were intact. His long-term memory regards events before surgery was fine. His short-term memory was also fine. He could, for example, memorise eight-digit numbers, and retain information for up to 30 seconds.

> *Right now, I'm wondering. Have I done or said anything amiss? You see, at this moment everything looks clear to me, but what happened just before? That's what worries me.*
>
> *It's just like waking from a dream; I just don't remember."*
>
> HM

INTERACTIVES

Identify another case study where brain damage had a similar effect.

HM's problem was that he had lost the ability to convert short-term memories into new long-term memories. This condition HM has is called anterograde amnesia. Anterograde amnesia is the inability to learn new information after some trauma. In this case the trauma was the removal of parts of HM's temporal lobe, which inevitability affected his hippocampus. The hippocampus as we know is very important regards memory.

ONLINE INTERACTIVES

Read all about HM and 'The Day His World Stood Still' at:

www.brainconnection.com/topics/?main=fa/ hm-memory

A direct Link is available in the Chapter 2 section of Higher Psychology Learning Suite at **www.gerardkeegan.co.uk/index.htm**

Evaluation of STM theories of forgetting

Forgetting in STM occurs due to trace decay, interference and displacement, attentional diversion, and brain damage.

Most research in this area concerns trace decay and displacement. It is not easy to separate out trace decay from displacement as to why we forget in STM.

This is because it is difficult to judge the *individual* influences that trace decay and/or displacement has on information loss in short-term memory. Trace decay may be responsible for some but not all forgetting in STM (Shallice, 1967).

Displacement theory relies on the assumption that STM has a fixed and *limited capacity*. *Trace decay* theory alternatively assumes that STM has a fixed and *limited duration*.

These two assumptions are however questionable when we consider the likes of Shallice (1967), Jones (2002), and Baddeley *et al.* (1975). Their research, tells us that the capacity and duration of STM are each influenced by time. Shallice (1967) tells us that the faster the rate of presentation of digits, the less chance there is for displacement from STM, and the more one can retain and recall. Jones (2002) and Baddeley *et al.* (1975) indicate that the time it takes to pronounce words is of consequence. The longer the pronunciation times the smaller the capacity of STM.

STM is thus a fragile store from which information can be quickly lost or forgotten. How this occurs is still not clear. What is apparent is that displacement and decay are of some significance.

Forgetting in LTM

As we should now realise long-term memory or LTM involves us encoding and storing information primarily on the basis of its meaning.

A long-term memory can last anything between 20 seconds and a lifetime. Rehearsal and meaningful association helps in the transfer of information from short- to long-term memory. The biological term used to describe this process is called **long-term potentiation**. Long-term potentiation sees a more permanent physical change in the structure of neurons representing something we have come across in our environment that we want to remember.

Why we forget information in long-term memory may be due to trace decay, interference, cue dependent retrieval failure, and brain damage.

Trace decay in LTM

From our investigation of forgetting in STM we know that trace decay is the physical deterioration of a memory engram due to the passage of time. Trace decay may be apparent in LTM but is difficult to test specifically.

Jenkins and Dallenbach (1924) were the first to investigate trace decay in LTM. They conducted an experiment where two participants had to learn and recall nonsense syllables at retention intervals of between one and eight hours. The two participants learnt the nonsense syllables either at the beginning of the day, and thereafter remained awake, or at night just before they went to sleep.

Jenkins and Dallenbach discovered that their participants remembered more nonsense syllables after being asleep, than when awake. What is interesting about this is that in the non-sleep condition the two participants had a chance to rehearse, while in the sleep condition this was impossible.

Jenkins and Dallenbach (1924) concluded that trace decay as the cause of forgetting in long-term memory is dubious.

If trace decay *were* a factor there would have been no real difference in the amount of nonsense syllables recalled in the sleep and non-sleep conditions.

If trace decay theory were correct one would also expect decreased recall of nonsense syllables as the retention period increased *regardless* of whether participants were awake or asleep.

The results got by Jenkins and Dallenbach (1924) concerning forgetting in LTM are better explained by interference theory.

INTERACTIVES

1   What was the aim of Jenkins and Dallenbach (1924)?

2   Describe the procedure adopted by Jenkins and Dallenbach (1924).

3   What were their two conditions of the independent variable?

4   What was their dependent variable?

5   What did Jenkins and Dallenbach (1924) discover?

6   Why is trace decay a dubious explanation of why we forget long-term memories?

Interference theory

You may remember reading about interference earlier in this Chapter. One reason why we lose information in both STM and LTM is because of competing information. Competing information interferes and this causes a memory deficit.

Two kinds of interference can affect long-term memory, **retroactive interference**, and **proactive interference**.

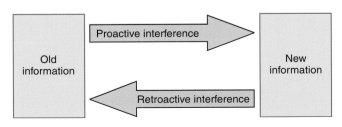

Figure 2.16 Interference and LTM deficit

Retroactive interference

Retroactive interference occurs when new information interferes with old information already stored in LTM. This later information causes previously stored material in long-term memory to be lost. Retroactive interference is also evident in STM (Waugh and Norman, 1965).

In an attempt to investigate retroactive interference in LTM McGeoch and MacDonald (1931) gave student participants a list of words to learn. They then divided them into groups and gave each group interference word lists to learn. After ten minutes they asked their participants to recall as many of the *original* list of words as possible.

McGeoch and MacDonald (1931) found that those participants who had been given an interference list of *similar* meaning words recalled on average 12.8 per cent less than those given an interference list of *unrelated* words (21.7 per cent), or *nonsense syllables* (25.8 per cent).

Best recall was found with the control group. These were the group of participants who got *no interference* task, and were not subject to any change or manipulation of the independent variable. They remembered 45 per cent of the original word list.

> ### INTERACTIVES
>
> 1 What was the aim of McGeoch and MacDonald (1931)?
>
> 2 Describe the procedure adopted by McGeoch and MacDonald (1931).
>
> 3 Identify four conditions of their independent variable?
>
> 4 What was their dependent variable?
>
> 5 Define the term 'control group'.
>
> 6 What were the results of this experiment?
>
> 7 What can we conclude regards forgetting and long-term memory from the work of McGeoch and MacDonald (1931)?

Proactive interference

Proactive interference occurs when old information already in LTM interferes with new information being processed to LTM. Interference affects both storage and retrieval of information.

A classic research example of proactive interference would be Ebbinghaus (1885, 1913), whom we came across earlier in this Chapter. In his experiments into memory Ebbinghaus discovered when trying to learn and remember new lists of nonsense words, old lists of nonsense words he had previously learnt interfered with new list recall.

Underwood (1957) confirmed the influence proactive interference could have on LTM recall. He found that the greater number of nonsense syllable lists learnt previously by participants, the greater their forgetfulness of new nonsense syllable lists presented 24 hours later. Proactive interference saw the new nonsense syllable lists becoming confused with the old ones.

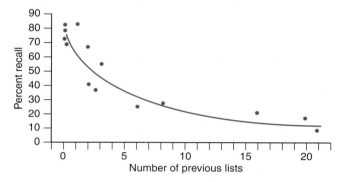

Figure 2.17 From Underwood, B.J. (1957) 'Interference and forgetting' *Psychological Review*, 64, 49–60

Wickens *et al.* (1963) found that proactive interference disappeared when the *nature* of the stimulus was changed. When, after a 24-hour delay, numbers replaced nonsense syllables, they discovered that participants were able to recall both sets of information.

Research evidence thus suggests that proactive interference is more likely to occur in LTM when the information to be recalled is similar.

Evaluation of interference theory and forgetting in LTM

The main criticism of interference theory concerns its ecological validity.

This is because research into interference as the cause of forgetting in LTM has traditionally been conducted in a laboratory setting. However many laboratory experiments do not reflect a real-life situation. The learning of nonsense syllables, as in

Ebbinghaus (1885, 1913), Underwood (1957), and Wickens *et al.* (1963), clearly demonstrates this.

There have been some studies done into interference in more real-life ecologically valid situations. For example, Baddeley and Hitch (1977) found that the more intervening games rugby players took part in, the less likely they were to remember names of teams played some time previously.

Interference theory can be used to our advantage.

As we know proactive interference occurs when previously learnt information interferes with later learnt information. In researching into proactive interference Gunter *et al.* (1981) presented news items to participants.

They found participants remembered more news items when successive news stories were dissimilar to each other rather than when they were similar.

As a student you can avoid proactive interference by studying *dissimilar* topics one after the other rather than similar ones. Remember Gunter *et al.* (1981)!

Cue-dependent forgetting

Forgetting may occur because the information to be recalled no longer exists in memory. It is not available for retrieval. Alternatively, forgetting can occur because desired information cannot be found. It is inaccessible. This type of forgetting is called cue-dependant retrieval failure, or cue-dependent forgetting.

Cue-dependent forgetting has been investigated by Tulving and Perlstone (1966). Tulving and Perlstone found their participants often forgot lists of learnt words. Their recall was enhanced however when they were given appropriate information, or a cue, to help them. An example would be saying 'It's a fruit' when the word to be recalled was 'pear'.

Cue-dependent forgetting occurs when we temporarily forget information due to missing stimuli or cues that were present at the time the memory was first encoded.

Psychologists have identified two types of cue-dependent forgetting, context-dependent forgetting, and state-dependent forgetting.

Context-dependent forgetting

Abernathy (1940) investigated the effect changed environmental conditions had on college examination results. He concluded that we recall information better, if when asked to remember it, it is in the same situation or context as when it was first encoded to memory.

Consequently, at exam or assessment time it is important to study in exam type conditions. Bear in mind context-dependent forgetting and sit on a wooden chair behind a desk, rather than lie on your big comfy bed!

State-dependent forgetting

In their research into state-dependent forgetting Goodwin *et al.* (1969) conclude we are more likely to remember information, if when asked to do so we are in the same physical or emotional state as when we first learnt it.

Goodwin *et al.* (1969) had male volunteers perform four memory tasks either sober or intoxicated. Twenty-four hours later they were tested for memory recall under the same, or the alternative condition.

They discovered memory recall was better when their participants were intoxicated during both sessions, rather than when intoxicated only during one.

Recognition, being our realisation of a previously encountered experience, was not significantly affected by changing state.

Goodwin *et al.* (1969) thus conclude that alcohol appears to produce a state-dependent effect, but not all forms of memory are equally sensitive to the phenomenon.

INTERACTIVES

1   What was the aim of Goodwin *et al.* (1969)?

2   What were the two conditions of their independent variable? (A context-dependent hint would be 'Hic!')

3   What was the procedure adopted in this experiment?

4   What did Goodwin *et al.* (1969) conclude?

5   Identify two forms of remembering investigated by Goodwin *et al.* (1969).

Emotion and forgetting in LTM

Our emotions concern how we feel about our world, which can be happy, sad, angry etc.

We all express the same emotions. Consequently our emotions are **innate**. This means we all share a universal set of feelings due to common genetic inheritance. Something that is innate generally has a high survival value for us.

Psychology teaches us that our emotions can help us remember or help us forget.

Flashbulb memory and repression are good examples of this. Flashbulb memory may prevent forgetting, while repression possibly encourages it.

Flashbulb memory

 For a recollection to be considered a flashbulb memory, it must involve not only a live quality accompanied by recall of minutiae, but also preserve details of the reception events and remain unchanged over long periods of time."

(Conway, 1995).

Brown and Kulik (1977) tell us that a flashbulb memory is a very vivid episodic memory. 'Flashbulb' memory is apparent when we can remember exactly what we were doing when an important, exciting or emotional event occurred. Try the following.

Brown and Kulik (1977) asked American participants questions about major world events during the 1960s and 1970s. Nearly 90 per cent reported flashbulb memories of personal shocking events, such as the assassination of President John F. Kennedy in Dallas, Texas on 22 November 1963.

It is important to note that *personal relevance* is important for flashbulb memory.

Seventy-five per cent of black American participants, in stark contrast to three per cent of white American participants, remembered the assassination of Malcolm Luther King, the famous Nobel Prize winning civil rights activist in Memphis, Tennessee on 4 April 1968.

Similarly Conway *et al.* investigated flashbulb memory following the resignation of British Prime Minister Margaret Thatcher in 1990.

ONLINE INTERACTIVES

Watch historical YouTube Video footage of Margaret Thatcher's resignation at:

www.youtube.com/watch?v=sTDS23DY670

A direct Link is available in the Chapter 2 section of Higher Psychology Learning Suite at **www.gerardkeegan.co.uk/index.htm**

INTERACTIVES

1 On what day and in what month did this event happen?

2 Describe what happened.

3 What were you doing on the day this happened?

4 Why do you think you can remember a lot about this day in particular? Use your knowledge of both flashbulb memory and encoding to LTM to help you.

Figure 2.18 The World Trade Centre, New York

Conway *et al.* (1995) report a year later more than 80 per cent of British participants could be classified as having a 'vivid and consistent' flashbulb memory of this momentous event.

This compares with less than 30 per cent of non-British participants remembering her resignation in vivid and consistent detail.

The importance of personal relevance to flashbulb memory cannot be underemphasised.

Brown and Kulik believe flashbulb memory to be a unique and distinct form of memory. They suggest emotionally important events trigger neural mechanisms that result in these significant episodes becoming deeply engrained in long term memory.

Whether we have possess 'flashbulb memory' has been questioned by McCloskey *et al. (1988)*.

ONLINE INTERACTIVES

Listen to this online episode about flashbulb memory from the BBC 4 'All in the Mind' series by Dr Raj Persaud.

www.bbc.co.uk/radio4/science/allinthemind_20030212.shtml

A direct Link is available in the Chapter 2 section of the Higher Psychology Learning Suite at **www.gerardkeegan.co.uk/index.htm**

STUDY

McCloskey, M., Wible, C. G., and Cohen, N. J. (1988). 'Is there a special flashbulb-memory mechanism?' *Journal of Experimental Psychology: General*, 117, 171–81

Aim: To test the accuracy of flashbulb memory.

Method: Interview.

Procedure: American participants were interviewed a few days after the Challenger space shuttle disaster in 1986 about what they remembered about the tragedy.

Nine months later they were similarly re-interviewed about what they remembered.

Results: McCloskey *et al.* (1988) found inaccuracies in participants' memories. There were discrepancies in what they remembered over the two occasions. People were inconsistent regards what they first remembered about the Challenger disaster, and what they later remembered about it nine months subsequently.

Conclusion: 'Flashbulb' memories are as prone to inaccuracy and inconsistency as other types of memory.

McCloskey *et al.* (1988) believe flashbulb memories are not a special species of memory but a stronger type of ordinary long-term memory.

Evaluation: McCloskey *et al.* (1988) has good ecological validity in that it was not an experiment and took place outwith the artificial setting of a psychology laboratory. As it took place in the real world it better reflected real life thoughts, feelings and behaviours.

Conway *et al.* (1994) reject McCloskey that flashbulb memories do not exist. Conway *et al.* argue this was not a study into flashbulb memory, as it did not meet the criteria for what flashbulb memory is.

Evaluation of Flashbulb Memory

Neisser (1982) says flashbulb memories are no different to other episodic memories. The event is just thought about and discussed more by us.

Consequently we better remember John F. Kennedy's death, Margaret's Thatcher's resignation, and 9/11 etc.

Neisser does not believe that any special neural activity occurs when a detailed episodic memory is formed. For Neisser, levels of processing theory better explains why we can remember more about some things that have occurred. We remember more about certain things because they are *personally meaningful* to us. Therefore we attend to them better, and process them more deeply into LTM.

Figure 2.19 The Hillsborough disaster

Further, as indicated by McCloskey *et al.* (1988), and with Wright (1993) in his study following the Hillsborough football disaster, the detail of 'flashbulb' memories have been found to be no more accurate than our memory of other events.

Thus studies supporting us having a 'vivid and consistent' flashbulb memory are inconclusive.

Freud and forgetting

Sigmund Freud founded the psychoanalytic approach around 1900. The aim of the psychoanalytic approach is to understand thoughts, feelings and behaviours by analysing our unconscious mental processes formed by early childhood experiences.

The diagnosis and treatment of any dysfunction we might acquire as a result, is carried out in psychoanalytic psychotherapy. Here the psychoanalytic psychotherapist helps the patient understand him- or herself by exploring their unconscious.

Psychoanalytic psychotherapy involves the patient being made aware of the unconscious drives that make him or her think, feel and behave the way he or she does.

Freud called an aspect of this **repression**.

Repression is an **ego-defence mechanism** that helps explains why and how we forget traumatic events. To understand this we need to look a little more at the psychoanalytic approach itself.

Who was Freud?

Sigmund Freud was born into a Jewish family at 6.30pm on the sixth of May 1856, at 117 Schlossergasse, Freiberg, Moravia, now part of the Czech Republic. He died from cancer of the mouth on the 23 September 1939, at 20 Maresfield Gardens, London, at the age of 83. During his lifetime he developed psychoanalytic theory and its related psychoanalytic psychotherapy as a means of helping people in psychological distress. He is probably the best-known psychologist in history, and his ideas have had a huge impact on Western culture.

Figure 2.20 Sigmund Freud

What is the psychoanalytic approach?

The psychoanalytic approach is a theory and a therapy, the two being closely linked.

Central to psychoanalytic theory is the need to understand that unconscious mental processes formed by early childhood experiences influence our thoughts, feelings, and behaviours. The application of a theory in everyday clinical practice in psychology is called psychotherapy. Those who seek the help of a psychoanalyst (someone trained in Freud's psychoanalytic theory and techniques) would then be undergoing psychoanalytic psychotherapy, which is the application of psychoanalytic theory in everyday clinical practice.

Neurosis and the unconscious

Freud thought that the causes of all mental and behavioural difficulties lie deep within the unconscious, and that our personality is influenced from birth by the contents of the unconscious. Any mental and behavioural difficulties that arise, he termed neuroses. A neurosis is a mental condition with no known medical (physical/biological) cause. A neurosis is distressing to the individual and influences their life in a negative way. Examples of neuroses that originate in our unconscious include phobias, compulsions, anxieties, panic disorders and hysterias.

We are unaware of our unconscious and what it contains. The purpose of psychoanalytic

psychotherapy is thus to access – in order to bring to the patient's conscious awareness – the unconscious causes of their neurosis. This will hopefully help the patient, as the client is termed in psychoanalysis, to understand the causes and symptoms of their distress. The psychoanalytic approach aims to restore the patient's personality to health. Knowing the cause of a neurosis is immensely helpful in coming to terms with its mental, emotional and social effects. You can deal with yourself better and become psychologically healthier.

> **Neurosis**
>
> Neurosis is a general term used to denote a wide range of disorders and is characterised by the following:
>
> Unrealistic anxiety is accompanied by associated problems such as phobias or compulsions.
>
> The neurotic individual retains complete contact with reality (in contrast with psychosis).
>
> The disorder tends not to transgress wider social norms, although it is recognised as unacceptable to the neurotic individual.
>
> Source: Mike Cardwell (2000) *The Complete A–Z Psychology Handbook*. 2nd edn, Hodder and Stoughton.

The structure and function of the unconscious

As emphasised above psychoanalytic theory is concerned with the unconscious mind.

Using what is called the iceberg analogy, the mind can be likened to an iceberg. Only the tip of an iceberg can be seen above the surface of the ocean, while the great remainder is hidden under the water line. The part of us of which we are aware is our conscious mind. Freud believed that people are only consciously aware of this small part of themselves. The greater parts of the mind – our deepest thoughts, instincts, traumas, fears and passions – are hidden from us in our unconscious. Our hidden unconscious is full of these forces that have much more influence over our behaviour than we might at first think.

The iceberg analogy

Our conscious/consciousness is our awareness. Consciousness is the rational decision-making part of our mind. Our preconscious is our dream state. Often we wake up aware of what we have just dreamt about. By remembering dream content we have brought some of our preconscious to our conscious awareness. R.M. Ryckman, in his *Theories of Personality* (2000), says that our preconscious is also that part of our mind that contains information we could bring to conscious awareness with little effort. This includes recent experiences, an example being remembering what you had for breakfast yesterday. We are not normally aware of our unconscious at all, probably because it is too scary! It contains our instincts (sex and aggression), traumas, fears and passions. As we age the sea of life gets choppier and choppier. This sees the iceberg of our mind thrown about. Parts of the iceberg – previously hidden under the water line – can then break off and float to the surface. In psychoanalytic terms, as life progresses parts of our unconscious can fragment and manifest themselves in our conscious awareness as phobias, compulsions, anxieties, panic disorders and hysterias.

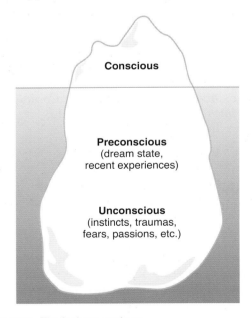

Figure 2.21 The iceberg analogy

The psychodynamic structure of personality: id, ego and superego

According to Freud, our personality is the pattern of thoughts, emotions and intellectual skills that makes us unique. He also believed personality to be largely unconscious.

Personality

Although our personality is what prompts each of us to act in the ways we do, we cannot study it directly. This is because personality is internal to us. Since it does not exist as a tangible reality, personality is another hypothetical construct. Freud thought he could investigate the influence of the unconscious on personality indirectly, by listening to people's free associations (thought associations), and reports of their dreams. From notes made of these sessions with his patients, Freud put together various theories where experiences in childhood are seen as central to the development of personality.

For example, Freud came up with a theory concerning the structure of personality. For him personality is made up of three parts: the id, the ego and the superego. Id means 'it' in Latin, and ego means 'I'. Id, ego and superego comprise the psychodynamic structure of personality.

Id

The id is the most primitive part of our personality. Present from birth, the id is the centre of an instinctive psychic energy Freud called libido. Libido constantly demands to be satisfied. The id, which is found in the unconscious, in order to satisfy libido, operates on what is called the pleasure principle. The pleasure principle drives us to seek pleasure and avoid pain. This can be seen in babies who demand that their needs are satisfied immediately. If they are hungry, need changing or are uncomfortable, they cry, and we respond immediately to satisfy their id desires. A baby's personality consists principally of id. The id continues to function throughout life, and its job is the immediate satisfaction of instinctive needs. Selfishness, sex and aggression are three manifestations of the demands of the id. They can be seen in our behaviours.

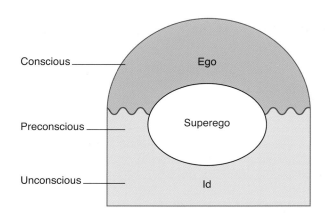

Figure 2.22 The psychodynamic structure of personality

Ego

From about two or three years of age the second more conscious part of our personality, the ego, starts to emerge. Our ego is influenced by our real-world experiences. At this stage personality structure is beginning to change. The ego part of our personality deals with those activities needed to get the demands of our id satisfied. The ego thus operates according to the reality principle. In obeying the reality principle the ego tries to find a realistic and socially acceptable solution to the demands of the id.

A child discovers that the whining id demand of 'Muuuum! I want sweets!' often accompanied by a tantrum doesn't work after a while. Their ego manages this id demand by coming up with a more 'acceptable' solution to what it wants, such as the child using the strategy of 'Mum, if I behave will you buy me sweets?' The id gets what it wants, but in an acceptable manner, based on the ego's experience of how other people get things.

> *The ego seeks to bring the influence of the external world to bear upon the id and its tendencies. For the ego, perception plays the part, which in the id falls to instinct. The ego represents reason and common sense, in contrast to the id, which contains the passions."*
>
> *(Freud, 1923)*

Superego

The third part of our personality to emerge at around four to six years is the superego. Like a watchdog, or internalised parent, over our entire personality the superego is our conscience. It holds a model of what we think, largely unconsciously, we

ought to be like. It punishes us with feelings of guilt if we do not come up to these expectations. The superego is formed as a result of our upbringing. The superego is not dominated by the need to satisfy instinctive drives. However it is not as rational as the ego, and can keep us in tight moral check by producing such feelings of guilt that result in anxiety and irrational behaviour. The superego operates on what is called the morality principle.

Id, ego, and superego: a psychodynamic relationship

A maturing, and mature, personality is the result of continuing clashes and compromises between these three parts of our personality. The id, ego and superego are therefore in a changing, or psychodynamic, relationship with one another. Sometimes the id will make demands of the ego that the ego cannot satisfy in an acceptable way. There is no 'safe' realistic solution to these id demands. We then may act in ways we know are 'bad'. This could include underage drinking, truanting from school, taking drugs, or having an affair. If we engage in these activities, the superego produces feelings of guilt as a consequence of our id-driven quest for pleasure.

A healthy adult personality is never entirely id or entirely superego. The diplomatic ego is continually working out solutions to square the conflicting pulls of id and superego. For Freud the all-id or all-superego personality is seen as psychologically unhealthy.

The component parts of personality, id, ego, and superego are in a psychodynamic relationship with each other. This is because the ego has to try to keep an even balance between the demands of the id and, at the same time, the demands of the superego. Achieving a healthy balance between id, ego and superego is not easy. It takes time.

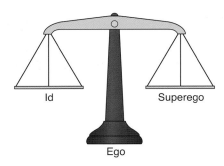

Figure 2.23 The psychoanalytic view of a healthy adult personality is that that person will be a delicate balance between their id and their superego. Their ego tries to balance each antagonistic demand in a realistic manner.

Ego-defence mechanisms

The ego has a number of defence mechanisms that it uses to protect itself (us) from unpleasant feelings of anxiety or guilt. These feelings can arise because we feel threatened by a real danger, or because our id or superego becomes too demanding of us. We use ego defence mechanisms to reduce these anxieties.

It is important to understand that the use of defence mechanisms is not under our conscious control. Defence mechanisms are then **non-voluntaristic**.

In conjunction with the ego, the unconscious will use one or more ego-defence mechanisms to protect us when we come up against a stressful situation in life. As suggested earlier Freud identified repression as an ego defence mechanism, which is influential regards why and how we forget traumatic events of the past.

Repression

Repression would happen when you experience something so painful and traumatic that you push it out of your conscious awareness. You permanently forget that it ever happened.

What is interesting is that the 'affect' (or emotion) attached to the memory cannot be repressed. It is still evident in your behaviour, perhaps as neurotic symptoms. Freud used **dream analysis**, slips-of-the-tongue (**parapraxes**) and **free association** to uncover patients' repressed information on the origin of their problems. This repressed information gave him a clue as to the cause of their psychological distress.

Repression is thus the unconscious act of forgetting a deeply disturbing trauma or event. Someone who has suffered the trauma of child sexual abuse may understandably use repression as an ego-defence mechanism. It is just too horrific for them to contemplate.

For Freud ego-defence mechanisms such as repression were natural and normal. When they get out of proportion, neuroses develop, such as anxiety states, phobias, obsessions or hysteria. These disorders affect emotional and intellectual functioning, relationships, health, well-being and quality of life.

Evaluation of repression as a cause of forgetting

It is difficult to evaluate whether repression causes forgetting because it is hard to prove that ego-defence mechanisms such as repression exist!

This is because a lot of Freudian theory concerns hypothetical constructs. A hypothetical construct is something that does not exist in reality. Consequently it is not easy to support scientifically.

Levinger and Clark (1961)

Notwithstanding, Levinger and Clark (1961) investigated the influence of emotional factors on forgetting.

Participants were shown 60 emotionally charged negative words such as '*war*' and '*fear*', and 60 neutral words, such as '*window*' and '*tree*'. Participants were then asked to try and remember each word by verbally associating it with something else. Examples would be 'war-soldier', 'fear-spider', 'window-house', 'tree-leaf' etc. These 'free associations' were recorded.

A short time later they were shown the emotionally charged and neutral words again. They were asked to remember the word with which they had earlier associated it. For example 'tree' and 'leaf'.

The longer this took the more repressed the associated word was thought to be. An objective record of participants' galvanic skin response (GSR) was also taken. GSR occurs when we are in a state of emotional arousal and sweat.

Levinger and Clark (1961) found that participants took longer to recall emotionally charged negative word associations than neutral word associations. For example when shown the word 'window' participants' recalled the associated word 'house' quicker than when shown the word 'spider' and asked to recall its associated word of 'fear'. They found that emotionally charged negative words such as 'fear', 'war' etc., also produced a higher GSR.

Consequently Levinger and Clark (1961) conclude that the delayed recall of emotionally charged negative words was due to repression. Emotionally charged negative words also produced higher levels of anxiety as measured by increased GSR.

Levinger and Clark (1961) imply that anxiety is reduced through the ego-defence mechanism of repression.

While Levinger and Clark's research support Freud's view that repression helps us forget unpleasant memories, the position is not entirely clear.

The 'weapons focus effect'

Loftus and Burns (1982) conducted an experiment where two groups of participants watched different versions of the same bank robbery. The independent variable, being the variable the researcher controls or manipulates, was the degree of violence used in the robbery. The version shown to the experimental group saw a young boy being shot in the face, while the version shown to the control group did not.

Loftus and Burns found that the experimental group were unable to recall as much detail about the robbery than the control group. They did however remember great detail about the young boy being shot in the face. This is called the 'weapons focus effect'.

The weapons focus effect occurs when witnesses to a crime focus on a weapon that is being used. This impairs their memory of other details of the crime such as the criminals face (Loftus *et al.*, 1987).

Participants in Loftus and Burns experimental group did not repress and forget the memory of the boy being shot. Indeed they remembered much more about it that anything else that happened. Forgetting due to repression of unpleasant memories is therefore questionable.

INTERACTIVES

1   What was the aim of the experiment conducted by Levinger and Clark (1961)?

2   Outline the procedure adopted by Levinger and Clark (1961)?

3   What were the results of their experiment?

4   What conclusions can be drawn from Levinger and Clark (1961)?

5   Do you agree with these conclusions? Give reasons for your answer.

Now let us turn to some applications of what we know about memory.

Memory and police investigations

Geiselman and Fisher developed the cognitive interview technique in Los Angeles in the 1970s and 1980s. The cognitive interview technique is a structured interview where knowledge of cognitive processes is used to maximise witness recall of an event. The CIT particularly concerns perception, attention and memory. We should here note, as we did in the introduction to this Chapter, the integrative and active nature of our information processes.

Information is the most important element in any criminal investigation. The ability of police to get accurate and useful information from witnesses and/or victims of crimes is crucial. Often an eyewitness will tend to focus on what they think is important.

Given the importance of personal meaning to our perception, attention and memory, this is understandable; however, important detail can become lost or forgotten and this can frustrate the efficiency of the police investigation.

Leading questions

Important information can also be lost if an interviewer uses leading questions. Leading questions can result in an accusation of interviewer bias.

Psychological research has demonstrated how the language used in a question can affect the answer given. Two classic examples of retroactive interference come from Loftus.

In Loftus and Palmer's (1974) study participants were asked to estimate the speed of a car that was involved in an accident.

When their participants were asked the question 'How fast were the cars travelling when they hit each other?' they reported a lower speed estimate than when asked 'How fast were the cars travelling when they smashed into each other?' In this instance they reported a higher speed.

The use of the words 'hit' and 'smashed', which were the their two conditions of the independent variable, appeared to influence the participants' perception of the speed of the car.

In another study, Loftus and Zanni (1975) demonstrated how the use of the words 'a' or 'the' in a question can change the way people answer a question.

ONLINE INTERACTIVES

Read the summary of the Loftus and Palmer (1974) study 'Reconstruction of automobile destruction' by Mark Holah at **www.holah.karoo.net/loftusstudy.htm** and then answer the following questions.

A direct Link is available in the Chapter 2 section of the Higher Psychology Learning Suite at **www.gerardkeegan.co.uk/index.htm**

1 What was the aim of Loftus and Palmer (1974)?

2 What method and procedure did they adopt in their first experiment?

3 What were the five conditions of the independent variable?

4 What were their results?

5 How did Loftus and Palmer explain these results?

6 What method and procedure did they adopt in their second experiment?

7 What were the three conditions of the independent variable?

8 What were their results?

9 How did Loftus and Palmer explain these results?

10 Evaluate the overall procedure used by Loftus and Palmer.

11 What evidence is there for the 'reconstructive hypothesis'?

12 What criticisms can be made of the 'reconstructive hypothesis'?

Loftus and Zanni asked different participants two slightly different questions about a car accident. The first question asked 'Did you see the broken headlight?' which assumes that there was a broken headlight in the situation. The second question was 'Did you see a broken headlight?' which is more open.

Participants had been shown a film of a car accident. There was no broken headlight in the film, but seventeen per cent of those asked about 'the broken headlight' said there was one, while only seven per cent of those asked about 'a broken headlight' reported they had seen one.

The cognitive interview technique (CIT)

The cognitive interview concerns how people remember. We store memories on the basis of particular aspects associated with them, most especially the context, or where the event happened, and just how personally meaningful the event was for us.

CIT encourages the eyewitness to (1) reconstruct the circumstances, (2) report everything, (3) recall the events in a different order, and (4) change perspectives. The method is systematic, and thus the sequence used (i.e. (1), (2), (3) and (4)) is important.

Reconstruct the circumstances

Here the officer would ask the witness to reconstruct the circumstances of the event in general. The witness essentially tells their story. This will give a general overview of the incident. The starting point might be the story of their day well before the incident itself. You ask them what they were doing, feeling or thinking.

Report everything

With an eye to the personal nature of attention and perception here the officer would encourage the witness not to withhold any detail, however trivial it might seem to be. Interestingly the interviewer here uses statements in the present tense like: 'What do you see? What is your immediate reaction?' They are trying to make the person relive the incident.

Recall the events in a different order

Here the police officer gets the witness to recount the story in different ways. This could mean from the beginning to the end, then the end to the beginning, or from a particular point from which the witness remembers a lot of detail. Other variations on this are the use of questions like: 'Of what you have told me, what stands out?' This is related to something in the study of perception called figure and ground. In order to make perceptual sense of our world we often unconsciously put aspects of a stimulus to the background, and other aspects of it to the foreground. Often this is done on the basis of what is important to you (foreground) and what is less important to you (background).

Recalling events in a different order is also a good lie detector! Lies are created and told in a logical order. Having a witness start at various stages confuses that order. Different order recall is most useful in catching out criminals, and naughty children too, for that matter!

Change perspective

The fourth general principle behind the CIT is where the police officer tries to get the witness to recall the incident from the perspective of where another person was standing, and involves asking questions like 'What was Richard doing while he was sitting in the Kay Park Tavern?' or 'If you were sitting where Richard was sitting, what would you have seen?'

Having a witness mentally change perspectives like this enhances the quality of remembered information about the incident or event. Often a witness has a variety of perspectives on the incident, but most people will report what they remember from only one perspective, their own! Changing perspective should avoid this.

Uncannily, figure and ground work in two dimensions as well. Take this image called Rubin's Vase. What aspect of it is to the front, what aspect of it is to the back? Ask others what they see. Do you share the same figure and ground perspective, or point of view?

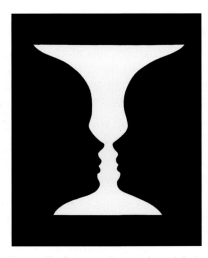

Figure 2.24 Uncannily, figure and ground work in two dimensions as well. Take this image called Rubin's Vase. What aspect of it is to the front, what aspect to the back? Ask others what they see. Do you share the same figure and ground *perspective*, or point of view?

The effectiveness of CIT

Geiselman *et al.* (1986) compared the cognitive interview with the standard interview technique. Fifty-one participants saw a film of a simulated violent crime and were questioned about it two days later.

The table below shows their results, comparing the mean (average) number of items recalled using the cognitive and standard interview methods.

	Cognitive interview (CIT)	Standard interview (SI)
Items correctly recalled	42	35
Items incorrectly recalled	9	9

Table 2.5 Effectiveness of CIT

No difference was found in the number of errors made by participants undergoing the SI in comparison to the CIT. However witnesses questioned using SI recalled 35 correct items, whereas those questioned using the cognitive interview recalled 42 correct items.

In another set of trials based on real crime, Fisher *et al.* (1989) and Fisher and Geiselman (1988) compared the interview performance of pre- and post-CIT trained detectives. Results showed a 47 per cent gain in information got from witnesses after training. Further, in comparing information from witnesses elicited by CIT trained and untrained detectives, results showed those who used CIT got 63 per cent more information than their untrained colleagues. What CIT appears to indicate is that people often remember more than they think! The form of questioning that is used is one of the critical factors to eyewitness testimony in the reconstruction of memory.

The cognitive interview technique has come under criticism of late. Memon and Stevenage (1996) outline a number of mainly theoretical issues that concern CIT.

These include the generalisability of the term itself, and the fact that in many police forces the CIT, as first proposed, has become a random and haphazard amalgam of different interview techniques.

Memory improvement techniques

This book is delighted to contribute to the Scottish Government's school and College achievement agenda. This is because the study of memory helps us learn things more easily.

Students of psychology are more aware of how memory works. We are better able to encode, store and retrieve important information. We know, for example, that organising and ordering such information has a significant effect on what we can later remember.

So here are some useful memory techniques to enhance your grades!

Get ready, get set, and then go!

It is essential to get organised before studying. Here are some basic tips.

Set aside a study timetable for your subject/course, and adhere to it.

Allocate around three hours a week to each subject that you do. This should be over and above any homework you have. If you have a busy social life, family commitments, or work finding regular blocks of time is challenging but essential.

If you miss a 'shift' make it up. The less you do, the less chance you have of passing whatever it is you are (not!) studying.

Find a suitable working environment. If home is too distracting use the school/college/university/local library.

What does studying entail?

What does *studying* actually mean? Studying involves a number of activities. The first is getting your class or lecture notes organised. You should write/type these out in full, making them as coherent as possible. Look things up that you don't understand. Elaborate on your notes where appropriate. Keep notes for each subject that you do in separate folders.

Lay out notes by using boxes, headings, underlining, and bullets. Highlight the important points by using capitals, colour etc.

The more you put into these earlier, the more useful they will become later on when it comes to studying for assessments and exams.

If you are an organised person, it is also a good idea to make up summaries of lectures and classes as you go along. Postcard-sized lined cards, available from a stationer are ideal for this.

Again use boxes, headings, underlining, and bullets. Little pictures are useful as well. Highlight the important points using capitals, colour etc.

Review notes and summaries on a regular basis. When the assessments or exams come around you will then have your 'crib' notes/cards already made up.

Exclusively study these time and time again to get the essential information into your head! Anything you don't understand look it up in your now excellent notes, or read up on it. If in doubt consult your teacher or lecturer.

Take breaks

Getting such information into memory is a fundamental part of studying. When we have to do this activity it is important to remember the cognitive benefit of taking regular breaks.

As a rough rule of thumb when studying take a five-minute break every 20 to 25 minutes or so.

This allows your brain time to absorb and process what you have just been trying to put into it!

A good example of someone using regular breaks while studying is the nineteenth century explorer Sir Richard Francis Burton.

He learned new languages by carrying a list of new words in his pocket. He did not 'look at it for any longer than fifteen minutes at a time because after this the mind loses its freshness.'

Burton mastered 29 Languages and twelve additional dialects on this basis.

Organisation by category and hierarchy

When information is stored *methodically*, it is easier to retrieve from memory. Psychologists like Tom Bower tell us that information can be accessed better if it is first organised by category and hierarchy. Using a repeated measures design Bower *et al.* (1969) presented the same group of participants with two word lists that were arranged randomly and hierarchically.

> A repeated measures design is when in an experiment the one group of participants repeat the measure of performance under the differing conditions of the independent variable.

After a while they were asked to recall as many of the words from each list as they could. The results showed that participants remembered two to three times more words from the hierarchical list than from the random list.

Bower (1969) indicates that organised information is easier to retrieve from memory than disorganised information. Information is therefore easier to remember if first organised in categories or in a hierarchy.

INTERACTIVES

1   What was the aim of Bower *et al.* (1969)?

2   What do you understand by the term a 'repeated measures design'?

3   What were the two conditions of their independent variable?

4   What were their results?

5   What conclusions did Bower *at al.* reach?

Organisation by imagery

Imagery is memory of a 'thing' in picture form. Imagery is useful because the brain has unlimited potential for remembering images. Encouraging participants to use imagery Nickerson (1965) found they could later remember 9996 pictures out of the 10,000 shown to them.

After studying patients with damage to one of their temporal lobes, Paivio (1971) proposed the **dual coding hypothesis**.

> *Human cognition is unique in that it has become specialised for dealing simultaneously with language and with nonverbal objects and events. Moreover, the language system is peculiar in that it deals directly with linguistic input and output (in the form of speech or writing) while at the same time serving a symbolic function with respect to nonverbal objects, events, and behaviours. Any representational theory must accommodate this dual functionality."*
>
> *Paivio (1986)*

The dual coding hypothesis suggests that we process words and images separately. Concrete words, which can also be images, e.g. house, carrot, spade etc., are encoded twice in memory; once as verbal symbols and then again as image-based symbols.

Such dual coding increases the likelihood of us remembering such information.

Logogens and imagens

According to Paivio we have two cognitive subsystems. One processes information as verbal entities represented as **logogens**. Logogens are similar to 'chunks' as described by Miller (1956).

The other cognitive subsystem processes information in nonverbal form using representations called **imagens**. Imagens are mental entities of images.

Logogens are organised in terms of associations and hierarchies, while imagens are organised in terms of part-whole relationships. These aspects of Paivio's dual coding hypothesis are illustrated in Fig. 2.25.

You may like to reference Paivio with the phonological loop that we came across earlier?

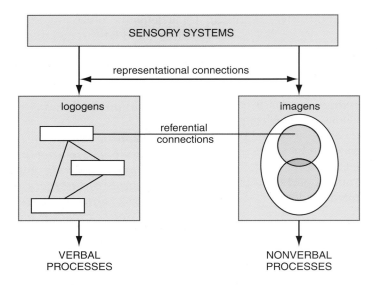

SENSORY SYSTEMS

representational connections

logogens

imagens

referential
connections

VERBAL
PROCESSES

NONVERBAL
PROCESSES

Figure 2.25 Paivio (1986) Schematic representation of dual coding theory from tip.psychology.org/paivio.html

Creating imagery

How do you create an image to remember something? It is a good idea to think in terms of adding movement, exaggeration, association, humour, symbolism, pleasant imagery, combining objects, and order and sequence.

You should try to keep the images as clear as possible so that they cannot be confused as representing something else.

To illustrate, here is an example that helps to remember the psychologist J. Ridley Stroop of Stroop Effect fame.

This image is a combination of the letter S, and a symbol to represent 'troop' resulting in S-troop… or Stroop!

Another example is this representation for Freud's structure of personality; id, ego and superego!

Association

As was seen with logogens *association* is an important aid to memory. This is where we remember something by associating it with something already in our mind.

Association and imagery can both be used to enhance later memory recall. An excellent example of this is the Memory Palace, or Roman Room

The memory palace

The ancient Greek poet Simonides of Ceos (556 BC–469 BC) was first to emphasise imagery, association and *loci* as aids to memory in his tale of an evening dinner that ended in tragedy.

Dinner was progressing well when one of the diners went outside to get a breath of fresh air. This was fortuitous as moments later the building collapsed! Relatives of the diners searched the rubble for survivors, but sadly only found dead bodies laying where they once had sat. No one was able to identify the deceased. A dispute then arose between the various families, as they did not want to make funeral arrangements for someone else.

The sole survivor agreed to try and remember who was sitting where. He found that if he took a mental walk around the dining table, he was able to picture in his head exactly where everyone was sitting.

The man later elaborated on this strategy. He began taking mental walks around his own home. He would imagine a journey through the various rooms in his house and designate certain items as 'hooks'. These designated hooks were permanent, such as stone pillars, and could then be associated with something that he wanted to remember. If he wanted to get his sword sharpened he would, for example, imagine it hanging on a pillar. He also found that if he imagined the sword swinging and making grinding noises against the pillar, this made the fact that he needed to get it sharpened even more memorable for him.

Thereafter when he imagined a walk through his house, he would remember the objects he had placed on his various hooks, and why. He discovered that he could use this method to remember any amount of information. All he had to do was make more hooks. Through the use of *loci*, or place where something happens, imagery and association the famous Roman room technique, or memory palace was born.

You may wish to try the memory palace system to remember your psychology.

ONLINE INTERACTIVES

For more on memory techniques go to:

www.gerardkeegan.co.uk/index.htm/sandt/memorytech.htm

A direct Link is available in the Chapter 2 section of the Higher Psychology Learning Suite at **www.gerardkeegan.co.uk/index.htm**

Organisation by context

It has been found that we can remember things better if we are in the same context, or situation, as when we first encountered it (Estes, 1972).

Godden and Baddeley (1975) asked divers to learn a series of words in two different environments, being on land or under water. They found the divers forgot around 40 per cent of the words when asked to recall them in the alternative environment. The presence of external environmental cues aid recall. This is related to **context-dependent** forgetting, which we came across earlier.

Internal biological cues are also of interest here. Related to **state-dependent** forgetting, what state we are in when first learning something appears to influence later recall.

Goodwin *et al.* (1969) report state-dependent effects regarding alcohol. Similar state-dependent recall has been found with the ingestion of marijuana (Eich, 1975), and amphetamines (Bustamente *et al.*, 1970).

Active techniques

Active learning helps us attend to, process and recall essential information. There are all sorts of active learning techniques. Whatever one appeals to you may depend on your learning style.

ONLINE INTERACTIVES

Find out more about learning styles at:

www.gerardkeegan.co.uk/index.htm/sandt/learningstyles.htm

A direct Link is available in the Chapter 2 section of the Higher Psychology Learning Suite at **www.gerardkeegan.co.uk/index.htm**

Here are a few of them.

PQRST

Research by Thomas and Robinson (1982), Spache and Berg (1978), and Robinson (1970) have demonstrated that a simple study method known as PQRST can significantly improves understanding and memory.

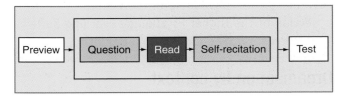

Figure 2.26 PQRST

PQRST is an acronym for preview, question, read, self-recitation and test. An acronym is a type of abbreviation, which uses an invented combination of letters from a phrase to helps us remember it.

PQRST techniques rely on three basic principles for improving memory:

➤ organising information to be learnt

➤ elaboration of information to be learnt

➤ practising of retrieval of information to be learnt

PQRST is particularly useful when you have read material such as this book!

Stage P (preview)

When you preview what is to be learnt you look at the material you need to study. This could be this Chapter on memory!

Get a feel for the topic, by seeing how it is organised. Read the Introduction. Then skim through the Chapter paying attention to the headings of the main sections and subsections. Finish your preview by reading the Chapter summary, or conclusion, at the end.

A preview helps you organise the material to be learnt. Your ability to later retrieve it is enhanced.

Stage Q (question)

During the question stage the headings and subsections of the Chapter should be read, and changed into questions.

An example would be 'What are Mnemonics?'

These questions should then be answered during the next stage.

Stage R (read)

Each section should be read first to grasp its meaning.

While reading, think about the questions posed at stage Q. Highlight key words. This will make the main ideas stand out when you later review the material. Try to avoid taking notes until you have finished reading a section. This way important ideas and concepts, necessary to answer the question asked at the Q stage, will not be missed.

Stage S (self-recitation)

Self-recitation, or saying things over to oneself is an excellent way to embed information into memory. You should try to recall and recite the main ideas of the topic that you are studying. Put the main ideas into your own words as much as possible.

Self-recitation helps organise material you have stored in memory. It is better to spend time attempting to recall and recite ideas than to read and re-read a section or sections in a book.

Ebbinghaus (1895) found that the more he repeated something to be learnt initially, the less time it took him to relearn the same information at a later date.

This is related to the need to rehearse essential information to pass exams and assessments. The schedule below should therefore be of some help.

Review information after	To keep it for a further
10 minutes	24 hours
24 hours	Week
1 week	Month
1 month	6 months
1 year	Year

Remember that stages Q, R, and S should be applied to each section until the entire Chapter is finished. It is important continually to:

➤ Make up questions.

➤ Read sections to answer these questions.

➤ Then recite and recall the main ideas.

Stage T (test)

The final stage is the test stage. This should come at the end of the Chapter once all the material has been subject to QRS.

You should try to recall all the facts read throughout the Chapter, and how they relate to one another.

PQRST is a better approach to study than straightforward reading. The Preview and Test stage apply to the Chapter as a whole, while the QRS stages apply to each section of the chapter as they are encountered.

Mnemonics

Mnemonics have been used to aid memory since the time of the ancient Greeks. A mnemonic is a memory trigger using prompts such as visual imagery or sounds.

In general mnemonics are a combination of imagery, associations, and *loci*.

Loci refer to the occurrence, or the context where things are found.

Using mnemonic devices like imagery, association and *loci* Themistocles was able to remember the names of all 20,000 people in Athens! Xerxes in similar fashion could recall every soldier's name in his 100,000 strong army.

While many are familiar with the use of simple mnemonics such as 'Richard of York gave battle in vain' to help remember the colours of the rainbow, mnemonics, as can now be appreciated are a bit more sophisticated than that.

Grouping as a mnemonic

Grouping, as an aid to memory is where we classify the things we need to know on the basis of a common characteristic. We essentially put things into categories.

Simple examples would be where we would group things on the basis key elements such as colour, size, function, likes/dislikes, good/bad, etc. A more complex example would be grouping species of trees under their two general categories of deciduous or evergreen.

Rhymes as a mnemonic

Rhymes are often used to help us remember things. The sound the rhyme makes enhances memory recall.

Examples would be:

➤ 'I before E except after C.'

➤ '30 days hath September, April, June and November….'

➤ 'In fourteen hundred and ninety two, Columbus sailed the ocean blue.'

Acrostics as a mnemonic

An acrostic is an invented sentence where the first letter of each word is used as a cue to an idea you need to remember.

Earlier we came across the acrostic '**R**ichard **of Y**ork **g**ave **b**attle **in v**ain.' to help us remember the colours of the rainbow. Being of course red, orange, yellow, green, blue, indigo, violet.

> ## INTERACTIVES
>
> Make up a narrative chain mnemonic to remember the fifteen stations on the Glasgow Underground:
>
> Hillhead, Kelvinbridge, St. George's Cross, Cowcaddens, Buchanan Street, St. Enoch's, Bridge Street, Shields Road, Kinning Park, Cessnock, Ibrox, Govan, Partick, Kelvinhall.

Chaining as a mnemonic

Narrative chaining is a mnemonic where we create a nonsense story to remember important words, ideas, concepts etc. Key words in the story cue further key words in the story that we need to remember.

The value of narrative chaining has been investigated in psychology. In 1969 Bower and Clark got participants to make up stories from lists of ten unrelated nouns. Ninety-three per cent later recalled the unrelated lists of nouns accurately.

Memory maps

Made famous by the likes of Tony Buzan, a memory map is a diagram used to represent words, ideas, tasks or other items, linked to and arranged around a central key word or idea. It is used to generate, visualise, structure and classify ideas.

It is an aid in study, organisation, problem-solving, and decision-making. You might like to begin to use memory maps to help you with your psychology.

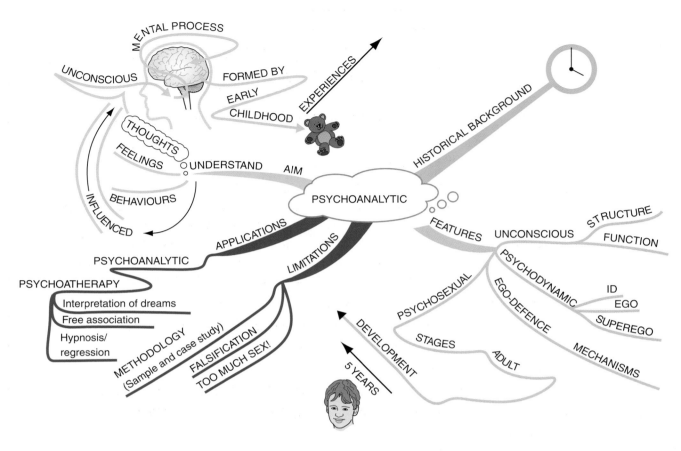

Figure 2.27 An example of a memory map that helps illustrate the psychoanalytic approach

Evaluation of mnemonics

While excellent in assisting us to remember essential information mnemonics as aids to memory can be criticised.

Copeland and Robertson (2004) rightly tell us that mnemonics do not help us *understand* whatever it is we are trying to remember.

'Better be right or your great big venture goes west' is an acrostic, and refers to the ohms value of the colour bands on resistors. The dark band comes first, and the light band last. Black, brown red, orange, yellow, green, blue, violet, grey and while.

But *what* is an ohm, and *what* is a resister? What significance do ohm values have? Unless you know this, acrostics like this are meaningless.

Mnemonics can also be time consuming to construct and then learn. In a stressful situation like an examination or assessment, the mnemonic may be forgotten, and the information it contains lost to us.

Chapter summary

This chapter has investigated encoding, capacity and duration of memory. It has also examined and evaluated the multi-store and working models of memory. Forgetting has been discussed in terms of trace decay, displacement, and interference. Cue and context dependent forgetting has also been outlined, as has eye witness testimony and other applications of memory.

STRUCTURED QUESTIONS WITH ANSWER GUIDELINES

1   Describe and explain the Atkinson and Shiffrin (1968) multi-store model of memory.

With reference to the preceding pages, structure your answer as follows:

● start by saying that Atkinson and Shiffrin (1968) highlight memory as separate stores: sensory register, STM and LTM. Model concentrates particularly on STM. At each of its three stages of memory information is filtered, further selected and even altered, supporting the earlier work of Bartlett (1932) who saw what we remember as influenced by personal experience. Then expand on the following features of their multi-store model of memory. Remember to refer to research studies where appropriate:

  ➤ how we remember: acoustic, visual and semantic encoding

  ➤ sensory register: encoding (iconic/echoic memory), pattern recognition

  ➤ STM: duration (Peterson & Peterson, 1959)

  ➤ STM: acoustic encoding

  ➤ STM: size (immediate memory span), Miller (1956), Baddeley et al. (1975)

  ➤ STM: forgetting (decay and displacement), Waugh and Norman (1965)

  ➤ LTM: semantic encoding, visual encoding

  ➤ LTM: duration and capacity

  ➤ LTM: types – eidetic memory, procedural and declarative memory, episodic memory, semantic memory

  ➤ LTM: forgetting – interference

2 Evaluate the Atkinson and Shiffrin (1968) multi-store model of memory.

With reference to the preceding pages structure your answer as follows:

● Secondary evidence for the Atkinson and Shiffrin (1968) multi-store model that we have two separate and distinct memory stores comes from research into brain damaged people. Primary evidence comes from studies Atkinson and others conducted using free recall tasks. Then elaborate on the following:

  ➤ Brain damage: HM and Clive Wearing case studies

  ➤ Free recall tasks: what are these?

  ➤ Describe Atkinson and Shiffrin (1968) free recall experiment and results

  ➤ With reference to Atkinson and Shiffrin (1968) explain the primacy effect, the asymptote, and the recency effect

  ➤ Mention Glanzer and Cunitz (1966) experiment into interference

  ➤ Give criticisms of Atkinson and Shiffrin (1968) multi-store model

ONLINE INTERACTIVES

1   Go to the Higher Psychology Learning Suite at **www.gerardkeegan.co.uk/index.htm**. Click Chapter 2 'Cognitive Psychology: Memory' and do the interactive crossword. But don't cheat!

2   Go to the Higher Psychology Learning Suite at **www.gerardkeegan.co.uk/index.htm**. Click Chapter 2 'Cognitive Psychology: Memory' and do the online interactive hangman game.

3   Go to the Higher Psychology Learning Suite at **www.gerardkeegan.co.uk/index.htm**. Click Chapter 2 'Cognitive Psychology: Memory' and print off the crossword for homework.

4   Go to the Higher Psychology Learning Suite at **www.gerardkeegan.co.uk/index.htm**. Click Chapter 2 'Cognitive Psychology: Memory' and do the online interactive quiz.

GLOSSARY

Attention: Our cognitive ability *to attend to one thing at a time, or all things all the time* (Keegan, 2003). The former concerns focused attention, the latter divided attention. Focused attention is the kind of attention we use when we *actively* attend to something. It is our ability to attend to one thing to the exclusion of everything else. Focused attention is physiologically tiring. Our more natural attentional state is divided attention. This is our ability to attend simultaneously to lots of things. We switch from divided attention to focused attention all the time.

Classical conditioning: Made famous by the Russian animal physiologist Ivan Pavlov (1849-1936) classical conditioning is learning stimulus–response units of behaviour as a result of association. If we want to make a bus stop, we learn to stick out our hand. See www.gerardkeegan.co.uk/index.htm

Cognitions: Another name for our mediational or information processes of perception, attention, language, memory and thinking.

Computer analogy, the: The computer analogy illustrates why we think, feel, and behave as we do. The cognitive approach likens the workings of our mind to a computer. Input is what our senses pick up about stimuli in our world (S). This information is then relayed to our brain. Here it is further processed using our cognitions of perception, attention, language, memory, and thinking (X). We then respond towards the stimulus/stimuli in terms of our behaviour, or output (R). Perception, attention, language, memory and thinking are then the mediational processes that come between stimulus and response [S->(X)->R]. As a consequence the cognitive approach believes that we are active processors of information. Not passive learners as the behaviourist approach suggests.

Input	→	Processor	→	Output
S	→	(X)	→	R
Stimulus		Mediational process		Response

(X) = Our active information processes of perception, attention, language, memory, and thinking that come between stimulus and response.

Dependent variable: The name given to the variable in experimental research that measures/observes any change in animal or human thoughts, feelings or behaviours as a result of their exposure to the independent variable. As a consequence we can discover if the change or manipulation of an independent variable has caused, or had an effect on how we think, feel, or behave; this change being measured as the dependent variable.

Deterministic: Another criticism of behaviourism is that it is deterministic. This means the behaviourist approach believes we passively respond to stimuli in our environment. We have little free will, or exercise of control over our environment, or the objects, events, and people within it. Not so!

Ecological validity: A criticism often levied at the cognitive approach in psychology is that it is accused of lacking in ecological validity. This is because it often uses the laboratory experiment in research. Laboratory experiments can often be accused of lacking in ecological validity as they do not reflect a real-life situation. This is a problem for psychology in that it is a subject interested in our real-life everyday behaviours. Lab experiments by their very nature often get human participants behaving in an abnormal manner. This leads to distorted data, and thus weak psychological conclusions.

Empirical data: Objective, factual data such as a count or measure of something we experience.

Gestalten: Innate abilities that help us make sense of our world. Koffka, Kohler and Wertheimer, the founders of the long gone gestalt school of psychology, first identified them around 1910 in Germany with their Laws of Pragnänz (laws of perceptual grouping). They said we have a natural ability to tidy up a stimulus in terms of 'wholeness' to understand it better. Particular gestalten include proximity, similarity, continuity, closure, texture and common fate. Visit www.gerardkeegan.co.uk/index.htm/ glossary/gloss_g.htm#gestalten and find out more.

Independent variable: The variable (thought, feeling, behaviour) a psychologist changes or manipulates when using the experimental method of research. This is to try and discover a cause-effect relationship with the dependent variable.

Information processes: Name used to describe our cognitions of perception, attention, language, memory, and thinking. Cognitions are what make us uniquely human, and are the workings of the mind. Our information processes come between stimuli in our environment, and our response(s) to it. Our cognitions, individually and collectively, actively process stimulus information. They thus help us make appropriate behavioural responses to our world. See the computer analogy.

Language: Our ability to communicate.

Mechanistic: A criticism of behaviourism, mechanistic means we merely respond to our environment, having little control over it. Behaviourism favours an ABC model of behaviour viz. *Antecedent -> Behaviour -> Consequences*

Memory: The cognition that helps us to organise, store, retrieve, and recognise information about our world. Input to memory is called encoding, and is done on the basis of its content (viz. acoustic encoding, visual encoding, semantic encoding). We store memories in short-term memory (STM) and long-term memory (LTM). Types of memory include episodic memory, our autobiographical memory; and semantic memory, which is our general knowledge about our world. Semantic memory is where all your knowledge about psychology should be!

Operant conditioning: Idea progressed by American psychologist B.F. Skinner (1904–1990) who said learning is influenced by reward or unpleasant consequence. This is known as reinforcement. Positive reinforcement, or reward, should encourage the repetition of behaviour. Negative reinforcement, or unpleasant consequence, strengthens behaviours that result in their removal or avoidance.

Past experience: Individual past experience is important to the difference between our sensation of a stimulus and our perception, or understanding, of it. When two individuals come across a stimulus they both sense it in the same way. They will perceive it differently however as a result of their past experience of it. Two young people seeing a police officer visually sense the same person, but may perceive and react to him/her differently. Why? Past experience. One may have never been in trouble, the other a regular in police custody.

Perception: An active information process, which allows us to *organise*, *interpret*, and ultimately act upon or behave towards sensory information coming to us from our outside world. Perception is different from sensation. We may all sense the same stimulus, but our individual perception of it can be different. This is a consequence of our perception, where our senses, gestalten, and past experience of the stimulus combine. What makes the difference between what we sense, sensation, and perception is *past experience*.

Senses: We have at least six senses. These are touch, smell, taste, sight, hearing and balance. *Touch* is our tactile sense. *Smell* our olfactory sense. *Taste* our gustatory sense. *Sight* our visual sense. *Hearing* our auditory sense, and *balance*, which is our kinaesthetic sense. Our kinaesthetic sense is a result of our visual, auditory, and tactile senses working together. Each sense has a particular accessory structure equipped with special transducer cells, which convert the incoming energy of what we touch (pressure), see (light), hear (sound) etc. into electrical, or electrochemical energy. Electrical/electrochemical energy is the only type of energy our bodies can understand at an internal level. This is then sent to particular parts of our brain associated with each sense. Here the sensation is further organised, analysed and acted upon. For example what we visually sense hits our retina in terms of light energy. This is converted into neural signals (electrochemical pulses) that leave the back of each of our eyes via each optic nerve. Eventually this information arrives at our visual cortex, a part of our brain just above our neck. Here the degree and intensity of electrochemical signal is compared to previous input in visual memory. We then put meaning on what it is we have visually sensed. Individual experience makes the difference between sensation, or what our senses pick up, and perception, the *meaning* on we put on what it is our senses pick up.

Thinking: Our ability to problem-solve, and is a 'whole brain process.'

CHAPTER THREE

Developmental Psychology: Early Socialisation

BY THE END OF THIS CHAPTER YOU SHOULD BE ABLE TO:

● Demonstrate a knowledge and understanding of early socialisation

● Analyse and evaluate early socialisation

Early socialisation is the study of certain important influences from infancy and early childhood that help us understand our later emotional and cognitive development.

As previously, let us first examine the topic of *early socialisation* in its parent domain, developmental psychology.

What is developmental psychology?

Developmental psychology is the branch of psychology that studies psychological changes that happen to us during our lifetime.

Developmental psychology is the area in psychology that examines changes that happen to us from pre-birth to death, and what these may mean for us.

These changes: *which occur at different ages and stages throughout our lifetime*: are *continuous* and *progressive,* and fall into the following four categories: physical, cognitive, social and emotional

" *What do we study in developmental psychology?"*

Physical development concerns the major changes to, and development of, our body's **anatomy** (bodily

structure), and **physiology** (bodily processes) during our life.

Developmental psychology studies how these physical developments influence how we think, feel and behave as we age. What they find out about our physical development is **universal** in its application.

This is because, with some slight variation, we all physically develop at approximately the same age the world over.

Cognitive development concerns the study of perception, attention, language, memory and thinking (or problem-solving). As we read in Chapter Two these are called our *mediational, cognitive, or information processes.*

An investigation of cognitive development in developmental psychology almost exclusively concerns the growth and development of our thinking ability.

Social development is enquiry into what influences our development as social beings.

Here, as we shall see, developmental psychology looks at **socialisation**. Note also that **sociability**; child-rearing practices, moral development, groups and **peer group** influences etc. are also significant to social development.

Emotional development, which is closely related to our social development, concerns the nature of the

attachments we form with others, our temperament, our personality, what motivates us to aggression, our identity and our search for meaning in life.

Physical, cognitive, social, and emotional changes should not be seen as separate and distinct from each other in developmental psychology. They are interdependent in that there is much overlap. Change in one area often leads to change in another. Physical changes in infancy impact on cognitive development; physical changes in adolescence impact on social development; physical changes in adulthood impact on emotional development, and so on.

The lifespan approach

The study of continuing and progressive changes in the above four areas is called lifespan development theory or the **lifespan approach**.

The German psychologist Baltes first discussed the lifespan approach in 1980.

Baltes *et al.* (1980) divide the human lifespan into stages. Thus developmental psychology identifies important age-stages across the human lifespan as:

- **Conception to birth**: often referred to as the **prenatal stage** of development
- **Infancy**: often referred to as the **neonatal stage** of development
- Childhood
- Adolescence
- Adulthood
- Old age

Particular age-stages sometimes emphasise one aspect of development and change over another. So developmental investigation at the prenatal stage almost exclusively concerns the physical or biological changes a foetus will undergo during pregnancy.

Infancy

Similarly investigation of infants during the neonatal stage places more emphases on physical and cognitive development, rather than on social or emotional factors.

Childhood

Alternatively the period we call childhood has developmental psychologists look at our social, moral and intellectual development.

Adolescence

Adolescence sees us study the emotional development and social behaviours of teenagers. This is related to the great physical and cognitive changes a young person experiences during this time.

Adulthood and old age

Adulthood and old age are concerned with physical and cognitive development and change, personality and social development.

The lifespan approach: three underlying assumptions

The *lifespan approach* is different from other 'approaches' in psychology, such as psychoanalysis or behaviourism. This is because the lifespan approach does not favour any particular psychological theory, or theorist.

However the lifespan approach *does* make certain assumptions about human development.

Biological maturation

The first assumption made by the lifespan approach is that biological **maturation**, as determined by our **genetics**, must take place before any physical, and then cognitive, social, and emotional changes occur for us.

Sequence

The second assumption held by the lifespan approach is that we all experience the same sequence of physical, cognitive, social and emotional change and development over our lifetime.

Environment

The third and final assumption made by the lifespan approach is that our **environment** helps shape these physical, cognitive, social, and emotional changes

Biological influences on development

As it states above, a major assumption made in developmental psychology concerns biological maturation.

Biological maturation is driven by our genetics. Biological maturation must occur before other physical, cognitive, social and/or emotional changes take place for us.

So what is meant by genetics and biological maturation?

Genetics

Genetics is the study of inherited biological characteristics. In human terms these inherited biological characteristics are got from our mother and father.

Inherited biological characteristics account for the colour of our eyes, our hair, and our height and body shape. Genetics have been found to also influence our intelligence, personality and physical and mental health.

Our genetics further determine our physical development during the course of our life. Genetics thus affect our body's anatomy (physical structure), and physiology, (bodily functions). A good example of the influence genetics have over our physical development would be puberty.

The study of developmental psychology tells us that genetics are crucial to biological maturation (physical/bodily aging) that can help or hinder cognitive, social and emotional development as we grow.

> **Puberty**
>
> A sequence of genetically driven events where a child becomes a young adult. Puberty is characterised by secretions of hormones, development of secondary sexual characteristics, reproductive functions, and growth spurts.

An example of a genetic disorder is where an infant has an extra chromosome 21, resulting in Down's syndrome. Another is phenylketonuria or PKU. PKU is an inherited genetic disorder affecting body chemistry that, if untreated, can cause mental retardation.

Chromosomes

A chromosome is a threadlike structure found at the centre or nucleus of all cells. All species have a set number of chromosomes. In the case of humans it is 46.

This is because the normal human baby inherits 23 pairs of chromosomes from their male and female biological parents. The 23rd pairing determines a baby's sex. During fertilisation when male chromosomes in the sperm combine with female chromosomes in the ovum, an XX 23rd pairing will produce a female baby, and an XY, a male.

Chromosomes contain genes, essential to building a molecule called protein. Our body is constructed of proteins.

It is estimated that each chromosome contains from 10,000 to 20,000 genes. A gene carries biological information in the form of **deoxyribonucleic acid** – DNA – to build the developing organism.

DNA

DNA contains the biological instructions to form cells necessary for any living organism to develop, grow, and function.

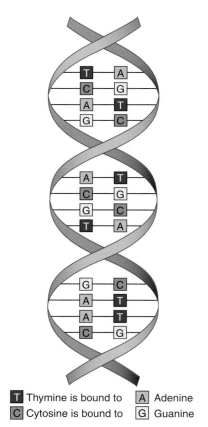

T Thymine is bound to   A Adenine
C Cytosine is bound to   G Guanine

Figure 3.1 DNA

DNA carries the body's protein-building instructions in a code, made from a four-letter string: A, T, C and G.

These initials stand for four nucleotide bases, adenine, thymine, cytosine and guanine. Each rung in our DNA chain consists of these four bases, with particular bases always pairing with another: A with T, C with G, T with A, and G with C. The order of pairings differs from rung to rung. What sequence these letters take forms our genetic code.

Until very recently it was thought that we share 99.9 per cent of the same genetic code, and that it was the 0.1 per cent difference in our genetic code that made uniquely different from one another. However Canadian geneticist Steven Scherer has discovered as much as a ten per cent genetic variation in the human genome (Scherer, 2006). There could be anything up to a 30-million-nucleotide difference between one individual and the next.

While this may seem a lot one should note that it is estimated that the human body, or genome, consists of 3,000,000,000 nucleotide base pairs!

Genotype

Our genetic inheritance or genotype is a mixture of both our biological parents' genes. Genotype is a sort of blueprint or plan of what we will be like as we develop and grow. *Genotype is our inherited genetic potential.* As said earlier genotype accounts for the colour of our eyes, hair, and height and body shape.

Genotype is also an important factor regards our physical and mental health, intelligence, and to some extent our personality. Whether you attain your genetic potential or genotype depends on your environment.

Our biological predispositions, or genetic potential, represent the influence of *nature*, and our environment represents *nurture*. The influence of genetics and environment in psychology is called the nature–nurture, or nativist–empiricist debate.

The interaction of genotype and environment produces **phenotype**. We shall look at the influence of environment on genotype shortly.

> **Genotype** is our genetic potential when born.
>
> **Phenotype** is what this genetic potential becomes.
>
> This is largely due to the influence of our environment.

Biological maturation and developmental sequencing

Biological maturation is the process of physical growth or physical ageing. Biological maturation starts at conception and lasts a lifetime.

All normal human foetuses develop at the same rate. We all learn to manipulate our hands and fingers; to move (or *orientate*) our heads; to crawl and to walk at approximately the same time. This progressive rate of development is the same for all children, and is genetically determined.

It is important to note that we can only learn to adapt our behaviour when we are maturationally, or biologically, ready to do so. This is evident in infants about one year old, who can crawl like champions and stand up with support; but because of their body shape cannot yet walk. Quite simply, their legs have not yet straightened enough to support upper body weight. Walking can only occur when the infant is physically – or maturationally – ready.

Human beings do not mature very quickly. For the first few years of life we are the most helpless of all species. Almost 25 per cent of our lives are spent as an immature child. No other animal spends as long preparing for adulthood as we do.

The age stage or non-age-stage question

Developmental psychology wants to discover what, and whether, physical, cognitive, social and emotional changes are related to particular age-related stages in our life; or if certain developmental changes are non-age-stage related.

This is because developmental psychology has seen some debate as to whether language; personality; moral values; intelligence etc. are developed at, and through, fixed and identifiable age stages, or whether they develop continuously across the human lifespan.

Language: an age-stage example

Where certain skills, abilities, or behaviours *do* develop during a particular age-stage we look for certain boundaries to differentiate its development.

This differentiation is evident in, for example, the development of language in infancy where:

Each phase of an emerging skill or ability displays a particular kind of behaviour not found previously.

Infants between the ages of about three and five weeks start to coo, producing vowel-like sounds (e.g., 'ooooh') over and over again. Between four and six months of age, infants start to babble.

Babbling consists of combinations of vowels and consonants that seem to lack meaning. The babbling of infants up to about six months of age is similar in all parts of the world. Babbling is universal.

Most interestingly babbling is evident in hearing impaired infants, as well as hearing ones. However, by about eight months of age, hearing infants begin to articulate language they have heard around them.

The kind of behaviour (and associated thinking) that goes with each phase of an emerging skill or ability is different.

At around eight months the developing infant begins to associate particular sounds with particular objects in their environment. As a consequence they begin to develop specific vocabulary e.g. *daddy, mummy, teddy* etc.

They realise that particular sounds have a particular meaning. Particular sounds represent things in their environment. As this develops they acquire more words that allow even more meaningful communication with those around them. They begin ask questions and can state preferences. They could not do this earlier in life.

All children go through similar phases of skill or ability development, in the same order, at approximately the same age, and generally at the same rate.

The development of language clearly demonstrates this. We can identify when particular phases in the development of language occurs during infancy.

This *universal* sequence of language development is the same for all children. It is this combination of *mental activity, and actual behaviour* that is the subject matter of developmental psychology.

The development of language: an age-stage-related process	
Identified behaviour	**Identified common age**
Babbling	Four months to one year
Using words	One year to eighteen months
Using simple sentences	Eighteen months onwards

Table 3.1 Language: An age-stage related process

The lifespan approach: conclusion

When taking a lifespan approach in developmental psychology we investigate what type or kind of physical, cognitive, social and/or emotional development is occurring, when; and whether it is age-stage related, or develops gradually across the human lifecycle.

ONLINE INTERACTIVES

Language development starts in the womb. Visit Baby Talk at **http://babyparenting.about.com/od/childdevelopment/a/babytalk.htm** to discover more.

A direct Link is available in the Chapter 3 section of Higher Psychology Learning Suite at **www.gerardkeegan.co.uk**

Nature–nurture

Nature–nurture, or the influence of genetics, environment, or both genetics *and* environment is evident in many areas of developmental psychology.

Take for example language, the development of which is understood in terms of the interaction of nature and nurture.

The famous psycholinguist Noam Chomsky thinks language is determined by our biology. On the other hand the renowned behaviourist B.F. Skinner believed we acquire language in terms of learning in environment.

As you should remember from Chapter One the degree to which nature, our innate abilities, and/or nurture, experiences in our environment, explain why we think, feel and behave as we do is known as the nature–nurture debate.

Also known as the heredity–environment, or nativist–empiricist debate, the influence of heredity, environment, and their interface are studied in many areas of psychology.

Interactionism

Consequently the interface of nature and nurture is called **interactionism**. An interactionist is someone who believes that *both* nature *and* nurture contribute to an understanding of our thoughts, feelings and behaviours.

The interactionist view is particularly relevant in developmental psychology when we look at such things as language, personality, cognitive development etc. Each to some degree can be explained iin terms of our biology interacting with our environment. The theme of nature–nurture is constant throughout developmental psychology. Developmental psychologists have a great interest in the environmental factors that influence genotype to produce phenotype.

This is because human development is largely explained in terms of both biological and social factors.

ONLINE INTERACTIVES

Read 'The Magic School Bus: From Genes To Traits: How Genotype Affects Phenotype' at:

www.pkblogs.com/themagicschoolbus/2006/ 05/from-genes-to-traits-how-genotype.html

A direct link is available in the Chapter Three section of Higher Psychology Learning Suite at **www.gerardkeegan.co.uk/index.htm**

Environmental influences

Three key environmental factors that influence our development are our family, our school and our culture.

Family

In Western culture, a family is determined as being a group of people affiliated through blood, or legal ties such as marriage or adoption.

A vast body of psychological research exists that emphasises the importance of the family. How a family, and particularly parents, behave towards their offspring affects almost every aspect of their development. A child's physical, cognitive, social and emotional development can be helped or hindered due to family relationships, situations, and circumstance.

School

A school is an educational institution where young people learn. Mostly all children in Scotland are legally obliged to attend school between the ages of five and sixteen.

Our school experience also help shape our physical, cognitive, social and emotional development. As mine did at Holyrood Secondary in Glasgow! (*Hoc Vince.*)

Culture

A culture is taken to be a particular society at a particular time and place.

A culture helps transmit common knowledge and values that are shared by all in a society. Culture influences our general and individual behaviours, values, attitudes, beliefs, morals etc. This process is known as **socialisation**.

Socialisation is the process where the individual learns to conform to the moral standards, codes of conduct, role expectations etc. of a specific society.

Our family and our school play an important role in our socialisation, as do cultural institutions and organisations such as the mass media, religion, the Scottish Government, Westminster parliament etc.

INTERACTIVES

Give as many examples as you can of how family environment can influence a child's physical, cognitive, social and emotional development.

It is to the psychological process, influence, and outcome of **early socialisation** that we now turn.

Early socialisation

Early socialisation is the study of important influences from infancy and early childhood that help us understand a person's later emotional and cognitive development.

> **Infancy** is a period of time from birth to age two.
>
> **Childhood** refers to a period of time from age two to adolescence.

Accordingly 'early socialisation' sees developmental psychology look at **sociability** and **attachment**.

As we shall discover *sociability* is the building block to our personality; while *attachment* concerns the bonds and relationships we have with others around us.

Both sociability and attachment are related to one another. Both are important developmental issues during infancy and early childhood, the outcomes of which can last a lifetime.

Temperament

Sociability refers to one of three dimensions of temperament, the other two being emotionality and activity. All are present within us at birth and are inherited. In order to understand sociability, we must first look at 'temperament'.

Our *temperament* is our inner disposition or nature, and is innate to us all. It is the genetically based part of our personality we have when born. Whatever temperament we have when we come into the world influences the development of our personality.

The study of temperament can be traced back to the ancient Greeks. In 190 AD the physician Galen identified four humours, or personality types found within the Greek population. Galen thought we behaved the way we do because of one of four bodily fluids in our body: blood, phlegm, black bile and yellow bile. An excess of one of these fluids or humours gave rise to a particular temperament or general personality. Thus according to Galen, excess blood would lead to a sanguine personality; excess phlegm – a phlegmatic personality; excess black bile – a melancholic personality, or excess yellow bile – a choleric personality.

Galen's personality temperaments live on today in Eysenck's Personality Inventory (EPI). The EPI has four personality types into which we all fit.

Eysenck's stable extrovert reflects the traits of Galen's sanguine personality; his unstable extrovert, Galen's choleric traits; his unstable introvert, Galen's melancholic traits and his stable introvert, Galen's phlegmatic personality traits.

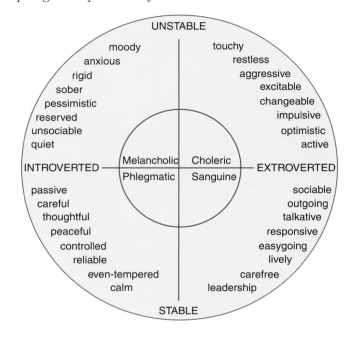

Figure 3.2 Dimensions of personality (from Eysenck, 1965)

Galen's four humours are also similar to Keirsey's four temperaments of artisan, idealist, guardian, or rational. To discover which of these four temperaments you exhibit do the Interactive below.

ONLINE INTERACTIVES

To discover what type of temperament and general personality type you are please complete the online questionnaire at:

http://www.keirsey.com/sorter/register.aspx

A direct link is available in the Chapter Three section of Higher Psychology Learning Suite at **www.gerardkeegan.co.uk/index.htm**

Buss and Plomin

In 1984 Buss and Plomin conducted a study into temperaments, which they believe indicate early personality traits.

Avoiding the bodily fluid model of personality(!), Buss and Plomin alternatively identified **sociability** as an important temperament.

In addition, and as alluded to above, they discovered **emotionality** and **activity** as other dimensions to temperament evident in infancy, which are also influential on the developing personality.

Buss and Plomin tell us that someone who has an infant temperament high on emotionality will have a tendency to become strongly aroused in upsetting situations.

This would be evident in the amount of distress, anger or fear they showed.

Alternatively someone who has a high-energy output in infancy will have a temperament or disposition to be active.

They are a personality who would prefer to play tennis rather than chess etc.

Sociability

Sociability refers to the degree to which we as individuals need and prefer to be with others.

In their investigation into sociability Plomin and Rowe (1979) measured sociable behaviours shown by 21-month-old male and female monozygotic and dizygotic twins.

> **Mz** means monozygotic (identical) twins derived from the one egg.
>
> **Dz** means dizygotic (non-identical) twins derived from two separate eggs.

Four of these sociable behaviours were the degree to which the **Mz** and **Dz** twin pairs looked at a stranger, approached a stranger, showed proximity or nearness to a stranger, and vocalized or talked to a stranger.

Plomin and Rowe (1979) discovered that Mz or identical twins showed a far higher degree of similar sociability than Dz or non-identical twins. This implies that temperaments such as sociability are genetically inherited.

While this study can be criticised, as Plomin and Rowe themselves say, what is interesting is the similar sociability behaviour shown by identical twin pairs. If one Mz twin demonstrated a high degree of sociability, so did the other. If one demonstrated a low degree of sociability so did the other etc. This was in contrast to the non-identical pairs who did not behave as consistently as each other.

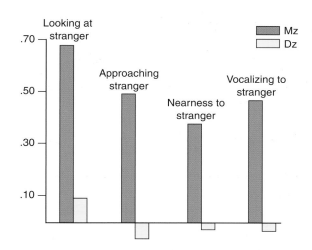

Figure 3.3 Sociability of Mz and Dz twin pairs (Plomin and Rowe, 1979)

Sociability and genetic heritability

What Plomin and Rowe's Mz twins' data illustrates is known as the **heritability coefficient**. This is the degree of *sameness* shown in thoughts, feelings and behaviours thought due to genetic similarity, rather then environment.

A high heritability coefficient, of for example 0.70 regards both Mz twins looking at a stranger, allowed Plomin and Rowe (1979) to conclude that the degree of sociability we exhibit is genetically inherited.

> INTERACTIVES
>
> Why do the high heritability coefficients found by Plomin and Rowe (1979) help us to conclude that sociability is genetically inherited?

Sociability: a prerequisite to attachment

Sociability is innate. It is thought that the uterine environment influences sociability. Consequently what the foetus is exposed to in its uterine environment during pregnancy will affect its later social development as a human being.

This social side to being human is our inbuilt need to want, and to be with others. Sociability is important in that it helps us build these relationships with others. These interactions nurture our biological, cognitive, social and emotional development.

A baby who has a sociable temperament is more likely to form a secure attachment, with its subsequent benefits, rather than a baby who is not as sociable. Sociability is thus a *prerequisite* to attachment. As sociability is obvious from birth, the process of attachment can be said to begin at conception.

Sociability: nature and nurture

Each person's individual nature and nurture influences the *degree* of sociability they have.

From infancy one individual may be naturally shy and reserved, while another is friendly and open. Each will be brought up in a particular environment, their experience in which will further influence how sociable they are. Sociability, and personality, is a dance between *nature* and *nurture*.

Thus our social experiences, and what we learn as a result, are influential in determining our sociability towards other people. If someone is shyer than others in early infancy, and this is continually commented upon negatively, this person may very well grow up showing introverted adult personality traits later on in life (Kagan, 1989).

> **Introversion** is 'the state of or tendency toward being wholly or predominantly concerned with and interested in one's own mental life' (Merriam Webster Dictionary).
>
> Introverts are quiet, low key, deliberate, and relatively non-engaged in social situations.
>
> They take pleasure in solitary activities such as reading, writing, watching movies, inventing, and designing.
>
> An introverted person is likely to enjoy being alone rather than with large groups of people.
>
> They enjoy one-to-one, or one-to-few interactions with close friends.

Sociability suggests we all share a need for others, but we do not all share the same *degree* of need for others. Thus some people who are very outgoing will be most at home being in the company of others. Whereas some will be equally as happy just being part of the group, or not part of any particular group at all. At the same time others will be content being on their own, thinking or reading to themselves.

These behaviours indicate the degree of need each of us has towards being sociable with others.

Sociability or 'a child's willingness to engage others in social interaction, and to seek their attention or approval' (Schaffer, 1989) is, as we shall see, an important foundation to attachment.

Attachment

According to Ainsworth (1989) an attachment is an affectional bond involving 'a relatively long-enduring tie in which the partner is important as a unique individual and is interchangeable with none other.'

> **Who can be a primary caregiver?**
>
> In developmental psychology a primary caregiver is anyone who nurtures or cares for an infant, child or adolescent. A primary caregiver may also be involved in the care of an adult who is infirm or incapacitated
>
> A primary caregiver can be mum, dad, aunt, uncle, grandmother, grandfather, elder brother, sister, foster parent etc.

Kagan *et al.* (1978) suggest attachment to be 'an intense affectional relationship that is specific to two people, that endures over time, and in which prolonged separation from the partner is accompanied by stress and sorrow.'

Alternatively, Schaffer (1993) says attachments are the 'close emotional bonds that form between two people, characterised by mutual affection and a desire to maintain proximity.' Proximity refers to closeness.

While attachments can arise between two people at any time, developmental psychology is particularly interested in attachment in early infancy.

Attachment in early infancy usually occurs between a baby and its mother. It is important to note that in the absence of a mother an infant can form a close attachment to any **primary caregiver**.

Whomever a baby forms an attachment with, the quality of the attachment bond formed is of crucial importance to its later social and emotional development.

ONLINE INTERACTIVES

Read 'What is attachment' at:

www.toddlertime.com/dx/rad/what-is-attachment.htm

and then answer the following questions:

1   Define 'attachment'.

2   Why, in a developmental sense, is attachment important?

3   Identify three causes of attachment problems in infancy.

4   Describe and explain three behaviours associated with problematic attachment.

Fantz and face recognition

In 1961, developmental psychologist Robert Fantz published some fascinating research into infant form perception. Fantz showed infants aged between four days and five months pairs of face-shaped discs. Using pictures of realistic faces, scrambled faces, and blank faces he measured the amount of time each infant spent fixating on each type of face.

This style of research is known as the preference method. The preference method is where a researcher observes and measures which of two stimuli is looked at most. Preference here is measured in terms of the time a baby spent looking at one face over another. This would indicate their ability to discriminate between them.

INTERACTIVES

Why do you think a baby's early ability to identify human faces is important?

Fantz (1961) discovered that infants of all ages looked most at the realistic face and least at the blank face. This suggests that an infant's ability to recognise human faces is either innate or learned shortly after birth.

Whatever the reason behind a baby's ability to recognise human faces, this preference is significant in the development of an attachment to a primary caregiver.

INTERACTIVES

Why did Fantz have to conclude the possibility that face recognition could be learned?

Early attachment behaviours

In 1980 Macoby identified four behavioural characteristics of attachment shown by infants and toddlers.

➤ An obvious desire to be near the primary caregiver.

➤ Distress when separated from the primary caregiver.

➤ Joy on being reunited with the primary caregiver.

➤ Visible behaviours directed towards the primary caregiver.

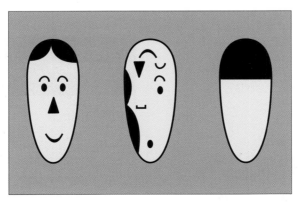

Figure 3.4 Types of faces used by Fantz (1961) in his study of infant form perception

At birth general attachment behaviours, or behaviours indicative of wanting others, include crying, eye contact, grasping, and being comforted. Reciprocal attachment behaviours that are evident from two to three months onwards include arm waving, smiling back, and reaching out to others.

As well as showing a specific recognition and preference for human faces (Fantz, 1961), by three months of age babies also respond to human sounds.

Stern (1977) identifies **mutual reciprocity** in mother–infant verbal interactions. *Mutual reciprocity* is noticeable when a mother talks to her infant. The infant looks intently at her, makes noises and then stops, as if inviting her to continue talking. Mutual reciprocity is where it appears a two-way conversation is taking place.

From birth to three months, infants will behaviourally respond in the same way to anyone showing an interest in them. From three months onwards they will begin to behaviourally discriminate, and by six or seven months they will show a special preference for one or two people. This should be noticeable in their behaviours. This is because attachment in infancy is a strong, long lasting and close emotional bond with a primary caregiver, which causes the baby distress when broken.

But how do we know?

How do attachments develop?

In an attempt to generate empirical evidence regards attachment, and attachment behaviours, Schaffer and Emerson (1964) carried out a **longitudinal study** in Glasgow of 58 babies from five weeks to 23 weeks of age through interviews, dairies, and naturalistic observation of mostly mother–infant interactions.

They visited the babies in their homes at monthly intervals during the first year and then again at eighteen months. The babies' attachment to their mothers was measured on the basis of *social referencing*, and '*separation upset*', as illustrated by fear of strangers and separation anxiety.

> **Naturalistic observation** involves observing participants' behaviours in their natural environment without attempting to influence or control it.

Social referencing

Social referencing was the degree to which the infant looked to the person to whom they were attached to see how he or she responded to something new. They then took their cue from them regards how to react to the new situation. Social referencing is very obvious in babies, toddlers and young children.

Separation upset

Fear of strangers concerned the infant's response to the arrival of a stranger, whether or not their mother was present. Separation anxiety was the amount of distress shown by the infant when separated from their mother, and the degree of comfort and pleasure shown when they were reunited.

Attachment and sensitive responsiveness

Schaffer and Emerson (1964) discovered that infants are more likely to form attachments with people who respond *sensitively* to them. Interacting with babies is a learned skill, rather then something innate that only mothers possess. The implication is that fathers can acquire these skills just as mothers do.

Schaffer and Emerson also found that the strength of an attachment is due to the amount of 'sensitive responsiveness' that the carer shows to the infant, rather than the amount of time spent with the infant.

Specific attachments are formed at around seven months. After the first attachment has been created infants develop 'multiple attachments' with others. Schaffer and Emerson found that several of the infants were as attached to their fathers as to their mothers. Some, too, had developed an attachment to the father but not to the mother, even though it was the mother who was looking after them most of the time.

In all instances of father attachment it was the father who had responded most sensitively to the baby.

Age/stage of attachment	Percentage of babies attached to more than one person
Initial stage	17
Four months later	50
At eighteen months	87

Table 3.2 Schaffer and Emerson (1964)

Thus, as well as identifying specific ages and stages in the development of attachment behaviours Schaffer and Emerson (1964) emphasise that the infant–mother attachment is not the only attachment to develop early on.

The fact that they also highlight the importance of sensitivity shown by the carer in the development of an infant attachment makes this a landmark study.

STUDY

Schaffer, H.R. and Emerson, P.E. 'The development of attachment in infancy'. *Monographs of the Society for Research in Child Development*, 1964, no.94.

Aim: To investigate ages and stages in the development of infant attachments, and to discover to whom and how these attachments are made.

Method: Large-scale, longitudinal study in Glasgow investigating 58 infants over two years using interviews, diaries and naturalistic observation.

Procedure: Researchers observed infants once a month for one year, then again at eighteen months. Mothers were also asked to keep 'diary-style' records. Attachments were measured in two ways. Separation anxiety/protest, which was measured naturalistically e.g. what did the baby do when left alone, being babysat, being put to bed, left in pram outside house, or shops etc. Stranger anxiety where in playing the role of a stranger the researcher(s) approached the infant and observed their behaviour.

Results: Schaffer and Emerson discovered specific ages and stages in the development of attachment behaviours in infants.

The **asocial stage** from 0–6 weeks saw no specific attachments being formed, or associated attachment behaviours evident.

The **indiscriminate attachment stage** from six weeks to six months saw the babies attaching indiscriminately to whoever was interacting with them. They seemed to enjoy being held by anyone and protested when put down.

The **specific attachment stage** from seven months to one year sees the emergence of one specific attachment, usually to the mother. Infants' show a demonstrative fear of strangers, and also separation anxiety when mother/primary caregiver is absent. This lasts from between three to four months. 50 per cent of the Schaffer and Emerson sample showed specific attachment behaviours at between six and eight months of age. By the end of the specific attachment phase 65 per cent of the infants were deemed attached to their mother, 30 per cent to the mother and another person, and three per cent were attached to the father alone.

The **multiple attachment stage**, where from one-year-old infants begin to show attachment behaviours towards others important in their life. By eighteen months of age as few as thirteen per cent of the sample were exclusively attached to one person. 33 per cent were attached to five or more people.

Conclusion: Schaffer and Emerson confirmed that there are related ages and stages in the development of infant attachments. Further, in 39 per cent of cases it was a primary caregiver other than the mother who formed the most intense attachments. Thus the individual who shows the most sensitive responsiveness to a baby is the one to whom they attach most deeply.

Questions:

1   What were the aims of Schaffer and Emerson (1964)?

2   What method and procedure did they adopt?

3   What were their results?

4   What were the conclusions reached by Schaffer and Emerson (1964)?

Shaffer's phases in the development of attachments

In a retrospective on earlier work Schaffer (1996a) says the attachment process can be divided up into various phases.

The pre-attachment phase: birth to three months

From six weeks babies show preference for human beings over and above physical aspects of their environment. This was evident earlier when we looked at the work of Fantz (1961). Preferences are seen in behaviours such as nestling; gurgling and (social) smiling directed at people in their world.

The indiscriminate attachment phase: three to ten months

From three to ten months babies start to discriminate between familiar and unfamiliar people, becoming more animated and excited in the presence of those they have a previous knowledge about. The social smile previously directed at anybody has disappeared. They will allow strangers to pick up and cuddle them as long as this is done in a caring considerate manner.

The discriminate attachment phase: seven/eight/nine months

The beginnings of a specific attachment become evident from seven/eight months as seen in proximity behaviours to, and separation anxiety from the primary caregiver.

The discriminate attachment phase parallels the onset of object permanence in babies.

Object permanence is the dawning realisation by infants that objects, events, people etc. do still exist even when they cannot directly see or experience them.

The multiple-attachment phase: nine months plus.

This is the phase where strong additional attachments are made with other important caregivers e.g. dad, grandparents, siblings (brothers and sisters), and the developing peer group of other children. Proximity behaviours and separation/stranger anxiety begin to diminish. However the strongest attachment bond is still the mother, or primary caregiver.

Earlier explanations of attachment

Cupboard love theories

For the first half of the twentieth century, developmental psychology understood attachment on the basis of **'cupboard love'** theories.

Cupboard love theories involve an explanation of attachment from both a psychoanalytic and the behaviourist perspective.

The psychoanalytic view of attachment

Why the psychoanalytic and behaviourist explanations of attachment are called *cupboard love theories* are because they both concern food.

Freud, as we know, was the founding father of the psychoanalytic approach. He thought infants become attached to their mothers during the oral stage of personality development. When a mother breastfeeds her baby Freud thought her baby experiences '*oral gratification*', and thus a reduction in its instinctual drive to be fed.

> *The reason why the infant in arms wants to perceive the presence of its mother is only because it already knows that she satisfies all its needs without delay."*
>
> *(Freud, 1926)*

Freud surmised, wrongly as it happens, that healthy attachments come about due to instinctual needs. For him, being breastfed satisfies the baby's need for food, security and oral gratification.

The implication here is that the attachment bond can be frustrated when a baby does not get its oral stage needs satisfied, or if its oral needs are satisfied too much.

This can result in the development of what Freud called an **oral retentive personality**; later evident in the adolescent and adult nail biter, finger chewer, lip chewer, smoker etc.

To understand this better let us briefly look at the first stage of Freud's psychosexual theory of adult personality development.

Freud's psychosexual theory of adult personality development

The oral stage (birth to twelve months)

In the first year of life, a baby's mouth is the centre of its universe. Look at any baby's oral behaviour to confirm this! They are constantly putting things into their mouth and getting much satisfaction as a result.

Freud thought these oral behaviours come about because, when born, a psychic energy known as libido is centred on our mouth.

If you cast your mind back to Chapter Two you may remember that the id is the part of our personality that is present from birth. Libido fuels our id that then sees us engage in related behaviours to reduce instinctual needs.

As libido is initially centred in our mouth we thus see id-driven oral behaviours in babies such as sucking, biting and breastfeeding. The obvious satisfaction got by such oral activities is evidence of oral gratification demanded by libido.

Oral gratification sees a **drive reduction** in id driven behaviours, as instinctual needs, such as our essential desire to be fed, have been reduced.

Fixations

If an infant becomes stuck in the oral stage, because of too much or too little oral stimulation, Freud (1917) said they could grow up orally fixated. This is because 'early interactions set the pattern for later personality and social development.'

Thus, as suggested earlier, oral fixations are apparent in people who like to put things into their mouths, as seen in the smoker, the nail-biter, the finger-chewer, the lip-sucker etc.

Freud thought that oral fixations came about because of too much/too little breastfeeding when a baby. He would be very interested in the current fashion among young people for tongue piercing! He would say that this, and other oral behaviours, displayed an oral personality. Our oral fixations often surface when we are under stress. On leaving an exam hall the nail-biters have no fingernails left, while the student smoker reaches for a cigarette.

Freud was correct in his assumption that attachment is important regards later social and emotional development. However, his psychoanalytic view of attachment developing because of an infant's inner drive to satisfy an instinctual need to be fed has not been supported.

This will become obvious when we look at the work of Harry Harlow.

The behaviourist view of attachment

ONLINE INTERACTIVES

Read much more on Freud and the psychoanalytic approach. Visit:

www.gerardkeegan.co.uk/index.htm/resource /psychoanalytical.htm

A direct link is available in the Chapter Three section of the Higher Psychology Learning Suite at **www.gerardkeegan.co.uk/index.htm**

For different reasons behaviourists also see food as important in the attachment process.

To appreciate why, we must first look at how the behaviourist approach understands why we act or behave the way we do.

Learning theory

The behaviourist approach believes we *learn* to behave in response to our environment, either by **stimulus–response** association, or as a result of **reinforcement**.

For behaviourists, we learn or become *conditioned* to behave the way we do. They say we form learnt behaviours as a result of *associating* a particular *stimulus* with a particular *response*. Thus we learn that if we want a bus to stop, on seeing it, we stick out our hand.

All Behaviours are learned

It is important to realise that the behaviourist approach understands *all* our behaviours in terms of stimulus response learning.

The founding father of behaviourism J.B. Watson in the *Behaviourist Manifesto* of 1915 tells us that when born, we are **tabula rasa**, which means that our mind is like a blank slate. What we come to understand as our mind, and what is in it, for the behaviourist comes about as a consequence of learning in our environment.

All behaviour is learned. When born our mind is *tabula rasa*.

We learn how to behave in response to our environment, by forming stimulus–response (S–R) units of behaviour.

Behaviours can be 'unlearned' by breaking these previously formed, stimulus–response (S–R) connections.

What behaviourism discovered concerning stimulus–response learning in animals is equally applicable to human beings.

The mind is private and personal and consists of concepts difficult to study in a scientific way. An organism's observable outcomes – their behaviour – should therefore be the focus of study in psychology.

For psychology to be thought a true science, its theories need to be supported by empirical data obtained through the careful and controlled observation and measurement of behaviour in an experimental setting.

Table 3.3 Key points of the Behaviourist Manifesto, 'Psychology as the behaviourist views it' Watson (1915)

Behaviourism believes that we consist of learning experiences, called stimulus–response units (S–R) that we use, then and thereafter, to navigate our way through life.

Behaviourists consequently fall on the 'nurture', or empiricist, side of the nature–nurture debate, because for them it is our environment that makes us what we are. The influence of the environment on what we teach and learn led Watson (1925) to write:

> *Give me a dozen healthy infants ... and my own specified world to bring them up in and I'll guarantee to take any one at random and train him to become any type of specialist I might select – doctor, lawyer ... and yes even beggar man and thief."*

Reinforcement

Very often reinforcement helps in the formation of stimulus–response units of behaviour. Our behaviours can be encouraged by reinforcement. The importance of reinforcement in the learning process was first emphasised by Ivan Pavlov in his theory of **classical conditioning**, and then by BF Skinner in his theory of **operant conditioning**.

Classical conditioning

The beginnings of behaviourism are credited to the famous Russian Ivan Pavlov (1849–1936). Pavlov was an animal physiologist, who studied the reflex response of salivation in dogs. As a consequence of his research he gave to the behaviourist approach his theory of classical conditioning.

Classical conditioning means learning by association. For Pavlov, an organism learns to behave towards its environment because of stimulus–response associations. This had a profound effect on J.B. Watson in America and the subsequent development of behaviourism on a global scale.

Stimulus–response

Let us remind ourselves that a stimulus is any person, event or object, which causes us to respond to or behave towards it in some way.

According to the behaviourist approach, we act or behave as we do because we have formed stimulus–response units of learned behaviours. We behave, or respond to stimuli coming to us from our environment in terms of S–R learned units of behaviour formed from the time we are born. The behaviourist approach thus attempts to understand our behaviour from the point of view of stimulus response units of learned behaviour. One way these S–R units of behaviour come about is considered in the theory of classical conditioning, which concerns learning by association.

Learning by association: S–R

In his laboratory Pavlov noticed two things about his dogs' behaviours. The first was that when they were given food (a stimulus) they proceeded to salivate (a response), and second, that they often salivated in anticipation of getting fed. They seemed to know when they were to be fed, in that they salivated when they saw a light flashing above the locked door of the laboratory. It flashed, of course, to alert Pavlov to the keeper's arrival with their food. Up until then salivation was thought to be a reflex response in animal and human organisms that only occurs on the eating or smelling of food, not in its anticipation. His dogs had, however, learned to associate the light with the imminent arrival of food and being fed. Salivation in this instance was not a reflex, but a learned response by his dogs. Pavlov thought his dogs salivated because they had become conditioned to associate the light with the onset of food. It was from these observations that Pavlov set up an experiment to investigate learning by association. This work led to Pavlov's theory of classical conditioning, which rapidly caught up, and began to overshadow his earlier work on the physiology of dogs that was to win him the Nobel Prize for medicine and physiology in 1904.

'The experimental psychology and psychopathology of animals'

In 1903, at the 14th International Medical Congress in Madrid, Pavlov read a paper on 'The experimental psychology and psychopathology of animals'.

This laid down the underlying principles behind his theory of classical conditioning, which suggests that animals and humans learn to behave in response to their environment in terms of conditioned, or learned, reflex actions. These conditioned behaviours are called S–R units. A stimulus–response unit of learned behaviour, or conditioned reflex action, is the mechanism that explains why we behave the way we do when we encounter stimuli in our environment. Pavlov said

one way we react to our world is by associating a stimulus (S) with innate bodily reflexes (R). How we learn associated stimulus–response units of learned behaviour is illustrated below.

Pavlov's theory of classical conditioning

Ivan Pavlov's theory of classical conditioning (stimulus–response learning by association) uses some strange and unusual vocabulary.

In his classic experiment with his dogs, food is known as the *unconditional* stimulus, the US, and salivation, the *unconditional* response, or UR.

Unconditional means 'not learned' in that salivation is an innate reflex action found in dogs when food is presented to them. No learning is needed for this stimulus–response (S–R) link, so both stimulus and response are said to be unconditional. The tone of the bell is the *neutral* stimulus or NS. Dogs show no innate reflex reaction in response to a bell ringing.

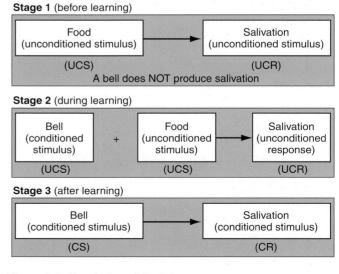

Figure 3.5 The apparatus used by Pavlov

Stage 1 (before learning)

Food (unconditioned stimulus)	→	Salivation (unconditioned stimulus)
(UCS)		(UCR)

A bell does NOT produce salivation

Stage 2 (during learning)

Bell (conditioned stimulus)	+	Food (unconditioned stimulus)	→	Salivation (unconditioned response)
(UCS)		(UCS)		(UCR)

Stage 3 (after learning)

Bell (conditioned stimulus)	→	Salivation (conditioned stimulus)
(CS)		(CR)

Figure 3.6 Classical conditioning

Pavlov (1927) wanted to find out if he could condition his dogs to salivate in response to a previously neutral stimulus of the tone of a bell. He set up his apparatus (see Figure 3.6) and in **Stage one** rang the neutral stimulus of the bell. The bell elicited no response from his dogs. He then presented the unconditional stimulus of food, and his dogs salivated (the unconditional response).

In **Stage two** he presented the bell (NS) and food (US) *contiguously*, or together in time. Known as the **law of temporal contiguity**, this simultaneous pairing of the NS of the bell with the US of the food saw the unconditional response (UR) of salivation.

In **Stage three** he rang the bell *only*. The now conditional stimulus of the bell resulted in the conditional (learned by association) reflex response of salivation.

In behaviourist terms when a NS and US occur together they can become associated with each other, until eventually the NS causes the UR, which is here salivation. When this happens, the NS becomes known as the learned, or conditional stimulus (CS), and the reflex action, the learned or conditional response (CR).

Pavlov discovered that a conditional stimulus could produce a desired conditioned (learned) reflex response. The implications of this are immense in that Pavlov's work showed that one way we learn to respond to stimuli in our environment is by classical conditioning, or learning by S–R association. Further, classical conditioning tells us it is possible to produce S–R units of learned behaviours by associating two previously unconnected variables. In Pavlov's experiment these were the stimulus of the bell and the response of salivation.

Classical conditioning is all about how a diverse range of previously neutral stimuli can come to trigger a reflex response in animal and humans.

Extinction

After a while Pavlov discovered his dogs stopped salivating in response to the bell ringing. The conditioned S–R learned behaviour of bell–salivation no longer occurred. Because they were no longer getting fed, the conditional response of salivation was *inhibited* by the non-appearance of the US of food. The dogs no longer salivated in response to the bell alone. Not responding after conditioning is called *extinction*.

Reinforcement

After extinction, to *resurrect* the conditioned S–R response of bell–salivation Pavlov had to repeat Stage two of the classical conditioning process. He found the occasional re-occurrence of bell (NS) and food (US) together, brought back the conditioned response of salivation to the bell alone (CS). In order to avoid extinction Pavlov found that **reinforcement**, the occasional representation of the NS and US together, was necessary. In classical conditioning such reinforcement makes a learned association between a stimulus and a response more permanent.

Spontaneous recovery

Pavlov discovered that if he waited up to several hours after extinguishing the conditioned S–R unit of bell–salivation (by not using reinforcement), on *later* ringing of the bell he *sometimes* saw the conditioned response of salivation re-occur. Albeit weaker than before, Pavlov called the reappearance of the conditioned response of salivation *spontaneous recovery*. What spontaneous recovery suggests is that we never entirely forget the things we learn in life. Behaviours can be modified, but never extinguished completely.

> INTERACTIVES
>
> If behaviourism is correct and that all 'behaviours can be modified, but never extinguished completely' what importance does this have regards early attachment in infancy?

Skinner and operant conditioning

Burrhus Frederic Skinner was born on 20 March 1904, in Susquehanna, Pennsylvania. His contribution to the behaviourist approach was the concept of operant conditioning. **Conditioning** means learning. An **operant** is something that reinforces our behaviours as we operate in our world.

Operant conditioning occurs where 'the behaviour is followed by a consequence, and the nature of the consequence modifies the organism's tendency to repeat the behaviour in the future' (Skinner, 1938).

Reinforcers: an environmental response

Skinner's theory of operant conditioning concerns the use of *reward* and *unpleasant consequence* in the learning process. In operant conditioning a reward/unpleasant consequence is the *environmental response*, or operant, that encourages or discourages us in the learning of behaviour. The operant of reward given to encourage a desired behaviour is called a positive reinforcer, while an unpleasant consequence is called a negative reinforcer.

According to Skinner, the process of positive reinforcement can encourage the repetition of behaviours, probably because it becomes connected with a positive outcome for an organism.

Primary reinforcer: a stimulus from our environment, whose ability to reinforce our response is based on an innate biological drive, e.g. our need for food, water and warmth

Secondary reinforcer: an environmental stimulus that has become associated with a primary reinforcer. Secondary reinforcers help precipitate primary reinforcers, e.g. we use money to purchase food

Alternatively, the process of negative reinforcement sees a behavioural response that removes or provides an escape from an unpleasant consequence.

Positive reinforcement

According to Skinner, the use of positive reinforcement increases the likelihood of a similar response to the stimulus in the future.

Positive reinforcement occurs where a positive reinforcer, such as a reward, is given following a desirable behaviour. It is the situation of a behaviour followed by a positive consequence or outcome.

We have all experienced positive reinforcement from parents, primary caregivers and teachers, to encourage us to learn particular behaviours. We also use positive reinforcement to encourage positive behaviours in others. An example of this would be where a child shows a parent or primary caregiver a piece of schoolwork they have done. If the adult shows interest and praises the child's efforts, operant conditioning tells us that this positive reinforcement of praise should encourage the continuation of schoolwork.

Classical and operant conditioning theories have each contributed to a cupboard love understanding of attachment.

Classical conditioning and attachment

In classical conditioning there is always a naturally occurring reflex action. With Pavlov's dogs it was salivation. With babies, their pertinent reflex actions are a rooting reflex, sucking reflex, and their ability to swallow.

> **Rooting reflex:** A reflex seen in newborn babies, who automatically turn their face toward the stimulus and make sucking (rooting) motions with the mouth when the cheek or lip is touched. The rooting reflex helps to ensure breastfeeding.

Attachment can be explained in terms of classical conditioning theory because the person providing a baby with sustenance, usually the mother becomes *associated* with the provision of food, and the subsequent conditioned response of pleasure. Infants begin to associate this feeling of pleasure with the person who provides it with food, even when no food is on hand. '*This eventually generalises into a feeling of security whenever the caregiver is present, and is the basis of the attachment bond*" (Copeland and Robertson, 2004).

Operant conditioning and attachment

Skinner's theory of operant conditioning can also be applied to the attachment process in terms of cupboard love theory.

This is because Dollard and Miller (1950) tell us that we are born with primary drives that motivate us to reduce our hunger and thirst. We are biologically driven to satisfy these drives otherwise we will die.

With regard to operant conditioning theory an infant will find breastfeeding rewarding. This is because the infant is driven to reduce its feelings of hunger and consequently its drive reduction behaviour of breastfeeding is positively reinforced. Subsequently, when feeling hungry the infant will look to their mother. They learn to associate the secondary reinforcer of their mother with being breastfed, and the positive reinforcement or reward that come with this. As a result the infant–mother attachment bond is forged.

Self-image

Attachment sees the infant want to be around the attachment figure. This is because the attachment figure gives those forming the attachment security, comfort, and confidence. The strength and worth of this relationship will ultimately influence their **self-concept**,

Our self-concept is our self-image or personal identity. Our self-concept is who we think we are as a person, and, as a result why we think, feel and behave as we do. Our self-concept is greatly influenced by those around us. This is because we come to believe what these others think about us as being true.

From as young as age two, children begin to develop their self-concept. They become increasingly aware of who they are as individuals, and who they are in relation to other people. Most will know their name, and that they are part of a family. They will know who comprises their family.

By age five most children's descriptions of who they are will be very categorical and rigid. This is especially true in terms of their age, their gender, and associated behaviour patterns. For example a child of six will be very precise as to whether they are six, six and a half or nearly seven! Further, a girl or boy of this age will usually display their gender through gender-related play.

Developing self-image and such things as related sex role identification is greatly influenced by the messages young children receive from their environment, and those in their environment.

Between ages five and twelve a child's self-concept begins to widen out. The primary school years see children begin to describe themselves *qualitatively*. They use terms such as 'nice', 'smart', 'tall', 'small', and 'pretty' etc. to describe themselves and others. This indicates that they are beginning to compare, contrast, and most importantly evaluate themselves in comparison to other children in their peer group.

During childhood, and beyond, social comparison is hugely influential on our self-image. It helps or hinders self-confidence, or how good one feels about oneself. It helps or hinders our self-esteem or how much we have come to value, respect, and appreciate the individual that we are.

The role of the attachment figure is of immense importance in the formation of a healthy positive self-image. This is because the attachment figure, or primary caregiver represents a secure base from which the 'attached' infant or child can safely explore the unknown, unfamiliar or threatening. If this is frustrated or upset an infant may develop a dysfunctional personality.

Why this may happen, and the beginnings of a more modern theoretical understanding of attachment, has its origins in a subject called **ethology**.

Ethology

Ethology is the scientific study of animal behaviour in a natural setting. Influenced by Charles Darwin ethology is particularly interested in the *evolution* of animal behaviours, or how and why it is that animals have adapted to behave in the ways that they do.

Ethology tells us that if an animal has a biological characteristic that helps it to more successfully reproduce then this biological characteristic is more likely to stay in that species genetic make-up.

Ethology confirms the importance of the mother–infant bond in the animal kingdom, and its contribution to ensuring the survival of the infant into adulthood. The process involved in the establishment of the mother–infant bond in the animal world is called **imprinting**.

Imprinting sees infant animals 'attach' to the first large moving object they see on birth. This is usually their mother. Imprinting is an adaptive behaviour, and is a genetically determined biological characteristic innate in all prosocial animals. An adaptive behaviour is an evolved behaviour that ultimately aids successful reproduction, and as a result species survival. What is important is that imprinting occurs without any feeding taking place. Consequently imprinting casts doubt on cupboard love theories of attachment.

Imprinting

Konrad Lorenz, the famous Austrian zoologist, ornithologist, and animal psychologist, was the first to popularise the idea of imprinting in prosocial animals. A prosocial animal is an animal that lives in a group.

Lorenz divided a clutch of greylag goose eggs into two groups. He had the mother goose hatch one group, while the other group were hatched in an incubator.

When born the group that had been hatched by the mother goose followed her around, while the incubated group followed Lorenz. This was because Lorenz had been the first large moving object his incubated goslings had seen on birth. On hatching they had imprinted on *him*. Later in life they preferred his company to that of adult geese.

Figure 3.7 Lorenz and his imprinted ducks

In his book *King Solomon's Ring*, published in 1952, Lorenz wrote about similar behaviours he also found in young mallard ducks, kittens, hedgehogs, horses, fish etc.

He believed that the need of many animals to imprint on another soon after birth was genetically determined. Imprinting is innate.

The reason why is because the object they imprint upon and follow is usually their mother. She teaches them the essential survival skills necessary to reach adulthood and reproduce themselves. 'The attachment of animals to their mothers is of crucial importance for later social and mating behaviour' (Lorenz, 1952).

Consequently imprinting makes it more likely that the offspring will reach sexual maturity to allow it to pass on its species genes to the next generation.

ONLINE INTERACTIVES

Read more about Konrad Lorenz. Visit: en.wikipedia.org/wiki/Konrad_Lorenz

A direct link is available in the Chapter Three section of the Higher Psychology Learning Suite at www.gerardkeegan.co.uk/index.htm

The critical period

From his observations Lorenz thought that many animals have between four and 24 hours to imprint upon an adult figure. He called this a **critical period**.

If imprinting does not occur during this time then an animal can become socially and sexually damaged. Lorenz thought the effects of this were irreversible.

Imprinting is therefore crucial to individual and general species survival.

The sensitive period

The idea of a short critical period during which imprinting *must* occur is nowadays less vital than Lorenz first thought.

Sluckin (1964) reran Lorenz's experiment, but with duckling eggs. He kept each egg in individual incubators isolated from one another. He found that his ducklings could imprint on a parent-figure, or any large moving object as late as four to five days after hatching. Sluckin explains this by saying that Lorenz's incubated hatchlings had imprinted on each other. Because Sluckin's ducklings had been kept isolated from one another their period of imprintability has lasted up to five times longer.

While Lorenz's four to 24 hour period is thought to be the optimum time for imprinting to occur Sluckin believes it is not as narrow a window as Lorenz believed. For this reason Sluckin renamed the critical period, the **sensitive period**.

Lorenz's claim as to the permanent effects of imprinting has also been disputed.

The yellow rubber gloves

Guiton (1966) reared some young male chicks in isolation from each other for 47 days. During this time an assistant wearing yellow rubber gloves fed them. Her yellow rubber gloves were all they saw coming through their feeding hatch every day. On their release from isolation the chicks then attempted to mate with the yellow rubber gloves! They appeared to have imprinted on them.

Guiton then put the male chicks into a pen with normally reared female hens of the same age. Although well past the sensitive or critical period for imprintability, the change in company seemed to have an effect. The males and females successfully mated with each other. The male chicks no longer seemed to yearn after the yellow rubber gloves.

The detrimental effects of faulty imprinting, at least for chicken fowl, appear to be neither permanent nor irreversible. For Guiton, dysfunctional sexual behaviour arising from faulty imprinting would only arise if the male chicks had *never* had the opportunity to mix with others of the same species.

Lorenz's work prompted similar investigations into imprinting in other species. From the point of view of psychology in general, and attachment in particular, the most notable must be the research conducted by American psychologist Harry Harlow.

The end of cupboard love theory: Harlow's monkeys

In 1959 Harry Harlow of the University of Wisconsin took eight infant rhesus monkeys and reared them in isolation from each other in their own individual cages.

In each cage were two model 'mothers'. One model had a large round monkey-type head with eyes and ears, and was covered in terry towelling. The other model was a bare wire mesh affair, with a rectangular 'crocodile'-type head.

Each type of model – soft cloth and wire mesh – had a feeding bottle protruding from their chest. Four of his monkeys were fed via the bottle coming from the soft cloth mother; the other four via the bottle coming from the wire mesh model.

Figure 3.8 An infant rhesus monkey with Harlow's model 'mothers'

Harlow was interested in whether his rhesus monkeys would develop an attachment to one of the model mothers. He was particularly intrigued if food had a part to play in the process.

Harlow hypothesised that if the old 'cupboard love' theory of attachment was correct, and food was vital to the attachment process, then the first four monkeys would become attached to the soft cloth model, and the other four to the wire mesh model.

All eight monkeys developed an attachment to the soft cloth model, even although four of them were fed from the bottle coming from the wire mesh model. All would clamber onto the cloth-covered model in their cages and cling to it. Only if appropriate did four of the monkeys occasionally go to the wire mesh model to be fed. To test attachment Harlow observed what happened when the models were taken away.

Attachment and the importance of tactile comfort

The removal of the wire mesh model produced no response, while the removal of the soft terry-towelling model saw all of the young rhesus monkeys engage in distress behaviours. They would throw themselves on the floor, clutch themselves, rock back and forth, and scream in terror. When a wind-up teddy bear was put into the cage each monkey ran and clung onto the soft terry-towelling model burying their head in its chest. After a while they would look over their shoulder and 'keek' towards the teddy, while still clinging firmly to the soft model.

The presence of the soft cloth mother in an 'open field' test saw the young monkeys explore quite happily. If the soft model mother was not present, or was removed, the monkeys became distressed and cowered in a corner. Harlow's research tells us that attachment is not dependent on food. It is much more dependent upon *who* gives the baby *tactile* or *contact* comfort.

Attachment and privation

In 1962 Harlow produced another paper on his eight rhesus monkeys. In this he reported that they had grown up physically well, but that they were emotionally damaged. They were timid, frightened of new experiences, and lacked social skills when around normally reared monkeys. Sexual reproduction was also a big problem.

Harlow thought his monkeys' emotional and sexual difficulties were due to **maternal deprivation** in infancy. Maternal deprivation assumes a mother is present initially but is then absent, either temporarily or in the long term.

But as his monkeys never had their natural mother around when they were brought up, it is probably better to understand their psychological difficulties arising as a result of social **privation**.

Privation means never having that 'something' in the first place. Social privation is therefore the absence of social contact with others of the same species. Harlow's monkeys had been reared in complete isolation from both their mothers and other rhesus monkeys.

Harlow concluded that a rhesus monkey has a critical period of around 90 days during which time it had to form attachments with other monkeys. If this is frustrated, as was the case in his study, then their social, emotional and sexual development becomes seriously impaired.

INTERACTIVES

What is the difference between privation and deprivation?

Monkey island

To try and alleviate these problems Harlow put his experimental monkeys into 'group psychotherapy'. He moved them to a zoo that had a monkey island; a natural habitat populated entirely with monkeys. Six months later he returned to gauge any improvements.

He found slight developmental improvements in his monkeys' social behaviours. They were able to mix with others but were still very timid in comparison. Sexual reproduction still eluded them, as none had been able to mate successfully. Harlow concluded that the psychological effects of social privation in infancy are permanent.

In 1975 Novak and Harlow revised their view on the permanency of the effects of social deprivation after working with other rhesus monkeys in similar circumstances

ONLINE INTERACTIVES

Read a fascinating excerpt from Harry F. Harlow's, 'Love in Infant Monkeys,' (1959) at:

darkwing.uoregon.edu/~adoption/archive/HarlowLIM.htm

A direct link is available in the Chapter Three section of the Higher Psychology Learning Suite at **www.gerardkeegan.co.uk/index.htm**

They now believe the possibility of reversibility, or complete psychological recovery, from the effects of social isolation in infancy. We should be cautious however in extrapolating such a conclusion onto ourselves due to the huge differences between infant rhesus monkeys and human babies.

Dr John Bowlby

Dr John Bowlby (1907–1990) is a famous British developmental psychologist who was schooled in the psychoanalytic tradition. He is most noted for his pioneering work into attachment theory, and the psychological effects attachment has for human beings. For Bowlby 'Prolonged deprivation of maternal care may have grave and far-reaching effects on the child's character' (Bowlby, 1951).

Deprivation means having 'something' and then having that 'something' taken away.

Maternal deprivation means once having a mother, who is then taken away or removed from you.

In his **maternal deprivation hypothesis** written in 1958 Bowlby proposed that a human infant has a critical period of between six months and five years of age to form an attachment with their mother or caregiver figure.

Influenced by ethology and psychoanalysis Bowlby understood that all children have an instinctual need for a comforting, secure adult figure. So much so that they become distressed in their caregiver's absence, and comforted upon their return. They are also more active and exploratory when the caregiver is present, than when he or she is not.

Monotropy

Bowlby called a human baby's innate tendency to become attached to a particular individual, most usually their mother, **monotropy**. Monotropy can be defined as 'turning towards one person'.

Most of us form a monotropic bond at birth with our biological mothers. This first relationship acts as a template for all other subsequent relationships. The monotropic bond establishes an '**internal working model**' in our mind (Bowlby, 1981). This is a mental model of the world that we use to predict, control and manipulate our environment. The quality of our monotropic bond affects this for good or ill.

The monotropic bond is unlike any other relationship we may have in life. It develops in stages to age five. For Bowlby its frustration or absence can cause a child social and emotional difficulties then and thereafter.

The strength and worth of the monotropic bond ultimately influences a person's self-concept. As, 'it is because of this marked tendency to monotropy that we are capable of deep feelings' (Bowlby. 1988).

Age	Behaviour
Phase 1	
0 to five months	Responds similarly to anyone
Phase 2	
five to seven months	Responds more (e.g. smiles) to significant others i.e. primary caregiver,
Phase 3	
seven months to three years	Shows proximity to primary caregiver when strangers around; shows separation anxiety
Phase 4	
three to five years	Goal-corrected behavioural partnership with primary caregiver; takes account of caregiver's needs
Phase 5	
five years+	Has developed an internal working model of the world, proximity to primary caregiver is less important

Table 3.4 Five phases of attachment (Bowlby 1969, 1988)

Social Releasers

Bowlby wrote that babies display instinctual behaviours like smiling, sucking, gesturing and crying. Such behaviours have evolved to maximise the chances of a baby being noticed, looked after, and surviving. Smiling, sucking, gesturing and crying are called social releasers, and their function is to trigger an instinctive parenting response from adults. The interplay between social releasers and parenting response is the process that builds the attachment bond between infant and carer. 'Babies' smiles are powerful things, leaving mothers spellbound and enslaved. Who can doubt that the baby who most readily rewards his mother with a smile is the one who is best loved and cared for?' (Bowlby, 1957)

The origins of Bowlby's maternal deprivation hypothesis

The origins of Bowlby's maternal deprivation hypothesis lie in a study he published in 1946 while working for the Tavistock Clinic in London. As Head of its Children's Unit he worked with dysfunctional, or disturbed, teenagers.

He was able to compare the backgrounds of 44 disturbed teenagers who had been identified as thieves by the authorities, with a similar group of teenagers, who showed dysfunctional behaviour, but were not criminal.

The results of the study, contained in his report 'Forty-four Juvenile Thieves: Their Character and Home Life', indicated that among the 44 thieves, seventeen had been separated from their mothers in early infancy. By comparison the control group contained two teenagers who had been separated from their mothers in early infancy.

The behavioural indicators of **'affectionless psychopathy' are** an inability to form meaningful emotional relationships with others, chronic anger, poor impulse control, and a lack of remorse.

He also found that among the seventeen maternally deprived teenage thieves, there were fourteen who exhibited behaviours that were even more cognitively, socially, and emotionally dysfunctional than their peers. These behaviours included juvenile delinquency, low IQ, and affectionless psychopathy.

Further, in comparison to the control group many of the maternally deprived group were unable to form close relationships with others. They had little or no moral values, and had a very casual approach to crime. Most worryingly they demonstrated 'affectionless psychopathy' in that they did not care about the effects their crimes had on their victims.

INTERACTIVES

According to Dr John Bowlby what three problems can arise due to maternal deprivation in infancy?

Give reasons for your answer.

Nowadays this type of person would be referred to as a sociopath. They suffer from an antisocial personality disorder.

ONLINE INTERACTIVES

Investigate the symptoms and treatment of antisocial personality disorder. Visit:

allpsych.com/disorders/personality/ antisocial.html

A direct link is available in the Chapter Three section of the Higher Psychology Learning Suite at **www.gerardkeegan.co.uk/index.htm**

Bowlby concluded that the root cause of his 44 juvenile thieves' problems stemmed from their experiences in early infancy.

Seventeen had suffered from maternal deprivation, and consequently as '...*mother love in infancy and childhood is as important for mental health as are vitamins and proteins for physical health*', it was maternal deprivation that had caused their later problems. They had been deprived of their mother and vital mother love in infancy.

For Bowlby it was this inability to form a monotropic bond in infancy that had caused their juvenile delinquency, low IQ, and affectionless psychopathy in their later teenage years.

Maternal care and mental health

Bowlby also explored the effects of maternal deprivation in 1949, when he was commissioned by the World Health Organisation (WHO) to investigate the psychological effects of the Second World War (1939–45) on the thousands of displaced children who were wandering Europe at the time.

In his paper *Maternal Care and Mental Health* presented to the UN in 1951 he confirmed much of his earlier findings. These being that a lack of mother love in infancy can jeopardise intelligence, and also create social and emotional difficulties that are carried through into adolescence and beyond.

Is Bowlby correct?

The implications of Bowlby's maternal deprivation hypothesis were immediately felt. His work had profound effects in the Britain of the 1950s and 1960s.

Hayes (2000) tells us that Bowlby's maternal deprivation hypothesis rapidly assumed social and political dimensions. His research was used by some post-war pressure groups to argue that women should stay at home and look after their children full time. Maybe not coincidently the subsequent movement by women back into the home helped free up jobs for returning ex-servicemen from the Second World War!

Bowlby's research received a large amount of publicity, which was inevitably sensationalised by the popular press. The question must then be asked as to whether Bowlby is correct in his assumptions. This being that a lack of mother love in infancy causes a child major cognitive, social and emotional difficulty later on in life. In order to do this we have to look at his theory at two levels. We ask questions concerning its **internal validity**, and also **external validity**.

In questioning a theory's *internal* validity we ask just how convincing the theory is in the light of the research that generated it. We investigate whether the research been conducted in a scientific manner, and whether any contributory theories used to support the research are appropriate or inappropriate.

Alternatively, when questioning a theory's *external* validity we ask questions about just how convincing the theory is when compared and contrasted with alternative theories concerning the same topic.

Internal validity
Bowlby's supporting research

In constructing his theory on the effects of maternal deprivation in infancy Bowlby used two sources. First, he cites research done by William Goldfarb.

Goldfarb

Goldfarb (1943) investigated the cognitive, social and emotional development of two groups of children in New York. Goldfarb's experimental group were a group of children who were in care, or *institionalised*, until the age of three and a half.

His control group were another group of children who were fostered immediately at birth. Goldfarb's findings were startling regards later cognitive, social, and emotional development. He discovered that his experimental group, when compared to the control group, consistently scored lower on IQ tests, had problems with moral rule keeping, lacked social skills, and had difficulties forming long lasting relationships with others.

Crucially however, Goldfarb took no account of his children's race, gender, sociability, physical appearance etc. These factors or *extraneous variables* may have been why those in his control group had been fostered at birth, while those in the institutionalised group had not.

Such **individual differences** rather than pure chance could have been the reason why one child had been fostered immediately and another had not.

Race, gender, sociability, physical appearance etc., rather than institutionalisation alone, could have been the reason for the experimental group's later social and cognitive problems.

Bowlby also relied on research conducted by Rene Spitz and Katherine Wolf.

INTERACTIVES

What do you understand by the term 'individual differences'?

STUDY

Goldfarb, W. (1943) 'The effects of early institutional care on adolescent personality' *Journal of Experimental Education*, 12, 106–29

Aim: To assess the extent to which a deprived upbringing can influence a child's subsequent cognitive, or intellectual, development.

Method: A longitudinal study using a matched pairs design. Two groups of children were matched on a number of characteristics such as genetic factors, their mothers' education and occupational status etc.

Procedure: This longitudinal study, which is one that lasts for a year or more, compared the cognitive development of two groups of children.

The experimental, or 'institionalised' group of fifteen children [n=15] were raised in children's homes from six months until age three and a half and were then fostered. The control group of fifteen children [n=15] were fostered straight from the biological mother's home at about six months.

The two groups were assessed at the age of three, and then again between the ages of ten and fourteen. They were tested on intelligence, abstract thinking, social maturity and their ability to make friends and follow rules.

Results: At age three the experimental, or institutionalised, group were found to perform worse than the fostered group on all of the above measures. All fifteen in the fostered group were found to be average in language development compared with only three in the institutionalised group. The institutionalised group were characterised by their inability to follow rules. They lacked an ability to feel guilt, craved adult affection, and were unable to form lasting relationships.

At ages ten to fourteen the institutionalised group performed more poorly on IQ tests, scoring on average of 72 compared with 95 for the fostered group, they lacked in social maturity, language development and were still unable to form lasting relationships.

Conclusions: Goldfarb (1943) was later used as support for Bowlby's maternal deprivation hypothesis.

This was because Goldfarb's institutionalised children had impaired cognitive development thought due to their lack of attachment in early infancy to a mother or mother substitute.

Questions

1   What was the aim of Goldfarb (1943)?

2   What do you understand by the terms a) a longitudinal study and b) a matched pairs design?

3   What did Goldfarb discover about the effects of early institutionalisation on later cognitive and social development?

4   What factors, other than early institutionalisation could have led to the differences in the two group's cognitive and social development?

5   Who later was to use Goldfarb (1943) to support their own theory of attachment in early infancy?

Spitz and Wolf

Spitz and Wolf propose that young children who suffer the loss of a parent can suffer mental health problems in later life.

This was discovered as a consequence of their research into **anaclitic depression**.

ONLINE INTERACTIVES

Anaclitic Depression is a type of depression that occurs primarily in infants who have been separated from, or lost, their mother or primary caregiver. If a child suffers from anaclitic depression there is a high risk of serious intellectual, social and emotional problems developing. There is also some evidence of physical deficit.

Although anaclitic depression has been identified almost exclusively in infants, psychologists have found it in adults and even monkeys.

If you want to learn more about anaclitic depression visit:

www.findarticles.com/p/articles/mi_g2602/is _0000/ai_2602000035

A direct link is available in the Chapter Three section of the Higher Psychology Learning Suite at **www.gerardkeegan.co.uk/index.htm**

Spitz (1945), and Spitz and Wolf (1946) investigated the psychological development of 123 babies in a South American penal institution who were being looked after by their unmarried mothers.

When the babies were between six and nine months their mothers, due to overcrowding, were temporarily moved to another institution. The babies were then cared for by the other young mothers, or pregnant girls who remained behind.

During separation the infants did not see their mothers, or at best saw them once a week. Spitz and Wolf noted the changes in the infants' behaviour. They cried more than before, lost their appetites, and failed to make the usual weight gain.

Spitz and Wolf termed this state of affairs 'anaclitic depression'. Anaclitic depression becomes evident at around six to twelve months of age, and symptoms include weeping, withdrawal, apathy, weight loss, and sleep disturbance (Rutter, 1986). When their mothers returned, the infants went back to how they had been before the separation.

Spitz and Wolf hypothesised that anaclitic depression is the child's response to maternal loss. If not addressed within three months recovery is impossible. Anaclitic depression can result in major intellectual, social and emotional problems in later life (Spitz, 1945, 1946; Spitz and Wolf, 1946).

As we now appreciate Bowlby used Goldfarb (1943), Spitz (1945), and Spitz and Wolf (1946) in support of his theory of maternal deprivation.

Their work is however less useful than Bowlby first thought. This is because the institutions they studied were deficient in a variety of ways. The children in them suffered from a severe lack of adult attention and intellectual stimulation *over and above* being maternally deprived.

Goldfarb's findings on the origins of his sample's reduced IQ etc., and the conclusions reached by Spitz, and Spitz and Wolf concerning anaclitic depression may then have been due to a number of other factors, and not just maternal deprivation.

In relying on research conducted by theorists such as Goldfarb, and Spitz and Wolf, Bowlby should also have taken account of the effects of institutionalisation on the intellectual, social and emotional development of children. Rather, he assumed that maternal deprivation *alone* was the root cause of his own sample's low IQ, juvenile delinquency and affectionless psychopathy.

Bowlby's research methodology

In consideration of the internal validity of Bowlby's theory of maternal deprivation his own research methodology is flawed. This is because he used a **retrospective case study** approach with his 44 thieves.

Retrospective case study

Retrospective case studies see participants reflecting back on their lives. As a result retrospective case studies are prone to problems such as a participant's selective memory, or incomplete records.

Selective memory is where an individual tells an interviewer only those things they want them to know! Incomplete records make it impossible to check the truth of such statements.

Consider that Bowlby's sample consisted of 44 teenagers who had been convicted of criminal offences. Teenagers exaggerate, and criminals are notorious for telling lies. Funny that!

Another problem with the retrospective case study is that the sample is able to pre-select itself.

A retrospective case study is not a good research technique. It would have been better if Bowlby had been able to conduct a *longitudinal* case study. An example of a longitudinal case study would be where a researcher takes a whole group of children born on the same day and researches them over at least the next year.

Of Bowlby's 44 thieves, 27 were not separated from their mother at birth or in infancy. Questions must arise therefore as to why *they* became criminal.

A psychoanalytic approach

Bowlby was a psychoanalyst. In taking a psychoanalytic approach Bowlby concentrated too much on what happened to his participants in the first five years of their lives. He generally ignored what happened to them in their later years.

Developmental psychology would recommend we find out about a person's *whole* life when trying to understand why and where in their lifetime things happened that made them what they are.

Changing child-rearing practices

Finally Bowlby ignored the changed reality of family life in Britain.

Bowlby advocated a 'constant care' mother–child relationship as the *only* way to avoid cognitive, social and emotional difficulties in later life. This would necessitate a mother staying at home 24/7 to raise her children Such a constant care mother–child family situation may have been possible in the Britain of the 1950s and 1960s, but certainly not today.

Bowlby did not, and could not, take account of the millions of children who are nowadays brought up in a situation where mum is absent for one reason or another – and who do not suffer low IQ, juvenile delinquency or affectionless psychopathy, as his theory would predict.

He also ignored the different child-rearing arrangements we have in Britain like the use of relatives in helping to look after children if mum/dad are absent; the employment of nannies and nursery nurses; situations where both parents work; single-parent families; cultural child-rearing differences and practices and alternative child-rearing strategies.

We shall look more at the relationship between attachment and social and cultural variations in child-rearing styles shortly.

ONLINE INTERACTIVES

Read a summary of Dr John Bowlby's maternal deprivation hypothesis at:

http://en.wikibooks.org/wiki/Applied_History_of_Psychology/Attachment#Maternal_Deprivation

A direct link is available in the Chapter Three section of the Higher Psychology Learning Suite at www.gerardkeegan.co.uk/index.htm

---

External validity

Juvenile delinquency

When psychologists examine a theory's *external* validity they ask about just how convincing the theory is when it is compared with alternative theories concerning the same topic.

We will thus first look at the external validity of Bowlby's theory in the light of what other theorists have to say about the causes of juvenile delinquency.

Michael Rutter

While generally supporting Bowlby, Professor Sir Michael Rutter is critical of Bowlby's error in confusing maternal deprivation with maternal privation.

He has said 'maternal deprivation is too general a term and there needed to be a clear distinction made between maternal deprivation and maternal privation' (Rutter, 1981).

Rutter himself concentrates on the effects of maternal deprivation. To remind us again, maternal deprivation is a situation where a child has had a mother but becomes separated from her in the short or long term.

In examining the causes of juvenile delinquency in 1972, 1979, and again in 1981, Rutter concluded that the main factor leading to delinquent behaviour was whether or not a teenager's earlier home-life had been stressful and unhappy. What he means by this is discord and disharmony in the home.

Rutter (1972) tells us that when estranged from a mother or mother substitute not only does a child feel stressed because they are separated from an attached figure; they also feel anxious because they find themselves with strange people in strange and unfamiliar surroundings. An example of this would be a stay in hospital.

Rutter's (1976) Isle of Wight Study

In 1976 Rutter interviewed 2000 boys aged between nine and twelve, and their families, who lived on the Isle of Wight. Some of his sample had experienced maternal separation due to being in hospital with a physical illness, or on the death of their mother. Others had had a psychiatric illness or had suffered disharmony within their family. Rutter found that the latter group were four times as likely to become delinquent than the former. He concluded that family disharmony rather than maternal separation causes juvenile delinquency and psychiatric problems.

Robertson and Robertson

James and Joyce Robertson were colleagues of Bowlby. In the 1950s they noticed that many children in hospital showed high levels of distress. This was because they were separated from their 'attachment objects', being their mother or primary caregiver. In those days hospitals did not encourage parents to visit their children too often. They interfered too much with the militaristic hospital regime!

James Robertson made a series of films called 'Young Children and Brief Separation' that he showed to the National Health Service. Gradually hospital policy changed, and by the end of the 1960s most children's hospitals had come into line with the Robertsons' recommendations – that parents and children should not be separated.

On the basis of the Robertsons' research we can identify five variables that influence the effects of such a separation, both on the child, and on the mother or primary caregiver:

● Just how secure the original attachment bond was.
● The more secure the original attachment; the more difficult the effects of the separation on the child.
● The temperament of the child: a child who is generally resistant to cuddles, or who is slow to respond to parental approaches, or who is more independent, will probably suffer less
● The child's previous experiences of separation: if for example the separation is one of many stays in hospital the child has undergone the effects will probably not be as badly felt.
● The age of the child: older children can understand why the separation has to occur and are better able to cope
● The length of the separation: the longer it is, the worse the emotional distress may become.

(Robertson and Robertson, 1989)

Maternal deprivation and stress

The effects of such anxiety, stress and unhappiness can be reduced if, when separated, the child is allowed to have familiar objects and people around them. What also helps is if the child can first become acquainted with their new surroundings. This leads to a happier separation, and less stress and anxiety as a result.

ONLINE INTERACTIVES

Read how and why Yorkhill Hospital in Glasgow helps prepare children for their stay at the 'Sick Kids'.

www.yorkhill.scot.nhs.uk//parents_and_visitors/ in_patients/in_patients.asp

Go on a Virtual Tour of Glasgow's 'Sick Kids'. Visit:

www.yorkhill.scot.nhs.uk/virtual_tours/ virtual_tours.asp

A direct link is available in the Chapter Three section of the Higher Psychology Learning Suite at **www.gerardkeegan.co.uk/index.htm**

Powers, Ash, Schoenberg and Sorey lend support to Rutter's view that a stressful home life can precipitate juvenile delinquency.

Powers, Ash, Schoenberg and Sorey (1974) looked at why you get one-off juvenile offenders and recidivists. (A recidivist is a continual or *habitual* offender.)

Powers *et al.* (1974) believe that the main factor behind habitual offending, particularly among teenagers, is stress in the home. An unstable and stressful family environment seems to be important in the development of juvenile delinquent behaviours.

INTERACTIVES

1 Explain the difference between maternal deprivation, and maternal privation.

2 What for Professor Sir Michael Rutter is the root cause of juvenile delinquency?

3 Give an example of a situation where a child might experience maternal deprivation. What effects can this separation have? How might these effects be reduced?

External validity: affectionless psychopathy

Rutter (1972, 1979) argues that Bowlby's affectionless psychopathy is not the result of maternal deprivation but maternal *privation*. Maternal privation is never having had a mother or primary caregiver to become attached to in the first place. Affectionless psychopathy is thus as a consequence of an infant's initial difficulty in forming any attachment to a primary caregiver.

When reviewing Bowlby's 44 thieves research Rutter realised that those who had been institutionalised in Children's Homes, and had developed dysfunctional behaviours, *never* had had the experience of maternal love in the first place. Maternal privation rather then deprivation was at the root cause of their dysfunctional behaviour.

Pringle and Bossio (1960) also examined the effects of maternal privation on personality development. They looked at two groups of children who were institutionalised. One group, whom they labelled 'maladjusted' had come into care soon after birth; while the other, whom they labelled 'stable', were a more developmentally normal group of children who had spent at least one year in their family home.

Pringle and Bossio discovered that the maladjusted group showed traits similar to those associated with affectionless psychopathy. They showed complete indifference towards others, and did not care how their behaviours affected those around them.

Privation, or not having the opportunity to form close relationships with others in early infancy, seems to lead to the formation of a personality that we call affectionless psychopathy.

Low intelligence

We know that Bowlby relied on a number of other people's research to frame his own theory on maternal deprivation. One of these was Goldfarb. Goldfarb (1943) argued that children who suffered from maternal deprivation would end up less intelligent than their peers, who had a more normal family life (a peer is a counterpart of the same age).

However the development and maximisation of intelligence, or the skills or abilities that we have, are not *solely* due to the presence or absence of mother love in infancy. Intellectual stimulation in our early years is much more important.

Dennis and the Iranian orphanage

In 1969 Dennis investigated children in an Iranian orphanage. This institution seemed to produce children who were less intelligent than others. He found that the children, although well cared for physically, lacked much in the way of intellectual stimulation. They had little interpersonal interaction with their carers. For Dennis a lack of intellectual stimulation in infancy is more important to the development of intelligence than maternal love, or lack of it.

CASE STUDIES

Genie

Curtiss (1989) reports on the disturbing case of Genie. In 1970 Genie, then thirteen, was found by the State authorities in Temple City, Los Angeles strapped to a potty-chair in her home.

She had spent most of her life like this locked in a room in her home. She had had little contact with anyone, and had been discouraged from making any sounds.

Despite possessing the necessary biological attributes to vocalise, she was unable to speak. She also could not understand spoken language.

After considerable therapy she was able to perform tasks that did not need language. Her verbal language skills remain very poor, and she prefers to communicate by signing.

For more about Genie visit:
www.feralchildren.com/en/showchild.php?ch=genie
A direct link is available in the Chapter Three section of the Higher Psychology Learning Suite at
www.gerardkeegan.co.uk/index.htm

Dennis also believes that there is a *critical period* up to age two where intellectual stimulation, as found in the 'normal' family home, *must* occur otherwise children will suffer a permanent intellectual deficit.

Psychology appreciates the connection made by Dennis regarding early intellectual stimulation and the development of intelligence. However, there is debate over his idea of a critical period for intellectual stimulation, and the permanency of any detrimental effect a lack of intellectual stimulation may have (Koluchová, 1976).

Take the work of Skeels for example.

Are the effects of privation permanent?

In 1939 Skeels came across two baby girls aged thirteen months and sixteen months in an American orphanage

Both were both very intellectually challenged. Due to overcrowding they were transferred to an institution for mentally retarded adult women, as such were referred to in the 1960s.

At the time of their transfer the children's IQ was estimated at between 35 and 46. They were categorised as being moderately to severely mentally handicapped.

> *The youngsters were pitiful little creatures. They were tearful, had runny noses, and coarse, stringy, and colourless hair; they were emaciated, undersized, and lacked muscle tone or responsiveness. Sad and inactive, the two spent their days rocking and whining."*
>
> *(Skeels, 1939)*

Within three months the change in the two children was dramatic. They were more alert, intelligent and sociable. Skeels found that because the children had been so young when transferred they had been 'adopted' by the others in the home. They had been cuddled; talked to and encouraged to play much more than before. Ward attendants had purchased toys and books for the girls, and residents had played and talked with them continuously.

After living with the older women for six months, the girls' IQs were measured at 77 and 87 respectively. A few months later both had IQs in the mid-90s. The average person has an IQ of 100.

Skeels believed that the tactile and intellectual stimulation the girls had received from the adults around them had caused the amazing improvement in their intellectual, social, and emotional abilities.

Skeels and Dye (1939)

Skeels was very excited with these findings. They indicated that the detrimental effects of maternal privation need not be permanent, and can be reversed.

Children receiving tactile and intellectual stimulation from adults, in a caring and loving environment, can result in intellectual, social and emotional deficits being overcome, and indeed gains being made.

Sensing the possibilities Skeels and Dye convinced the state authority in Iowa to allow them to conduct an unusual longitudinal experiment.

The experimental group

Thirteen one- to two-year-old children were selected to form their experimental group. Eleven of the thirteen children were deemed 'mentally retarded', having an average IQ of 64. Because of a state law in Iowa at the time all had been judged unsuitable for adoption due to their low intellect.

The experimental group children were removed from their unstimulating Children's Home and put into an institution where they were looked after by mentally retarded teenage girls.

The teenage 'mothers' were taught how to provide and care for 'their' baby. They were shown how to hold, feed, talk to, and stimulate them. The babies also attended a nursery for half a day each week. Such was the experimental group's treatment' that distinguished it from those in the control group.

Put another way, you may remember that the independent variable, or IV, is what the researcher controls or manipulates in an experiment

INTERACTIVES

1. What is an independent variable in an experiment?

2. What is a dependent variable in an experiment?

3. Describe the independent variable manipulated by Skeels and Dye (1939).

4. Describe the dependent variable measured by Skeels and Dye (1939).

Skeels and Dye's independent variable was whether or not their participants had experienced an intellectually stimulating and loving environment in childhood.

The control group

To assess the influence of such a manipulation a control group of twelve children, also less than three years of age, was formed from those left in the Children's Home.

These children received sufficient medical and physical care, but got little in the way of individual attention. At the beginning of the study the children in the control group were estimated as having an average IQ of 86. Only two were classified as mentally retarded. In this instance IQ score was the dependent variable.

The dependent variable in an experiment sees a researcher observe or measure the effect changing or manipulating the independent variable may have. Two years later, both groups were reassessed.

The results

The children in the experimental group showed an average *gain* of 27.5 IQ points. Under then Iowan state law this was enough for eleven of the thirteen to become eligible for adoption.

Alternatively the children in the control group, who had stayed in the Children's Home, were found to have *lost* an average of 26 IQ points.

Skeels and Dye Revisited

More than 25 years later, Skeels (1966) traced all the participants who had taken part in his original study. What he discovered was astonishing. Of the thirteen children in the experimental group, eleven had married. Their marriages had produced nine children. All nine children were of normal intelligence.

Most of the experimental group had attained the educational standard required of a seventeen-year-old. Four had gone on to attend college. All were either homemakers, or employed. Of those employed most worked in professional or business type occupations. The two who had not been adopted held down jobs in domestic service.

In startling contrast were the stories of the twelve children in the control group who had remained in the Children's Home. Skeels found that even as late as 1965 four of the control group participants were still institutionalised.

Of the remaining eight who were non-institutionalised all but one worked as an unskilled labourer. Most had only achieved the educational standard of an eight-year-old. They were unable to earn enough to be self-supporting, and were still regarded as mentally retarded.

Skeels suggests that it is the quality, content, and amount of intellectual stimulation we receive in early childhood that is important to later intellectual, social, and emotional development.

Our intellectual, social and emotional development is not, as Bowlby thought, *solely* due the amount of maternal love we receive. A poor environment stifles intellectual development. This has a detrimental affect on our personality, intellectually, socially, and emotionally.

INTERACTIVES

Outline the Aim, Research Method, Procedure, Results, and Conclusions of Skeels and Dye (1939). What ethical criticisms can be made of this study?

The father's role

Bowlby thought fathers played no role as attachment figures. They only had indirect value offering love and financial support to their child's mother. This view has some support within modern day sociobiology. Sociobiology thinks that mothers have a greater parental investment in their offspring. Consequently they are better prepared for child rearing and attachment (Kendrick, 1994).

However, according to Parke (1981) 'both mother and father are important attachment objects for their infants, but the circumstances that lead to selecting mum and dad may differ.'

For as Crooks and Stein (1991) suggest in their review of the literature, rather then being inconsequential as an attachment figure, fathers make their own unique contribution to the physical, cognitive, social and emotional upbringing of their children (see the Info box below).

The father–child bond

Many fathers form close emotional bonds with their babies shortly after they are born (Greenberg and Morris, 1974).

Some twelve-month, and older, infants are equally or even more attached to dad than mum (Kotelchuk, 1976).

Although fathers seem to spend less time with their children than mothers, the time they do spend with them is play rather than care-orientated (Easterbrook and Goldberg, 1984).

When fathers become primary caregivers, they interact with their infants in a nurturing, gentle manner typical of mothers (Field, 1978).

In general, while there may be a difference in mother/father style of interaction, there are no real differences in the quantity or quality each give to their offspring (Yogman *et al.*, 1977).

Adapted from Crooks and Stein (1991)

Bowlby: conclusion

In evaluating Bowlby's theory of maternal deprivation, Rutter (1981, 1989) highlights Bowlby's confusion regards deprivation and privation. For Rutter it is *maternal privation* that should be emphasised. Maternal privation can result in major intellectual, social, and emotional difficulties for a child.

Consequences and causes of maternal privation (Rutter, 1981)

➤ Intellectual retardation due to a lack of stimulation and essential life experiences.

➤ Affectionless psychopathy due to failure to form an attachment in infancy.

➤ Developmental dwarfism due to nutritional deficiencies in infancy.

➤ Delinquency due to dysfunctional family relationships.

➤ Enuresis (bed wetting) due to stress up to age six.

Rutter believes children's **developmental pathways** into adulthood can be affected if they are not raised in a stable, caring, loving and stimulating environment,

Rutter also suggests that the amount of sensitivity, support and warmth got from others in our early years is related to our ability to show similar sensitivity, support and warmth to others in our later adult years.

Rutter emphasises that our early attachment experiences impact on our social and emotional stability as adults. The quality of early attachment experience is crucial. To avoid later social and emotional difficulties he recommends that our home-life should be harmonious and relatively stress-free.

In his analysis Rutter confirms that any negative effects arising from a child's inability to form an attachment with a primary caregiver need neither be permanent, nor irreversible.

Low IQ is not just as a result of maternal deprivation, or privation. Other variables play a part such as growing up in an intellectually sterile and poor environment.

The psychological effects of maternal *deprivation* in infancy can be both short and long term.

INTERACTIVES

Please answer the following three questions using research evidence where appropriate.

1 Outline Dr John Bowlby's theory of maternal deprivation.

2 What criticisms may be made of his theory on the basis of its internal validity?

3 What criticisms may be made of his theory on the basis of its external validity?

The short-term effects of maternal deprivation

The short-term effects of maternal deprivation can result in a '**syndrome of distress**' (Hill, 2001). Symptoms associated with the syndrome of distress include infant protest, despair and detachment.

Infant protest is where the baby or toddler exhibits irrational anger, fear, and frustration.

Despair is where the baby or toddler shows apathy and signs of depression, such as avoiding others.

Detachment occurs when interaction with others is resumed. These interactions are however superficial, and the infant shows no preferences between people. Re-attachment is resisted, and a temporary delay in intellectual development is also apparent (Hill, 2001).

General characteristics of the poorly attached child

- ➤ Manipulative
- ➤ Controlling
- ➤ Defiant
- ➤ Poor eye contact
- ➤ Rage-filled
- ➤ Not affectionate on parents' terms but often affectionate with strangers
- ➤ Incessant questions
- ➤ Acting incapable
- ➤ Lying and/or stealing
- ➤ Mean to pets
- ➤ Interest in blood/gore

The long-term effects of maternal deprivation

The long-term effects of maternal deprivation are evident in separation anxiety. Children who suffer from **separation anxiety** are prone to increased aggression. They are also very 'clingy' in their attachment behaviour towards any caregiver, as evidenced in a refusal to go to school.

A **psychosomatic disorder** is a medical condition without any medical or physical cause.

The cause is emotional or psychological in origin.

They can become increasingly detached in their social interactions, and often develop psychosomatic disorders such as skin and stomach problems.

Research also shows that children who are maternally deprived in infancy are more likely to suffer from depression after the death of their biological attachment figure in comparison to those who were not not maternally deprived (Hill, 2001).

Social and cultural variations in child rearing

Early socialisation is interested in social and cultural variations in child rearing, or the different ways children are brought up.

INTERACTIVES

In no more than 500 words describe and explain the short- and long-term effects of maternal deprivation?

What do we mean by a *culture*?

As was mentioned earlier in this Chapter a *culture* 'refers to a set of rules, morals and methods of interaction that bind a group of people. These rules, morals, values, beliefs and norms, or common ways of behaving, are the products of socialisation. We learn these through **enculturation**, or social interactions with other members of our culture' (Flanagan, 1999).

Socialisation

We all come from various cultures. Within each culture are subcultures, which themselves are separated by class, ethnicity, religion, economic opportunity, education etc. Cultural, and subcultural differences account for variations in the *socialisation* process. Socialisation as we may have realised earlier is a major factor in the way children are 'brought up'.

How we are socialised has generated research regards cultural variations in child rearing practices, and the effects this has on attachment and other aspects to personality.

Mary Ainsworth

By far the most important theorist in this area is Mary Ainsworth (1913–1999). She was an American developmental psychologist who contributed much to modern day attachment theory because of a famous study she conducted called 'The Strange Situation'.

Born in Ohio, USA, Ainsworth moved to England in 1950. She took up a post at the Tavistock Clinic in London where she worked on the effects of maternal separation on child development. It was here that she began to realise that a child's lack of a mother figure has adverse developmental effects.

In 1954 she left the Tavistock Clinic for Uganda in Africa. With the support of the East African Institute for Social Research she then began her famous studies into mother–infant interactions.

ONLINE INTERACTIVES

Read about the fascinating professional relationship between John Bowlby and Mary Ainsworth in 'An Ethological Approach to Personality Development' at

www.psychology.sunysb.edu/attachment/online/ainsworth_bowlby_1991.pdf

A direct link is available in the Chapter Three section of the Higher Psychology Learning Suite at www.gerardkeegan.co.uk/index.htm

INTERACTIVES

Outline the Aim, Research Method(s), Procedure, Results, and Conclusions of Mary Ainsworth's (1967) Ugandan study into specific attachments.

The Uganda study

In 1967 Mary Ainsworth investigated the interactions of 28 Ganda babies and their mothers who lived near Kampala in Uganda. When her study began the babies were aged from fifteen weeks to two years. They were all breastfed. Ainsworth observed each mother–infant dyad, or pair, in their home for two hours once a fortnight over a nine-month period.

Using data got from such **naturalistic observation**, and also from interviews with the mothers, Ainsworth identified *three* different types of mother–infant attachment behaviours. These were derived on the basis of correlations made between each mother's own sensitivity rating got from interview, and the amount of cuddling each mother gave their baby during naturalistic observation.

Maternal sensitivity and attachment

One group of babies she labelled as *securely attached*; the second *insecurely attached,* and the third *not-yet-attached*.

Crucially Ainsworth discovered that the type of attachment bond formed depends on the degree of **maternal sensitivity** mothers show towards their offspring.

Ainsworth's studies in Uganda allowed her to conclude that there are specific types of attachment behaviors. She also felt that babies go through a number of stages in the development of an attachment to a primary caregiver, and that some patterns of parenting are more likely to lead to secure attachments; and others to insecure attachments.

The Baltimore study

In 1978, Ainsworth, along with Blehar, Waters, and Wall, decided to replicate her Ugandan study in Baltimore, USA. This particular study is of immense significance. It has been called 'the most important study in the history of attachment research' (Van Ijzendoorn and Schuengal, 1999).

As in Uganda, Ainsworth *et al.* used naturalistic observation and interviews, this time with 26 mother–infant dyads. The infants were all around one year old. Each of the 26 pairs was visited at home every three to four weeks, for three to four hours at a time. Each mother–infant pairing generated 72 hours worth of data.

The Strange Situation

In order to make sense of all this information Ainsworth *et al.* used a previously set standard against which to compare her observations of attachment behaviours. This was the 'Strange Situation' scenario that had been devised earlier by both herself and a colleague (Ainsworth and Wittig, 1969).

The Strange Situation was altered in the Baltimore study to allow for mother–infant behavioural patterns to be identified and recorded. These included episodes of crying, and maternal responsiveness to crying; close body contact between mother and infant; face-to-face encounters between them; separation and reunion behaviours, and infant co-operation or disobedience.

Ainsworth's Strange Situation occurred in a playroom environment. Each of the 26 infants was put into a situation of mild stress. This was to encourage them to seek comfort from their mothers. They were also placed in a novel situation. This was to encourage exploratory behaviour. The 26 infants and their mothers were placed in the following eight strange situations.

Figure 3.9 Eight strange situations

Episode	People present	Length of time	Description
1	Mum, baby observer	30 seconds	Observer brings mum and baby into room then leaves.
2	Mum, baby	3 minutes	Mum sits passively while baby explores, if needed play stimulated/encouraged after two minutes.
3	Stranger, mum, baby	3 minutes	Stranger comes in. first minute quiet. second minute stranger talks with mum. third minute stranger approaches baby. After three minutes mother leaves without being seen by baby.
4	Stranger, baby	3 minutes or less*	First separation episode. Stranger involved in active play with baby.
5	Mum, baby	3 minutes or more**	Stranger leaves. Mum greets/comforts baby. Attempts active play then leaves. 'Bye, bye.'
6	Baby	3 minutes or less*	Second separation episode.
7	Stranger, baby	3 minutes or less*	Continued separation. Stranger tries active play with baby.
8	Mum, baby	3 mins	Mum returns, greets and picks up baby. Stranger leaves without being seen.

*Episode stopped if baby very distressed

** Episode continued if baby became distracted

Table 3.5 Eight strange situations in Baltimore (Ainsworth *et al.* 1978)

The Strange Situation gives four behavioural measures that help indicate the type and quality of the mother child attachment bond:

➤ Separation anxiety

➤ Proximity

➤ Stranger anxiety and

➤ Reunion behaviours

Separation anxiety
Separation anxiety was measured by the distress the infant showed when their mum left, as in Episodes 4 and 6.

Proximity
A measure of infant proximity was seen in the infant's willingness to explore, as in Episode 2.

The attached infant was happy to explore as long as mum was present, or nothing unusual happened. If the infant's attachment was not so strong, they tended to be more clingy and proximal to their mother. They were less likely to explore.

Stranger anxiety
Stranger anxiety was where the attached infant showed distress when left in presence of stranger, such as in Episode 4 and 7.

Here Ainsworth *et al.* were particularly interested in the types of **reunion behaviours** shown by the babies on the return of their mothers.

Reunion behaviours
Ainsworth felt reunion behaviours were and are an indication of the *quality* of attachment that exists between a mother and her baby. She saw a connection between reunion behaviours, the quality of the attachment bond, and the emergent infant personality.

Reunion behaviours would have been evident during Episode 5 and 8.

INTERACTIVES

Describe how separation anxiety, proximity, stranger anxiety and reunion behaviours were measured in the Strange Situation.

Ainsworth's findings

Ainsworth found that two-thirds of her Baltimore babies were 'securely attached'. Those who were securely attached cried less at home, and more in the Strange Situation. In the Strange Situation, on reunion they immediately went to their mothers to be picked up. They were easily soothed, and when put down began to explore again.

The Baltimore study confirmed what Ainsworth had discovered in Uganda. This was that a mother's *maternal sensitivity* towards their baby is *the* variable that most influences the quality of the attachment bond.

Sensitive mothers have securely attached babies and insensitive mothers have insecurely attached babies. Insecurely attached babies fall into two categories: those who are anxious avoidant/detached, and those who are anxious resistant/ambivalent.

Type A insecurely attached anxious avoidant

In the Strange Situation the *Type A insecurely attached anxious avoidant* infant cared not one jot if mum was absent; they showed little stranger anxiety; and no reunion behaviours on mum's return.

In Ainsworth's Baltimore Study 22 per cent of the Baltimore babies fell into the *insecurely attached anxious avoidant* category.

Type B securely attached

Alternatively the *Type B securely attached* infant played happily in the Strange Situation when their mum was present. They ignored her presence while playing, and also when the stranger was around or absent. The type B securely attached infant got distressed when mum left. Their play reduced. They sought comfort and proximity immediately on her return. They then calmed down and resumed play.

Ainsworth found that any distress the securely attached Type B infant showed came about due to their mum's absence. Being left alone did not cause it. Sixty-six per cent of the Baltimore babies fell into the *securely attached* category.

Type C insecurely attached anxious resistant

In the Strange Situation the *Type C insecurely attached anxious resistant* infant showed distress when mum left, and was not easily comforted on her return. They sought out and rejected cuddling at the same time.

Mum was seen to be inconsistent in her behaviours. Sometimes they were insensitive, angry and rejecting; or over-sensitive in their responsiveness to their baby. These children engaged in limited exploratory play. They tended to be more proximal to their mother. Twelve per cent of the Baltimore babies fell into the *insecurely attached anxious resistant* category.

Main and Solomon (1986) later added the *Type D insecurely attached disorganised* infant to the typology. The Type D infant shows no set pattern of behaviour, either when separated or reunited with their mother. Flanagan notes that 'this kind of behaviour is associated with abused children or those whose mothers are chronically depressed.'

Attachment and adult romantic relationships

Most interestingly Ainsworth's three-fold classification of attachment styles has been applied to adult romantic relationships.

Hazan and Shaver (1987) discovered that secure adults find it relatively easy to get close to others. They are comfortable depending on others, and have others depend on them. Secure adults don't worry too much about being abandoned, 'chucked' or 'fired', or about someone getting too close to them.

Alternatively, avoidant adults are a bit uncomfortable being close to others. They find it difficult to trust others completely, and find it hard in depending on others. Avoidant adults are nervous of others when they get too close, and when love partners want them to be more intimate than they feel comfortable being.

The anxious–ambivalent adult find that others are hesitant to get as close as they would like. The anxious–ambivalent adult often worries that their partner doesn't really love them, or won't stay with them. The anxious–ambivalent adult wants to join completely with another person, and this sometimes scares the other person away.

Hazan and Shaver (1987) have been criticised due to their research methodology.

Notwithstanding, you may at this point want to examine any romantic encounters you have had to discover your own attachment type!

ONLINE INTERACTIVES

Read more about Hazan and Shaver's (1987) research into attachment and romantic relationships at:

www.psych.uiuc.edu/~rcfraley/measures/measures.html

A direct link is available in the Chapter Three section of the Higher Psychology Learning Suite at **www.gerardkeegan.co.uk/index.htm**

Evaluating the Strange Situation

Ainsworth's Ugandan and Baltimore studies confirmed that maternal sensitivity is the key variable to the development of secure or insecure attachments. However in both studies a relatively small sample of participants was used.

From a methodological point of view it is maybe adventurous to generalise Ainsworth's conclusions on types of attachment as applying the world over.

However an important supporting study comes from Van Ijzendoorn and Kroonenberg (1988).

STUDY

Van Ijzendoorn, M.H., and Kroonenberg, P.M. (1988). 'Cross-cultural patterns of attachment: A meta-analysis of the Strange Situation'. *Child Development*, 59, 147–56

Aim: To investigate cross-cultural variation in attachment.

Method: They conducted a meta-analysis of 32 studies from eight countries involving 2000 children. All had used the Strange Situation to measure and assess attachment.

Procedure: Databases from eight different countries were searched to compare and classify studies into the Strange Situation. These included Western cultures such as America, Britain, and Germany, and non-Western cultures such as Japan, China, and Israel.

Results: A large degree of consistency in types of attachment was found across all cultures.

In all eight countries secure attachment was the most common type found. Significant differences were found regards types of insecure attachments. In Western cultures the insecure anxious avoidant is prevalent. In non-Western cultures the insecure anxious resistant is the more common. The only exception to this was in China where the insecure anxious avoidant and the insecure anxious resistant were found to be equally distributed.

A key finding was that there is 1.5 times greater variation in attachment types within cultures than between cultures.

Conclusion: The general consistency found in attachment types suggests there may be universal characteristics that underpin infant-caregiver interactions. However, the significant variations in insecure attachment types indicate that universality is limited. Van Ijzendoorn and Kroonenberg believe that such cultural variation is as a result of different child-rearing practices. Further, the greater variation they found regards attachment types within cultures leads us to suggest that subcultural comparative studies would be more valid than cross-cultural comparisons. These significant differences also throw into question the validity of the Strange Situation scenario itself as a global assessment tool.

Questions

1   What was the aim of Van Ijzendoorn and Kroonenberg (1988)?

2   What method and procedure did they adopt?

3   What were their results?

4   What were the results of their study?

5   What conclusions did they reach?

Cross-cultural variation in secure and insecure attachment

In 1988 Van Ijzendoorn and Kroonenberg conducted a **meta-analysis**. A meta-analysis is a statistical technique that is used to analyse the results of a number of independent studies into the same topic. Their meta-analysis saw them review 32 studies of attachment that had used the 'Strange Situation' with 2000 children in eight countries.

They found that different cultures and subcultures emphasise different factors in the raising of children. They discovered that socialisation influences attachment type, and its incidence.

Variations in child rearing practice, both between and within different cultures, also saw different weightings of Type A, B and C infants emerging.

For example, of the two studies conducted in Japan, one showed an absence of type A insecurely attached anxious avoidant infants, but a high number of type C insecurely attached anxious resistant infants.

In the other the results were more consistent with Ainsworth's Baltimore types and spread.

Look at the overall percentage distributions of attachment types in Table 3.6 below. Compare these with those of the United States of America. It is clear

Country	Number of studies analysed	Type A Insecurely attached anxious avoidant percentage anxious	Type B Securely attached percentage	Type C Insecurely attached resistant percentage
West Germany	3	35	57	8
Great Britain	1	22	75	3
Netherlands	4	26	67	7
Sweden	0	22	74	4
Israel	2	7	64	29
Japan	2	5	68	27
China	1	25	50	25
USA	18	21	65	14
Overall average		21	65	14

Percentages above to the nearest whole number as reported by Van Ijzendoorn and Kroonenberg (1988).

Table 3.6 Summary of Van Ijzendoorn and Kroonenberg's meta analysis

that Van Ijzendoorn and Kroonenberg's meta-analysis helps to confirm Ainsworth's belief in a worldwide pattern of type A, B and C securely–insecurely attached infants.

However they dispute the weighting and universality of type A, B and C securely–insecurely attached infants that her work predicts. This is because of cultural and subcultural differences in the socialisation process.

Regards cultural differences and the attachment process, in Japan mothers seldom leave babies less than one year old alone. Takahashi (1990) says that it was this cultural difference in child rearing that gave rise to Japanese babies' significant distress behaviours at Episodes 4, 6 and 7 of the Strange Situation.

As a result fewer babies in Japan were classed as 'securely attached', in comparison with a higher percentage of babies in Sweden or Great Britain.

As for subcultural differences Van Ijzendoorn and Kroonenberg found that America had a greater variation of attachment types than anywhere else. This was, and is, because of the hugely diverse cultural backgrounds found in the USA. America is a microcosm of global cultures.

Van Ijzendoorn and Kroonenberg also found cross-cultural differences in that while Type B securely attached infants are found worldwide, type A insecurely attached anxious avoidant infants are more common in Western European societies like Great Britain and the Netherlands.

Alternatively type C insecurely attached anxious resistant infants are more common in non-Western societies such as Japan and Israel.

INTERACTIVES

Discuss reasons as to why there are cross-cultural differences in attachment types.

Challenges to Ainsworth

Family circumstance and attachment types

Vaughn *et al.* (1980) discovered that a child's attachment type could alter as their family circumstance change. Attachment type and all that follows is not fixed.

Vaughn *et al.* investigated the children of lone parents at twelve and eighteen months of age. They found a significant difference in a child's attachment type dependent on their changing home life.

A reduced income, associated poorer housing, and increased stress levels experienced by their mother saw some infants change from being securely attached to insecurely attached. Vaughn *et al.* (1980) suggests attachment types are not as permanent as Ainsworth's theory might imply.

Temperament and attachment types

Earlier on in this Chapter we came across the notion of temperament.

Temperament concerns our emotions. Temperament is the building block to personality, and comes to us as a consequence of our genetics. Temperament is innate. Consequently, 'the most emotionally intense preschoolers tend to be relatively intense as young adults' (Larsen and Diener, 1987).

Innate, or genetic, differences in temperament could then explain the types and quality of attachment bond a baby can form. Babies with a difficult temperament may experience problems in forming an attachment with a primary caregiver when compared to a baby with a more amiable temperament (Larsen and Diener, 1987).

Why do you think this might be the case?

Ecological validity and attachment types

Both Melhuish (1993) and Lamb *et al.* (1985) criticise Ainsworth's Strange Situation as being too artificial. While it may be considered by to be useful in investigating socio-emotional development in infancy, it does not reflect a real-life situation, and thus lacks *ecological validity*.

The Strange Situation was created and tested in the USA. This means that it could be culturally biased, or **ethnocentric**. In other words the Strange Situation reflects the norms and values of American culture. It is underpinned by a belief that attachment is related to anxiety on separation. There is an assumption by all who use the Strange Situation that behaviour has the same meaning in all cultures.

This is not the case, as we saw earlier when reviewing the incidence of infant mother separation in Japan when compared with America or Great Britain. Social constructions of behaviour differ across and between cultures.

Melhuish, and Lamb *et al.* also think that the Strange Situation is limited in terms of the information it obtains. It fails to take account of the mothers' behaviour. There is also the ethical issue of the Strange Situation in that it deliberately puts infants under stress.

Despite these challenges to Ainsworth, Scroufe *et al.* (1983) comment that 'securely attached infants are likely to be more confident, enthusiastic, and persistent in problem-solving later on as young children.'

It is felt that the more securely attached an infant can be, the more socially competent an adult they will become.

> ## INTERACTIVES ?
>
> Outline three challenges to Ainsworth's findings on attachment.

Applications of early socialisation

Family and working patterns have changed dramatically in Britain over the last 20 years.

In his keynote speech to the Daycare Trust on 11 November 2004 the then Prime Minister Tony Blair told delegates that nearly two-thirds of women with children were now in paid work. A quarter of children were living in a lone parent family compared to just eight per cent in 1972, and the employment rate was at a all time high of 75 per cent compared to 68 per cent 20 years ago.

> ## ONLINE INTERACTIVES
>
> Read a summary of a study by NICHD examining the relationship between childcare experiences and developmental outcomes at:
>
> **secc.rti.org/summary.cfm**
>
> A direct link is available in the Chapter Three section of the Higher Psychology Learning Suite at **www.gerardkeegan.co.uk/index.htm**

Having to work and raise children simultaneously is now an obvious fact of life in modern Britain.

But from what we have read so far it seems clear that a mother's absence can be damaging to a young child. Bowlby himself said that, 'approximately 50 per cent of young children spend time in day care and this disrupts the maternal bond and could impair development' (Bowlby, 1965).

Mothers of young children must then be in a dilemma when faced with the necessity of going out to work. They have to hand their child over to another, albeit for a short time.

Day care

Day care is care for infants and children that includes crèches, day nurseries, childminders, nannies and grandparents, but excludes foster and institutionalised care (Scarr, 1998).

Developmental psychology in the USA tells us:

> *Quality day care from infancy clearly has positive effects on children's intellectual, verbal, and cognitive development, especially when children would otherwise experience impoverished and relatively unstimulating home environments. Care of unknown quality may have deleterious effects.*"
>
> *(Lamb, 1998)*

> ## ONLINE INTERACTIVES
>
> Want to find out more about the psychological effects of day care on preschoolers? Go to:
>
> **www.nlm.nih.gov/medlineplus/ childdaycare.html**
>
> A direct link is available in the Chapter Three section of the Higher Psychology Learning Suite at **www.gerardkeegan.co.uk/index.htm**

But what is the situation in the UK?

Is day care harmful?

In 1988 Belsky and Rovine used the Strange Situation to assess 149 infants between 12 and 13 months who had received more than 20 hours a week day care in their first year of life. The sample consisted of 90 males and 59 females. They were from working class and middle class families and each had both married parents at home. Belksy and Rovine (1988) discovered these children to be more insecurely attached to their mother in terms of reunion behaviours than those who had not received such intense day care in early infancy.

Similarly Violata and Russell (1994) in a meta-analysis of 88 studies found that children who got more than 20 hours a week day care suffered in terms of socio-emotional development and insecure attachment behaviours.

In 2001 in an extensive study of 1153 mothers and their babies in 9 American states the NCIHD reported that the use of non-maternal care did not make a significant difference in children's attachment security. They did discover however that infants were less likely to be secure when low maternal sensitivity and responsiveness to them was combined with poor-quality childcare. Insecure attachments were also more likely if the child got more than more than minimal amounts of child care, or were subject to more than one care arrangement. Boys who got many hours of care, and girls who got minimal hours of care were somewhat less likely to be securely attached than others.

In 1977 Mayall and Petrie interviewed a non-random sample of 39 registered childminders in inner London. They also interviewed 28 of the mothers who had put their children, aged between two and three, in the care of the childminder. They tested 27 of the children for language development, and conducted 20-minute observations of childminder–child, and mother–child interactions with 28 of the children.

They found a considerable difference in the quality of care given by the childminders. All the childminders looked after their children's physical needs, but some did little to intellectually stimulate the children in their charge.

Mayall and Petrie saw a connection between this lack of involvement by the childminder and a lack of security shown by the child when back in the parental home. These children also demonstrated a worrying intellectual deficit when compared to intellectually stimulated children of the same age and stage.

Such research indicates that it is the poor quality of day care got by a child from their childminder that can cause social, emotional, and intellectual problems, rather than because of being maternally deprived when separated from their mother.

Kagan et al. (1980) also investigated the quality of day care and its psychological effects. Kagan et al.

conducted a five-year longitudinal study with preschool children who were in day care for seven hours a day, five days a week.

The children were tested at regular intervals regards attachment to their mothers. They also had their cognitive and social development assessed corresponding with their age and stage.

A control group of preschool children who were brought up by their mums at home was similarly tested. Kagan et al. (1980) found no significant difference in psychological development between the two groups. For Kagan et al. it is the quality of day care rather then maternal separation that is important.

Kagan et al. say there should be no developmental difference between under-fives raised at home, and those who attend day care if the day-care facility is staffed by experienced carers who have frequent and lengthy contact with the children in their care.

Kagan et al. further recommend that child day-care centres be well equipped to allow for stimulating intellectual activities. They should also have a good child-to-carer ratio, and have low staff turnover in an environment where children experience familiar routines.

We can conclude on the basis of Belsky and Rovine (1988), Mayall and Petrie (1977) and Kagan et al. (1980) etc. that minimal good quality day care has no serious effects on a child's cognitive, social or emotional development.

Promoting positive parenting

While non-examinable, *Higher Psychology* is delighted to promote good parenting. This is because an understanding of early socialisation can help us become better parents.

Take our study of attachment. We know that a primary caregiver's sensitive responsiveness and intellectual stimulation can influence a child's cognitive, social, and emotional development. We also know that parents play a huge role in the socialisation of their children. Their particular child-rearing style has a large part to play in this.

Psychology believes there is then a relationship between a parent's child-rearing style, and the personality their child can become.

Child-rearing styles

There is a range of child rearing styles evident in the UK. Generally we can identify the following:

The authoritarian parent: is the parent who does not consult with their child. This parent makes all decisions concerning their child independently of what their child wants.

The democratic parent: is the parent who consults with their child. At the end of the day they will decide what is best for their child but will often take on board their view.

The permissive parent: is the parent who allows their child to make their own decisions.

The laissez-faire parent: is the parent who leaves their child to go their own way. They are not involved in any decisions the child may make. They do not guide their child. They neither praise nor blame them for good or bad behaviours.

The difference between the above parenting styles is the degree of independence they allow their child (Baumrind, 1966, 1967).

Parenting style, child independence and personality

In the mid-1960s Diana Baumrind tried to establish a connection between parenting style and independence shown by children.

After interviewing parents, and observing their children at home and at school, Baumrind analysed a number of parents' approaches to child rearing. She was able to identify three different styles of child rearing, that she called authoritarian, authoritative and permissive.

The psychological effect of parenting styles

Baumrind found that children of authoritarian parents were fairly self-reliant, but withdrawn and mistrustful. Children of authoritative parents were mature, competent, and independent. Children of permissive parents were immature, and lacked independence and self-discipline.

Baumrind (1966, 1967) concluded that a parent's child-rearing style could influence how independent their child becomes. The authoritative style seems best. This is where a child is given responsibility but is guided by their parent(s) regards the decisions that they make, and the things that they do.

A criticism of this study, and studies like it, is that in using the interview method of research we can never be sure if we have correctly identified the variable, or thing, that is causing the observed effect. In this instance differing parenting styles, and amount of independence shown by children. There may be more to the independent personality that child-rearing style alone.

One final observation of Baumrind (1966, 1967) concerns the consistency of parenting style. A parent might be authoritarian about good manners, but more democratic about pocket money etc. This confuses the relationship between parenting style and independence of personality their offspring might show.

The personality outcomes of Baumrind's three parenting styles

Authoritative parenting

➤ Lively and happy disposition

➤ Self-confident about ability to master tasks

➤ Well developed emotional control

➤ Developed social skills

➤ Less rigid about gender-type traits e.g. sensitivity in boys/independence in girls).

Authoritarian parenting

➤ Anxious, withdrawn, and unhappy disposition

➤ Poor emotional reactions to frustration e.g. girls are particularly likely to give up, and boys become especially hostile

➤ Do well in school

➤ Unlikely to engage in antisocial activities like drug and alcohol abuse, vandalism, gangs.

Permissive parenting

➤ Poor emotional control

➤ Rebellious and defiant when desires are challenged

➤ Low persistence to challenging tasks

➤ Antisocial behaviours.

ONLINE INTERACTIVES

Find out if any of the three Baumrind parenting categories apply to you.

Are you or would you be an authoritarian, authoritative of laissez-faire parent? Go to:

childrentoday.com/resources/articles/parent. htm and complete the online questionnaire.

A direct link is available in the Chapter Three section of the Higher Psychology Learning Suite at **www.gerardkeegan.co.uk/index.htm**

INTERACTIVES

Reflect on how you have been raised. What parenting style have you experienced? How do you think this has influenced your personality? Give reasons for your answer.

The psychological effects of leadership styles

In a classic study in 1938 Kurt Lewin, Ron Lippitt, and Ralph White investigated the effects of leadership styles on ten-year-old boys.

The boys all went to an after-school model making club. They were allocated to one of three groups. Each group was tasked with making model masks. Each group contained the same number of boys, and were balanced regards boys' IQ, their popularity, apparent energy etc.

In this experiment the independent variable was the leadership style to which the boys were exposed. The dependent variable was group productivity. An authoritarian leader ran the first group. He remained aloof from his boys, and in directing his group's activities issued orders without any consultation. A democratic leader ran the second group. He offered guidance, encouraged his boys, and actively participated in the group A *laissez-faire* leader ran

the third group. He gave his boys information regards the task. He did not become involved with them, nor did he participate much in his group's activities.

The results of the experiment showed that the boys in the authoritarian group worked the hardest. They were polite and respectful towards their leader. However, when they were left alone they stopped working, and quarrels were seen to break out.

The boys in the democratic group were a lot more cheerful in comparison! They didn't quarrel as much. They were interested in their work, and when speaking to their leader asked him questions about it. When he was absent, the boys continued to work. If a problem arose they all tried to find a solution to it.

The boys in the *laissez-faire* group were very disorganised and lazy. If they encountered a problem with what they had to do, they just gave up. They rarely asked for help. In contrast with the other two groups they were the most noisy and quarrelsome.

To ascertain what was causing their good/bad behaviours Lewin *et al.* changed the leaders around. They concluded that it was not the boys who were the problem; it was the style of leadership to which they were exposed.

However, an evaluation of Lewin, Lippitt and White (1938) should consider that the boys had been brought up for ten years by parents who had their own child-rearing style. The boys' good/bad behaviours in the three model making groups may have been a reaction to a *change* of leadership style, rather then the style itself.

INTERACTIVES

Reflect on your earlier years in secondary school.

Identify teachers you have had who adopted an authoritarian, authoritative or laissez-faire leadership style in the classroom.

Did you behave differently in these classes?

Using the likes of Baumrind, (1966, 1967), Lewin, Lippitt and White (1938) etc. why do you think this was the case?

Cultural variations in early socialisation

As we should now realise socialisation concerns the way we are reared. Child-rearing practices, or the socialisation process, differs from one country to another. This is to assist children to adjust to their *particular* culture. We must then appreciate the beliefs and customs of other peoples in the context of their own culture rather than our own. This is known as cultural relativism.

One of the most famous researchers in this field is Margaret Mead (1901–1978). Mead, a **cultural anthropologist**, is best known for her book entitled *Coming of Age in Samoa* (1928).

Figure 3.10 Margaret Mead

ONLINE INTERACTIVES

Read more about Margaret Mead. Visit:

en.wikipedia.org/wiki/Margaret_Mead and www.loc.gov/exhibits/mead/field-sepik.html

A direct link is available in the Chapter Three section of the Higher Psychology Learning Suite at **www.gerardkeegan.co.uk/index.htm**

In it she writes eloquently about cultural influences on human development among the tribes' people of Samoa, New Guinea, and other remote Pacific Islands. She contrasts Polynesian family structure, education, and child-rearing practices and its effects with that of Western cultures such as the United States of America. Take her observations of different child rearing practices observed in three tribes in the region.

The Arapesh tribe live in the mountains of New Guinea. They are a poor people who live in an egalitarian society. They grow crops and raise animals communally. As a culture they demonstrate co-operation and gentleness. Babies are regarded as soft, vulnerable and precious. They are cared for and nurtured with extreme affection by both parents. Their tantrums are appeased. Marriage reflects the passivity of childhood. Men take a child bride, and feed and protect her. He is replaying the role his parents played for him as a child. Among the Arapesh arguments and aggression are rare.

This is in stark contrast to the Mundugumor tribe who live in the Sepik region of New Guinea. Nowadays known as the Biwat, they are fierce, aggressive and intolerant. Babies have to struggle for their mother's breast. They are fed while the mother is standing, and are never cuddled. Children have to assert themselves with others. Compared to the Arapesh child many would say they live very Spartan lives.

While the Arapesh five-year-old is gleefully playing, the Mundugumor five-year-old can is sent to a rival tribe's village as a hostage in the event of war! There they grow up very independent and self-reliant.

The third tribe Mead investigated were the Samoans. She found them a balanced and stable people interested in the pursuit of knowledge. They avoid excess. All the women in a household nurse any infants. They are later cared for by girls as young as six-years-old. The emphasis on child rearing among the Samoans is on natural, gradual development. Children are never punished. If they become irritating or annoying to adults the six-year-olds 'nurse's' job is to remove them. Infants are fed and cuddled on demand. They are allowed to sleep whenever they want. Around age six they adopt gender roles and behaviours, in that little girls become child nurses, and little boys learn to swim, fish etc.

Mead observed that as adults the Samoans are gentle, balanced and serene. They have a very stable family structure, with little disturbance in their society. While Freeman (1983) suggests Mead overemphasises the influence of culture on the development of personality, Ballard (1983) believes her conclusions hold good.

INTERACTIVES

Describe the differing Arapesh, Mundugumor and Samoan cultures. Why did Mead think differences arose? Give reasons for your answer.

Because of cultural relativism it is apparent that there are great variations in socialisation and child rearing practices worldwide.

In 1973 Urie Bronfenbrenner compared child-rearing practices in the then Union of Soviet Socialist Republics, with that of the United States of America. Bronfenbrenner found many differences. The main one being that the USSR had more of a planned approach to child rearing.

Because upwards of 20 million Soviet citizens were killed during the Second World War children were seen as incredibly precious. Soviet society was much more conscious that they were raising the adults of the future. As a result they took much more of an interest in the process.

Bronfenbrenner discovered that the peer group had a pronounced influence in moulding younger children's behaviour.

In America, teenagers and their peer group worked against society's values, while in the USSR the peer group embraced society's values. This might have been because in the USSR children and teenagers were not as cut off from the adult world as they were and are in the USA.

Factories in Russian towns and cities often adopted a class in a primary or secondary school. Mutual visits were then arranged. Children and adults had a better perception of the others' place in the broader society.

Bronfenbrenner was moved to report one particular incident that he saw. It concerned a little boy who was running along the street obviously escaping from his mum! A group of Russian teenage boys, rather then ignore him or worse, picked him up and duly returned him to his grateful mother.

Bronfenbrenner suggests that in the USA children are not regarded as so valuable. They often have to take second place to their parents' interests. According to the American Bureau of Labour Statistics, more than 25 million Americans work more than 49 hours a week. Of that, eleven million spend 60 hours or more at work each week.

Americans also have shorter holiday entitlements, the national average being thirteen days per year. They also have longer working days.

According to the 2001 census, and taking account of part-time working, in the UK women work on average 31.4 hours per week, and men 42.2 hours per week. The UK also has a statutory maximum working week of 48 hours.

With parents working long hours Bronfenbrenner was concerned that they and their children become even more alienated from one another. He thought that insufficient parental involvement was related to the increasing levels of vandalism in the USA.

With an eye to the need for quality intellectual stimulation, and related cognitive, social and emotional growth, he also saw a danger in television replacing parent–child interactions.

He has a point when one considers the following...

The box in the corner

AC Neilson and Co. is one of the worlds leading marketing companies. AC Neilson and Co. reports that American parents spend 3.5 minutes per week in meaningful conversation with their children. Their children watch on average four hours of TV per day. That's 28 hours a week, or two months a year. By age 65, nine years will have been spent in front of the TV.

By age twelve an American child will have seen 8000 murders on television. By age eighteen, they will have seen 200,000 scenes of violence. Seventy-nine per cent of Americans believe there is a relationship between TV and real-life violence.

Not that we in the UK should be too smug!

According to Sigman (2007) by the time a child in Britain reaches the age of six they will have spent a year in front of the television.

In a meta-analysis of 35 previous studies, Sigman found that watching TV suppresses the production of the hormone **melatonin**. Melatonin is important regards the workings of our immune system; sleep cycle and the onset of puberty. He posits that the lower melatonin levels found nowadays in pre-secondary school females may be the cause of girls reaching puberty earlier than in previous generations. Sigman's research indicates that watching TV in early childhood may trigger autism, and can precipitate the onset of Type II diabetes. He also says that in adulthood excessive TV viewing can increase the chance of developing Alzheimer's disease.

Social variations in early socialisation

Our position in society influences how we are brought up. This affects our personality and life chances.

Our position is measured in terms of socio-economic status. In Britain socio-economic status or SES is ascertained on the basis of census data using a sophisticated occupational coding system (Meier and Moy, 1999). After the last census of 2001 the Office of National Statistics coded everyone's socio-economic status as below.

The National Statistics socio-economic classification analytic classes
1 Higher managerial and professional occupations
1.1 Large employers and higher managerial occupations
1.2 Higher professional occupations
2 Lower managerial and professional occupations
3 Intermediate occupations
4 Small employers and own account workers
5 Lower supervisory and technical occupations
6 Semi-routine occupations
7 Routine occupations
8 Never worked and long-term unemployed

Table 3.7 UK socio-economic status

Figure 3.11 Eton schoolboys

For our purposes SES refers to a person's class, wealth, and economic position in society. A parent's socio-economic status affects how their children are raised. Socio-economic status is reflected in the socialisation process we each undergo.

Kohn (1977) tells us that parents in lower level routine occupations (e.g. 5, 6, 7 and 8) are more likely to want obedience, neatness and good manners from their children. Their children lack confidence about what the future holds for them. It is likely that these children are raised in the more authoritarian household, in that these traits support the earlier findings of Baumrind, and Lewin, Lippitt and White etc.

Alternatively, children whose parents are of intermediate socio-economic status, and who were formerly known as the 'middle class' (e.g. 2, 3, and 4), have higher expectations of their offspring. They place greater emphasis in developing their children's independence. Their children tend to have a more positive and optimistic outlook regards what the future holds for them. It is more likely these children are exposed to an authoritative parenting style.

The research suggests that the value a middle-class parent places in independence facilitates their children's upward social mobility, while the working-class parents' emphasis on obedience prohibits it (Kohn, 1977).

Socio-economic status and educational success

The Office of National Statistics tells us that parental and family circumstance impacts upon educational success. Socio-economic status affects cognitive achievement.

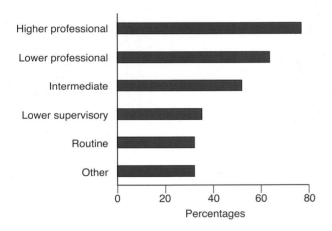

Figure 3.12 Attainment of five or more GCSE grades A* to C: by parental NS–SEC, 2002, England and Wales

In 2002, 77 per cent of 16 year olds in England and Wales whose parents were employed in higher professional occupations got five or more A* to C grade GCSEs. This was more than double the proportion for children with parents in routine occupations (32 per cent).

Like attainment at school, participation in further or higher education is strongly influenced by people's social and economic background. In 2002, 87 per cent of sixteen year olds with parents in higher professional occupations were in full-time education. This compares with 60 per cent of those with parents in routine occupations, and 58 per cent of those with parents in lower supervisory occupations.

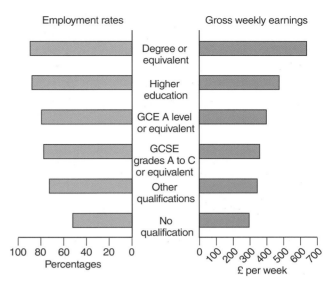

Figure 3.13 Employment rates and gross weekly earnings for full-time employees of working age: by highest qualification, spring 2003, UK

There is a distinct relationship between higher qualifications and higher earnings. As can be seen the earnings potential for possessing a degree is particularly high. In April 2003 the average gross weekly income of full-time employees in the UK with a degree was £632. This was more than double the weekly income of £298 for those with no qualifications. The likelihood of being employed is also higher for those with higher qualifications.

In April 2003, 88 per cent of working age adults with a degree were in full-time employment. This was in comparison to 50 per cent of working age adults with no qualifications.

Education is also a key to explaining the inequality gaps between advantaged and disadvantaged groups in terms of health, living standards and social participation.

Socio-economic status and health

In March 2007 the Scottish Executive issued figures indicating that one in five children in Scotland were living in poverty. A poor household in Scotland is one where the weekly income is less than 60 per cent of the national median wage. Poverty in Scotland is rising year on year. In 2006 there were 100,000 children living in poverty. In 2007 110,000 were living in poverty. Such families are blighted by chronic illness and disability, mental ill health and drug or alcohol addiction. They appear to be trapped inside a *cycle of poverty that is being passed on from one generation to the next.*

It has been known for quite some time that socio-economic status has a major impact on health. There is substantial evidence that a lower socio-economic status is associated with increased risks of certain diseases, infant mortality, and recently, a reduced life span.

Specter (2006) discovered that low social status accelerates the ageing process by about seven years.

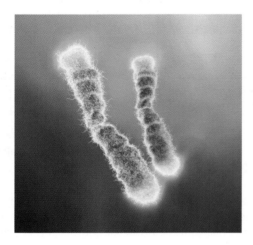

Figure 3.14 Telomeres

Specter's joint UK/US team analysed pieces of DNA called telomeres from 1552 female volunteers.

Their data revealed that people of lower socio-economic status are biologically older than those of higher socio-economic status.

In a very clever piece of research Specter compared, or correlated, the social class of his volunteers with the average length of their telomeres.

Telomeres are thought to indicate biological age, and are repeat sequences of DNA that sit on the ends of chromosomes, protecting them from damage.

As people age, their telomeres become shorter and shorter, leaving cells more susceptible to damage and death, which are the causes of ageing and disease.

Adjusting their data to account for factors such as chronological age, body mass index, smoking, and exercise Specter discovered that his volunteers' telomere length corresponded to their social class.

Specter thinks telomere length is stress related. According to him people of a lower social class suffer from an effort–reward imbalance in their work. Their self-esteem is lower. They have less control over their lives.

Specter believes all this may have a biological impact on the body, making cells divide more quickly. Ageing is accelerated.

Consequently the lower social class die seven years earlier than their higher social class counterparts.

ONLINE INTERACTIVES

Read 'Ageing linked to social status' at:
http://news.bbc.co.uk/2/hi/health/5188742.stm

What evidence does Specter (2006) use to counter claims that genetics cause telomeres to shorten prematurely?

A direct link is available in the Chapter Three section of the Higher Psychology Learning Suite at **www.gerardkeegan.co.uk/index.htm**

Postscript to promoting positive parenting

Kaye (1984) gives us good advice on positive parenting. Borrowing from the Soviet psychologist Lev Vygotsky, Kaye views infants and young children as 'apprentices'. They learn cognitive, social, and emotional mastery of their world from their parents. Parents provide 'scaffolding' or frameworks around which a child grows.

This includes caring for a child's physical and emotional well-being; protecting them from danger, but allowing them to safely explore their world; helping them manage, adapt, and cope with new experiences; giving them positive feedback on their behaviours to improve performance or avoid danger; acting as role models to demonstrate desirable skills and attitudes; encouraging meaningful communication; and acting as a memory aid to assist children organise information and plan ahead.

Sounds easy, but not so! Being a parent is one of the most difficult roles imaginable. There is no 'manual' to help us become the perfect parent. Given that most will one day have parental responsibilities it is important that we try to avoid inappropriate or ineffectual child rearing practices. The best advice is to seek advice from more experienced people or organisations.

These would include our own parents, brothers and sisters, grandparents, GPs, practice nurses, health visitors, social workers etc. Getting involved in a mother and toddler group is also a good idea. Talking to others is the key, which should continue until our children are well into adolescence.

The Royal College of Psychiatrists has published 36 excellent fact sheets on 'Mental Health and Growing Up' available from the link below.

ONLINE INTERACTIVES

The Royal College of Psychiatrists 'Mental Health and Growing Up' fact sheets are available at:

www.rcpsych.ac.uk/mentalhealthinformation/ mentalhealthandgrowingup.aspx

A direct link is available in the Chapter Three section of the Higher Psychology Learning Suite at **www.gerardkeegan.co.uk/index.htm**, which is probably just as well!

Chapter summary

This Chapter concerned early socialisation. Early socialisation is interested in sociability and attachment in infancy. We looked at what sociability and attachment is, how attachments develop, and what factors affect the quality of the attachment bond between an infant and their primary caregiver. The differences between privation and separation were examined in depth. Child rearing practices within and across different cultures were discussed, as was parenting styles and their effects. Theories and research concerning sociability, attachment, privation, deprivation, child rearing, and parenting styles were described, explained and evaluated. All are useful in our understanding of the various issues involved in early socialisation.

STRUCTURED QUESTIONS WITH ANSWER GUIDELINES

1   **Describe and explain Ainsworth *et al's*. (1978) Baltimore study.**

    With reference to the preceding pages, structure your answer as follows:

    ● Indicate this was a replication of Ainsworth's 1967 Ugandan study into attachment. What did she discover in Uganda?

    Then expand on the following features of the Baltimore study:

    ➤ Ainsworth *et al.* used 'the Strange Situation' to help compare her earlier observations of attachment behaviours

    ➤ describe 'the Strange Situation'

    ➤ describe the four behavioural measures the Strange Situation produced: separation anxiety, proximity, stranger anxiety, and reunion behaviours

    ➤ describe Ainsworth *et al's* findings (attachment types A, B and C)

STRUCTURED QUESTIONS WITH ANSWER GUIDELINES CONTINUED

2 Evaluate Ainsworth *et al*'s. (1978) Baltimore study.

With reference to the preceding pages structure your answer as follows:

● Ainsworth *et al*. (1978) confirmed that maternal sensitivity is the key variable to the development of secure attachments. A methodological criticism would be that in both the Ugandan and Baltimore studies a relatively small sample of participants took part. However, others support her work.

Then elaborate on the following remembering to refer to research studies where appropriate:

➤ Cross-cultural variations in attachment types: Van Ijzendoorn and Kroonenberg (1988) – aim, method, procedure, results, conclusion

➤ Family circumstance and attachment types

➤ Temperament and attachment types

➤ Ecological validity and attachment types

ONLINE INTERACTIVES

1 Go to the Higher Psychology Learning Suite at **www.gerardkeegan.co.uk/index.htm**. Click Chapter Three 'Developmental Psychology: Early Socialisation' to access direct links to all websites mentioned in this chapter.

2 Go to the Higher Psychology Learning Suite at **www.gerardkeegan.co.uk/index.htm**. Click Chapter Three 'Developmental Psychology: Early Socialisation' and do the online interactive crossword. But don't cheat!

3 Go to the Higher Psychology Learning Suite at **www.gerardkeegan.co.uk/index.htm**. Click Chapter Three 'Developmental Psychology: Early Socialisation' and do the online interactive hangman game. Try and beat the executioner!

4 Go to the Higher Psychology Learning Suite at **www.gerardkeegan.co.uk/index.htm**. Click Chapter Three 'Developmental Psychology: Early Socialisation' and print off the hard copy crossword. When finished you might like to hand it into your teacher as homework.

5 Go to the Higher Psychology Learning Suite at **www.gerardkeegan.co.uk/index.htm**. Click Chapter Three 'Developmental Psychology: Early Socialisation' and do the online interactive quiz. Try and win the prize!

GLOSSARY

Affectionless psychopath: (a *sociopath*): Someone who lacks conscience regards their often criminal activities.

Attachment: Active, emotional and mutual relationship between two people (usually infant and parent/primary caregiver) with interaction reinforcing and and strengthening the link or monotropic bond.

Critical period: A set time where something must occur otherwise a deficit is experienced.

Developmental pathways: The physical, cognitive social and emotional paths we journey along in life influenced by experience.

Enculturation: The learning of society's norms, values or ways of behaving.

External validity: Ability of a theory/piece of research to sustain itself when confronted with alternative explanations for the phenomenon under investigation.

Gender: Roles and behaviours regarding the significance of being male or female.

Internal Validity: The ability/inability of contributory pieces of research to sustain a proposed theory.

Longitudinal study: A (case; observational) study that lasts more then one year.

Matched pairs design: An experimental design where groups of participants are matched for extraneous physical, cognitive social and emotional confounding variables.

Monotropy: The attachment/affectional bond formed (usually) between mother and infant.

Nature: Aspects of an individuals physical, cognitive, social and emotional make-up influenced by genetics.

Nurture: Aspects of an individuals physical, cognitive, social and emotional make-up influenced by environment.

Primary caregiver: Person who qualitatively and quantitatively nurtures a baby, infant child etc. in the absence of the biological mother.

Reinforcement: Something which increases/decreases the likelihood of a behaviour being repeated i.e. a reward or punishment.

Self-concept: Knowledge of personal identity – who you are and who you are in relation to other people.

Self-esteem: How much we value, respect and appreciate whom we have become.

Self-image: A person's sense of self or personal identity.

Sex-role identification: Sex-role and associated gender behaviour: behaving in a masculine or feminine way evident from ages two to five.

Sociability: The particular temperament we have at birth. Influenced by genetics and foetal environment and is the building block to personality.

Socialisation: Process of developing the habits, skills, values, and motives shared by members of a particular society or culture.

CHAPTER FOUR

Biological Psychology: Stress

BY THE END OF THIS CHAPTER YOU SHOULD BE ABLE TO:
- Demonstrate a knowledge and understanding of stress
- Analyse and evaluate stress

Before turning to our subject proper, let us first locate *stress* in its parent domain.

Stress is a topic studied in **physiological psychology**, which is part of the **biological approach** as to why, and how, it is we think, feel and behave as we do.

Stress is our body's uncertain response to demands placed upon it.

What *is* the biological approach to psychology?

As suggested in Chapter One the biological approach in psychology analyses us from the point of view of our **genetics** and **physiology**.

Thus the study of psychology from a biological approach can be divided into two areas; evolutionary psychology and physiological psychology.

The biological approach: evolutionary psychology

Evolutionary psychology emphasises the influence of our genetics on our thoughts feelings and behaviours.

Our genetics are those individual biological characteristics that we inherit from our natural

parents, and also those evolved biological characteristics that we commonly share.

As was suggested in Chapter One, evolutionary psychology with its emphasis on genetics has been very much influenced by the work of Charles Darwin.

The biological approach also concerns the influence of our physiology

The biological approach: physiological psychology

Our physiology refers to our physical being, or bodily processes and functions.

The study of stress emphasises **physiological psychology**, and is largely understood from this point of view.

Overview of physiological psychology

Generally physiological psychology investigates where behaviours occur in our brain, and looks at associated topics like emotion, motivation, stress, dreams and dream states, etc. Physiological psychology is also concerned with our **central nervous system (CNS)** and our **endocrine system**.

Our CNS consists of our brain, spinal cord and bodily nerve fibres that connect with our sense organs, muscles, glands, and internal organs. Our central nervous system controls our bodily functions.

Our brain's **hypothalamus** and the **pituitary gland** direct our **autonomic nervous system** to activate the endocrine system in its release of hormones. Our endocrine system is the network of glands that manufacture and secrete chemical messengers called **hormones** throughout our bloodstream. These hormones consequently act on structures and functions throughout our body. Hormones, the consequence of the endocrine system, direct bodily functions, and prompt puberty for example.

In order to better understand this it is important we have some knowledge of our bodily structures and functions.

Physiological psychology and the nervous system

 ... Biopsychology's uinique contribution to neuroscientific research is a knowledge of behaviour and of the methods of behavioural research ... the ultimate purpose of the nervous system is to produce and control behaviour."

(Pinel, 1993)

Physiological psychology understands us as a result of our nervous system.

The nervous system of the human body consists of a number of divisions and subdivisions. The two interrelated divisions of the human nervous system are the central nervous system, or CNS, and the peripheral nervous system, or PNS.

Before looking at the nervous system in particular, it is important to introduce a major aspect to our physiology, the neuron.

Neurons help communication in the body.

Neurons

We receive information about our environment via our sensory organs, which are our eyes, ears and nose etc.

This information is transmitted to the brain, which sees us react almost instantaneously in some way.

How this happens is that our nervous system picks up and sends this information to our brain, and then to the rest of the body, through an intricate network of between ten and twelve billion specialised nerve cells called **neurons**.

Neurons receive, process, and/or transmit information to, and from, the brain to all parts of our body.

Neurons have two major functions:

➤ to transmit environmental information that impinges on our senses to our brain

➤ and to then transmit information from our brain to our body's organs to initiate action

Eighty per cent of neurons are to be found in the outer layer of the brain known as the cerebral cortex. The only energy our brain and internal body understands is electrical energy. When an external energy is picked up by the physiology of our senses, be it pressure, light or sound, it is converted into electrical energy. It is the job of our neurons to convey this information to our brain to be processed, understood and acted upon.

Our nerves are made up of bundles of neurons. Most neurons receive information from other neurons, and pass this information on.

Types of neurons

We have three types of neuron.

Sensory neurons

Also called afferent neurons respond directly to external stimuli from our environment. Sensory neurons carry messages from our sense organs to the spinal cord and brain.

Motor neurons

Also called efferent neurons carry messages from the brain and spinal cord to our muscles and glands.

Interneurons

Also called connector or association neurons, these link neuron to neuron, and integrate sensory and motor neurons. Only very occasionally do motor and sensory neurons connect directly.

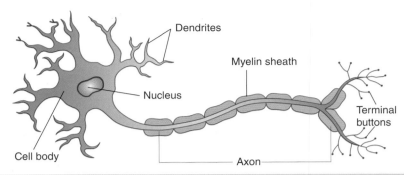

Nucleus: The cell body, or soma, of a neuron consists of its nucleus, which houses our genetic code, and cytoplasm, from which the nucleus feeds.

Dendrites: The dendrites help each neuron make electrochemical contact with its neighbours.

Axons: The axon, a thin cylinder of protoplasm, carries signals received by dendrites to other neurons, muscles or glands.

Myelin sheath: With some neurons, a white fatty substance called the myelin sheath surrounds the axon and insulates it, which helps in the transmission of electrochemical signals to the terminal buttons, or synaptic knobs.

Terminal buttons: Terminal buttons or synaptic knobs transmit neural impulses directly from the axon of one neuron to the dendrites of another.

Figure 4.1 Anatomy of a neuron

Organisation of the nervous system

As we now know the human nervous system consists of our central nervous system, the brain and spinal cord, and our peripheral nervous system.

The **peripheral nervous system** sends information about our environment, via the senses, to our central nervous system, and also assists the CNS to send information to our muscles and glands.

The peripheral nervous system

Our peripheral nervous system consists of two subdivisions, the somatic and the autonomic nervous systems, and connects our brain to our outside world.

What is the somatic nervous system?

The somatic nervous system deals with our external environment and controls our sensory and motor nerves, which account for our voluntary movements and actions.

What is the autonomic nervous system?

The autonomic nervous system controls our internal world, or internal bodily environment.

The somatic nervous system and the autonomic nervous system together make up the nerves in our body that connect our brain and spinal cord to our senses, our internal organs, and our glands.

Two types of nerves are found in the somatic nervous system, **sensory nerves** and **motor nerves**.

Sensory nerves and motor nerves

Sensory nerves transmit information about our external environment to our central nervous system, which make us aware of pain, pressure and temperature variation.

Motor nerves of the somatic system carry impulses from the central nervous system to the muscles of the body, where they initiate action.

The motor nerves of our somatic nervous system control all of those muscles that we use to engage in voluntary actions and movements such as walking and smiling.

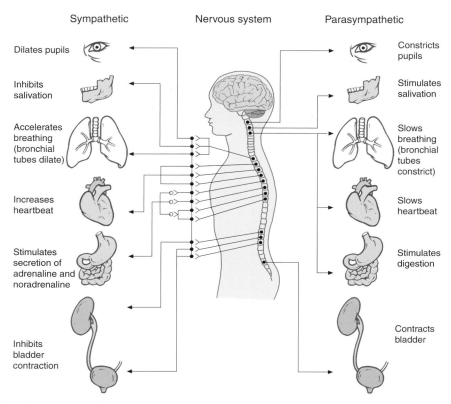

Figure 4.2 The autonomic nervous system

These motor nerves also govern the involuntary movements we make to adjust our posture and balance.

The autonomic nervous system

The **autonomic nervous system** or ANS controls our internal organs and glands, over which we have little voluntary control.

The function of our ANS is to regulate our internal bodily environment by sending information to our CNS, which then directs any necessary adjustments.

The ANS is subdivided into two branches, the sympathetic branch, and the parasympathetic branch.

The sympathetic branch of the ANS

The **sympathetic branch** of our ANS moves us to action in our world.

What this means is that the sympathetic branch of the ANS operates when we have to use, or expend, energy.

The parasympathetic branch of the ANS

The **parasympathetic branch** of our ANS operates when we have to restore this expended energy to our body.

The sympathetic and parasympathetic branches of our autonomic nervous system are therefore said to be *antagonistic* to each other. Simply put, as one pulls in one direction, the other pulls in the other direction. This is to return the body to a state of **homeostasis**, or internal balance.

The sympathetic and parasympathetic branches and homeostasis

The sympathetic branch of our ANS is made up of bundles of neurons that run up either side of our spinal cord to our brain.

The ANS directs and drives our bodily response to stressful environmental situations, such as emergencies. This is called our fight or flight response (Cannon, 1927).

In an emergency such as fight or flight we can often become aware of our sympathetic branch as it increases our heart rate, dilates our pupils, increases our breathing and dries our mouth. All this is necessary to focus energy outwards to deal with the situation.

When the emergency has passed, this additional energy is no longer required and the parasympathetic branch of our ANS takes over to return our body to its natural state of *homeostasis*.

To achieve homeostasis, which is a constant, calm, comfortable internal bodily environment, the parasympathetic branch constricts the pupil, stimulates salivation, constricts our bronchial tubes, etc.

The endocrine system

As suggested earlier the endocrine system is a network of glands that manufacture and secrete chemical messengers called **hormones** into our bloodstream. These powerful chemical messengers act on structures and functions throughout our body.

Our endocrine system is important to our physical development and complex psychological behaviours.

Although the endocrine system is not part of the human nervous system as such, it is related to the activities of our autonomic nervous system.

Our brain's **hypothalamus** and the **pituitary gland**, known as our master gland, direct the autonomic nervous system to activate the endocrine system to stimulate the release of hormones in our body.

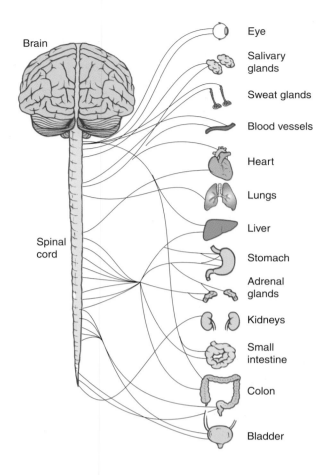

Figure 4.3 This diagram illustrates those organs of our body that are affected by the sympathetic and parasympathetic branches of our autonomic nervous system.

These hormones are secreted into the blood, and then travel throughout our body to control a wide variety of bodily activities.

The Pituitary Gland

The pituitary gland is our most important gland, in that it produces the largest number of hormones, and also controls the release of hormones by other endocrine glands.

Gonadotrophin is a hormone, produced by the pituitary gland, which ends up at the gonads. In the gonads it stimulates the production of oestrogen, progesterone and some testosterone in females, and of testosterone in males.

During puberty, oestrogen stimulates breast development and causes the vagina, uterus (womb) and fallopian tubes (that carry eggs to the womb) to mature. It also plays a role in the adolescent growth spurt and alters the distribution of fat in females, resulting in more fat being deposited around the hips, buttocks, and thighs. Oestrogen is important in preparing a female's body for childbirth. Testosterone helps to promote muscle and bone growth, and is linked to aggression.

Hormones

Probably the most common of hormones is adrenaline, which we came across above in relation to flight or fight.

Adrenaline is central to emotions such as fear, anger and aggression. The ANS, hypothalamus and pituitary gland all have a role in the production of adrenaline.

The effects of adrenaline

The effects of adrenaline include:

> increase in heart rate.

> increase in oxygen intake and breathing patterns.

> the release of sugar stored in the liver and muscles into the bloodstream as glycogen – this is our inner fuel or energy to help us fight or flight.

> the reduction of blood supply to less important parts of the body, by the hypothalamus and ANS, to focus energy outwards towards dealing with the stimulus that has got us into this emotional state (fear, anger, aggression).

Another important hormone is somatotrophin, which is our growth hormone. Its effect is evident throughout infancy, childhood, adolescence, and adulthood.

Somatotrophin is secreted by our pituitary gland and influences the growth of our bones and muscles, and is ultimately responsible for our adult height. Too much somatotrophin can lead to gigantism, while too little can lead to pituitary dwarfism.

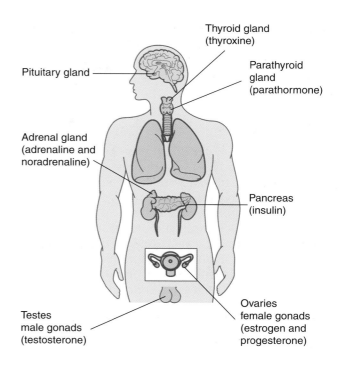

Figure 4.4 Major glands in the endocrine system

Oxytocin is secreted by the hypothalamus and acts on the uterus, or womb, stimulating contractions during childbirth, and lactation when breast-feeding.

Insulin is produced in our pancreas to control our blood-sugar levels. Too much sugar in the bloodstream occurs in diabetes, which is potentially fatal unless treated.

Hormone	Function
Oestrogen	Important for puberty in girls
Adrenaline	Important to fight or flight
Gonadotrophin	Prompts puberty in both sexes
Somatotrophin	Growth hormone
Insulin	Controls blood-sugar levels
Testosterone	Important for puberty in boys
Oxytocin,	Aids childbirth

Table 4.1 Hormones and functions

The central nervous system

The central nervous system consists of our brain and spinal cord.

The spinal cord

Our spinal cord travels all the way down our back and connects our brain with the rest of our body. Our spinal cord is like a fibre optic cable that allows communication between our central nervous system and our peripheral nervous system. Any damage or accident to the vertebrae and nerves in the spinal cord can have devastating results. A damaged spinal cord effectively cuts off the communication link between the brain, spinal cord, peripheral nervous system, and the muscles. The effect can be widespread paralysis.

The brain

The function of our brain is threefold.

➤ Our brain takes in information, via our senses, about stimuli in our external environment.
➤ Our brain processes and interprets this information to allow us to make sense of it, and then;
➤ Our brain directs us, consciously or unconsciously, to think, feel, and/or behave in a particular way towards these stimuli.

Information received by us about our outside world, and from the rest of the body, converges at the brain to be processed, understood and acted upon.

Our brain is a hugely complex information-processor. Its power is due to its make-up. It comprises between eight and twelve billion neurons, each of which will have between 1000 and 10,000 synapses connecting with other neurons.

Remembering that the body communicates on the basis of neurotransmitters, or electrochemical signals, the permutations here are awesome.

The number of ways neurons in a human brain can be connected and interconnected exceeds the estimated number of atoms that go to make up our universe.

Via nerve impulses, communication occurs between the brain and the spinal cord, and also between the brain and twelve pairs of cranial nerves. Some of our cranial nerves are mixed, containing both sensory and motor axons.

Some, like the optic and olfactory nerves, contain sensory axons only, while others contain motor axons only, an example here being the cranial nerves that control the muscles of our eyeball!

The structure and functions of the brain

The human brain has three parts: the forebrain, the midbrain and the hindbrain.

The forebrain is at the top of our head, the midbrain is hidden, while the hindbrain is at the bottom of our head and extends into the top of our spinal cord.

The forebrain

The cerebrum is the largest part of the human forebrain and is divided into two separate cerebral hemispheres: the right cerebral hemisphere and the left cerebral hemisphere. The visible part of our cerebrum, or the outermost layer of our brain, is called our cerebral cortex.

The cerebral cortex

The two hemispheres of the cerebrum have numerous interconnections, especially through the hidden corpus callosum, a bundle of about 200 million nerve fibres that transfers information back and forth between the two hemispheres. Most of the nerve fibres connecting the brain to the various parts of the body cross from left to right, or from right to left. This means that the right cerebral hemisphere receives sensory messages from, and controls movement, on the left-hand side of the body, while the left cerebral hemisphere receives sensory messages from, and controls movement on, the right-hand side of the body.

Frontal lobe

The frontal lobe is important regards planning, initiative and voluntary motor control. The frontal lobe is a highly developed area of the brain in humans compared to animals. Damage to the frontal lobe causes lack of insight, spontaneity and an inability to adjust behaviour to a given situation.

Parietal lobe

The parietal lobe is important regards sensation and monitoring of body parts. The parietal lobe integrates information from different sensory areas, e.g. pairing up the *sight* and *sound* of an object. Damage to the parietal lobe can cause a wide range of difficulties depending on which area is damaged.

Damage to the parietal lobe due to physical trauma or a stroke can result in paralysis.

Temporal lobe

The temporal lobe is responsible for our hearing, language and memory.

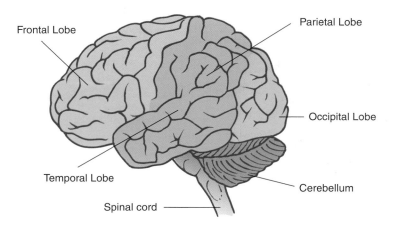

Figure 4.5 The brain

Damage to the temporal lobe may cause impairment of any of these functions.

Occipital lobe
The occipital lobe is concerned with vision. Damage to the occipital lobe may cause a variety of visual disturbances, depending on where damage occurred.

Spinal cord
The spinal cord is part of the central nervous system that extends from the base of our skull and through the vertebrae of our spinal column. Neurons in the spinal cord connect neurons in the brain to neurons in the body via 31 pairs of spinal nerves, which communicate with the body as a whole.

Cerebellum
The cerebellum is responsible for the coordination of movement and balance.

Cross-sectional structures of the brain

The thalamus
The thalamus is found at the centre of our forebrain and straddles the left and right cerebral hemispheres. The thalamus is a pivotal structure in the direction of information throughout our nervous system, and governs the flow of sensory information around our brain. It can be seen as a kind of relay station for all our senses. Its centre, called the thalamic nuclei, also relays commands between the motor cortex and our skeletal muscles.

The hypothalamus
The hypothalamus is a small nucleic structure situated just below the thalamus, which plays an important role in controlling the satisfaction of our physical needs. Important parts of the hypothalamus include the dorsal hypothalamus, concerned with pleasure seeking, the posterior hypothalamus concerned with sex drive, and the ventromedial hypothalamus, concerned with hunger. The hypothalamus consequently influences eating, drinking and sexual activity.

As indicated earlier when we considered the sympathetic and parasympathetic nervous system, the hypothalamus also governs homeostasis in our body. It does this by monitoring our bodily functions, and setting off homeostatic mechanisms if the internal environment begins to deviate from optimum levels. For instance, if our bodies overheat, we sweat in order to cool down. Sweating is a homeostatic mechanism. The hypothalamus also plays an important role in our bodily reaction to stress.

Cerebral cortex
The cerebral cortex is the outer layer of the brain.

The corpus callosum
The two hemispheres of the cerebrum have numerous interconnections, especially through the hidden corpus callosum, which is a bundle of about 200 million nerve fibres that transfers information back and forth between the two hemispheres.

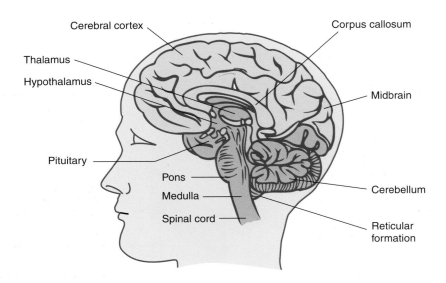

Figure 4.6 The brain in cross-section

The midbrain

The midbrain occupies only a small part of the human brain. The midbrain in other species is much larger. Structures in out midbrain include the reticular formation, the substantia nigra which helps coordinate our bodily movements, and the ventral tegmental area (VTA) associated with our pleasure-seeking behaviour. Problems with the substantia nigra contribute to Parkinson's Disease.

The reticular formation

Structures in out midbrain include the reticular formation, which gathers input from higher-level brain centres and passes it on to motor neurons.

Medulla

The middle or marrow of bone.

The pons

The pons is the bridge between the midbrain and the medulla. The pons connects our spinal cord with our brain, and parts of our brain with each other. It integrates movement on both sides of our body, and is important to functions such as breathing, alertness, sleep and attention.

Pituitary gland

Our master gland responsible for an array of hormones.

The cerebellum

The cerebellum lies behind the pons underneath our two cerebral hemispheres. The cerebellum is very wrinkled, much like a cauliflower. It is responsible for muscle tone, balance, and the coordination of our voluntary movements. The cerebellum assists in controlling our physical activity. The cerebellum operates our complex motor behaviour, leaving the rest of our brain free for more conscious and deliberate activities.

Before turning to our topic of 'Stress' test yourself on related biological structures and functions by doing this crossword

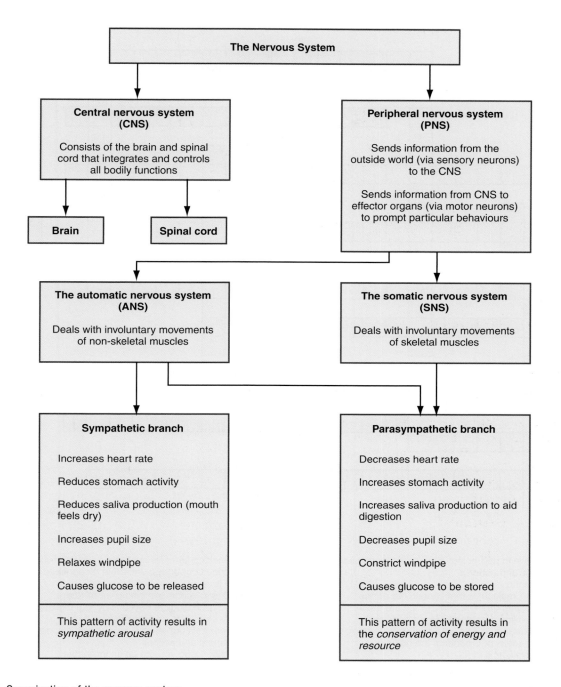

Figure 4.7 Organisation of the nervous system

Interactive crossword

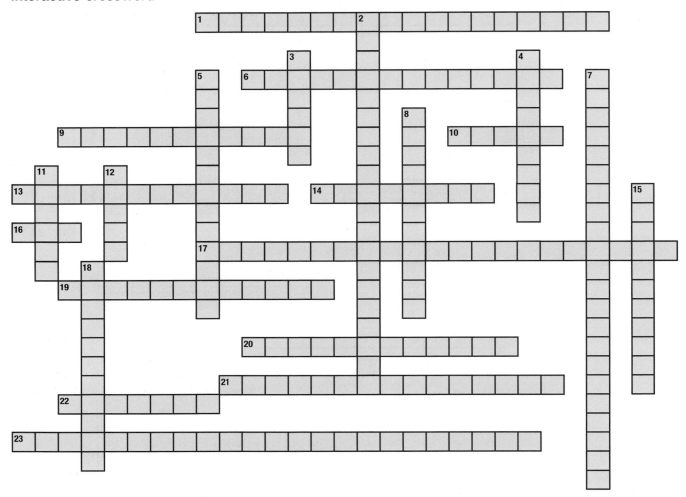

Across

1 The perspective in psychology that understands us in terms of our physiology and genetics
6 Our master gland
9 Very long DNA molecules that contain our genes
10 Adenine, cytosine, guanine and thynine are these
13 Involved in sensing and monitoring of body parts
14 Chemicals produced in one area of cells (or organ), which act at another place (cells or organs) of the body
16 Deoxyribonucleic acid
17 An area of study in psychology that looks at personality, atypical behaviour, and intelligence
19 The part of the brain that regulates body temperature, blood pressure, heartbeat, metabolism of fats and carbohydrates, sugar levels in the blood, hormonal secretions, and is also important regards our emotions
20 Word to describe the branch of Biological Psychology that explains our thoughts, feelings, and behaviours in terms of our inherited biological characteristics
21 Is said to be antagonistic to the sympathetic branch of the ANS
22 Cells in our body that mostly make up our nervous system
23 Connects our brain and spinal cord (CNS) to our outside world

Down

2 The medical term for our brain and spinal cord
3 Describes our body's uncertain response to demands placed upon it
4 Used to describe something we all share
5 Branch of Biological Psychology that explains us in terms of bodily structures and functions
7 This controls our internal organs and glands, involuntary movement and actions
8 Describes who you are as an individual
11 Told us about fight or flight
12 Controls our hereditary characteristics
15 Our body's natural state
18 The branch of ANS responsible for fight or flight response or the branch of PNS which prepares our body for emergencies

Answers are on p174

What is stress?

Stress can be defined as a feeling we experience when 'demands exceed the personal and social resources the individual is able to mobilise' (Lazarus, 1984).

For Lazarus, stress is a state of anxiety produced when events and responsibilities exceed our ability to cope.

Alternatively stress can be seen as *'the nonspecific response of the body to any demand made upon it'* (Selye, 1956).

For Selye these demands can be a threat, a challenge, or any kind of change that requires our body to adapt. Our body's response is automatic and immediate.

It is important to note that both Lazarus and Selye see stress in both a *positive* and *negative* light. On the one hand stress is good, on the other is is not so good!

Positive stress is called eustress, while negative stress is called distress.

ONLINE INTERACTIVES

Go to:

www.breathingspacescotland.co.uk

to find out more about stress; why it can be bad for us, and what we can do about it.

A direct link is available in the Chapter 4 section of the Higher Psychology Learning Suite at **www.gerardkeegan.co.uk**

Eustress and distress

Eustress is a positive form of stress, and is usually related to desirable events in our life. Generally eustress helps us to perform better.

Distress is the more common type of stress, with which we associate negative outcomes. Distress causes us upset and makes us unwell.

Symptoms of distress:

➤ Bad tempered/irritable

➤ Persistent headaches

➤ Persistent backache

➤ Worse than normal lack of concentration

➤ Feelings of panic

➤ Feelings that you can't get your breath properly

➤ Feelings of unhappiness or despair

➤ Feelings of pointlessness

➤ Stomach ache

➤ Dizziness

INTERACTIVE

Look at the symptoms of distress.

Under what circumstance did you last experience some or all of these symptoms?

Both eustress and distress are equally taxing on our body.

Their effects can be cumulative, depending on our ability to adapt to the changes or events that have triggered it.

What causes stress?

Stress can be caused by events or changes in our environment that requires us to psychologically adjust in response.

These life shaping events or changes are called **stressors**. Our body has us respond to such stressors physically, mentally and emotionally.

Types of stressor

Anderson (1991) distinguishes between three types of stressor:

Level 1 Chronic stressors: like racism, overcrowding, poor housing, noise etc.

Level 2 Major life events: see SRRS below.

Level 3 Hassles: see Hassles and Uplifts below.

We all cope with stressful situations differently.

Unemployment is a good example of this, in that what would be distress for one may be eustress for another. Why might this be the case?

Unemployment and the threat of redundancy may cause one individual to become physically, mentally and emotionally unwell. They perceive it as a threat that will have major negative consequences for them.

Another individual may react completely differently. They become physically, mentally and emotionally elated at the prospect!

This is because *they* see it as an opportunity to move on and try new things in life.

The cause of stress and our response to it thus varies from person to person.

Internal and external stressors

As we now know a *stressor* is a cause of stress. Stressors are both internal and external to us.

> **Examples of internal stressors**
>
> ➤ Lifestyle choices: caffeine, not enough sleep, overloaded schedule 'burning the candle at both ends'.
> ➤ Negative self-talk: pessimistic thinking, self-criticism, over-analysing.
> ➤ Mind traps: unrealistic expectations, taking things personally, all-or-nothing thinking, exaggerating, rigid thinking.
> ➤ Individual personality traits: Type A, perfectionist, workaholic, and pleaser etc.
>
> Do any of these internal factors cause you stress?
>
> Compare your answers with someone else if possible.
>
> **Examples of external stressors**
>
> ➤ Physical environment: noise, bright lights, heat, confined spaces.
> ➤ Social interactions with other people: rudeness, bossiness, aggressiveness, harassment, bullying etc. on the part of someone else.
> ➤ Organisational: rules, regulations, changes.

> ➤ Major life events: death of a relative, lost job, promotion, and new baby etc.
> ➤ Daily hassles: commuting, misplacing keys, mechanical breakdowns.
> ➤ Do any of these external factors cause you stress?
> ➤ Compare your answers with someone else if possible.

In psychological terms, stress is then a process where internal and external events or changes threaten our individual well-being. This has physiological and biochemical, psychological, and behavioural consequences for us.

Models of stress

Groesch and Fuller (1995) identified three models of stress:

➤ The **engineering model**, which sees stress as a **stimulus**.

➤ The **physiological model**, which sees stress as a **response**.

➤ The **transactional psychosocial model**, which sees stress as an **interaction** between our environment and ourselves.

The engineering model

The *engineering* model understands stress as an excess load or demand placed upon a person, which exceeds their ability to adapt to it.

The engineering model sees us as subjects of stress rather than actors. We become stressed because of external events that are outside our control.

Examples of situations outwith our control that could cause us stress would be the bus being late, the car not starting, the family pet dying, being 'restructured' in the workplace etc.

Stressors like these can place demands on individuals that are beyond our adaptive limits.

The physiological model

Of importance to Higher psychology is the *physiological* model of stress.

The physiological model understands stress in terms of our emotional response to whatever has caused it. Our emotional response to environmental stressors

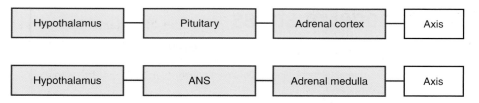

Figure 4.8 The hypothalamic-ANS-adrenal medulla axis and the hypothalamic-pituitary-adrenal cortex axis

is governed by our physiology, in particular our hypothalamus and autonomic nervous system.

Both operate individually and together to allow us to cope better in stressful situations. How our body responds to stress is understood in terms of two physiological pathways or routes that are regulated by our hypothalamus in our brain.

These two pathways, routes or *axes* produce biochemical hormones that influence how our body feels and behaves towards whatever is stressing us in the first place.

They are called the hypothalamic-ANS-adrenal medulla axis, which drives our short-term response to stress, and the hypothalamic-pituitary-adrenal cortex axis, which drives our long-term response to stress.

INTERACTIVE

Please answer the following questions.

1   What is the hypothalamus?

2   What is the pituitary gland?

3   What is the autonomic nervous system?

The adrenal glands

The two axes are linked in our body by way of our adrenal glands, which are to be found just above each of our kidneys.

Our adrenal glands are part of our endocrine system, and like it are controlled by our hypothalamus. Our adrenal glands have two parts: the adrenal cortex and the adrenal medulla.

The adrenal cortex, which is the outer part of our adrenal gland, releases a series of hormones called **Glucocorticoids** into our bloodstream.

The adrenal medulla releases hormones such as **Adrenaline** and **Noradrenaline** into our bloodstream.

All help us deal with stress in the short- and long-term.

The hypothalamus is found at the base of the brain, and has a small structure sitting above it called the pituitary gland. They control the endocrine system in our body.

The endocrine system secretes hormones in to our bloodstream, which act as chemical 'messengers' instructing our body what to do. Hormones can have dramatic effects on our behaviour and emotions.

In a stressful situation our pituitary gland or 'master gland' secretes certain hormones into our bloodstream. These travel via our bloodstream to various parts of our body e.g. the kidneys, where they initiate the release of further hormones, which have us behave in particular ways.

143

The physiological model of stress

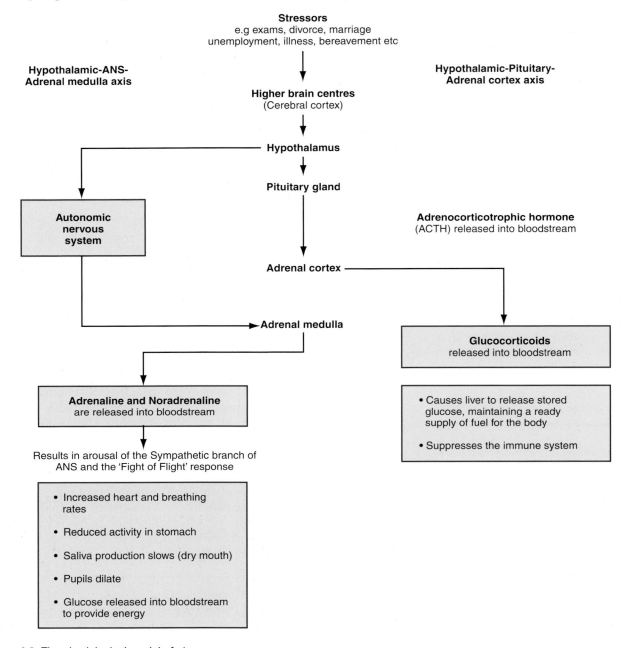

Stressors
e.g exams, divorce, marriage
unemployment, illness, bereavement etc

Hypothalamic-ANS-Adrenal medulla axis

Hypothalamic-Pituitary-Adrenal cortex axis

Higher brain centres
(Cerebral cortex)

Hypothalamus

Pituitary gland

Autonomic nervous system

Adrenocorticotrophic hormone
(ACTH) released into bloodstream

Adrenal cortex

Adrenal medulla

Glucocorticoids
released into bloodstream

Adrenaline and Noradrenaline
are released into bloodstream

- Causes liver to release stored glucose, maintaining a ready supply of fuel for the body

- Suppresses the immune system

Results in arousal of the Sympathetic branch of ANS and the 'Fight of Flight' response

- Increased heart and breathing rates

- Reduced activity in stomach

- Saliva production slows (dry mouth)

- Pupils dilate

- Glucose released into bloodstream to provide energy

Figure 4.9 The physiological model of stress

The physiological model of stress: short-term response

Our immediate and short-term response to an environmental stressor involves the hypothalamic-ANS-adrenal medulla axis, or pathway.

Our *immediate* response to a stressor shocks the sympathetic branch of our autonomic nervous system into action. Regards our body's physiological response to stress, five things occur in the short term.

➤ The sympathetic branch stimulates the adrenal medulla in our adrenal glands.

➤ The adrenal medulla then secretes two hormones: adrenaline, and noradrenaline.

➤ These hormones arouse activity in our sympathetic nervous system and reduce activity in the parasympathetic nervous system.

➤ Arousal of the sympathetic nervous system leads to the 'fight or flight' response (Cannon, 1914). The 'flight or fight' response prepares the body for action, which can be either fighting or fleeing the threat or danger.

➤ Once the 'threat' is over the parasympathetic branch takes control and brings the body back into a balanced state. This is called homeostasis.

No adverse physiological effects are experienced by our short-term response to stress. Indeed this innate ability, which is outwith our conscious control has survival value for us.

INTERACTIVES

Please read this scenario and answer the question that follows.

You are walking through a wood near your home. Suddenly a large ferocious dog appears yards in front of you.

From a physiological point of view explain your body's short-term response to this situation.

Structure your answer as follows:

● Define the physiological model of stress.

● Identify the stressor in the above situation.

● Briefly explain the elements that go to make up the hypothalamic-ANS-adrenal medulla axis.

● Describe the body's short-term reaction on this basis.

The physiological model of stress: long-term response

Our more prolonged long-term response to an environmental stressor involves the hypothalamic-pituitary-adrenal cortex axis, or pathway.

Prolonged exposure to a stressful situation demands that our body expends vast amounts of energy. Our body's counter-shock response helps minimise any damage that might be done to it due to prolonged exposure to stress.

➤ The pituitary gland produces an adrenocorticotrophic hormone (ACTH).

➤ ACTH then stimulates the adrenal cortex in our adrenal glands to produce other hormones called glucocorticoids. An important one being cortisol, which affects our glucose metabolism. Cortisol is our 'stress hormone'. When stressed cortisol is found in large amounts in our urine. Hormones like cortisol help us produce glucose, our body's internal fuel.

The physiological effects of our body's long-term response to stress are similar to those in the short-term.

However such long-term maintenance of increased heart and breathing rates, and associated physiological changes to our body do have negative health consequences for us.

To discover what these negative health consequences are Hans Selye conducted experiments with rats where he measured their physiological responses to external stressors such as heat and cold, prolonged restraint, and surgical procedures. Selye (1956) then extrapolated his findings to human beings.

He identified our body's defence mechanism against the effects of stress as the general adaptation syndrome (GAS). GAS is a descriptive term.

Life's a GAS

Hans Selye was an Austrian born physician who went to Canada in 1939. Here he studied the General Adaptation Syndrome.

> *'I call this syndrome general because it is produced by agents, which have a general effect upon large portions of the body. I call it adaptive because it stimulates defence... I call it a syndrome because its individual manifestations are co-ordinated and even partly dependent upon each other.''*
>
> *Selye (1956)*

Stress is one cause of the general adaptation syndrome.

The consequences of unrelieved stress include tiredness, irritability, lack of concentration and difficulty in sleeping. We may also experience hair loss.

Over and above stress itself, the general adaptation syndrome is further influenced by our general health and bodily well being, our sex, our age, our ethnic or racial background, our level of education,

our socio-economic status (SES), and genetic makeup, etc.

Some of these variables are biological in origin and difficult or impossible to change.

Selye thought that the general adaptation syndrome involved two major systems of the body, our nervous system and our endocrine (or hormonal) system.

He then went on to outline three distinctive stages in the evolution of the general adaptation syndrome.

Selye called these the alarm reaction stage (AR), the stage of resistance (SR), and the stage of exhaustion (SE).

Stage 1: Alarm reaction (AR)

The first stage of the general adaptation syndrome is called alarm reaction. Alarm reaction is our *immediate* reaction to a stressor. In the initial phase of stress, we demonstrate a '**fight or flight**' response, which prepares our body for physical activity.

However, our alarm reaction response to stress can *decrease* the effectiveness of our immune system, particularly if prolonged. We can thus be more susceptible to illness during this phase.

Overview of Stage 1 Alarm Reaction (AR)

- ➤ Presence of stressor registered
- ➤ Stress response systems activated
- ➤ ACTH secreted
- ➤ Glucocoticoids secreted
- ➤ Adrenaline and noradrenaline secreted

Alarm reaction gets our body to prepare to expend energy

When a stressful situation happens our body is thrown into a state of shock.

Physiological changes occur, and our body temperature and blood pressure are initially lowered. Physiological arousal to fight or flight takes over.

Stage 2: Resistance (SR)

Stage 2 of the GAS *could* be renamed a stage of adaptation, instead of the stage of resistance.

This is because during prolonged periods of stress our body *adapts* to the continued stress placed upon it. Such physiological adaptation allows us to survive better.

If for example the stressor was starvation, possibly due to anorexia, during the stage of resistance it is likely the person would experience a reduced desire for physical activity. This is in order to conserve energy. The person's body would also further adapt to maximise the absorption of nutrients from any food that they *do* ingest.

Overview of Stage 2: Resistance (SR)

- ➤ Body's stress response is fully activated in trying to cope with the stressor.
- ➤ 'Fight or flight' response less effective.

During the resistance stage our body tries to maintain 'normal' functioning. If stress is prolonged our body will remain in a high state of arousal in order to cope with it.

Continued exposure to the stressor (or additional stressors) eventually drains the body of its resources and leads to the third stage.

Stage 3: Stage of exhaustion (SE)

At this third and final stage stress will have continued for some time. Selye says that consequently our body's resistance may gradually reduce, or collapse altogether.

Generally, this means that our immune system, and our body's ability to resist disease, may be almost totally destroyed.

This sounds dramatic but patients who experience long-term stress have been found to be more vulnerable to heart attacks or severe infection due to their reduced immunity.

This makes sense, in that someone with a stressful job may experience long-term stress that might lead to high blood pressure, and an eventual heart attack.

Overview of Stage 3: Exhaustion (SE)

- ➤ Energy reserves depleted.
- ➤ Hormone levels depleted.
- ➤ Immune system collapses.
- ➤ Stress related illnesses become more likely

During this stage our bodily resources become so depleted that exhaustion occurs and our susceptibility to illness increases.

INTERACTIVE

Do you know of anyone who may have been prone to Stage 3 of Selye's GAS?

Give reasons for your answer.

Stress isn't all bad!

Selye did not regard stress in a purely negative light. He frequently pointed out that stress is an inevitable part of life, which can result in pleasure, as well as fear or anxiety.

As he says 'Stress is not even necessarily bad for you; it is also the spice of life, for any emotion, any activity, causes stress' (Selye, 1956).

Later researchers coined the term 'eustress', or pleasant stress, to reflect that positive experiences such as a promotion, completing a degree, a training programme, getting married, foreign travel, etc. while stressful are also joyful.

Selye also tells us that our perception of stress and our response to it is highly individualised.

A job or sport that one person finds anxiety provoking or exhausting, may be appealing and enjoyable to someone else. As said earlier what is distress for one, is eustress for another.

In *The Stress of Life* (1956) Selye suggests we deal with stress by 'living wisely in accordance with natural laws.'

How to deal with stress

➤ Adopt an attitude of gratitude toward life rather than seek revenge for injuries or slights.

➤ Act toward others from altruistic rather than self-centered motives.

➤ Retain a capacity for wonder and delight in the genuinely good and beautiful things in life.

➤ Find a purpose for your life and express your individuality in fulfilling that purpose

➤ Keep a healthy sense of modesty about your goals or achievements.

After Selye (1956)

INTERACTIVE: THE GENERAL ADAPTATION SYNDROME

Please answer the following statements as either True or False

1 Hans Selye identified the General Adaptation Syndrome in 1956.

2 Selye discovered the GAS after his experiments on cats.

3 The GAS involves our nervous system.

4 There are three stages regards the GAS.

5 Alarm reaction prepares our body to expend energy.

6 Flight or fight firstly occurs at the SE stage.

7 The resistance stage could be renamed the adaptation stage.

8 Prolonged stress can seriously affect out immune system.

9 Eustress is bad for us.

10 Eustress for one person may be distress for another.

For answers see page 174.

Evaluating Selye

Selye's GAS is a useful approach to the physiology of stress. However its application to human beings is weak. The GAS ignores the role of our cognitive processes in a stressful situation.

This is because, unlike animals, *we* apply our higher-level cognitive processes of perception, attention, language, memory, and thinking to our analysis and response to stressors.

Thus while the physiological model understands stress in terms of our biological response to it, the more appropriate transactional psychosocial model sees stress in terms of an interaction between our environment and us.

The transactional psychosocial model of stress

Lazarus and Folkman (1984) are credited with the development of the transactional psychosocial model of stress.

Their view focuses on stress as being a transaction between individuals' and their external environment. The transactional model thus combines aspects of both the engineering and physiological model. Accordingly, the transactional model believes stress arises due to a combination of external and internal factors. The transactional model emphasises the role our cognitions play in influencing our individual perception of stress, and our response to it.

> Perception is an active information process, which allows us to *organise*, interpret, and ultimately act upon sensory information coming to us from our outside world. Our previous past experience greatly influences our perception of stimuli in our world.

The transactional model understands stress in terms of how we first appraise a stressor, and then how we appraise our individual resources to cope with it.

In developing their transactional psychosocial model of stress Lazarus and Folkman (1984) tell us that stress should be thought of as resulting from an 'imbalance between demands and resources' or as occurring when 'pressure exceeds one's perceived ability to cope'.

Stress is 'a particular relationship between the person and the environment that is appraised by the person as taxing or exceeding his or her resources and endangering his or her well-being."

Lazarus and Folkman (1984)

Their rationale was then to go on and develop some stress management techniques, some of which we will look at shortly.

'*Transactional*' refers to the interaction between an individual's environment and themselves, while '*psychosocial*' are the triggers and consequences of such an interaction in terms of the individual's thoughts, feelings, and behaviours.

Examples of psychosocial events that can cause stress can be seen below.

ONLINE INTERACTIVES

Go to:

www.onlineclassroom.tv/psychology/catalogue/psychology_critical_issues/stress_management/preview1

to see how stress is measured and managed.

A direct link is available in the Chapter 4 section of the Higher Psychology Learning Suite at www.gerardkeegan.co.uk

Categories of psychosocial events that can cause stress

Parkes (1993) cites three general categories of psychosocial events that can cause us stress and damage our health:

➤ Events that force us to make major changes to the way we view the world.

➤ Events that has lasting consequences for us.

➤ Events that happen relatively quickly and allow us little time to adjust.

The transactional psychosocial model and primary appraisal

The transactional psychosocial model has us first use our cognitive processes in a primary appraisal of a stressor.

This is to help us decide its *positive* or *negative* implications for us.

The transactional psychosocial model and secondary appraisal

The transactional psychosocial model then says we engage in a secondary appraisal of the stressor.

This sees us decide whether we have the necessary resources or ability to cope or overcome the stressor.

Put another way the transactional model believes that in a stressful situation cognitive, emotional, and physiological factors interact to determine three things:

➤ Whether a situation is positively stressful or negatively stressful.

➤ Whether we can or cannot cope with the situation.

➤ What coping strategy should we then adopt?

An example would be when a stressor is perceived as positive or challenging. If we are confident that we have the resources to cope with it, eustress will result.

Alternatively when we perceive a stressor as negative or threatening, and are not confident about our ability to deal with it, then distress will result.

The transactional psychosocial model and our psychological reaction

Let us remind ourselves that psychology concerns how we think feel and behave. Psychology consequently studies the cognitive, emotional and behavioural components regards what it means to be human.

Unsurprisingly then, the transactional psychosocial model of stress indicates that our *psychological reaction* to stressors take three forms.

➤ A **cognitive** response

➤ An **emotional** response, and

➤ A **behavioural** response

Our cognitive response to stress

Lazarus and Folkman believe that stress reduces our ability to process information properly. Our cognitive response to stress involves distractibility and impaired task performance. This is because we just can't '*think straight.*' If stress is short-lived this is not too problematic. If stress is longer term it is.

Long-term stress can result in *negative* and *catastrophic thinking*. Both can have disastrous consequences for us. Both can even increase the probability of us experiencing *more* stress.

Negative thinking

Negative thinking is viewing yourself and your world in a pessimistic light. Such negative self-perception can change who you are. A person who was always known as a 'go-getter' may become a person who is utterly dependent on medication and on others. Their previous self-assurance has been replaced by self-pity. Prolonged self-pity can lead to depression.

Negative thinking may then be the stimulus for, or response to, mental health problems such as stress, anxiety and depression.

Catastrophic thinking

Catastrophic thinking is where we exaggerate the pain and discomfort a negative outcome will have for us. Catastrophic thinking is evident when we view ourselves as totally helpless to deal with negative outcomes. We imagine things as catastrophic, rather than unfortunate or a frustration that can be overcome. As with negative thinking, catastrophic thinking can be the stimulus for, or response to, mental health problems such as stress, anxiety and depression.

Turning negatives into positives!

See how you can change negative thoughts into more positive ones.

Apply your psychology and try to do this in real life from now on!

(-) Focusing only on the problems: One category and example of negative thoughts is when we dwell on the problem, instead of the solution.

(+) Instead: Always think that most problems have a solution, and ask 'How could I make this situation better?'

(-) Expecting the worse: Another category and example of negative thoughts is where we always expect the worse. Examples here might be 'What if I put on weight?' 'What if he doesn't like me?' Expecting the worse only promotes anxiety.

(+) Instead: Always give yourself a more positive thinking outcome. 'What can I do to prevent myself from putting on weight?'

'How can I make a good impression on him?'

(-) Thinking in absolutes: Another category and example of negative thinking is when we use absolutes. We often exaggerate reality with words like 'always,' 'never,' and 'everyone'. 'I will never be slim because I always eat too much.'

(+) Instead: Replace the exaggerations with more accurate and positive words. 'I often eat more than I need, but I can change that.'

Our emotional response to stress

Emotion or a change in the way we feel *always* accompanies stress.

Our emotional response to stress is a result of physiological factors interacting with our appraisal of the stressful situation. A stressor first triggers our physiological *fight or flight* response.

According to Lazarus and Folkman (1984) we then impose the transactional model, where we assess the situation to decide on its positive or negative implications for us. Finally we decide whether we have the necessary resources or ability to deal with it. We feel emotional as a result. We experience stress responses such as anger, hostility, embarrassment, depression, fear, anxiety, excitement, elation etc.

What our stress response will be is influenced by our individual differences. What is distress for one is eustress for another. We will look at this area in a little more detail shortly in our examination of coping strategies

Our behavioural response to stress

Stress with its cognitive and emotional components also often gives rise to a change in our behaviour: These behavioural changes can take a variety of forms.

INTERACTIVES

In light of the cognitive response to stress why might negative and catastrophic thinking be problematic?

Structure your answer as follows:

- Define the transactional psychosocial model of stress
- What are our three psychological reactions to stress?
- Describe and explain our cognitive response
- Describe and explain with examples negative and catastrophic thinking
- Outline some health related outcomes

ONLINE INTERACTIVES

Go to:

www.oaktreecounseling.com/stress.html

and do the emotional stress quiz.

A direct link is available in the Chapter 4 section of the Higher Psychology Learning Suite at **www.gerardkeegan.co.uk**

Facial expression: our emotional response to stress may show in our non-verbal communication of anger, fear, disgust, shock, anxiety, etc.

Body language and posture: our emotional response to stress may be evident in our body language and posture. A stressed person may appear nervous, or adopt an aggressive stance; their voice may change in pitch and tone. Alternatively, extreme stress can also result in lethargy.

Avoidance behaviour: when a stressor is intense, we may come to fear it, and try to avoid it. Confronting stressors needs courage. Courage as a resource is in short supply, and it is often easier for us to *avoid* the stressor altogether. Examples of avoidance behaviour to stressors include drug and alcohol abuse, and in extreme cases suicide.

Anti-social behaviour: Many of us attempt to deal with stress by transferring our negative emotions and thoughts onto others. If we are frustrated in our inability to deal positively with the stressor we act aggressively towards others.

INTERACTIVE: EMOTIONAL MOOD STATES

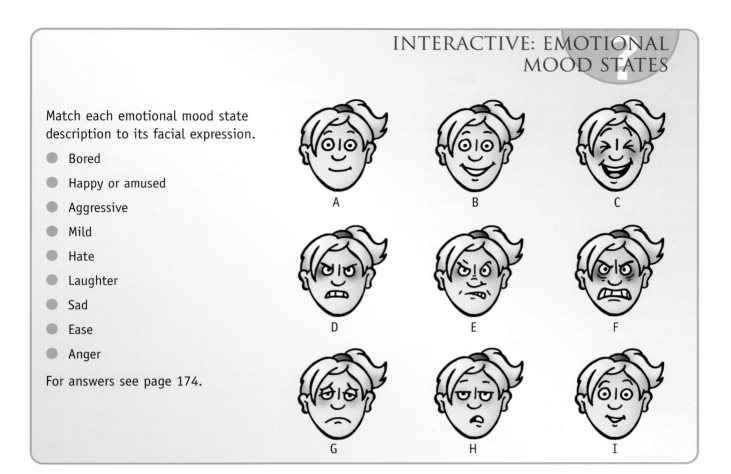

Match each emotional mood state description to its facial expression.

- Bored
- Happy or amused
- Aggressive
- Mild
- Hate
- Laughter
- Sad
- Ease
- Anger

For answers see page 174.

Sources of stress

We all differ in the things we perceive to be stressful. We view situations differently, and possess different resources to deal with them. Consequently one person may experience distress, another eustress.

It is generally accepted that whatever one's perception, and whatever one's resources *certain* situations are likely to act as stressors for the majority of us.

Frustration as stress

We often become stressed when we are frustrated in our desire to do something. Failure to achieve something can be due to internal or external factors.

Examples of *internal factors* that can contribute to an inability to achieve goals include ability, personality, sensitivity towards others etc.

Examples of *external factors* that can contribute to an inability to achieve goals include personal resources, transport, family circumstance etc.

The frustration–aggression hypothesis

Frustration is an emotion we experience when something gets in the way of us achieving a goal. According to the frustration–aggression hypothesis (Dollard *et al.* 1939), there is a far greater chance of aggression in situations where individuals think that someone/something is barring the way to them getting something.

Later studies suggest that the frustration–aggression hypothesis is over-simplistic. Frustration alone doesn't necessarily produce aggression (Miller, 1941). Berkowitz (1989) has developed an interesting aggressive-cue theory on this basis. Aggressive-cue theory says that two conditions must come together to produce aggression when frustration occurs. The first condition is anticipation by the individual that aggression might be needed in their frustrating situation. The second condition is an environmental cue that precedes any aggressive behaviour. A kind of red rag to a bull! Both of these conditions combine and aggression occurs.

An illustration might be someone at the end of his or her tether with officialdom. Frustration at *not* getting something done may have built up over a long period. They may have tried everything but to no avail. They finally get a meeting with someone. They tell their story, but again don't seem to be getting through. Worse, the official is sending non-verbal and verbal cues that they really don't care. They've got a pressing golf game. Twenty minutes later, the official is in the hands of two paramedics, and the complainer in the hands of two policemen!

Aggression allows us to protect ourselves, and others, when in danger. Aggression is a biological predisposition common to us all, which sees our physiology respond in a particular way when under threat.

Aggression is thus an innate, inherited biological characteristic. It is exacerbated by environmental factors, but is, as a general rule, recognised as unacceptable in modern society.

INTERACTIVE

How might the transactional psychosocial model of stress explain the frustration-aggression hypothesis?

Structure your answer as follows:

- What is the transactional psychosocial model of stress?

- What is the frustration–aggression hypothesis?

- With reference to an example what elements of the frustration–aggression hypothesis can be applied to the transactional psychosocial model of stress?

Conflict as stress

Conflict as stress occurs when we have to decide between contradictory goals or courses of action.

Lewin (1935) identified three patterns of conflict:

Approach–approach conflict occurs when we have to choose between two alternative courses of action both of which are equally attractive. Since both goals are desirable, this is the least stressful situation.

An example would be if you had to make a choice between going on a date with someone you have fancied for a very long time on the same night that your friends want to take you to a concert.

Avoidance–avoidance conflict occurs when we have to choose between two equally unappealing options. Both are negative, or repellent to us. This causes stress.

An example would be the ultimatum from your mum when she says, 'Either you do your homework or you are not going out this weekend.'

Approach–avoidance conflict occurs when we are faced with a situation that has both desirable and undesirable outcomes for us.

An example would be the timid man who wants to propose to his girlfriend. He hopes she will accept but also fears rejection. This conflict of the desirable and the undesirable causes him stress.

INTERACTIVE

Interview three people. Ask them if they have ever had any goals or ambitions thwarted. What were these? Ask them why this happened.

Were they frustrated in achieving these goals or ambitions because of internal or external factors, or a combination of both?

Life events

It should come as no surprise to learn that major life events cause us stress.

In 1967 psychiatrists Holmes and Rahé discovered a relationship between major life events and the later onset of physical illness and psychological health problems. These included heart disease, cancer, stress, anxiety and depression.

They also found that the effects of major life events are *cumulative*. The more upheavals we experience in life the more likely it is we will become ill.

They discovered that people who had experienced an unusually high number of stressful life events during a given period were very much more likely to experience a prolonged illness in the following year compared to people who had not.

On the basis of examining 5000 medical case histories and conducting interviews with a large number of people who were suffering, or had suffered, from extreme stress Holmes and Rahé developed their Social Readjustment Rating Scale or SRRS.

STUDY

Holmes and Rahé, (1967) 'The Social Readjustment Rating Scale', *Journal of Psychosomatic Research*, Vol. 11, p 213–18

Aim: The aim of Holmes and Rahé' was to create a scale of measurement to assess the impact of major life events in terms of associated stress.

Method: Case histories, interviews, survey questionnaire.

Procedure: From information obtained from 5000 medical case histories and interviews with patients who had or were suffering from stress-related illness Holmes and Rahé identified 43 life events that commonly cause stress. The list or Social Readjustment and Rating Questionnaire (SRRQ). was then given to an opportunity sample of 394 participants. The participants were asked to rate each event on the list for the amount of stress they thought each produced.

Standardised instructions were given to each participant who completed the SRRQ. For example, marriage was given the arbitrary value of 500 by the researchers.

Asked to use personal experience where applicable and also drawing on the experience of others, participants had to rate whether events on the SRRQ required more or less readjustment than marriage.

Values for each event were awarded relative to the 500 value given to marriage. If participants thought an event needed a greater/longer readjustment than marriage a higher score was awarded, if participants thought an event needed a smaller/shorter readjustment than marriage a lower score was awarded.

Results: All the participants' values for each item were averaged and divided by 10 to arrive at individual scores for each event e.g. Trouble with boss 23, Son or daughter leaving home 29 etc. In order to check consistency, participants were divided into several subgroups, e.g. male and female, single and married. A correlation indicated a strong degree of agreement among and between participants on values given to life events.

Conclusion: On the basis of the SRRQ results Holmes and Rahé went on to develop their Social Readjustment Rating Scale (SRRS). This scale helps adjudge the amount of stressful life events and life readjustment an individual has experienced in a given period and whether they could be susceptible to stress-related illness in the short to medium term. Coping strategies could then be recommended.

Their SRRS ranks life events according to how much stress they give people. Marriage has a nominal stress value of 50, divorce 65, bereavement 100 etc. Not every life event is the same. Getting married, going through a divorce or suffering bereavement is very much more stressful than changing one's eating or sleeping habits.

On its basis Holmes and Rahé observed that people who scored between 200 and 300 points in a given year were statistically more likely to develop stress and anxiety problems the following year; while those scored over 400 points were likely to suffer a major illness such as heart problems, cancer or depression (Cohen, 1998).

INTERACTIVE: CONFLICT AS STRESS

Match the components to complete the grid below.

Type of conflict	Description
	Occurs when we have to choose between two alternative courses of action both of which are equally attractive
Avoidance-Avoidance Conflict	
	Occurs when we are faced with a situation that has both desirable and undesirable outcomes for us.

Components

- Approach-Avoidance Conflict
- Occurs when we have to choose between two equally unappealing options.
- Approach-Approach Conflict

For solution see page 174.

Holmes and Rahé suggest this happens because of the effect repeated stress has on the body's general adaptation to long-term stress. As we now know from Selye's stage of exhaustion if the immune system becomes seriously impaired people become a lot more susceptible to illness.

The Social Readjustment Rating Scale

How to use the SRRS

To measure the amount of stress caused by social readjustment the SRRS first gets individuals to identify the number of 'life change units' that have befallen them in the last year. All these life change unit scores are added up, and the final score gives a rough estimate of how such stress might affect their health.

It is suggested that someone with a score of more than 300 is at risk of serious illness; someone with a score of 150 to 299 has a moderate risk of illness and someone with a score less than 150 has only a slight risk of illness.

To test the reliability of their stress scale as a predictor of illness Rahé (1970) gave the scale to 2500 US sailors. They were asked to rate their life events for the previous six months. Over the *next* six months, detailed records were kept of the sailors' health.

Rahé found a +0.118 correlation between previous stress scale scores and later physical and psychological illness. This seemingly small *statistical* *relationship* is felt to be significant and supports the Holmes and Rahé hypothesis of a link between life events and illness.

ONLINE INTERACTIVES

Do an online SRRS at: www.geocities.com/beyond_stretched/holmes.htm

A direct link is available in the Chapter 4 section of the Higher Psychology Learning Suite at www.gerardkeegan.co.uk.

Hassles and uplifts

Not all of the stress we experience comes from major life events. Lesser events can also be stressful, such as when we have to give a speech or a presentation, lose our keys during a busy day, or have our peace disrupted by noisy neighbours.

These everyday events are called hassles.

Kanner, Coyne, Schaefer and Lazarus (1981) constructed a scale to measure people's experiences of such day-to-day events.

Called the Hassles Scale it lists 117 everyday events that range from minor annoyances, such as 'silly practical mistakes,' to major problems, such as 'not enough money for food.' Respondents are asked to indicate hassles that have occurred to them in the past month and rate each as 'somewhat,' 'moderately,' or 'extremely' severe.

Life event	Life change units	Life event	Life change units
Death of a spouse	100	Trouble with in-laws	29
Divorce	73	Outstanding personal achievement	28
Marital separation	65	Spouse starts or stops work	26
Imprisonment	63	Begin or end school	26
Death of a close family member	63	Change in living conditions	25
Personal injury or illness	53	Revision of personal habits	24
Marriage	50	Trouble with boss	23
Dismissal from work	47	Change in working hours or conditions	20
Marital reconciliation	45	Change in residence	20
Retirement	45	Change in schools	20
Change in health of family member	44	Change in recreation	19
Pregnancy	40	Change in church activities	19
Sexual difficulties	39	Change in social activities	18
Gain a new family member	39	Minor mortgage or loan	17
Business readjustment	39	Change in sleeping habits	16
Change in financial state	38	Change in number of family reunions	15
Change in frequency of arguments	35	Change in eating habits	15
Major mortgage	32	Vacation	13
Foreclosure of mortgage or loan	30	Christmas	12
Change in responsibilities at work	29	Minor violation of law	11
Child leaving home	29		

Table 4.2 Holmes and Rahé Social Readjustment Rating Scale

In developing the Hassles Scale Kanner, Coyne, Schaefer and Lazarus tested 100 middle-aged adults monthly over a nine-month period. The half-dozen most frequent hassles reported were:

➤ Concerns about weight

➤ Health of a family member

➤ Rising prices of everyday items

➤ Home maintenance

➤ Too many things to do

➤ Misplacing or losing things.

In the course of developing the Hassles Scale, Kanner, Coyne, Schaefer and Lazarus found that having good experiences in life made hassles more bearable and reduced their impact on health.

They then went on to develop another instrument called the Uplifts Scale.

The Uplifts Scale lists 135 events that bring us peace, satisfaction, or joy. This was administered along with the Hassles Scale to the same 100 middle-aged adults. They were asked to indicate which uplifts they had experienced in the past month, and whether each event had been 'somewhat,' 'moderately,' or 'extremely' strong.

Some of the most frequently occurring uplifts reported were:

➤ relating well to your spouse or lover

➤ completing a task

➤ feeling healthy

Both were combined into the Hassles and Uplifts Scale, which is nowadays in widespread use throughout the world as an indicator of life events as a cause of stress.

In comparison to the SRRS, Hassles and Uplifts has been found to be a *better* predictor of health. It allows for continuous daily monitoring of everyday hassles, and has enabled a causal link to be made between such stressors and poor physical and psychological health (Stone *et al.,* 1987).

The workplace

Work and the workplace are major contributors to stress and associated health problems. Workplace stress comes about because of pressures of work and the work environment.

Hayward (1996) has investigated work-related stress. He reports workers regularly feel under intense pressure. This is exacerbated by impossible deadlines, conflicting and confusing information about what is expected of them, poor interpersonal relationships with colleagues, fear of redundancy/unemployment and a general lack of control over work and the work environment.

Certain jobs have been found to be particularly stressful.

> **The four most stressful jobs in the UK**
>
> ➤ Nursing
> ➤ Social Work
> ➤ Teaching
> ➤ Police
>
> **Why do you think this is? Give reasons for your answers.**

The work environment does not help either. Many workers like oil-rig workers, fishermen, fire fighters etc. are exposed to danger on a daily basis. Many others face hidden stressors working with radiation, pesticides, toxins and chemicals.

Environment

There are a number of important environmental factors that affect workplace stress: These include:

➤ Overcrowding

➤ Background noise

➤ Pollution

➤ Excessively bright or dim light

➤ Temperature

The European Agency for Safety and Health at Work and our own Health and Safety Executive recommend that employers take the impact of the work environment on people's physical and psychological health seriously.

The EHSE say an employer could be found failing if they do not have a safe, clean, well laid out, easy-on-the-eye working environment. They should encourage a calm workplace, and have a 'quiet' room for thinking/relaxation. They should give workers breaks every 90 minutes or more frequently if they are doing intense tasks such as keyboard or screen work. They also need to ensure workers work reasonable hours, or no more than eight hours a day except in cases of dire need

INTERACTIVES

Compare and contrast the Social Readjustment Rating Scale with the Hassles and Uplifts Scale.

Structure your answer as follows:

● What do the two scales attempt to do?

● Describe the development of the SRRS.

● Briefly describe the content of the SRRS.

● Briefly describe evidence to support the SRRS.

● What criticisms can be made of the SRRS?

● What is the difference between the SRRS and the Hassles Scale?

● Describe the development of the Hassles Scale.

● Briefly describe the content of the Hassles Scale.

● What did Kanner *et al.* discover about good experiences?

● Describe the development of the Uplifts Scale.

● Briefly describe the content of the Uplifts Scale.

● Briefly describe evidence in support of the Hassles and Uplifts Scale.

Degree of control

Several studies indicate that the more unpredictable a situation, and the less control people feel they have, the more stress they experience.

A classic study by Langer and Rodin (1976) found that the mortality rate among elderly patients in a residential home was lower amongst those given greater control than those with relatively little control over their lives.

A similar situation exists in employment. Workers who have little or no control over decisions that affect them have been found to be more prone to low self-esteem, anxiety, depression, apathy, exhaustion, and the symptoms of coronary heart disease (Hayward, 1996).

Interpersonal factors

Mattson and Ivancevich (1982) found that an inability to get along with others was the most common source of stress in the workplace. Poor interpersonal relationships and support from others have been found to influence high anxiety, job tension, and low job satisfaction in some workplaces. Unsurprisingly bullying and violence at work are associated with stress, absenteeism, and poor mental health.

This is in contrast to those organisations that encourage positive interpersonal relationships and interpersonal support, which promotes good physical and mental health in the workplace (Hayward, 1996).

Role ambiguity/commitment

Role ambiguity occurs when an employee is unclear about what they are meant to be doing. This triggers frustration and anxiety.

Role conflict occurs when a worker is asked to do something that conflicts with what they think they are there to do. Role conflict is associated with cardiovascular disorders and peptic ulcers.

Having too much to do and not enough time to do it also causes role conflict. Sales (1969) reported that stress increases when workers have to choose between quantity and quality of work.

Shift work

Shift work negatively influences our body clock. Disrupted body rhythms can make people feel unhappy, fatigued, or ill, and can increase the incidence of industrial accidents. Czeisler *et al.* (1982) found a correlation between shift work among manual labourers and raised accident rates, absenteeism, and ill health.

Poor health

Poor health itself can be very stressful, particularly if the illness is chronic or terminal. The pain and discomfort suffered from an infection, virus etc. can be physiologically and psychologically stressful. Our immune system is greatly weakened and we become more prone to further illness. We may have a poorer quality of life, an enforced reduction in opportunities for social interaction with others and can become fearful for the future.

Home and family life

Home and family life can also be very stressful. Research by Dennerstein (1995) indicates that trying to keep up with the traditional role of being a wife and mother is responsible for the highest rates of stress and mental health problems in women.

We shall explore this shortly when we look at gender and stress.

Stress and physical illness

Selye himself categorised certain diseases, ranging from cardiovascular disorders to inflammatory diseases and mental disorders as '*diseases of adaptation*', regarding them as '*largely due to errors in our adaptive response to stress*'.

Consequently stress has been related to a number of medical problems including:

➤ Headaches

➤ Infectious illnesses (eg influenza)

➤ Cardiovascular disease

➤ Diabetes

➤ Asthma

➤ Rheumatoid arthritis

There are several ways in which stress can cause such physical illness:

Stress and endorphins

Prolonged and repeated exposure to stress inhibits our body's production of endorphins, which are natural painkillers manufactured by the pituitary gland.

Goetsch and Fuller (1995) tell us endorphins play a vital role in helping the body cope with stress. Participants who were given a drug that inhibited the production of endorphins later showed increased anxiety, depression, a lack of concentration, and poorer levels of general functioning.

Stress and white blood cells

Prolonged and repeated exposure to stress also inhibits the action of lymphocytes in our body. Lymphocytes are types of white blood cells that help us fight off viruses and infections.

Stress and ill health

Stress may cause people who are already ill to become even more so. Being ill leads to stress, which causes further physical decline and more stress and more illness.

Stress and behaviour

Stress can cause people to behave in ways detrimental to their health. Stress related behaviours include poor eating habits, smoking, sleep loss, drinking too much alcohol, self-medicating drugs etc. This leads to even more ill health and an increased susceptibility to stress.

Stress and physiological change

Research by McEwen (1997) indicates that exposure to prolonged stress can permanently change the structure of the hippocampus in the brain. The hippocampus is an area found deep in the temporal lobe in the middle of our brain that is important for learning and memory. It is also associated with our emotions.

Stress and early childhood experience

A study conducted by Nemeroff *et al.* (2000) discovered that abuse in early childhood can lead to permanent changes in the brain chemistry of its female victims. Nemeroff thinks that such abuse over stimulates stress hormones to such an extent that abused girls are incapable of having a 'normal' stress response in later life. Many suffer impairment of cognitive functioning, depression and anxiety. The outlook for such individuals mental and physical health is quite poor. Nemeroff *et al.* think that male victims of such abuse can also be similarly affected. It should be noted that the study has been criticised in failing to account for the influence of other extraneous variables throughout people's lives that could account for the same results (Kilpatrick, 2000).

Individual differences and the stress response

Our personality, disposition, self-esteem and gender have all been found to influence individual response to stress.

Personality

Friedman and Rosenman are two American cardiologists who in 1974 found a link between personality type, stress and coronary heart disease. While coronary heart problems are traditionally associated with smoking, obesity, diabetes, lack of physical activity and old age Friedman and

Rosenman felt these variables did not account for *all* its occurrences in their patients.

What had put them on to this was a furniture problem. The leather seats in their waiting room were getting worn away much faster than they should. This was because a number of their cardiac patients were very agitated when sitting on them. They just couldn't sit still!

Friedman and Rosenman wondered if there was a connection between this type of personality, and coronaries. They discovered that there was. A lot of their cardiac patients shared the same behaviour

The Type A behaviour pattern
Impatience
Competitiveness
Easily irritated
Quick to anger
Suspicious
Hostile
Driven to achieve
Aggressive
Perfectionists
Highly successful but dissatisfied
Try to do more than one thing at a time
Preoccupied with deadlines
Rapid, loud speech
Often interrupt others

Table 4.3 Friedman and Rosenman's Type A behaviour pattern

patterns. They had the same type of personality, as described in Table 4.3.

They recognised the above traits in individuals as showing a Type A behaviour pattern, and their absence, a Type B. Friedman and Rosenman reported that as many as 50 per cent of the (US) population can be classified as Type A personalities.

Typologies

Friedman and Rosenman tell us that Type A personalities are two and a half times more likely to develop coronary heart disease than Type B personalities. Type A personalities are prone to high blood pressure and high cholesterol levels.

In comparison to Type As, Type B personalities are usually relaxed, not excessively competitive, emotionally stable and psychologically secure.

In a stressful situation the Type B personality is likely to be less hostile than their Type A counterpart, and consequently suffer fewer heart-related health problems.

Today Type C, D and ER personalities have also been identified.

Temoshok (1987) proposed that a Type C personality has problems expressing emotions, particularly negative ones like anger. The Type C personality is also more prone to cancer but there is no evidence to suggest the Type C personality *causes* cancer.

The Type D personality is anxious, gloomy and socially inept. Burne (1999) reports the Type D personality as four times more likely to have recurring heart attacks as other personality types who have just one.

The Type ER personality is the *emotional responder*. These individuals demonstrate wild mood swings going from great elation to deep despair. Such mood swings reduce blood flow to the heart The Type ER personality are four times more likely to suffer a heart attack as a result (Burne, 1999).

ONLINE INTERACTIVES

Download and listen to a PsyCast about personality and stress

www.psychlotron.org.uk/podcasts/stressperso nalitypsycast.zip

A direct link is available in the Chapter 4 section of the Higher Psychology Learning Suite at **www.gerardkeegan.co.uk**

Friedman, M. and Rosenman, R. H. (1974) *Type A behaviour and your heart*. New York: Knopf

Aim: To test the hypothesis that Type A individuals are more likely to develop coronary heart disease than Type B individuals.

Method: Medical case histories, interview and observation.

Procedure: 3200 healthy young men aged 39-59 from the San Francisco area were assessed for their personality type. All were found to be free from coronary heart disease at the start of the research. Any change in this situation was recorded for the next eight and a half years.

Assessing Type A/B behaviour patterns: This was done by means of a structured interview using two kinds of information.

a) Answers given to pre-set interview questions such as how participants reacted to queuing, driving in slow traffic, deadlines at work, and problems at home.

b) Observation of participants' behaviour during the interview such as their way of speaking e.g. loudness, speed of talking, and their tendency to show impatience and hostility calculated by their reaction to the interviewer deliberately interrupting them from time to time.

On the basis of these measures the participants were classed as A1 (Type A), A2 (not fully type A), X (equal amounts of Type A and B) and B (fully Type B) personalities.

Findings: 70 per cent of the 257 who developed coronary heart disease during the study had been assessed as Type A individuals at the beginning of the study. This association remained significant even when risk factors known to be associated with heart disease such as smoking and obesity were taken into account.

Conclusion: The Type A personality is an independent risk factor regards heart disease. Men characterised as Type A personalities are roughly twice as likely to develop coronary heart disease as their Type B counterparts.

Disposition

Our *disposition* is our outlook on life. Generally people are either optimistic or pessimistic.

There is a lot of evidence to suggest that optimism has important health benefits. Scheier *et al.* (1989) found that optimistic coronary heart-bypass patients healed quicker than pessimistic ones.

In a study of woman who underwent mastectomies because of breast cancer Greer *et al.* (1979) found that those with a positive fighting spirit were significantly more likely to be free of cancer five years later in comparison to those who felt helpless when diagnosed.

Of significance to Higher psychology students, Aspinwall and Taylor tell us that optimistic students experience fewer physical symptoms of stress at the end of term than pessimistic ones.

Pessimists tend to suffer poorer physical and mental health. They are more likely to respond emotionally to stressors, and experience negative emotions of guilt, distress and shame. They react defensively rather than positively in stressful situations.

Is the glass half full or half empty?

If you answered 'half full' you are probably an optimist. An optimist is a person disposed to take a favourable view of things. If you answered 'half empty' you are probably a pessimist. A pessimist is a person who takes an unfavourable view of things.' Being one or the other can positively or negatively influence your physical and mental health.

ONLINE INTERACTIVES

Read about the benefits of optimism at: **stress.about.com/od/ optimismspirituality /a/optimismbenefit.htm**

A direct link is available in the Chapter 4 section of the Higher Psychology Learning Suite at **www.gerardkeegan.co.uk**

ONLINE INTERACTIVES

How do you rate on self-esteem? Complete the Rosenberg Self Esteem Questionnaire at:

eib.emcdda.europa.eu/attachements.cfm/ att_7983_EN_rosenbrg.pdf

A direct link is available in the Chapter 4 section of the Higher Psychology Learning Suite at **www.gerardkeegan.co.uk**

Self-esteem

Related to disposition is self-esteem.

Individuals with high self-esteem are likely to have a positive outlook on life. Their greater confidence affects the way they interact with their environment, and the way their environment interacts with them. They are more likely to achieve their goals and are thus less likely to experience stress (Kreger, 1995).

Those with low self-esteem show less confidence and therefore have more problems in achieving their goals. They tend to experience stress and as a consequence adopt defensive coping strategies (Smith, Zhan, Huntington, Washington, 1992).

Gender, mortality and morbidity

At every age from birth to 85+ more men die than women.

Of interest here is that despite having a lower mortality rate than men, women have a higher morbidity rate. Morbidity rate refers to the occurrence of disease and illness within a particular population.

Women are more prone to diabetes, amnesia, gastrointestinal problems, and rheumatoid arthritis. They visit their doctor more, and take more prescribed drugs than their male counterparts. They are however less likely to succumb to life-threatening health problems such as coronary heart disease.

The reason for this may be biological. Women produce the hormone oestrogen, the effect of which has been found to protect against heart disease. However an alternative explanation may be related to stress, or the lack of it.

Frankenhauser (1983) compared the adrenaline output of male and female students' when they were asked to do an intelligence test. Frankenhauser found females produced less adrenaline than males. A female's lack of physiological responsiveness in such stressful situations *could* then be a factor regards their greater life expectancy. They are less prone to heart problems.

Later Frankenhauser *et al.* (1991) found that males and females in traditional male professions such as engineering and driving buses showed the same level of adrenaline output in response to job related stressors. This suggests that socialisation and gender account for the different stress response, rather than biological factors.

Generally males and females learn to respond differently to stressors because they undergo a different socialisation process.

Eisler and Blalock (1991) suggest that women suffer less stress than men because they are less likely to be Type A personalities. They are less *hostile*.

A Type A personality reflects the traditional male gender role. This includes such things as high achievement drive, a need to have power over others, competitiveness, individualism, being unemotional, and being roused to anger when frustrated.

Davison and Neale (1994) think these personality characteristics are associated with men's greater tendency to heart disease and other stress-related disorders.

However, other theorists state that women actually suffer more stress than men, because of their traditional role. This is because women are encouraged to be compliant and passive, while men are encouraged to be assertive, competitive and unemotional. It may be that male frustration manifests as stress and aggression, while women's stress manifests as depression and anxiety.

ONLINE INTERACTIVES: STRESS AND GENDER

Read this article on 'Stress and Gender' at:

www.webmd.com/balance/ stress-management/features/stress-gender

1   How do women appear to deal with stress?

2   How do men appear to deal with stress?

3   Give evidence as to how Mr and Mrs Seller deal differently with stress.

4   What two hormones do men and women produce when under stress?

5   What are their effects?

6   What hormone do women then secrete more than men?

7   What is its affect?

8   Why does it not affect men the same?

9   Why do the researchers at UCLA think these stress-related mechanisms have developed?

10 What strategy could men adopt to minimise the onset of stress-related health problems?

A direct link is available in the Chapter 4 section of the Higher Psychology Learning Suite at **www.gerardkeegan.co.uk**

For answers see page 175.

Locus of control (LOC)

The notion of locus of control (LOC) was developed by Rotter (1966).

Originally called locus of control by reinforcement, LOC concerns our perception about the underlying causes of events in our life. Put more simply, do you believe that your destiny is controlled by at an *internal* personal level, or by *external forces* such as fate, God, or powerful others?

We discovered earlier that life events and situations outwith our control cause us the most stress. We have a strong desire to control our own destiny and behaviour. We do not enjoy being at the mercy of

External LOC

Someone with a high external LOC is an individual who believes that his/her behaviour is guided by fate, luck, or other external circumstances

Internal LOC

Someone with a high internal LOC is an individual who believes that his/her behaviour is guided by his/her personal decisions and efforts.

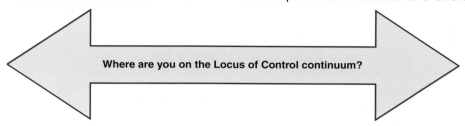

Where are you on the Locus of Control continuum?

external forces. Our own *locus of control* is associated with stress.

LOC is measured on a scale that runs from high external to high internal control.

Does your LOC matter?

Having a high internal locus of control is generally thought more desirable that having a high external locus of control. Kim (1997) found children with an internal locus of control showed fewer signs of stress when their parents divorced.

If someone has a high internal locus they:

➤ take responsibility for their own actions

➤ see themselves as being in control of their own destiny

On the other hand if someone has a high external locus of control they:

➤ tend to see their fate as lying in the hands of others

➤ attribute both their success and failures to others

Stress, depression and anxiety are associated more with people who have a high external locus, than those with a high internal locus (Johnson and Sarason, 1978). People with a high external locus of control are more prone to stress-related illness.

We should be wary however in seeing external locus as 'bad' and internal locus as 'good'. As Wade and Tavris (1999) caution:

 Believing that an event is controllable does not always lead to a reduction in stress, and believing that an event is uncontrollable does not always lead to an increase in stress. The question must always be asked: Control over what?"

Wade and Tavris further distinguish two types of control, each of which is culture bound. Each is learned as a consequence of the socialisation process. These are primary control, and secondary control.

Primary control

Some researchers have pointed out that people in different cultures have different kinds of perceived control. The Western approach emphasises the importance of primary control. When faced with a problematic situation, people in Western cultures tend to focus on changing the situation so that the problem no longer exists.

Secondary control

A different approach, seen in many Asian cultures, emphasises secondary control. When faced with a problematic situation, people in these cultures focus on accommodating the situation by changing their perspective on it. Both kinds of control can be beneficial.

Locus of control is also related to learned helplessness (Seligman, 1975). This refers to the learned belief that nothing we do can make any difference to our situation. This is an external locus of control in the extreme.

ONLINE INTERACTIVES

Assess your own locus of control at:

stress.about.com/od/selfknowledgeselftests/a/locus.htm

A direct link is available in the Chapter 4 section of the Higher Psychology Learning Suite at www.gerardkeegan.co.uk

Are you coping?

For Lazarus and Folkman (1984) coping with stress involves:

 constantly changing cognitive and behavioural efforts to manage specific external and/or internal demands that are appraised as taxing or exceeding the resources of the person."

Cohen and Lazarus (1979) classified coping strategies into five general categories.

Category 1 **Information-seeking:** Trying to learn more about the nature of the problem and what can be done to deal with it.

Category 2 **Taking direct action:** Any action to reduce the stress level e.g. taking alcohol or drugs, becoming aggressive/fighting or removing an environmental factor.

Category 3 **Using intrapsychic (cognitive) processes:** Altering perspective on the problem e.g. by reappraising your attitude towards it, possibly going into denial.

Category 4 **Turning to others:** Seeking help or emotional support from others.

Category 5 **Inhibiting action:** Refraining from taking an action e.g. holding back from having an argument or a fight, where another person might have acted.

Table 4.4

These reflect Lazarus and Folkman's (1984) problem-focused and emotion-focused coping strategies that we will turn to shortly. The former involves some kind of plan being made by us to deal with the stressor. We implement the plan until the stressor has been dealt with satisfactorily. Problem-focused coping strategies are found in Category 1, 2, and to some extent 5 in Table 4.4 above.

As we will discover emotion-focused coping gets us to adopt cognitive and behavioural strategies to deal with stressors. These are useful in the short term. They reduce the negative thinking associated with stress, but do little to deal with it in the long term. Category 4 in our table is a good example of emotion-focused coping strategies.

Stress management

Stress management is an ability we learn based upon our previous past experience. Stress management needs effort on our part. Sometimes an individual needs help to recognise when they get stressed, how they negatively cope with stress in the present, and how they might better cope with stress in the future.

As introduced above Lazarus and Folkman (1984) identify two main types of coping skills; problem-based coping, and emotions-focused coping.

Problem-based coping

Problem-based coping skills get us to focus in on the stressor. Problem-based coping skills have us deal *directly* with the issue. In so doing we restructure the problem in such a way that it no longer is a problem! Examples of problem-based coping strategies would be information gathering, planning and taking action.

It is a fact of life that we are often given bad news about our health. Being told you have a serious medical condition invariably leads to physiological and psychological stress. Many cope with this by taking a problem-focused approach. They find out as much as they can about the problem, make plans for themselves and others regards the future, and then take action on this basis by beginning intensive treatment etc.

Emotions-focused coping

Emotions-focused coping involves us in an emotional response to deal with a stressor rather than directly tackling the stressor itself.

Emotions-focused coping has us use ego defence mechanisms to protect us from the harsh realities of life.

Ego-defence mechanisms

Sigmund Freud tells us that we use ego-defence mechanisms to protect ourselves from feelings of stress, anxiety or guilt, which often arise because we feel threatened, or our world becomes too demanding.

Ego-defence mechanisms are not under our conscious control. They are thus non-voluntary. We use them unthinkingly to protect us from stressful situations in life.

Ego-defence mechanisms are natural and normal. When we use them too often and they get out of proportion, neuroses develop, such as anxiety states, phobias, obsessions, or hysteria.

Types of ego-defence mechanisms include repression, which happens when you experience something so painful and traumatic that you push it out of your conscious awareness. You permanently forget that it ever happened.

Repression is the unconscious act of forgetting a deeply disturbing trauma or event.

Displacement involves the transfer of ideas and impulses from one object or person to another. For example, you may feel hostile and aggressive towards your boss as a result of getting the blame for something you did not do. You feel like lashing out, verbally, physically, or both. This is not realistic. You could lose your job. You use displacement and snap at and criticise a colleague instead.

Regression occurs when a person behaves in a manner more suitable to an earlier stage of life, e.g. adults who resort to childish behaviours like stamping, kicking, and or shouting in an effort to get their own way.

Regressive behaviours such as thumb sucking can be seen when individuals are in a stressful situation, like examination time!

Other ego-defence mechanisms include denial, rationalisation, projection, and suppression.

ONLINE INTERACTIVES

Go to:

allpsych.com/personalitysynopsis/defenses.html

and then answer the following question.

Describe and explain the ego defence mechanism we might use if we were diagnosed with cancer.

A direct link is available in the Chapter 4 section of the Higher Psychology Learning Suite at **www.gerardkeegan.co.uk**

Psychologists caution against using the wrong coping style in the wrong context. An emotions-focused coping strategy would be inappropriate if we were faced with a work-based problem.

Consequently there a variety of stress management questionnaires available that help us identify our own coping strategies. This may lead us to change how we cope with stressors in the future, particularly if how we do is not appropriate to the situation.

ONLINE INTERACTIVES

Folkman, Lazarus, Dunkel-Schetter, DeLongis, and Gruen (1986) developed 'The Ways of Coping Questionnaire'. It asks people to respond to a specific stressor, such as street crime, and then indicate the degree to which they have used each particular coping method to deal with it.

Read Folkman on her revised 'Ways of Coping Questionnaire' at:

www.caps.ucsf.edu/tools/surveys/pdf/Ways%20of%20coping.pdf

A direct link is available in the Chapter 4 section of the Higher Psychology Learning Suite at **www.gerardkeegan.co.uk**

Physiological interventions to combat stress

Physiological interventions combat how we *feel* when stressed.

Most physiological interventions are emotion-focused. They address the relationship between bodily arousal and emotional response to environmental stressors and tackle our bodily reaction to such external stimuli.

Physiological measures address our body's emotional response to stress.

Physiological interventions include drugs, biofeedback and relaxation techniques.

Psychological interventions to combat stress

Psychological interventions deal with negative thinking and faulty perception. We should note that not all psychological interventions are problem-focused.

Psychological interventions include stress inoculation and increasing hardiness.

Review of the physiological effects of stress

It is useful to remember that the physiological effects of stress are measures taken by the body to tackle the stressful situation.

Functional adjustments or the physiological effects of stress

➤ Diversion of blood from less vital to more vital organs of the body.

➤ Increase in the heart rate to supply more blood quickly.

➤ Increase in the blood pressure to supply blood efficiently.

➤ Increase in our breathing rate to get more oxygen from the atmosphere.

➤ Breakdown of glycogen stores in our liver and muscles to access even more glucose.

➤ Formation of more glucose from non-carbohydrate substances.

If our body's internal homeostasis is disturbed, then compensatory adjustments take place. If the disturbing factor is stress, then our body secretes stress hormones to tackle the situation with what we call the fight or flight response.

Fight or flight

When our body is stressed, the hypothalamus secretes a adrenocorticotrophic releasing hormone (ARH). ARH stimulates our pituitary gland to produce the adrenocorticotrophic hormone (ACTH).

ACTH stimulates our adrenal glands to secrete stress associated hormones such as adrenaline and cortisol. Adrenaline and cortisol are responsible for the physiological effects of stress or the 'fight or flight response'. They do so by triggering certain functional adjustments within our body.

The consequence of such physiological adjustments is to prepare our body to tackle stress by providing more energy for it in the form of increased oxygen and glucose. We are *then* in a position to fight or flight.

Physiological interventions: drugs

There are generally two classes of drug prescribed for stress. The first are anti-anxiety benzodiazepines, such as Librium and Valium. The second are beta-blockers such as Propranolol.

Benzodiazepines, or 'benzos', are mild tranquillisers that slow down our central nervous system. The long-term use of benzodiazapines can cause physical dependence.

Beta-blockers slow own heart rate and reduce high blood pressure. They make a physiological response to stress difficult. Beta-blockers help protect people from heart related problems associated with stress. They should only be used in the short-term.

All drugs influence our bodily processes involved in the stress response, i.e. they intervene in the activity of the ANS. They are easy to use and effective but should only be taken in the short term.

Drugs only tackle the symptoms of stress and not the real problem. They can produce unpleasant side effects such as an upset stomach, drowsiness, blurred vision, irregular heartbeat etc.

Physiological interventions: biofeedback

In biofeedback electrodes are attached to various parts of the body. This is to monitor various physiological functions like heartbeat, pulse, and blood pressure etc. These of course increase in stressful situations. Results are fed back to the individual. If results are abnormally high the person is asked to adjust their behaviour to make them lower. A muscle monitor can indicate if a person is tense. If they are, they are asked to relax and continuous monitoring helps indicate to them when this tension has reduced.

Dworkin and Dworkin (1983) used biofeedback to teach sufferers of scoliosis to control their back muscles and alter their posture. Scoliosis is a medical condition where a person's spine is curved from side to side, or may also be rotated

In a somewhat dubious study Miller and DiCara (1967) investigated the relationship between biofeedback and positive reinforcement. They paralysed 24 rats and kept them alive using artificial respiration. Half were rewarded when their heart rate slowed down. Half were rewarded when their heart rate speeded up. In order to keep getting their reward the rats learned to adapt their heartbeats accordingly.

Biodots

Biodots are often used in biofeedback

Biodots are small self-adhesive, temperature sensitive discs that are placed on the skin to monitor changes in skin temperature.

Such changes are due to changes in the amount of blood flowing through our body. More blood flow, the skin is warmer; less blood flow, the skin is cooler.

When we are tense blood vessels in our skin constrict, reducing our blood flow. When this happens a biodot would appear as yellow, amber or black.

When we are calm and relaxed blood vessels in our skin dilate, increasing blood flow. Biodots then appear turquoise, blue or violet.

Biodots are particularly useful as biofeedback in relaxation training. They help motivate the user to reduce tension, and give reassurance and instant feedback that they are becoming more relaxed. A colour interpretation chart is used. Users quite simply relate the colour of the biodot to the level of relaxation and tension that they are experiencing.

As a physiological intervention for stress biofeedback has no side effects. It can be used in the long term. It is non-invasive. It can however be expensive and time consuming. Being emotion-focused, biofeedback treats the symptoms not the problem

Physiological interventions: relaxation techniques

There are numerous relaxation techniques. What they all have in common is that they train us to reduce our physiological arousal response in reaction to environmental stressors.

Adopting relaxation techniques can improve our physical response to stress by:

➤ slowing our heart rate

➤ lowering our blood pressure

➤ slowing our breathing rate

➤ reducing our need for oxygen

➤ increasing blood flow to major muscles

➤ reducing muscle tension

According to the prestigious Mayo Clinic, relaxation techniques have us experience fewer physical symptoms, such as headaches and back pain; our emotions are better controlled; we are less prone to anger and frustration; we have more energy, an improved concentration, a greater ability to handle problems, and are deal more efficiently with everyday life.

Any type of relaxation technique usually involves us refocusing our attention onto something calming, while increasing body awareness. There are several types of relaxation techniques, such as autogenic relaxation, progressive muscle relaxation, and visualisation.

Autogenic relaxation

Autogenic means something that comes from within.

In **autogenic relaxation** you use both visual imagery and body awareness to reduce stress.

You repeat words or suggestions in your mind to help you relax and reduce muscle tension.

You may imagine a peaceful place and then focus on controlled, relaxing breathing, slowing your heart rate, or different physical sensations, such as relaxing each arm or leg one by one.

Progressive muscle relaxation

Using progressive muscle relaxation you focus on slowly tensing and then relaxing each muscle group in your body.

This helps you focus on the difference between muscle tension and relaxation, and you also become more aware of physical sensations.

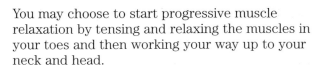

You may choose to start progressive muscle relaxation by tensing and relaxing the muscles in your toes and then working your way up to your neck and head.

PMR suggests that we tense each group of muscles for at least five seconds and then relax for 30 seconds, and repeat. When fully relaxed we should then move onto another muscle group in our body.

Visualisation

With visualisation you form mental images that take you on a visual journey to a peaceful, calming place or situation.

If you want to try it, close your eyes, sit in a quiet spot and loosen any tight clothing.

Use as many of your senses and associated sensations as possible, such as smells, sights, sounds and textures.

For example, imagine relaxing at the ocean. Think about the warmth of the sun, the sound of crashing waves, the feel of the grains of sand between your feet, and the smell of salt water.

INTERACTIVES: RELAXATION TECHNIQUES

Now try to name another five relaxation techniques that set out to achieve the same physical and psychological purpose.

Go to page 175 and find out if you got any not on this list!

Psychological interventions: stress inoculation training

Psychological interventions are generally problem-focused strategies that help us cope better with stress.

A well known psychological intervention is called SIT, or stress inoculation training. Stress inoculation training was designed by Meichenbaum (1977) to help increase our resistance to stress. It is a cognitive-behavioural psychotherapy.

Cognitive-behavioural psychotherapy or CBT combines cognitive therapy and behavioural therapy. In cognitive therapy people learn how to change or manage how they think, while in behavioural therapy people learn how to change unwanted or undesirable behaviours.

Cognitive-behavioral therapy combines these two approaches, using techniques from each approach that are best suited to the needs of the individual client. The ultimate aim of any CBT is to change the way the client thinks, feels and behaves.

ONLINE INTERACTIVES

Read 'Stress Inoculation Training for Coping with Stressors' by Donald Meichenbaum at:

www.apa.org/divisions/div12/rev_est/ sit_stress.html

and then answer the following questions:

1   Identify its three phases.

2   Describe the first phase of SIT.

3   What is the purpose of phase two?

4   What is the purpose of phase three?

5   What is the normal length of treatment for anyone learning SIT?

6   Identify three situations where SIT has been successfully applied.

For answers see page 175.

A direct link is available in the Chapter 4 section of the Higher Psychology Learning Suite at **www.gerardkeegan.co.uk**

Is SIT effective?

To assess the effectiveness of the SIT, Meichenbaum (1977) compared it to systematic desensitisation. Systematic desensitisation is a behavioural psychotherapy.

Meichenbaum's clients had both snake and rat phobias. One phobia was treated using either stress inoculation training or systematic desensitization.

Meichenbaum found both methods were effective but SIT was better as it *also* reduced the non-treated phobia. This suggested that his SIT clients had learned *general* strategies for coping with anxiety, and had applied it accordingly.

In another study into the effectiveness of SIT, Fontana (1999) found that students benefited in the medium term from a six-week stress inoculation programme. When they were advised to apply SIT to stressful situations in their lives most who did were found to have a lower heart rate six months later.

Psychological interventions: increasing hardiness

Increasing hardiness is another cognitive-behavioural technique used to combat stress, and was developed by Kobasa (1979).

Hardiness is a term that describes our personal resilience to cope with the rigours of life. Hardy individuals are healthier than others (Kobasa, 1979).

> **Hardy persons are considered to possess three general characteristics: (a) the belief that they can control or influence the events of their experience, (b) an ability to feel deeply involved in or committed to the activities of their lives, and (c) the anticipation of change as an exciting challenge to further development.**
>
> *Kobasa (1979)*

Kobasa and Maddi (1977) discovered that hardy people cope better with stress. This is down to their outlook on life. For Kobasa, Maddi and others cognitive hardiness can be learned.

Kobasa and Maddi (1977) studied 200 male executives at the Illinois Bell Telephone Company who were exposed to inordinate stress because of a takeover by another company. They faced possible demotion, loss of seniority, and even loss of employment.

Kobasa and Maddi found one reason as to why half were able to avoid stress-induced illnesses, while the other half were subject to a host of stress-related problems: 'Their different way of looking at the stressful events.'

Neither group had control over the takeover, but they did have control over their *reaction* to it.

The ones who seemed immune to illness saw the drastic changes, not in a positive or negative light, but as an inevitable part of life. They viewed the changes as opportunities for new growth and experiences, rather than as threats to their security.

Their optimistic appraisal of the situation influenced their ability to control their reaction to it. This reduced their stress levels.

Further, Kobasa and Maddi found this group had a deep commitment to their families as well as to their work, which gave their lives a greater sense of meaning, direction, and excitement. This enabled them to develop what Kobasa calls 'hardy personalities.'

Increasing hardiness teaches people to focus better in order to become more aware of stressors and stress. They are taught to control a stressful situation by *reconstructing* it to make it less threatening then it might be. They are encouraged to engage in *self-improvement* compensating for the negative physiological and psychological effects of stress. And to first do tasks that are easily done, which gives them confidence that they can cope with life.

Evaluation of 'increasing hardiness'

Wiebe (1991) found that individuals who rated higher in hardiness showed lower heart rates in stressful tasks in comparison to others. Maddi (1999) found that hardy individuals had lower blood pressure and reported less stress.

However Funk (1992) argues that low hardiness is same as negativity, and it is *negativity* that leads to stress. Increasing one's hardiness also needs considerable effort and determination.

A major criticism is that the Kobasa and Maddi (1977) study into increasing hardiness was conducted only with middle-aged white business people.

While increasing hardiness may be a useful psychological intervention in the reduction of stress, it would be wrong to suggest on the basis of this biased sample that increasing hardiness is applicable to everyone.

Stress management: conclusion

Stress is best dealt with by using a combination of problem-focused and emotion-focused strategies. What works best depends upon the source of the problem, an individual's personality, and their perception and consequent physiological and psychological reaction to the stressor.

INTERACTIVES

Using research evidence where appropriate describe, explain, and evaluate physiological and psychological stress management techniques.

Structure your answer as follows:

- What is stress?
- How to cope with stress
- Stress management
- Problem-based coping
- Emotions-focused coping
- Ego defence mechanisms
- Physiological interventions
- Drugs
- Biofeedback
- Relaxation techniques
- Psychological interventions
- Stress inoculation
- Increasing hardiness

Remember to evaluate each element throughout. Use research evidence to help you.

ONLINE INTERACTIVES

Go to:

www.onlineclassroom.tv/psychology/catalogue/psychology_critical_issues/stress_management/preview2

to see stress management in action.

A direct link is available in the Chapter 4 section of the Higher Psychology Learning Suite at www.gerardkeegan.co.uk

Chapter summary

This chapter has emphasised the physiological basis to stress, and the biological processes we undergo when confronted by it. This includes sympathetic and parasympathetic arousal of the autonomic nervous system, the fight-or-flight response, and the General Adaptation Syndrome. We have looked at models of stress, in particular the physiological view, and individual differences in peoples' susceptibility to stress. It is evident that stress has short- and long-term effects on physical and mental health. To address this we have also examined and evaluated a variety of stress management techniques.

ONLINE INTERACTIVES

1. Go to the Higher Psychology Learning Suite at www.gerardkeegan.co.uk. Click Chapter 4 'Biological Psychology: Stress' to access direct links to all websites mentioned in this chapter.

2. Go to the Higher Psychology Learning Suite at www.gerardkeegan.co.uk. Click Chapter 4 'Biological Psychology: Stress' and do the online interactive crossword. But don't cheat!

3. Go to the Higher Psychology Learning Suite at www.gerardkeegan.co.uk. Click Chapter 4 'Biological Psychology: Stress' and do the online interactive hangman game. Try and beat the executioner!

4. Go to the Higher Psychology Learning Suite at www.gerardkeegan.co.uk. Click Chapter 4 'Biological Psychology: Stress' and print off the hard copy crossword. When finished you might like to hand it into your teacher as homework.

5. Go to the Higher Psychology Learning Suite at www.gerardkeegan.co.uk. Click Chapter 4 'Biological Psychology: Stress' and do the online interactive quiz. Try and win the prize!

STRUCTURED QUESTIONS WITH ANSWER GUIDELINES

1   **Describe and explain how we cope with stress.**

With reference to the preceding pages, structure your answer as follows:

● Define stress. Indicate that how we cope with stress is called stress management. Stress management is an ability we learn based upon our previous past experience. Stress management needs effort on our part. Lazarus and Folkman (1984) identify two main coping mechanisms: problem-based coping and emotions-focused coping. On this basis we use physiological and psychological interventions to help us cope with stress.

Then elaborate on the following remembering to refer to research studies where appropriate:

➤ problem-based coping

➤ emotions-focused coping – ego defence mechanisms

➤ how do physiological and psychological interventions help us cope with stress?

➤ review the physiological effects of stress: functional adjustments and fight or flight

➤ physiological interventions: drugs

➤ physiological interventions: biofeedback and biodots

➤ physiological interventions: relaxation techniques - autogenic relaxation, progressive muscle relaxation and visualisation

➤ psychological interventions: stress inoculation training

➤ psychological interventions: increasing hardiness

2   **Evaluate physiological and psychological stress management techniques.**

With reference to the preceding pages structure your answer as follows:

● outline the part physiological and psychological interventions play in the reduction of stress

● advantages and disadvantages of physiological interventions: drugs

● advantages and disadvantages of physiological interventions: biofeedback and biodots N. B. Dworkin and Dworkin (1983), Miller and DiCara (1967)

● advantages and disadvantages of physiological interventions: relaxation techniques

● advantages and disadvantages of psychological interventions: stress inoculation training N. B. Meichenbaum (1977), Fontana (1999)

● advantages and disadvantages of psychological interventions: increasing hardiness N. B. Kobasa and Maddi (1977), Wiebe (1991), Funk (1977)

Adrenaline: Is hormone or neurotransmitter produced by the adrenal medulla that is secreted in moments of crisis. It stimulates our heart to beat faster and work harder to increase the flow of blood to our muscles. It causes increased alertness, and produces other changes to prepare our body to deal with an emergency.

Atypical behaviour: Behaviour that is deemed abnormal.

Autonomic nervous system/ANS: The ANS is a major division of our peripheral nervous system that controls our internal organs and glands, involuntary movement and actions.

Biological approach, the: The biological approach understands thoughts, feelings, and behaviours as caused by our biology. In particular, our physiology and genetics.

Cannon (1927): Cannon is famous for overturning the James-Lange theory of emotion. According to Cannon (1927) we feel emotions first, and then feel physiological changes, such as muscular tension, sweating, etc. In neurobiological terms, the thalamus receives a signal and relays this to the amygdala, which is connected with our emotions. The body then gets signals via the autonomic nervous system to tense muscles, etc. Cannon's famous example is 'I see a bear. I feel afraid. I tense in readiness to run away.' See also *fight or flight*.

Central nervous system/CNS: This is the medical term for our brain and spinal cord, which along with the peripheral nervous system makes up the human nervous system.

Ego defence mechanisms: Any of various usually unconscious mental processes, including denial, projection, rationalisation, and repression, that protect us or our ego from shame, anxiety, conflict, loss of self-esteem, or other unacceptable feelings or thoughts.

Endorphins: Hormone-like substances produced in the brain that reduce our sensitivity to pain and stress.

Evolutionary psychology: Evolutionary psychology is a ranch of Biological Psychology, which explains our thoughts, feelings, and behaviours in terms of our inherited biological characteristics. Or genetics.

Fight or flight response: Our fight or flight response was investigated by Cannon (1927). Cannon discovered that our sympathetic branch of the ANS is responsible for our flight or flight response. When we are startled or threatened, it reacts by quickly releasing hormones such as epinephrine (aka adrenaline), which has several effects on our body. It increases our heart and breathing rates, it changes our circulation so that more oxygen goes to the muscles needed for running or fighting, and it increases alertness and perception. Our senses, nerves, and muscles go into high gear to allow us to perceive any threat or danger much more quickly and. accurately than normal. We respond to it faster and with more agility. On this basis we decide to take flight, or alternatively stay and fight. When the danger is over our parasympathetic branch, antagonistic to the sympathetic branch, returns our body to its more natural state of homeostasis, or internal balance.

General adaptation syndrome (GAS): The general adaptation syndrome (GAS) was discovered by Hans Selye in 1956. It is a term used to describe the body's short-term and long-term reactions to stress.

Glucocorticoids: A class of hormones produced by the adrenal cortex, an example of which is cortisol.

Hippocampus: A part of the brain important for learning, memory and emotion.

Homeostasis: Homeostasis determines our body's internal balance.

Hormones: Hormones are chemicals produced in one area of cells (or organ), which act at another place (cells or organs) of the body. Hormones get around via our blood stream. Hormones have five functions:

- They help maintain homeostasis and maintenance of internal bodily conditions.
- They prompt growth and development.
- They are essential for reproduction.
- They allow us to produce, store and use energy.
- They are related to a range of human behaviours.

Interestingly hormone secretion is usually controlled by negative feedback viz. glucagons are released from the pancreas when our blood glucose levels drop. Glucagons stimulate cells to synthesis glucose from amino acids and glycerol. Glucagons stimulate cells to breakdown glycogen to glucose. Rising blood glucose levels inhibits the release of Glucagons from the pancreas.

Hypothalamus: The hypothalamus is situated in our brain below the thalamus and posterior to the optic chiasm. It is an immensely important part of our brain that regulates body temperature, blood pressure, heartbeat, metabolism of fats and carbohydrates, and sugar levels in the blood. Through its direct attachment to the pituitary gland, the hypothalamus also regulates hormonal secretions. The role of the hypothalamus is also important to our ability to experience pain and pleasure, and is involved in emotions, such as fear and rage, and in sexual behaviours. Despite its numerous vital functions, the hypothalamus in humans accounts for only 1/300 of total brain weight, and is about the size of an almond. Structurally, it is joined to the thalamus; the two work together to monitor the sleep–wake cycle.

Individual differences: An area of study in psychology that looks at personality, atypical behaviour, and intelligence. Individual differences are thus those things we share, but differ around. Individual differences are thought influenced by our genetic inheritance. Or put another way, personality, abnormal behaviour, and intelligence are to some degree a consequence of our biology.

Learned helplessness: Learned helplessness is a tendency in animals and humans, where they learn to be helpless towards things they cannot escape (Seligman, 1976).

Lymphocytes: Lymphocytes are types of white blood cells that help us fight off viruses and infections.

Morbidity rate: The morbidity rate is the rate at which sickness and injury occur within a defined group of people.

Neurons: Neurons are the cells in our body that mostly make up our nervous system.

Noradrenaline: Noradrenaline is a hormone produced by the adrenal medulla which has wide ranging effects on many parts of the body. It is often referred to as a 'fight or flight' chemical, as it is responsible for the body's reaction to stressful situations. Noradrenaline normally produces effects such as increased heart rate, increased blood pressure, dilation of pupils, dilation of air passages in the lungs and narrowing of blood vessels in non-essential organs. This enables the body to

perform well in stressful situations.

Parasympathetic branch: The human nervous system is divided into the peripheral nervous system (PNS) and the central nervous system (CNS). Our peripheral nervous system is divided into two branches, the sympathetic branch, and the parasympathetic branch. The parasympathetic branch of our PNS returns our bodily functions to normal after they have been altered by sympathetic stimulation. In times of danger like 'fight or flight', the parasympathetic branch reverses previous sympathetic changes when the danger is over. Both branches of our PNS thus operate on the principle of homeostasis.

Peripheral nervous system: The peripheral nervous system connects our brain and spinal cord (CNS) to our outside world. This is as a result of its two branches, the somatic nervous system and the autonomic nervous system.

Personality: Who you are as an individual.

Physiological psychology/physiology: Physiological psychology is a branch of biological psychology, which explains us in terms of structures and functions in our brain, and bodily structures, processes, and functions. Greatly influenced by the founding father of American psychology William James.

Pituitary gland: The pituitary gland is our master gland. The pituitary gland produces the largest number of hormones in our body, and also controls the release of hormones by other endocrine glands.

Somatic nervous system: A major branch of our peripheral nervous system, the somatic nervous system consists of two types of nerves. The first sensory nerves transmit information about our outside world to our CNS. Sensory nerves allow us

to experience pain, pressure and changes in temperature. The somatic nervous system also has motor nerves, which carry impulses from the CNS to the muscles of the body, prompting us to do things, such as walk, smile and balance.

Stress: Stress is our body's uncertain response to demands placed upon it.

Stressor: Anything in our internal or external environment that causes us stress.

Sympathetic branch: The human nervous system is divided into the peripheral nervous system (PNS) and the central nervous system (CNS). Our peripheral nervous system is divided into two branches, the sympathetic branch, and the parasympathetic branch. The sympathetic branch of the PNS prepares our body for emergencies, such as 'fight or flight'. In fight or flight, the sympathetic branch distributes the release of noradrenaline. This stimulates our heart, raises our blood pressure, dilates the pupils, dilates our trachea and bronchi, stimulates the conversion of liver glycogen, shunts blood away from the skin and viscera to the skeletal muscles, brain, and heart, inhibits peristalsis (smooth muscle contractions) in the gastrointestinal tract, and inhibits contraction of the bladder and rectum.

Universal: Term often used in psychology to refer to those thoughts, feelings, and behaviours that apply to us all. Universal abilities are innate. This means that they come to us by way of genetic inheritance. If something is innate it usually has a high survival value for us. This is the reason it is innate in the first place! Universal abilities include such things as the fight or flight response.

Answers

Crossword p.140

Across / Down answers (from grid):

1. BIOLOGICAL APPROACH
2. CENTRAL NERVOUS SYSTEM
3. STRESS
4. UNIVERSAL
5. PHYSIO...
6. PITUITARY GLAND
7. AUTONOMIC NERVOUS SYSTEM
8. PERS...
9. CHROMOSOMES
10. BASE
11. C...
12. GENES
13. PARIETAL LOBE
14. HORMONE
15. HOMEOSTASIS
16. DNA
17. INDIVIDUAL DIFFERENCES
18. S...
19. HYPOTHALAMUS
20. EVOLUTIONARY
21. PARASYMPATHETIC
22. NEURONS
23. PERIPHERAL NERVOUS SYSTEM

Interactive: The general adaptation syndrome p.147

1 True

2 False Selye discovered the GAS after his experiments on rats.

3 False The GAS involves our nervous system and our endocrine system.

4 True

5 True

6 False Flight or fight first occurs at the alarm reaction stage.

7 True

8 True

9 False Eustress is 'pleasant' stress.

10 True

Interactive: Emotional mood states p.151

1H, 2B, 3F, 4I, 5E, 6C, 7G, 8A, 9D

Interactive: Conflict as stress p.154

Type of conflict	Description
Approach-Approach Conflict	Occurs when we have to choose between two alternative courses of action both of which are equally attractive
Avoidance-Avoidance Conflict	Occurs when we have to choose between two equally unappealing options.
Approach-Avoidance Conflict	Occurs when we are faced with a situation that has both desirable and undesirable outcomes for us.

Interactive: Stress and gender p.162

1 Women use 'tending and befriending' to deal with stress.

2 Men deal with stress by using the 'fight or flight' response.

3 When Mrs Sellers comes home from work she plays with her son, and then calls friends to tell them about her stressful day. When Mr Sellers comes home he doesn't talk about how his day has been. He keeps his feelings to himself.

4 Cortisol and adrenaline.

5 Cortisol and adrenaline raise blood pressure and cholesterol levels and suppress the immune system.

6 Oxytocin.

7 Oxytocin helps scale back the production of cortisol and adrenaline, minimizing their harmful effects.

8 Men produce lesser amounts of oxytoxin than women, and its effects are inhibited by male hormones such as testosterone.

9 These stress-related mechanisms have developed because of evolution. They each better ensure male and female survival and the survival of the species overall.

10 Men should nurture people close to them, and talk to others more about the stresses and strains of daily life.

Interactive: Relaxation techniques p.168

Yoga, Tai chi, Music, Exercise, Meditation, Hypnosis, Massage.

Interactive: SIT p.168

SIT is used to help individuals cope in the aftermath of stressful events and to make them more immune to the effects of stress in the future.

1 The conceptualisation phase, the skills acquisition and rehearsal phase, and the application and follow through phase.

2 In the initial *conceptualisation phase* a working relationship is established between the clients and the therapist. A dialogue is used to educate clients about the nature and impact of stress, and the role of both primary and secondary appraisal processes and the transactional nature of stress where clients may inadvertently, unwittingly, and perhaps, even unknowingly, exacerbate the level of stress they experience. Clients are encouraged to view perceived threats and provocations as problems-to-be-solved and to identify those aspects of their situations and reactions that are potentially changeable and those aspects that are not changeable. They are taught how to 'fit' either problem-focus or emotion-focus to the perceived demands of the stressful situation. The clients are taught how to breakdown global stressors into specific short-term, intermediate and long-term coping goals. As a result of interviewing, psychological testing, client self-monitoring, and reading materials, the clients' stress response is reconceptualised as being made-up of different components that go through predictable phases of preparing, building up, confronting, and reflecting upon their reactions to stressors. The specific reconceptualisation that is offered is individually tailored to the client's specific presenting problem e.g. anxiety, anger, physical pain, etc. As a result of a collaborative process a more hopeful and helpful model is formulated; a model that lends itself to specific intervention.

3 The purpose of phase two is to acquire and practice appropriate coping skills such as relaxation training.

4 Phase three provides opportunities for clients to apply their coping skills across increasing levels of stressors.

5 In most instances, SIT consists of some eight to fifteen sessions, plus booster and follow-up sessions, conducted over a three to twelve month period.

6 Any three from *acute time-limited stressors* such as in preparation for medical examinations; chronic *intermittent stressors* such as military combat or recurrent headache; chronic *continual stressors* such as medical illness (asthma, hypertension, Type A behaviour, chronic pain, cancer, burns, rheumatoid arthritis); or *stressor sequence* that results from exposure to stressful events (e.g., divorce, unemployment, rape).

CHAPTER FIVE

Investigating Behaviour: Research Methods

● **Demonstrate a knowledge and understanding of psychological research methods.**

Unit 2 of Higher Psychology is called Investigating Behaviour, and in the following three Chapters we will do just that!

In this Chapter we will look at Research Methods. In Chapter 6 we will address Methods of Collecting Data, while in Chapter 7 we will turn our attention to Analysing Data and the Research Investigation.

The table below illustrates the 'methods' and 'skills' components of this Unit, and how they relate to the SQA Investigating Behaviour internal assessment, and SQA Higher Psychology external exam.

Higher Psychology candidates should note that SQA change the Research Investigation projects every year. Research project briefs and logbooks *must* be got from your teacher/lecturer/centre.

Research methods

Research methodology, or how we go about doing research, is what makes psychology different from other social sciences such as history, philosophy, politics, sociology, etc. These other subjects do not claim to be sciences in the same sense as psychology and therefore don't need to adopt a rigorous scientific approach.

Psychology concerns itself with individuals, their environment, and the interaction of both.

As you will discover, psychology's principal scientific research method is the experiment. However, because of what we are interested in – people, and their behaviours in their world – the experimental

	Internal Assesment	External Assessment
Research Methods	30-minute National Assessment Bank supervised test	Section B of exam paper
Practical Research Skills	Practical Portfolio: Plan and log of a experimental or non-experimental research investigation	Report of a research investigation. It is recommended that this is based on the Practical Portfolio plan and log from the internal assessment opposite

Table 5.1 Methods and skills of Unit 2 Higher Psychology

method is often not the most appropriate method of enquiry to use. Put simply, experiments can be too artificial. Any experimental research that doesn't reflect our real-life behaviours is said in psychology to lack **ecological validity**.

Ecological validity

Ecological validity is something we have come across before. We will return to it once again in our next Chapter, when we consider the advantages and disadvantages our different research methods attract.

At this juncture it is enough to say that if an experiment, or any other research method, is said to lack *ecological validity*, this means that critics are having difficulty in accepting that its results and conclusions can be generalised to real-life situations.

It is clear that psychology encourages research. All the psychological topics that we have examined so far, their underlying approaches and associated branches have strongly emphasised this fact. It is very likely you yourself will conduct research for a practical investigation. What all students of psychology have in common is that they use a research method in the carrying out of any practical work that they do. They are methodical in investigating phenomena, whatever research method they use. This is because a method gives your research purpose, and a route to achieve an aim. Each has a recognisable procedure, which is important, as data needs to be collected.

Qualitative and quantitative data

The research information or *data* we collect can be of two kinds, qualitative or quantitative.

Qualitative data

Qualitative data is *descriptive* detail about an issue.

An example of qualitative data would be detail about what people thought or felt about a topical issue such as embryo research, membership of the European Union etc. Qualitative data in psychology is thus opinionated and personal. The interview and case study methods of research often derive qualitative data.

Quantitative data

Quantitative data is *factual* and *objective* information.

Quantitative data is a count or measurement of some kind. In psychology this would be about the behaviour under investigation. An example of quantitative data would be where a count was taken of the number of times a rat pressed a lever to obtain a reward. Another example would be where a count was taken of the number of aggressive acts observed in children after they had viewed a violent cartoon.

In psychology, quantitative data is often also called **empirical data**. Empirical data are those facts about our world achieved through sensory experience. The experimental, observational, and survey methods of research often derive quantitative data.

INTERACTIVE

Think you know the difference between qualitative and quantitative data? Go to:

www.psychlotron.org.uk/resources/research/AS_ANY_research_qualorquant.pdf

to find out!

A direct link is available in the Chapter 5 section of the Higher Psychology Learning Suite at www.gerardkeegan.co.uk

Validity and reliability

Any type of data collected for psychology must be scrutinised for validity and reliability.

This is because data is used to back up our **hypotheses** and theories.

As psychology is a subject that tries to be as scientific as possible, psychologists are instinctively wary of accepting the results, explanations and conclusions of any research.

Validity

Validity in psychology asks the question, 'Is the criterion in this research measuring the psychological phenomena it *claims* to evaluate?'

An example of validity would be assessing whether an intelligence test *actually* measures an individual's intelligence.

Reliability

Reliability is slightly different and concerns the question, 'Is the criterion in this research *consistently* measuring the psychological phenomena it claims to evaluate?'

An example of reliability would be asking if an intelligence test is consistent in its measure of an individual's intelligence at different points in time.

As you will discover, some research methods are more valid and reliable than others. This can strongly influence the value of what they discover, and whether or not a researcher can generalise their conclusions to a wider population. Validity and reliability are often used to determine the strengths and weaknesses, advantages and disadvantages, of a piece of research and its resultant theory.

INTERACTIVE

Extend yourself and read about the difference between external and internal validity in psychological research. Do the accompanying exercises at:

www.psychlotron.org.uk/resources/research/AS_ANY_research_qualorquant.pdf

A direct link is available in the Chapter 5 section of the Higher Psychology Learning Suite at www.gerardkeegan.co.uk

Participants and subjects

In psychology human beings who help us in our research are called *participants*, while non-human animals are called *subjects*. Often in research reports, etc. participants are abbreviated to Ps, and animals, Ss.

Samples and populations

Whether a P or an S, each individual in our research forms part of a research sample. Your research sample should be representative of the **target population** onto whom you want to generalise your results. A representative sample is thus one that reflects the characteristics of the target population. If it were representative, it would then not reflect **sampling bias**.

If a sample is not **representative** of the target population, another reason might be **volunteer bias**.

Volunteer bias

A lot of research in psychology takes place in universities, and very often the participants who take part are students. Indeed, they are usually psychology students, and as participants they illustrate volunteer bias. Psychology students who volunteer for psychological research are not representative of the general student population, and neither are their teachers and lecturers!

Volunteer bias is a further consideration in whether you can generalise your research results and conclusions to a wider population.

Sampling

In research sampling is the participant/subject selection technique that allows for generalisation of your results onto the target population from which your sample was drawn.

You can *infer thoughts, feelings and behaviours from a sample* and thus for example how target population might think, feel, behave.

A sample must therefore be as representative of the target population as possible. We achieve this by adopting a particular type of sampling *technique*, examples of which are below.

Sampling techniques

Opportunity sampling sees your sample made up from whoever is available and around at the time. If you need 20 participants an opportunity sample is the first 20 people you find willing to assist. Opportunity sampling is particularly popular in student research because it is convenient.

Quota sampling is popular in consumer research. Quota sampling is having a sample from a particular stratum or subcategory in society, in equal proportion to their occurrence in the target population. If consumer researchers were interested in finding out the buying habits of 16- to 21-year-old males who made up ten per cent of a city's population of 100,000, a quota sample survey would survey only this age group and stop when the quota of 10,000 of the required age group were reached.

Random sampling is where every member of a target population has an equal chance of being chosen to take part in your research e.g. one in ten. This could be achieved by drawing straws or pulling names from a hat. An example of random sampling would be if you wanted to get information from a college community about their potential use of a new college sports centre. You could use random sampling by previously deciding that every tenth person to come through the main entrance during a certain time is asked to participate in the survey. The people who complete the survey are your random sample. It is random because every person coming through the main entrance had an equal chance (1:10 in this instance) of being chosen for the survey.

Sampling method	Advantages	Disadvantages
Random sampling	If the random sample is large enough, random sampling gives the best opportunity for everyone in a target population to participate in your research. In a target population of 2000, a representative random sample of 1:20 would be more representative than one of 1:200. 1:20 as a representative random sample of 2000 would be an unbiased random sample. 1:200 would be a biased sample.	The bigger the target population, the more difficult it is to randomly sample in it. You are unsure who the target population is. If it were a town of 60,000, for example, looking in the phone book and choosing every 1000th person would be a problematic random sample. Not everyone is in the phone book, people are ex-directory, thousands of people use only mobiles whose numbers are not listed.
Stratified sampling	When it is important that characteristics/subcategories/strata of a target population be investigated, stratified sampling is most useful. Stratified sampling gives you a truly representative sample of your target population on the basis of those identified characteristics you want to investigate.	Stratified sampling is time-consuming because characteristics in the target population have to be identified, and a calculation of their ratio of occurrence worked out. This is to ensure the correct ratios in your stratified sample.
Opportunity sampling	Opportunity sampling is extremely quick and economical. It is the most common method of sampling because it is convenient.	It is an unrepresentative method of sampling. There is a difficulty when using opportunity sampling to generalise your results to a meaningful target population. If your opportunity sample was 10 first-year pupils from a large secondary school, anything you might infer from a survey could only be applied to this small unrepresentative group.
Quota sampling	Quota sampling is a quick and efficient way to gather information on specific strata within a population. If you were a consumer intelligence firm and a client were a large fashion chain catering to females in the 16–25 age group, quota-sampling females in this age group above would be ideal from the point of view of efficient market research.	How the quota sample is chosen is often left up to the researcher. If 100 16–25-year-old females were to be the quota sample, an opportunity sample of 100 16–25-year-old female students might be used. This quota would not reflect all 16–25 year old females in the target population.

Table 5.2 The advantages and disadvantages of sampling

Stratified sampling occurs when you look at your target population and decide to make up a sample for your research reflecting the make-up of the target population. At a simple level, if your target population were 60 per cent male, and 40 per cent female, your stratified sample would reflect this gender balance. In a stratified sample of 100, 60 would have to be male and 40 female. You 'stratify' on the basis of the variables you think are important to your research.

INTERACTIVE: SAMPLING TECHNIQUES ?

Go to:

www.psychlotron.org.uk/resources/resdes.html

and download a Powerpoint presentation on sampling techniques courtesy of Psychlotron.

A direct link is available in the Chapter 5 section of the Higher Psychology Learning Suite at **www.gerardkeegan.co.uk**

Extraneous variables

Sampling bias and volunteer bias are examples of **extraneous variables** in psychological research. Extraneous variables are variables from the outside that can creep into any research investigation and pollute results. Extraneous variables thus give rise to an alternative explanation for your results.

Alongside validity and reliability, extraneous variables are factors to be considered in the examination of any research done in psychology, by whatever method. We shall consider extraneous variables in our next Chapter when we look at the experimental method of research.

Research design and research methods

Our different research methods fall into two categories.

The laboratory experiment, field experiment and quasi-experiment are *experimental* in design.

The observational, interview, case study and survey methods are *non-experimental* in design.

What determines whether a research method is experimental, or non-experimental, is just how scientific it is. Does the research method follow what is called the scientific method?

The scientific method

The key element of any form of research is that the methodology, or research method, should be as rigorous and as objective as possible. The main way to do this is to adhere to what we call the scientific method, where:

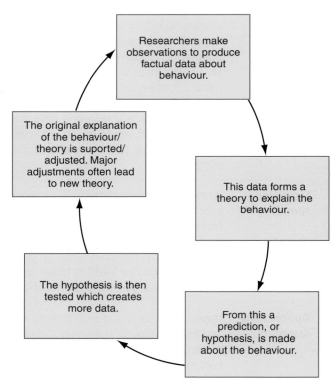

Figure 5.1 The scientific method, and the cyclical nature of how science progresses

The scientific method has researchers make observations that go to produce factual data about a particular behaviour. That data then forms a theory to explain such behaviour. From any theory a prediction, called a hypothesis, is made about the behaviour. The hypothesis is then tested, which generates more data. In the light of this new data the original explanation of the behaviour, or theory, is consequently supported or adjusted. Major adjustments often then lead to a brand new theory explaining the behaviour.

The scientific method, and the cyclical nature of how science progresses, is back to square 2!

A bit more on hypothesis testing

A *hypothesis* is a testable statement derived from a theory.

A hypothesis makes a specific prediction about what is expected to happen under certain circumstances. All sciences test such hypotheses under controlled conditions. To discover whether the prediction is correct, measurements of the extent of their prediction are taken. This factual data helps to support the hypothesis or otherwise. If the hypothesis has generated supporting evidence, this gives a measure of confidence in accepting any theory from which the hypothesis came.

There are two types of research hypothesis used in psychology, the experimental hypothesis and the correlational hypothesis. You will meet both types in greater detail shortly.

Suffice to say an experimental hypothesis is a statement of cause and effect between two *variables*. A correlational hypothesis is a statement that suggests a statistical relationship between two *co-variables*.

Both the experimental and correlational hypothesis share a similar feature called the null hypothesis.

The null hypothesis

A null hypothesis is a statement of no effect in an experiment, or no relationship in a correlation.

This is explained in greater detail in our next two Chapters, when we consider the experimental method of research.

Variables

To test a hypothesis underlying a theory you have to first identify the variables to be investigated. According to Mike Cardwell a variable 'is literally anything whose value is free to change'. Variables, then, include intelligence, depression and aggression. The next stage is to operationalise these variables.

The operationalisation of variables means finding a physical objective measure to observe and record their occurrence. The variable of intelligence could be measured by way of an IQ test. An IQ test gives you a quantifiable score. Depression could be measured using the BDI (Beck's Depression Inventory) also giving you a quantifiable score.

The operationalisation of hypothetical constructs is particularly difficult. This is because the construct itself doesn't exist in reality. Difficulties abound in finding an agreed definition of constructs from which we can identify variables to then operationalise.

Ethics

'Ethics' are a set of values that define right from wrong.

All of us who are involved in psychology are bound to adhere to certain values in any research that we do. That includes you in conducting your Higher Psychology Research Investigation!

So, what are psychology's ethics?

The BPS Ethical Guidelines and Code of Conduct

The following is based on the British Psychological Society (BPS) Ethical Guidelines and Code of Conduct (1985).

General consideration: always ensure that the research you do is carried out from the standpoint of the participants/subject taking part. Research should never be offensive to anyone. This means that you should do nothing that threatens a person's/animal's health, well-being, or dignity. You should also be aware that you live in a multicultural society with a range of diverse ethnic communities. Research should be considered from a socially inclusive, non-sexist, anti-racist and non-ageist perspective.

Consent: wherever possible consent should always be obtained from participants. If participants are under sixteen then consent should be obtained from a parent or guardian.

Deception: deception is not allowed if participants would be unlikely to co-operate without it. It in doubt the researcher should seek advice from a teacher, lecturer, etc.

INTERACTIVE

Know your ethics by completing this crossword. Test yourself against the clock.

Across
4 Wherever possible this should always be got from participants
5 Deluding participants is not allowed
6 Participants should be told they can do this at any time during the research process
7 Consent is difficult to get in this type of study
9 The opportunity to discuss outcomes with participants
10 Ethics apply to this for you
11 Who in psychology should adhere to our ethical principles?
12 The type of validity missing if results and conclusions cannot be generalised to real-life situations
13 A testable statement which all type of psychological research, experimental and non-experimental, will have

Down
1 You must avoid giving this
2 Researchers must do this with all their participants
3 To be observed at all times
8 The British Psychological Society
14 They give you data collection purpose and a recognisable procedure

See p.184 for the solution

Debriefing: any research should provide participants with an opportunity to discuss the outcomes of it. This is called debriefing, and allows discussion of the specific purpose of the research; interpretation of the participant's particular performance scores, answers, etc., and gives them an opportunity to ask questions.

Withdrawal from the investigation: all participants should give their permission to take part in your research. They should also be allowed to withdraw at any time if they so wish.

Confidentiality: unless subject to Scots law and UK statute, e.g. the Data Protection Act (1998), confidentiality between participant and researcher should be observed at all times. It in doubt get advice from your teacher lecturer, etc.

Protection of participants/subjects: all participants taking part in research should be protected from any physical or mental harm.

Observational research: any observation should observe the privacy and psychological well-being of those studied. If consent to be observed is not possible, observations should only occur where it would be normal that those observed would/could be by others. If in doubt consult your teacher or lecturer.

Giving psychological advice: sometimes during research, the researcher will be asked their advice concerning a psychological matter that is of concern to a participant. The golden rule is not to give advice if not qualified to do so. If in any doubt you should seek advice from your teacher or lecturer.

Colleagues: everyone who studies psychology should abide by the above set of ethical principles. It is our duty to encourage others who carry out psychological research to observe these ethical guidelines at all times.

ONLINE INTERACTIVES

1   Go to the Higher Psychology Learning Suite at **www.gerardkeegan.co.uk**. Click Chapter 5 'Investigating Behaviour: Research Methods' to access direct links to all websites mentioned in this chapter.

2   Go to the Higher Psychology Learning Suite at **www.gerardkeegan.co.uk**. Click Chapter 5 'Investigating Behaviour: Research Methods' and do the online interactive crossword. But don't cheat!

3   Go to the Higher Psychology Learning Suite at **www.gerardkeegan.co.uk**. Click Chapter 5 'Investigating Behaviour: Research Methods'

and do the online interactive hangman game. Try and beat the executioner!

4   Go to the Higher Psychology Learning Suite at **www.gerardkeegan.co.uk**. Click Chapter 5 'Investigating Behaviour: Research Methods' and print off the hard copy crossword. When finished you might like to hand it into your teacher as homework.

5   Go to the Higher Psychology Learning Suite at **www.gerardkeegan.co.uk**. Click Chapter 5 'Investigating Behaviour: Research Methods' and do the online interactive quiz. Try and win the prize!

GLOSSARY

Ecological validity: Ecological validity is a criticism often directed at the experimental method in general and the laboratory experiment in particular in psychology. They do not reflect a real-life situation. This is a problem for psychology in that it is a subject interested in our real-life everyday behaviours. Laboratory experiments by their very nature often get human participants behaving in an abnormal manner. This leads to distorted data, and thus weak psychological conclusions.

Empirical data: Objective, factual data obtained by sensory experiences.

Extraneous variables: Variables, or things from the outside that can contaminate a piece of research. Extraneous variables give rise to alternative explanations for your results.

Hypothesis: A hypothesis is a testable statement. All type of psychological research, experimental and non-experimental, will have a hypothesis. ('Hypotheses' is the plural of *hypothesis*.)

Null hypothesis: A statement of no effect, or no relationship.

Opportunity sampling: A type of sampling technique used to get a group of people to take part in research. An opportunity sample consists of those who are/were available to take part in research as it happens.

Quota sampling: A type of sampling technique where the sample chosen proportionally reflects the demographic characteristics of the target population onto which the research results are to be generalised.

Random sampling: A type of sampling technique that gives everyone in the target population an equal chance of being selected to be part of the research sample.

Representative: Mirroring, reflecting.

Research hypothesis: A testable statement.

Sampling bias: A situation where due to poor construction, a sample is not representative of the target population.

Stratified sampling: A type of sampling technique where the target population is divided into subpopulations or strata, and random samples are taken of each stratum.

Target population: The population onto which research conclusions are generalised.

Volunteer bias: Researchers have to be aware that volunteers in psychological research have personal characteristics that set them apart from individuals in the general population. They volunteer! Such volunteer bias means that a sample may not be representative of the population upon to which a researcher may wish to generalise their results.

Answers

Crossword, p182

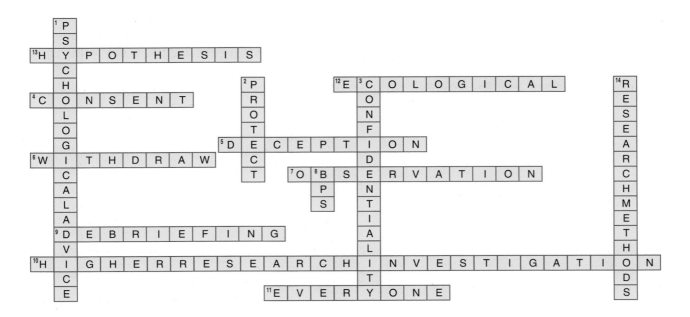

CHAPTER SIX

Investigating Behaviour: Methods of Data Collection

- **Demonstrate a knowledge and understanding of psychological research methods.**
- **Analyse and evaluate these psychological research methods.**

As suggested in the previous Chapter, psychology uses a number of research methods to collect information on our thoughts feelings and behaviours.

These are categorised into experimental and non-experimental methods, as shown below.

Experimental methods	Non-experimental methods
Laboratory experiment	Observational method
Field experiment	Survey method
Quasi- experiment	Interview method
	Case study

Table 6.1 Research methods in psychology

The experimental method

The experimental method is a research procedure well known to traditional sciences such as physics and chemistry. In this chapter the experimental method is presented as the most powerful and scientifically vigorous method of investigation used in psychology.

In using the experimental method you are adhering to its essential principles: the manipulation of an **independent variable**; the observation of any effect this has on a **dependent variable**; and the control of extraneous variables.

Importantly, the experimental method allows us to generate data that gives scientific support to the experimental hypothesis being tested. An experimental hypothesis is a testable prediction of a cause and effect relationship between an independent and dependent variable. This shall be examined in detail. We will further discover that there are three types of experiment – laboratory, field, and quasi – that reflect the experimental method. These will be illustrated, as will their advantages and disadvantages.

What is the experimental method?

The experimental method of research is a controlled procedure involving the manipulation of an independent variable (IV) to observe and measure its effect on a dependent variable (DV).

The experimental method of research is the major method of enquiry in psychology. The behaviourist, cognitive and biological approaches particularly favour the experimental method. The experimental method generates all-important empirical data upon which these approaches and related topics base a lot of their theories and ideas. Theories or ideas can be converted into an experimental hypothesis, a claim that one thing causes another. The experimental method tests this in a scientifically rigorous fashion.

Generalisation, replication and validity

The experimental method sets three standards. These include the ability to generalise your results to a wider population: the procedure you follow should be standardised (set down step by step) allowing others to replicate the experiment and get the same results; finally any measure you use to record the behaviour under investigation should be valid. This means that your measure must be related to the behaviour under investigation. Using 'kilograms' would not be an appropriate measure of running ability! Neither would the use of the Weschler Intelligence Scale for Children (WISC) (a measure of intelligence) to investigate the capacity of short-term memory – WISC would just not be valid.

> A variable is anything that can vary in its quantity or quality. It is any measurable characteristic, such as a type of behaviour, a physical entity, a way of thinking, feeling, or anything else that can be counted.

The experimental hypothesis is tested by the experimental method by manipulating something called an *independent variable* (IV). This is to measure or observe the effect this manipulation might have on a *dependent variable* (DV). The experimental method further requires us to control all other factors which might influence the effect of any manipulation of the IV on the DV. These other factors are called *extraneous variables*. One way to control for extraneous variables is to use a particular *experimental design*.

Experiments are of three main types: *laboratory*; *field*; and *quasi-experiment*. The difference between the three is their *location*. Location, or where the experiment takes place, also affects the degree of *control* the researcher has over extraneous variables.

Key features of the experimental method

The independent variable and the dependent variable

In an experiment, the researcher manipulates or changes one factor to measure or observe any effect this has on another factor. What is changed or manipulated is called the independent variable. What is observed or measured as a result is called the dependent variable. Take the following example.

Imagine the Scottish government were interested in a total ban on alcohol consumption for all drivers. This would not be a popular move, despite the dangers associated with drinking and driving. The Scottish government would need to come up with convincing scientific evidence to support a ban, and would fund some research to help their case. The researchers would be asked to investigate what effect drinking alcohol has on driving ability. They could set up an experiment where alcohol is given to participants. Participants would then sit a driving simulation test to measure the effect alcohol has on driving ability. The *manipulation* – of giving alcohol to participants – is the independent variable. The effect of this manipulation – measured by the number of errors made on the driving simulation test – is the *dependent variable*.

Control group and experimental group

The researchers would want to be sure that any observed effect on driving ability is caused by alcohol and no other factor. To be confident that it is alcohol alone that influenced driver ability they could set up a situation where they have a **control group** and an **experimental group**. Volunteers would be randomly allocated to each group.

The control group and the experimental group would then undergo different **conditions** of the independent variable. The control group would get the no-alcohol treatment and take the simulation test. The experimental group would get the alcohol treatment and likewise take the simulation test.

The **treatment**, or condition of the independent variable, is here the giving/not giving of alcohol.

> ## INTERACTIVE
>
> Identify the independent and dependent variable in the experimental hypothesis below. The independent variable is the one you manipulate or change. The dependent variable you observe or measure as a result. Libido is a free-floating sexual energy identified by Freud.
>
> H_1: 'That Viagra will have a significant influence on libido'.

The dependent variable: An observed effect

A key feature of the experimental method is the observation and measurement of the dependent variable. In an experiment the experimenter controls any manipulation of the independent variable and has no control over the dependent variable.

The dependent variable is always a measurable aspect of a human's or an animal's behaviour. We observe and measure the effect of a manipulation of the independent variable using whatever measure is most appropriate. In our example the dependent variable would be measurable in terms of errors made on a driving simulation test.

It is important that what you want to observe should be measurable in terms of number or category. Number or counts in a category later allow you to use statistics to discover if your results mean anything. Let's say in our example that the average number, or **mean**, of driver errors in the non-alcohol condition was 6.5, and in the alcohol condition 16.5.

With a mean error difference of 10 there has clearly been some kind of effect. Measurement of any observed effect is important to the experimental method. It allows you to draw conclusions that your manipulation is the cause of the observed effect. We shall return to the measurement of the dependent variable when we look shortly at the null hypothesis, probability and significance.

It is worth noting that it would be ethically wrong to conduct this type of experiment in a real-life situation. You could not give a group of drivers alcohol, let them loose in public, and observe them breaking the law! The use of simulation ensures safety in a controlled environment in the investigation of a serious issue.

INTERACTIVE

?

Your school/college thinks drinking water during examinations has a positive influence on examination performance. They have asked you to write up an experimental procedure to test this idea. Include in your report reference to your independent variable, dependent variable, the different conditions of the independent variable and treatment.

The experimental hypothesis

Experimental hypothesis: a testable scientific prediction of cause and effect between an independent and a dependent variable.

An experimental hypothesis has two features. It must be a prediction, and this prediction must be testable. Any experimental hypothesis will predict that the manipulation of an independent variable will have a measurable effect on a dependent variable.

Taking our example of alcohol and driving ability, our experimental hypothesis could be:

H_1: Alcohol affects driving ability.

The giving/not giving of alcohol to our participants is the treatment, or manipulation, of the independent variable. Driving ability, as measured by the number of errors made on the driver simulation test, is our dependent variable. As an experimental hypothesis, or cause and effect prediction, it is ready to be tested.

We should note that an experimental hypothesis is also called a research hypothesis or alternative hypothesis. While psychologists using non-experimental methods would have a research hypothesis, the only procedure where you can say you are using an experimental hypothesis is in an experiment. An experimental/alternative/research hypothesis in a true experiment must predict some relationship between a dependent variable and an independent variable. This is the experimental method in essence.

The IV and the DV: A cause and effect prediction

Since an experimental hypothesis predicts a cause and effect relationship between an independent and dependent variable, the experimental method emphasises that all other aspects of the investigation be kept constant, to ensure that an identifiable cause did indeed create the effect. This will be more fully explored when we turn to *extraneous variables*.

To establish cause and effect in our example we would give participants differing levels of alcohol (the IV) and measure their performance on the driving simulation test (the DV). The independent variable which we control is 'cause' and the dependent variable is 'effect'. If a significant number of errors were made on the driver simulation test, levels of alcohol would be our IV, or cause; errors made on the simulation, our DV, or effect.

The independent variable is the one the experimenter controls or manipulates. The independent variable or IV is the cause in an experimental hypothesis.

The dependent variable, or DV, is the one the experimenter measures or observes as a result of the manipulating the IV. The DV is the measurable effect in an experimental hypothesis.

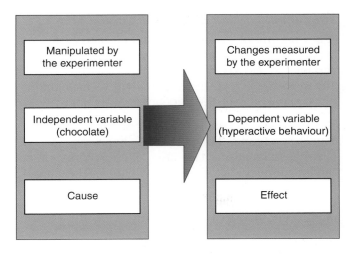

Figure 6.1 The independent and dependent variable and the experimental method

INTERACTIVE

1 What type of experiment is this?

2 Construct a hypothesis for Asch (1955).

3 What were the two conditions of the independent variable in this experiment?

4 What lessons can we learn from Asch (1955)?'.

STUDY

Asch (1955)
'Opinions and social pressure.'
Scientific American, 193, 31–5

Aim: To test how we conform to others' points of view when we find our judgement is questioned.

Method: Laboratory experiment.

Procedure: Participants were individually taken into a psychology laboratory and shown a straight line drawn on a card. They were then shown another card with three straight lines drawn on it. They were asked which of these matched the length of the first single line. All got the answer correct.

The same participants were then put into a room with a number of other people who were confederates of the experimenter. The same question was asked again of the participants, but the confederates, who were to answer first, were instructed to give wrong answers.

Results: Seventy-four per cent of the original participants (who had as individuals previously given correct answers) changed their answers in the group situation. When asked why, they said they knew they had given incorrect answers.

Conclusion: Social pressure from others influences conformity in that here each individual bowed to group pressure and gave incorrect answers they clearly knew were wrong. The issue was completely unimportant, i.e. the length of lines.

One- and two-tailed experimental hypotheses

In the framing of an experimental hypothesis we can make it one- or two-tailed.

A *one-tailed experimental hypothesis* predicts the *direction* of the result, or effect. Generally a one-tailed hypothesis would state that one condition or manipulation of the IV is *better* than another condition or manipulation of it; or, that there is a *positive* or *negative* relationship between the IV and the DV.

A *two-tailed experimental hypothesis* simply predicts that there will be an effect. This can be a predicted difference between our different conditions of the independent variable. It can also be stated in terms of a cause–effect relationship between the independent and dependent variable.

In our example we could have H_1: *Alcohol will have a negative effect on driving ability*. This experimental hypothesis indicates the predicted direction of the results (a negative effect) and is therefore a one-tailed hypothesis.

Alternatively we could have H_1: *Alcohol will affect driving ability*. This is a two-tailed experimental hypothesis. We are predicting that there will be an effect, but not indicating the direction, i.e. whether it is going to be positive or negative.

INTERACTIVE

Which of the following are examples of a one- and a two-tailed hypothesis? Give reasons for your answer.

1   H_1: Alcohol will have a positive effect on reaction time.

2   H_1: Those in the no-alcohol condition will do better on reaction time tests than those in the alcohol condition.

3   H_1: There will be a difference in reaction time between the non-alcohol condition and the alcohol condition.

The null hypothesis

Another feature of the experimental method is the null hypothesis. We came across the null hypothesis in our previous Chapter.

The null hypothesis is important from the point of view of statistics. In an experiment we have *both* an experimental and a null hypothesis. Remember that an experimental hypothesis is a prediction of an effect due to the manipulation of an independent variable. A *null hypothesis* states there is *no observable effect* with regard to the IV and the DV. Taking our example, our null hypothesis would therefore be:

H_0: Alcohol will not have an effect on driving ability.

A null hypothesis is an assumption that the experimenter takes to be true. If the experimenter comes up with evidence that contradicts this assumption, i.e. our data indicates that the null hypothesis is untrue, this allows the experimenter to do a very clever thing. They can take it that because the null hypothesis is false, the experimental hypothesis must be 'true'.

To use the jargon, if you find evidence to reject your null hypothesis, this allows you to *accept* or *support* your experimental hypothesis. If, on the other hand, you find evidence to support your null hypothesis, you must accept this and reject your experimental hypothesis. By attempting to prove a null hypothesis you also show that your experiment is unbiased, which improves the **validity** of your experimental conclusions.

If, in our experiment, we found evidence to say that alcohol had an adverse effect on driving ability we could conclude our research by saying: *On the basis of the supporting evidence, the null hypothesis, H_0: 'Alcohol does not have an effect on driving ability' is rejected, and the experimental hypothesis H_1: 'Alcohol affects driving ability' is accepted.*

If we found that the group in the alcohol condition performed better than the no-alcohol group you would however have to conclude: *On the basis of the supporting evidence, the null hypothesis, H_0: 'Alcohol does not have an effect on driving ability' is accepted and the experimental hypothesis H_1: 'Alcohol affects driving ability' is rejected.'*

If you did get this highly unlikely result, it is possible that it could have been caused by other factors you did not take into account when you were designing your experiment. These other factors are called extraneous variables. Before we turn to this, let us consider the $64,000 question. If you reject your null hypothesis, is your now accepted experimental hypothesis significant? Does your cause and effect relationship really mean anything?

Probability and significance

A null hypothesis, as was said earlier, is always assumed primarily to be true. It is a testable statement about a belief i.e. H_0: *Alcohol does not affect driving ability*. If you came up with evidence to reject this H_0: and consequentially accepted the experimental hypothesis, H_1: *Alcohol affects driving ability*, how sure could you be of your results and conclusions?

To have confidence in your conclusions you would place a bet on yourself that your results were not down to chance factors. Chance factors are referred to as *probability*. Probability is the likelihood of an event happening – like Scotland getting through to the second round of the World Cup, or even the first (!), or it snowing on Christmas Day, etc. If you went to a bookie you could get odds on the likelihood of these events happening. If they do, you've won some money. If you are over eighteen of course!

The likelihood of results in a psychological experiment being due to chance factors other than the manipulation of the IV, are expressed in terms of levels of significance. Levels of significance indicate the probability level (p value) of chance factors being the cause of your results. You choose your p value, or level of significance. It is normal in psychological experiments to set a p value, or level of significance, at $p = 0.05$. This means that you accept that there is a 1:20 chance that any result you get is due to factors other than the manipulation of your IV. Consequently our null hypothesis would be written:

H_0: Alcohol will have no effect on driving ability at the 0.05 level of significance.

Having a level of significance also allows you to use powerful inferential statistics to test the results that you generate. If you found evidence to reject the above null hypothesis and thus support the experimental H_1: *Alcohol affects driving ability*, with a 0.05 level of significance in your null hypothesis, you are accepting that there is a five per cent, or one chance in 20 that your results are wrong. You are also, however, accepting that there is 0.95, 95 per cent or 95 chance in 100 that your results are correct.

INTERACTIVES ?

Indicate the percentage and chance factor associated with the levels of significance below:

Level of significance	Chance factor	Percentage
0.05	1:20	5%
0.01		
0.005		
0.001		

Table 6.2

If your doctor prescribed you a new drug, what would be the highest level of significance you would want it to have been tested at? Give reasons for your answer.

Extraneous variables

An extraneous variable is, as we read earlier, something that can creep in and give rise to an alternative explanation for your results. An extraneous variable can be the cause of any effect that might result from your experimental procedure. Extraneous variables also influence the outcome of correlations and structured observation, both of which are non-experimental methods of research. Extraneous variables (*coming from the outside*) are of two main types – random and confounding.

Random variables

Random variables are extremely difficult to control. Using our alcohol/driving ability example, a random variable would occur if a participant were feeling unwell on the day and didn't perform as they might. You have little control over this. Random variables just happen. Another example of a random variable would be if, during our driving simulation test, a radiator in the room starting making strange noises – so strange that people were distracted. Random variables like these are almost impossible to anticipate; they can, however, give rise to an alternative reason for any cause–effect conclusion that the manipulation of your IV gives you.

Confounding variables

Confounding variables are variables that can be anticipated, and controlled. Let us look at three types of confounding variable that occur when using the experimental method.

Situational variables

Situational variables refer to *the experimental situation* itself. The environment, or where the experiment takes place, may influence our results. This is especially the case with laboratory experiments. Situational variables concern the physical environment of the experiment. In order to control situational variables, all taking part in our alcohol/driving ability experiment should experience the *same* environmental situation. Temperature, lighting, background noise, etc. would therefore be kept *constant* throughout our experimental procedure.

Experimenter variables

Experimenter variables unsurprisingly refer to the experimenter(s) themselves. You, the experimenter can be a confounding variable. One experimenter variable known as the **experimenter effect** has suggested that experimenter characteristics such as age, sex and general behaviour may have subtle effects on participants' performance (Eagly and Carli, 1983).

Experimenter bias is a more common confounding variable in experimental research. Experimenter bias happens when the expectations of the experimenter influence the participants' behaviours. A classic example of experimenter bias is the **expectancy effect** discovered by Rosenthal and Fode (1963).

Rosenthal and Fode (1963) asked students to train rats to run through a maze. They told one group of students that they had been given particularly smart rats that would learn to run the maze quickly. The other group were told that they had dull rats that would be slow to learn to run the maze. Rosenthal and Fode actually had no idea how clever or otherwise their rats were.

The group who were told they had smart rats later reported that they had quickly learned to run through the maze, while those who had been told their rats were dull reported theirs to be slow. The smart rat group produced data showing a better maze running performance in comparison to the dull rat group.

Rosenthal and Fode (1963) say that the students' (false) expectations about whether a rat was smart or dull had had an effect on the results. The group with the smart rats got the result they did, either because they put more effort into training their rats to run the maze, or because their recording of the rats maze running abilities was affected by expectations.

In order to control for experimenter variables many experiments first do a **pilot study**, or a rehearsal of the experiment. A pilot study, which can involve the researchers as the 'participants', helps iron out confounding variables such as the experimenter and expectancy effect. Pilot studies give you an opportunity to develop an even more controlled experimental procedure, which we generally refer to as standardisation. When you do any research, if appropriate conduct a pilot study as 'good practice'.

Participant variables

Remember that a confounding variable concerns other factors that could account for your result.

A participant variable could then be the cause of any observed effect on your dependent variable, other than the manipulation of your independent variable.

Participant variables are confounding variables that come from the participants themselves. In our alcohol/driving ability example participant variables include whether participants were male or female. This is because men and women have different metabolic rates and break down alcohol differently. Other participant variables that could interfere with our results are body fat, which influences the breakdown of alcohol, drinking experience, or lack of it, etc.

We can control for such participant variables using a standardised experimental procedure called an **experimental design**. Experimental designs help control for confounding variables.

At this juncture two participant variables deserve explanation: the *Hawthorne Effect*, or participant expectancy; and *demand characteristics*.

The Hawthorne Effect: Participant expectancy

Participant expectancy was discovered in 1939 by probably the world's first occupational psychologists, Roethlisberger and Dickson. Their study is better known as the Hawthorne Effect.

Roethlisberger and Dickson were interested in the relationship between factory pollution and productivity levels at the Hawthorne electrical generating plant in America. Their independent variables included changing the lighting conditions in the factory and the times the workers could take their breaks. They assessed the output of five female workers under differing working conditions for two years. Much to Roethlisberger and Dickson's surprise productivity increased, rather than decreased, when they manipulated their IV of worsening working conditions. They discovered the women had worked harder because they wanted to please the psychologists. It was this 'wanting to please the psychologist' that produced their strange results.

Knowing that you are a participant in an experiment, and wanting to please the researchers can create the Hawthorne Effect. This is because the Hawthorne Effect sees participants behave in an unnatural way.

Demand characteristics

Demand characteristics are any features of an experiment, which help participants work out what is expected of them, and consequently lead them to behave in artificial ways. These features 'demand' a certain response. Participants search for cues in the experimental environment about how to behave and what (might) be expected of them.

How did the workers in the electricity generating factory work out they were taking part in an experiment? Psychology tells us they most likely picked up cues that gave the game away. Cues that give away the nature of an experiment are called **demand characteristics,** a term first coined by Orne in 1962.

ONLINE INTERACTIVES

Please now go to the British Psychological Society at:

www.bps.org.uk/thesociety/code-of-conduct/code-of-conduct.home.cfm

and read 'The Code of Ethics and Conduct' (2006).

Demand characteristics, or giving participants too many clues about what we are interested in, are some of the main reasons why psychologists are never entirely truthful with participants who take part in our research! If you tell someone, consciously or unconsciously, about what you are really after, you can never be sure of your results; they might be caused by demand characteristics. As a result we very often use deception in experimental work – we do not tell participants the true nature of our research. This raises ethical issues, which should not be avoided. If you have to deceive your participants you must at least get their consent that they want to

take part and give them a debriefing on the true nature of your work at the end of your study.

You can also minimise demand characteristics in experimental work by using a **single-blind technique**. This is where the participant does not know to which condition of the independent variable (control or experimental) they have been allocated. There have been reports that cannabis helps alleviate symptoms of multiple sclerosis and Parkinson's disease. To test this in a scientific experiment using a group of MS or Parkinson disease participants, half of the experimental group would be given the cannabis pill, while the other half, the control group, a harmless sugar pill or **placebo**. No participant would know whether they had been given the cannabis or the placebo. All nonetheless record any effect. This is a good example of the single-blind technique where the participant doesn't know to which condition of the IV they have been allocated.

Experimental designs

An experimental design refers to the controlled structure, form or plan of the experimental procedure. Experimental designs help narrow down confounding variables, especially those concerning the participant. Designs also reflect an important principle of the experimental method, which is an ability to make sense of any data that is produced. This is because experimental designs allow us to compare one treatment of the independent variable with another. As we read earlier this produces data, the significance of which we test using statistics.

Experimental designs fall into two categories: related and unrelated. A related design generates data that are related; unrelated designs generate data that are unrelated.

Related experimental designs

There are two types of related designs used in experimental research – repeated measures, and matched pairs design.

Repeated measures

A repeated measures design (RMD) repeats the measure of performance, the dependent variable, under the differing conditions of the independent variable. A repeated measures design is particularly appropriate if you want to do a 'test–retest' comparison with two, and sometimes more, manipulations of the independent variable. A repeated measure is a **within-subjects design**, because each participant provides data for all manipulations of the independent variable.

To use an RMD in our alcohol experiment we would use one group of participants. They would first undergo condition A of the independent variable, no alcohol, and be asked to do the driving simulation test. They would then undergo condition B of the independent variable, alcohol, and repeat the simulation test. We are clearly repeating the measure with our group of participants – the measure being the number of errors made on the simulation test under the two conditions of the IV. This is a repeated measures design.

Mention must be made here of another *participant variable* called **order effect**.

Order effect

Order effect refers to the influence on your results of practice, fatigue, or boredom. Order effect can pollute an RMD because you are asking participants to do something at least twice, in this instance a driver simulation test. What if, whether drunk or sober, they learned to do the simulation test better in condition B as a result of practice in condition A? In an RMD, practice can influence results, as can other order effects such as tiredness and boredom.

ABBA and counterbalancing

If you use a repeated measures design and want to control for order effect, the trick is to use **counterbalancing**.

Counterbalancing evenly distributes any order effect across the two conditions of the independent variable. In our example with ten participants, counterbalancing would see us randomly allocate participants 1–5 to undergo condition A first (no alcohol), then condition B (alcohol). Alternatively, participants 6–10 would be allocated to condition B first, and then condition A. Counterbalancing is an ABBA presentation to the two conditions of the IV. This means condition A then B for one half of our participants, and condition B followed by A for the other half. Counterbalancing using an ABBA exposure cuts down the likelihood of order effect in an repeated measures design.

INTERACTIVE

?

Why are repeated measures and matched pairs designs said to be related?

Advantages and disadvantages of a repeated measures design

The repeated measures design is very popular with psychology students in their experimental research. Its advantages include good control of participant variables and fewer participants are needed in comparison with a matched pairs design. Needing fewer participants probably helps its popularity with students! This is because with an repeated measures design you are of course asking the same group of participants to do something twice. Using a repeated measures design also distributes any individual differences the participants may have across the two conditions of the IV. Any individual differences will cancel each other out across condition A and condition B. In our example individual differences could be drinking experience, or lack of it, length of driving experience, sex of participant, body fat, and so on.

The main disadvantage of the repeated measures design is order effect – counterbalancing should be used to control for this. Another disadvantage is that of demand characteristics. The participants could guess the true purpose of our alcohol research and decide that it was not in their interests to behave as they might.

Matched pairs design

Another related design, termed a matched pairs design, is used when a test–retest procedure is difficult because of order effect. It is characterised by matching participants on the basis of the participant variables you think could give rise to an alternative explanation of any results you get. What are relevant confounding participant variables differs from experiment to experiment. In our alcohol study participants would be matched on the basis of sex, body fat, drinking experience, etc. Other participant variables like IQ (intelligence quotient), and socio-economic status (what you do, where you live, and how well off you are) are maybe not as relevant in this instance, but could be in others. Once matched, participants are randomly allocated to the control and experimental group conditions. Applying a matched pairs design to our example, we would match participants on the basis of relevant confounding variables, then randomly allocate each matched participant to either the control condition A, or the experimental condition B of the independent variable, and ensure that each group mirrors the other as far as possible. The control group would get no alcohol and does the driving simulation test. The experimental group would get alcohol and similarly does the simulation test. The scores obtained by each group under each condition of the IV would then be compared.

Advantages and disadvantages of a matched pairs design

The main advantage of the matched pairs design is that you avoid order effect. Participants, in whatever condition, are only asked to do one thing once. Here participants only undergo one manipulation of the IV (no alcohol, alcohol) and then do the driver simulation test. If you have matched participants properly on the basis of relevant confounding variables, it is a reasonably good procedure to control for participant variables. An MPD also gives you access to powerful inferential statistics such as the related t test.

The main disadvantage attached to an MPD is the question of whether you have matched on the basis of relevant confounding participant variables. You can never be entirely sure that you have accounted for all the important differences between people that may influence the results of your study. As a result it is difficult to control totally for all participant variables. Other disadvantages are the time and resources required to find out what individual differences are relevant to your study. These of course you have to match. You also need twice as many participants as in a repeated measures design.

Unrelated experimental designs

The main unrelated experimental design is an independent group design (IGD). An independent group design is also referred to as an independent sample, or independent measures design. An unrelated design creates a situation where any data obtained is unrelated. This is because the participants undergoing each condition of the independent variable are unrelated to one another; they are 'independent' groups.

Independent groups design

An independent group design is a **between-groups design**. Each participant in each group experiences only one condition of the independent variable, and provides data for one manipulation of the independent variable.

To create an independent groups design as an example you could use two independent groups of participants, say the Kilmarnock History Club and Kilmarnock FC Supporters Club; you would toss a coin and randomly allocate one group to the control condition (no alcohol), and the other to the

experimental condition (alcohol). Both groups would do the driving simulation test and you would compare their results.

An independent groups design is also appropriate where there is more than one condition of the independent variable. Take this example.

The participants of one group are each given a list of words and asked to repeat each word several times before going on to the next one. Participants in the second group are asked to form vivid mental images of each word, making links between that word and its successor. Both groups are then tested on memory recall.

There are two different conditions of the IV above: two different forms of remembering, rehearsal and imagery. The dependent variable in both instances is the number of words remembered under each of these conditions.

INTERACTIVE

1 What do you think is the aim of the above piece of research?

2 What do you think the outcome would be?

3 If one form of remembering were found to be better than the other, how confident would you be of your results (using an IGD)? Give reasons for your answer.

Advantages and disadvantages of an independent groups design

Order effects, such as practice, fatigue or boredom, do not arise because participants are allocated to only one condition of the independent variable.

As you may have worked out from the above Interactive, the main disadvantages of the IGD are participant variables, or individual differences. In our alcohol-driving ability investigation with the Kilmarnock History Club and the Kilmarnock FC Supporters Club you would definitely not be comparing like with like! The two groups differ entirely in the number of males and females involved, drinking experience, body fat and so on. Your results, comparisons and conclusions would be rather meaningless.

Another disadvantage of an IGD is that you need more participants in comparison to a repeated measures design. This is because you need two groups.

Look at the data charts below. Identify the designs of these two experiments. Give reasons for your answer. Explain these designs, and give two advantages and two disadvantages for each.

Design 1 Participant number	Condition A results	Condition B results
1		
2		
3		
4		
5		
6		
7		
8		
9		
10		

Design 2 Condition A results	Condition B results
P1	P11
P2	P12
P3	P13
P4	P14
P5	P15
P6	P16
P7	P17
P8	P18
P9	P19
P10	P20

Types of experiments

There are three types of experimental procedure that adhere to the experimental method. These are laboratory, field and quasi-experiments. Each involves:

- the manipulation of an independent variable
- the observation of any effect this manipulation has on a dependent variable
- the control of extraneous variables

The difference between the three types of experiment is their *location*. Location, or where the experiment takes place, affects the amount of *control* the researcher has over extraneous variables.

Laboratory experiments

The **laboratory experiment** involves the manipulation of an independent variable and the subsequent measurement/observation of the dependent variable. Laboratory experiments take place in the closed, heavily controlled setting of a psychology laboratory.

To ensure better control, a laboratory procedure standardises any instructions given to participants. Standardisation means that instructions to participants are agreed and checked for ambiguity before the experiment proper. Any ambiguities should have come to light in an earlier pilot study.

Standardised instructions ensure all participants are told exactly the same thing. Standardised instructions are also important where participants are involved in non-experimental methods of research such as observation and the correlational technique. Read the next Study for an example of a laboratory experiment.

Blakemore, C. and Cooper, G.F. (1970) 'Development of the brain depends on the visual environment.' *Nature*, 228, 477–8

Aim: To investigate environmental influence on the development of perception.

Subjects: Kittens (non-human animals are called 'subjects' in psychological research).

Method: Laboratory experiment.

Independent variable: Independent variable: being raised in either a vertical or horizontal environment. Dependent variable: kittens' response to vertical and horizontal visual line stimuli.

Procedure: Blakemore and Cooper raised kittens from birth in complete darkness. For five hours each day the kittens were put into either a horizontal or vertical striped drum. Using an inverted cardboard funnel around their necks, the kittens were also sensorily deprived from seeing their own bodies. They could only look forward, so that stripes – horizontal or vertical – were the only stimuli they encountered.

At five months old, the kittens were tested for line recognition by being presented with a moving pointer going in either a horizontal or vertical direction.

Results: The results showed that kittens raised in a vertical world only reacted to vertical line stimuli, while those kittens brought up in a horizontal world only responded to horizontal line stimuli.

The vertically raised kittens showed 'behavioural blindness' towards horizontal stimuli, and the horizontally raised kittens were 'behaviorally blind' towards vertical stimuli. Blakemore and Cooper discovered that this behavioural blindness corresponded with 'physiological blindness'. By placing electrodes in the kittens' visual cortex they found that the kittens raised in a vertical environment did not possess cells that 'fired' in response to horizontal line stimuli. On the other hand kittens raised in a horizontal stimuli did not have cells that fired off in response to vertical stimuli.

Conclusion: Environment affects the development of perception in some species at a physiological level. If an environment does not nurture aspects of perception, the species can suffer a deficit physiologically, which in this instance was behavioural/physiological blindness in either a horizontal/vertical environment.

Figure 6.2 Blakemore and Cooper's cats

INTERACTIVE

1   What was the aim of Blakemore and Cooper's (1970) study?

2   What was the IV and what was the DV?

3   Is this a repeated measures, matched pairs or independent groups/samples design? Give reasons for your answer.

4   What ethical issues does Blakemore and Cooper's (1970) study raise?

Field experiment

As we should now appreciate the laboratory experiment is often accused of lacking in ecological validity. This means that they are 'unreal' and don't reflect a real-life situation. To avoid the question of ecological validity very often the experimental method is applied to a field experiment.

A **field experiment** also sees the manipulation of an IV and subsequent measurement/observation of a DV, but takes place away from the laboratory, indoors or out. A field experiment can occur in the natural environment of the participant, e.g. a school classroom, a playground, or the street.

Quasi-experiments

A **quasi-experiment** also occurs outside the laboratory but there is no manipulation of an independent variable, as the IV is already 'in place'. Measurement/observation of a DV does however follow. 'Quasi' means 'nearly' or 'almost'. A quasi-experiment is then *nearly* an experiment, but differs in one important respect. Participants are not randomly assigned to conditions of the IV by the experimenter. In a quasi-experiment the conditions of the independent variable are already in place.

Take the following example. You might be interested in the impact developmental changes have on intelligence. The development of intelligence is affected by biological, cognitive, social and emotional factors. Put another way, intelligence is affected by our nature (genetics), nurture (environment), and the outcome of the interaction of both. Nature and nurture, the changing factors that influence intelligence, are here your independent variables; they are already in place and, as such, cannot be manipulated. This is the scenario of a quasi-experiment.

To conduct this quasi-experiment you would need to find a sample of participants and using a valid and reliable test, measure their intelligence at age 20, 30, 40, 50, 60 and 70. Any significant differences in participant intelligence scores would be put down to

STUDY

Bickman L. (1974) 'The social power of a uniform'.
Journal of Applied Social Psychology, 1, 47–61

Aim: To investigate obedience in a real-life setting.

Method/Procedure: Experimental method. Field experiment. Bickman wanted to investigate obedience in the streets of New York. He asked different confederates to wear a) a security guard's uniform b) a milkman's uniform and c) civilian dress. These were the different conditions of his independent variable. They were then observed on the streets of New York asking passers-by to pick up a paper bag, give a dime to a stranger, or move away from a bus stop.

Results: Bickman found that 80 per cent of passers-by obeyed the guard in comparison to 40 per cent who obeyed the confederate dressed as a civilian. The number who obeyed the milkman was the same as the number who obeyed the civilian.

Conclusion: We learn from our culture and social world to be more obedient to certain authority figures than others.

changing biological, cognitive, social and/or emotional factors in their life. These are in place and you have no control over these independent variables. You can measure their influence nonetheless.

Using other non-experimental techniques such as survey, interview and case study, it would be possible to track individual genetic and environmental changes that might suggest a link with intelligence, were you to live long enough to conduct this longitudinal study. A longitudinal study in psychology lasts more than one year. This one stretches that a wee bit!

Another example of a quasi-experiment is Namikas and Wehmer (1978) who were interested in aggression shown by males and females in litters of mice. The independent variable was the number of male and female mice born to each litter. The IV (male/female ratio) was 'in place' and varied naturally from litter to litter. It is a quasi-experiment because they had no control over this. Namikas and Wehmer (1978) observed that a male mouse born in an overwhelmingly female litter was more aggressive than male and female mice born and raised together in a mixed litter.

INTERACTIVE

Find another two laboratory experiments in this book. Write a short report on each identifying the name, date, aim, method (experimental: laboratory), procedure (what did the psychologist(s) do), results and conclusion(s).

Natural experiments

Confusingly, a natural experiment is often included under the heading of the 'experiment' in psychology. In a natural experiment the researcher usually observes an animal or human in their natural environment. There is no manipulation of an independent variable in a natural experiment. The researcher does not, and cannot, have one. As a result the 'natural experiment' is not a procedure that reflects the experimental method.

Enough of all this talk about experiments – why not now try one?

STUDY

An investigation into taste perception or Scotland's other national drink

Aim: The aim of this investigation is to assess the influence of visual cues on taste perception.

Experimental hypothesis: H_1: When visual cues are frustrated, taste perception will be adversely affected.

This is a one-tailed hypothesis.

Null hypothesis: H_0: The frustration of visual cues will have no adverse effect on taste perception at the 0.05 level of significance.

Independent variable: egg yellow food colouring in lemonade in Condition B.

Dependent variable: observation and measurement of participant response to the Condition B manipulation of lemonade/egg yellow.

Method: Laboratory experiment. Repeated measures design.

Apparatus:

500ml of quality lemonade

500ml of quality orangeade

Disposable cups (four per participant)

38ml of egg yellow food colouring

Data response sheet (see later)

Preamble: Earlier in the cognitive approach, we looked at a cognitive process called perception. We enjoy visual perception, auditory perception, taste perception, etc. Taste perception is a result of our sense of vision, taste and smell all working together. Previous past experience is also an issue. Questions in this experiment are, is taste perception frustrated when visual cues are absent?, and does previous past experience influence taste perception?

Procedure: Arrange to get participants from your school, college, workplace, etc. This is a random sample obtained by opportunity sampling because the participants are easily available! Ten would be a good number. If you have ten participants you will need 40 disposable cups. Ask the participants beforehand if they mind taking part in an experiment on taste perception. If they say yes, you have their consent to proceed. Also brief them as to the general nature of your research (an investigation into taste perception). At the end it would also be a good idea to debrief your participants telling them the precise purpose of your experiment, and what it was you found out.

Before they arrive do the following. Mix up some egg yellow with lemonade until it resembles the colour of Scotland's other national drink. Then get four cups per person and put a little lemonade into the first, orangeade into the second, orangeade into the third and lemonade with egg yellow into the fourth. For the second participant have the sequence orangeade, lemonade, lemonade/egg yellow, orangeade, and so on. What you are doing, as our chart illustrates, is counterbalancing in each condition of the IV to avoid order effect.

Participant	Condition A		Condition B	
1	Lemonade	Orangeade	Orangeade	Lemonade/egg yellow
2	Orangeade	Lemonade	Lemonade/egg yellow	Orangeade
3	Lemonade	Orangeade	Orangeade	Lemonade/egg yellow
4	Orangeade	Lemonade	Lemonade/egg yellow	Orangeade
5	Lemonade	Orangeade	Orangeade	Lemonade/egg yellow
6 etc.	Orangeade	Lemonade	Lemonade/egg yellow	Orangeade

Table 6.3 Counterbalancing chart

Invite your participants into your laboratory one at a time. A classroom will do. Get them to taste each cup in the sequence above and ask them what they think the liquid is that they are drinking. Note any comment they make. Any comment made by a participant is called introspection. These are useful in the writing up of psychology reports, over and above the discussion of empirical data. It is likely in the lemonade/egg yellow manipulation people say they can't taste anything much, or that it is a well-known Scottish soft drink. Which it is not of course!

Give one point for each drink correctly identified in each condition of the IV, i.e. 'lemonade' or 'orangeade'. If participant number one identifies both drinks in Condition A as lemonade and orangeade they get two points. If they identify only one as correct they get one point, if none, no points. Do the same for Condition B. Enter participants' responses in a data chart as below. Participant scores have been entered as an example.

Participant	Condition A Score	Condition B Score	B–A Sign of difference
1	2	1	−
2	2	1	−
3	1	2	+
4	2	1	−
5	2	1	−
6	2	1	−
7	2	1	−
8	2	1	−
9	2	1	−
10	2	1	−

Table 6.4 Data sheet: taste perception

You are testing your experimental hypothesis using a statistic called the 'sign of difference' test, also called the Binomial Sign Test. Work out the sign of difference for each participant by subtracting the B score from the A score and entering the sign of difference (+ or −) in the last column of your data response chart. If there is no sign of difference, i.e. if you get 1 in condition A and 1 in condition B, or 2 and 2, or 0 and 0, leave the right-hand-side sign of difference column blank for these participants. You can ignore these.

Count up the number of times a sign of difference occurs (either + or −). Call this N. In our example above N = 10. This is because there is one (+) and nine (−) in our B–A column. 1+9=10.

Count up the sign that occurs least frequently and call this calculated s. In the above example, with ten participants calculated s = 1, because there is only one +. Then consult the Binomial Sign Table.

Run your finger down the left-hand column until you find your N. In our example N = 10. Go across to your level of significance, which in this example is 0.05 for a one-tailed hypothesis.

Here we find the critical value is 1. Calculated s must be equal to, or less than, this critical (tabled) value. Our results show that calculated s = 1, and with N = 10 the critical value at the 0.05 level is 1.

In this instance because calculated s is equal to its critical value we can therefore reject our null hypothesis and accept our experimental hypothesis, being: When visual cues are frustrated taste perception will be adversely affected.

Level of significance for one-tailed test					
N	0.05	0.025	0.01	0.005	0.0005
Level of significance for two-tailed test					
	0.10	0.05	0.02	0.01	0.001
5	0	--	--	--	--
6	0	0	--	--	--
7	0	0	0	--	--
8	1	0	0	0	--
9	1	1	0	0	--
10	1	1	0	0	--
11	2	1	1	0	0
12	2	2	1	1	0
13	3	2	1	1	0
14	3	2	2	1	0
15	3	3	2	2	1
16	4	3	2	2	1
17	4	4	3	2	1
18	5	4	3	3	1
19	5	4	4	3	2
20	5	5	4	3	2
25	7	7	6	5	4
30	10	9	8	7	5
35	12	11	10	9	7

Table 6.5 Binomial sign test table

An interesting aspect to this experiment being done in Scotland would be the influence of culture on taste perception, remembering that perception is understood as our senses, plus gestalten, plus meaningful past experience. Can you see why in this example?

Calculated s must be EQUAL TO or LESS THAN the table (critical) value for significance at the level shown.

Source: F. Clegg, *Simple Statistics*, Cambridge University Press, 1982. With the kind permission of the author and publishers.

ONLINE INTERACTIVES

Once you have done the above, go to:

www.gerardkeegan.co.uk/resource/ research1.htm

for help on how to write up a report on the

investigation. Use the recommended headings as much as possible.

A direct link is available in the Chapter 6 section of the Higher Psychology Learning Suite at **www.gerardkeegan.co.uk**

Advantages of the experimental method

The advantages of the experimental method are fourfold: the ability to establish cause and effect, the control of variables, objectivity, and replication.

Cause and effect and control

The experimental method is the only method of enquiry where a *cause–effect* relationship can be established between variables. This is because the experimental method emphasises the *control of variables*. When, using a particular experimental design, we control confounding variables and get data to support our experimental hypothesis; we can draw a cause and effect conclusion between our independent and dependent variables.

Objectivity, validity and measurement of the dependent variable

The validity of any conclusion we may reach on cause and effect is founded on objectivity. Precise measurement of the dependent variable helps produce objective and factual data, and this empirical data is the most scientific. We can thus be more confident of the results and conclusions of experiments in comparison to non-experimental research procedures, where data is more descriptive and subjective.

Standardisation, replication and generalisation

The standardisation of experimental procedure and instruction is another advantage attached to the experimental method. Standardisation of design and instructions to participants helps in the *replication* of your experiment. If others follow your standardised procedure, replicate your experiment and get the same results, all can be more confident of a probable cause and effect relationship regards the IV and the DV. With careful sampling of participants, the experimental method also allows you to generalise your results to the population from which your sample was drawn.

Disadvantages of the experimental method

Ecological validity

Lack of *ecological validity* is the main disadvantage of the experimental method. The situations for which psychological experiments try to establish a cause–effect relationship very often do not reflect real life. This was illustrated in our examination of the behaviourist approach in particular. Is there really no difference between the animal and human species? Do animals learn in the same way as we humans? By comparing animals with humans regarding how species learn, are behaviourist experiments lacking in their ecological validity?

Sampling bias

Sampling bias can also be a disadvantage in that a poor sample can prevent you from generalising your results to a larger population. A great number of psychological experiments involve student participants – indeed student participants who study psychology. Relying on participants from such a closed group shows sampling or *selection bias* (the exclusion of others).

Extraneous variables

Extraneous variables are also a major disadvantage of the experimental method. The situation, the experimenter, and the participant can all give rise to other explanations for the results. Absolute control of extraneous variables is an almost impossible task. One type, *random variables*, cannot be controlled, as they cannot be anticipated. They just happen. Other *confounding variables* such as the experimenter him/herself can influence results.

Confounding variables

Experimenter expectations, giving rise to experimenter bias, can be a problem. He or she can consciously or unconsciously create an experimenter effect (Rosenthal and Fode, 1963).

Participant variables are a particular confounding variable in experiments that can cause difficulty. Those concerning individual differences, even when controlled using a design, can never be entirely anticipated. *Participant expectancy*, or the Hawthorne Effect, can see participants behave in an unnatural way because they know they are the subjects of an experiment. How they know is because of the *demand characteristics* of the experimental situation. Cues are picked up that can reveal the true purpose of the experiment, and this can interfere with the thoughts, feelings, and behaviours of those taking part.

Advantages of the experimental method	Disadvantages of the experimental method
Cause and effect	Question of ecological validity
Control of variables	Control of extraneous variables
Objectivity	Confounding variables (participant)
Replication	Demand characteristics

Table 6.6 Advantages and disadvantages of the experimental method

Advantages and disadvantages of different types of experiment

Advantages of the laboratory experiment

The main advantage of the laboratory experiment is that it gives a clear *cause and effect* relationship between an independent and dependent variable. This is because it is easier to control extraneous variables in a laboratory than in other experimental situations.

The laboratory experiment also ensures greater accuracy in the measurement of our dependent variable. Devices to precisely measure behaviours are far easier to use in a laboratory than elsewhere. These objective measures of observed behaviour guarantee the *validity of our empirical data*. The laboratory experiment's standardised procedure also allows others to replicate what has been done. If after *replication*, this new empirical evidence is supportive, we can be even more confident that any cause and effect relationship is as a result of the manipulation of the IV on the DV, and not other extraneous chance factors.

Disadvantages of the laboratory experiment

The control of all extraneous variables is impossible. *Random variables*, for example, just happen, and cannot therefore be controlled. You can try to anticipate and control for *confounding variables* but can never be entirely certain that you have accounted for them all, until after the experiment, and then it is too late. The laboratory experiment is also often accused of lacking in ecological validity. This is because the results are often from an unreal situation, which is difficult to find in real life.

Who is to say that in our alcohol and driving ability example, our participants in real life would drink and then get behind the wheel of a car? Only an idiot would do this. *Generalisation* of results into a real world situation is therefore sometimes difficult because of a laboratory experiment's lack of real-life, ecological validity.

Advantages of the field experiment

A field experiment yields greater ecological validity than a laboratory experiment; and because it takes place in a real-life setting, any behaviour it observes is more likely to be natural. You avoid sampling bias because you access in the field a more representative sample of the population to whom you want to generalise your results. Demand characteristics can be minimised.

Disadvantages of the field experiment

It is more difficult to control for extraneous variables in a field environment than in a laboratory. Imagine designing a field experiment to investigate types of play behaviour in children from age four to eight years. The most appropriate field environment for this would be a primary school playground. You arrange everything, and on the day your field experiment is due to take place it rains! You have to call it off – yet the project is due in the next day! This is an example of a random variable in a field experiment.

Controlling for confounding variables in a field experiment is equally hazardous, there are just so many. An example of this is Feshbach and Singer's (1971) study.

Feshbach and Singer were interested in the influence violent/non-violent TV programmes had on male teenage behaviours. They predefined programmes such as 'Batman' as violent. Boys aged between nine and fifteen from seven residential schools were randomly assigned to either condition of the independent variable, which was to watch either violent or non-violent TV. Each group within each home was instructed to watch at least two hours of television per day for six weeks, watching in either condition of the IV.

For three of the seven schools tested, levels of aggression among those exposed to violent programmes were found to be *lower* than those of participants exposed to non-violent TV. According to Feshbach and Singer, this supports the *catharsis hypothesis*. The catharsis hypothesis says that watching violent TV provides a safe fantasy outlet for aggressive impulses and helps to reduce aggressive behaviours. This is in sharp contrast to Bandura *et al.*'s (1961) findings on naturally aggressive children. Bandura *et al.* found naturally aggressive children to be more aggressive as a consequence of observing and imitating aggressive adult models.

You might think Feshbach and Singer would appear to have made an important discovery. However Liebert and Sprafkin (1988) criticise Feshbach and Singer on two counts. Boys in the non-aggressive TV group in the three institutions where the catharsis effect appeared had rebelled against being told they could not watch 'Batman'. To keep the peace no doubt, Feshbach and Singer then proceeded to let them watch their 'banned' programme. This constitutes an important difference in comparison to the treatment of all the other groups. Further, Liebert and Sprafkin (1988) say:

> **An important alternative explanation ... for the fact that some control subjects were more aggressive is that they resented being restricted to non-aggressive programmes, and this resentment was expressed in an increase in violence."**

Resentment alone could have accounted for more violent behaviour in the non-aggressive control group.

INTERACTIVES

How many confounding variables can you find in the Fesbach and Singer firld experiment that could provide an alternative account for their catharsis hypothesis?

Advantages of the quasi-experiment

The biggest advantage of the quasi-experiment is its high ecological validity. Quasi-experiments are more 'natural'; the IV is one that naturally occurs; the participants you access are in their natural environment. Their thoughts, feelings and behaviours are deemed to be more normal and natural as a result. In a quasi-experiment sampling bias disappears, as do demand characteristics. This is of course as long as participants are unaware they are part of a psychological experiment.

Disadvantages of the quasi-experiment

You have no control over the independent variable. In a quasi-experiment it is also extremely difficult to infer a cause–effect conclusion due to an inability to control extraneous variables. These could be other factors that give rise to your results (see earlier Feshbach and Singer, 1971).

Quasi-experiments are almost impossible to replicate. They take place at a particular time, a particular place and with a particular group of participants. Consequently a quasi-experiment has only spatio-temporal validity.

Quasi-experiments can also attract participant expectancy in that the demand characteristics of the situation might give participants a clue that they are taking part in an experiment. On the other hand, if participants do not know they are the subject of an investigation, the quasi-experiment can attract ethical criticism concerning privacy, disclosure, consent and debriefing.

Because of an inability to control the IV and extraneous variables, and an inability to replicate to confirm/deny the original results, the quasi-experiment is least like a procedure that adheres to the experimental method. Procedures that are recognised as 'true' experiments must see the manipulation of an independent variable, the observation and measurement of any effect of this manipulation on a dependent variable, and the control of extraneous variables.

Type of experiment	Advantages
Laboratory experiment	Cause and effect can be better established
	Objectivity and precision measurement of DV
	Control of confounding variables
	Replication due to standardised procedures (design/instructions)
Field experiment	High ecological validity
	Avoids sampling bias
	Demand characteristics minimised
Quasi-experiment	Great ecological validity
	Little, if any, sampling bias
	Participants less influenced by demand characteristics

Table 6.7 Advantages of types of experiments

Type of experiment	Disadvantages
Laboratory experiment	Impossible to control for all extraneous variables
	Lack of ecological validity due to artificial laboratory environment
	Sampling bias, demand characteristics, experimenter expectancy can all influence behaviours, results and conclusions
	Ethics (deception, etc.)
Field experiment	Difficult to control extraneous variables
	Difficult to replicate
	Precision measurement problematic
	Ethics (consent, deception, privacy, etc.)
Quasi-experiment	Cause–effect difficult to establish between IV and DV
	No control over IV
	Little control over extraneous variables
	Impossible to replicate
	Only spatio-temporal validity
	Ethics (consent, deception, privacy, etc.)

Table 6.8 Disadvantages of types of experiments

Summary

The experimental method of research is a controlled
procedure that sees the manipulation of an
independent variable (IV) to observe and measure
any effect this has on a dependent variable (DV).
The essential features of the experimental method
are the control, observation and measurement of
variables. Having the hallmarks of a science, the
experimental method makes us more confident
about the validity of any cause–effect relationship
established between an independent and dependent
variable. The experimental method also makes us
more assured about the generalisation of its results
to a wider population. The experimental method's
emphasis on strict procedures helps others replicate
the experiment to confirm, or otherwise, the original
research findings. This is how scientific knowledge
grows. The experimental method sets out to test a
null hypothesis, which if rejected allows the
researcher to accept the experimental, or research,
hypothesis. Hypotheses will, more often than not, be
tested at a level of significance. A level of
significance is the wager, probability, or p value, a
researcher places on themselves that their results
happened by chance. Students of psychology
generally set themselves a level of significance of
0.05, which means they are happy to accept that in
the rejection of their null hypothesis, there is still a
1:20 chance that any cause–effect relationship
established is due to chance or random factors.

These chance or random factors, which can be an
alternative explanation for results in psychological
research, are called extraneous variables and are of
two kinds. Random variables just happen, making
them impossible to control, and confounding
variables, which can be anticipated and controlled.
Examples of confounding variables would be any
situational variable found in the experimental
setting, experimenter variables, such as
experimenter and expectancy effect, and participant
variables, which are those participant peculiarities
that can influence results. These include participant
expectancy and demand characteristics.

To control for extraneous variables, the experimental
method uses one of two kinds of design procedure, a
related or within-subjects design (like repeated
measures or matched pairs), or alternatively, an
unrelated independent group/sample/measures
design. Each category, and each type of design, has
particular features. For example, the repeated
measures design, where participants experience all
conditions/manipulations of the independent
variable, can attract order effect.

Counterbalancing can control order effect. What
design is adopted is often decided in anticipation of
confounding variables that can arise in the different
experimental situations, which are the laboratory,
field and quasi-experiment. They differ in their
location, and thus the degree of control a researcher
has over confounding variables.

The laboratory experiment often attracts criticism
on the grounds of ecological validity. The further
away from the laboratory a researcher goes,
however, the more likely it is that the (more
ecologically valid) quasi- or field experiment will
attract random and confounding variables. As a
research method, the experimental method is
assuredly the most rigorous of methodologies in
psychology.

To get an even better understanding as to why this
can be said, let us now examine non-experimental
designs.

STRUCTURED QUESTIONS
WITH ANSWER GUIDELINES

1   Describe and explain the experimental method of research.

With reference to the preceding pages, structure your answer as follows:

● Define the experimental method of research as being a controlled procedure that sees the manipulation of an independent variable (IV) to observe and measure its effect on a dependent variable (DV).

Then using examples to help you, identify and explain the following features of the experimental method:

➤ generalisation, replication and validity.

➤ the experimental hypothesis, one and two-tailed.

➤ the independent and dependent variable.

➤ the null hypothesis, probability and significance.

➤ extraneous and confounding variables.

➤ situational, experimenter and participant. Types, examples, control.

➤ experimental designs: RMD and IGD.

➤ types of experiment: laboratory, field and quasi.

➤ features of laboratory, field and quasi-experiments. Location and degree of control over IV and confounding variables.

2   Evaluate the experimental method of research in terms of its advantages and disadvantages.

Structure your answer as follows:

● Define the experimental method of research as being a controlled procedure that sees the manipulation of an independent variable (IV) to observe and measure its effect on a dependent variable (DV).

Then using examples to help you, identify and explain advantages of the experimental method, i.e.

➤ cause and effect.

➤ control of variables.

➤ objectivity.

➤ replication.

- Then describe the specific advantages attached to specific types of experimental method.

- Next identify and explain disadvantages of the experimental method:

  ➤ ecological validity.

  ➤ control of extraneous variables.

  ➤ participant variables.

  ➤ demand characteristics.

- Finally describe specific disadvantages attached to specific types of experimental method.

Non-experimental research designs

The observational method

From your first introduction to research methods in our previous Chapter, you may remember that the observational method is a non-experimental research design – as are the interview, survey, and case-study methods.

When using the observational method there is no manipulation of an independent variable. As a consequence no cause–effect relationships can be made concerning your observations as to why the behaviour(s) may have occurred.

What all observations share is their use of a standardised (planned and systematic) approach in order to obtain accurate data on whatever behaviour is being observed. This gives the researcher accurate and detailed data from which to draw conclusions.

We find five types of observation used in psychological investigations:

➤ Participant observation

➤ Non-participant observation

➤ Structured (controlled) observation

➤ Unstructured (uncontrolled) observation

➤ Naturalistic observation.

In all five, observation involves the planned gathering, analysis and interpretation of data on observed behaviour.

The observational method has both advantages and disadvantages as a research tool in psychology. Ethics and the issue of disclosure can be major headaches, but if the researcher adheres to the observational method – to plan, structure and conduct their observation in a disciplined way – the observational method may be seen as one of the purest forms of non-experimental research, as it taps directly into behaviour, rather than perceptions of it as might happen in a case study or interview.

What is the observational method?

The observational method of research concerns the planned watching, recording and analysis of observed behaviour as it occurs in a natural setting.

The study of naturally occurring behaviour

Given that psychology is the study of human behaviour and mental processes, it seems logical to suggest that in order to study the *behavioural* aspect of psychology we need to observe the behaviours of those around us. Indeed, much research that psychologists conduct involves observing behaviour at some stage in the research process.

The observational method requires careful planning

The theme that runs through procedures using the observational method concerns the careful planning of *how* the behaviour under scrutiny is to be observed and recorded. We all observe each other on a daily basis. Indeed, your interest in psychology might encourage you to observe others much more closely than you did before! If you are in a supermarket you may glance at the purchases of other shoppers. While sitting in a café you may observe the interactions between people, their eating habits or their clothes. You cannot tell anything much from these casual observations of behaviours, although they may sow the seeds for later hypothesis testing, as the following exercise illustrates.

Figure 6.3 Observing!

Key features of the observational method

Generating empirical data

The observational method requires us to pre-plan our approach to those behaviours we want to watch. A major part of this preparation involves us in deciding how our observations are to be recorded. This is because our records, and/or our recordings, can give us factual and objective measurements of our observed behaviour, i.e. empirical data. This empirical data is later analysed in order to draw factual conclusions on the behaviours observed.

A good example of the generation of empirical data from an observation in everyday life is that of an athlete running 100 metres. All involved agree beforehand on the measurement of 100 metres. The athletes line up and start when they hear the gun. Electronic devices are used to identify false starts. The athletes' time to run 100 metres is objectively and factually recorded in seconds using stopwatches. The athlete who crosses the line first wins. By comparing times we are able to say how an athlete has performed in relation to the others in the race, and 100-metre athletes in the athletic world at large. We are able to draw many more conclusions about the athletes' running behaviour due to the generation of empirical data. This data tells us, for instance, who was fastest off the block, who was first to 50 metres, whether the athletes have achieved their personal best, and so on. Data from observations can either be quantitative or qualitative. We have already met these terms. But let us remind ourselves about them.

Quantitative data

Quantitative data is objective, factual information about behaviours.

Quantitative data, in an observation, provides us with a *quantity* or *number* concerning the behaviours of people. We could observe, for example, the sex and film choice of people using a particular cinema complex during a particular period of time. You could decide to observe the first hundred people entering the cinema and record their sex and which film they go in to see. After this data has been collected, you would be able to quantify, or give a *measurement* to the sex of participants and their particular film choice.

Qualitative data

Qualitative data gives emotional details concerning behaviours. It is subjective, i.e. 'How was it for you?'

If you wanted to find out what those hundred people *thought* of the film you could also give them a short exit interview or survey that would allow you to collect *qualitative* data. Qualitative data is the rich, detailed, personal information provided by each individual on, here for example, the strengths and weaknesses of the acting, the story, the direction, the special effects and so on.

Data-gathering techniques

To get the most meaningful measurements of behaviour in observational studies some important questions should be considered. What is to be observed; why is it being observed; by whom; where and when is the observation to be conducted, and how is the recording of our observations to be carried out?

What?

The types of behaviours that can be observed in psychology are varied, and can be those of either human or non-human subjects, i.e. people or animals.

Why?

At the outset it is important to have an understanding of the topic under investigation and why you are conducting your research. You have to determine its purpose; you may begin by trying to answer a question out of simple curiosity, e.g. what is the sexual behaviour of people in a particular group? This would gradually become more specific as you refine your initial observations, such as, what are the specific behaviours of the male in this group; who attracts the most females, or what do men in this group do in social situations to attract a female. Or indeed *vice versa*.

By whom, and where?

The observational method of research is particularly appropriate for social psychologists, developmental psychologists and animal behaviourists, primarily because of the participants/subjects used in their studies, i.e. social groups, children and animals. In each case, valid and reliable results would be more likely if behavioural observations occurred in the *natural environment* of the participants/subjects.

When?

When to observe can be problematic. To help us there are two methods of recording observed behaviours – continuous recording and time sampling. Continuous recording means recording all behaviours all the time. Time sampling records snapshots of behaviour.

Continuous recording

Continuous recording allows for an exact record of behaviours with the time they occurred (for events), or the time at which the behaviour started and finished (for states of behaviour, e.g. aggression).

Time sampling

Time sampling involves the periodic recording of behaviour, e.g. recording a situation at five-minute intervals. Time sampling gives you less information, and an exact recording of the behaviour you are interested in is not necessarily obtained. You could be recording the wrong five minutes! However, time sampling is a way of condensing information in observational research, and with good prior planning

a sample of the behaviour(s) you are interested in can be captured and recorded.

How?

How you get data from your observation is important to the generation of objective empirical data. Observations often use precise measures, such as audio/visual recordings and/or observation schedules.

Video recordings provide an exact audio and visual record of behaviour. They are particularly useful in situations where behaviours are being recorded over a lengthy period. Video recordings are also helpful when the behaviour under investigation is too fast, or too complex, to be analysed in real time. Tapes and recordings can then later be slowed down, stopped or freeze-framed to give a better idea as to why the behaviour may have happened.

Written records are also often used in observations, either on their own, or to complement audio and visual recordings. Called observation schedules or check sheets, they are carefully constructed in order to get an accurate picture of the behaviour under investigation. Codes and a behaviour index might also be used, as we can see in our example below.

Date/time xx/xx/xx 1pm	Kitten A	Kitten B	Kitten C	Kitten D
Intervals				
0.30	F	S	Mw	S
1.00	F	S	S	S
1.30	F	S	S	T
2.00	F	S	Aw	T
2.30	S	S	Aw	F
3.00	F	S	Aw	F
3.30	F	F	P	F
4.00	S	F	P	F
4.30	F	F	F	F
5.00	F	F	F	F

Table 6.9 An observation schedule: check sheet using time sampling

Behaviour index:

S = kitten is sleeping

F = kitten is feeding from mother

P = kitten is playing or fighting with others in litter

Mw = the mother is washing the kitten

T = the mother is toileting the kitten by licking

Aw = the kitten is awake but still.

Figure 6.4
How would you categorise the behaviour on the right?

Using time sampling, this observation schedule check sheet has been used to record behaviours of very young kittens. The date and time of recording would normally be inserted in the top left box. For recording purposes the four kittens in the litter were given a letter A–D. The time interval sampled was every 30 seconds over a five-minute period. The behaviour index allowed the observer to quickly and accurately record what each kitten was doing at each particular time sampled. This is excellent quantitative empirical data essential for analysis and a considered conclusion.

INTERACTIVES ?

Why would the above observational check sheet give you quantitative data? Why would qualitative data be impossible in this situation?!

Obtrusive and unobtrusive measures

An **obtrusive measure** in an observation is where an observer uses a check sheet or observation schedule, 'scoring' the behaviours as they happen in front of them. A video camera or camcorder would also be deemed an obtrusive measure if in sight of those who are taking part.

An **unobtrusive measure** in an observation is a *hidden* measure of behaviour, such as the use of a one-way mirror, hidden camera/recorder, etc.

The use of obtrusive measures can be an extraneous variable in an observation, and give rise to an alternative explanation as to why the behaviour you observed has occurred.

Control of extraneous variables

Despite careful planning, extraneous variables or *variables from the outside* can give rise to alternative explanations in observations of behaviour. Extraneous variables are unavoidable and infinite. As researchers, we must try to make sure that extraneous variables are anticipated and controlled in our research procedures.

As we saw earlier in this chapter regards the experimental method, extraneous variables are of two types. **Random variables** are extraneous variables that 'just happen'. You have no control over random variables. Examples would be the weather, or how a participant was feeling on the day.

The other type of extraneous variable that can be anticipated and controlled is called a **confounding variable**. An obtrusive measure in an observation could be a confounding variable because the presence of an observer with a check sheet or camcorder could influence the behaviour of those being observed.

One of the most effective types of observation used to avoid extraneous variables is, as we will see, a structured observation. Structured means controlled. Structured observations can give rise to a common type of confounding variable in observational research called observer bias, which we came across earlier when we looked at the work of Rosenthal and Fode (1963).

Observer bias

Observer bias can occur if more than one observer is used, for instance, if different observers are recording data at the same time, or working on a shift basis over an extended time period.

Observer bias would be a confounding variable if one observer has a different understanding of what the codes used in a behaviour index mean, and fills in the schedule wrongly. Another example of observer bias would be where one observer has their own hypothesis and, consciously or unconsciously, selects *only* those observations for recording to substantiate this.

In order to control for observer bias there are two types of reliability check that can be used. These are called within-observer reliability, and between-observer reliability.

Within-observer reliability

Within-observer reliability measures the extent to which each individual observer obtains consistency when recording scores or ratings of the same behaviour on different occasions. Their video recordings and check sheet records of the 'same' behaviour on a number of occasions can verify this.

Between-observer reliability

Between-observer reliability measures the extent to which two or more observers obtain the same results when measuring the same behaviour on the same occasion. This can again be confirmed, or otherwise, using their video recordings and check sheets.

Within- and between-observer reliability can be further tested by correlating the records of different observers. The greater the statistical relationship of within- and between-observers' scores/ratings, the greater the level of **inter-rater reliability** an observational study is said to have. This strengthens the reliability of any conclusions that may be made.

You – the observer – can thus be a confounding variable in your own observational research. Guard against this by agreeing on what goes to make up the behaviour you want to observe. Agree a common coding system for this, construct a behaviour index and check sheet/observation schedule. You could increase the inter-rater reliability of your study by verifying your own, and others' coding of observed behaviour by using a correlation.

Types of observation

There are as indicated earlier five different types of observations that adhere to the observational method: participant observation; non-participant observation; structured observation; unstructured observation; naturalistic observation.

Participant observation

Participant observation sees the observer(s) set up and take part in the behaviour under investigation.

Participant observation can give an accurate record of what is actually happening in a situation. However, while the behavioural information may be accurate, it is also possible that the presence of an observer may alter the behaviour of those taking part. This is known as the **observer effect**, and is an example of another confounding variable in observational studies. You can avoid the observer effect by deciding not to disclose who you are. Called covert observation, this attracts obvious ethical criticisms, in that you are not being open and honest about your true purpose with fellow 'participants'. If your observation is known about, this is an **overt observation**. You are being open about what you are doing. Now please read the Rosenhan Study and do the Interactive that follows.

STUDY

Rosenhan, D.L. (1973). 'On being sane in insane places'. *Science*, **179, 250–8**

Aim: To find out if those characteristics that lead doctors and other professionals to a diagnosis of mental illness are a result of the patient's actual condition, or because of the environment and context within which the patient is observed and diagnosed.

Method: Eight sane people presented themselves for admission to twelve different hospitals in the USA (participant observers). They complained of hearing voices such as 'empty', 'hollow' and 'thud'. Other than this symptom the eight pseudo-patients complained of no other ailments. After admission to the hospital they stopped complaining about hearing voices. They took part in the activities on the ward, and in their role as participant observers, wrote notes about staff and patients.

Results: Seven of the eight pseudo-patients received a diagnosis of schizophrenia. They were kept in hospital for between seven and 52 days (average nineteen). They were all released with a diagnosis of schizophrenia in remission. The only people who suspected that they were not genuine patients were some of the other patients in their ward.

Conclusion: Psychiatric professionals saw note-taking by the pseudo-patients as an aspect of their condition. Outside the context of a psychiatric ward this, and other behaviours, would not be seen as abnormal. David Rosenhan concluded that 'normal' behaviours were reinterpreted as 'abnormal', based on the context of the situation, psychiatric hospitals, and therefore the subsequent expectations of the staff. These expectations existed because of the labels they attached to the sane and insane.

From the perspective of participant observation it should also be noted that accounts given by the pseudo-patients of their experiences within a psychiatric ward are not necessarily representative of the experiences of 'real' patients, who do not have the comfort of knowing that they have been possibly misdiagnosed. It may be apparent that here it would have been difficult to use anything but participant observation.

INTERACTIVES

1   What evidence is there to indicate that Rosenhan's (1973) study is a participant observation?

2   Did Rosenhan (1973) generate empirical data? Give reasons for your answer.

3   Why is Rosenhan's study not a structured observation?

Non-participant observation

Non-participant observation sees no participation on the part of the observer.

Non-participant observation is where the observer does not take part in the behaviour under investigation and observes and records what occurs from a distance. This eliminates the possibility of observer effect, and is usually a covert observation in that your measures would be hidden, or just too far away for anyone to be aware of them.

The behaviours being observed are thus prone to subjective interpretation on the part of the observer, and this could show itself in the form of observer bias which should be anticipated and controlled.

An example of non-participant observation is the study by Piliavin *et al.* (1969). It should be noted that here, observation was used in conjunction with the experimental method, since the researchers controlled a number of *independent* variables. Independent variables are, of course, a feature of any procedure that uses the *experimental method*.

Piliavin, I.M., Rodin, J. & Piliavin, J.A. (1969). 'Good Samaritanism: An underground phenomenon?' *Journal of Personality and Social Psychology*, 13, 289–99

Aim: In order to investigate passenger-response to an emergency in a real-life situation of a New York subway train and to ensure ecological validity, Piliavin et al. used non-participant observation within a field experiment. They were interested in the speed, frequency, and rate of passenger response to a manipulated 'emergency' involving stooges who were told to act in a particular way. Other aspects to helping behaviour (altruism) that were of interest were the number of passengers in the carriage where the emergency occurred, their race, and whether there was any difference in them offering help if the 'victim' was perceived as drunk or visually impaired.

Method: Incidents such as a black/white victim drunk or sober (with a cane) collapsing in a carriage of a New York subway train were staged at set times over a period of two months. Passengers on the trains were the participants. Each train carriage contained an average of 43 passengers, with a racial mix of 45 per cent black and 55 per cent white. The researchers were four students (two male and two female). The females were the non-participant observers of the incidents enacted by their two male colleagues.

The observers recorded the race, age, sex and location of each passenger on pre-prepared sheets. They then recorded who and how many people helped the 'victim' and how long it took for them to respond.

Results: The cane victim received help on 62 of 65 trials. The drunk victim received help on 19 of 38 trials. On 60 per cent of all trials the victim received help from two or more helpers. On close analysis the sex of the 'first helper' was more likely to be male.

Conclusion: Passengers were more helpful than Piliavin had predicted and he attributed this to a delicate balance on the part of the helper between personal cost and personal reward. The cost of helping may be embarrassment; the cost of not helping, guilt. The rewards associated with helping may be praise and respect, while those associated with not helping may be 'no time wasted' in a busy day.

Piliavin *et al.* thought that what motivates someone to help is not altruism – a drive within us to help for helping's sake – but our need to remove/avoid a negative emotional state if we don't help. We feel bad about it.

ONLINE INTERACTIVES

1 Why is Piliavin *et al.*'s (1969) study an example of non-participant observation?

2 What type of experimental design is also being used?

3 Can you identify any independent variables?

4 What do you understand by the term 'ecological validity'?

Structured observation

Structured observation is the planned watching and recording of behaviours as they occur within a controlled environment.

Structured observation sees the researcher first identify the behaviour(s) in which they are interested, and then observe its type or frequency over a set period of time using a pre-coded data-gathering instrument, such as a check sheet. Generally a structured observation would follow the following procedure.

In a structured observation you need to:

➤ define the behaviour or type(s) of behaviours to be studied

➤ identify the time frame during which the behaviour is to be observed

➤ develop a data-gathering instrument, e.g. observation schedule

➤ select an observer role – what is it you want the observers to do

➤ train observers if more than one is to be used

➤ conduct the observation(s) using your data-gathering instrument(s)

➤ verify data for reliability

Structured observations: a controlled environment

If you were interested in toy preference among girls and boys in the under-five age group, a structured observation would be ideal. Having obtained the necessary permission to conduct your research you would find out prior to the observation those toys familiar to the participating children. You would then introduce an equal number of familiar and unfamiliar toys into the nursery situation, having also discovered from an independent source whether they were considered 'male toys' or 'female toys'. This could be done by contacting manufacturers, or by surveying members of the public and asking their opinion on which toy they thought more appropriate for which sex.

Once all this has been determined, you could enhance your structured observation of pre-five toy-preference by using a range of obtrusive measures such as a check sheet, plus utilise unobtrusive measures like a hidden video recorder or CCTV.

Structured observations and ethics

Structured observations are often used to protect the welfare of those being observed. In Ainsworth *et al.*'s (1978) study a naturalistic observation of an infant's reaction to being separated from his/her mother would have been unsafe and unethical. The natural environment of a supermarket or park would have been just too dangerous. The situation in Ainsworth *et al.*'s Strange Situation study is 'natural,' in so far as the child and mother could expect to find themselves in a similar situation at some time or another because it took place in an environment akin to a doctor's surgery. As we read in Chapter 3, an important feature of this structured observation was the eight changing environments that occurred during the course of the observation.

STUDY

Ainsworth, M.D.S., Blehar, M.C., Waters, E. & Wall, S. (1978) *Patterns of attachment: A psychological study of the strange situation*. New Jersey: Lawrence Erlbaum Assoc. Inc.

Aim: To observe the emotional reactions of infants to brief separations from their caregivers in the presence of strangers, and of their behaviour when the caregiver returned.

Method: Using a structured observation procedure and a specially prepared observation room, interactions between infants and their caregivers, while in the presence/absence of a stranger/caregiver, were observed and recorded through a two-way mirror. There were eight stages (or strange situations) in the process. Each of the eight stages lasted approximately three minutes.

Observers recorded the reactions of the baby and the mother in each of the stages. They were interested in four types of behaviours evident during the strange situation, which they coded accordingly, i.e.

1 Separation anxiety – any distress the infant showed when mother left.

2 The infant's willingness to explore.

3 Stranger anxiety – anxiety shown by the infant when approached by the stranger.

4 Reunion behaviour – reaction of the infant after separation when mother returned.

Results: As a result of their observations, Ainsworth *et al.* concluded that there were three main types of attachment behaviours found between mothers and their infants: **Type A – Anxious–avoidant** (infant is ambivalent to mother's presence; they are more distressed by being left alone than by the mother's departure and find comfort with the stranger). **Type B – Secure attachment** (infant plays happily in the mother's presence, they are distressed at the mother's departure rather than because of their isolation. Although the stranger can offer some comfort, there is a clear difference between the comforts obtained from the caregiver and the stranger). **Type C – Anxious–resistant** (the infant is wary in mother's presence, they play and explore less than types A and B children. On the mother's return anxious–resistant infants both seek and reject her comfort at one and the same time. The stranger cannot comfort them).

Conclusion: Of the mother/infant pairings studied, 15 per cent showed type A anxious–avoidant behaviour; 70 per cent, type B secure attachment behaviour; and 15 per cent, type C anxious–resistant attachment behaviours. Sensitive mothers have infants who can tolerate short separations and explore strange environments independently, who seem safe in the knowledge that they can return to the mother for security (Type B). Insensitive mothers have infants who lack secure attachment to the mother, and demonstrate this by either ambivalence or anger at being separated from her (Types A and C).

INTERACTIVES

Read the Ainsworth *et al.* (1978) structured observation and consider the following questions.

1 What was the purpose of the study?

2 What procedures were undertaken to ensure this was a structured observation?

3 What ethical reasons might have prompted the use of structured observation in this instance?

4 Describe the coding system used by the researchers.

Naturalistic observation

Naturalistic observation is the planned watching and recording of behaviours as they occur within a natural environment.

Naturalistic observation is often associated with **ethology**, a branch of psychology that studies the behaviour of animals in their natural environment. They do this in order to make species–species comparisons with humans in, for example, mother–infant attachment behaviours, aggression, etc. Naturalistic observation, or observations of real-life behaviours in a real-life natural setting, gives ecological validity to what you discover. This means behaviours are real because they have been naturally observed – but in a planned and systematic fashion.

An example of a naturalistic observation would be if we wished to see the behavioural reaction of an animal to a new food source. We would obtain the most valid results if we observed food source changes in the animal's natural environment. Consider a troop of monkeys living in an area of the forest where their main food is banana. Researchers may wish to test if the monkeys can adapt to another food source, e.g. berries not native to the forest. They would provide quantities of the berries within easy reach of the monkeys and observe and record the monkeys' behaviour in relation to the new food source.

Figure 6.5 The feeding behaviour of monkeys could be studied by naturalistic observation

Naturalistic observation and children

Naturalistic observation is also often used with children. Children react to the slightest change in their environment as was evident in Ainsworth *et al.* (1978) and their Strange Situation. In order to observe children's *natural* behaviours, psychologists would want to observe them in an environment familiar to them. Thus with infants and children, a *naturalistic* observation could take place in the home, school, playground, etc.

Naturalistic observation can be applied to our earlier example of toy choice among girls and boys in the pre-five age group. To be a naturalistic observation, you would arrange to go to the nursery, then using a pre-planned system; you would record the sex of each child, and length of time you observe each child play with the toys normally available to them. At the end of this you might be able to conclude that boys preferred particular toys, while girls preferred others. Your knowledge of Early Socialisation should give you an idea as to why this might be.

Extraneous variables in naturalistic observations

There are problems with deducing too much from what you naturally observe in this situation. The boys' and girls' toy preference could have been influenced by a variety of confounding variables such as the toys available, their prior knowledge and experience of particular toys, and your presence as a stranger in the nursery.

Random variables could also occur in that something may have happened to the child/children, which may have influenced their mood, and thus their behaviour, on the day of your observation.

Unstructured observation

Unstructured observation is the unplanned, informal, watching and recording of behaviours as they occur in a natural environment.

An unstructured observation is a form of observational study where the behaviour of interest,

> ## INTERACTIVES
>
> How might observer bias influence an unstructured observation?

and/or the method of observation have not been clearly specified in advance. Unstructured observations are used when a specific behaviour being studied cannot be clearly identified, and when it is important to observe participants in their own environments rather than in, say, a laboratory setting. An example of an unstructured observation is that of a social psychologist going undercover to observe the behaviours of a gang of football casuals.

All that unstructured observations do is give the researcher a sense of *what is going on here?* The investigator does not have any measuring or recording instrument other than a notebook or memory. Particular attention must be paid to observer bias in unstructured observations. In the above example it would be foolhardy for the social psychologist to pull out a notebook and start taking the 'firm's' details! His later recall of events can however be influenced by personal opinion. Observations would not have been recorded in a planned, systematic and objective manner.

Examples of unstructured observations include Whyte in 1943 when he joined an Italian street gang in Chicago. He used a cover story that he was writing a book about the area. His true purpose was to observe the gang from a psychological point of view. He is remembered for his famous statement on his experiences:

> *I began as a non-participating observer. As I became accepted into the community, I found myself becoming a non-observing participant.*"

Observation as a technique

Bandura *et al.* (1961)'s study is a classic piece of psychological research where a Canadian research team, led by Alfred Bandura, conducted an experiment and a non-participant observation into the transmission of aggressive behaviours from adults to children. As we can see from the study that follows they had three conditions of the independent variable.

They used observation as a technique, rather than a method in its own right. Observations occurred within a laboratory experiment. In their experiment they observed and recorded children's behaviours from behind a one-way mirror, later coding and analysing their recordings. On this evidence Bandura *et al.* (1961) concluded that children observe, then imitate and model themselves on the adult behaviours that they see.

Stanley Milgram's work into blind obedience is another example of structured observation being used as a technique to gather data within an experimental design. His 1963 laboratory experiment used film to observe and record his participants' emotional reactions to orders from an authority figure to inflict apparently lethal doses of electricity on another person.

Bandura, A., Ross, D., & Ross, S.A. (1961). 'Transmission of aggression through imitation of aggressive models'. *Journal of Abnormal and Social Psychology*, **63, 575–82**

Aim: To discover if aggression in children is influenced by observation, imitation and modelling of aggressive adult behaviour.

Method: Three groups of children were shown an adult being either rewarded, not rewarded or punished for aggressive behaviour towards a Bobo doll. Each child was then observed in an identical play environment with any resultant aggressive behaviour recorded onto film and later analysed, on a frame-by-frame, child-by-child basis.

Results: Children who had watched adult models engage in aggressive acts went on to exhibit more aggressive behaviours than those who had watched non-aggressive acts. Boys showed more aggression than girls. Male models induced more aggression in boys than female models. Male models induced more physical aggression, and female models, more verbal aggression in girls.

Conclusion: Children learn aggressive behaviours as a result of observing, imitating and modelling themselves on adults.

Figure 6.6 The aggressive behaviour of a female model, and the subsequent behaviour of a boy and girl who watched her (from A. Bandura *et al.*, 1961)

INTERACTIVES

1   Describe the features of this research that Bandura *et al.*'s (1961) study shares with the experimental method.

2   Identify the independent variables in this study.

3   What was the dependent variable in this study?

4   What did Bandura *et al.* discover?

5   Identify features of the observational method in this experimental situation.

INTERACTIVES

Identify any ethical considerations you think are relevant to *three* observational studies detailed in this Chapter. Give a reason, or reasons, for your answer. Please adhere to psychological conventions in your answer, i.e. 'Piliavin *et al.* (1969)', etc.

Advantages of the observational method

As a research tool the observational method can lead to a hypothesis for further study, and in so doing can save time and money being spent on a badly designed experiment, or other method of research.

The observational method provides 'real-life,' ecologically valid information, in that in an *ideal* situation, the researcher observes behaviour unobtrusively as it happens. Being in their natural environment, and *unaware* of the observer's

Observational method	Advantages
Naturalistic observation	Particularly good for observing certain subjects
	Provides ecologically valid recordings of naturally occurring behaviour
	Spontaneous behaviours are more likely to occur
Structured observation	Allows control of extraneous variables
	Reliability of results can be tested by repeating the study
	Provides a safe environment to study contentious concepts such as infant attachment
Unstructured observation	Gives a broad overview of a situation
	Useful where situation/subject matter to be studied is unclear
Participant observation	Gives an 'insiders' view
	Behaviours are less prone to misinterpretation because researcher was a participant
	Opportunity for researcher to become an 'accepted' part of the environment
Non-participant	Avoidance of observer observation effect

Table 6.10 Advantages of particular types of observation

presence (a covert observation), those being observed are more likely to behave naturally. The observational method can therefore avoid the problem of people behaving in a unnatural way if they know they are taking part in a piece of psychological research, if participants/subjects are unaware that they are being observed. There are some subjects for whom the observational method is the only ethical method to use, e.g. young children and animals (outside captivity).

The standardisation of observational procedures gives sound evidence in the form of empirical data from which to draw conclusions about why participants/subjects behave as they do.

Disadvantages of the observational method

The main disadvantage of the observational method of research concerns replication. Replication of research allows for confirmation of results – or otherwise. Getting the same results the second, etc. time around allows you to be more confident of any conclusions

you have previously drawn. Replication of observations is almost impossible. By their very nature future observations take place in a different time and space.

You cannot in any observation draw any cause–effect conclusions. There is no independent variable. These only occur in procedures that use the experimental method.

Another disadvantage is the lack of control of variables in most observational situations. You can never be *entirely* sure that you have identified, anticipated and controlled all confounding variables that could influence the behaviours you have observed.

Observational method	Disadvantages
Naturalistic observation	Ethics: Where research is undisclosed, consent will not be obtained; where consent is not obtained, details may be used which infringe confidentiality
Structured observation	The implementation of controls may have an effect on behaviour
	Lack of ecological validity
	Observer effect
	Observer bias
Unstructured observation	Only really appropriate as a 'first step' to give an overview of a situation/concept/idea
Participant observation	Observer effect
	Possible lack of objectivity on the part of the observer
Non-participant observation	Detachment from situation so relies on perception which may be inaccurate

Table 6.11 Disdvantages of particular types of observation

ONLINE INTERACTIVES

Read a one-page summary of the observational method at:

www.gerardkeegan.co.uk/resource/observatio nalmeth1.htm

A direct link is available in the Chapter 6 section of the Higher Psychology Learning Suite at **www.gerardkeegan.co.uk**

Summary

The observational method is non-experimental in design. The absence of an independent variable does not allow any cause–effect conclusions to be drawn from observational research. Sound evidence is however important to the observational method. Indeed, the observational method's key feature is a standardised, planned, and systematic approach to observe and record behaviour objectively. This is of course to generate all-important data upon which to base any conclusions. Observations, which can be overt or covert, are of five main types: participant observation, non-participant observation, structured observation, unstructured observation and naturalistic observation. Each involves the planned gathering, analysis and interpretation of mostly empirical data on observed behaviour. Each type of observation has its own features, advantages and disadvantages. Participant observation, for example, sees the researcher set up, and take part in the observation of behaviour under investigation. Non-participant observation sees no involvement on the part of the researcher, with recordings of observed behaviours being taken from afar. The observational method has both advantages and disadvantages as a research design in psychology. Covert observations can be problematic as to ethics and disclosure. Confounding variables also plague observations. These are infinite, and include observer bias and the observer effect. If the researcher plans, structures, and conducts their observations appropriately, the observational method can be seen as a most valid and reliable form of non-experimental research in psychology mainly due to its high ecological validity.

ONLINE INTERACTIVES

Play The Observational Method Hangman Game at:

www.gerardkeegan.co.uk/resource/games/han gman/observational_method/hangman.php

A direct link is available in the Chapter 6 section of the Higher Psychology Learning Suite at **www.gerardkeegan.co.uk**

STRUCTURED QUESTIONS WITH ANSWER GUIDELINES

1 Describe and explain the observational method of research.

With reference to the preceding text, structure your answer as follows:

- Define the observational method of research as concerning the planned gathering, analysis and interpretation of data on observed behaviour, as it occurs in a natural setting.

- Identify and explain the following features of the observational method:

  ➤ non-experimental in design. Generally no IV, therefore no cause–effect.

  ➤ the need for empirical data. Types. Examples.

  ➤ detail of data-gathering techniques such as continuous recording, time sampling, audio-visual recorders, observation schedules, coding, behaviour index, and obtrusive and unobtrusive measures.

  ➤ control of extraneous variables, e.g. observer bias.

  ➤ types of observation, i.e. participant, non-participant, structured, unstructured, and naturalistic. Give definition of each.

Describe some features of each type.

Refer to examples of research that use the particular type(s) of observational method you are writing about.

2 Evaluate the observational method of research in terms of its advantages and disadvantages.

Structure your answer as follows:

- Define the observational method of research as the planned gathering, analysis and interpretation of data on observed behaviour, as it occurs in a natural setting.

- Identify and explain advantages of the observational method, i.e.

  ➤ To help decide on behaviours for further study by other means, e.g. an experiment or a survey.

  ➤ It gives us accurate detail of natural behaviours. Ecological validity.

  ➤ Appropriate for the study of infants and animals (say why: refer to research).

  ➤ Avoids unnatural behaviours (say why this is so).

  ➤ Standardisation (of what?) – gives valid and reliable results (why?).

**STRUCTURED QUESTIONS WITH ANSWER GUIDELINES
CONTINUED**

Then describe the specific advantages attached to specific types of observational method.

● Identify and explain disadvantages of the observational method:

➤ Replication.

➤ No IV (implications: no cause–effect).

➤ Control of extraneous variables, i.e. confounding – observer bias, observer effect; random – weather, mood state of participants.

➤ Ethics and covert observations.

➤ Then describe specific disadvantages attached to specific types of observational method.

The survey method

The **survey method** gathers quantitative data on those thoughts, feelings and behaviours we have in common, or on which we differ. The survey method asks a representative sample of people the same questions about particular attitudes, opinions, values and beliefs. If the sample is truly representative, this allows generalisation of results to the population from which the sample came. Surveys can be used on their own or with other research methods such as the experiment, observation and the interview. The survey method shares an important feature with the more structured methods of interviews and observations. This is the gathering of data by self-report from a respondent or interviewee. Surveys can be conducted by post, face to face, by telephone, videophone and the Internet. A good survey will be designed well with **standardised** instructions and questions. A **pilot survey** is often conducted to allow this to occur. Survey questions can be either open or closed. **Open questions** give rise to candid, descriptive answers, while **closed questions** restrict respondents' choice of answer. Open questions can give you too much qualitative, descriptive information in answers, which makes defining our common or differing attitudes, opinions etc. difficult. Closed questions, which give quantitative or numerical answers, are useful, especially if a **Likert scale** of measurement is used. Advantages of the survey method of research are that it is cheap, easily administered, replicable, and a large amount of data can be got from a lot of people in a fairly short time. Most importantly, a well-designed survey, if given to a representative sample, allows the researcher to generalise results to the population from which this sample came. Disadvantages include poor design, GIGO, reliability and validity, **acquiescence response**, a tendency to give socially desirable answers, and response and sampling bias.

What is the survey method of research?

The survey method of research asks a representative sample of people oral or written questions to find out about their attitudes, behaviours, beliefs, opinions and values.

The survey method of research is non-experimental in design. In psychology the survey has two functions. It gathers quantifiable data on the behaviours of a target population, and it is also used to test hypotheses.

Surveys and quantifiable behaviour

An example of the former is the 1999 Glasgow University Social and Public Health Unit survey. This was a two-year longitudinal survey into psychological development in early adolescence. In 1993–4 a survey was given to a large number of children in Primary 7 in West Central Scotland about their thoughts and feelings. Two years later in 1996–7, the children were again given a similar questionnaire.

The children were now in their second year (S2) in 43 secondary schools in and around the city of Glasgow. The number reporting feeling nervous, worried or anxious in P7 jumped from 40 per cent to over 50 per cent by S2. Those reporting feeling irritable and bad-tempered *went* from 40 per cent to 48 per cent over the same period. Those feeling sad and unhappy increased from 35 per cent to 40 per cent. Glasgow University concluded that respondent symptoms were indications of psychological ill health, which appears to increase during adolescence. The survey concluded that a substantial number of teenagers in Scotland suffer from low self-esteem during their early teenage years. Only time will tell if this low self-esteem is permanent and is related to mental ill health in the medium to long-term.

It is worthwhile to note that the Audit Commission, in their 1999 report, deemed young people to be at greater risk of developing mental health problems than their peers when they were:

➤ Living with only one natural parent, either in a step-family or with a lone parent

➤ Living in families where the main breadwinner was unemployed

➤ Experiencing some form of learning disability

➤ Looked after by the local authority.

Surveys and hypothesis testing

An example of the survey method being used to test hypotheses is Adorno *et al.*'s (1950) study, which aimed to find out about the authoritarian personality. Psychology in general and social psychology in particular, wanted to know whether we were all capable of terrible atrocities, or was such horror the result of a particular and unique personality – an authoritarian one. As is explored in Chapter 8, Adorno *et al.* wanted to confirm whether there was an authoritarian personality, and, if so, to investigate how it came about.

Adorno and his colleagues designed a survey to reveal prejudice, which they thought was an important personality trait in the authoritarian personality. They posted it off and got two thousand replies from people from all sorts of backgrounds. The **volunteer sample** who returned the questionnaire included school and university students, nurses, prison inmates, psychiatric patients and workers. They were all white, native-born, lower middle, and middle-class Americans.

Eighty were then invited to attend a clinical interview. On the basis of their completed surveys, these were the ones Adorno *et al.* had thought were the more prejudiced. At a subsequent clinical interview they were each asked a selection of more detailed, open questions about their background and upbringing. Initial survey and subsequent clinical interviews helped to then construct the famous Adorno F-Scale. The F-Scale is a measure of just how fascist and authoritarian an individual might be. This personality came about as a consequence of upbringing and environment.

The volunteer sample

A volunteer sample is problematic in all types of psychological research. A volunteer sample is one made up of those people who decide they want to participate in the research programme. Volunteers are not representative of the normal population. Rosenthal and Rosnow (1975), in *The Volunteer Subject*, New York: John Wiley, pp. 195–6, identify 22 characteristics of those who volunteer for research such as:

➤ Volunteers tend to be better educated than non-volunteers.

➤ Volunteers tend to have higher social-class status than non-volunteers.

➤ Volunteers tend to be higher in need of social approval than non-volunteers.

➤ Volunteers tend to be more sociable than non-volunteers.

➤ Volunteers tend to be more intelligent than non-volunteers when volunteering is for research in general, but interestingly not when volunteering is for somewhat less typical types of research such as hypnosis, sensory isolation, sex research, small-group and personality research.

A volunteer sample can therefore give rise to volunteer bias in research.

Survey design

What makes a good survey is good design. This is easier said than done and demands some expertise. To begin to think about a survey as a method of research it is essential that you first clarify its purpose. Knowing exactly what it is you are trying to find out from any survey will shape the questions you want to ask. Having a clear purpose will help you in the design and standardisation of your survey.

Standardisation concerns the instructions and questions that you give to people to help them complete your survey. These should be worded so that your respondents know what is required of them. In essence, instructions and questions should be easily understood. Care should also be taken over the type of questions used. Open questions encourage respondents to give open or descriptive answers. Closed questions restrict respondents to give closed answers.

The type of question asked influences the usefulness of the data collected. If you ask open questions you get a lot of descriptive, opinionated answers, which are difficult to analyse. Closed or restrictive answers are easier to analyse but sometimes don't mean very much. Surveys are cheap and easy to administer, and can generate a lot of useful information, but have their disadvantages. We have seen that surveys can suffer from volunteer bias. They can also attract other extraneous variables like participant response set, acquiescence response set, social desirability, sampling, and interviewer bias. If constructed well, surveys are an excellent research tool, and it is to this that we now turn.

Key features of the survey method of research

The survey method includes any type of research that involves asking people *oral or written* questions about their thoughts, feelings and behaviours. It is thus important to realise that key features of the survey apply to questionnaires, structured/semi-structured/clinical interviews, and the more structured of observations.

Whatever their form, surveys aim to collect standardised data from a representative sample of people. As a method of enquiry the survey is passive, in that there is no manipulation of an independent variable. As a result no cause and effect conclusions can be made on the basis of a survey. As emphasised above the main feature of the survey method is that it is structured. As will be explained, a **structured survey** will feature the standardisation of instructions and questions, often after a pilot survey has been done. The types of questions asked, which can be either open or closed, can affect the type of data a survey can generate. This as we will see has implications for any conclusions made.

The unstructured survey

With all this emphasis on structure it seems odd to suggest that a survey can be unstructured. The unstructured survey is more commonly known as the clinical interview, which is examined in more detail shortly. The reason the clinical interview is sometimes called an unstructured survey is it will always have a pre-prepared set of core questions that an interviewer will want to ask. These questions will have been developed beforehand, often after refinements have been made following a pilot study. The standardisation of oral questions in clinical interviews is as important as the standardisation of written questions in surveys.

The structured survey

The structured survey is used in all areas of life such as consumer research, psychological enquiry, politics, health, etc.

Surveys can be done by post, face to face, by telephone, videophone and the Internet. Their usefulness depends on how well the survey was designed, and the sample to which it was given.

What do I want to know?

In order to design a survey, you need to know what you want to do. Clarifying 'What is it exactly I am interested in, and what in particular am I trying to find out?' helps you design relevant questions. You could design a survey to find out about attitudes to lowering the voting/driving age to sixteen, legalising cannabis, sex/violence on TV, what the silent majority of pupils think about bullying in school, etc. A survey could examine health-related behaviours such as under-age drinking, investigate religious beliefs and church attendance, collect opinions on social and moral issues such as the ethics of genetic engineering, and so on.

Survey item design

Once you have decided on the purpose of your survey you must design the questions you want to ask. This is called item design. There are two types of item, or question, that the researcher can use in a survey – the open question and the closed question.

Open questions

An open question is a question that can have many different answers. An example of an open question in a survey is, 'What is the biggest problem facing Scotland today?' If this were given to a thousand different people you could get a thousand different answers. Concluding what these thousand people have in common would be impossible. Open questions like this are to be avoided. They give you too much descriptive or *qualitative* information with which you can do very little. To be of any value to the researcher data in a survey should be amenable to measurement. It should be quantifiable.

Closed questions

You can get measurable, quantitative answers to questions in a survey when you use what are called 'closed questions'. Closed questions are questions which offer *a restricted choice of answer or response* for the participant, probably the simplest example being 'yes' or 'no'. Closed questions, which have restricted answers, include questions on gender, age, where you live, occupation, etc. As can be seen below there is only one answer to these types of closed question. These answers are then counted or *quantified* by the researcher, against the relevant item. Examples of closed questions might be:

➤ Are you male or female?

➤ What age are you?

➤ Are you employed/unemployed?

➤ What is your postcode?

➤ What is your occupation?

Closed questions like this often appear at the beginning of a survey, and give valuable quantitative information. The answers to closed questions help the researcher work out how many men and women took part in the survey, their age, what district they live in, their occupation, etc. Postal codes can reveal all sorts of things, the most important, certainly in consumer research, probably being your socio-economic status. Closed questions can generate very useful data that can have interesting results. In 2002 the Halifax plc bank was much embarrassed by the leak of a document based upon internal survey research advising their staff to be wary of doing business with taxi drivers, window cleaners and market traders. People reported being offended by what the Halifax's data analysis of customer occupations seemed to imply. What do you think that was?

Closed questions fall down when they try to get answers to complex questions. Consider the following closed question:

> **Please answer the question below.**
> **Please circle your response.**
>
> The biggest priority
> facing Scotland today   Yes   No
> is qualifying for the
> World Cup?

Figure 6.7

Here *you* are deciding that qualifying for the World Cup is Scotland's biggest priority, as opposed to say, the Health Service, education, housing, transport, etc.

The forced-choice nature of the response, *yes* or *no*, further does not allow people who genuinely *do not know* how to answer. You can add up and measure yes/no answers to questions, but if the question doesn't really apply to people's actual thoughts, feelings and behaviours then what you get is meaningless.

In summary, surveys hope to generate manageable quantitative data on complex issues. To do so, closed questions will be used, certainly at the beginning of the survey, to get numerical data on your sample. They are of less use in the body of a survey because of their forced-choice nature. Closed questions don't generate quality answers. Open questions only can do this, but these are notoriously difficult to analyse because of the many different responses you can get. This can be overcome by using a scale of measurement for your item/question responses.

Scaling items: the Likert scale

One way around the problem of generating meaningful quantitative answers to restrictive closed questions is to use a Likert scale. This is named after Renais Likert who designed it at the University of Michigan Institute for Social Research in the 1960s. It is often used in surveys today and is recognisable when you are asked to indicate your strength of feeling about a particular issue on a rating scale. Taking the above question 'The biggest priority facing Scotland today is qualifying for the World Cup?' by using a Likert scale you would indicate your strength of feeling on the matter by circling 1, 2, 3, 4, or 5 on a rating scale. Circling 1 would mean you strongly agree; circling 2, agree; circling 3, don't know; 4, disagree, and 5, strongly disagree.

Please indicate your strength of feeling about the question below by circling 1, 2, 3, 4 or 5.

	Strongly agree	Agree	Don't know	Disagree	Strongly disagree
'The biggest priority facing Scotland today is qualifying for the World Cup?'	1	2	3	4	5

Figure 6.8 Likert scale

This would allow other maybe more important questions on unemployment, homelessness, education or the National Health Service, to be asked elsewhere. At the end of the day *scaling* the answers to closed questions can generate statistical measurements of people's attitudes and opinions, such as those they feel are important in the Scotland of the twenty-first century. The use of a Likert and other scales of measurement in a survey yield both qualitative *and* quantitative data, and are nowadays relatively obvious and widespread. A survey's use of a Likert scale allows people to agree/disagree on the basis of their strength of feeling on an issue. It also allows people to say they have no opinion if the question isn't an issue for them. Likert scales help avoid forced-choice compliance.

Using a Likert scale, those numbers circled are used by the researcher as quantitative data. If 10,000 people circled 1 in the above example this would be analysed as a major priority in Scotland. If 10,000 people circled 5, this would be analysed as a non-priority. Just how much of a non-priority would also depend on the Likert score obtained from other items in the survey hopefully covering unemployment, homelessness, education, and transport and the National Health Service.

The parental authority questionnaire

Our study of early socialisation tells us that parenting style influences the development of a child's personality. 'Questionnaire 1' is an example of a Likert scale being used in a psychological test called the parental authority questionnaire, which is used to assess parenting style. The PAQ is a 30-item (question) questionnaire. The questionnaire is given separately to both the mother and the father. When all the items are complete, a score can be obtained. A permissive mother/father is measured by the likes of question 1, authoritarian mother/father by the likes of questions 2 and 3, and an authoritative mother/father by 4 and 5.

Likert scale warning!

If you are ever asked to complete a questionnaire that uses an even number of Likert-type response choices, i.e. 1, 2, 3, 4 instead of 1, 2, 3, 4 or 5 – this is a fixed-choice compliance survey. Because it does not have an odd number of item response choices there is no room for a 'don't know' answer. Without this DK filter it forces respondents to say that 'Yes indeed this is an issue about which I have an opinion' (when it may not be). Respondents then are forced to strongly agree/agree or disagree/strongly disagree. Take the following example.

Please indicate by circling 1, 2, 3 or 4 your strength of feeling about the question below.

	Strongly agree	Agree	Disagree	Strongly disagree
'Changes should be made to the Higher psychology examination.'	1	2	3	4

Why should you be wary of a fixed choice compliance survey, like the above?

QUESTIONNAIRE 1: THE PARENTAL AUTHORITY (PAQ)

Instructions: For each of the following statements, circle the number on the 5-point scale (1 = strongly disagree, 5 = strongly agree) that best describes how the statement applies to you and your mother. Try to read and think about each statement as it applies to you and your mother during your years growing up at home. There are no right or wrong answers, so don't spend a lot of time on any one item. We are looking for an overall impression regarding each statement. Be sure not to omit any items.

1 While I was growing up my mother felt that in a well-run home the children should have their way in the family as often as the parents do.

1   2   3   4   5

2 Even if her children didn't agree with her, my mother felt it was for our own good if we were forced to conform to what she thought was right.

1   2   3   4   5

3 Whenever my mother told me to do something as I was growing up, she expected me to do it immediately without asking any questions.

1   2   3   4   5

4 As I was growing up, once family policy had been established, my mother discussed the reasoning behind the policy with the children in the family.

1   2   3   4   5

5 My mother has always encouraged verbal give and take whenever I have felt that family rules and restrictions were unreasonable.

1   2   3   4   5

From Buri, J.R. (1991) ' Parental authority questionnaire'. *Journal of Personality Assessment*, 57 (1), 110–19, Lawrence Erlbaum Associates.

Standardisation

Standardisation concerns the careful construction of instructions and questions. The standardisation of instructions and questions asked of anyone in any type of research is vital. This is because respondents/participants at the very least need to know what is required of them. If the instructions are confusing, or the questions ambiguous and difficult to understand, then a survey is not particularly effective. Neither is any other procedure where the standardisation of instructions and questions is an issue. This would include the experiment; the structured, semi-structured and clinical interview; and structured observation.

Principles of survey design

In the box on the right is a 12-step survey design. To achieve this, the following principles should be borne in mind.

➤ Keep the language simple. Ask yourself 'Who is the audience?' and write your questions and instructions to this level. Parten (1950) suggests that language an eleven-year-old would understand is appropriate.

➤ Keep questions short and on one issue. Keep the number of questions to a minimum. The longer the questionnaire, the less likely a respondent will feel like filling it in. If what you need to find out is necessary, ask the question. If it isn't, then leave it out.

➤ Avoid technical terms, e.g. performance criteria, jargon or abbreviations such as SQA. This is unless you know for sure that your respondents understand these sorts of terms.

➤ Avoid leading questions. Leading questions are questions worded in a way that lead the respondent to a particular answer. An example of a leading question might be: 'Have you stopped smoking cannabis?' Yes/No. Whichever way the respondent answers, he/she is 'admitting' to having broken the law! Think about it.

➤ Avoid emotive or moral questions. The respondent may feel your survey is getting too personal. The 'best' and 'worst' example the author has ever seen of this was a survey given to female members of the public, by a non-psychology student, asking respondents for their names and addresses; and then Question 1 asked 'Have you ever had an abortion? Yes or No.' This is definitely to be avoided. If you must use personal or emotional questions, place them at the end of the questionnaire. If in doubt always ask your teacher or lecturer.

The should–would question

Should–would questions are interesting. Selltiz *et al.* (1963) suggest that survey respondents answer 'should' questions from a social or moral point of view, and answer 'would' questions in terms of their personal preference. Having should or would as part of questions on social, moral and personal issues can skew results and conclusions.

Taking our earlier issue:

'Would you legalise cannabis? Yes Don't Know No'

could produce a different answer to what at first appears an almost identical question:

'Should cannabis be legalised? Yes Don't Know No.'

12-step survey design

If you decide to use a survey as a research method you could adopt the following design model.

1 Select an area of psychological interest.

2 Research the topic area to get ideas about what questions to ask.

3 Write the questions down.

4 Use closed questions at the beginning of the survey to generate good quantitative data on your sample.

5 For better item analysis, use a Likert scale to get quantitative data on answers to your questions.

6 Decide on a sequence of questioning. What is to be Question 1, Question 2, etc.? It is always best to randomise your sequence in case the survey attracts response acquiescence set (see Disadvantages of the Survey Method).

7 Write down your standardised instructions. These should come at the beginning of your survey and make clear what is expected of the respondent. They should also make reference to the general purpose of the survey, confirming that the respondent agrees to take part, their right to withdraw etc. Please see www.bps.org.uk/the society/code-of-conduct/code-of-conduct.home.cfm for 'The Psychologists' Code of Conduct'.

8 Conduct a pilot survey with a small group of people. It is best if they are from the group who will complete the final survey. Their job is to tell you if they understand the instructions, the questions, etc. Put simply, they highlight flaws.

9 Redraft the survey, and if necessary pilot it again.

10 Conduct your survey.

11 Debrief your respondents, and give them an opportunity to find out the results.

12 Analyse your results.

INTERACTIVES

Try the should-would question out. Ask only one respondent one question! Get 20 responses for the first question, and 20 for the second. Make sure all respondents come from the same population, i.e. students in S5 and S6, students in a college etc.

Compare your results. Did you get a should–would effect?

Survey modes

Face to face

Survey mode refers to the way a survey is done. The most common survey mode used by psychology students is face to face with respondents. The face-to-face survey can attract extraneous variables such as interviewer bias and the interviewer effect. This is explored more fully in our next chapter on the interview method and concerns the subtle communication of 'expected' answers in face-to-face questioning situations. Face-to-face surveys can take place in the street, at your door, in your workplace, at your school or college, etc.

Figure 6.9 A face-to-face survey

Postal survey

The postal survey is also very common. Postal surveys are often used to find out about consumer behaviours, attitudes and opinions. They suffer from a very high non-return rate. A low return rate in a postal survey can throw doubt on its results. Unfortunately non-return rates in postal surveys are notorious. The very best of surveys can get a 65 per cent return rate, but it is much more usual for a postal survey to have a return rate of between 15 and 25 per cent. This would be seen as a good result!

To increase the likelihood of return, it is a good idea to prepare people about the survey they are going to be asked to complete. Census 2001, the National Report for England and Wales saw a TV and billboard advertising campaign prior to the census taking place.

A respondent would also nowadays expect their postal survey to include a stamped-addressed envelope, allowing them to return it at no expense. Consumer surveys may further entice completion by enclosing a pen, and/or some sort of return incentive, like a prize. Postcard and telephone follow-ups are also helpful in increasing return rates, as is collecting the survey directly from the respondent at their home. If households do not return their national census, they are visited by a series of census officials, and if they still don't hand it over, this can result in criminal prosecution. The national census prides itself on its very high return rate!

Postal surveys and volunteer bias

Because of their long-standing problem of low return rates, postal surveys suffer from volunteer bias, which we came across earlier when we looked at the problems of the volunteer sample. Because of the postal survey's very high non-return rate, volunteer bias and thus the unrepresentative nature of the respondents who actually do return them, the results of postal surveys are questionable.

Telephone, videophone, and online surveys

To avoid problems associated with the volunteer sample it is common nowadays to find surveys being done by telephone, videophone, the Internet, and e-mail.

An example of an online survey

During November 2001 to March 2002 the British Psychological Society was interested in finding out what school and FE college students in the UK thought of their psychology courses. Students were asked to complete the following online survey.

ONLINE INTERACTIVES

Please go to www.onlinepsychresearch.co.uk and discover the huge range of online surveys currently being conducted by psychologists in the UK.

A direct link is available in the Chapter 6 section of the Higher Psychology Learning Suite at www.gerardkeegan.co.uk

PSYCHOLOGY STUDENT QUESTIONNAIRE

The British Psycological Society is interested in how students respond to their school and college courses in psychology. Please complete the following questions about the course in psychology that you are taking this year.

Please enter your age (in years)

☐

Please select your sex

☐ Male   ☐ Female

What course are you on?

☐ AQA AS/A Level

☐ EDXCEL AS/A Level

☐ OCR AS/A Level

☐ SQA Higher Level

☐ Other

Why did you choose this course?

☐ want a career in psychology

☐ sounded interesting

☐ something different to study

☐ heard about the teacher

☐ my friends had chosen it

☐ I had read about it

☐ other

PSYCHOLOGY STUDENT QUESTIONNAIRE CONTINUED

If 'other' please state the reason

Compared to other subjects I am studying or have studied, psychology is:

- much more interesting
- slightly more interesting
- about the same
- slightly less interesting
- much less interesting

Compared to other subjects I am studying or have studied, psychology is:

- much more relevant to my life
- slightly more relevant to my life
- about the same
- slightly less relevant to my life
- much less relevant to my life

Compared to other subjects I am studying or have studied, psychology is:

- much more difficult
- slightly more difficult
- about the same
- slightly less difficult
- much less difficult

PSYCHOLOGY STUDENT QUESTIONNAIRE CONTINUED

Compared to other subjects I am studying or have studied, psychology requires:

☐ much more work

☐ slightly more work

☐ about the same

☐ slightly less work

☐ much less work

My psychology course is:

☐ very much as I expected

☐ fairly much as I expected

☐ different to what I expected

Do you want to study psychology further (after you have finished the course you are on)?

☐ yes

☐ maybe

☐ no

My favourite topic in my psychology course is ...

My least favourite topic in my psychology course is ...

PSYCHOLOGY STUDENT QUESTIONNAIRE CONTINUED

What do you think would make the psychology course better?

What advice would you give to a friend who was thinking of studying psychology?

Who do you think are the three most important or influential psychologists?

one

two

three

I am glad I chose to study psychology.

1	2	3	4	5

Strongly agree   Strongly disagree

Thank you for completing this questionnaire. Please click the SUBMIT button.

Sampling

As we read in the previous Chapter, sampling is crucial to any psychological research. In order to conduct research, psychology needs participants to study. It is usually impossible to study everyone of interest in your target population (group of interest), so psychologists sample from it instead. Poor sampling however will give you poor results and poor conclusions. Any sample used in any kind of research in psychology should therefore reflect the target population onto which the researcher wants to generalise their results and conclusions. Sampling issues are of critical importance to the survey method of research. This was vividly illustrated in the 1992 UK General Election. In the run-up to the 1992 election, national poll after national poll published by firms such as NOP, MORI and System 3 all pointed to a narrow Labour victory under Neil Kinnock. On polling day itself, four polls published that morning agreed that Labour were still one point ahead. In the election itself, the Conservatives were found to be eight points ahead. It was the biggest ever discrepancy in British polling history between what the polls had anticipated and what actually transpired (Butler and Kavanagh, 1992).

One reason for the psephologists' mistake was poor sampling. They did not access those who went out and voted Conservative at the last minute. And just in case you ever appear on a quiz show, a psephologist is someone who studies political opinion polls.

Good sampling allows for the generalisation of your results onto the target population from which your sample is drawn. You can infer certain things, i.e. how the population of a country might vote. Because of the desire to generalise results and conclusions, a sample must be as representative of the target population as possible.

INTERACTIVES

1   What do you understand by the term 'sampling'?

2   Why is it important we use a representative sample of people in psychological research?

3   Give an advantage and disadvantage of four different types of sampling method. You may wish to refer to Chapter 5 to help you.

Advantages of the survey method

The advantages of surveys are that large amounts of standardised information can be obtained from a large number of people in a short space of time. If designed well and completed by a representative number of people, survey results can be generalised onto the population from which the representative sample came.

Surveys are highly replicable, and can be used on a longitudinal basis to update us constantly on questions of interest. The BPS survey above should be permanently 'up' for this very reason. Such a longitudinal survey also allows for trends and changes in opinion to be gauged over time.

Surveys are also easy to score, unless of course open-ended questions are used. We get quantifiable data from a survey that can be useful to help develop and support hypotheses. A survey can also generate empirical data giving a measurement of behaviours, attitudes, opinions, beliefs and values of a target population.

One final advantage of the survey method is that it is cheap! If a survey is well designed it is a most useful tool of research in its own right, or as rich soil for future research using other methods of enquiry.

Disadvantages of the survey method

If a survey is poorly designed, as a credible research tool it can attract a wide variety of problems. Students of Higher psychology should be extremely cautious if considering designing their own survey for their practical investigation. Be warned!

Any research method that uses oral or written instructions/questions must first standardise them. This is to ensure that all participants/respondents get the same instructions/questions, and that these instructions/questions are clear and unambiguous. Unless this happens the issues of validity and reliability will arise.

Validity concerns *whether the questions measure what they claim to measure.* A question of reliability would also arise if researchers didn't standardise instructions/questions beforehand. If left to their own devices to give instructions and ask questions, researchers would be inconsistent in what they said to different individuals. Any information got from such a non-standardised situation, and any claims made as a result, are questionable. It is not reliable as data to lend support to hypotheses, or as objective facts about behaviours, attitudes, opinions, beliefs or values. What you put into a survey by way of careful design, you get out of it in terms of valid and reliable data. Poorly designed instructions and questions see a survey suffer from the GIGO effect. Quite simply, 'Garbage in, garbage out'!

Earlier it was suggested that when a survey is designed the questions in the body of the survey should be scaled and randomly presented. This helps avoid acquiescence response, socially desirable answers, and response set. Acquiescence response is a tendency people have to agree, or say yes, especially to things that they think don't affect them that much. Consequently, surveys can be very prone to acquiescence response. Response set arises when respondents think they see a pattern of desired answers to survey questions, and answer accordingly. To avoid response set, scaling and the randomisation of questions are recommended. Scaling and randomisation also help prevent acquiescence response, and a tendency by people to give socially desirable answers.

As emphasised, features of the survey method also apply to other research methods where the asking of (oral or written) questions is important. What can jeopardise all these procedures, even when researchers adhere to good research design, is sampling bias. If your sample does not reflect a target population, you cannot make generalisations to this population because your sample is not representative of it. There are, as we know, different types of sampling techniques, such as random, stratified, opportunity and quota sampling. Each of these has particular advantages and disadvantages, which should be taken into consideration if thinking about using the survey method of research.

INTERACTIVES

Read over the advantages and disadvantages of the survey method of research and in no more than 50 words design a study aid to remember what they are.

ONLINE INTERACTIVES

Read:

www.socialresearchmethods.net/kb/survwrit.php

for some very useful tips on survey design.

A direct link is available in the Chapter 6 section of the Higher Psychology Learning Suite at www.gerardkeegan.co.uk

Summary

The survey method of research is non-experimental in design. It is a method of enquiry that asks a representative sample of people oral or written questions. Surveys are often used in the likes of social and consumer psychology to support or develop hypotheses on our attitudes, opinions, beliefs, values and behaviours. A good survey is well designed, considering in its structure the use of open and closed questions, and scales of measurement such as a Likert Scale. To ensure a survey is worthwhile it is important to standardise the instructions to be followed beforehand and the questions you want to ask. Standardisation reduces ambiguity and respondents' acquiescence response. One way to achieve standardisation is to do a pilot survey, the purpose of which is to point out flaws.

Surveys are nowadays conducted face to face, by post, telephone or online. These different survey modes can help reduce sampling bias, and increase your 'return' rate. Advantages of surveys are that they are cheap and generate a large amount of standardised information from a lot of people, which if quantifiable can be used as measurements upon which to base conclusions. Disadvantages of the survey method are that poor design gives poor results. If a survey is badly constructed, its results and conclusions can be accused of being invalid and unreliable.

ONLINE INTERACTIVES

Read a one page summary of the survey method at:

www.gerardkeegan.co.uk/resource/surveymeth 1.htm

A direct link is available in the Chapter 6 section of the Higher Psychology Learning Suite at **www.gerardkeegan.co.uk**

ONLINE INTERACTIVES

Play The Survey Method Hangman Game at:

www.gerardkeegan.co.uk/resource/games/han gman/survey_method/hangman.php

A direct link is available in the Chapter 6 section of the Higher Psychology Learning Suite at **www.gerardkeegan.co.uk**

STRUCTURED QUESTIONS WITH ANSWER GUIDELINES

1 **Describe and explain the survey method of research.**

   With reference to the preceding chapter, structure your answer as follows.

   ● Define the survey method of research as one that asks questions in oral or written form of a representative sample of people, to find out about their attitudes, behaviours, beliefs, opinions, and values.

   ● Identify and explain the following features of the survey method of research:

   ➤ non-experimental in design. Gathers information on behaviours, etc. (give example), and to support/develop hypotheses (give example). Importance of good survey design.

   ➤ open questions and closed questions. Pros and cons. Likert scale of measurement.

   ➤ standardisation of instructions and questions. Pilot studies. The should–would question.

   ➤ survey modes (how surveys are conducted nowadays).

STRUCTURED QUESTIONS WITH ANSWER GUIDELINES CONTINUED

2   **Evaluate the survey method of research in terms of its advantages and disadvantages.**

Structure your answer as follows.

● Define the survey method of research as one that asks questions in oral or written form of a representative sample of people, to find out about their attitudes, behaviours, beliefs, opinions, and values.

● Identify and explain advantages of the survey method, i.e.

➤ great deal of standardised information, etc. in a short space of time. Give example.

➤ replicable. What does this allow?

➤ easily scored quantifiable data. What does this allow the researcher to do?

➤ cheap.

● Identify and explain disadvantages of the survey method, i.e.

➤ poor design gives poor results.

➤ lack of standardisation of instructions/questions leads to questions of validity and reliability of the survey.

➤ GIGO effect.

➤ acquiescence response, socially desirable answers and response set. Suggest how these can be avoided.

➤ sampling bias. Volunteer samples/bias. Importance of a representative sample. A good answer would indicate this could affect the results and conclusions using any research method.

The interview method

The interview method of research is used in psychology to get personal accounts of individual experiences. The purpose of the interview method is neatly captured in the phrase 'a conversation with a purpose'. Interviews are also often used in conjunction with other research methods as part of a larger investigation. As we will see, there are two categories of interview, structured and unstructured. The structured interview also includes the semi-structured interview and the clinical interview. The major difference between the categories is the ability to ask spontaneous questions of the client/participant/patient. This affects what kind of

data that can be collected, whether the data can be generalised beyond those people being interviewed, and whether the data is valid and reliable. These advantages and disadvantages of the interview method will now be explored, as shall advantages and disadvantages of particular types of interview.

What is the interview method of research?

The interview method of research is a conversation with a purpose.

The interview method of research is non-experimental in design. It is a conversation with a purpose. The interview has the researcher collect detailed personal information from individuals in a one-to-one setting using oral questions. The interview is used widely in psychology, often alongside the survey, to supplement and extend our knowledge about the person or psychological issue under investigation. As in surveys, interview questions will be either 'open' or 'closed'. An open question is one that can have a variety of answers. A closed question is one that restricts the answer given. Whatever types of questions are asked, interview data should be recorded using pre-prepared scales, notes, audio or videotape. Unless using a measure like a scale, interviews give us mostly qualitative, or descriptive, data about people's thoughts, feelings and behaviours. This is mainly due to the free-ranging nature of questioning in the less structured types of interview, which makes obtaining numerical or quantitative data difficult.

Open and closed questions

An example of an open question could be 'Why do you enjoy studying Higher psychology?' Ask this of a thousand students and you would get many different answers. Because answers would be very *descriptive*, this *qualitative* data would be very difficult to analyse. Open questions can give you too much data to analyse in a meaningful way.

A closed question could be 'Do you enjoy studying higher psychology, yes or no?' With closed questions you get *numerical*, or quantitative data. Here you might find 700 out of 1000 students enjoyed studying Higher psychology. Closed questions can give you too little data to analyse in a meaningful way. You would probably want to know why 700 enjoyed Higher psychology. And more importantly why the other 300 didn't!

Key features of the interview method

There are two categories of interview in psychological research, the structured interview and the unstructured interview.

The structured interview

The structured interview means you plan beforehand what questions are to be asked of those taking part. This standardisation, or your prior preparation, of

interview questions, is a key feature of the structured interview. The questions asked will depend on the issue to be investigated.

Another recent feature, certainly of the structured interview, is its mode or setting. Interviews nowadays can be conducted face to face, by telephone, videophone and the Internet.

There are three types of structured interview used in psychology, the structured interview itself, the semi-structured interview and the clinical interview. What they share is the *standardisation* of questions asked. Where they differ is the degree of freedom the interviewer has to deviate from these pre-set questions.

The unstructured interview

The other category of interview is the unstructured interview. The key feature of the unstructured interview is the free-ranging nature of the interview questions asked. You do not have to have, or stick rigidly to, any pre-set questions.

As we shall see when we look at advantages and disadvantages of the interview method, whether you pre-arrange your questions in a standardised format, or have a free-ranging discussion are both an advantage and disadvantage of the interview method. Standardisation in structured interviews versus free-ranging questioning in a less structured situation can influence the reliability and validity of your results and conclusions.

Structured interview

Structured interview: where the researcher plans and carefully constructs pre-set questions. These are the only ones asked.

A structured interview attempts to obtain a detailed understanding of a particular aspect of a person's mental processes and behaviours. To achieve this, the structured interview will have the researcher use pre-planned, carefully constructed and pre-set questions.

Structured interviews are often used to conduct research looking at a unique group of individuals who share a particular condition or problem. We also come across them in those structured interviews conducted by market research companies in our high streets. Very often they are collecting data on our attitudes and opinions on a wide range of subjects.

Standardisation of structured interview questions

The structured interview therefore consists of a pre-prepared set of specific questions.

Standardisation in a structured situation does not allow the interviewer to ask any questions other than those prepared beforehand. They could not inject anything 'extra' into the interview, and as a result the structured interview is mostly a 'question and answer' session. If the questions are pre-set, interviewers may well have a response sheet, or scale, which they score as the interview progresses. This numerical data is later used to give *quantitative* data upon which to base any results and conclusions. In a structured setting the interviewer attempts to be objective and tries not to influence the participant's replies.

Standardisation gives quantitative data

Di Nardo *et al.* (1994) point us to the Anxiety Disorder Interview Schedule (ADIS) used in the USA to help diagnose obsessive–compulsive disorder (OCD). In the United Kingdom OCD affects one in 50 people. In a good example of a structured interview that generates quantitative data, clients using ADIS are asked about their obsessions and compulsions. An obsession is a constant, often irrational, thought or feeling. A compulsion is a behaviour that you repeat over and over again, which is connected to your obsession. On an eight-point scale the client scores the frequency of their compulsive behaviours from 'never' through 'occasionally' to 'constantly'.

This would see someone who is obsessed with hygiene probably 'constantly' wash his or her hands, or 'constantly' marking the same homework hour after hour, night after night.

The structured interview's ability to generate quantitative data is also found in personnel selection. Take someone who is applying for a job as a psychology lecturer in an FE college! To find out about their psychological knowledge, a structured interview *could* contain the following structured questions:

➤ What are the symptoms of depression from the biological point of view in psychology?

➤ What stages are involved in Piaget's theory of cognitive development in young children?

In each case there is a correct answer. Each candidate's answers to these pre-prepared pre-set questions could be scored on a scale of one to ten to give the college a better understanding of someone's knowledge of psychology. This would be useful data on which to base a decision.

Asking an individual a set of pre-arranged pre-set questions is thus called standardisation. The issue of standardisation in the *framing* of oral and written questions was explored when we looked at the survey method of research. As we discovered the construction of questions for structured interviews/surveys is not easy. These issues should also be taken into account when considering the interview as a research method.

Obsessive–compulsive disorder (OCD)

Obsessive–compulsive disorder is a psychological condition characterised by high anxiety. Symptoms include hand washing, constantly checking, i.e. that the gas is off/door is locked, ruminating – or thinking endlessly about things – being overly neat, tidy and ordered, hoarding and fearing harm. Body dysmorphic disorder also shares similarities with OCD. This is an obsession with how you look. OCD takes up a lot of a sufferer's time. It can also seriously affect their family relationships, work and social life. While the cause of obsessive–compulsive disorder is not known, it is thought by OCD support organisations to be possibly a result of a chemical imbalance in the brain. Symptoms seem to have nothing to do with the sufferer's basic personality. Nor is it likely OCD is caused by childhood experience. A Freudian analysis is inappropriate. People with OCD are usually aware that their compulsions and obsessions are irrational. Their perceptions of reality are usually not distorted in other ways. They 'function' normally in all other respects. It is other people's perception of their obsessive–compulsive behaviours that unfortunately adds to their problems. Others, put simply, write them off as 'mad'.

Dedicated to A.M.

Replication and generalisation

Standardisation of questions is also important because it allows the same questions about the same issue to be asked of different individuals. This *replication* of the same questions is another feature of the structured interview. When you give the same set of questions to a sample of individuals you are able to make *generalisations* about what you have found out to the population from which they came.

We shall return to this when we look at advantages of the structured interview.

Structured interview modes

The mode or setting of the structured interview has, as indicated earlier, begun to be of interest to psychologists. Mode concerns whether the interviewer is present and face to face with the participant, or absent as when conducting the interview by telephone.

Donovan *et al.* (1997) compared information about personal health obtained face to face or by telephone interview from people in Perth, Western Australia. Two samples were put together; 1000 in the face-to-face group, and 222 in the telephone group. From each group, a stratified sample was drawn. Each individual in each stratified sample took part in a number of interviews over a three-year period. All were asked the same structured questions, the only difference being the interview mode used – face to face, or telephone.

Telephone respondents reported significantly lower levels of smoking and higher levels of drinking behaviours when compared to those interviewed face to face in their homes. Donovan *et al.* (1997) conclude we should be cautious about the results different structured interview modes can generate. Different modes can throw up different results even though the same questions are asked.

Semi-structured interview

Semi-structured interview: where the researcher prepares pre-set questions, but will occasionally ask some spontaneous questions.

The semi-structured interview still has pre-arranged pre-set questions but the interviewer is a bit freer to explore the more interesting answers given by the client or participant.

Semi-structured interviews are used to diagnose affective, or mood disorders such as clinical depression. As we shall discover shortly when we look at atypical behaviours, clinical depression is a disorder that affects 20–30 men per thousand, and 40–90 women per thousand in the UK. In its diagnosis the clinician would use a semi-structured interview to confirm five of the symptoms shown below.

In order to be said to be suffering from clinical depression, a person should have experienced a number of the following symptoms together over a period of time.

A   Persistent low mood (for at least two weeks)

plus

B   At least five of the following symptoms:

1   Poor appetite or weight loss, or increased appetite or weight gain (change of 1 lb [450 g] a week over several weeks or 10 lb [4.5 kg] in a year when not dieting).

2   Sleep difficulty, or sleeping too much.

3   Loss of energy, fatiguability or tiredness.

4   Body slowed down or agitated (not mere subjective feeling of restlessness or being slowed down, but observable by others).

5   Loss of interest or pleasure in usual activities, including social contact or sex.

6   Feelings of self-reproach, excessive or inappropriate guilt.

7   Complaints or evidence of diminished ability to think or concentrate such as slowed thinking or indecisiveness.

8   Recurrent thoughts of death or suicide, or any suicidal behaviour.

Table 6.12 Symptoms of clinical depression (based on Spitzer *et al.*, 1978)

The semi-structured interview is also used for personnel selection in the workplace. In order to get the best person for the job, a personnel department would put together structured interview questions matched to the job specification. All candidates would be asked these questions, but if someone says something particularly interesting, the interviewer(s) might ask them to expand on this. Very often, in this now semi-structured situation, a candidate discloses interesting personal detail that gets them the job. Or doesn't.

Clinical interview

Clinical interview: where the researcher has some pre-set questions, but will ask spontaneous questions. What spontaneous questions are asked depend on the previous answer given by the participant.

A clinical interview is similar to a structured and semi-structured interview. It has some pre-arranged pre-set questions and also an option to ask free-ranging questions. However it would go further and get respondents to expand even more on their interesting answers.

Piaget used the clinical interview to discover whether four-year-old children had acquired the ability to conserve volume. Indeed it was he who coined the phrase 'clinical interview'.

Piaget had a one-to-one clinical interview with four-year-olds. He put equal amounts of liquid into two identical beakers, A and B (Figure 6.xx). He then poured the contents of A into a same-shaped glass C, and the contents of B into a different-shaped glass D. Each child was then asked which one they wanted (C or D) and why. They invariably chose the tall thin glass D over the short fat one C.

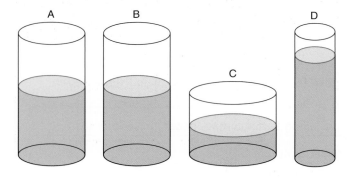

Figure 6.10 Beakers used in Piaget's experiment

Piaget (1952) believed this was because at four, children have not yet acquired the ability to conserve volume. This means that they are mentally unable to consider two aspects of an object

simultaneously. They can only take on board that the tall thin glass looks bigger than the small fat one. They are unable to use **transformation**, to move the liquid back and forth from glass to glass, to work out that both contain the same amount of liquid. With different children Piaget slightly varied the questions asked in response to their last answer given. This is what makes this a clinical interview.

Sigmund Freud also used the clinical interview method. The detail he got went on to form many of his case studies. Believing that most of our psychological problems lie in our unconscious Freud used connected, free-ranging but focused oral questioning with many of his patients to get to their specific fears and worries. He believed these fears and worries were to blame for their hysterias or phobias. Once exposed, and these connections made, Freud hoped his patients would have a greater understanding of why they were thinking or behaving in a dysfunctional way. As a consequence they could overcome their problem better. Freud's use of what would be recognised today as a clinical interview laid the basis for such important works as *The Interpretation of Dreams*.

The unstructured interview

Unstructured interview: where the researcher has no pre-set questions. He or she asks free-ranging questions.

The 'unstructured' interview does not have pre-arranged pre-set questions and as such is freer ranging. The unstructured interview is used to explore an issue or area of enquiry generally. It may throw up some interesting ideas to be researched later using more structured research methods.

In an unstructured interview the researcher can ask the same sort of questions as with a structured interview, but their style is free-flowing rather than rigid. It is much more conversational. Questions can be adjusted according to how the interviewee is responding. The interviewer may even inject their own opinions, humour or ideas to stimulate the interviewee's responses. The unstructured interview requires much more skill and is much more complex in process and analysis than a structured interview.

The humanistic approach with its use of the client-centred interview is a good example of an unstructured interview. In the past in humanistic psychotherapy the client-centred interview was entirely non-directive. It was an unstructured interview in extreme form where the client led the pace. It was they who decided what was to be talked about. The counsellor helped the client to explore their inner personality or self, using humanistic strategies of **genuineness**, **empathy** and **unconditional positive regard**. Nowadays humanistic psychotherapy is more direct. This is because the non-directive interview method was found to be rather wasteful of time. It was just too loose and free-ranging. Nobody got anywhere particularly fast. The unstructured interview will probably nowadays have some direction to it, as is illustrated below.

> **Examples of unstructured interview questions**
>
> 'Could you tell me more about …'
>
> 'I'm not sure I understood what you meant by …, could you explain that in a bit more detail?'
>
> 'I find that fascinating! Tell me more.'
>
> 'What was happening in your life when this problem started?'
>
> 'How did you feel then?'
>
> 'How did this all start?'
>
> Unstructured interviews are useful for general information gathering.

Training

Whatever types of interview used – structured or unstructured – the interviewer, researcher or psychologist will have undergone lengthy training.

A clinical psychologist will have studied for over six years completing undergraduate and post-graduate study in psychology. They will also have undergone supervision as a probationer clinical psychologist.

Many careers officers in Scotland will also have studied and trained in interview techniques at postgraduate level. This is in order to give considered careers advice when interviewing young people and adults who require their assistance. Training is essential to conduct interviews.

As a method of research for a Higher psychology practical it is not really recommended!

Advantages of the interview method

Generally interviews allow for the production of a large amount of data about individuals, which can be very detailed. Depending on the interview method used, i.e. structured or unstructured, this data can be quantifiable (numerical), or qualitative (descriptive). This very much depends on the type of question asked. That is, whether it is an open or closed question, and whether it was planned or asked on the spur of the moment. Closed questions can be quantified. Open questions cannot. Planning to ask a question gives you an opportunity to prepare a measure to quantify an answer. Spontaneous questions lead to open answers, which are notoriously difficult to quantify and analyse.

Further, the more structured the interview the more able the researcher is to generalise their results to whatever population their interview sample came.

Disadvantages of the interview method

The interview method is unreliable as it is based on self-report from patients/clients/participants. They could be lying or economical with the truth. At a job interview, are you likely to inform the panel of your past misdeeds?!

Another disadvantage associated with the interview method is that no cause–effect relationship can be made. There is no manipulation of any independent variable upon which a cause–effect relationship can be based.

Interviewer inexperience or lack of training is often seen as an extraneous variable with the interview method of research. The **interviewer effect**, produced by their manner, style of questioning, type of questioning, and so on, may not encourage a natural response from participants. As a consequence, replies obtained may be biased by the interviewee responding to the interviewer's behaviours. This could influence any results and conclusions that might be drawn.

Advantages of the interview method	Disadvantages of the interview method
Large amount of quantitative/ qualitative data obtained	Self-report by the interviewee is an unscientific method of gathering data
Gives detailed understanding of issue under investigation	Cannot make any cause and effect relationship
Generates further research	Inexperience and lack of training of interviewer can be an extraneous variable

Table 6.13 Advantages and disadvantages of the interview method of research

Advantages and disadvantages of different types of interview

Advantages of the structured interview

As it asks the same questions of different individuals, a structured interview can give you quantifiable data. In using structured interviews market researchers ultimately get a count of the types of cars people own, the shops they frequent, their buying habits, and so on. Standardisation of questions allows researchers to be confident that any data they generate is reliable. *Reliability* means that you are asking successive individuals the same questions assured that the issue is being investigated *consistently*.

> **Reliability**
>
> Investigating the issue by way of an interview in a consistent manner.

Another advantage of the structured interview is that because you are asking the same questions of a group of individuals, you can generalise your results out to the population from which the interview sample was drawn.

Disadvantages of the structured interview

The structured interview restricts those being interviewed to answer only the questions asked. It is an insensitive way to conduct research in that people don't enjoy answering questions in an automatic fashion.

Further, the rat-a-tat-tat manner of structured interview questions does not allow for the rich qualitative data people often prefer to give you about their life. It may be in this descriptive data that a better clue to the issue under investigation is lurking. Because of the stilted nature of the questions asked, structured interviewing needs substantial training. This is to try and avoid it becoming too awkward or too uncomfortable for those taking part.

In a structured interview, indeed any interview, the researcher gets to make up the questions. A structured interview could then be accused of lacking *validity* if the researcher asks the 'wrong' questions in their search for the 'right' answer. See also the survey method.

Advantages of the semi-structured interview

The freer ranging nature of the semi-structured interview overcomes the insensitivity of the structured interview. You may, at least occasionally, allow participants to express themselves.

The semi-structured interview gives *reasonably* reliable results, in that the majority of questions are pre-set and asked consistently of everyone. This makes these answers easier to quantify and analyse.

Disadvantages of the semi-structured interview

Its free-ranging nature encourages qualitative answers. Descriptive answers are difficult to quantify and analyse. In a job interview, the occasional spontaneous question asked of some candidates may be seen as unfair to others.

Advantages of the clinical interview

The clinical interview is flexible and responsive to where the client/patient/participant is coming from. It is sensitive to what they are saying and what they would like to say. Information got from a clinical interview is reasonably valid in that the core questions concerning the issue will be prepared beforehand. Answers/responses to these can then be analysed relatively easily.

Disadvantages of the clinical interview

Spontaneous questions in clinical interviews can give rise to problems of replication and generalisation. Being too sensitive, or flexible and wide-ranging in spontaneous questioning makes replication of the same clinical interview with others difficult. If you had to give a clinical interview to twelve people and came up with useful spontaneous questions with interviewee number 8, what do you do about those already interviewed and those still to be interviewed? Indeed, does your spontaneous question have relevance to what you are investigating? Is it valid? Further, if you can't replicate the same procedure you cannot generalise your findings out to the population from where your sample came.

The occasional nature of spontaneous questions could be seen as bias on the part of the researcher, and is a further disadvantage of the clinical interview. The client may say something that fits the researchers' 'pet' theory, and the researcher encourages this with a spontaneous question or two! This is known as interviewer bias.

Interviewer bias and the interviewer effect

Interviewer bias and the interviewer effect thus describe situations where the interviewer affects the kind of responses given in an interview. The interviewer may subtly communicate expectations in the same way as an experimenter might with experimenter bias. This we came across earlier in the Rosenhan study and the self-fulfilling prophecy.

Psychology has discovered that participants search for clues about how to behave in a research study and are prone to being influenced by a researcher's expectations. This is especially so of child participants. Interviewer bias is also a problem in unstructured interviews, where the interviewer thinks of questions as he/she is going along.

Leading questions

Interviewer bias can be explained in terms of leading questions. Psychological research has demonstrated how the language used in a question can affect the answer given. Two classic examples come from Loftus. In Loftus and Palmer's (1974) study participants were asked to estimate the speed of a car that was involved in an accident. When participants were asked 'How fast were the cars travelling when they *hit* each other?' they reported a lower speed estimate than when asked 'How fast were the cars travelling when they *smashed* into each other?' In this instance they reported a higher speed. The use of the words 'hit' and 'smashed' appeared to influence the participants' perception of the speed of the car.

In another study, Loftus and Zanni (1975) showed how the use of the words 'a' or 'the' in a question can change the way people answer a question. Loftus and Zanni asked participants two slightly different questions about a car accident. The first question was 'Did you see the broken headlight?' which assumes that there was a broken headlight in the situation. The second question was 'Did you see a broken headlight?' which is more open. Participants had been shown a film of a car accident. There was no broken headlight in the film, but seventeen per cent of those asked about '*the* broken headlight' said there was one, while only seven per cent of those asked about 'a broken headlight' reported they had seen one.

Advantages of the unstructured interview

An unstructured interview can give you highly detailed data on an individual. Its more relaxed atmosphere can capture their particular point of view. It is an extremely flexible non-experimental method that has high ecological validity because it is more natural for those taking part.

Disadvantages of the unstructured interview

The free-ranging nature of the unstructured interview gives rise to problems of reliability, replication and generalisation. Because questions are 'non-standardised', an unstructured interview if given to a series of individuals could be accused of inconsistency or unreliability. This is because different individuals would be asked different questions. For this reason, unstructured interviews cannot be replicated.

An inability to replicate the unstructured interview means you cannot generalise out, or apply your findings, to a wider population from those interviewed. Unstructured interviews given their free-ranging and spontaneous nature also make what participants reveal difficult to quantify and analyse. Another disadvantage to the unstructured interview is the validity of the unplanned question asked. Does it investigate what you want it to investigate?

Wiesner and Cronshaw (1988) analysed 151 employment studies conducted by government bodies in the UK, USA, Canada, Europe and Australia. They wanted to compare the effectiveness of the unstructured and structured interview techniques as a predictor of later job performance. Applying a correlation of category of interview against later job performance, Weisner *et al.* found the validity of structured interviews to be higher ($p = 0.34$ in 10,080 cases) when compared to unstructured interviews, where $p = 0.17$ in 5,518 cases. Wright *et al.* (1989) further report the validity of category of interview against job performance at 0.14 for unstructured interviews and 0.39 for structured interviews.

What both these studies highlight is the thorny issue of the validity of spontaneous questions asked in the less structured kind of interview. A question that is particularly problematic for the unstructured interview is 'Are these spontaneous and free-ranging questions actually investigating the issue?' In Wiesner and Cronshaw's (1988) and Wright *et al.*'s (1989) studies, the issue was what category of interview gave you a better chance of getting the right employee. The unstructured interview was not particularly helpful in the prediction of actual job performance when later compared to the structured interview.

Given that a perfect positive correlation is when $p = +1.00$, both the structured and unstructured interview would here appear to fall short of the mark, if their purpose was to predict conclusively future ability to do the job.

Type of interview	Advantages	Disadvantages
Structured interview	Standardisation of all questions can give quantifiable data Replication Data is more reliable as the issue is being investigated in a consistent way Allows generalisation of results/conclusions to the population from which the sample was drawn	Restrictive questioning leads to restrictive answers Insensitive to participants' need to express themselves Validity of questions asked. Are they the right ones?
Semi-structured interview	Standardisation of most questions gives quantifiable data Replication Data is therefore reasonably reliable Ability to ask some spontaneous questions is sensitive to participants' need to express themselves	Its use of an occasional spontaneous question makes these answers difficult to quantify and analyse Spontaneous questions asked of some and not of others can be seen as unfair, especially in personnel selection
Clinical interview	Flexible, responsive and sensitive to participants Preparation of core questions should ensure validity Core questions and responses should be reliable and analysed easily	Difficult to replicate As a result, an inability to generalise your findings to a wider population Possible interviewer bias in their use of leading spontaneous questions
Unstructured interview	Flexible, responsive and sensitive to participants Relaxed and natural for those taking part Highly detailed and ecologically valid qualitative data	Difficult to replicate As a result, an inability to generalise your findings to a wider population Possible interviewer bias in 'selective' use of leading, and spontaneous questions

Figure 6.14 Advantages and disadvantages of different types of interview

Figure 6.11 Do spontaneous and free-ranging questions actually investigate the issue?

Summary

The interview method of research is a conversation with a purpose. It is non-experimental in design. The interviewer on a one-to-one basis collects detailed personal information from individuals, using oral questions. The interview is used widely to supplement and extend our knowledge about individual(s). Interviews can give us both quantitative and qualitative data about participants' thoughts, feelings and behaviours. This is due to the standardisation and/or free-ranging nature of questions asked. The more structured or standardised interview questions are, the more able you are to get quantitative data. Quantitative data is reliable and easy to analyse. The less structured and freer ranging the interview questions, the more qualitative your data becomes. Qualitative data is difficult to analyse and is not as reliable.

There are two categories of interview, the structured interview and unstructured interview. The key feature of the structured interview is the pre-planning of all the questions asked. Structured interviews also allow for replication of the interview with others, which further enables generalisation of what you find out to the population from which your interview sample came. Structured interviews are conducted in various modes: face to face, by telephone, videophone and the Internet. There are three types of structured interview. The structured interview, the semi-structured interview and the clinical interview. A major feature, and difference, is the degree to which each uses standardised and unplanned questions. Standardisation helps the

reliability of your results and conclusions. The greater the use of unplanned questions, the less structured the interview becomes. Unplanned spontaneous questions are a key feature of the unstructured interview. Spontaneous questioning is more responsive to the participant. However spontaneous questioning does not allow for generalisation. Spontaneous questions can also be accused of generating invalid results and conclusions. Thus standardisation versus the free-ranging nature of questions is both the main advantage and disadvantage of the interview method of research, in general and in particular.

ONLINE INTERACTIVES

Play The Interview Method Hangman Game at:

www.gerardkeegan.co.uk/resource/games/hangman/interview_method/hangman.php

A direct link is available in the Chapter 6 section of the Higher Psychology Learning Suite at www.gerardkeegan.co.uk

STRUCTURED QUESTIONS WITH ANSWER GUIDELINES

1   **Describe and explain the interview method of research.**

With reference to the preceding chapter, structure your answer as follows:

● Define the interview method of research as a conversation with a purpose. Explain its purpose in terms of getting personal accounts of individual experiences. Then go on to identify and explain the following features of the interview method:

➤ categories of interview. Structured and unstructured.

➤ three types of structured interview. Structured, semi and clinical.

➤ explain structured interviews. Definition, purpose, standardisation, quantitative data (with examples), generalisation, modes.

➤ explain semi-structured interviews. Definition, similarity and difference to structured interviews, examples of their use.

STRUCTURED QUESTIONS WITH ANSWER GUIDELINES
CONTINUED

➤ explain clinical interviews. Definition, similarity and difference to structured/semi-structured interviews, examples of their use.

➤ explain unstructured interviews. Definition, purpose, features (free flowing spontaneous questions), examples of their use.

➤ need for interviewer training in whatever interview situation.

2 Evaluate the interview method of research in terms of its advantages and disadvantages.

Structure your answer as follows:

● Define the interview method of research as a conversation with a purpose. Explain its purpose in terms of getting personal accounts of individual experiences. Then go on to identify and explain the following:

● Identify and explain advantages of the interview method, i.e.

➤ generates large amounts of detailed information on the person(s) or psychological issue under investigation.

➤ often prompts more structured research by other means, e.g. an experiment or a survey.

➤ depending on interview method used, obtains quantitative and/or qualitative data.

➤ standardisation (of what?) – may give valid and reliable results (why?)

➤ the specific advantages attached to specific types of interview method.

● Identify and explain disadvantages of the interview method, i.e.

➤ self-report unscientific. Why?

➤ no IV (implications: no cause–effect).

➤ interviewer as an extraneous variable. Why?

➤ the specific disadvantages attached to specific types of interview method.

The case-study method

The case-study method of research is a detailed in-depth investigation into a single-case happening.

Idiographic in nature, a case study can be about a person, a family, an organisation or an event. The case study is often used by the psychoanalytic approach, developmental psychology, and in the study of individual differences such as personality, intelligence and atypical behaviour.

The case study is a method of enquiry that generates rich, mostly qualitative, descriptive detail about a unique individual, episode or situation. As a method of research, the case study is said to be ecologically valid, in that it is true to life.

A case study can be **retrospective** or **longitudinal**, and can involve the use of case histories, interviews, questionnaires, **psychometric tests**, diaries, observation and experimental research. These features will now be addressed, as will the advantages and disadvantages of the case-study method.

What is the case-study method of research?

The case-study method of research is a detailed in-depth investigation of a single case happening concerning a person, a family, an organisation, or an event.

Because it investigates the 'single case', as a research method the case study is idiographic in nature. It is centred on the individual or unique situation or event. Sigmund Freud, the founding father of the psychoanalytic approach, made the case study famous. He used the **retrospective case-study method** in the development of his theories about the unconscious and personality. His two most renowned case studies were Little Hans (1909) and Anna O (1910). These case studies were *retrospective*, which means that Freud collected rich, qualitative, descriptive detail about his participants' *pasts*. These case studies required his participants to *self-report* from their point of view. Also known as **introspection**, self-report is an individual's personal subjective account of an experience. Subjective self-report is however one of the main criticisms of the case study, as we will see.

Case studies can also be *longitudinal*. This type of case study follows a unique occurrence, episode, or situation for at least a year into the future. An example of a longitudinal case study could be one investigating the psychological impact on an individual, family, or organisation following the 11 September 2001 attack on the World Trade Centre.

INTERACTIVES

Gregory and Wallace (1963) discovered that a 52-year-old patient, SB, blind almost from birth, was to have an operation to restore his sight. They were particularly interested in his newfound visual abilities, but also became intrigued by the influence the restoration his sight had on his emotions. They studied his past hospital records, and examined his developing visual sense in controlled experimental conditions. They found that SB perceived more and more
detail about a stimulus as a result of greater experience and exposure to it. Perception is more than merely 'seeing' or visually sensing. What we perceive involves the biology of the eyes, gestalten and past experience, plus cognitions such as attention, language, memory and thinking. Gregory and Wallace also interviewed SB. A great deal of qualitative data was recorded about SB's cognitive and emotional change after his operation. SB told them that he was initially delighted with his new ability but had became depressed. Vision was not all that it was cracked up to be. He had thought the sighted community could see
a lot better than they did. He thought sight meant a better ability to see in the dark, and that what the sighted saw equated with beauty. He could not understand acceptance of impure visual surfaces like chalk marks on a board, flaky paint, and so on. Gregory and Wallace (1963) say SB's case lends support to the development of visual perception being an interaction of nature, our biology, and nurture, our experiences in our environment.

1   What features indicate that Gregory and Wallace's (1963) study is a case study?

2   What was the purpose of this case study?

3   Was this a longitudinal or retrospective case study? Give reasons for your answer.

4   What did Gregory and Wallace discover about SB's visual, perceptual and emotional development?

5   According to Gregory and Wallace (1963), how does perception develop?

Figure 6.12 Professor Lord Robert Winston

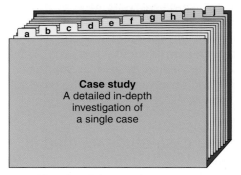

Case study
A detailed in-depth
investigation of
a single case

a   Experimental research
b   Observation
c   Diaries
d   Psychometric tests
e   Questionnaires
f   Interviews
g   Case histories
h   Longitudinal or retrospective
i   Subject: person, family,
    organisation or event

Figure 6.13 The case-study method

Another is the BBC's Child of Our Time, which is a longitudinal study into the psychological development of a group of Millennium babies born during the year 2000. Presented by Lord Robert Winston, one of Britain's leading scientists, the series will be broadcast annually until 2020. It is of much interest to developmental psychology. This is because developmental psychology is all about biological, cognitive, social, and emotional development in and across the human life span. This series looks at such developments in infancy, childhood, adolescence and early adulthood, and is a must for anyone with an interest in psychology.

Key features of the case-study method

We have identified the case-study method as a detailed in-depth investigation of a single case happening concerning a person, a family, an organisation or an event. The subject of a case study is anything or anyone who is found to be unique in some way. What psychologists use to construct a case study will differ from participant to participant, subject to subject, issue to issue. Before we turn to these elements, let us look at first feature of the case-study method, its subject matter.

The case study: a single case happening

The case study is usually about a single case concerning an individual. It can also be applied to organisations and even animals, as the following should illustrate.

Case study: the individual

Koluchová (1972, 1976, 1991) is a classic longitudinal case study of identical twin Czechoslovak boys, PM and JM, born in 1960. Their mother died when they were born and the babies were fostered for the first eighteen months of their lives. They were then returned to their father and stepmother, who subjected them to an extremely cruel regime. They were isolated from everyone, kept malnourished, given no exercise or intellectual stimulation and beaten severely. When again found at age seven they were physically, cognitively, socially, and emotionally retarded. Medical records indicated that they were small for their age, had rickets and had little speech. Their new social surroundings terrified them. They were put into a home, assessed by interview and natural observation, and sent to a school for children with severe learning difficulties. Due to being unable to read, write or speak very well, their intelligence had to be estimated. They were assessed as having the intelligence of a three-year-old.

Figure 6.14 A case study concerns an individual who is unique in some way

PM and JM were then adopted by two sisters, who immediately started to nurture, love and cherish them. Over the next seven years, they gradually began to catch up with physical, cognitive, social, and emotional developments of children of their own age. When Koluchová revisited the boys at age fourteen, and using intelligence tests and questionnaires, interviews with the boys, interviews with the sisters and school, she concluded they showed no sign of atypical behaviour or physical abnormality. They attended a normal secondary school and were average pupils. When they left school they did a technical apprenticeship, later going to an FE college to study electronics. Both served in the army, got married and had children. Another visit by Koluchová in 1989, when the twins were 29, saw her report them as entirely normal, stable, and in a permanent, loving relationship with their respective wives and children.

Case study: the organisation

Hayes and Lemon (1990) used the case-study method to examine the successful management of change within an organisation. Their clients were a small computing firm in the UK who had got into a rut. The biz and the buzz associated with a computer company were missing. This is fatal to any business, but more so for one at the cutting edge of new technology. They needed some help. After observing the day-to-day running of the business, they conducted interviews with the management and workers, the conclusions of which went into a report. The report recommended that management work more as a team to promote an internal and external company identity. It also recommended that shop-floor issues be addressed concerning the future of the business. The management agreed to implement all the recommendations. The researchers revisited the firm six months later. They again observed the day-to-day running of the business, but this time to gauge the degree and effect of change. They also conducted more interviews to see how happy the workers and management were with what had been implemented. Hayes and Lemon reported that most of the earlier suggestions had been successfully implemented. Management were more cohesive. Everyone worked more as a team. Management, the workers and the company had found their common identity, and this was paying dividends on the business front. Management spoke to the workers more and took more of their concerns on board. They were more aware of the importance of good management–employee relations in the successful running of a business.

INTERACTIVES

1   Is Hayes and Lemon's (1990) study a retrospective or longitudinal case study? Give reasons for your answer.

2   How did Hayes and Lemon generate their reports for this case study?

3   Do Hayes and Lemon adopt a case study approach? Give one reason for your answer.

Case study: the animal

Gardner and Gardner's (1998) study, which looked at teaching sign language to chimpanzees, is a good example of a case study of a non-human animal. The use of the case study to investigate animals is by no means exceptional in psychology. The method has been used with non-human animals such as Gua the chimpanzee (Kellogg and Kellogg, 1933), the peppered moth (Kettlewell, 1955) and Koko the gorilla (Patterson, 1978).

Elements of the case study

A retrospective case study gathers in information about the past.

A longitudinal case study gathers in information for at least a year into the future.

Case studies, which can be retrospective or longitudinal, are made up from a variety of sources. These include case histories, interviews, questionnaires and psychometric tests, diaries, observation and experiments. As we will see, almost all research methods looked at previously in this chapter can be used in the construction of a case study.

Case histories

Case histories are records of case notes from the past that have a bearing on the present issue under investigation. Examples of sources for a case history could be school and college records, medical records held by a GP, records held by other professionals such as social workers, the police and the criminal justice service. A researcher sifts through these for relevant information concerning the matter under scrutiny. An example of this could be with a person thought to be schizophrenic. The researcher, or mental health professional, would read relevant records to look for previously reported symptoms such as signs of withdrawal, loss of friendships, voice hearing, reporting messages from strange sources telling him/her to do things, or paranoia.

Interviews

An individual is often interviewed to find out how things from their past, or present, have influenced their thoughts, feelings, and behaviours. This information can contribute, in whole or in part, to a case study. An example of interviews being used to form a retrospective case study was illustrated earlier with Freud's Little Hans and Anna O.

Investigations into the impact of tragic events on individuals, communities or organisations often use interviews as a major part of any programme, report, or piece of research on those affected. These interviews could contribute to a longitudinal case study, with the programme makers, reporters or researchers revisiting and re-interviewing the individual, community or organisation at a later date.

It should also be noted that interviews could also take place with relatives, friends, doctors, social workers or teachers, concerning the individual subject, or **target**, of the case study.

STUDY

Sign Language Studies of Human-Fostered Chimpanzees, Gardner & Gardner (1998)

Aim: Gardner and Gardner raised an infant chimpanzee named Washoe in a home as close as possible to the home of an infant human being to see how the chimpanzee would develop like a human child. Washoe lived in a human house, slept in a human bed, and played with human toys. She ate human food at a human table with forks and spoons, and she had to help set the table and clear up after. She learned to use a human toilet, undressing herself, wiping herself, flushing the toilet, and even asking to go the toilet during lessons and chores. A human member of her foster family was with her all her waking hours every day of the year.

Procedure: Earlier Hayes & Hayes (1951) raised chimpanzee Viki like a child, but they only spoke English to Viki and a chimpanzee vocal tract cannot make the sounds of English. The modern human vocal tract evolved over millions of years. True human fostering requires a common human language. Instead of speech, Gardner and Gardner spoke to Washoe in American Sign Language, ASL, the visual-gestural language of the deaf in North America, because chimpanzee hands are so much like human hands. Using a human language permitted Gardner and Gardner to compare Washoe with human infants acquiring ASL. Gardner and Gardner replicated Project Washoe with four more infant chimpanzees, Moja, Pili, Tatu and Dar, who were human-fostered from birth.

Gardner and Gardner taught ASL the way human parents teach human infants. They modelled ASL for the infants, named interesting objects and events, and asked and answered questions.

Skinner's operant conditioning was obviously inappropriate for human-fostering. Later, a student of Skinner attempted to teach a caged chimpanzee by strict operant conditioning with very little success (O'Sullivan & Yeager, 1989).

Results: Extensive daily records showed that Washoe, Moja, Pili, Tatu and Dar signed to friends and to strangers. They signed to each other and to themselves, to dogs and to cats, toys, tools, even to trees. Along with their skill with cups and spoons, pencils and crayons, their signing developed stage for stage much like the speaking and signing of human children (Gardner & Gardner, 1998). They also inflected their signs in the elementary ways that deaf children inflect their signs. They performed far above chance on tests in which observers could see the chimpanzees but could not see what the chimpanzees were naming.

Later in a communal laboratory setting, Fouts and Fouts introduced ten-month-old Loulis to the human-fostered chimpanzees. Humans ceased signing when Loulis could see them, which was nearly all the time. Under these conditions, Loulis learned over 50 signs of ASL that he could have learned only from other chimpanzees (Fouts *et al.*, 1989).

Conclusion: Treated like human children, chimpanzees develop like human children in all ways, including conversation in American Sign Language. Conversational skill develops in stages that are parallel to the stages of human development, only slower.

Interviews that contribute to a case study are fairly loose and unstructured. A clinical interview may be given to an individual or group of individuals. As we read earlier, a clinical interview would feature some pre-set core questions asked of all being interviewed. The clinical interview gives a researcher flexibility to explore issues that arise from the interviewees' more interesting answers. An unstructured interview would have some idea about what questions could be asked by a researcher, but is even more flexible in style when compared with the clinical interview. The questions asked in the unstructured interview really depend on the previous answer given by the participant. Or any answer at all.

As we saw when we looked at the interview method of research, interviews give us mostly qualitative, or descriptive data about peoples' thoughts, feelings and behaviours. This is mainly due to the free-ranging nature of questioning in the less structured types of interview, which makes obtaining numerical, quantitative data difficult.

Questionnaires and psychometric tests

Questionnaires and psychometric tests, on the other hand, do give a researcher quantitative, numerical data. These *facts* are useful in any case study.

A case study concerning an organisation would almost certainly use a survey to assess the organisation and those individuals in it. A survey is a pre-prepared standardised written questionnaire. Surveys give a researcher quantitative data on the issue being investigated. The survey could be used to find out why an organisation is at it is, and how this might be changed. The results of the survey would generate empirical data. This would be used as empirical evidence to identify problem areas and suggest remedies.

Case studies of individuals often use psychological questionnaires and psychometric tests to assess attitudes, intelligence, personality, and so on. A **psychometric test** gives you *a measurement of a human characteristic* such as personality and intelligence.

Take, for example, the psychometric measurement of intelligence. Intelligence is normally distributed in a population. What this means is that relatively few people are extremely intelligent, the vast majority are of average intelligence, and the relatively few are unintelligent. The vast majority have an IQ, or intelligence quotient, of around 100 (the average) as measured by psychometric tests. Giving someone a psychometric test of intelligence allows their score to be compared with others in and outside their age group. In Koluchová's case the twins were initially assessed as having an IQ of 40. In comparison with other seven-year-olds, the twins had a comparable intelligence more like that of a three-year-old. This is valuable in a case study in that it can be used as a baseline to measure any improvement in intelligence as a consequence of change in environment or dedicated learning programme. In Koluchová's case, the love, care and affection given to the twins by the sisters was the key variable to their improvement from 'abnormal' to 'normal' in less than seven years. These dramatic changes were measured by psychometric tests of intelligence, amongst other things.

Diaries

The case study can also involve a participant being asked to keep a diary. This would be used to record how they thought, felt and behaved over the course of the study. A pharmaceutical company may ask volunteers in a new drug trial to keep a diary and a doctor might do the same with a patient being put on new medication. A family might be asked to keep a diary if piloting a new product for a company. New technology has seen the advent of palm-held electronic diaries where participants in a study enter data on whatever the case study concerns.

Electronic diaries have begun to be used by native trackers in the South African bush to help in animal conservation work. The trackers are trained to record the many different species of animal they come across by pressing a particular picture icon on their hand-held palm tops. Video diaries are the basis of the success of a lot of fly-on-the-wall TV programmes. Individuals often use video diaries to vent their frustrations and reveal how they *really* feel during the course of the programme. This everyday realism is most attractive to us, the TV audience!

Observation

Observation can be another element to a case study. The observational method of research concerns the planned watching, recording and analysis of observed behaviour as it occurs in a natural setting. Observation, as a method of research can be structured or unstructured, participant or non-participant. More usually, however, any observation that is used in a case study is naturalistic. Something happens that the observer sees as an important element to their research. The importance of Freud's natural observation of Anna O's hysterical attacks laid the foundation to his theories and the psychoanalytic approach. Gardner and Gardner's observation in the wild that chimpanzees communicated by gesture laid the basis of an important contribution to the psychology of language, research that continues to this day.

Experiments

An experiment, or series of experiments, can also contribute to a case study. These experiments would be laboratory-based in the main. Excellent examples of would be in cases of anterograde amnesia. In anterograde amnesia a victim is unable to remember anything after a particular point in time. Such serious memory loss is caused by brain infection, as we discovered in Chapter Two in the case of Clive Wearing, the former chorus master with the London Sinfonietta, or as a result of a surgical operation, as with HM, a case study conducted by Milner *et al.* (1968).

To recap, HM's *medical case history* indicated that he had suffered massive and frequent epileptic fits from age sixteen. When he was 27 he underwent radical surgery. This involved the removal of his hippocampus on the left and right-hand side of his brain. His life-threatening epilepsy was cured, but he suffered anterograde amnesia as a result of the operation, where he could remember mostly everything about life before his operation, but nothing thereafter. To discover the extent of his memory deficit, and gain an insight into the role of the hippocampus and memory, Milner *et al.* set HM various *laboratory*-based memory tasks. They report that his short-term memory (STM) is normal and has a normal duration of around fifteen seconds. However he is unable to transfer much information from STM into his long-term memory (LTM). The very limited information he can transfer into LTM he cannot retrieve and use later on. From *observations* they also suggest that HM cannot learn anything from the present. Any news item he reads or sees cannot be recalled. He has no concept of time unless he looks at a clock and cannot remember family details, such as the death of his father, since his operation. The present is meaningless. He greets everyone he has come across since the removal of his hippocampus as complete strangers, even though they may meet him many times a day. As Blakemore writes:

> *... new events, faces, phone numbers, places, now settle in his mind for just a few seconds or minutes before they slip, like water through a sieve, and are lost from his consciousness.*"
>
> *(Blakemore, 1988)*

INTERACTIVES

1   Why, in your opinion, is this study of HM a case study?

2   What causes anterograde amnesia? What are the effects on memory?

3   What radical surgery did HM undergo?

4   What were the consequences for him?

5   Identify three different research elements that contributed to the case study on HM by Milner *et al.* (1968).

Advantages of the case study

The main advantage of the case study is that it can give excellent in-depth, mainly qualitative information about a single case happening concerning an individual, organisation or animal. It is a very useful research tool that is used to investigate one-off phenomena in a rich and detailed way. It treats those whom it investigates with respect, and has the welfare of the individual at heart. This is one of the reasons why a case study is a more appropriate research method to use when investigating controversial topics such as child abuse.

Case studies usually give researchers information high in **ecological validity**. What this means is that the information a case study generates is real. It is an investigation into a happening that has an individual self-report on an actual experience as it has affected them. In recent years case studies of similar rare occurrences have begun to be pooled on a global basis. The pooling of information helps contribute to our overall knowledge of something of unique interest. The study of the paranormal is maybe an obvious example.

Throughout the course of history, some individuals have been reported to possess paranormal powers, such as telepathy, clairvoyance, extra-sensory perception (ESP) and psychokinesis. The study of ESP includes *precognition*, or the ability to foresee the future. Psychokinesis, or PK, is a paranormal ability to move and manipulate objects without touching them. Individuals with paranormal powers are rare in any one country. One way of investigating the paranormal is to use a meta-analysis of pooled case studies of individuals from all over the world. A meta-analysis examines a number of reported cases of these exceptional individuals. Meta-analysis is then a 'study of all the studies'. It aggregates and averages the results of a large number of similar, but independent studies of a particular phenomenon.

Disadvantages of the case study

The main disadvantage of the case-study method is that it is idiographic in orientation. This means that because the case study is geared towards the individual and the single case, its findings cannot consequently be applied to everyone. As a case study is about a unique happening concerning an individual or organisation, any generalisation of results and conclusions to the population from which the individual or organisation comes is impossible.

Further, because the case study is about a single case happening it cannot be replicated. Replication helps confirm earlier results and conclusions. The ability to replicate a case study, to find support or otherwise for *its* earlier results and conclusions is impossible. The difficulty in the replication and confirmation of results is related to another disadvantage to the case-study method, its subjectivity.

A case study gathers in mainly qualitative, descriptive information about an individual. This information is obtained from case histories, interviews, diaries, etc. and is subjective because it is based on an *individual's personal feelings and opinions*. Another flaw with subjective self-report data is that its worth depends on the individual being truthful. We should be circumspect about self-reported information for all sorts of reasons, the main reason being that we are never entirely truthful! We forget things, we miss out things that we think are irrelevant, we lie (even to ourselves), we are 'economical with the truth', we exaggerate, we disclose some things about ourselves and keep other things hidden. The reliability of information got by self-report is therefore suspect.

The case study can also attract ethical concerns about the *privacy* of individuals whose life histories may be publicised after their death. If a case study is to be carried out, it is advised that the individual/organisation's real names are not revealed. *Confidentiality* should also be observed, with aliases for participants being used wherever possible.

Each component used by the case study also attracts its own disadvantages, a number of which we came across in earlier chapters. The unstructured interview forms the main element to a number of case studies. Unstructured interviews are prone to interviewer bias. Interviewer bias occurs where the interviewer subtly communicates his or her expectations to the interviewee, which are then reflected in the responses given to the questions asked. Leading questions can also be a problem in the more unstructured of interviews, particularly when the interviewer asks spontaneous questions. Could these questions be leading the interviewee to give an answer that fits the researcher's theory or idea? Fisher and Greenberg (1977) think that Freud had a tendency to select or emphasise information that fitted psychoanalytic interpretation. Also, a lot of psychoanalytic ideas came to Freud as he naturally observed his patients. He took no notes during his psychoanalytic sessions, thinking this would distract his patients in therapy. Instead, he wrote up the case notes for his case studies several hours after his patients had left. His case studies were his memories of what had happened in therapy some time after the event. Nothing exists to substantiate what Freud says he observed. Such subjective or opinionated observation as the foundation to theory is not good science. The case study then lacks scientific validity. It is not an objective, controlled method of research and is prone to bias. One final disadvantage is that because it is a non-experimental method of research, *no cause–effect* conclusions can be drawn from any data generated in a case study.

Advantages of the case-study method	Disadvantages of the case-study method
Detailed in-depth information obtained of a single case concerning a person, a family, an organisation or an event	Cannot generalise results
High ecological validity	Replication impossible, to confirm earlier results
Sensitive to the individual, and sensitive issues concerning the individual	Reliability of information got by self-report
	Interviewer/observer bias
	Lack of scientific validity: no cause–effect conclusions can be drawn

Table 6.15 Advantages and disadvantages of the case-study method

ONLINE INTERACTIVES

Read a one-page summary of the case-study method at:

www.gerardkeegan.co.uk/resource/casestudy meth1.htm

A direct link is available in the Chapter 6 section of the Higher Psychology Learning Suite at **www.gerardkeegan.co.uk**

Summary

The case-study method of research is a detailed in-depth investigation into a single-case happening concerning an individual, organisation or animal. Because of its interest in the single case the case study is said to be idiographic in nature. It is a method of enquiry that generates rich, mostly qualitative, descriptive detail about a unique individual, episode, situation, etc. The case study has been used in the psychoanalytic approach, examples being Freud's Anna O and Little Hans. Developmental psychology has also used the case study as with Koluchová (1972, 1976, 1991), while the study of individual differences sees its use in single cases of interest concerning intelligence, personality, and atypical behaviour. A case study can be retrospective or longitudinal, and can involve the use of case histories, interviews, questionnaires, psychometric tests, diaries, observation and experimental research. As a method of research the case study's main advantage is its ecological validity. It is true to life. It gets detailed in-depth information about a single case happening concerning an individual, organisation or animal in a humane manner. Its disadvantages include an inability to generalise results, difficulties of replication and confirmation of earlier results, and

the subjectivity and reliability of information got by self-report. Interviewer and observer bias further reduces its usefulness as a scientifically credible method of research.

ONLINE INTERACTIVES

Play The Case-Study Method Hangman Game at:

www.gerardkeegan.co.uk/resource/games/hangman/case_study_method/hangman.php

A direct link is available in the Chapter 6 section of the Higher Psychology Learning Suite at **www.gerardkeegan.co.uk**

STRUCTURED QUESTIONS WITH ANSWER GUIDELINES

1   **Describe and explain the case-study method of research.**

With reference to the preceding chapter, structure your answer as follows:

- Define the case-study method of research as a detailed in-depth investigation of a single case happening concerning a person, a family, an organisation, or an event.

- Identify and explain the following features of the case-study method:

  ➤ non-experimental in design. Idiographic. Give examples of its use.

  ➤ retrospective and longitudinal. Explain.

  ➤ elements: case history, interviews, questionnaires, psychometric tests, diaries, observation and experiments. Give some detail.

2   **Evaluate the case-study method of research in terms of its advantages and disadvantages.**

With reference to the preceding chapter, structure your answer as follows:

- Define the case-study method as a detailed in-depth investigation of a single case happening concerning a person, a family, an organisation, or an event

- Identify and explain advantages of the case-study method, i.e. detailed in-depth information of a single case happening concerning a person, a family, an organisation, or an event. Illustrate with examples.

  ➤ high ecological validity. Why?

STRUCTURED QUESTIONS WITH ANSWER GUIDELINES CONTINUED

➤ sensitive to the individual and sensitive in its investigation of issues concerning the individual.

● Identify and explain disadvantages of the case-study method:

➤ inability to generalise results. Why?

➤ impossible to replicate. Why?

➤ information got by self-report of doubtful reliability. Why?

➤ extraneous variables: interviewer and observer bias. Explain.

➤ lack of scientific validity. No IV (implications: no cause–effect).

➤ ethics and confidentiality.

Chapter summary

This chapter examined the cyclical nature of the research process in psychology. Types of hypotheses and hypothesis testing were considered, as were ethics in psychological research. The experimental method was emphasised including types of experiment and features of the experimental method. Advantages and disadvantages of the experimental method were illustrated generally and specifically. The control of extraneous variables was discussed, as were the merits and demerits of related and unrelated experimental designs. Non-experimental methods were also examined as were their features and individual and comparative advantages and disadvantages.

ONLINE INTERACTIVES

1 Go to the Higher Psychology Learning Suite at **www.gerardkeegan.co.uk**. Click Chapter 6 'Investigating Behaviour: Methods of Collecting Data' to access direct links to all websites mentioned in this chapter.

2 Go to the Higher Psychology Learning Suite at **www.gerardkeegan.co.uk**. Click Chapter 6 'Investigating Behaviour: Methods of Collecting Data' and do the online interactive crossword. But don't cheat!

3 Go to the Higher Psychology Learning Suite at **www.gerardkeegan.co.uk**. Click a Chapter 6 'Investigating Behaviour: Methods of Collecting Data' and do the online interactive hangman game. Try and beat the executioner!

4 Go to the Higher Psychology Learning Suite at **www.gerardkeegan.co.uk**. Click Chapter 6 'Investigating Behaviour: Methods of Collecting Data' and print off the hard copy crossword. When finished you might like to hand it into your teacher as homework.

5 Go to the Higher Psychology Learning Suite at **www.gerardkeegan.co.uk**. Click Chapter 4 'Biological Psychology: Stress' and do the online interactive Quiz. Try and win the prize!

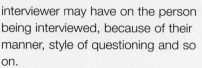

GLOSSARY

Acquiescence response: A psychological tendency people have to agree with what is asked of them.

Behaviour index: An index used in observations to record the behaviour of subjects/participants.

Between-subjects design: An unrelated design such as an independent groups design. Also called independent subjects/samples design.

Closed question: A question whose answer is restricted in some way, e.g. 'what age are you?' is a closed question. It only has one possible answer.

Continuous recording: The recording of all behaviour during the observation period.

Counterbalancing: A technique used in an experiment to control for order effect, e.g. ABBA.

Covert observation: Observations that take place without the subject's knowledge.

Demand characteristics: Clues from the research situation that help the participant work out its purpose. Demand characteristics alter behaviour, and thus influence results.

Dependent variable: In an experiment the DV is the variable that is measured or observed as a consequence of changing or manipulating the independent variable.

Double-blind technique: A technique in which neither the researcher–observer nor the participant knows to which condition of the independent variable they have been allocated. This helps avoid confounding variables.

Ecological validity: Research that reflects real life. Laboratory experiments are often accused of lacking in ecological validity.

Empathy: Empathy is where the counsellor (or facilitator) appreciates where his/her client is coming from.

They do this verbally and non-verbally. Or through the use of encouraging noises and body language.

Ethology: The study of animals in their natural environment.

Experimental design: The procedure adopted to control for participant variables in an experiment, e.g. repeated measures, independent groups.

Experimental method: A research design only applicable to a laboratory, field or quasi-experiment. The experimental method is identified by the manipulation of an IV, the observation of any effect this has on a DV, and the control of extraneous variables.

Experimenter effect: An aspect associated with the experimenter in research e.g. their behaviour, manner, age, sex, age etc. that influences the behaviour of the participant in some way.

Field experiment: An experiment that takes place away from the laboratory in a more natural setting. The experimental method of control, observation and measurement of variables still occurs.

Genuineness: In humanistic psychotherapy the counsellor or facilitator will be genuine about themselves. In doing so it is hoped the client will be genuine about him or herself, which helps them towards psychological good health.

GIGO: Garbage in, garbage out. GIGO is the result of poor survey design.

Idiographic: An investigative approach centered on a unique or single case happening concerning a person, an organisation, a family or an animal.

Independent variable: In an experiment the IV is the variable that is changed or manipulated to measure/observe its effect on the dependent variable.

Interviewer effect: The influence an interviewer may have on the person being interviewed, because of their manner, style of questioning and so on.

Introspection: Self-reporting of experience by participants in research. Used by Sigmund Freud and Wilhelm Wundt.

Laboratory experiment: Traditional setting of an experiment that adheres to the experimental method of control, observation, and measurement of variables.

Likert scale: A scale of measurement often used in a survey that allows for a person's strength of feeling on a matter to be expressed. Likert scales also generate good quantitative (numerical) data on issues.

Longitudinal case study: A case study following the future of a participant/subject/organisation.

Longitudinal study: Research of a year or more.

Mean: A statistical average, e.g. the mean of $2 + 3 + 4 + 1 + 2 + 5 + 1$ is 2.571 (18 divided by 7).

Observer bias: May occur in that the observer may be influenced by prior knowledge/experience or expectations of the subjects/situation under investigation.

Observer effect: Any changes in a participant's behaviour as a result of the observer's presence.

Obtrusive measures: Devices used to measure performance/behaviour that can be seen by the participants of observational studies, and can thereby affect behaviour, e.g. a video camera.

Open question: A question that has a variety of possible answers.

Order effect: The influence of tiredness, fatigue or boredom on participants in an experiment. Controlled by counterbalancing.

Overt observation: Open observation, where all who take part know they are participating.

Pilot study: A practice run of an experiment to identify any flaws, snags or ambiguity of instructions before conducting the experiment proper.

Pilot survey: A practice run of a survey to identify any flaws, snags or ambiguity of instructions/questions before conducting the survey proper.

Placebo: A placebo is the control condition of the IV that has no effect, e.g. a sugar pill.

Pseudo-patient: As in Rosenhan's (1973) study, where researchers pose as patients in order to record observations.

Psychometric test: A psychological test that measures psychological factors, e.g. personality, intelligence, aptitude and so on.

Quasi-experiment: A situation that is 'nearly' an experiment, which takes place in a real-world environment. The main difference between a quasi- and a field/laboratory experiment is that participants are already found in those conditions of the IV you are researching.

Retrospective case study: A case study investigating the past of a participant/subject/organisation.

Single-blind technique: Used in experimental research where the participant does not know to what condition of the independent variable they have been allocated.

Standardised instructions: Agreed instructions to be given to participants in an experiment, usually formulated after a pilot study has been conducted.

Structured survey: A survey whose instructions/questions will be standardised, usually after a pilot survey has been conducted.

Survey method: The survey method of research asks a representative sample of people oral or written questions to find out about their attitudes, behaviours, beliefs, opinions, and values.

Target: The subject (person, organisation, family, animal) of a case study.

Time sampling: The recording of behaviour at particular set times

Transformation: This is the cognitive ability we develop to move and manipulate objects, etc. in our minds.

Treatment: The conditions or manipulations of an independent variable.

Unconditional positive regard: Unconditional positive regard is the love we get from other people for who we are as a person, warts and all. Most usually unconditional positive regard comes from our parents.

Unobtrusive measures: Observational methods of measurement and recording that are hidden and as a result do not impact on the subject's behaviours, e.g. CCTV, video recordings.

Volunteer sample: A sample made up of people who volunteer to take part in your research. Can give rise to volunteer bias.

Within-subjects design: Related designs such as repeated measures and matched pairs.

CHAPTER SEVEN

Investigating Behaviour: Analysing Data and the Research Investigation

TOPICS

● **Demonstrate practical research skills, and carry out a psychological research investigation.**

Levels of measurement

In psychology whenever possible we *quantify*, measure or count any data we collect. Such quantifiable data can be measured at three levels.

1 Nominal data

Nominal data is quantifiable information that is *categorised*. Nominal data is *named* data.

Nominal data sees a researcher establish named categories for the information they collect. A variable is measured or counted when it falls into this category.

Examples of nominal data would be:

➤ The number of males and females in a psychology class.

➤ The number of monolingual, bilingual and multilingual students in a school or college etc.

2 Ranked/ordinal data

Ranked data is quantifiable data that is put into some kind of order.

A ranked or ordinal level of measurement has us rank order such information to see how it relates to each other.

An example of ranked or ordinal data would be placing athletes first, second, third etc. after they had run a 100m race.

3 Interval/ratio data

Interval or ratio data is our most sophisticated quantified level of measurement. The difference between interval data and ratio data is that interval data does not have a natural zero, while ratio data does. Interval data can also include negative values. Examples of interval data would be temperature and dates. Examples of ratio data would be height, weight, age, length, and time.

In our 100m race example below, the finishing *times* of runners would be ratio data e. g.

Interval data	Ratio data
Temperature	Height
Dates	Weight
	Length
	Time

Table 7.1 Types of data

We can tell on the basis of such ratio data that Keegan was first, Keating was second and Kerr last.

Runner	Time (secs)
Keegan, G	11.4
Keating, L	11.9
Kerr, P	12.1

Table 7.2 Ratio data for a 100m race

We can also adjudge just how much better Keegan performed in relation to Keating and Kerr. And indeed how Keegan, Keating and Kerr's performance compares to other 100m runners in their club, county, country etc.

It is thus not surprising to learn that interval/ratio data is much more useful and informative than nominal and ordinal data.

INTERACTIVES: NOMINAL, ORDINAL, INTERVAL

Read the following statements and decide whether you think they describe nominal, ordinal or interval data.

1   The number of Ps who only read the *Herald*, *The Scotsman* or *The Sun*.

2   Participants rating of their own self-worth using a scale ranging from 1–50.

3   Fifteen photographs arranged by participants according to level of attractiveness.

4   Results of Higher Psychology assessment (marked out of 45).

5   A set of clinical records which classify patients as 'acute' or 'chronic'.

6   Participants' ratings on how interesting they found a particular Psychology lesson using a scale of 1–100 where 100 was 'Fascinating'.

7   The number of aggressive acts observed in a *Tom and Jerry* cartoon.

Answers on page 293.

Descriptive statistics

In psychology we use descriptive statistics to *describe* the basic features of the data we collect. Descriptive statistics help provide simple summaries in our investigations regard how our sample thinks, feels, or behaves.

Together with graphical representations of our results, such descriptive statistics form the basis of most quantitative **analysis** of data in psychology.

Measures of central tendency

When we have a collection of scores calculating the 'average' is a way of indicating where most of the scores lie.

In statistics there are three different types of average known collectively as measures of central tendency.

Measures of central tendency include the *mean*, the *median* and the *mode*.

The mean

The mean is the most common type of average in statistics. Sometimes called the arithmetic mean, a mean is the value that occurs most frequently in a data set.

Adding up all the scores in a data set and dividing this sum by the number of scores that occur help calculate the mean.

The formula to calculate the mean is:

$$\bar{x} \text{ (Mean)} = \frac{\Sigma x \text{ (sum of all scores/values)}}{N \text{ (number of scores/values)}}$$

Participant	Time taken to read word list (secs)
1	12
2	12
3	13
4	13

Table 7.3 Partial Raw data table for Stroop Effect experiment

INTERACTIVE: MEDIAN

Calculate the median number of words recalled by 10 participants in an experiment into short-term memory.

Participant	1	2	3	4	5	6	7	8	9	10
Words recalled	5	8	9	7	7	6	5	8	5	6

Answers on page 293.

To calculate the mean time it took our four participants in the Stroop experiment to read a word list we add up their total times and divide by four i.e.

$$\overline{x} = \frac{\sum x}{N}$$

$$\overline{x} = \frac{12 + 12 + 13 + 13}{4} = \frac{50}{4}$$

$$\overline{x} = 12.5 \text{ seconds}$$

The median

The median is a statistical term for another type of average. The median is the *middle* score in a set of data.

The median is the value that divides the distribution of all our scores in half. To find the median, you put the scores in ascending order. If there is an odd number of scores, the median is the middle score. If there is an even number of scores, you average the two middle scores.

In either case, half of the scores in the data set or distribution will be above the median and half will be below it.

Take our partial raw data chart above.

Our participants median time is 12.5 seconds, or the two middle scores in the array divided by two, i.e. 12, 12, 13, 13.

$$\frac{12 + 13}{2} = 12.5$$

The mode

The mode is our third measure of central tendency. The mode is the most *frequently occurring value* in a data set. Or the score most often obtained.

Look at the data set below. To work it out the mode you quite simply count the number of times each value occurs and enter it into a frequency table.

Participant	1	2	3	4	5	6	7	8	9	10
Number of words recalled	5	8	9	7	7	6	5	8	5	6

Table 7.4 A data set

Number of words recalled	5	6	7	8	9
Frequency	3	2	2	2	1

Table 7.5 The frequency table for the above data set

The mode is 5 as this occurred three times, in comparison to the frequency of times six words were recalled (twice), seven words (twice) etc.

While extremely useful, knowing the mean, median, or mode in a data set is often not enough in psychological research. We *also* need to know how 'spread out' our scores are. This area of descriptive statistics concerns 'measures of dispersion'.

ONLINE INTERACTIVES

Go to this BBC GCSE Bitesize website and do some online exercises on the mean, median, and mode.

www.bbc.co.uk/schools/gcsebitesize/maths/data/measuresofaveragerev1.shtml

A direct link is available in the Chapter 7 section of the Higher Psychology Learning Suite at **www.gerardkeegan.co.uk**

Measure	Description	Advantages	Disadvantages
Mean	The **mean** is the sum of all the results or scores got by a sample divided by the number of observations	Quick and easy to calculate. Most sensitive to all values. The numerical centre of all actual values.	May not be representative of the whole sample. Greatly affected by extreme scores.
Median	The **median** is the middle value of all the results or scores got by a sample. In other words, the median is the value that divides the set of data in half, half of the observations being above (or equal to) it and half being below (or equal to) it	Takes all results or scores into account equally. Generally unaffected by extreme scores.	May not be an actual value as appears in the data set. More tedious to calculate than the mean or mode. Can be influenced by a few very large (or very small) numbers
Mode	The **mode** is the most frequently observed value of the results or scores got by a sample. By its very nature there can be more than one mode or no mode.	Fairly easy to calculate. Generally unaffected by extreme scores.	Tedious to find for a large sample which is not in order

Table 7.6 Measures of central tendency at a glance

Measures of dispersion

One measure of dispersion we need to know about in Higher psychology is the range.

The range

The range is the distance in units from the top to the bottom value in any data set. A simple formula we can use to calculate the range is:

Top value – bottom value + 1

Look again at the number of words recalled by our participants in their experiment into STM. To calculate the *range* of scores recalled by them we merely work out the difference between the highest and the lowest number of words recalled and add one.

Participant	1	2	3	4	5	6	7	8	9	10
Recalled	5	8	9	7	7	6	5	8	5	6

Table 7.7 A data set

Thus: $9 - 5 + 1 = 5$

The range is 5. This is because there are five values that occur between the bottom score of 5 and the top score of 9 viz. 5, 6, 7, 8, 9.

INTERACTIVES

Work out the range for the following data set:

57, 63, 72, 77, 81, 86.

Evaluation of range

The main weakness with a descriptive statistic like the range is that it tells us nothing about how spread out our scores are within a data set.

Another criticism is that the range does not give an accurate reflection of results when a group of scores contains a peculiar score that is obviously higher or lower than the rest.

One way to address such skew is to use another measure of dispersion called the *standard deviation*.

Standard deviation

Standard deviation (SD) refers to the average amount that all scores in a data set deviate from the mean. Standard deviation measures the distribution of scores around the mean.

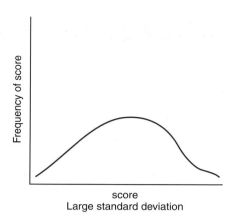

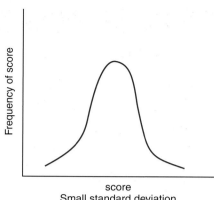

Figure 7.1 Examples of large and small standard deviations

If the standard deviation of a group of scores is large, this indicates that the scores are widely distributed, with many scores occurring a long way from the mean.

If the standard deviation of a group of scores is small, this means that the scores are closely distributed, with most if not all scores occurring close to the mean.

Definition of normal distribution

A *normal distribution* describes and illustrates the frequency distribution for a set of variable data, usually represented by a bell-shaped curve symmetrical about the mean.

If scores for a particular population are normally distributed, as illustrated by our normal distribution curve for IQ (intelligence quotient), 68.26% of all scores will lie between +1 and -1 SD from the mean, or between one standard deviation above the mean and one standard deviation below the mean; 95.44% of all scores will lie between +2 and -2 SD from the mean; and mostly all scores will lie between +3 and -3 SD of a sample's IQ scores or whatever else is being measured.

The value of Standard Deviation (SD) is always given in terms of the score that you are measuring.

Regards IQ the mean or most common score got by people on IQ tests are 100, and the SD is 15.

Remembering that *standard deviation* is the average amount all scores will deviate from the mean, in a measure of IQ as suggested above roughly 68% or two-thirds of a population's scores will lie between 85 and 115 IQ points, while 95% of the same population's scores will lie between 70 and 130 IQ points.

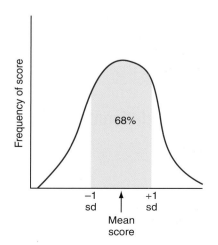

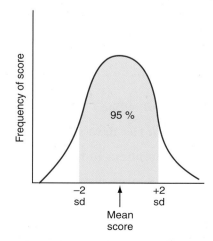

Figure 7.2 A normal distribution curve illustrating the percentage for scores that fall between 1 and 2 standard deviations from the mean

ONLINE INTERACTIVES

Go to:

www.youtube.com/watch?v=cLTSenQotqw

and watch 'Standard Deviation Man' on YouTube!

A direct link is available in the Chapter 7 section of the Higher Psychology Learning Suite at **www.gerardkeegan.co.uk**

Evaluation of standard deviation

Standard deviation is the most sensitive measure of dispersion. It uses and accounts for *all* scores in a data set.

Standard deviation can be used to relate the sample to the population's parameters. A parameter is the boundaries or extremes within which something is set.

However a standard deviation can be time consuming to calculate.

How to calculate the standard deviation

In order to calculate the standard deviation, the difference between each score is worked out. The mean of those scores is calculated and then squared. This is to avoid negative or minus values.

These squared deviations are then added together and *their* mean calculated to give a value called the *variance*.

The squared root of the variance gives us the standard deviation of the scores.

The formula for the standard deviation is:

$$S = \sqrt{\frac{\Sigma(x - \bar{x})^2}{N}}$$

S = **standard deviation**

√ = **square root**

Σ = **sum of (Greek symbol sigma)**

x = **each score/number in the data set**

x̄ = **mean of the scores/numbers in the data set**

N = number of times the scores occurred

Worked example

To find the standard deviation of the following data set:

14, 22, 11, 19, 30, 24

First find the mean

14 + 22 + 11 + 19 + 30 + 24 = 120

$$\frac{120}{6} = 20$$

Then take the mean away from each number and square the answer

$14 - 20 = -6, -6^2 = 36$

$22 - 20 = 2, 2^2 = 4$

$11 - 20 = -9, -9^2 = 81$

$19 - 20 = -1, -1^2 = 1$

$30 - 20 = 10, 10^2 = 100$

$24 - 20 = 4, 4^2 = 16$

Add all those squared numbers together

36 + 4 + 81 + 1 + 100 + 16 = 238

Now divide 238 by $N - 1$.

N is the total number of participant scores. Here $N = 6$ so $N - 1 = 5$

$$\frac{238}{5} = 47.6$$

Then find the square root of 47.6

$\sqrt{47.6} = 6.9$ to 1 decimal place

The Standard Deviation of this set of data = 6.9

INTERACTIVE: STANDARD DEVIATION

Please calculate the standard deviation of the following data set:

2, 3, 3, 5, 8, 9

Answer on page 293.

The correlational technique

Correlation is a statistical technique used to indicate the degree of relationship between two covariates.

Correlation is not a research method but a statistical technique used to discover the degree of relationship between two covariates, or **covariables**. A covariate could be an individual or group behaviour, an event, or a situation that is itself free to vary. Examples would be hours spent studying, hours spent watching TV, levels of aggression, delinquent behaviours, etc.

> **Correlations and hypotheses**
>
> As with an experiment, a correlational study will have a null hypothesis. The null hypothesis was earlier explored when we looked at the experimental method.
>
> In a correlational study the null hypothesis (H_0) would predict that there is no relationship between two covariates. If a correlation coefficient were being used, the level of significance (p value) would also be stated.
>
> Further, as with an experimental hypothesis, a correlational research or alternative hypothesis (H_A or H_R) would indicate whether the hypothesis was either one- or two-tailed. In a correlation a one-tailed hypothesis predicts the direction the relationship between the covariates is expected to go. A two-tailed hypothesis does not predict the expected direction. A one-tailed H_R would predict that there was a positive or negative relationship expected between the covariates. A two-tailed H_R would predict a relationship, but not its direction.

Correlations are widely used in psychology to discover the extent to which two independent behaviours might be related. If you find you *do* have a correlation, this allows you to make a prediction about a behaviour/event/situation in the future. We will discover that a correlation can establish a relationship between one covariate and another and this allows predictions to be made.

Examples of correlations, or relationships between two covariates, could be: hours spent studying, and examination performance; amount of violent TV programmes watched, and levels of aggression; physical punishment in the home, and delinquency; finger length, depression, and fertility; and even levitation and crime levels! Let us take an example of a possible correlation between the number of hours studied by ten students, and their subsequent scores in a psychology assessment.

To get a correlation you obtain a measurement of each covariate from the individuals/groups in your sample. You then tabulate this paired data as shown below.

To discover whether there is a correlation between the number of hours studied and scores in an assessment, we would tabulate our data as above, and then plot our pairings onto a **scattergram**. A scattergram is a descriptive statistic that helps illustrate a statistical relationship, such as a correlation. The patterns our plots form indicate whether a correlation exists. Number of hours studied is the x-axis value, plotted on the horizontal, and score in the assessment, is the y-axis value, plotted on the vertical.

Positive correlations

We can see from the plots on the scattergram that as the number of hours spent studying increases, the student's assessment score increases. When, as here, one covariate *increases*, and the other similarly *increases*, we have a **positive correlation**. This is because there is a positive relationship between hours spent studying and assessment scores. We can tell this from the pattern our plots make. Our plots are going in an upward, positive direction, as indicated by the trend line, which you will note in a scattergram, does not 'join the dots'! It runs through them as a 'line of best fit'. The direction, and the degree of elevation in our trend line, indicates the strength and degree of correlation between our two covariates. Here we have a *picture* of a **near perfect positive correlation** between the two covariates on our x and y axes; hours spent studying, and assessment scores.

Participant	1	2	3	4	5	6	7	8	9	10
Hours studied (*x*)	8	3	2	5	9	2	1	4	6	8
Psychology assessment score (*y*)	83	34	32	48	76	40	27	36	56	81

Table 7.8 Covariate measurements

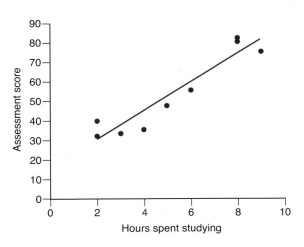

Figure 7.3 Scattergram illustrating a near perfect positive correlation

From our scattergram we are able to predict future assessment performance by suggesting, on the basis of our trend line, that a student who puts in two hours studying will do less well than a student who works for ten hours. We are also able to project our line of best fit to accommodate a prediction of results based on more/fewer hours studied by individuals. If someone studied for 20 minutes their predicted score would be less than 20. If someone studied for between eleven and twelve hours their predicted result would be over 90.

The correlation coefficient

We can also take our correlational data one step further and use a statistical sum such as Spearman's *rho* to calculate a **correlation coefficient**. While non-examinable in Higher psychology it is useful to know that a correlation coefficient is a mathematical calculation that tells us the degree of relationship between two covariates. A Spearman's rho calculation would give you a correlation coefficient answer of between –1 and +1, somewhere along the following range:

The nearer rho (p) is to +1, the more perfect the correlation you have, and thus the more certain you are that there is a positive relationship between your two covariates. You can infer that one is positively related to the other. A correlation coefficient of around +1 is diagrammatically represented in Figure 7.3. If a Spearman's rho was calculated on the basis of our data, p would be somewhere between 0.8 and +1. This would be confirmation of our strong positive correlation pattern as seen in Figure 7.3. Absolutely perfect positive correlations, having a calculated correlation coefficient of $p = +1$, are extremely rare in psychological research.

Another useful property of a correlation coefficient is that it allows you to test the significance of your results. Levels of significance are more fully explored in our next chapter on the experimental method.

The nearer p is to 0, the less likely there is to be any correlation between the independent covariates.

Negative correlations

We can also generate a *negative* correlation between two covariates. What this means is that as one covariate increases, the other decreases. There is thus a negative relationship between the two covariates. Again a negative correlation can be represented by a scattergram, and also calculated using Spearman's rho. Let us take our example above of hours spent studying and assessment scores. Our data could be:

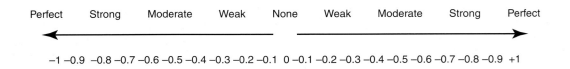

Figure 7.4 Correlation coefficient parameters

Hours	1	2	3	4	5	6	7	8	9	10
Score	83	76	74	67	56	48	36	34	32	27

Table 7.9

Our scattergram would then look like Figure 7.5:

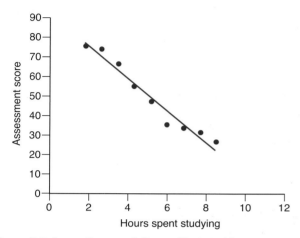

Figure 7.5 A negative correlation as illustrated by a scattergram

The pattern got with our plots in the scattergram Figure 7.5 is an example of a **near perfect negative correlation**. This is because as one covariate *increases* (hours spent studying), the other consequently *decreases* (assessment scores). In a negative correlation, as in Figure 7.5, the trend line is going in a downward, negative direction. We can say that our scattergram here illustrates a strong negative correlation between hours spent studying, and scores in a subsequent assessment. On the basis of this trend line you could predict that someone who studied a lot would not do as well as someone who did not! If we were to apply Spearman's rho to this data it would give rise to a negative correlation coefficient of p being between –0.8 and –1.0.

A negative correlation like the above does not sound as absurd as it might seem. It would be true to say that the author was not known for his academic ability in S5 and S6 at Holyrood Secondary School, Glasgow. His mother would say this was an understatement. His mother would be right. Studying was for swots, and aged seventeen or so he did not want this tag. No chance. The night before his Higher Modern Studies examination in 1974, when others were hard at work in their bedrooms, he was watching TV! Panorama ran a documentary entitled '*The Social, Political and Economic Effects of Scottish Oil.*' The first question your author saw in his Higher paper the next day was

'*Discuss the social, political, and economic effects of Scottish oil.*' The invigilator had to get a bucket of water in case his script burst into flames, because of the fury and speed at which he wrote. He got an A band 1, the only thing that impressed at his university interview for social sciences, and his introduction to the subject of psychology. This book is a result of a negative correlation!

The point to this story is that you can get correlations between almost anything. There could be other factors, as identified earlier, called *extraneous variables* that might influence your results, which you have not taken into account. Hours spent studying and assessment performance may indeed be related, but our positive/negative relationships could have arisen because of other factors. Our negative correlation may have arisen because the students who put in a lot of hours 'studying' could just have been dossing on their bed for hours 'reading' pages of notes from their big fat psychology folder. Our topic of Memory would tell you why these students didn't do as well as others, who did not study (badly) like this, but instead watched dedicated TV programmes, building upon, and enriching, their previously learned knowledge of psychology. The study of cognitive psychology in general and memory in particular can improve your examination performance. Definitely.

Correlations should then never be taken as scientific 'truths'. They can only indicate that there *might* be a positive or negative relationship between two behaviours or situations. They cannot ever show that one covariate *causes* another. Very often the general public can be lulled into believing a correlation is scientific 'proof' that one thing causes another.

Any cause–effect relationship in psychology can *only* be established using the experimental method. Correlation is a statistical technique that can only be used to establish the degree and strength of a relationship between two things; never that one covariate *causes* another.

Later we will look at a good, and a circumspect (or dodgy) correlation; for the moment using the data in Table 7.10, look at Figure 7.6 over the page for an illustration of a 'no correlation' situation using our 'hours studied/assessment performance' example.

Hours	1	2	3	4	5	6	7	8	9	10
Score	83	32	34	56	67	48	36	74	76	27

Table 7.10

In Figure 7.6 there is no correlation. We cannot establish a trend line, or line of best fit between the paired covariate data. An interpretation of this scattergram pattern would be that no relationship exists between hours spent studying, and assessment performance.

Spearman's rho

It is useful to remind ourselves that a sum like Spearman's rho helps us to calculate the strength and degree of relationship, or correlation, between sets/pairs of ranked data. It produces a numerical value or *correlation coefficient* of between –1 and +1, from which you can tell the degree of positive or negative relationship. The nearer our answer is to +1, the more positive the relationship between the covariates. They are each increasing in a positive direction. The nearer our answer is to 0, the less chance of a relationship, while the nearer it is to –1, the more negative the relationship that exists between the covariates. As one goes in one direction, the other goes in the other.

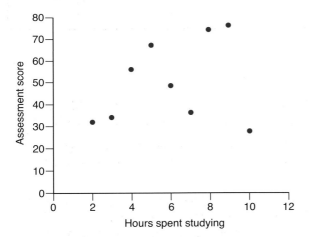

Figure 7.6 Scattergram illustrating no correlation

Using rho also allows us to test our null hypothesis (H_0) for significance. We use levels of significance to test the **probability** that our results happened by chance or random factors. Let us here however try to work out a correlation coefficient for the above data based upon the following correlational hypotheses.

Alternative hypothesis H_A: 'That there is a positive relationship between the number of hours a student studies and their subsequent assessment score.'

Null hypothesis H_0: 'That there is not a positive relationship between the number of hours a student studies and their assessment score at the 0.05 level of significance.'

Our alternative (or research) hypothesis, H_A, is one-tailed. This is because it is predicting the direction of expected relationship, i.e. as the number of hours spent studying increases, a student's assessment score should similarly increase. It is predicting a positive correlation, or relationship.

Our H_0 predicts that there will be no relationship. If the data, when applied to Spearman's rho, does produce a calculation to support a relationship, testing to a level of significance of 0.05 indicates that the researcher is willing to accept that there is a 1:20 likelihood that any statistically supported relationship has happened because of chance or random factors.

Using our original data in Table 7.8 (from page 267) that produced our first scattergram, you calculate rho as follows.

Hours studied	1	2	2	3	4	5	6	8	8	9
Score	27	40	32	34	36	48	56	81	83	76

Table 7.11

How to do a Spearman's rho

Lay out the data in the following way:

Column 1	Column 2	Column 3	Column 4	Column 5	Column 6	Column 7
Participant	Hours studied (x)	Psychology assessment score (y)	Rank x	Rank y	Difference d (between values in columns 4 & 5)	Difference multiplied by the power 2 (d^2)
1	8	83	8	10	−2	4
2	3	34	4	3	1	1
3	2	32	2	2	0	0
4	5	48	6	6	0	0
5	9	76	10	8	2	4
6	2	40	2	5	−3	9
7	1	27	1	1	0	0
8	4	36	5	4	1	1
9	6	56	7	7	0	0
10	8	81	8	9	−1	1
						$\Sigma d^2 = 20$

Table 7.12

Then:

1 Enter participants, e.g. 1–10 in column 1.

2 Enter in your x values in column 2 (number of hours each studied), e.g. participant 7, 1 hour, etc.

3 Enter in your y values in column 3 (psychology assessment scores), e.g. participant 7, 27, etc.

4 Rank order your x values in column 4. Rank the smallest score 1 (first), etc.

5 Rank order your y values in column 5. Rank the smallest score 1 (first), etc.

6 Subtract each y value from each x value, as in column 6, e.g. participant number 2, 4 − 3 = 1.

7 Find the difference 'squared' for each $(x − y)$ value, as in column 7, e.g. participant number 2, 1 × 1 = 1.

8 Add up all the values in the d^2 column to get Σ. The symbol Σ (sigma) means 'sum of'. So Σ means that you add up all the figures in the d^2 column. In this instance in column 7, $\Sigma = 20$.

You now have all the necessary data to 'plug' into the Spearman's rho formula, which is:

$$r_s = \frac{1 - 6\ (\Sigma d^2)}{N(N^2 - 1)}$$

r_s = Spearman's rho

Σ = sum of

d^2 = difference $(x - y)$ squared

N = number of participants

N^2 = number of participants squared

$$r_s = \frac{1 - 6(20)}{10(100 - 1)}$$

$r_s = 1 - 0.12$

Calculated $r_s = 0.88$

This is your calculated rho. One last step is to find critical rho. Consult the Spearman's rho critical value table shown on page 271. Run your finger down the n column – 'n' means the number of participants in your correlation. So here, $n = 10$.

Remember our null hypothesis H_0: 'That there will not be a positive relationship between the number of hours a student studies and their assessment score at the 0.05 level of significance.'

You then run your finger along until you find the 0.05 level of significance for a one-tailed test. Here you find critical rho. Critical rho at the 0.05 level of significance for a one-tailed test, where n = 10 is 0.564.

Then merely follow the instruction at the bottom of the table, which is:

'Calculated r_s, must EQUAL OR EXCEED the tabled (critical) value of significance at the level shown.'

Our r_s of 0.88 does indeed 'equal or exceed' the critical value of 0.564 at the level of significance shown in our null hypothesis (0.05) for a one-tailed test. As a result we can reject the null hypothesis, and accept the alternative hypothesis H_A: 'That there is a positive relationship between the number of hours a student studies and their subsequent assessment score.'

Our Spearman's rho correlation coefficient calculation of 0.88 now clearly supports this conclusion. Remembering that our null hypothesis has a probability (p) value of 0.05, please appreciate that while being able to reject the H_0 and accept the H_A we must accept that there is a 1:20 likelihood that this positive correlation has arisen because of chance or random factors.

Level of significance for a two-tailed test			
0.10	0.05	0.02	0.01
Level of significance for a one-tailed test			
0.05	0.025	0.01	0.005
$n = 4$ 1.000			
5 0.900	1.000	1.000	
6 0.829	0.886	0.943	1.000
7 0.714	0.786	0.893	0.929
8 0.643	0.738	0.833	0.881
9 0.600	0.700	0.783	0.833
10 0.564	0.648	0.745	0.794
11 0.536	0.618	0.709	0.755

Level of significance for a one-tailed test (*continued*)			
12	0.503	0.587	0.671	0.727
13	0.484	0.560	0.648	0.703
14	0.464	0.538	0.622	0.675
15	0.443	0.521	0.604	0.654
16	0.429	0.503	0.582	0.635
17	0.414	0.485	0.566	0.615
18	0.401	0.472	0.550	0.600
19	0.391	0.460	0.535	0.584
20	0.380	0.447	0.520	0.570
21	0.370	0.435	0.508	0.556
22	0.361	0.425	0.496	0.544
23	0.353	0.415	0.486	0.532
24	0.344	0.406	0.476	0.521
25	0.337	0.398	0.466	0.511
26	0.331	0.390	0.457	0.501
27	0.324	0.382	0.448	0.491
28	0.317	0.375	0.440	0.483
29	0.312	0.368	0.433	0.475
30	0.306	0.362	0.425	0.467

Table 7.13 Spearman's rho table of critical values

Calculated r_s must EQUAL or EXCEED the table (critical) value for significance at the level shown.

Source: J.H. Zhar, 'Significance testing of the Spearman Rank Correlation Coefficient', *Journal of the American Statistical Association*, 67, 578–80. With the kind permission of the publishers.

Depression, fertility and fingers

Interesting research based upon correlations done by Dr John Manning of the School of Biological Sciences at the University of Liverpool has uncovered a relationship between the length of our fingers, depression, and also fertility rates.

Manning, Martin & Dorwick (2001) studied 50 men and 52 women from different socio-economic backgrounds. They took a number of physical measurements such as wrist size, ear size, height, and the length of their fingers. The also gave each participant the Beck Depression Inventory (BDI), widely used in the clinical diagnosis of depression.

With men, the results showed that the length of their ring finger (fourth digit) positively correlated with a high BDI score. To control for the fact that tall men have longer limbs, fingers and feet dividing finger length by height, gave an even stronger basis for predicting that male participants with long ring fingers would score highly on the depression inventory. The 50 male participants on average scored 5 on the BDI. The ten male participants with the shortest ring fingers had a mean score of 1.56, while the 10 longest-fingered males averaged 8.5. (The BDI 'depressed' range starts at 10.)

The key to this strange relationship appears to be prenatal testosterone, which is produced from the eighth week of pregnancy. According to Dr Manning:

> *Foetal testosterone plays a key role in the development of the male genital system. It also impacts on the development of fingers and thumbs, and the central nervous system. Men who experienced high concentrations of foetal testosterone have relatively long fingers – in particular, fourth digits, which are longer than their second digits.*"

Conversely, men who experienced low concentrations of foetal testosterone have shorter fourth digits than their second digits. Interestingly, the study's results suggest that depression in women has a different, and as yet undetermined origin.'

What this work suggests is that high foetal testosterone levels in males (as indicated by the length of the ring finger) biologically predisposes them to be more susceptible to depression than males with low foetal testosterone levels (who have short ring fingers).

It isn't all bad news for long-ring-fingered males however. Men with long ring fingers have higher fertility levels than their shorter ring-fingered male counterparts. So, if having lots of babies is important to you, you might consider the length of fingers from now on! Please note however that Dr Manning warns that much more research is needed in order to be more confident in any relationships suggested by his amazing correlations.

Circumspect correlations

Followers of the Maharishi Mahesh Yogi in the UK have established the transcendental meditation TM–Sidhis programme. It is more commonly known as yogic flying, first brought to the British public's attention by the not unrelated, and now defunct, Natural Law Party in the mid-late 1990s. Yogic

flying is attempting to levitate, or jump, into the air from a squat position. Yogic flying is thought to bring 'bubbling bliss for the individual' and 'positivity and harmony in the environment'. T–m.org.uk suggests that when yogic flying is practised in groups, it produces a 'field effect on the level of human consciousness'. Through this field effect apparent 'coherence radiates throughout the environment, dissolving stress, reducing negativity and creating a positive and harmonious influence in society'. This has seen them allege something called the 'Maharishi effect'. A graphical representation of the 'effect' is reproduced here.

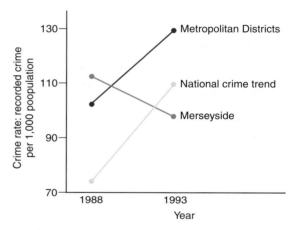

Figure 7.7 Maharishi effect

The organisation claims that during a five-year period into a study of the Maharishi effect, crime in Merseyside 'fell by 15 per cent while crime in the rest of the country rose by 45 per cent, a relative decrease of 60 per cent'.

The reason for the fall in crime in the Merseyside area, t–m.org.uk says, was down to the transcendental influence of a group of 200 yogic flyers. This was because they had been yogic flying in nearby Skelmersdale from 1998, at around the same time the fall in crime rate on Merseyside began (see Figure 7.7). According to the now defunct Natural Law Party this negative correlation between yogic flying and the crime rate known as the Maharishi Effect, is the best established of all findings in the social sciences.

The Maharishi effect

This is an excellent example of why we should be wary of correlations. While yogic flying may indeed bring bubbling bliss, it cannot claim to cause a fall in crime rate just because people were jumping up and down from a squat position at the time the crime rate began to fall. There are just far too many other extraneous variables.

Figure 7.8 Yogic flyer

The variable that precipitated the fall in crime rate in Merseyside during this time happened a few years earlier. This was the Toxteth riot that erupted during a very hot summer spell in 1981 in an area of Liverpool known as Liverpool 8. The Toxteth riot sparked similar riots in Moss Side, Manchester and Brixton in London. The Conservative government was so concerned that all police leave throughout the UK was cancelled during the summer of 1981. The author was in Sheffield and Brixton at the time, and can guarantee that revolt was in the air. Thousands spilled onto the streets of major cities in Britain 'waiting', and/or posturing aggressively towards the hundreds of riot police opposite, themselves 'waiting', and/or posturing back. A heady cocktail for someone with an interest in social psychology!

Toxteth led to the then Home Secretary Michael Heseltine setting up the Scarman Enquiry, which consequently saw a massive sea change in police–community relations in Merseyside. There was a vast increase in financial investment in police–community affairs in Merseyside from the mid-1980s onwards. Maybe this better explains the drop in crime rate, as opposed to the alleged negative correlation called the Maharishi effect. You can make up your own mind.

Figure 7.9 The Toxteth riots

Advantages of the correlational technique

The correlational technique is useful in situations where an experiment would be impractical. This is because no manipulations of behaviour are required. The behaviour, over which you as a researcher have no control, is already occurring/has just occurred. This is why the correlation is an *ex post facto* research technique. *Ex post facto* means 'after the fact', the fact being the covariates you are now measuring in retrospect.

Correlation is also used in situations where other research methods would be unethical. It is correlations, for example, that have established the relationship between cancers and smoking. To conduct an experiment in which one group was encouraged to smoke, and another not, and then to measure any effect on health would be unethical.

Correlations are a good basis for more rigorous experimental investigations to be carried out later on. Strong relationships between behaviours are always worth exploring in a more scientific fashion. We could conduct an experiment to discover what the cause might be behind any strong relationship suggested by a correlation. Using a correlation coefficient can also indicate and help you decide whether it is worth exploring the phenomenon further using the more controlled experimental method.

This is because techniques like Spearman's rho give you a *numerical* indication of the type and strength of relationship between two covariates (–1.0/+1.0). Inferential statistics like rho turn the descriptive data on your scattergram into *quantifiable* data, in the form of a correlation coefficient. This gives you more precise information to decide what to do next. A coefficient of near –1 or +1 would be worth investigating further, while a coefficient of say –0.2, or 0.3 would not.

Disadvantages of the correlational technique

The main disadvantage of the correlational technique is that it lacks the power and rigour of the experimental method in that it establishes *only* a relationship. It is a statistical technique that can never specify a cause and effect relationship between its covariates. This is in contrast to the experimental method, which as we will shortly discover does allow cause–effect conclusions to be reached – if they are scientifically justified.

Consequently, in a correlational study any apparent relationship that is suggested may well be due to factors *other* than those being claimed, as with our yogic flying/crime rate example earlier.

Graphical representations

Graphical representations refer to how information is visually displayed. This can be in a variety of forms.

Frequency distributions

If you have collected a set of scores from participants you could plot these results on a frequency distribution curve or chart.

There are of two kinds of frequency distributions - histograms and frequency polygons.

Histograms and frequency polygons

When you have a set of scores, you can illustrate their frequency distribution using a histogram or frequency polygon. A common name for a frequency polygon is a *line graph/curve.*

A histogram illustrates the number of times each value occurs in a data set. The frequency of such values must have originally been measured as interval data. If data has been collected in terms of categories, a histogram should show *frequencies* of occurrences for each of these categories. Plotting *frequencies* on the *y*-axis is the essential difference between a bar chart and a histogram. A histogram is a special type of bar chart.

A histogram uses the width of its bars to represent a class or type of information, and the height of its bars to represent their relative frequencies. The column width for each category interval is equal; consequently the area of the column is proportional to the number of cases it contains of the sample.

Here is an example.

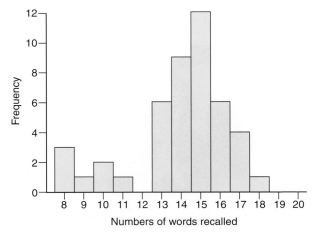

Figure 7.10 Histogram of memory scores (N = 15)

The width of each bar in the histogram above represents the number of words recalled by participants in a memory experiment, while the height of each bar illustrates the frequency of number of words recalled e. g. 8 words were recalled three times, 9 words once, 12 words never etc.

A histogram represents the frequency distribution of *all* data in continuous form, even those with zero values.

A variation of the histogram is the frequency polygon or line graph.

A frequency polygon or line graph has the same purpose as a histogram. A line graph illustrates the same frequency and distribution of data, but uses lines to connect the mid-points of each column plotted regards the frequencies of each class or value measured.

We can use a frequency polygon to illustrate the number of words recalled by participants in our memory experiment.

A frequency polygon or line graph also allows us to illustrate two or more sets of data in the one graph. This could be one line showing the frequency of scores got by participants in a test under Condition A of the independent variable, and another line showing the frequency of scores got by participants in the test under Condition B of the independent variable (Figure 7.11).

In both instances of the histogram and frequency polygon, the variable under investigation is laid out along the horizontal *x*-axis, while the frequency or number of times the variable occurred is laid out along the vertical *y*-axis.

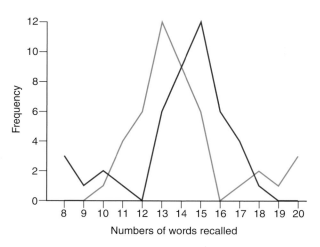

Figure 7.11 Frequency polygon of memory scores (*N* = 15)

It is important that you remember to *label* the axes of all your graphs so that others can understand your work.

Bar chart

As indicated above a histogram is a special type of bar chart. While the columns of a histogram must always represent *frequencies* of events, columns in a bar chart can show totals or percentages for each category of event, ratios, group means etc.

Unlike a histogram, with a bar chart each column is separated from one another. This is because each category on the *x-axis* is discrete from one another. There are no values that occur between them. In our example below a Monday is a Monday etc.

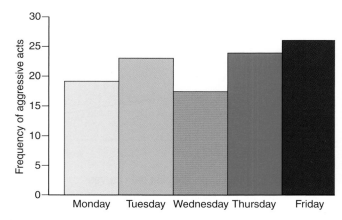

Figure 7.12 Bar chart illustrating number of aggressive acts observed in a primary school playground during one week.

A bar chart is also useful because it can illustrate data for only those categories in which a researcher is interested in comparing. With an eye to your Higher psychology research investigation a bar chart

would be an excellent descriptive statistic to show what happens under the different conditions of an independent variable in an experiment etc.

Data curves

If you have to take measurements of behaviour from the same participants at different points in time this information can be graphically represented using a data curve.

Below we can see a data curve illustrating the effect of different amounts of practice on the number of errors made in a mirror-writing task.

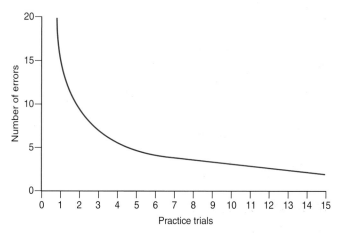

Figure 7.13 Data curve representing the effect of different amounts of practice on the number of errors made on a mirror-writing task

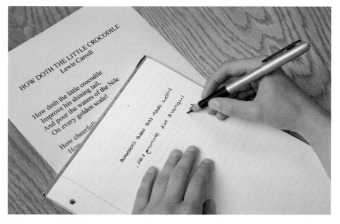

Figure 7.14 Mirror writing

It is clear from this data curve that participants made fewer errors as a consequence of the number of times they performed the mirror-writing task. In the first trial on average 20 errors were made. In the fifteenth trial on average one error was made. Practice did make perfect in this instance!

INTERACTIVES: GRAPHICAL REPRESENTATION

Look at the graph below and answer the questions that follow.

1 What does it represent?

2 What is the *x*-axis value?

3 What is the *y*-axis value?

4 Is this a bar chart or histogram? Give two reasons for your answer.

Answers on page 293.

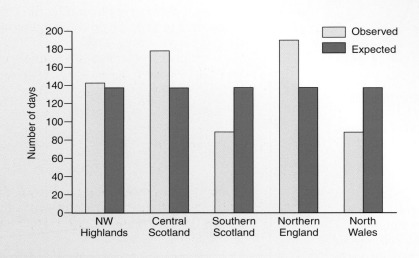

Figure 7.15 Days with snow cover

Overlapping data curves

You can also use *overlapping* data curves on the one graph to illustrate comparisons.

This allows us to illustrate two sets of results simultaneously.

In our example of an overlapping data curve the dark blue line represents the number of altruistic or helpful acts observed in one group of children over a four-week period after being shown a video that encouraged helping behaviour.

Alternatively, the light blue line represents the number of altruistic or helpful acts observed in another group of children over the same period who were shown a neutral video that did not show helpful or unhelpful behaviour.

If as in our example a relevant experiment has been conducted, both types of data curve allow us to see at a glance the effect the independent variable has had on the dependent variable over a particular period of time.

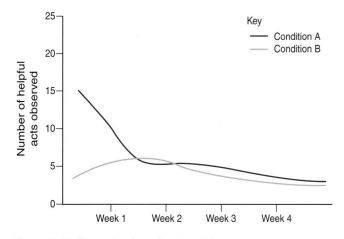

Figure 7.16 Example of overlapping data curves

In this case, we can see the number of helpful acts performed by Condition A children immediately increased after being shown the helping behaviour video. Over the next month we can also appreciate their helping behaviour reduced to a level close to that observed in the Condition B group children who had been shown the neutral behaviour video.

INTERACTIVES: GRAPHS

Please answer the following questions

1   What research method does Figure 7.16 suggest?

2   Look at the overlapping data curves and suggest an experimental hypothesis for this investigation.

3   What were the two conditions of the independent variable?

4   What was the dependent variable?

Answers on page 294.

Pie charts

Pie charts represent the proportion of all scores, values or number of times an event occurs that is got by various categories or classes in a piece of research.

This is illustrated below.

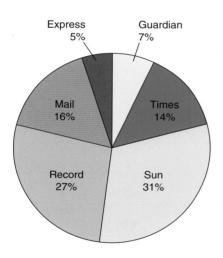

Figure 7.17 Percentage of people who spend more than ten minutes a day reading particular newspapers

To construct a pie chart wee need to know the total occurrences of the variable under investigation, and then how often it occurs for each group being studied.

Summarising results

Tables

The most basic way we present our information in psychological investigations is in table or tabular form. A hugely important table in our investigations is our *raw data table*.

Raw data are data that have not yet been summarised. Raw data are our initial measurements got from our participants prior to any calculations or graphical representations being done.

INTERACTIVES: PIE CHARTS

Make up a pie chart on student destination based on the following information.

There are 200 students in the fifth and sixth years at your school.

Sixty intend going into employment. Fifteen are going to University to study Criminology. Twenty-five are going to University to study Psychology. Thirty are going to University to study Arts.

Thirty-five are going to University to study Social Science. Five are going to University to study Geography. Ten are going to University to study History. Six are going to University to study French. Four are going to University to study Accountancy. Five are going to University to study Law. Five are going to University to study medicine.

See below an example of a raw data chart recording the number of eye contacts made by participants at one and three metres in a repeated measures design experiment.

The table reveals that more eye contacts were made at three metres than at one metre. Note that Participants are just numbered rather than named in our first column. Note further that each participant's scores are recorded under the two conditions of the independent variable.

Participants	Condition A at 1 metre	Condition at 3 metres
1	8	20
2	12	18
3	10	30
4	5	12
5	10	21

Table 7.14 Raw data table

INTERACTIVE: HISTOGRAMS AND FREQUENCY POLYGONS

Please study the table below.

Person	Height	Self-esteem
1	68	4.1
2	71	4.6
3	62	3.8
4	75	4.4
5	58	3.2
6	60	3.1
7	67	3.8
8	68	4.1
9	71	4.3
10	69	3.7

Person	Height	Self-esteem
11	68	3.5
12	67	3.2
13	63	3.7
14	62	3.3
15	60	3.4
16	63	4.0
17	65	4.1
18	67	3.8
19	63	3.4
20	61	3.6

Your first task is to create two histograms.

The first one is to illustrate the frequency of heights occurring in the data set. Remember that height is plotted on the *x*-axis, while the frequency of times a *particular* height occurs is plotted on the *y*-axis.

The second histogram will illustrate the frequency of self-esteem scores occurring in the data set. Remember that self-esteem score is plotted on the *x*-axis, while frequency of times a *particular* self-esteem score occurs on the *y*-axis.

When you have finished your two histograms please then draw a frequency polygon representing the same information.

In all instances remember to *label* your graph axes correctly. It is also a good idea to give each graph a *Legend*. Or an idea what it is the graph represents. This comes in the top right hand corner of your graph.

INTERACTIVES: THE CORRELATION

Covariate																				
Height	58																			75
Self-esteem	3.2																			4.4

There may well be a statistical relationship between height and self-esteem. Why don't you try and find out?

To discover if such a correlational research hypothesis is correct please complete the above data table. You will use this later to help you draw a scattergram. The first and last is done for you.

Now, letting height values equal the *x-axis* and self-esteem values equal the *y,* construct a scattergram to discover if any type of correlation exists between these two co-variables. Remember to insert your *line of best fit*.

What type of correlation have you discovered between height and self-esteem?

Do you think that there is a *direct* relationship between these two co-variables? Is the correlational hypothesis supported?

The research investigation

A major part of your Higher Psychology course demands that you carry out a Research Investigation. This is externally marked and goes towards your overall grade.

What you have learned previously in this Chapter will stand you in very good stead.

SQA change the Higher Psychology research investigation topics every year. It is **vital** that you liaise with your teacher or lecturer to complete essential paperwork, and to find out exactly what it is you need to do.

General advice

If you want to get as many marks as possible for your investigation then presentation is important.

While a number of exam boards say it can be handwritten, a typed report produced on a pc looks far better. You can also present superior graphical and numerical information.

Use a standard font throughout e.g. Times New Roman Size 12. Write on one side of the page only; use double margins and 1.5 line spacing.

ONLINE INTERACTIVES: GET THAT TODAY!

Before doing your research investigation download the Higher Psychology Investigating Behaviour Support Pack currently available from: **www.sfeu.ac.uk/subject_ networks/social_science/nq_psychology_supp ort_materials**

A direct link is available in the Chapter 7 section of the Higher Psychology Learning Suite at **www.gerardkeegan.co.uk**

Have a contents page correctly linked with appropriate page numbers inside. Make sure you have a detailed introduction and discussion.

Ensure your graphs are correctly labelled and identified, and any other numerical information given is both appropriate and correct.

It is essential to refer to your results in your discussion.

Be careful citing references.

How to write up the research investigation

Research is one of the most interesting aspects to the study of psychology. For a little while we get to be 'real psychologists'! The key to successful research investigations lies in thinking, feeling, and behaving like a scientist, which almost guarantees good marks at the end of the day.

A scientific report should contain the following sections:

➤ Title

➤ Abstract

➤ Introduction

➤ Method

➤ Design

➤ Participants

➤ Apparatus/materials

➤ Procedure

➤ Results

➤ Discussion

➤ Conclusion

➤ References

➤ Appendices

Let us now turn our attention to an example.

Title

'An investigation into the influence of gender on perceived intelligence.'

The title should be short and to the point. It should indicate the variables under investigation. In this *experiment* gender is the independent variable, perceived intelligence the dependent variable.

Prior to settling on the title as above, you would of course have done an extensive literature search to find out as much as possible about your topic. In our example you would have researched into gender, self-image, perception, and intelligence, and looked at for example:

Hogan, H. (1978). 'IQ self-estimates of males and females'. *Journal of Social Psychology*, 106, 137–8.

In doing so you will have discovered that Hogan (1978) reports on eleven different studies, which all made use of American college students. In some studies, participants were asked to estimate their own IQs, while in others, they were also asked to estimate their parents' IQs, and yet in others, the IQs of males and females in general.

Compared to the males, the females underestimated their IQ scores (50 per cent of the time significantly so), and nearly all believed their fathers had higher IQs than their mothers.

This hopefully would have prompted you to delve even deeper into the topic, and as a consequence you could also have read:

Furnham, A., & Rawles, R. (1995). 'Sex differences in the estimation of intelligence'. *Journal of Social Behaviour and Personality*, 10, 741–5.

And even:

Furnham, A., (2000) 'Parents' estimates of their own and their children's multiple intelligences'. *British Journal of Developmental Psychology*, 18, 583–94.

In so doing you would have come across lots of useful psychology that you would use in the introduction and discussion sections of your research investigation report. The whereabouts of these are found on your contents page. Here is an example.

Contents page

Contents	Page number
Abstract	1
Introduction	2
Method	3
Design	and so on
Participants	
Apparatus/materials	
Procedure	

Results

Discussion

Conclusion

References

Appendices

Make sure your page numbers on your contents page correspond with the page numbers used within the rest of your report!

Abstract

Your **abstract** should be about 250 words long. An abstract should succinctly summarise the aim, background; design; sample; measures; results and statistical conclusions of your study.

Write it in the past tense, and **please** avoid personal references like 'I'.

Your abstract should first state the aim of the study e.g., 'In the light of Hogan (1978) the aim of this investigation was to investigate the effect of gender on perceived intelligence.'

You should then state the **research hypothesis** H_1: 'That gender has an effect on perceived intelligence,' and whether or not this is a **one** or **two tailed hypothesis**. Our example is a two-tailed hypothesis. We are saying gender does have an effect on perceived intelligence, but not giving the direction of the expected effect.

Now tell the reader your research method by saying, as in this example, that this was an **experiment** using a **repeated measures design**. Identify the two conditions of your **independent variable** i.e. in condition A male and female participants were asked to judge their mother's IQ, while in condition B their father's.

You would then state that to eliminate **order effect**, **counterbalancing** was used using the **ABBA** procedure.

Now state how your **sample** was selected, the number of participants used, generally who they were, and where they were obtained. For example,

'Using opportunity sampling XX participants, comprising AA males, and BB females aged 16–18, were selected from S5 and S6 at Queen Margaret Academy, Ayr to participate in the study.'

Say that your results were analysed using **descriptive** statistics, and what type you used.

Conclude your abstract by stating your statistical conclusions, i.e. as in our example the **mean** and **median** values of IQ estimate in each condition. And say how these influenced results.

Say what this means i.e. if mean/median in one condition is higher than mean/median in the other then you can reject your null hypothesis H_0: 'That gender does not have any effect on perceived intelligence' and thus by **counter intuition** accept your research or experimental hypothesis H_1: 'That gender does have an effect on perceived intelligence.'

Alternatively if you think there is no difference between the two conditions of the IV you must say so, indicating what this means in the light of your hypotheses.

This would be to say that you accept the null hypothesis, and by counter-intuition reject the experimental.

A very useful tip is to write your abstract *after* you have written up the rest of the report. You will then be much better acquainted with its essential elements.

Introduction

An **introduction** must tell the reader a bit about the topic that is being investigated, and give an account of some relevant research.

An Introduction in a psychology report is shaped like a funnel going from the general at the beginning to the specific, or what it is **you** are actually investigating towards the end.

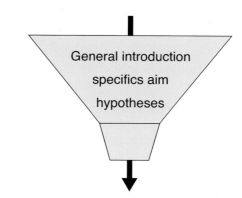

Figure 7.18 Introduction funnel

For your research investigation first tell the reader what it is about, and where you are coming from. If you were to do an investigation into gender and perceived intelligence you would first discuss what you mean by intelligence and perceived intelligence, then report on Hogan (1978) giving details of this work. You might then go on to generally explain sex-role stereotyping/gender, perception and the self-concept.

You conclude your introduction by telling the reader your aim and the **hypotheses**.

Your hypotheses could be:

Research hypothesis H_1: 'That gender has a effect on perceived intelligence.'

Null hypothesis H_0: 'That gender does not have an effect on perceived intelligence.'

Declare H_1 to be a two-tailed hypothesis, and say **why**. (NB No specific *direction* of results predicted).

Method

The method section concerns how we go about our research investigation.

Design

In this subsection you state the research method and design that used. Taking *our* example you would thus say that you used a repeated measures experimental design. Because it is an experiment you would also state the two conditions of the IV. Thus here, participants in Condition A first estimated their mother's and then their fathers IQ. Condition B participants first estimated their father's IQ and then their mother's.

Also in your design subsection when conducting an experiment identify your **dependent variable** or DV, which in this instance are individual participant's IQ estimates.

It is a good idea to then describe the design that you used.

Here you would say what a repeated measures design is, and how it was implemented. Give its advantages and disadvantages. As an RMD was used remember to also describe and explain the extraneous variable of order effect, and how using counterbalancing or the ABBA procedure this was overcome e. g. 50 per cent of participants underwent Condition A then B, while the other 50 per cent underwent Condition B then A.

Participants

Here you say how your sample was selected, in this example by using **opportunity sample**, why you used this method (availability!), how many

participants took part, and their make-up (i.e. males and females, ages, no prior knowledge of psychology etc.)

Apparatus

In an apparatus section you list all the apparatus used while conducting your research investigation. See below the apparatus that was used for our exemplar investigation into gender and perceived intelligence. You would have much the same thing.

- Consent form
- Standardised intelligence estimate forms A and B
- Debriefing statement
- Raw data table

Remember to indicate in your report at what page, and in what Appendix the consent form (*Appendix i*), the standardised intelligence estimate forms (*Appendix ii*), the raw data table (*Appendix iii*) and the debriefing statement (*Appendix iv*) can be found.

Note above that we have used lower case roman numerals to indicate each appendix. Please do the same in your research report for your Appendices.

Procedure

The procedure subsection is by far the most important part of any research investigation report. This is because anyone using the design, sampling technique and apparatus as indicated above should by following your procedure be able to replicate your experiment and come up with the same results.

If using your own questions to get for example participants to estimate their own IQ, it is wise to conduct a **pilot study** of them first. All this means is that you give your questions to six or so people, and ask them if they understand them. If they don't, you change them and pilot again until there is no ambiguity. In so doing you have standardised your questions. This is good practice.

If a psychologist in another research investigation has already used your questions, say so. State that they have been previously standardised by him or her.

If you do a pilot tell the reader in your procedure section that you did. Show off!

Remember that your procedure section tells a reader what happened with each participant from the minute they entered your laboratory until the minute they left.

Example of a procedure subsection

Procedure

An opportunity sample of XX participants was assembled at Loudoun Academy, Galston. They were then told the general purpose of the experiment, which was to estimate the IQ of another person. All were asked to complete a consent form (see *Appendix i*, Page 18) and informed that they could withdraw at that, or any other future stage.

Half of the sample was then taken into another room to undergo condition A of the independent variable. This was to estimate first their mother's intelligence quotient, and then their fathers. This they did using the standardised intelligence estimate forms (*Appendix ii*, Page 19)

The half that remained underwent condition B, which was to estimate first their father's intelligence, and then their mothers. This they did using the standardised intelligence estimate forms (*Appendix ii*, Page 19)

The dependent variable was measured in terms of the numerical response each participant estimated his or her parents' intelligence to be, and entered into the Raw Data Table (*Appendix iii*, Page 20).

On completion all participants were thanked for taking part in the experiment. All were given the debriefing statement (*Appendix iv*, Page 21), and advised that if they wished to read it a copy of the report would be available from any of the researchers from 30th April.

Participant	Gender Male/Female	Condition A IQ estimate mother	Condition B IQ estimate father
1	Male	102	106
2	Female etc.	100	110 etc.
3			
4			
5 etc.			

Table 7.15 Example of a raw data table

Results

This is the scary bit, but fear not!

What you do in a results section is present your results in a meaningful way, and then make some sense of them in the light of your null hypothesis. To do this at Higher level we use descriptive statistics. Before you do anything though, you need to have made up and completed a raw data table like the one above.

As suggested in the procedure make sure in any study you include a completed raw data table as an appendix.

It is always a good idea before you present a statistic in a results section to say what each statistical term means e.g. what *is* meant by the *mean* or *median*

of anything, what is the purpose of a histogram, frequency polygon, bar chart etc.

When you have a completed raw data table you can then begin to make statistical sense of it. In your results section you could for example:

➤ Work out the *mean* and *median* values of IQ estimate in each condition.

➤ Construct *histograms* of each gender's IQ estimate for each parent. Estimated IQ score would form the x-axis, the frequency or occurrences of an estimated IQ score the y-axis.

➤ Construct *frequency polygons* of each gender's IQ estimate for each parent. One line would form Condition A, the other Condition B.

➤ Construct a *bar chart* comparing male and female IQ estimates for their male and female parents. The *x*-axis would comprise of bars representing male and female participants' estimates of their mother's and father's IQ. The *y*-axis, the mean of the participants' IQ estimates for their male and female parents.

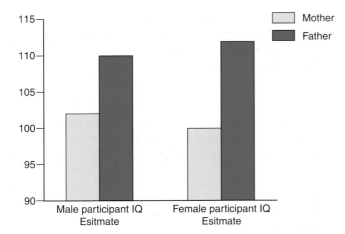

Figure 7.19 Example of a bar chart illustrating male and female IQ estimates for their mothers and fathers

Whatever you do make sure axes are labelled; the diagram is given a name, and a figure number etc.

Discussion

A discussion is as structured as any other section of your report. Certain elements are meant to be in it. If they aren't you lose valuable marks. This would be a pity after all your hard work! To avoid this make sure you write it in something like the following sequence.

Refer back to your introduction, briefly reminding the reader the purpose of your investigation.

Tell the reader what your results are (e.g. mother/father mean and median scores) and using our IQ example discuss what this all means.

a) In the light of your hypotheses, (null and experimental).

b) In the light of Hogan (1978).

c) In the light of comparable studies as reported by Furnham (1995, 2000) etc.

Then explain your findings referring to some psychology e.g. intelligence, sex-role stereotyping/gender, perception and the self-concept.

It is also useful in a discussion section to refer to your descriptive statistics (graphs and charts) to back up what you say – otherwise what was the point of doing them! Use language like 'As can be seen from Figure x on page y, ….'

Identify shortcomings in your investigation e.g. disadvantages with your design, method, sampling technique etc.

Identify remedies/suggest improvements on these for the future. It may for example have been better to use an independent groups design. If so, say so and why.

It may have been better to use a larger more representative sample, using a more robust sampling method. Again if so, say so and why etc.

If you only used a sample of S5 and S6, your results can only at this stage be generalised to the whole population of S5/S6 in your school. Nobody else. You may wish to avoid this in the future. If so, say so and why etc.

Finally, try to identify future research you might like to do. Pose other research questions like 'As a consequence of this study an interesting avenue to explore in the future would be whether there is a gender influence on perceived IQ evident across all age groups in society.'

You have now just about finished your research investigation report.

Lastly comes your conclusion.

Conclusion

Your Conclusion section is a brief non-numerical statement on your findings. Here is an example of a full mark conclusion in a psychology practical investigation.

It would be a good idea at Higher level to do something very similar!

References

This is where you state in the globally accepted format known as the Harvard referencing system the primary source of any psychologist, psychological theory, or study directly referred to in your report.

If you, for example, used a statistics book to help you do your 'sums' this would go in a bibliography underneath the reference section.

Where things go e.g. surnames first, initials etc. is the Harvard Referencing system. Also note that

Conclusion

This experiment was based on J. Ridley Stroop's (1935) study on interference on serial verbal reactions. Its aim was to determine whether interference could influence performance on a recall task.

Analysis of recorded results gave a mean value in Condition A of 14 seconds, and mean value in Condition B of 18 seconds. The median in Condition A was 14 seconds while in Condition B was 18 seconds. This allowed rejection of the null hypothesis and acceptance of the experimental hypothesis H_1: 'That there will be a difference in participants' information processing times under two conditions of the independent variable as a consequence of the Stroop Effect.'

These results support the findings of J. Ridley Stroop (1935) and conclude that interference does influence performance on a serial recall task.

References

McLeod, G.M. (1991) Half a century of research on the Stroop Effect: an integrative review. *Psychological Bulletin* 109, 163 – 203.

Stroop, JR. (1935) Studies of interference in serial verbal reactions. *Journal of Experimental Psychology* 18, 643 – 622.

Bibliography

Atkinson et al. (1990) *Hilgard's Introduction to Psychology*, Harcourt College Publishers.

Cardwell, M. (2000) *The Complete A – Z Psychology Handbook*, Hodder and Stoughton.

Coolican, H. (1999) *Research Methods and Statistics in Psychology*, Hodder and Stoughton.

Eysenck, MW. (1999) *Principles of Cognitive Psychology*, Psychology Press.

Gleitman, H. (1991) *Psychology*, W.W. Norton & Company.

references to journal articles are cited slightly differently from references taken from books. The use of italics as below is thus deliberate. If worried about references talk to your local/school/college/university librarian. They are your resident experts on such things as this.

Last of all in a psychology report is your appendix.

Appendix

An **appendix** is where you have your raw data chart, measures of central tendency/dispersion calculations, materials, consent form etc.

Enumerate and label each element e.g. Appendix *iv* 'Measures of central tendency calculations'.

Note the use of *roman numerals* to identify each appendices. Please do the same.

Make sure each appendix has a page number which corresponds with your contents page e.g. On the contents page you would see 'Measures of central tendency calculations page 14'.

If you have adhered to what is said above you should get a good mark in your investigation.

But to make this even more certain it is recommend that you cannot read and edit it often enough before you hand it in. You want to produce something that could be published. If you intend going on to study psychology at University, a good report taken along to an interview is brilliant psychology to smooth your path into a faculty! Show it to the interviewer and they will be very impressed. They may ask you questions about it – so make sure you refresh your memory about what you did.

1   Go to the Higher Psychology Learning Suite at **www.gerardkeegan.co.uk**. Click Chapter 7 'Investigating Behaviour: Analysing Data and the Research Investigation' to access direct links to all websites mentioned in this chapter.

2   Go to the Higher Psychology Learning Suite at **www.gerardkeegan.co.uk**. Click Chapter 7 'Investigating Behaviour: Analysing Data and the Research Investigation' and do the online interactive crossword. But don't cheat!

3   Go to the Higher Psychology Learning Suite at **www.gerardkeegan.co.uk**. Click Chapter 7 'Investigating Behaviour: Analysing Data and the Research Investigation' and do the online interactive hangman game. Try and beat the executioner!

4   Go to the Higher Psychology Learning Suite at **www.gerardkeegan.co.uk**. Click Chapter 7 'Investigating Behaviour: Analysing Data and the Research Investigation' and print off the hard copy crossword. When finished you might like to hand it into your teacher as homework.

5   Go to the Higher Psychology Learning Suite at **www.gerardkeegan.co.uk**. Click Chapter 7 'Investigating Behaviour: Analysing Data and the Research Investigation' and do the online interactive quiz. Try and win the prize!

GLOSSARY

Abstract: An abstract is a summary of the important points found in a psychology research report. It should be about 250 words long, and should succinctly summarise the aim, background; design; sample; measures; results and statistical conclusion of your study. Write an abstract in the past tense, and avoid personal references like 'I'.

Aim: The aim of your investigation should be found at the end of the introduction section in your research report. Your aim concludes with the proper presentation of your null and experimental hypotheses. For further details see 'null hypothesis'.

Apparatus: In the method section of a psychology research investigation you would have the subheading 'apparatus'. Here you list any apparatus you used in your investigation.

Appendix: This is the last section in a research investigation where you have the likes of your raw data chart,

apparatus, mean, median, materials, consent form, debriefing forms etc.

Case study: A non-experimental research method used in psychology, the others being the observational, survey, and interview methods of enquiry. A case study is a detailed in-depth investigation of a single case happening concerning a person, a family, an organisation, or an event. Because of its interest in the single case the case study is idiographic in nature. It is a method of enquiry that generates rich, mostly qualitative, descriptive detail about a unique individual, episode, situation etc.

Conclusion: Your conclusion section in your research investigation is a brief non-numerical statement on your findings.

Confounding variables: These are variables that if anticipated could be controlled in an experimental situation. If they are not controlled they can give rise to an alternative explanation of results. Examples of confounding

variables would be situational variables and participant variables.

Correlation coefficient: A statistical sum that calculates the strength and degree of relationship between two seemingly unconnected events.

Consent: A big issue in psychology investigations! So make sure you prove you have it in your Higher psychology research investigation report.

Contents: Different examination bodies/institutions may have slightly different requirements as to the contents, or what should be contained in your psychology research reports. The layout in this Chapter is one that is globally recognised. Yours should be very similar. A contents page should obviously indicate where in a report things can be found.

Correlation: A correlation is a technique that tries to establish a statistical relationship between two covariables/covariates. An example of a correlation would be the relationship statisticians have found between smoking and cancer. A correlation can be illustrated using a descriptive statistic called a scattergram, and also measured using an inferential statistic like Spearman's rho.

Counterbalancing and ABBA: Counterbalancing is used to overcome order effect in a repeated measures design experiment. Counterbalancing helps control for practice, fatigue, or boredom when participants are exposed to the measure of performance or dependent variable on second and subsequent manipulations of the independent variable. Counterbalancing uses the ABBA procedure to control for order effect in a repeated measures design experiment. This is where half of the participants undergo Condition A followed by Condition B, while the other half undergo Condition B followed by Condition A of the independent variable.

Counter-intuition: Used in experiments, and is a hallmark of the experimental method. In an experiment if the null hypothesis is found to be untrue, our experimental or research hypothesis by counter-intuition is supported. Alternatively if the null hypothesis is found to be true, by counter-intuition our experimental hypothesis is rejected.

Covariables: Also known as covariates are independent behaviours etc. studied using the correlational technique.

Debriefing: Another issue regarding ethics. All who take part in psychological research deserve to find out what it was all about! This is often done at a debriefing, where, after an experiment, a participant is told about its true purpose, what it was all about, and when/where they can find out the results of the investigation proper.

Demand characteristics: Orne (1962) writes that demand characteristics are any features of an experiment, which help participants work out what is expected of them, and consequently lead them to behave in an artificial and unnatural way. These features demand a certain response. Participants search for cues in the experimental environment about how to behave and what might be expected of them. This sees them behave in an unnatural way and skews results.

Dependent variable: In an experiment the dependent variable is the one that is measured or observed as a consequence of changing or manipulating the independent variable. The dependent variable is the *effect* of any change or manipulation.

Descriptive statistics: This is the name given to numerical or graphical statistics that we use to describe or summarise any data we generate in our research.

Descriptive *numerical* statistics are those that indicate averages in data. These include such 'sums' as the mean, median, mode and standard deviation. Descriptive *graphical* statistics include graphs, charts, histograms, bar charts, frequency polygons, and scattergrams etc.

Design: The design is the research method you adopt. Research methods in psychology fall into two categories, those that adopt an experimental design and those that are non-experimental in design. Only the laboratory, field and quasi-experiment are experimental in design. Observation, interview, case study, and the survey are non-experimental. The reason is that the latter do not have an independent variable. The researcher in non-experimental procedures changes or manipulates nothing. As a result you can never make any cause-effect conclusions in non-experimental research. There is no IV if you use a non-experimental design.

Discussion: The part of a research investigation report where you refer back to your introduction, briefly reminding the reader the purpose of your investigation. Tell the reader what your results are and discuss what this all means.

Ecological validity: Laboratory experiments can often be accused of lacking in ecological validity. They do not reflect a real-life situation. This is a problem for psychology in that it is a subject interested in our real-life everyday behaviours. Lab experiments by their very nature often get human participants behaving in an abnormal manner. This leads to distorted data, and thus weak psychological conclusions.

Ethics: Rules, values and principles.

Expectancy effect: As you should have read earlier in this Chapter, expectancy effect was discovered by Rosenthal and Fode (1963) and is a great example of experimenter bias!

Experiment: An experiment is a scientific procedure that adheres to the experimental method of research. An experiment in psychology is the only research method that can claim a cause and effect relationship between two variables. The experimental method is thus a controlled procedure involving the manipulation of an independent variable (IV) in order to observe or measure its effect on a dependent variable (DV). The experimental method is particularly popular within the biological, cognitive and behaviourist perspectives, or approaches, in psychology. There are three types of experiments that use the experimental method, namely the laboratory experiment, the field experiment, and the quasi-experiment. The essential difference is their location, and thus the degree of control the experimenter has over variables.

Experimental hypothesis: Is a testable statement of cause and effect between IV and DV, and is used in laboratory, field, and quasi-experiments.

Experimental method: The method of scientific enquiry in psychology, the experimental method involves the strict control, observation and measurement of variables.

Extraneous variables: Variables, or things from the outside that can contaminate a piece of research. Extraneous variables give rise to alternative explanations for your results.

Field experiment: Like a laboratory experiment, the field experiment also sees the manipulation of an independent variable and the consequent/observation/measure-ment of a dependent variable. The difference is that a field experiment takes place *away* from a laboratory, most often in the participants' natural environment like a school classroom, a playground, or the street.

Hawthorne Effect: Also known as participant expectancy, the Hawthorne Effect is a type of confounding variable associated with the participant, and was discovered in 1939 by Roethlisberger and Dickson. Participant expectancy or the Hawthorne Effect is a very good example of demand characteristics in an experiment.

Histogram: A histogram is a descriptive statistic used to represent data in a meaningful way.

Hypothesis/hypotheses: a testable statement.

Idiographic: Unique to the individual.

Independent variable: An independent variable only occurs in an experiment, and is the variable an experimenter *changes or manipulates* to see what influence or affect this has on a dependent variable.

Inferential statistic: Inferential statistics are used to make inferences about a target population on the basis of data got from your sample. Inferential statistics are used to determine whether your results occurred by chance or random factor. Inferential statistics allow us to find out if our results are statistically significant (if there is a real effect/relationship, rather than a chance one), and allow us to reject or accept our null hypothesis. Using counter-intuition we can then accept or reject our research hypothesis.

Interview: A non-experimental research method used in psychological research. The interview method of research is a conversation with a purpose. The interviewer in one-to-one conversation collects detailed personal information from individuals using oral questions. The interview is used widely to supplement and extend our knowledge about individual(s) thoughts, feelings and behaviours. Or how they think *they* feel and behave.

Introduction: In a psychology research report your introduction must tell the reader a bit about the topic that is being investigated, and give an account of relevant research. An introduction in a psychology report is shaped like a funnel going from the general at the beginning to the specific, such as your aim or what it is you are investigating towards the end.

Laboratory experiment: A laboratory experiment involves the manipulation of an independent variable and the consequent

observation/measurement of a dependent variable. Laboratory experiments take place in the closed, heavily controlled setting of a psychology laboratory, most often found in universities.

Level of significance: A level of significance is the bet a researcher places that their results are 'real' and did not occur by chance or random factor. The level of significance is found within your null hypothesis. The convention in psychology is to opt for a 0.05 level of significance. 0.05 means that even if your results allow you to reject the null hypothesis you still accept a 1 in 20 probability that your results occurred by chance or random factor.

Line graph: A line graph is a descriptive statistic used to represent data in a meaningful way.

Mean: A statistical term for the arithmetic average.

Median: A statistical term for another type of average. The median is the middle score in a set of data.

Method: A method section in a psychology report is a heading that refers to how you conducted your research. Indented underneath come four sub-headings: design; participants/subjects; apparatus; and procedure.

Non-experimental method(s): This category of research in psychology includes the observational, interview, survey and case-study methods of research. They are 'non-experimental' in design because there is no independent variable involved. As a result no cause–effect conclusions can be drawn when using a non-experimental method of research.

Negative correlation: A negative correlation is said to exist when as one covariate increases the other covariate decreases. An excellent example of a negative correlation would be number of hours spent socialising by a group of students and their eventual examination mark. Going out too much seriously jeopardises your examination success.

Null hypothesis: A research statement of no observed effect between two variables or covariates, used by both the experimental method and correlational technique. Take the following examples of a null and experimental hypothesis in an experiment. Also note how you write an experimental/null hypothesis.

Null hypothesis H_0: 'That gender does not have an effect on perceived intelligence.'

Experimental hypothesis H_1: 'That gender does have an effect on perceived intelligence.'

An example of a correlational null hypothesis would be:

Null Hypothesis H_0: 'That there is no relationship between hours spent studying and examination performance.'

Correlational hypothesis H_1: 'That there is a relationship between hours spent studying and examination performance.'

Observational method: A non-experimental design in psychology where the researcher plans, observes, and later analyses behaviours as they occur in a natural setting.

One-tailed hypothesis: In experiments, we have an experimental or research hypothesis. These can be one-tailed or two tailed. A one-tailed experimental hypothesis is one that is uni-directional. *You are predicting the direction you expect the effect to be* as a consequence of the manipulation of your independent variable. Take the experimental hypothesis H_1: '*That alcohol has an adverse influence on driver performance*.' This is a one-tailed hypothesis because of the use of the word 'adverse'. You are indicating that alcohol will have a *negative* influence or effect on driver performance. When you do not predict the direction you expect the effect to go this is called a two-tailed hypothesis.

Opportunity sample: One of the methods available to us to get a sample of people from a target population to take part in our research. It is the most favoured of sampling methods used by psychology students because it is dead easy! An opportunity sample is quite simply those who are/were available to take part in your research. If you were running an experiment and needed 20 people to take part in it, going into various college/school classes and getting the first 20 folk you come across would be an example of an opportunity sample.

Order effect: Order effect is one type of extraneous variable that can arise in an experiment as a result of using a repeated measures design. Order effect occurs when participants' performance is influenced by practice, fatigue or boredom! This can be as a result of being asked to do the same thing twice, as in the repetition of a measure of performance. Order effect could occur in our alcohol/driving performance example. By using the same group of people in both conditions of the IV (alcohol/no alcohol) their performance on the driving simulation test could be influenced the second time around by previous past experience of the first time they did the test. Order effect can be controlled using a procedure called counterbalancing.

Operationalisation: concerns agreeing a precise definition of our variables in research, and then finding a suitable measure of their occurrence. This can be difficult. Consider the concept of 'intelligence'. What is intelligence? Can intelligence be measured?

Participants/subjects: In a research investigation detail of participants or subjects should be given under this subheading as part of your method. A *participant* in a psychology investigation is a *person*, while a *subject* is an *animal*. In a participant subsection, you would indicate the number of people who helped you in your research, how many were male, how many female, ages/age range, and any other pertinent detail about them. Personal stuff like participants' names should never be given.

Participant variables: An important extraneous variable that concerns the peculiarities individuals bring to the research situation. These '*participant variables*' can give rise to alternative explanations for your results and conclusions.

Pilot study/pilot survey: Essentially a 'dummy run' of your research. If you were conducting a survey you would get half a dozen people to complete your survey form. Their job is to tell you about any ambiguities they find, or any improvements they think could be made. You take their advice on board and pilot until you get something useful.

Procedure: This is the most crucial subsection of the method section of any psychology research report. It comes after stating your design, participants/subjects and apparatus. Anyone using the same design, sampling technique and apparatus should by following your procedure be able to replicate your research and come up with the same results. In your procedure section tell the reader exactly what you did from the minute they entered your 'laboratory' until the minute they left. Then say

you thanked your participants, that they were debriefed (given the true purpose and nature of the study), and that they got a chance to themselves read your report at a later date.

Population/target population: A population is a particular group of people that have something in common. In psychological research the target population is the one from which a sample of participants in psychological research is drawn. It is the population to which a researcher wants to generalise their results. This is only possible if the sample selected is representative of the target population.

Positive correlation: As one covariate increases in one direction, so does the other, e.g. number of hours studied/examination mark.

Probability: The likelihood of events occurring by chance or random factor.

Qualitative data: Descriptive information.

Quantitative data: Numerical information.

Quantitative analysis: Analysis of numerical information.

Raw data: Raw data is the information you collect regards participant performance in a research investigation. An example of raw data would be the time it takes a participant to read a word list. This should be entered into a *pre-prepared* raw data chart. In Higher psychology research investigations your raw data chart helps forms the basis of your descriptive statistics.

References: This is where you state in the globally accepted format known as the Harvard referencing system the primary source of any psychologist, psychological theory, or study directly referred to in the text.

Reliability: A major question of research, which asks if the research

is investigating what it claims it is investigating.

Repeated measures design: A within-subjects experimental design that repeats the measure of performance or DV with all participants.

Representative/representative sample: Reflecting a target population.

Research hypothesis: a research prediction or statement.

Results: In a results section of a research investigation you present your raw data in a statistically meaningful way, which if doing an experiment or correlation allows you to accept or reject your null hypothesis, and then by counter-intuition, reject or accept your research hypothesis. To do this, use some descriptive statistics.

Sample: Participants/subjects who take part in an investigation got from a target population.

Sampling bias: Where participants/subjects who make up a research sample don't mirror the target population. This makes generalisation of results onto the target population questionable.

Scattergram: A graphical representation of a correlation between two covariates.

Situational variables: Types of extraneous confounding variable found in the experimental setting. Situational variables influence behaviour/performance of participants over and above any manipulations of the independent variable, and include such things as temperature, lighting, background noise etc. The researcher controls such situational variables by keeping them constant.

Spatio-temporal: Something such as a quasi-experiment that takes place at one particular time and place.

Standardised/standardisation: To

ensure better control in psychological research it is important that any instructions or questions given to participants are standardised. This means that all receive the same instructions or questions after they have been rigorously checked for ambiguity before the research itself takes place. This is done using a pilot study.

Survey: The non-experimental survey method of research asks a representative sample of people oral or written questions to find out about their attitudes, behaviours, beliefs, opinions, and values.

Target population: The wider population from which a research sample is drawn and onto which one can then generalise any results.

Title: The title of a research investigation should reflect what it is about. It should be short, and indicate the area of psychology that is being investigated e. g. 'An investigation into serial verbal reactions: the Stroop Effect' etc.

Trend line: A trend line is the 'line of best fit' drawn to illustrate the type and direction of statistical relationship, or correlation, found between two covariates in a descriptive statistic called a scattergram.

Two-tailed hypothesis: In experiments we have an experimental or research hypothesis. These can be one-tailed or two tailed. A two-tailed hypothesis is one that is non-directional. If present in an experimental hypothesis you would be are predicting an effect, but not the direction you expect the effect to go. Take the experimental hypothesis H_1: '*That gender has an influence on perceived intelligence.*' This is a two-tailed hypothesis in that while you are predicting gender will have an influence on perceived intelligence of oneself/another, you

are not predicting whether the effect of gender will be positive or negative. When you do predict the direction you expect the effect to go this is called a one-tailed hypothesis.
Validity: Another question of research, which asks if the research is consistently investigating what it claims to be investigating.
Variables: Literally anything whose value can change e.g. temperature, heart rate, score on an IQ test, etc. There are three main kinds of variable in experimental research, i.e. independent, dependent and extraneous variables.

Volunteer bias: An interesting extraneous variable. Volunteers in psychological research have personal characteristics that set them apart from individuals in the general population. Thus they are not representative of the population upon whom you may wish to generalise your results.
Within-subjects design: An experimental design situation where each participant provides data for all manipulations of the independent variable. An example of a within-subject design is a repeated measures design.

X-axis: Name given to horizontal line that runs along the bottom of a graphical descriptive statistic like a histogram or scattergram.
Y-axis: Name given to vertical line that runs from top to bottom at the left-hand side of a graphical descriptive statistic such as a histogram or a scattergram.

Answers

Interactive: Nominal, ordinal, interval p.262

1 Nominal

2 Ordinal

3 Ordinal

4 Interval

5 Nominal

6 Interval

7 Nominal

Interactive: Median p.263

First put words recalled in ascending order:

| 5 | 5 | 5 | 6 | 6 | 7 | 7 |
| 8 | 8 | 9 | | | | |

As this is an even distribution of ten scores, to calculate the median find and add up the *two* middle scores, and then divide by two:

$$\frac{(6 + 7)}{2} = 6.5$$

Consequently the median number of words recalled by participants in our experiment into STM is 6.5.

Interactive: Range p.264

The range is 86 − 57 +1 = 30

Interactive: Standard deviation p.266

First calculate the mean:

$$\frac{2 + 3 + 3 + 5 + 8 + 9}{6} = 5$$

Then

$$\sum(x - \bar{x})^2 = (-3)^2 + (-2)^2 + (-2)^2 + (0)^2 + (3)^2 + (4)^2$$
$$= 9 + 4 + 4 + 0 + 9 + 16 = 42$$

$$\frac{\sum(x - \bar{x})^2}{N} = \frac{42}{6} = 7$$

$$S = \sqrt{\frac{\sum(x - \bar{x})^2}{N}} = \sqrt{7} \text{ (standard deviation)}$$

$$\sqrt{7} = 2.6$$

Consequently the standard deviation of scores from the mean for this data set varies on average by 2.6.

Interactive: Graphical representation p.278

1 The graph represents the number of days of expected/observed snowfall in five areas of the UK.

2 The *x*-axis value is the five different areas of the UK.

3 The *y*-axis value is the number of days snow was expected or observed in each of these five areas.

4 This is a bar graph because each value on the *x*-axis is illustrated as separate and discrete from one other. Central Scotland is not Southern Scotland etc. Further, snowfall is recorded on the *y*-axis in terms of 'number of days' rather than frequency of occurrence.

Interactive: Graphs p.279

1   An experiment.

2   Something like H_1: 'That altruism in children can be encouraged as a consequence of observing it in others.'

3   The control condition of the IV was one group watched a neutral video; the experimental condition of the IV was the other group watched an altruistic video.

4   The DV was recorded observations of helping behaviour seen in the children over a four-week period.

CHAPTER EIGHT

Social Psychology: Conformity, Obedience and Prejudice

BY THE END OF THIS CHAPTER YOU SHOULD BE ABLE TO: TOPICS
- Demonstrate a knowledge and understanding of conformity, obedience, and prejudice.
- Analyse and evaluate conformity, obedience and prejudice.

Before beginning our study of *conformity, obedience and prejudice* let us first examine their parent domain social psychology.

What is social psychology?

Baron, Byrne and Suls (1989) tell us that social psychology is 'the scientific field that seeks to understand the nature and causes of individual behaviour in social situations'.

Social psychology sees us study human behaviour in its social context. Social psychology is the domain, or area, in psychology that examines our thoughts, feelings and behaviours as influenced by social phenomena.

Consequently social psychology explains our behaviour as the interaction between our mental state and our immediate social situation.

This is illustrated by Kurt Lewin's heuristic, or *rule of thumb*, where $B = f(P, E)$.

This simply means that for social psychology, behaviour (B) is a function (f) of the person (P) and their environment (E) (Lewin, 1951).

The historical roots of social psychology

Historically, social psychology originates from the work of eminent philosophers and social scientists

such as Aristotle, John Locke, David Hume, Jean Jacques Rousseau, James Mill, Jeremy Bentham, and Auguste Comte.

Aristotle (384–322 BC) studied crowd behaviour at chariot races. He can be thought of as the world's first social psychologist.

John Locke (1632–1704) saw the human mind as being active rather than passive. He believed that when born our mind is *tabula rasa*, or 'like a clean slate'. Essentially there is little in it.

Locke said that we then learn to think, feel and behave as we do because we form representations in our mind about our world. These representations, or ideas about our external reality, come to us as a result of sensory experience. He laid the foundations of **associationism**, later developed by Jean Jacques Rousseau and James Mill.

Associationism is the notion that two cognitions, or thoughts, when put together are greater than each alone.

Auguste Comte (1789–1857) was fascinated with the sociology of power, leadership and authority. In the context of social psychology he is best remembered as being the first thinker to apply the scientific method to the social world. He thought that all knowledge should derive from scientific discoveries. He promoted objectivity in the research process by founding **positivism**.

Social psychology is the study of human behaviour in its social context. It involves the scientific investigation of how our thoughts [cognitions]; feelings [emotions] and behaviours [observable] are influenced by the actual, imagined or implied presence of others.

With growing confidence such thinkers asserted that human social cognition and related behaviour could be studied scientifically.

As a result social psychology favours the experimental method of research. This is because it likes to generate empirical evidence for its theories. The first social psychologist to use the experimental method was the American Norman Triplett.

Social facilitation and the experimental method

Triplett studied **social facilitation**. Social facilitation concerns what happens to our behaviours when individuals join together with other individuals.

Triplett (1898) was interested in how the presence of others influenced performance on a task. Using people such as cyclists and schoolchildren, Triplett discovered that it took the presence of just one other person to influence another individual's behaviour.

In a number of field experiments Triplett discovered that individual performance among competitive cyclists varied depending upon the type of race they were in. The *types* of race in which they competed were the different conditions of his independent variable.

In general, the fastest speeds were obtained when cyclists were pitted against one another. The worst performances occurred when a cyclist raced only against the clock. Triplett discovered that it was the *physical* presence of other competitors that contributed to such differences in individual performance.

Triplett then got school-age children to turn a fishing reel as fast as possible for a short period of time. He found that when the children worked in pairs their performance was superior to when they worked alone.

ONLINE INTERACTIVES

Read all about the first social psychology experiment into social facilitation conducted by Norman Triplett in 1898. Go to:

www.psychclassics.yorku.ca/Triplett/

A direct link is available in the Chapter 8 section of the Higher Psychology Learning Suite at **www.gerardkeegan.co.uk**

'The imagined or implied presence of others'

The famous American psychologist Gordon Allport (1897–1967) helps focus our study in that he tells us that social psychology investigates human behaviour in its social context.

For him, social psychology is 'the scientific investigation of how the thoughts, feeling and behaviours of individuals are influenced by the actual, imagined or implied presence of others' (Allport, 1935).

The term '*imagined*…presence of others' suggests that our behaviour is prone to the influence of others even when no other people are present. An example would be when we are watching television.

The '*implied* presence…of others' concerns why we act as we do because of the position, or role, we have in a society, culture, or subculture.

Social interaction

Social psychology concerns the cognitive, affective and conative outcomes of our interactions with others. Our social interactions are all about our social relationships with others. These get us to think, feel, and behave in particular ways. Social interactions happen in different physical, social and cultural contexts, all of which have an impact on how we behave, or act. Take the following.

The physical context

The environment around us, or the *physical context*, affects our social interactions. Different environments direct us to behave in particular ways.

Please do the Interactive below to appreciate this.

The social context

Our social interactions are further determined by
psychological mechanisms that become associated
with the situations where we find ourselves. These
mechanisms include scripts, roles, social schemata,
and social identity.

Scripts

A 'script' is a recognised and agreed way of acting in
a particular situation.

Investigated by Schank and Abelson (1977), a script
is a planned sequence of behaving, which we follow
automatically.

Like the lines of a play, scripts help regulate
behaviour. Scripts are particularly useful in awkward
social situations.

We learn 'the script' on the basis of experience.

Roles

Roles concern the parts we play in our world. Roles
can be likened to the characters actors play in a
drama. A role is an expected pattern of behaviour
that becomes associated with a person, or the
position they hold in society.

We play many different roles in the course of a day.
Almost simultaneously we can be a son, a daughter,
a brother, a sister, a mum, a dad, a partner, a
customer, a student, a teacher, a patient etc. These
see us become that particular character, and we
adopt the behaviours to suit.

Social roles are reciprocal, or two-way. When we are
in a particular social role the person with whom we
are engaging is in another. Examples would be
mum–son; dad–daughter; brother–sister;
husband–wife; teacher–student etc.

There are two types of roles, formal roles and
informal roles.

Formal roles

Formal roles are associated with a job or position in
society. Examples would be doctor, nurse, teacher,
police officer, psychologist etc.

An institution, organisation, professional body, or the
government very often define the expected pattern
of behaviour that goes along with such a formal role.

Take for example the influence of the British Medical
Association, the Royal College of Nursing, the
General Teaching Council, the Home Office, and the
British Psychological Society, and how each affects
the formal roles indicated above.

Informal roles

As groups *coalesce*, or come together, the informal
roles that people adopt become evident.

It is useful to know that an informal role is different
from a formal role, such as a chairperson secretary,
or treasurer. Individuals who take on informal roles
in a group are not elected, appointed, or otherwise
designated. They can however exert a bigger
influence on their group, and the group process,
than do those in more formal roles (Vrchota, 2005).
This influence can be either constructive
or destructive.

Mudrack and Farrell (1995) identify three types of informal roles that we as individuals adopt in a group or team situation. These are task-roles, maintenance roles, and disruptive roles.

Task roles

Task roles are informal roles that help move a group or team towards achieving their goal.

A task-role orientated member is the person who is focused on getting things done. They would say, for example, 'We've been discussing this for an hour and I don't hear any new ideas. Are we ready to come to a decision?'

According to Mudrack and Farrell (1995) task roles include:

➤ The '*information seeker*': this is the person who asks for clarification and seeks ideas and input from other group members.

➤ The '*opinion seeker*': this is the person who encourages other group members to express their viewpoints.

➤ The '*information giver*': this is the person who provides information on the basis of their experience or expertise.

➤ The '*initiator–contributor*': this is the person who offers many ideas and suggests the group or team consider moving in new directions.

Maintenance roles

Maintenance roles are informal roles that focus on social interactions within the group or team.

An example would be where a maintenance role member notices another group member looking puzzled, and asks how he or she feels about what is being discussed. People who adopt maintenance roles are socio-emotive in orientation. They aim to be friendly and supportive of others in order to keep harmony within the group.

Examples of maintenance roles identified by Mudrack and Farrell (1995) are:

➤ The '*supporter–encourager*': this is the person who praises others' ideas, and encourages quiet members to join in the discussion.

➤ The '*harmoniser–tension reliever*': this is the person who encourages members who are in conflict with one another to reconcile their differences. They often do this by making a funny observation, or cracking a joke.

➤ The '*feeling-expresser*': this is the person who is sensitive to the climate within the group or team, and suggests having a break when everyone's energy begins to fade.

Disruptive roles

Disruptive roles are informal roles that some adopt to promote their own individual needs or goals. Disruptive role behaviours interfere with a group or team's needs or goals.

An example of someone adopting a disruptive role would be the group member who spends time discussing a personal issue. Another example would be the group member who jokes, or carries on to the detriment of the group or team process.

Mudrack and Farrell (1995) classify disruptive roles as:

➤ The '*stage hog*': this is the person who prevents others from expressing their opinions by commandeering the discussion.

➤ The '*clown*': this is the person who continually fools around to interrupt and disrupt group or team business.

➤ The '*cynic*': this is the person who focuses on negatives and finds faults in everything.

➤ The '*blocker*': this is the person who continuously throws up barriers to group or team ideas in order to frustrate the decision-making process.

INTERACTIVES

Do you adopt a task role, maintenance role, or disruptive role in a group situation?

Give reasons for your answer.

It is important to note that we can go from one type of informal role to another, both within groups, and between groups. Put simply, it is possible to be task orientated at one point, and disruptive at another! Such is the sophistication of human behaviour.

How are roles acquired?

As we read earlier behaviourism believes that we learn behaviours as a consequence of our experience in our environment. We learn such stimulus–response units of behaviour through association or operant.

The behaviourist approach has a number of flaws,

which should become apparent after doing the Interactive below. Suffice to say that there are other theories that better explain how we learn our roles in life. One of these is Social Learning Theory.

INTERACTIVES

Refresh your memory on how the Behaviourist Approach understands how we learn to behave the way we do. Read the Behaviourist section, and work your way through the Interactives at:

www.gerardkeegan.co.uk/resource/ behaviourist.htm

A direct link is available in the Chapter 8 section of the Higher Psychology Learning Suite at **www.gerardkeegan.co.uk**

Social learning theory

Social learning theory (SLT) explains human behaviour in terms of a continuous reciprocal interaction between cognitive, behavioural, and environmental influences.

Social learning theory was first popularised by the Canadian psychologist Alfred Bandura in 1961.

Social learning theory suggests that we learn behaviours such as social roles, both formal and informal, as a result of observing, then imitating and ultimately modelling ourselves on significant others.

Bandura thought that for a child, a significant other would be an adult. For Bandura, we learn how to behave in a social context, or from observations of our social world.

Bandura came to this conclusion after observing the behaviour of young children during his famous study called 'Transmission of aggression through imitation of aggressive models' (Bandura *et al.*, 1961).

Perhaps you would now like to return to Chapter 6: The Experimental Method and refresh your memory on this seminal study?

Social learning theory is pertinent to the controversial Stanford Prison Experiment conducted by Haney, Banks, and Zimbardo in 1973.

The Stanford Prison Experiment is a study we shall return to later in this Chapter. At this juncture it is enough to know that Haney, Banks and Zimbardo

(1973) tell us that in unconsciously observing others playing their particular roles in life, we ourselves internalise these behaviours. We then use these behavioural templates upon which to model our own behaviour, if we find ourselves in a similar situation in the future.

INTERACTIVES

'Social learning theory suggests that we learn behaviours such as social roles as a result of observing, then imitating and ultimately modelling ourselves on significant others.'

Describe any role that you play in life. Explain how you learned this role in terms of social learning theory.

Social schemata

Schema (plural schemata) is a hypothetical construct held in our mind that describes an organized body of knowledge and/or abilities that changes due to experience.

Social schemata are flexible cognitive frameworks that hold our social knowledge about our world. Social schemata are found in the human mind, and like it are hypothetical constructs. They don't actually exist in reality.

As discussed above one type of social schemata is the script.

According to Hayes (2002) we use scripts 'to guide our behaviour when we are in established social situations requiring a definite sequence of interactions between the parties concerned.'

Other types of social schemata include role-schema, person-schema and self-schema (Baron and Byrne, 1984).

Role schema

Our *role schema* is more sophisticated than role knowledge itself.

This is because role schemata are dynamic. They are forever changing bodies of knowledge about the roles we play, or come across in our world. The *experience* of playing a particular social role gives us a deeper understanding of it.

Responding to a particular role also influences role schemata. This is because we come to know, or understand, a specific social role that bit better. Examples of role schemata at work would be the interactions between a teacher and a student, a parent and a child, a police officer and a member of the public etc.

Person schema

A person schema is a body of knowledge that we hold in our mind about someone in our world. This too is influenced by experience. The more we come to know that person, the deeper our knowledge of them becomes. Their person schema becomes increasingly more detailed and sophisticated. We use this when engaging with them. It allows us to interact with them better. We know what issues are best to avoid. We know their likes and dislikes etc.

Our person schema regulates our social actions and interactions with others.

Self-schema

According to Baron and Byrne another type of social schema is our self-schema, or who we think we are as a person.

As we read in Early socialisation, the self is our inner personality that is likened to the soul, or Freud's psyche. Self in psychology is generally attributed to the humanistic perspective, and is their term for who we as individuals are as a person.

Our self or self-schema is formed by our phenomenology, our acts of personal agency, and our existentialism.

> **Self-image** is how we see ourselves as individuals, which is important to good psychological health. At a simple level this might see you perceive yourself as a good or a bad person, beautiful or ugly. Self-image, and how it comes about, has an effect on how we as individuals think, feel, and behave in relation to our world.

Phenomenology

Our phenomenology is our personal, subjective interpretation of the positive and negative experiences we have in life. Phenomenology influences our self-esteem and self-image.

> **Self-esteem** is '… the evaluation the individual makes and customarily maintains with regard to himself … and indicates the extent to which the individual believes himself capable, significant, successful and worthy.' (Coopersmith, 1967, pp. 4–5)

Personal agency

Personal agency is the humanistic term for our exercise of free will. Personal agency refers to the choices we make in life, the paths we go down, and their consequences.

Existentialism

Existentialism is the influence of the environments we find ourselves in, which is sometimes as a result of exercising personal agency. Existentialism affects the self, and all that comes with it.

> ## INTERACTIVES
>
> To appreciate the influence of personal agency and existentialism on psychological health read the book, or watch the video. *Trainspotting* by gritty Edinburgh novelist Irving Welsh.

These formative influences on our self-schema affect our self-image and self-esteem, and thus who we think we are. We often have a negative self-image, and consequently low self-esteem. This is not psychologically healthy.

This need not be the case, for in unlocking experiences that have affected our self-schema, and thus our self-image and self-esteem, we can strive towards becoming our ideal self, or who we really are, or want to be, in terms of our personality.

Please read the study conducted by Coopersmith (1967). You should appreciate the power our social world has in influencing our self-esteem. This is because our interactions with others affect how much we come to regard, or value, ourselves as a person. Our self-esteem is influenced by the reaction of others to us, and the comparisons made of us by other people (Argyle, 1983). This all happens in a social context.

> **STUDY**
>
> ## Coopersmith, S. (1967) *The Antecedents of Self-esteem*. San Francisco, Freeman
>
> **Aim:** Coopersmith (1967) wanted to investigate the origins and assess the effects of levels of self-esteem in children.
>
> **Method/Procedure:** Coopersmith studied several hundred nine to ten-year-old white middle-class boys. He measured their self-esteem using the self-esteem inventory, teachers' ratings as to how each boy reacted to failure, the thematic apperception test, and an assessment of their confidence when in strange surroundings. On the basis of what he found, he then divided the boys into high-, middle- and low-esteem groups and examined the personality characteristics of the boys in each group via questionnaires and interviews. He also questioned and interviewed the boys and their mothers about their upbringing.
>
> **Results:** The results indicated that 'external indicators of prestige [measurements of the parents' status] such as wealth, amount of education, and job title did not have as overwhelming and as significant an effect on self-esteem as is often assumed' (Pervin, 1993). Parental attitudes and behaviours including acceptance of their children, giving them clear and well-enforced behavioural boundaries and giving them respect for their actions all contributed to the children's sense of self-esteem or self-worth (Pervin, 1993). Coopersmith found that of the three self-esteem groups, the high self-esteem group were more expressive, active, confident and successful (academically and socially) than the middle- and low-esteem groups. The middle self-esteem group were the most conforming. The low self-esteem group were underachievers and did not rate themselves too much at all. They were social isolates, shy and hurt by criticism.
>
> Coopersmith followed his participants into adulthood and found that those identified as having high self-esteem in childhood were more successful in both work and in their relationships than participants in the other two groups.
>
> **Conclusions:** Self-esteem is formed from childhood. It does not depend on family wealth or background. Important to self-esteem is upbringing. Parents who give **unconditional positive regard** and bring children up within firm boundaries are more likely to produce children with high self-esteem. Low self-esteem children are from overly strict, overly lax or unloving family environments. Self-esteem can have a long-lasting influence on work and social relationships in adulthood.

Social identity

Tajfel (1978, 1982), and Tajfel and Turner (1986), believe that the groups to which we belong are important to *social identity*.

According to their **social identity theory** our membership of social groups is integral to our self-concept, or who we think we are as a person.

This is because our social identity does two things. Social identity defines and evaluates us as being part of a group. An example would be being Scottish or Irish, Catholic or Protestant. Social identity also dictates behaviours associated with belonging to such groups.

Until recently our idea of the behaviours associated with being either a Northern Irish Catholic or

Northern Irish Protestant probably differed rather dramatically. From a west of Scotland perspective we may also have defined and evaluated our *own* social identity against that of the Northern Irish Catholic or Protestant.

INTERACTIVES

1   What type of school do, or did, you go to?

2   How does or did it differ from the other type of school available in Scotland?

3   What football team does/did the majority of people in your school support?

4   Did/does this differ from the football team supported by students at the other type of school in your area?

5   From the point of view of social identity theory why do you think this is?

Breakwell (1978) studied teenage football fans, some of who went to most games, while others did not. Those who did not go to games were more vehement in their loyalty to their team. They showed more in-group bias; presumably because they had a greater need to prove themselves as fans.

When on holiday abroad, we feel our nationality far more obviously than when we are at home. We tend to band together in national groups. We perhaps make adverse comments about the strangeness of the 'natives', or holidaymakers from other countries! Recognise anyone?

This is because when we belong to a group, the **in-group**, we are likely to derive our sense of identity, at least in part, from that group. We also enhance the sense of identity by making comparisons with **out-groups**.

Social identity is different from personal identity, or self, which is derived from our own personal characteristics and individual relationships. Social identity is derived from belonging.

We shall return to this later in this Chapter when we look at prejudice.

Social psychology so far...

> *The social psychology of this century reveals a major lesson: often it is not so much the kind of person a man is as the kind of situation in which he finds himself that determines how he will act."*

> *(Milgram, 1974)*

Social psychology assumes that all our behaviour happens in a social context, even when nobody else is physically present. Our society and other people greatly influences how we think, feel and behave.

Social psychology investigates the power of social influence in its study of conformity and obedience. Factors that determine social cognition and our social behaviour are addressed in the topic of prejudice.

It is to these we now turn. But before we do, please take a moment to do the Interactive below.

INTERACTIVES

Please use the following scale to rate how independent a person you think you are.

By circling 1 you are a person who is very easily led by others. By circling 10 you are a person not very easily led by others.

1   2   3   4   5   6   7   8   9   10

Conformity

The act of conformity has us behave in a way others want, particularly in a social situation. Conformity may not reflect what we truly want to do.

There are two types of conformity.

The first is *public conformity* or compliance where there is a change in our behaviour but not our opinion.

The other is *private change* or internalisation where there is a change in our behaviour and our opinion (Kelman, 1958).

Mann (1969) suggests 'the essence of conformity is yielding to group pressure.'

Alternatively Aronson (1985) says that 'conformity can be defined as a change in a person's behaviour or opinions as a result of real or imagined pressure from a person or a group of people'.

While Hayes (2000) tells us that conformity is 'the process of going along with other people… acting in the same way that they do.'

What all the above definitions of conformity share are a reference to groups and the pressure groups can exert on us as individuals.

But what are groups, and why do groups have such an influence on our behaviour?

Groups and group pressure

In sociology a group is a collection of people who share certain characteristics, interact with one another, accept any expectations and obligations from being members of that group, and share a common identity.

In psychology a definition of a group can vary depending on its size.

The large group

For large social groups, such as a society, or an ethnic grouping Lewin (1948) suggests their definition as '… the experience of common fate.'

This definition can be applied to large groups such as the Aztecs, and the Jewish people in Nazi Europe. The Aztecs were wiped out in 1521 by conquistador Hernán Cortés. This was as a consequence of the Spanish colonisation of Mexico. From 1933–1945 the Nazis killed around six million European Jews. This holocaust was because of Hitler's demented Final Solution.

The small group

According to Copeland and Robertson (2004) a small group consists of between two and 20 people.

Sherif and Sherif (1969) define a (small) group in terms of '…the existence of some formal or implicit social structure, usually in the form of status and role relationships.'

This definition would apply to a family or a workplace. This is because in each situation there are power and status differences. For example, grandma, grandpa, mum, dad, older brother, older sister etc., or Principal of a College, Director, Head of Faculty, Assistant Head of Faculty, and Lecturer etc.

ONLINE INTERACTIVES

Go to:

www.gendercide.org/case_srebrenica.html

Read the case study on the Srebrenica Massacre of July 1995. Is there any evidence in this study to support Kurt Lewin's 1948 definition of a large group?

Give reasons for your answer.

A direct link is available in the Chapter 8 section of the Higher Psychology Learning Suite at www.gerardkeegan.co.uk

---

A small group is formed when two or more people interact.. For Bales, groups '… consist of people in face-to-face interaction with one another.' For Turner (1982), a group occurs when '… two or more individuals… perceive themselves to be members of the same social category.'

Of interest to our membership of groups is the role of self-perception, or who we think ourselves to be. Self-perception is related to our self-schema, and social identity theory, both of which we came across earlier.

Self-perception may also apply to Brown (2000). He tells us that 'A group exists when two or more people define themselves as members of it, and when its existence is recognised by at least one other. These two or more individuals believe they have something in common, while another [*who is not part of the group being formed*] does not' (author's emphasis in parenthesis).

Group cohesiveness

Group cohesiveness is the 'social glue' that holds a group together. Important to group cohesiveness is mutual support, or just how well group members get on with one another in pursuit of their common goal.

Groups whose membership gels well and work to achieve a common aim are highly cohesive.

If there is an absence of mutual support and a common goal, such groups quickly disintegrate.

Group cohesiveness and conformity

The influence of group cohesiveness on group conformity should not be underestimated. Social psychology has applied its understanding of group cohesiveness to many areas of our life.

For example, Murray *et al.* (1984) discovered that school-based anti-smoking and drug initiatives had more success when run by peers rather than teachers and other adults. A peer is better able to offer mutual support to others of the same age and background than those perceived to be in positions of authority.

Burn (1991) investigated a group of neighbours who recycled waste. When compared to a postal campaign that had people drop a 'Recycle Waste' leaflet through neighbours' letterboxes, the common bond of collectively recycling waste saw this group go out and convert twice as many to their cause.

Crandall (1988) conducted a unique study into whether being a member of a female friendship group influenced a member's tendencies to binge eat. Binge eating is an eating disorder where people alternate between periods of great food consumption and bodily purging.

Crandall hypothesised that the female members in the study would become more like their peer group friends in regard to binge eating behaviours. The passage of time would see their friendship bonds strengthen, and they would become even closer because of their shared binge eating lifestyle. Crandall was proven correct. Why was this?

The more we like other people, the more we want to be like them. This is because we want to gain their approval. Their approval of us is our reward. Their disapproval of us is a sanction, and something we want to avoid. We are thus more prone to social pressure to behave like them, and to comply with their wishes etc.

We shall return to this when we look at the work of Herbert Kelman and compliance, internalisation and identification.

Group pressure

> **Social norms** are the expected behaviours associated with belonging to a particular group.

We often find ourselves under group pressure to conform with the membership groups to which we belong and the reference groups that we admire.

Both membership groups and reference groups see us adopt social norms to behave in particular ways.

The power of norms

There are three reasons as to why norms influence our behaviour.

We are motivated to be correct, and norms often provide us with information as to what is most likely right (Inkso *et al.*, 1983).

We are motivated to be liked by others. In a group situation adhering to established norms help facilitate this (Inkso *et al.*, 1983).

We learn from childhood onwards that supporting a group norm is good, and can earn us a reward. Railing against a group norm is bad, and can lead to a sanction (Levine, 1989). Thus norms hold a society together. Norms underlie social reinforcement and social sanction.

INTERACTIVES

From your own experience identify a norm of expected behaviour in a group situation. What reward did you or others get by adhering to it? What sanction was used when you or others did not adhere to this expected behaviour?

Social norms

Social norms are expected ways of behaving as a consequence of belonging or wanting to belong to a group. To choose not to adopt a particular group's norms could mean our continued membership of the group is denied, or access frustrated.

Social norms can be explicit, or expressed. An example of an explicit social norm, or declared rule of behaviour, would be the 'No smoking' signs now found in all enclosed public places in Scotland.

Social norms can also be implicit, or unspoken. An example of an implicit social norm, or assumed rule of behaviour, would be not standing too close to strangers.

Membership groups

Membership groups are groups of 'significant others' in our life. Membership groups include our peer group, family, clubs, societies etc.

Reference groups

Zimbardo *et al.* (1995) tells us that we often have ' a tendency…to adopt the behaviour, attitudes and values of a reference group'.

A reference group is then a group whose values we admire, or to which we want to aspire. A reference group could be a social circle, which is currently closed to us, or we are unable to access. Your mum might not let you!

Conformity and social pressure

Conformity occurs because of real or imagined group pressure, which is largely unspoken and indirect.

Zimbardo and Leippe (1991) say that we conform due to 'a change in belief and behaviour in response to real or imagined group pressure when there is no direct request to comply with the group nor any reason to justify the behaviour change.'

Consequently we conform because of social pressure.

Social pressure can be *real,* as in when others are physically present. There presence prompts us to act in a particular way, rather than how we would act or behave if they were not present (Aronson, 1976).

Social pressure can also be *imagined,* and occur when others are not physically present. We conform to be commensurate with expected social norms, or society's rules (Aronson, 1976). One reason we conform in this situation is because to do otherwise could result in some kind of social sanction, or disapproval.

An example of social pressure to conform would be the 'No Smoking in enclosed public places' ban that came into effect in Scotland on Sunday, 26 March 2006.

The presence of janitors at the entrance to Scotland's colleges on the morning of Monday 27th March, 2006 saw many smokers immediately conform to the national smoking ban. Smokers went instead to the new designated smoking area. The janitors' actual presence had discouraged smoking.

A day later, smokers adhered to the new rule, this time without any janitors present. There was no smoking to be seen at the front of Scotland's colleges. Any smoking that did take place was now confined to special designated places.

The 'no smoking in enclosed public places' ban had become the social norm. Smokers in Scotland now adhere to the new rule because of social disapproval or possible sanction.

Inducing compliance

Compliance, or our public conformity to act in a way others wish, need not necessarily be because of a *direct* request made for us to behave in a certain way.

Sales staff, politicians, social psychologists etc. have found that often the best way to induce compliance is first to ask the target for something else! This strategy can take one of three forms. Have you been a victim of any of these?

The foot-in-the-door technique

The foot-in-the-door technique consists of someone making small requests of us and then gradually working up to bigger ones. The strategy comes from a field experiment conducted in a Californian town by Freedman and Fraser in 1966.

Using an independent group design one group of residents were approached by a researcher and told about concerns over road traffic accidents in the area. They were then asked if they would like to put a large 'Drive Carefully' sign in their front garden. Seventeen per cent complied with this request.

A researcher also approached another group of residents. This group were asked to sign a petition to get the state legislature to work towards reducing road traffic accidents in the area. A few weeks later a different researcher went back to ask them to place the large 'Drive Carefully' sign in their front garden; 55 per cent complied with this request (Freedman and Fraser, 1966).

Subsequent research concerning the effectiveness of the foot-in-the-door technique seems to confirm this compliance strategy. The reasons are twofold.

First, people are more likely to comply with a request when personal cost in terms of time, money, effort or inconvenience is low.

Second, complying with a small request makes us think of ourselves as being supportive or committed to the source of the request. This makes us feel good. When the later larger request is made, to refuse would make us feel psychologically uncomfortable. We would be inconsistent in terms of our earlier thoughts, feelings and behaviours. This mental discomfort is known as cognitive dissonance. We want to avoid this, as we like to be in a state of cognitive consonance, or psychological comfort (Swartzwald, Bizman and Raz, 1983).

This underlies the 55 per cent compliance rate found by Freedman and Fraser when using the foot-in-the-door technique with their second group of participants, above.

The foot-in-the-door technique tries to persuade us to comply with what others want all the time. We often get letters from companies telling us we have won a free gift. In order to claim it all we need do is complete and send back the enclosed pre-paid postcard.

This everyday example of the foot-in-the-door technique often prompts a low level of compliance from us. It is made more likely because there is little effort and no cost involved in sending back the postcard. Our compliance is further encouraged by the prospect of receiving the free gift and getting something for nothing!

Sometime later we get our prize of a low value gift voucher through our letterbox. We discover it is only redeemable against items from the company's catalogue, which is unsurprisingly sent to us at the same time!

The door-in-the-face technique

The door-in-the-face technique is another strategy that gets us to comply with the demands of others. Cann, Sherman and Elkes (1975) tell us that this strategy begins when someone makes a very large request of us, which they know we are we are likely to reject. An example would be someone asking you for £100, and you telling them to get lost! The person asking for the £100 then concedes that was maybe a bit too much, and alternatively requests a lower amount i.e. £20. Because this is more modest sum we are more likely to comply.

The low-ball technique

The low-ball technique involves someone getting X by first asking for Y, X being what he or she wants, Y being a decoy.

With the low-ball technique the first step is to get a verbal agreement from someone to do something. The second step is to show that only a higher cost version of the original request will suffice, and the third step is then to make this higher cost request. The difference between the low-ball and the foot-in-the-door techniques is that with the low-ball approach the initial request is escalated once it has been agreed, but before it can be fulfilled.

Take the following example of a student that the author knows who got a lift to college from their student friend every Monday morning for their 9a.m. class. There was nothing unusual about this until you learn that the *driver's* first class on a Monday wasn't until 10.40a.m.! For 36 weeks the driver was nearly two hours early for their first class doing a favour for their non-driving friend.

The passenger had used the low-ball technique in that they had first asked their driver friend for a lift to college on a Monday morning. Their driver friend was only too happy to comply, as they too had to go to college on the same day. It was only once their agreement with the request had been got that the passenger's additional request of needing to be picked up at 8.30a.m. to make *their* 9a.m. class was made.

Bait and switch

Low-ball methods are often used in 'bait and switch' sales schemes. An example of bait and switch would be where you the customer see a flat screen HD television advertised at a special sale price of £499. You go in to the shop and agree to buy it. The salesperson goes off to the stockroom to get it for you but then returns to tell you there is none left in stock. They knew before they went that this model had sold out. They then say that there is another make available with a better specification but at the 'slightly higher price' of £699. All too often we fall for this bait and switch tactic and end up spending a lot more than we originally intended.

Herbert Kelman: Compliance, internalisation and identification

According to Herbert Kelman (1958) we conform, or yield to social pressure, because of compliance, internalisation, or identification.

Compliance

Compliance, as we should now appreciate is the type of conformity that occurs when there is a change in our behaviour but not in our opinion.

Compliance sees us act in a particular way because of a direct request from another. We change our behaviour to go along with the group, the crowd, the workplace etc. We do not however alter our private beliefs.

Thus compliance is an individual's public conformity to social pressure (Kelman, 1958).

Compliance occurs when we adjust our behaviour in response to a direct request from others. Compliance is aptly illustrated by our 'No smoking in public places' example above. We comply primarily because we want to gain a favourable reaction from others, or want to avoid an unfavourable one.

We also comply because we recognise the social consequences of agreeing or disagreeing with powerful others who can offer rewards and punishments for compliance or non-compliance.

Compliance and minority influence

Compliance usually occurs when the minority change their behaviour due to social pressure from the majority. This is called normative social influence. We will look at normative social influence in more depth shortly.

Sometimes a minority *can* influence a majority. This is particularly so when a minority opinion is expressed passionately, confidently and consistently. Such minority opinion is often embedded in strongly held attitudes and unshakable beliefs.

When this happens social conflict can arise. The minority place doubt and uncertainty in the minds of the majority. They can refuse to compromise. Resolution is only possible when the majority move towards *their* position.

Moscovici *et al.* (1969) presented participants with a series of blue-coloured slides. His participants had to say what colour each slide was.

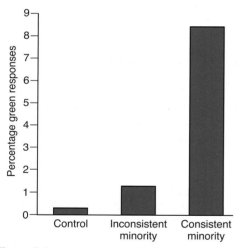

Figure 8.1

He placed two confederates in a group with four naïve participants. He primed his two confederates on seeing the slides to say green rather than blue. In so doing they were able to influence 32 per cent of naïve participants into making at least one incorrect judgement on the colour of slides they saw i.e. reporting they too saw green rather than blue.

Whether a minority can affect a majority to comply is difficult to assess, particularly in a real-life situation. It is much more likely a minority can influence a majority using another type of social influence termed internalisation.

Internalisation

Internalisation is a second type of social pressure to conform. Internalisation happens when there is a change in our behaviour *and* opinion. Internalisation is a more resilient kind of conformity to social pressure. This is because our internalisation of others views or opinions, majority or minority, are more likely to effect how we think, feel, and thus behave, as hopefully we shall now see.

Internalisation arises when we *agree* with the attitude or opinion of the group, the crowd, the minority, the workplace etc.

Internalisation as social pressure to conform is non-problematic. This is because we see others attitude or opinion as logical, reasonable, or compelling. Internalisation sees us privately change our behaviour or views (Kelman, 1958).

Internalisation is when a group's attitude or opinion coincides with our own broader values and goals. We need not be members of a group for our internalisation of their attitude or opinion to occur.

Identification

Identification is a third type of social pressure that sees us conform.

Identification occurs when we change our behaviour and opinion because we want to identify with a *particular* group. Identification happens because we want to be seen to agree with others we value. This is because we want to start, or maintain, a personal relationship with them.

The process of identification helps promote any personal goals we have regards forming social relationships with others, and in creating our social identity.

Identification can be likened to 'ingratiational conformity'. This occurs where 'a person tries to do whatever he thinks the other will approve in order to gain acceptance' (Mann, 1969).

Power, credibility and attractiveness

Kelman (1958) presented participants with a persuasive communication or appeal. He then got his 'influence agent' to use three distinct variables of personal power, personal credibility, and personal attractiveness in making the appeal.

Power

When Kelman had the influence agent exercise personal power, such as giving rewards or punishments, participants' agreement with the appeal reflected their *compliance*.

Their compliance occurred because his participants wanted to gain a favourable reaction or reward, and avoid an unfavourable reaction or sanction from the influence agent.

Credibility

When Kelman described the influence agent as a credible source, his participants' agreement with the appeal suggested their *internalisation* of the appeal message.

An example of a credible source influencing us on the basis of internalisation would be Nelson Mandela talking about world poverty, or HIV. Because of his previous track record we believe what he says.

Kelman found that internalisation was more likely when the attitude, opinion, or values articulated by the credible source coincided or supported those already held by his participants.

Attractiveness

When Kelman's influence agent was perceived as an attractive role model his participants wanted to

identify with the person making the appeal. They did not however necessarily agree with the sentiments of the appeal itself.

Advertising uses celebrity endorsement and product identification to persuade us to buy a vast range of products every day.

Evaluation of compliance, internalisation and identification

According to Kelman (1958) we yield to group pressure to conform to new norms of behaviour because of compliance, internalisation, or identification.

Of the three, compliance is the least effective form of social pressure. While rewards and punishments are important to compliance, they must be forever available to effect a permanent change in someone's behaviour.

Identification as a means of social pressure is only useful if we perceive the source that wishes us to conform and behave in a particular way as attractive. We may, or may not, wish to identify with them. Our own tastes and desires continually change, as does the cult of celebrity.

Internalisation of another person's, or group's, attitude or opinion is the most effective method of social pressure. We like to be right. When we internalise another's attitude or opinion, this bolsters and confirms our own thoughts on the matter (Turner, 1991).

Studies into conformity

Jenness (1932)

Jenness (1932) conducted one of the first studies into conformity. He was interested in how a majority view influenced our tendency to conform in a group situation.

He filled a glass jar with beans, and asked participants to individually estimate how many beans were in the jar. Each estimate was noted. The participants were then put into a group, and asked for a group estimate. After this the participants were again interviewed individually and asked if they would like to change their original estimate. Almost all changed their original estimate to conform closer to the group norm, or what the group had decided were the number of sweets in the jar.

Sherif (1935)

Sherif (1935) investigated the formation of group norms using a phenomenon known as the autokinetic effect. The autokinetic effect is the apparent, though not real, movement of a stationary spot of light (Adams, 1912).

Sherif put participants individually into a darkened room, and flashed a spot of light onto the wall in front of them. He again flashed the spot of light but this time asked each participant how far, and in what direction, they thought it had moved. The spot of light was stationary but participants assumed it had moved from the leading question asked by Sherif. Each participant then gave an estimate of the light's apparent movement.

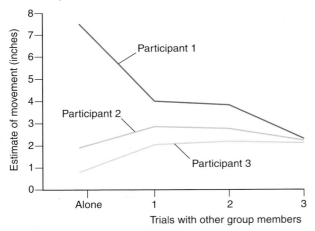

Figure 8.2

The procedure was carried out again, but this time with groups of three. Each participant in the triad was asked, in turn, how far and in what direction the light had moved. In the group situation all answers were found to be very close to the estimates provided by the first person. All participants also disregarded their previous individual estimates.

When put into new triads, and again asked how far and in what direction the spot of light had moved, participants reported the apparent movement of the light in terms of the previously established *group* norm, rather then their first individual estimates.

Evaluation of Sherif (1935)

Sherif (1935) can be criticised in that the autokinetic effect is difficult to measure. The researcher has to rely on the participant telling him or her how long or how short any apparent movement of the light might be. It is thus difficult to ascertain the degree of conformity that has taken place.

Wren (1999) also cautions that people's general health, age and eyesight must also influence the autokinetic effect. Sherif did not control for these extraneous variables.

Notwithstanding, Sherif (1935) illustrates the influence of others' opinion in the formation of a group norm, even when this opinion is wrong.

So why does this happen?

Informational social influence

In both Jenness (1932) and Sherif (1935) participants conformed to the group norm due to **informational social influence**.

Informational social influence is a type of conformity where we base our behaviours on what the majority of others think, feel or do. Informational social influence is particularly prevalent in unclear situations.

Informational conformity, or informational social influence 'occurs where the situation is vague or ambiguous, and because the person is uncertain, he turns to others for evidence of the appropriate response' (Mann, 1969).

Deutsch and Gerard (1955) believe informational social influence effects our behaviour because of our need for certainty in our world. We like to be right. Informational social influence can also be likened to internalisation (Kelman, 1958).

In ambiguous situations, such as guessing the number of beans in a jar or how far a spot of light has (not!) moved, participants relied on informational social influence from others because they were unsure of the answer. In similar situations we tend to do the same.

Informational social influence is evident in a crisis. Because crises do not happen to us that often we unquestionably do what a police officer tells us to do if we find ourselves in an emergency situation. We presume the police officer's judgement is more superior to our own. We presume that in a crisis situation he or she has more experience than we do.

Keeping up with the Joneses

The phrase 'keeping up with the Joneses' is very much associated with informational social influence and its effect this has on our behaviours. Informational social influence has us behave in particular ways because others around us are so doing.

This 'keeping up with the Joneses' is particularly relevant to our consumer behaviours. We see someone with something new and exciting, we want it as well! Think about how many mobile phones you have had and why you have upgraded time and again from one model to another. Have you changed their house phone as often? Why do you think there is such a difference in our behaviours concerning the same kind of technology?

In 2005 the American social psychologist Robert Cialdini conducted some fascinating research into how the peer group, or 'the Joneses', can influence conformity behaviours to help save energy, reduce global warming and minimise our carbon footprint.

Cialdini and his team from the University of Arizona conducted a telephone survey of more than 2000 Californian residents asking them to identify why they tried to conserve energy. Three overwhelming reasons emerged. They wished to protect the environment, they wished to be responsible citizens and they wished to save on energy costs. The lowest-rated reason given by respondents was because their neighbours were doing so.

At first glance 'Keeping up with the Joneses' seemed to have little influence on Californians' 'green' behaviours.

'However, what we found was that the lowest-rated factor—the belief that their neighbours were engaging in energy conservation—had the highest correlation with reported energy conservation on the part of the people surveyed,' Cialdini said. 'They were fooling themselves.'

Cialdini (2007) then applied these findings to persuade hotel guests to recycle their used towels.

He approached two hotels in Phoenix, Arizona and asked them if they could randomly put one of five cards in 260 guests' rooms. On the basis of the telephone survey above, each card had a slightly different explanation of how reusing towels can conserve energy and help save the environment:

➤ Card 1 said, 'Help the hotel save energy,' focusing on the benefit to the hotel.

➤ Card 2 said, 'Help save the environment,' emphasising environmental protection.

➤ Card 3 said, 'Partner with us to help save the environment,' highlighting environmental co-operation.

➤ Card 4 said, 'Help save resources for future generations,' stressing the environmental benefit to future generations.

➤ Card 5 said, 'Join your fellow citizens in helping to save the environment,' indicating what others were doing and why.

Cialdini found that card number 5 had the most impact. The *descriptive* or *informational norm* it contained told occupants of these particular rooms how other guests in the hotel were behaving. As an informational social norm it had a powerful effect on their behaviour in that 41 per cent who saw it complied and recycled their towels.

The least effective message was contained in Card number 1. This card, which emphasised the economic benefit of recycling for the hotel, only prompted 20 per cent of guests to comply.

Cards 2, 3 and 4, which focused on environmental benefits, saw around 31 per cent compliance from guests in whose rooms they were displayed.

Normative social influence

Deutsch and Gerard (1955) additionally tell us that another reason for conformity is normative social influence.

We came across normative social influence earlier when we looked at compliance. Normative social influence occurs in situations where we want to gain approval, or avoid disapproval, from others. Normative social influence concerns our need for social acceptance.

Normative social influence can be likened to Mann's (1969) ingratiational social influence or Kelman's (1958) compliance. With both we outwardly behave consistently with the majority view, but inwardly disagree with it. Normative social influence is similar.

Normative social influence sees a public change in our behaviour, but no change in our private opinion.

A good example of normative social influence on behaviour would be when we see bullying taking place in our school or workplace. Despite privately disagreeing with bullying, we stay quiet because we are scared the same thing will happen to us. While understandable this is not a good idea.

Read 'First they came…' by the famous Pastor Martin Niemöller to appreciate why.

> *First they came...*
>
> *First they came for the Communists,*
>
> *and I didn't speak up, because I wasn't a Communist.*
>
> *Then they came for the Social Democrats,*
>
> *and I didn't speak up, because I wasn't a Social Democrat.*
>
> *Then they came for the Trade Unionists,*
>
> *and I didn't speak up, because I wasn't a Trade Unionist.*
>
> *Then they came for the Jews,*
>
> *and I didn't speak up, because I wasn't a Jew,*
>
> *Then they came for me,*
>
> *and by that time there was no one left to speak up for me."*

Asch (1951, 1952, 1956)

A criticism of Jenness (1932) and Sherif (1935) is that both concerned the establishment of group norms in ambiguous situations. Estimating the number of beans in a jar, or how far a light may have moved is imprecise, unclear, and inexact.

Solomon Asch aimed to test group conformity in an unambiguous situation, or one where there was clearly only one answer.

Asch is *the* classic study relating to normative social influence. He wished to investigate 'the social and personal conditions that induce individuals to resist or to yield to group pressures when the latter are perceived to be contrary to fact' (Asch, 1951).

Asch ran a series of laboratory experiments with groups of male college students. Each group consisted of one naïve participant, and between seven and nine Asch confederates. One hundred and twenty-three naïve participants were used overall.

He had each person in each group sit on one side of a desk, and from right to left verbally state which of three unequal lines matched a given line (see Figure 8.3 below). The naïve participant was always seated next to last, and had to answer next to last.

The Asch paradigm

Previously Asch tested 36 participants individually on 20 presentations of line stimuli like the one below (Figure 8.3).

In this pilot study, when the 36 participants were asked to compare and identify the standard line with the three A, B, C comparison lines only three mistakes were made in 720 trials (0.42 error rate).

The purpose of the pilot study was to ascertain that the task was both simple and unambiguous. This procedure in social psychology is known as the Asch paradigm. It is the standard to which other social psychologists who replicate similar studies into conformity adhere.

In the experiment proper Asch's confederates were primed to give the wrong answer in twelve of his eighteen presentations. Thus for example when asked which line matched X, the six or so confederates who came before the naïve participant would answer C.

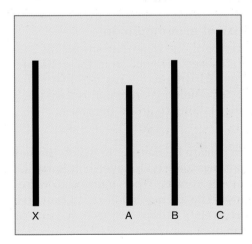

Figure 8.3 Example of Asch line stimulus

Asch was interested in how the naïve participant would answer in such circumstances. Would they give the right answer, and in our example answer B, or conform to the incorrect group norm, and answer C?

His dependent variable was the occurrence of a conformity response by his naïve participants when the erroneous critical trials occurred. Asch called the result of this the 'majority effect.'

The average rate of conformity or 'majority effect' was found to be 37 per cent, while 74 per cent conformed at least once, and 26 per cent never conformed.

Asch then varied the conditions of his independent variable to investigate other influences on group conformity.

ONLINE INTERACTIVES

Watch a You Tube video of an Asch's Conformity experiment. Go to: www.youtube.com/watch?v=R6LH10-38k

A direct link is available in the Chapter 8 section of the Higher Psychology Learning Suite at www.gerardkeegan.co.uk

Size of group

Asch discovered that as group size increased to a maximum of three others, conformity increased. After that there was little change. One naïve participant, one confederate: three per cent conformity. One naïve participant, two confederates: fourteen per cent conformity. One naïve participant, three confederates: 32 per cent conformity.

Unanimity of group opinion

The presence of one dissenter among his confederates saw a reduction in the conformity rate of naïve participants to 5.5 per cent. Group unanimity of opinion is crucial in regard to individuals yielding to group pressure.

Privacy

The more private the setting in which the naïve participant was allowed to give their answer, the less conformity there was. When allowed to write down their answer the average conformity rate among naïve participants dropped to from 37 per cent to 12.5 per cent.

Task difficulty

When the comparison lines were made similar in length to each other, this increase in task difficulty saw group conformity increase. The more ambiguous the task, the greater the likelihood an individual will conform to group opinion.

As the physical reality of a situation becomes less clear, people tend to rely more and more on others opinion (Shaw, Rothschild and Strickland, 1957).

Evaluation of Asch

The results of the Asch studies are a little misleading. They seem to suggest an obvious and constant conformity among those who took part. For example, Asch reports the average rate of conformity to be 37 per cent. This optimism can be criticised.

This is because many participants did not conform at all. Others were not consistent in their conformity behaviour. Twenty-six per cent of all participants remained independent from group pressure to conform, while at the other extreme five per cent yielded to group pressure on all twelve trials.

These variations suggest that a relationship between group pressure and individual conformity is more complex than Asch originally thought.

Methodology

Asch can also be criticised on methodological grounds. He used a biased sample in that it consisted entirely of male undergraduates from an American University. His sample did not reflect society at large. Generalising his conclusions about conformity onto society as a whole is adventurous.

His experiments also took place in a laboratory. As we know laboratory experiments in psychology lack ecological validity. Many do not reflect behaviours in a real life situation.

A child of its time

Further, Perrin and Spencer (1980, 1981) tell us that the Asch effect was a 'child of its time'. They carried out an exact replication of the original Asch experiment using engineering, mathematics and chemistry students as their participants.

Their results were clear-cut. On only one out of 396 trials did an observer join the erroneous majority. Perrin and Spencer argue that a *cultural* change has taken place in the value placed on conformity and obedience, and in the norms and values of students.

In America in the 1950s and 1960s students were generally conservative, unobtrusive members of society, whereas now they are much more libveral, free thinking, and individualistic.

Ethics

Lastly, The Asch studies saw some participants report feeling tense and uncomfortable. One said 'I felt disturbed, puzzled, separated like an outcast from the rest.' Another strong non-conformist reported 'It is more pleasant if one is in agreement.' Clearly they did not enjoy the experience.

INTERACTIVES

1   What was the aim of Asch (1951, 1952, 1956)?

2   What do you understand by the term normative social influence?

3   Outline the method and procedure adopted by Asch.

4   What was his dependent variable?

5   What were his results?

6   What other factors did he find influenced conformity in non-ambiguous situations?

7   What type of social influence do the Asch studies *generally* support? Give reasons for your answer.

8   Does Asch reflect compliance, internalisation, or identification? Give reasons for your answer.

9   What methodological criticisms does Asch attract?

10   What ethical criticism does Asch attract?

Consequently Asch raises ethical issues in regard to deception and participant distress. This should be avoided in psychological research.

Nonetheless Asch (1952) concluded that:

> *Independence and yielding are a joint function of the following factors; the character of the stimulus; the character of the group forces, in particular, the great importance of the factor of unanimity [and] the character of the individual".*

Crutchfield (1954)

Crutchfield felt the procedure used by Asch was too time consuming.

He thus set out a room with six cubicles to test participants six at a time. When seated in the cubicles his participants could not see, nor be seen, by others.

The aim of the Crutchfield (1954) experiment was to confirm if the privacy of the response situation reduced conformity. Asch (1952) had originally found that privacy of individual response reduced the occurrence of group conformity.

Each booth had an electronic screen and numbered buttons. Crutchfield had an image appear on the screen, such as a star and a circle. Participants were asked questions like 'What shape has the greater area, the star or the circle?' The circle was in fact about one-third larger in diameter. The participants answered by pressing one of the numbered buttons.

Participants thought they were answering in turn. However, the experimental manipulation was that all booths were allocated as number six. Crutchfield had all participants answer last and thus simultaneously. The cumulative answers chosen by the five 'previous' participants were false. Crutchfield made them up. This eliminated the need for Asch-type confederates. In this way Crutchfield manipulated group pressure.

Crutchfield carried out the same procedure with over 600 participants using varying stimuli: Asch's lines, stars, pictures etc. His results saw conformity levels rise to an average of 50 per cent (Crutchfield, 1954).

This was not what he had expected! Like Asch, Crutchfield had initially thought conformity levels would fall due to the privacy the booths gave to his participants.

One of the reasons for this was his sample. He got all his participants from military bases, and military personnel are trained to conform! This is an excellent example of an extraneous confounding variable at work in an experiment.

When the test was repeated, this time with a more typical group of ordinary people, the average conformity response returned to the 37 per cent level of the earlier Asch studies.

Crutchfield generally confirms similar work done by Asch and Sherif. It also shows that the physical presence of others is not necessary for conformity to occur.

However the occupational background of his sample, with their predisposition to obedience and conformity must be taken into account in any assessment of research into factors that give rise to conformity.

Factors that can influence or reduce conformity

Factors that can influence or reduce conformity include the size of the majority, cultural differences and gender.

Majority size and conformity

In 1955 Asch became interested in how the size of the majority might affect conformity.

He re-ran various trials of his experiment again, using between one and thirteen confederates each time. He found the naïve participants conformed most often when between three and seven confederates were used.

Any more than seven confederates had little or no effect on naïve participant conformity. When nine or more confederates were used, Asch reported conformity levels dropped.

The reason for this was that when a larger number of confederates were used the naïve participants become more aware something was afoot! They became suspicious that others were not independent observers, but part of a group of co-conspirators who were setting them up (Wilder, 1977).

In an Asch-type situation conformity is more likely to occur if other people's views are seen as independent of each other.

Cultural differences and conformity: Norway vs France!

Milgram (1961) adapted the Asch paradigm to investigate cultural differences and conformity.

He got groups of Norwegian and French participants to judge the duration of two tones of noise that they heard through earphones. Each participant was aware of the response of five others who they thought were also in their group. These five others were confederates of Milgram, and had been instructed by him to give the wrong answer on 16 out of 30 trails.

In this first experiment Milgram found a conformity rate of 62 per cent among his Norwegian participants, and 50 per cent among his French participants.

The second part of the experiment had a greater **ecological validity** in that it was more 'real life'. This was because both groups of participants were told that their answers would be used in the later design of aircraft safety signals. The tone would be used to optimise passenger safety. In this more vital situation Milgram found conformity rates to be lower in and between the two groups, but with the Norwegians still showing a higher level of conformity than their French counterparts.

In a third version of the experiment all participants were allowed to write down their answers in private. In this situation conformity levels in both groups dropped, but again the Norwegians conformed more than their French colleagues.

The fourth and final version of the experiment had previous non-conformers, or 'dissenters' targeted by the five confederates for not supporting their pre-arranged majority view. After being challenged Milgram saw the dissenters conformity levels rise significantly.

Across the four experiments the Norwegians demonstrated a 75 per cent conformity rate, while the French showed a 59 per cent conformity rate.

Milgram concluded such differences in conformity rates between the Norwegians and the French groups were due to culture. He saw the Norwegians as coming from a highly cohesive culture, whereas the French showed 'far less consensus in both social and political life.'

More modern comparative research investigating cultural differences and conformity support Milgram (1961).

In a **meta-analysis** of 31 studies Smith and Bond (1993) found cultural conformity rates of between 31.2 per cent and 44 per cent when comparing Fijian, African, and people from Western cultures on Asch-type line judgement tasks.

Smith and Bond conclude that the highest conformity levels are to be found in collectivist cultures, and the lowest in more individualistic cultures.

Gender and conformity

Psychologists have also given some consideration as to whether gender influences conformity.

Crutchfield (1954), and then Kretch *et al.* (1962) thought that women were more prone to conform because of differences between male and female **gender roles**. The basis to this claim lay in the psychological research of the time.

Earlier we read about Crutchfield (1954). In his variation of Asch he discovered that females had higher conformity rates than males. He found that high conformist females were 'characterised by easier acceptance of the conventional feminine role', while low conformist or dissenting females showed 'marked signs of conflict in their feelings about the conventional feminine role' (Gough, 1960).

Females were thought to have more 'persuadability' than males. This may not be the case today. What do you think?

Persuadability is an easier readiness to comply with social pressure from TV, magazines, peer group etc. In the 1950s and 1960s females were considered to be more submissive, and males more assertive. Hence the gender difference in conformity behaviours.

More recent research suggests that while females are more prone to conformity than males, the difference on the basis of gender is small. Indeed any difference may be due to other factors, such as what the task entails, and the gender of the researcher.

Javornisky (1979) discovered that females conform more than males when the task is male orientated and the researcher is male. This is supported by Sistrunk and McDavid (1971) who themselves conducted an interesting experiment on group conformity and gender. They got mixed male/female groups of participants to try to agree as to whether particular items were stereotypic male- or female-gender related objects.

The groups were shown male sex-stereotyped objects, such as a car wrench; female sex-stereotyped objects such as an eyebrow pencil, and non-sex stereotyped items such as pictures of popular singers that appealed to both male and females at the time.

Sistrunk and McDavid (1971) found males in their mixed groups to conform more on any female items shown to them; females in their mixed groups conformed more on male items, while on neutral items they scored the same.

A degree of informational social influence is evident in Sistrunk and McDavid (1971). This is because of their male/female participants' previous past experience of items related to their own gender. Generally females deferred to male opinion when shown a male orientated item, and males deferred to female opinion when shown a female orientated item.

Obedience

INTERACTIVES

Now that you have read what psychology has to say about conformity, please use the following scale to rate how independent a person you think you are.

By circling 1 you are a person who is very easily led by others. By circling 10 you are a person not very easily led by others.

1   2   3   4   5   6   7   8   9   10

If you completed this Interactive earlier in this Chapter you might like now to compare your scores. Is there any difference? Why do you think this is?

Obedience is our willingness to follow the express wishes of someone in a position of authority.

Conformity concerns a change in our behaviour or opinions because of real or imagined pressure from a person or a group of people. We conform due to compliance, internalisation, or identification.

Alternatively, **obedience** sees us submit to an explicit demand from an acknowledged authority figure. This is because of the power and status that they have. Examples of excessive obedience abound. After the Second World War, many Nazi soldiers said they had killed innocent civilians due to the direct orders given them by their superior officers.

Another example of excessive obedience occurred in 1978 in Guyana, South America. This was when around 1000 members of a sect called the Peoples Temple took poison and committed mass suicide when instructed to do so by their leader the Rev. Jim Jones.

The early twenty-first century has seen the emergence of suicide bombers. Many men, women, and in some instances children, have strapped bombs to their bodies. On the instructions of their superiors they have then killed themselves and hundreds of others by detonating their bombs in cafes, restaurants, hotel foyers, nightclubs, buses, trains etc.

Why do people do such things?

Psychology has tried to answer this question for quite some time.

ONLINE INTERACTIVES

What makes a respected US soldier torture and humiliate prisoners in an Iraqi jail? Why would a loving Hutu mother in Rwanda beat to death the Tutsi children next door? What could possibly compel ordinary German citizens to become slaughterers in Nazi concentration camps?

Listen to Andrew Marr in conversation with Philip Zimbardo on 'Start The Week' (16 April, 2007). Go to:

www.bbc.co.uk/radio4/factual/starttheweek_20070416.shtml

A direct link is available in the Chapter 8 section of the Higher Psychology Learning Suite at www.gerardkeegan.co.uk

Imagine…

Imagine you responded to an advert in a local newspaper asking you to take part in a psychological experiment at your local university. On arrival you find yourself in a room along with someone you think is another volunteer.

A psychologist comes in and you are both told that the purpose of the experiment is to assess the effect of punishment on the learning process. One of you – the learner – will be asked to learn a list of words. The other – the teacher – will assist the learner to remember the learnt words by giving him an electric shock whenever they make a mistake, forget a word, or get one wrong.

The researcher then turns to you and asks you to draw one of two cards from a box. You draw one that says 'teacher', probably very relieved that you have!

Public Announcement

WE WILL PAY YOU £20 FOR ONE HOUR OF YOUR TIME

Persons Needed for a Study of Memory

- We will pay five hundred London men to help us complete a scientific study of memory and learning. The study is being done at The University, London.
- Each person who participates will be paid £20 per hour (plus £5 bus fare) for approximately 1 hour's time. We need you for only one hour: there are no further obligations. You may choose the time you would like to come (evenings, weekdays, or weekends).
- No special training, education, or experience needed. We want:

Factory workers	*Businessmen*	*Construction workers*
City employees	*Clarks*	*Salespeople*
Labourers	*Professional people*	*White-collar workers*
Barbers	*Telephone workers*	*Other*

All persons must be between the ages of 20 and 50. High school and college students cannot be used.

- If you meet these qualifications, fill out the coupon below and mail it now to Prof. John Smith, Dept. of Psychology, The University, London. You will be notified later of the specific time and place of the study. We reserve the right to decline any application.
- You will be paid £20 per hour (plus £5 bus fare) as soon as you arrive at the laboratory.

- -

To:

Prof. John Smith, Dept. of Psychology, The University, London I want to take part in this study of memory and learning. I am between the ages of 20 and 50. I will be paid £20 (plus £5 bus fare) if I participate.

Name (please print) ....

Address ....

....

Telephone no. .... Best time to call you ....

Age ...... Occupation .... Sex *female* ❑ *male* ❑

Can you come: *weekdays* ❑ *evenings* ❑ *weekends* ❑

Figure 8.4 A typical advert for volunteers

Figure 8.5 Milgram's obedience experiment (1963)

The other volunteer or learner is then taken into an adjacent room and strapped into a chair. Electrodes are attached to his arm.

You are shown a shock generator with thirty switches. The switch on the left is marked '15 volts', with subsequent switches proceeding in 15-volt intervals, to the one on the extreme right marked 450 volts.

Underneath each series of switches are labels reading 'Slight shock', 'Moderate shock', 'Very strong shock', 'Danger – Severe shock', concluding with two ominously labelled 'XXX'.

The experimenter (E) then tells you (S) to use an intercom to read a list of word pairs, such as blue-box, nice-day, wild-duck etc. to the learner (A). You do so.

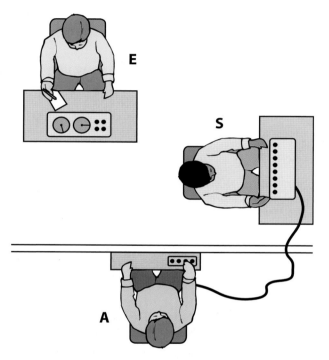

Figure 8.6

On completion you are instructed to read the list of words again, but this time only reading the first word of each pair. Your learner is told to indicate the associated word. When he makes his first mistake you are told to throw the switch marked 15 volts. Each time they make a mistake thereafter you are told to increase the shock in 15-volt increments.

When you reach 75 volts you hear him moan. At 105 volts he cries out in pain. At 150 volts he shouts and begs you to stop. You look at the experimenter who tells you to continue. You do. At 180 volts your learner is screaming and banging on the wall. You again look to the experimenter, who again tells you to continue.

What do you think you would do? Would you stop inflicting electric shocks to your learner? You might think 'yes'. Psychology suggests otherwise!

Stanley Milgram

Could it be that Eichmann and his million accomplices in the Holocaust were just following orders? Could we call them all accomplices?"

(Milgram, 1974)

In 1963 social psychologist Stanley Milgram began a series of such experiments at Yale University in America. He wanted to try and understand the mindset of those Germans who had taken part in the dreadful Nazi Holocaust of World War Two.

The Holocaust refers to a period of time where between nine and eleven million Jews, Socialists, Trade Unionists, gays, gypsies and others were gassed to death in the concentration camps of Auschwitz, Treblinka, and Birkenau to name just a few.

At the Nuremberg trials held after the war leading Nazis justified such actions by claiming they were obeying orders.

ONLINE INTERACTIVES

Go on a virtual tour of Auschwitz and Birkenau Concentration camps. Visit :

www.remember.org/auschwitz/

A direct link is available in the Chapter 8 section of the Higher Psychology Learning Suite at **www.gerardkeegan.co.uk**

The Court dismissed this 'excuse'. Subsequently many of the accused were sentenced to death or given long prison sentences.

At the time it was thought that such unquestioning obedience to authority was abnormal, and possibly due to some kind of mass character flaw evident in the German population at the time.

Milgram had a hunch that this was not the case. He thought that *everyone*, Americans, Germans etc. were all capable of committing such acts. His rationale being because we are all prone to obey others in authority.

Consequently in the 1960s and 1970s he investigated the extent to which ordinary people were willing to obey the orders of another person.

The question arises as to whether there is any connection between what we have studied in the laboratory and the forms of obedience we so deplored in the Nazi epoch."

(Milgram, 1963)

Obedience to authority (1963)

Milgram placed an advertisement in a New Haven newspaper to recruit 40 male participants to take part in the experiment outlined above. They were professional, white collar, or unskilled workers aged between 20 and 50. All were paid $4.50 for taking part.

A 31-year-old biology teacher, who introduced himself as Jack Williams, met each on their arrival at the University. Jack was dressed in a grey laboratory technician's coat, and was reputably of stern appearance. As indicated above, he duped each volunteer to be the 'teacher'. There were two cards marked 'teacher' in the box, which was always given first to the naïve participant.

The other person present was thought by the naïve participants to be another volunteer. He was however a 47-year-old Irish-American accountant called Wallace who had been trained to be the victim. He always played the 'learner'. He was reportedly mild mannered and likeable.

The experiment proceeded as illustrated. If a participant 'teacher' showed reticence in administering electric shocks Williams used standardised commands or 'Prods' such as 'Please continue' and 'You have no other choice, you *must* go on.'

Prod 1: 'Please continue' or 'Please go on';

Prod 2: 'The experiment requires that you continue';

Prod 3: 'It is absolutely essential that you continue';

Prod 4: 'You have no other choice, you must go on'.

The prods were always presented in sequence. Only if Prod 1 was unsuccessful could Prod 2 be used, etc. If a participant continued to disobey after Prod 4, the experiment was stopped. The experimenter's tone of voice was always firm, but not impolite.

If and when a participant asked if their learner could suffer permanent harm, a special prod was used. This read 'although the shocks may be painful, there is no permanent tissue damage, so please go on'. If necessary, Prods 2, 3 and 4, followed this.

If the participant said that their learner wanted to stop, another special prod was used. This read 'whether the learner likes it or not, you must go on until he has learned all the word pairs correctly, so please go on', Again, if necessary, Prods 2, 3 and 4, followed this.

The experiment ended when the 450-volt shock had been reached and administered, or when the teacher participant walked out.

Any participant who stopped prior to administering the highest shock of 450 volts was termed a *defiant* participant. Any who obeyed up to the 450 volts was called an *obedient* participant.

Forty sessions were filmed. Research assistants observed proceedings through a two-way mirror and took notes. The length of each shock given by the teacher participant to the stooge victim was timed. As was the latency or delay time taken to administer it. The results were astonishing.

Results

Not one of the 40 teacher participants stopped administering electric shocks before the 300-volt mark! At 300 volts just five or 12.5 per cent defiant participants protested and stopped.

Twenty-six or 65 per cent of obedient participants went on to inflict the maximum 450-volt shock to the learner-stooge.

In a large number of cases the degree of tension reached extremes that are rarely seen in sociopsychological laboratory studies. Subjects were observed to sweat, tremble, stutter, bite their lips, groan and dig their fingers into their flesh. These were characteristic rather than exceptional responses to the experiment...One sign of tension was the regular occurrence of nervous laughing fits...Full-blown, uncontrollable seizures were observed for three subjects. On one occasion we observed a fit so violently convulsive that it was necessary to call a halt to the experiment. In the post experimental interviews subjects took pains to point out that they were not sadistic types, and that the laughter did not mean they enjoyed shocking the victim."

(Milgram, 1963 from Hill, 2001)

Fourteen or 35 per cent backed out of the experiment before the end.

Milgram had previously asked his psychology students and fellow academics to give percentage estimates of how many participants they thought would inflict the maximum shock of 450 volts. Their average estimate was 1.2 per cent. They were only 63.8 per cent out in their estimation!

After the experiment, the participants were interviewed and debriefed using open-ended questions. To ascertain that his participants were not harmed Milgram gave them a number of psychometric tests. These included projective tests and attitude scales concerning how each participant felt.

The participant was also reunited with the victim. This was to show them that the victim was not harmed. It was also explained to obedient participants that their behaviour was normal. These extensive debriefing procedures were taken to ensure that the participants left the laboratory in as good a state of well being as possible.

Of his 1963 results Milgram said, 'The extreme willingness of adults to go to almost any lengths on the command of an authority constitutes the chief finding of the study and the fact most urgently demanding explanation' (Milgram, 1974).

ONLINE INTERACTIVES

Listen to a podcast on Obedience. Audio includes Definitions; key studies (Milgram and variations); factors that affect obedience (legitimate authority, responsibility); impact of Milgram's research. Go to:

www.psychlotron.org.uk/podcasts.html

A direct link is available in the Chapter 8 section of the Higher Psychology Learning Suite at www.gerardkeegan.co.uk

Factors influencing obedience

Milgram believed that such blind obedience to authority was determined by social factors. According to Milgram we obey the direct instructions of others for the following reasons.

Status and prestige
Milgram thought that his social status, and the prestige of the surroundings where the 1963 experiment took place had influenced the high levels of obedience obtained in his study. After all he was a Professor, and his experiment had been conducted at Yale, one of America's most prestigious 'Ivy League' Universities.

To test his 'Legitimate Authority' hypothesis, and measure the effect status and prestige has on obedience; Milgram then rented a house in Bridgeport, Connecticut.

As before, he put an advertisement in a local newspaper to get participants. This time he made no mention of himself or Yale University. Participants came forward and the experiment proceeded as before.

Under these less prestigious circumstances levels of obedience dropped, but to a lesser extent than Milgram expected.

Forty-eight per cent of Bridgeport participants continued to the maximum 450 volts, in comparison to 65 per cent in the original study.

Proximity
Milgram also thought the proximity of an authority figure to their subject affected obedience. To test this assumption Milgram got his experimenter to interact with his teacher participants in various ways.

He found that when his experimenter gave instructions by phone; only 20 per cent of teacher participants gave the learner the maximum shock of 450 volts. Others lied and said they had, but hadn't (Rada and Rodgers, 1973).

In another variation on proximity obedience levels remained high when the experimenter gave their instructions in person, and then left the room (Rada and Rodgers, 1973).

Obedience thus depends upon the closeness of the authority figure to the subject. The more proximal an authority figure to us, the more likely we are to obey their instructions.

The proximity of participant to victim also has an effect on obedience levels, but in a negative direction.

Milgram found that the nearer his teacher volunteers were to their learner, the less likely they were to inflict lethal doses of electricity. When the teacher and learner were in the same room 40 per cent of participants went to 450 volts. As proximity increased, obedience levels substantially decreased (Milgram, 1965).

Presence of others who disobey

Milgram also created a situation where he had three teachers (Milgram, 1965). Teacher 1 was a confederate of Milgram's. His task was to read the word lists to the learner. Teacher 2 was also a confederate of Milgram's. His task was to indicate when the learner forgot a word, or made an error. Teacher 3 was the actual participant. His task was to inflict the electric shocks.

On Milgram's previous instructions when 150 volts was reached Teacher 1 refused to participate further. Teachers 2 and 3 were then instructed to continue by the experimenter. By prior arrangement when 210 volts was reached Teacher 2 also pulled out. Teacher 3 was instructed to continue on alone. At this point in 90 per cent of cases Teacher 3, who was the real participant opted out.

The presence of others who disobey clearly reduces the likelihood of individuals continuing to blindly obey the direct orders of an authority figure.

Obedience to authority: Situation	Obedient participant rate (Those who inflicted up to 450v)
Original experiment at Yale University	65 per cent
Bridgeport, Connecticut	48 per cent
Teacher and learner in same room	40 per cent
Experimenter gives phone instructions	20 per cent
Presence of others who quit	10 per cent

Table 8.1

Milgram and ethics

Milgram's blind obedience experiments have long been the subject of controversy and criticism.

Baumrind (1964) believes his studies were unethical. Her criticisms include the following:

➤ Milgram caused distress to his participants.

➤ Milgram deceived his participants as to the true purpose of his research.

➤ Milgram did not receive his participants *informed* consent to take part

➤ Milgram abused his participants right to withdraw, in that they were told to continue inflicting electric shocks when they indicated they did not want to do so.

ONLINE INTERACTIVES

Read 'Lying in the Laboratory: Deception in Human Research' at: **www.asa3.org/asa/topics/ethics/JASA12-82Bassett.html**

and answer the following question.

1   Give reasons for and against the use of deception in psychological research.

A direct link is available in the Chapter 8 section of the Higher Psychology Learning Suite at **www.gerardkeegan.co.uk**

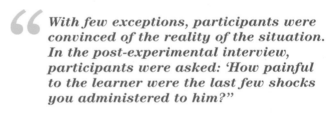

With few exceptions, participants were convinced of the reality of the situation. In the post-experimental interview, participants were asked: 'How painful to the learner were the last few shocks you administered to him?"

On a printed 14-point scale ranging from 1 ('not at all painful') to 14 ('extremely painful'), the mean was 13.42."

(Milgram, 1963)

In response, Milgram (1964) defended his research saying that:

➤ He believed his research was not unethical as his results were unexpected.

➤ He appreciated his participants got distressed, but did not come to any psychological harm.

➤ He did not physically stop his participants from leaving. They could have left at any time.

➤ He rigorously debriefed his participants. They were introduced to the learner and saw he was completely unharmed.

➤ He had them complete a survey one year later, and found that 84 per cent were 'glad to have been in the experiment.' Fifteen per cent were neutral, and only 1.3 per cent sorry that they had participated. Eighty per cent said there should be more research like it, and 74 per cent thought that they had learned something about themselves (Milgram, 1964).

➤ He had his participants undergo a psychiatric assessment one year later. No signs of psychological harm were found.

Recent world events have seen a more sympathetic reaction to Milgram's classic study. This author has never doubted his original analysis.

ONLINE INTERACTIVES

Read 'Could Abu Ghraib happen again?' by Princeton psychologists Fiske, Harris and Cuddy (2002). Go to: www.princeton.edu/pr/news/04/q4/1125-fiske.htm

A direct link is available in the Chapter 8 section of the Higher Psychology Learning Suite at www.gerardkeegan.co.uk

Explanations of obedience studies

There are two explanations as to why we show obedience to authority. Both concern social power. The first is Agency theory, as advocated by Milgram, and the second Social impact theory, as put forward by Latanè and Wolf.

Agency theory

Milgram thought that we when obey orders from others we lose personal responsibility for our actions. We perceive ourselves as the authority figure's *agent*, acting on their behalf.

Milgram believed the high levels of obedience attained in his studies were because his participants underwent a *cognitive shift* in viewpoint. His participants went from an autonomous state, which is one where they had personal control of their situation, to an agentic state, which is one where they felt themselves to be 'the instrument for carrying out another person's actions' (Milgram, 1974).

Milgram thinks our ability to do this is as a result of evolution. Our agentic ability has evolved because it

helps society to function better. Our ability to submit to the authority of others allows us all to achieve collective goals.

If everyone did his or her own thing and acted autonomously, society would collapse.

Social impact theory

Social impact theory is also applicable to an understanding of obedience and was first proposed by Latanè and Wolf in 1981.

Social impact theory suggests that we succumb to social influence because of three variables, strength, immediacy and number.

Strength

Strength refers to just how important the influencing agent, person or group of people are to us.

This was alluded to earlier. Milgram thought his social status as a Professor of Psychology, and the prestige of Yale University where his original 1963 experiment took place greatly influenced the high levels of obedience shown by the participants in his study.

Immediacy

Immediacy refers to just how close in time and space the influencing agent, person or group are to us when the influence attempt is made.

The more recent a request, the more likely we are to grant it. The nearer the person or group making the request is to us, the more likely we are to behave the way they want.

Again Milgram confirmed this. The more proximal, or nearer his teacher volunteers were to their learner, the less likely they were to inflict lethal doses of electricity. When the teacher and learner were in the same room 40 per cent of participants went to 450 volts. When the experimenter gave instructions over the phone 20 per cent of participants obeyed. These reduced obedience levels are in comparison to 65 per cent in the original study (Milgram, 1965).

Number

Latanè and Wolf tell us that the more people in a group who behave in a particular way, the greater the influence this will have on others to do the same. Such impact does however diminish as group size grows.

If you are giving a presentation to three people and a fourth one joins the group, this is more significant than if you were giving a presentation to 31 people and one more joined.

While each individual can influence others, the more people present, the less influence any one individual will have. We are more likely to listen attentively to a speaker if we are in a small group than if we were in a large group.

In Milgram's study, when there were a number of other people present participant obedience levels decreased. Milgram consequently confirms much of Latanè and Wolf's social impact theory.

INTERACTIVES

Please answer the following questions:

1 How did Milgram understand the results that he got in his study?

2 What is meant by an 'agentic state'?

3 How does an individual's agentic state help society function?

4 What do you understand by 'social impact theory'?

5 Why is social impact theory relevant to Milgram's study?

Milgram: Postscript

Milgram concluded that obedience, or our compliance with an explicit request from an authority figure, is an extremely powerful force behind why we often behave as we do; inside the laboratory and out.

Hofling et al. (1966)

For example Hofling *et al.* (1966) researched blind obedience to authority in an American hospital. They had an unknown doctor make telephone calls to 22 nurses instructing them to give patients twice the maximum allowed level of a drug. The drug was a placebo. The nurses did not know this, and thought it to be the real thing. The bottle that contained the 'drug' was clearly labelled with warnings about going over the maximum allowed dose. Twenty-one of the 22 nurses, or 95 per cent, blindly obeyed the unknown doctor, who could of course have been anyone!

This was in contrast to their response when asked directly by the researchers if they would ever do such a thing. Here 21 of the 22, or 95 per cent, said that they would not have obeyed the doctor, as it would have broken hospital rules regards administering drugs.

Later, Bickman (1974) investigated obedience in the streets of New York. He was interested in the different status and power society gives to authority figures. Read his study on 'The Social Power of a Uniform' in the Chapter on the Experimental Method on page 197.

Zimbardo et al. (1973)

In 1973 the United States Navy and US Marine Corps commissioned Philip Zimbardo and his colleagues to investigate allegations of brutality and violence in their military prisons.

At the time it was thought people in prison behaved the way they did because of dispositional attributes. Dispositional attributes refer to aspects of personality. Consequently particular personalities are attracted to become prison guards, a number of whom act in a brutal way. Similarly, particular personalities are attracted to become criminal, an aspect of which is to be violent.

Haney, Craig, Banks, Curtis and Zimbardo had a hunch that social role-playing, or situational attributes could *also* be the cause of such behaviours.

They set out to see whether this was the case.

The Stanford Prison Experiment

Zimbardo *et al.* (1973) put together a sample of 21 male volunteers from Palo Alto in California. They were invited to Stanford University and pre-screened for physical ailments and mental stability. They were told that they would be paid $15 a day for 14 days to take part in a study of prison life.

Using an independent group design they were allocated their role in the experiment. On the toss of a coin they became either a prison guard or prisoner. These were the two conditions of the independent variable. They were then sent home.

Shortly afterwards the local police arrived unannounced at the prisoners' homes. They were arrested, blindfolded, and then taken to a 'prison' in the basement of Stanford University.

Deindividuation

On arrival the prisoners were stripped, deloused, given a uniform with a prison number on it and put into ankle chains. Thereafter, they were identified only by this number e. g. 'Prisoner 3456…'

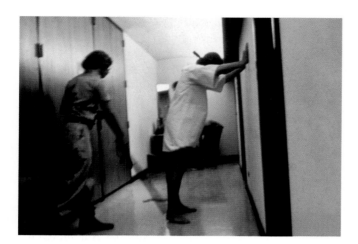

Figure 8.7 The Stanford Prison Experiment

To further encourage deindividuation, or the temporary loss of personal identity (Le Bon, 1895), the guards wore uniform and dark reflective sunglasses. They also carried long wooden staves, handcuffs and whistles.

Diener (1980) thinks deindividuation, or loss of self awareness and personal identity, results in:

➤ poor self-monitoring

➤ less concern for social approval

➤ increased impulsive behaviours

➤ reduced ability to think rationally.

Situational attributes

After just six days the study was stopped. The participants had become too immersed in their respective roles.

The guards would wake the prisoners during the night. They would lock them in cupboards. They were made to clean the toilets with their bare hands.

One prisoner went on hunger strike. Some asked for parole! Others broke down. Zimbardo *et al.* observed early signs of depression among their inmates.

Zimbardo *et al.* (1974) suggests that situational attributes caused the dramatic changes observed in their participants' behaviours.

Guard brutality or prisoner upset could not have been solely because of dispositional attributes. This was because guards and prisoners had been randomly allocated to their roles.

Each participant was seen to very quickly adopt the behavioural norms associated with the role they found themselves in. These norms would have been stored in their minds as social schema.

Normative social influence was evident. Publically participants behaved in the way they thought a prisoner or guard should, but privately they didn't feel comfortable in so doing.

Zimbardo *et al.* (1973) illustrates how a person's situation rather than their disposition can influence conformity to social norms.

Criticisms of Zimbardo *et al.* (1973)

The main criticism levelled at Zimbardo *et al.* (1973) concerns ethics.

It is clear participants were caused emotional distress. While the participants were all paid volunteers, those who were prisoners did not realise they would be arrested at home. They did not know they would be so dehumanised on arrival at the prison, or that the guards would treat them harshly.

The researchers should have foreseen this, and probably abandoned the research design.

It is evident that obedience to authority is a behavioural tendency that we *all* share.

Resisting social influence

Social influence is the effect other people have on our thoughts, feelings, and behaviours. Social influence is pertinent to both conformity and obedience.

In 'the Lucifer effect', which concerns why good men turn evil, we are reminded that 'social situations lead ordinary people to commit unimaginable acts of violence, discrimination, and indifference to the suffering of others.

 Many of us hope that if we were placed in such situations, we would be the courageous ones who resist unjust authority, who are immune to compliance tactics, and who never abandon our core beliefs and principles in the face of social pressures."

(Zimbardo and Wang, 2007)

Resisting social influence is thus immeasurably difficult. Examples of resistance in psychological research tend to reflect this. In Milgram (1963), for example, only 35 per cent of participant-teachers refused to give the maximum electric shock to the learner-victim.

ONLINE INTERACTIVES

Go to:
www.lucifereffect.org/index.html

to find out more about the Lucifer effect, and the Stanford Prison Experiment (1971).

Then answer the questions at:
www.prisonexp.org/discuss.htm

A direct link is available in the Chapter 8 section of the Higher Psychology Learning Suite at www.gerardkeegan.co.uk

Asch (1951) saw higher rates of resistance to conform. In his line judgement task 26 per cent of participants did not conform at all, while 100 per cent , or all 50, were resistant at least once in the original line test.

Having *social support* is crucial to resisting social influence.

Social support

In Asch (1951) having just one other person agree that the (stooge) majority view was wrong lowered conformity from an average 32 per cent to five per cent. With two other teachers present in Milgram (1963) participant obedience levels fell to ten per cent.

Rebellion

Gamson *et al.* (1982) set out to test the hypothesis that a group of people are more likely to rebel than one lone individual

Gamson *et al.* (1982) established 33 groups of participants. Twenty-five or 92 per cent refused, and sixteen or 50 per cent rebelled against unfair requests made of them from authority figures. This may have been because the groups were deliberately given plenty of breaks, and thus had time to discuss what they had to do and how they might react. They were able to *define the situation* and establish their own group norm. Groups provide an opportunity for dissent, and also give dissenting individuals social support for their actions.

Gamson *et al.* put the high levels of rebellion down to people complying rather then agreeing with those who initiated the rebellious behaviour. As you may remember compliance is a type of conformity that sees a change in an individual's public behaviour but not private beliefs.

Dissent and rebellion may also have been exacerbated due to *deindividuation*. Deindividuation is a feeling felt by members of a group that they have lost their personal identities to the greater group identity. They find they have merged into the group or crowd and become, to all intents and purposes, anonymous (Festinger, Pepitone, and Newcomb, 1952).

As we read earlier deindividuation was most apparent in Zimbardo *et al.* (1973).

Types of resistance

Independent behaviour: this is where person behaves consistently with his or her own attitudes regardless of social influence.

Anti-conformity: this is where someone resists social influence by opposing what the majority do. They deliberately behave differently. The non-conformist's behaviour is still affected by society however. Can you think why this is?

Why one person can resist social influence more than another

Why is it that some people are better able to resist social influence than others?

The answer lies in group identity, psychological reactance and socialisation.

Group identity

You may remember that we came across group identity earlier with reference to Tajfel (1978, 1982) and Tajfel and Turner (1986).

Our group identity is resistant to social influence from others.

This is because different groups have different goals from each other. Their norms also differ. To achieve particular goals it is unlikely one group would adopt another group's norms or expected ways of behaving. This would destroy the group's unique identity and purpose.

Psychological reactance

Psychological reactance is a emotional reaction to social pressure which threatens individual freedoms (Brehm, 1966). Telling someone they are no longer allowed to do something often prompts them to do it!

Throughout history people have resisted societal constraints on their freedom. The United States of America was founded on this principle.

First Amendment to The Constitution of the United States of America 1791

Congress shall make no law respecting an establishment of religion, or prohibiting the free exercise thereof; or abridging the freedom of speech, or of the press; or the right of the people peaceably to assemble, and to petition the government for a redress of grievances."

Figure 8.8

Psychological reactance has seen the emergence in the UK of groups like NO2ID. They are a highly organised single-issue pressure group dedicated to campaigning against the introduction of compulsory ID cards in the UK.

ONLINE INTERACTIVES

Visit:

www.no2id-scotland.net/

to find out more about NO2ID Scotland and their practical response to psychological reactance.

A direct link is available in the Chapter 8 section of the Higher Psychology Learning Suite at **www.gerardkeegan.co.uk**

Socialisation

Socialisation is the process we undergo where we learn to conform to the moral standards, codes of conduct, role expectations etc. of our society.

Socialisation can make you more or less resistant to social influence, in that how one is raised can affect the level of independence you have. We saw this earlier in our study of early socialisation.

In a cross-cultural **longitudinal** study Berry (1966, 1967) discovered that the Canadian Inuit show more independent behaviours than the Temne from Sierra Leone in Africa. This is because of the different socialisation process each culture undergoes.

From a very young age the Inuit are encouraged to be self-reliant. This is because as adults they have to hunt, fish etc. on their own. The Temne in comparison are encouraged to co-operate as children. This is because as adults they all work together farming their land.

Conformity concerns a change in our behaviour or opinions because of real or imagined pressure from a person or a group of people. We conform due to compliance, internalisation, or identification.

Obedience sees us submit to an explicit demand from an acknowledged authority figure. This is because of the power and status that they have.

Let us now turn to the psychology of prejudice.

Prejudice

Definition of prejudice

Prejudice can be defined as 'an attitude that predisposes a person to feel, perceive and act in favourable or unfavourable ways towards a group or its individual members' (Secord and Backman, 1974).

Prejudice predisposes a person to behave in a particular way. Prejudice demonstrates itself in two ways.

Firstly as *preferential treatment* for oneself or one's own **ingroup**.

Secondly as *disadvantaging* or discriminating against another person or persons' **outgroup**.

What is discrimination?

'Discrimination is the inequitable treatment of individuals considered to belong to a particular social group' (Secord and Backman, 1964).

Discrimination is the actual behavioural consequences of a person's prejudiced attitudes.

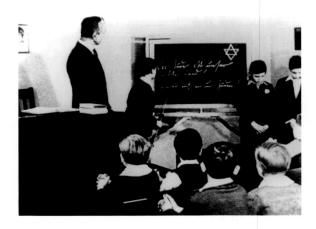

Figure 8.9 Germany circa 1935: two Jewish pupils are humiliated before their classmates. The inscription on the blackboard reads 'The Jew is our greatest enemy, beware of the Jew'

The frustration–aggression hypothesis

We experience frustration in our life because we are unable to achieve or reach desired goals.

Dollard *et al.* (1939) first put forward the frustration–aggression hypothesis.

The frustration–aggression hypothesis says the occurrence of aggressive behaviour always presupposes frustration, and that frustration always leads to some form of aggression.

Berkowitz (1969) later reformulated Dollard *et al.* to argue that frustration may result in aggression, and that the less the person who frustrates you is able to retaliate, the more likely you are to aggress against that person.

In the study of prejudice we are interested in the connection between such frustration, and subsequent aggression upon what is called a '**scapegoat**'.

Frustration, aggression, the scapegoat and prejudice

A **scapegoat** is an individual or group who are disliked or hated by others, and are made to take the blame for things for which they are not responsible. They are also relatively powerless to retaliate against inevitable acts of aggression.

In order to study links between frustration–aggression, the scapegoat and prejudice experimental studies in psychology first attempt to frustrate participants. This is done by, for example, insulting them, stopping them attain desired goals, or ensuring they fail on some task. The extent of any ensuing prejudice they might have is then measured on an attitude scale.

These results are then compared with those of a control group who did not go through the frustration experience, but just answered the attitude questionnaire.

Among the first to use such a procedure were Miller and Bugelski.

Miller and Bugelski (1948)

Miller and Bugelski (1948) initially asked their participants about their attitudes towards minority groups. Half were then frustrated when they were denied a desired film. This 'frustrated' group were then asked again about their attitudes towards minority groups. In comparison to the control group, they showed an *increase* in prejudice. Frustration when denied something seems to be related to prejudicial attitudes.

Weatherly (1961)

Later Weatherly (1961) selected two groups of non-Jewish white male college students. One group were made up of those who scored high on an anti-Semitic questionnaire, the other group low.

Half of those who scored high, and half of those who scored low on the initial questionnaire, were insulted while completing another questionnaire. The other two halves comprised the control group. They filled out the same second questionnaire but were not insulted.

All were then asked to write short stories about some pictures of men they were shown, two of which had Jewish names.

Two results were obtained. Highly anti-Semitic participants who were insulted directed more aggression onto the pictures with Jewish sounding names. The both halves of the group who had been insulted did not differ in the amount of aggression they directed at the pictures of people with *non-Jewish* sounding names.

Weatherly (1961) gives support to the idea that highly anti-Semitic people direct their aggression towards Jews, and not other groups of people.

Blaming a scapegoat arises as a result of a prejudiced person's frustration in regard to other factors. This may be because of economic climate, threats to status, or other socio-economic factors such as an inability to access services. This may account for the rise in popularity of the British National Party in recent years.

Generally when things go wrong we get frustrated. We may then look for some suitable scapegoat to blame for the situation other than ourselves.

INTERACTIVES

Please answer the following questions:

1   What was the aim of Weatherly (1961)?

2   What research method did Weatherly use?

3   What was the independent variable?

4   What was the dependent variable?

5   Outline the procedure used by Weatherly (1961).

6   What were the results?

7   What conclusion may we draw from Weatherly (1961)?

Forms of prejudice

Prejudice can take many forms, such as mild prejudice in terms of talking about or avoiding certain people, to extreme prejudice in terms of massacres and **pogroms**.

Conflict is an extreme form of discrimination where an intention to do harm is present, or harm is actually committed on another.

Sociology gives us the context within which prejudice occurs. Sociology emphasises its social, cultural and subcultural factors, and generally helps establish the background to our psychological enquiry. One should note however that we are concentrating almost exclusively on a psychological explanation of this phenomenon.

Approaches to prejudice

There are three psychological approaches to prejudice:

➤   the individual approach

➤   the interpersonal approach

➤   the intergroup approach

It should be appreciated that all three approaches are complementary to one another.

What is a stereotype?

A stereotype is a commonly held idea about what another person or group of people are like.

What stereotypes to you associate with the following?

➤   A Scotsman

➤   An Englishman

➤   An Irishman

➤   A Welshman

Are your stereotypical ideas about the above overexaggerated?

INTERACTIVE: THE PSYCHOLOGY OF PREJUDICE

Visit:

mentalhelp.net/psyhelp/chap7/chap7l.htm

A direct link is available in the Chapter 8 section of the Higher Psychology Learning Suite at **www.gerardkeegan.co.uk**

Read what Manchester United and England defender Rio Ferdinand thinks about racism in football at:

www.stopthebnp.com/

A direct link is available in the Chapter 8 section of the Higher Psychology Learning Suite at **www.gerardkeegan.co.uk**

The individual approach

The individual approach suggests the causes of prejudice to result from the emotional dynamics of a person. Prejudiced behaviour fulfils some people's psychological need to reduce tension, or gain control and order in their life.

The individual approach understands prejudice as resulting from an individual having a particular type of *personality*, or being rooted in the make-up of all human beings.

In the former prejudice is seen as arising due to differences in people's personality. In the latter people are regarded as essentially the same. The two types of explanation share a common behavioural feature called *externalisation*.

Externalisation means that we deal with our inner problems, conflicts, tensions etc. by discharging or *projecting* them onto other individuals or groups of people. We do not recognise the problem or conflict as being of our own making, but as external to us (Pettigrew, 1959).

Personality differences and prejudice

Is there a distinct personality associated with a prejudice?

Adorno, Fenkel-Brunswick, Levinson and Sanford (1950) suggested as much after investigating people whom they describe as having an **authoritarian personality**.

The authoritarian personality

Adorno *et al.* (1950) says someone with an authoritarian personality will submit to the authority of others they think higher in status and power to themselves.

They will alternatively be authoritarian with those they think to be 'beneath' or lower in status to themselves. The authoritarian personality is also typified as one that demonstrates blind and excessive obedience to authority.

In uncovering the authoritarian personality Adorno *et al.* (1950) were initially concerned with anti-Semitism. Anti-Semitism is a specific type of prejudice shown towards Jews. Their interest in this was because of the horrors visited upon European Jews in the 1930s and 1940s.

They developed a questionnaire to measure its elements. They then turned their attention to measuring **ethnocentrism**, or prejudice in general. Anti-Semitism is just one manifestation of ethnocentrism.

INTERACTIVES

Other than anti-Semitism
identify and describe three other ethnocentric behaviours that demonstrate prejudice.

The two questionnaires led Adorno *et al.* (1950) to identify the F-syndrome. The F-syndrome is an authoritarian personality. F equates with fascist.

Adorno et al's. F-Scale

Adorno *et al's.* F-scale, developed to help recognise the F-syndrome, is a questionnaire that helps indicate the degree of authoritarianism an individual may have. It measures nine component behaviours such as conventionalism, authoritarian submission, superstition, preoccupation with power, puritanical sexual attitudes etc.

The F-Scale asks respondents to indicate their agreement with four or five statements regarding each component behaviour. Take 'conventionalism':

'Obedience and respect for authority are the most important virtues a child should learn;'

Or 'superstition':

'Some day it will probably be shown that astrology can explain a lot of things;

Or 'puritanical sexual attitudes':

'Homosexuality is a particularly rotten form of delinquency and ought to be severely punished;' etc.

The F-scale is constructed in such a way that a positive answer to a statement such as 'agrees' scores a point. This is taken as an indicator of an authoritarian personality. The higher one's F score the more authoritarian one is thought to be.

Adorno *et al.* (1950) then looked at the extent to which a person with an authoritarian personality was likely to be anti-Semitic and ethnocentric. Both their original work, and subsequent research by Christie and Cook (1958), illustrates a consistent positive correlation between three factors.

There is a strong positive statistical relationship between authoritarianism and ethnocentrism, authoritarianism and political/economic conservatism, and authoritarianism and fascist potential. There are however methodological and conceptual criticisms of these findings.

Evaluation of Adorno et al. (1950)

Methodological issues

The main methodological problem with the Adorno *et al.* F-scale, and its antecedent anti-Semitic and ethnocentric questionnaires, is that answering 'yes' to a particular statement was taken as someone indicating agreement with it. This may not have been the case. It could have been that respondents were demonstrating **acquiescence response**.

Acquiescence response is our natural tendency to agree or say yes to things, especially when there is no personal cost involved. We cannot therefore be entirely sure that a high F-scale score *does* show high authoritarianism etc.

Respondents could have agreed with statements because they wanted to be helpful to the researcher!

Acquiescence response could be overcome by redesigning the questionnaire, using for example a **DK filter**. For more on this please read pages 00–00 of The Survey Method.

Conceptual issues

Conceptual problems regarding Adorno *et al.* (1950) are more difficult to overcome. The F-Scale lacks **internal validity**. This is because common agreement as on what 'personality' is, how it is formed, and thus how it can be measured is difficult to find in psychology.

Hyman and Sheatsley (1954) get around this conceptual difficulty by suggesting that a distinct personality type is not needed to explain ethnocentrism.

For them education and socio-economic situation provide a more plausible explanation for an authoritarian personality. This can be seen from Table 8.2 below.

Hyman and Sheatsley found an authoritarian personality more likely to exist among people who were less well educated and of lower economic status than others. This is evident from Table 8.2 where participant agreement with items on the F-scale *decreases* as their educational level increases.

A further conceptual problem with the Adorno *et al.* authoritarian personality is that an authoritarian personality is associated with someone who gravitates towards extreme right wing political views. This is not the case.

Rokeach and the individual approach to prejudice

Rokeach (1960) argued that the authoritarian personality could equally be found in those who have extreme left-wing political views. This is because of an important element to the authoritarian personality called dogmatism.

A dogmatic individual is someone who has a rigid style of thought, and demonstrates intolerance towards others. Life is very black *or* white, and their view is always the right one. Dogmatism is not just found in those who hold extreme right wing political views.

Item from Adorno *et al.* F-Scale Questionnaire	Level of schooling achieved by Hyman and Sheatsley (1954) respondent		
	College	High School	Grammar
The most important thing to teach children is absolute obedience to their parents.	35 per cent	60 per cent	80 per cent
Any good leader should be strict with people under him in order to gain respect.	18 per cent	31 per cent	45 per cent
Prison is too good for sex criminals - they should be publicly whipped or worse.	18 per cent	31 per cent	45 per cent
No decent man can respect a woman who has sexual relations before marriage.	14 per cent	26 per cent	39 per cent

Table 8.2

Rokeach administered a questionnaire to Conservative, Liberal, Labour, and Communist students in England. His results supported his hypothesis that dogmatism is an aspect of people's personalities who hold an extreme right *or* left political view. This was because he found both Conservative and Communist students to score higher on dogmatic attitudes than Liberal and Labour students.

Methodological problems arose however. All 40 items on the Rokeach (1960) questionnaire are worded in such a way that respondent agreement, or saying 'Yes', indicates dogmatism.

This recurring problem of acquiescence response throws doubt on the *validity* of the Rokeach questionnaire. Rokeach does however make an important point concerning the search for a prejudiced personality by separating its primarily authoritarian element from any political ideology.

Eysenck and the individual approach to prejudice

Professor Hans Eysenck (1954) proposed that two dimensions to personality were needed to characterise similarities and differences between those on the extreme left and extreme right of the political spectrum; and whether as a consequence prejudiced attitudes will result.

These two dimensions he termed tough minded/tender minded, and radical/conservative. Tough minded/tender minded refers to an individual's temperament, and radical/conservative to their political leanings.

Whether an individual is on the left or on the right of the political spectrum is based on where delegates sat in the French Legislative Assembly around the time of the French Revolution of 1789. Jacobins sat on the left and Girondists the right. They differed in their attitude to the redistribution of wealth in society. This is still very much the case today.

Eysenck developed a social attitudes inventory, or questionnaire, to assess respondents in each dimension. Such results can be graphically illustrated.

A tender minded person would indicate in their answers to questions in the SAI that they believed in such things as the abolition of the death penalty, re-education of criminals, pacifism etc.

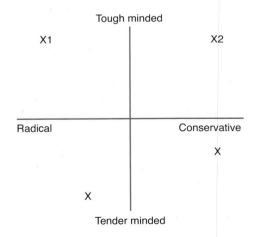

Figure 8.10

A tough-minded person would be in favour of the death penalty, prison and punishment, and compulsory sterilisation of people with serious hereditary defects.

It is worth noting that Eysenck's SAI was constructed in the mid-1950s. The questions it asks reflects debates current in Britain at the time.

Using his social attitudes inventory Eysenck then plotted the tough-minded/tender minded; radical/conservative attitudes of people from different political parties into his two dimensional model.

He found communists who are on the extreme left of the political spectrum to be radical and tough minded, and fascists on the extreme right to be conservative and tough-minded.

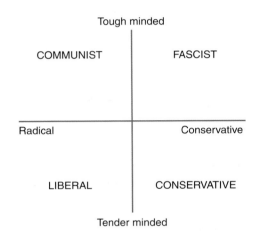

Figure 8.11

In terms of ethnocentrism generally, and prejudice in particular Eysenck concluded that prejudiced attitudes and discriminatory behaviour are more likely to stem from *tough-minded* people of *either* an extreme left, or extreme right wing political persuasion.

Eysenck's contention that Fascists and Communists share the common temperament of being tough minded, and that this tough mindedness results in prejudice and discrimination, has not received much support.

When we looked at Early Socialisation in Chapter Three we read that temperament is biological in origin. This being so, if Eysenck is correct many would be born with a biological predisposition to be Fascist or Communist. This is unlikely!

The individual approach to prejudice: conclusion

Adorno and his colleagues influenced the development of the individual approach to prejudice. Adorno *et al.* (1950) suggested prejudice occurs because of the F-syndrome. The F-syndrome describes the thoughts, feelings, and behaviours of someone with an authoritarian personality. An authoritarian personality was originally thought exclusive to people with extreme right wing political views. Subsequent research suggests otherwise. Eysenck and Rokeach found the authoritarian personality common in people at both ends of the political spectrum. Being tough-minded and dogmatic, emphasised by Eysenck (1956) and Rokeach (1960) respectively, are more important to an authoritarian personality than left- or right-wing political ideology. Dogmatism and tough mindedness illustrate how individuals at either end of the political spectrum are related in terms of an authoritarian personality. They are as equally prejudiced as each other towards those who do not hold the same beliefs as they do.

The interpersonal approach

Psychologists who take an interpersonal approach to prejudice look at two things.

They investigate whether we accept or reject others on the basis of similar religious belief or shared racial identity. They also try to assess the extent to which conformity to prevailing cultural stereotypes and/or values account for prejudice and discrimination.

Shared beliefs

Rokeach (1968) suggests that 'differences in belief on important issues are more powerful determinants of prejudice and discrimination than differences in race or ethnic membership.'

Discrimination suffered by Afro-Caribbean people in Britain in the 1950s and 1960s may then have been because Afro-Caribbeans held different beliefs to the indigenous British population. The interpersonal approach to prejudice believes race or ethnic membership to be irrelevant.

To test the shared beliefs hypothesis, Rokeach, Smith and Evans (1960) conducted an experiment where they asked participants to rate people according to whether they would like to be friends with them. Potential friends were described as having the same beliefs, or being of the same religion as participants. Participants were presented with descriptive pairs of statements like:

> A white person who believes in God.

> A black person who believes in God.

Or:

> A white person who is a Communist.

> A black person who is an anti-Communist.

Rokeach et al. (1960) found their participants to say they would like to be friends with people who believed in the same things as they did *regardless* of their race. Belief similarity was more important than race similarity.

To test the shared beliefs theory further, Rokeach (1968) conducted a field experiment where 26 black and 26 white males were invited for a job interview. Each was put into a waiting room with four experimenter confederates. The invitees thought they too were waiting for an interview.

The confederates were told by Rokeach to talk about how they thought mental heath patients should be treated. The conditions of the independent variable saw them discuss either a traditional or informal approach to treatment. The traditional approach concerned institutionalisation and drug therapy, while a more informal approach, care in the community and some kind of 'talking' therapy.

Things were arranged in such a way that two of the four confederates were of the *same* race as each participant. One held a different belief to the participant, the other the same. The other two confederates were of a *different* race to each participant. Again one held a different belief to them, the other the same.

After each participant had talked to the confederates for about ten minutes they were asked with which two out of the four confederates they would like to work.

Participants overwhelmingly chose potential workmates who shared the same beliefs *regardless* of their race. There was also a tendency for people to deliberately choose workmates of similar *and* different races, indicating a preference for mixed groups of workplace colleagues.

The shared beliefs hypothesis concludes that we positively discriminate in favour of those who have similar beliefs to ourselves, and negatively discriminate against those who don't. Rokeach concludes that belief similarity or dissimilarity is a more important factor to social discrimination than race similarity or difference.

In the light of racial tension in the UK evident since the 1950s is this in fact the case?

Shared identities

Does race *cause* prejudice?

Triandis was critical of the shared beliefs hypothesis. He thought race played an important part in our prejudiced behaviours. To discover if this were the case Triandis and Triandis (1960) developed their social distance scale. Their social distance scale measures the extent to which we would like to associate with others in different social situations.

Triandis and Triandis (1960) conducted an experiment where they gave participants descriptions of individuals. The descriptions differed on the basis of race, belief or occupation. Race, belief and occupation were the conditions of their independent variable.

In the light of these descriptions participants were then asked to indicate their agreement or disagreement with items on the social distance scale such as 'I would accept this person as my neighbour', 'I would not permit this person's attendance at a University' etc.

Triandis and Triandis found that the more dissimilar the description of the stimulus person was from the participant the greater the participant's social distance.

Analysis indicated that race was the main variable in the creation of social distance. Difference in terms of belief and occupation were found to be of equal, but minor, significance to social distance.

Triandis and Davis (1965) later revealed a more complex picture. In certain situations, such as marriage, race is more important in the creation of social distance than different belief. However belief is more important in the creation of social distance in less intimate circumstances.

Identification

One reason for this may be that in less intimate situations people do not identify strongly with their own race.

But is identification with ones own ethnic background not important?

In a classic study Clark and Clark (1947) presented white and black children with a white doll and a brown doll. They then asked the children which doll looked most like them. Ninety-nine per cent of white children identified with the white doll, as did 66 per cent of black children.

Hraba and Grant (1970) later repeated the study. They found an overwhelming majority of black children now identified with the brown doll.

The conclusion to this is that over the years, identification with one's race had become stronger. Thus the shared belief hypothesis proposed by Rokeach *et al.* is less significant than was once thought.

Thus from an interpersonal perspective race similarity/dissimilarity is more important in the understanding of social discrimination and prejudice than shared belief. This is due to increased identification with ones own ethnic background.

ONLINE INTERACTIVES

Go to:
www.holah.karoo.net/hrabastudy.htm

and read 'Black is Beautiful: A Re-examination of Racial Preference and Identification' by Hraba and Grant (1970).

Then please answer the following questions.

1 What was the aim of Hraba and Grant (1970)?

2 Why was this a quasi experiment?

3 What procedure did Hraba and Grant adopt?

4 What were their results?

5 What were their conclusions?

6 What criticisms might be made of this study?

A direct link is available in the Chapter 8 section of the Higher Psychology Learning Suite at www.gerardkeegan.co.uk

Let us now look at what the interpersonal approach can tell us about discrimination and prejudice, and conformity to prevailing cultural stereotypes and values.

Stereotypes

Allport (1954) says stereotyping is a grossly oversimplistic and overgeneralised abstraction about groups of people. These abstractions are usually highly inaccurate.

Stereotyping occurs when we categorise people on the basis of highly visible characteristics such as their race, sex, nationality, bodily appearance etc. All members of that social grouping are subsequently recognised as possessing these stereotypic characteristics.

According to Rokeach (1968) a stereotype is:

> *a socially shared belief that describes an attitude object in an oversimplified or undifferentiated manner; the attitude object is said to prefer certain modes of conduct which, by implication, are judged to be socially desirable or undesirable... A person's stereotype may contain an element of truth in it, but the stereotype is not qualified in any way.*"

Personal stereotype: Those attributes an individual thinks describes a group.

Consensual stereotype: Those attributes many people think describe a group.

Psychology has tried to measure stereotypes and its characteristics by giving people a list of adjectives together with a list of ethnic categories. They are then asked to score on a graded scale how these adjectives describe each particular group of people.

While people are less willing to engage in such an exercise nowadays, Karlins, Coffman and Walters (1969) have shown how stereotypes can change over time.

INTERACTIVES

Look at Karlins, Coffman and Walters (1969).

What evidence does this study present to help us conclude that while stereotypes change over time, the prevalence of stereotyping does not change?

Ethnic group	Trait	1933	1951	1967
		Percentage		
Americans	Industrious	48	NA	23
	Intelligent	47	NA	20
	Materialistic	33	NA	67
Jews	Shrewd	79	47	30
	Mercenary	49	28	15
	Ambitious	21	28	48
Negroes	Superstitious	84	41	13
	Lazy	75	31	26
	Musical	26	33	47

Table 8.3 Changing stereotypes of Americans, Jews and Negroes over a 40-year period. Karlins, Coffman and Walters (1969)

Putting measurement of stereotyping aside, the interpersonal approach then asks two questions.

What implications does stereotyping have for discrimination and prejudice?,

And what psychological function does stereotyping serve?

The psychological consequences of stereotyping

Campbell (1967) suggests stereotyping has four consequences.

First, stereotypes operate to *overestimate differences* existing *between* groups.

Second, stereotypes operate to cause *underestimation* of *differences within* groups.

Third, stereotypes *distort reality* since such overestimation of differences between groups, and underestimation of differences within groups, bear no relation to the truth.

Fourth, stereotypes are usually negative attitudes used by people to *justify* conflict and discrimination towards others.

The psychological function of stereotypes

What psychological function and purpose do stereotypes serve?

Psychology thinks stereotyping helps impose order on our potentially chaotic social world. Without such categorisation or pigeonholing of people it would be difficult for social interaction to proceed. We need a rough and ready system to guide us. Stereotyping and stereotypes do just that. They give us a basic belief system about our world that helps us interact in it. The stereotypes we form contribute to our social schemata.

Psychology also think stereotypes are formed by our conformity to prevailing social norms and values.

INTERACTIVES

Go back to pages 299–300, 332–334 and answer the following questions.

1   What are social schemata?

2   What role do social schemata play for us?

3   Identify two types of social schemata influenced by stereotypes. Give reasons for your answer.

4   Why should we be wary of stereotypes?

Conformity to values

Given the racism apparent in early 1950s America, and the inherent prejudice that existed at the time, Minard (1952) observed an inconsistency in the behaviour of white miners to black miners in a town in the southern USA. Below ground 80 per cent of white miners were friendly towards black miners, while above ground only 20 per cent were friendly to black miners.

Pettigrew (1958) calls this phenomenon **conformity to values**. Conformity to values occurs when *different* sets of norms or values operate between the same groups of people. Such difference is due to a change in social circumstance.

Literature is full of examples. Take the play *The Admirable Crichton* by JM Barrie where a group of upper class English people and their butler Crichton find themselves shipwrecked on a desert island. This dramatic change in their social situation very quickly sees new norms and values emerging to

enhance the group's survival. Servants become bosses, and bosses servants.

INTERACTIVES

To give a useful context to Pettigrew's conformity to values hypothesis download a free copy of the *The Admirable Crichton* by JM Barrie at:
www.gutenberg.org/etext/3490

A direct link is available in the Chapter 8 section of the Higher Psychology Learning Suite at **www.gerardkeegan.co.uk**

Generally, Pettigrew expects prejudice to depend upon the *social context* in which the behaviour takes place.

In presenting his conformity to values hypothesis Pettigrew believes that people who are more conforming are also more prejudiced.

In a study looking at racial tension in the Republic of South Africa, Pettigrew (1982) found that white South African students higher than average in prejudiced attitudes towards black and coloured South Africans also tended to conform more to prevailing social norms. The prevailing social norm in South Africa at that time was white supremacy and apartheid.

Further research by Pettigrew confirms conformity to values in its social context. He found that many southerners in America who displayed prejudice towards black people also regularly attended church. This was not the case in the northern USA. There was less prejudice, and no relationship between prejudice and church attendance.

Prejudice against blacks was less acceptable as a social norm in the north but not the south of the USA. Churchgoing in southern states in the USA is still a strong social norm even today.

The poacher-turned-gamekeeper hypothesis

Support for Pettigrew's conformity to values hypothesis and the interpersonal approach comes from Lieberman. Lieberman discovered that a person's attitudes and values *change* to conform to changing social norms.

Lieberman (1956) investigated the attitudes and values of factory workers, and how these changed after some were promoted or demoted. What emerged may be called the poacher-turned-gamekeeper hypothesis.

This is because when promoted new foremen and supervisors developed more favourable attitudes towards management than previously. Stronger pro union attitudes were also observed amongst those elected to shop steward positions. Demotion had the opposite effect. This quickly saw individuals return to previously held attitudes (Lieberman, 1956).

The work of social psychologists like Pettigrew and Lieberman gives weight to the intergroup proposition that conformity to prevailing norms and values strongly influence our thoughts, feelings and behaviours towards others.

If these norms and values include favouring one group at the expense of another then this is a realistic outcome. This is driven by the social context within which such norms and values are forged.

The interpersonal approach: Conclusion

We do not behave towards others in ways solely consistent with a distinct personality style, set of stereotypes, or shared race or belief similarity. This is because of pressures from our social environment. These forces cause us to conform to prevailing social norms, but norms change over time. Thus, while extremely useful, the Pettigrew conformity to values hypothesis does not offer sufficient explanation for *continued* prejudice and social discrimination evident in society.

The intergroup approach

The intergroup approach looks at whether membership of groups causes discrimination and prejudice.

The intergroup approach primarily investigates what happens when two groups are in competition with one another. This is known as the study of **intergroup conflict**.

They are also concerned as to whether group membership causes people to treat their own group more favourably than another. This is known as the study of **social categorisation**.

Intergroup conflict and social categorisation are factors in the intergroup's approach to an understanding of discrimination and prejudice

INTERACTIVES

Read 'Intergroup Conflict and Cooperation: The Robbers Cave Experiment' by Muzafer Sherif *et al.* at:
psychclassics.yorku.ca/Sherif/

A direct link is available in the Chapter 8 section of the Higher Psychology Learning Suite at www.gerardkeegan.co.uk

The Robbers Cave experiment

In 1954 social psychologist Muzafer Sherif investigated intergroup competition and conflict between eleven- and twelve-year-old boys attending a summer camp in Oklahoma in the USA.

His **field experiment** lasted three weeks and had two hypotheses.

Sheriff's hypotheses
When individuals who do not know one another are put together in a group; the aim of which is to achieve common goals, a hierarchical group structure will emerge, with members having a defined status and role.

When two such **in-groups** are brought into competition with one another intergroup conflict will arise.

Group selection
Twenty-four boys aged around eleven were pre-screened to take part in the experiment. Of these 22 were chosen. All came from similar stable lower middle class Protestant backgrounds. They were all in the same year at school, and according to the researchers were well adjusted psychologically, and of normal physical development.

Sherif put the boys into two groups of eleven. The two groups mirrored each other in terms of the physical, intellectual, and emotional talents of its members.

In the summer of 1954 each group was picked up on consecutive days and taken to a Boy Scouts of America camp situated in the Robbers Cave National Park in Oklahoma.

The experiment that then took place had three distinct stages.

Stages 1 and 2 was concerned with the development of conflict. Stage 3 was concerned with the reduction of conflict.

Figure 8.12 Robbers Cave National Park Oklahoma

Stage 1: In-groups and out-groups – the Eagles and the Rattlers

Stage 1 of the experiment lasted five to six days. Each group, and its membership, were unaware of the other's existence. Both were kept separate from each other. During this time members of each group bonded with one another by working together to achieve common goals. This demanded discussion, planning and execution. Both groups saw a leader come to the fore. Individual members took on differing roles. Status hierarchies emerged. Without prompting each group chose its own distinct name. One group called itself the Eagles; the other group called itself the Rattlers. This further strengthened group identity.

Gradually the Eagles and the Rattlers became aware of the other's existence. This seemed to reinforce group identity. Each group began to become defensive about 'ownership' of the camp's facilities. Both groups began to persuade Sherif and his staff to arrange intergroup competitions. In-group tasks such as putting up tents, baseball etc. became in themselves competitive. Each group streamlined their status hierarchies more efficiently in order to become more proficient at what they were asked to do.

By the end of Stage 1 the mere presence of an out-group had a psychological impact on in-group behaviours. The Eagles wanted to appear 'better' than the Rattlers, and vice versa.

Stage 2: In-group–out-group conflict

Stage 2 of the experiment lasted four to six days. Sherif wanted to create friction between the two groups using minor frustrations. Both groups were told that a series of competitions were being arranged. A group trophy and individual prizes such as medals and multi-purpose penknives were to be given to the winning group, with consolation prizes going to the losers.

The Rattlers immediately perceived themselves as winners! They spent the day talking about the competition. They went to the baseball field to train, where some suggested they erect a 'keep off' sign to dissuade the Eagles from using it. They erected a Rattlers flag at the edge of the pitch accompanied by threats about what they would to the Eagles if it were removed.

The two groups were then brought together in the dining hall. There was considerable name-calling ('stinkers', 'braggers', 'sissies'), teasing, and singing of derogatory songs! Before supper some Eagles said they didn't want to eat with the Rattlers.

Conflict escalated during the next day. Each rival group's flag was burned. Each group raided the other's cabin.

After the first contest, *which the researchers made sure the Eagles won*, the Rattlers were so incensed they invaded the Eagle's cabin and 'removed' their winners' medals and penknives!

In the dispute that followed the Rattlers and the Eagles nearly fought one another. Name calling greatly intensified. The environment became much nastier. If an out-group member walked by, the in-group would hold their noses etc. Neither group wanted to eat in the dining hall if the other was present.

Sherif comments:

 If an outsider had entered the situation at this point with no information about preceding events, he could only have concluded on the basis of their behaviour that these boys (who were the 'cream of the crop' in their communities) were a wicked, disturbed, and vicious bunch of youngsters."

(Sherif, 1966)

Sherif's main point is that group conflict, and thus discriminatory behaviour, arises because of competition between two groups for some prize, goal, resource etc. that can only be achieved by one group at the expense of another.

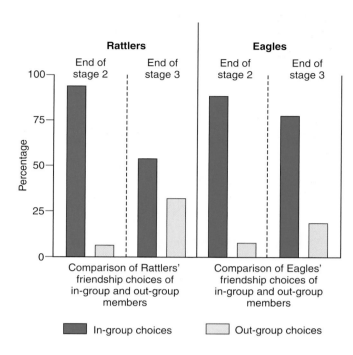

Figure 8.13 Comparison of Rattlers' (left) and Eagles' (right) friendship choices of in-group and out-group members at the end of Stage 2 and Stage 3.

Stage 3: The integration phase – all for one and one for all!

Stage 3 of the experiment lasted six to seven days. Called the integration phase, it was intended to reduce intergroup conflict.

Sherif arranged a number of get-togethers to get the two groups to reconcile their differences. These included a bean-collecting contest, the showing of a film, and the letting-off of fireworks to celebrate the Fourth of July, American Independence Day.

Rather than reducing tension, these events resulted in food fights! The Eagles and the Rattlers still displayed hostility towards each other.

The strategy of superordinate goals was then introduced. A **superordinate goal** is a goal that demands co-operation and teamwork. It cannot be achieved or solved by a small number of people. Superordinate goal setting creates co-operation.

These scenarios were played out at a new location in the belief that this would tend to inhibit recall of grievances that had been experienced at Robbers Cave.

The drinking water problem

The first superordinate goal concerned a common resource used by both groups; their water supply.

All of the drinking water in the camp came from a reservoir in the mountains north of Robbers Cave. The water supply had been stopped deliberately by Sherif, and blamed on 'vandals.'

The Eagles and the Rattlers investigated the extensive piping, and discovered that an outlet tap had had a sack stuffed into it. Almost all the boys gathered around the tap to try to clear it. Suggestions from members of both groups about how to unblock the obstruction were offered by both groups simultaneously. This led to cooperative efforts to clear the obstacle lasting over 45 minutes.

When the water finally came on there was common rejoicing. The Rattlers did not object to having the Eagles stand in the queue ahead of them to get a drink. The Eagles did not have canteens with them and were thirstier. No protests or 'Ladies first' type of remarks were made!

The film problem

The next superordinate goal to help in the reduction of prejudice concerned how all could get to see their favourite film.

In consultation with children's film experts' two films had been chosen, and brought to the camp by Sherif.

One afternoon, the boys were called together and camp staff suggested the possibility of watching either *Treasure Island* or *Kidnapped* written by Robert Louis Stevenson. Both groups yelled approval for both these films. After some discussion, one Rattler said, 'Everyone that wants *Treasure Island* raise their hands.' The majority of members in both groups gave enthusiastic approval to the Walt Disney classic *Treasure Island*.

The superordinate task was then introduced. This was when a member of staff said that hiring the film would cost $15, and that the camp could not pay the whole sum.

After much discussion involving all the boys it was suggested that both groups would come up with $3.50, and the camp would pay the balance. This was accepted even though, as a couple of homesick Eagles had gone home, the contribution per person per group was unequal.

At supper that night there were no objections to eating together. Some scuffling and sticking chewing gum on each other occurred between members of the two groups, but such carry-on involved fewer boys on both sides than previously.

Other problem-solving superordinate goals introduced in this phase included the joint use of a tug-of-war-rope when both groups of boys 'accidentally' came across a stuck-in-a-rut truck that was carrying food for both groups.

The joint pursuit of such superordinate goals saw a lessening of intergroup conflict. Sherif observed at breakfast and lunch on the last day of camp that the seating arrangements were considerably mixed insofar as group membership was concerned.

The departure

By the last day the majority of the boys agreed that it would be a good to return to Oklahoma City together on one bus. When they asked if this was possible, and were told yes, some of the boys actually cheered! When the bus pulled out, the seating arrangement did not follow group lines.

Just before the bus pulled into the town where a refreshment stop had been planned, a Rattler asked those in his group if they still had the five-dollar reward they had won in the bean contest. When all the boys were at the refreshment stand, the Rattler leader suggested that their five dollars be spent on soft drinks for *all* the boys in *both* groups. Several Rattlers nearby agreed; and the others approved the idea when asked.

Sherif's large scale Intergroup Relations Project, clearly established support for his hypotheses. That, firstly, when individuals who do not know each other are brought together as a group to achieve common goals, a hierarchical group structure with defined status and roles will emerge. This makes the achievement of such goals more likely.

That, secondly, when two groups are competing for limited resources hostility by each will be shown towards the other. Such prejudice and discrimination displayed towards the out-group- will be standardised and shared in varying degrees by in-group members.

In short, the findings suggest the various methods used with limited success in reducing intergroup hostility may become effective when employed within a framework of co-operation among groups working towards goals that are genuinely appealing and require equitable participation and contributions from all groups."

Note however:

That the superordinate goal must have genuine appeal to both groups, and, that there must be equitable participation and contribution from both groups. Reduction of intergroup hostility will not occur when one group is of higher status or in command, and one of lower status or subservient"

(Sherif, 1966)

INTERACTIVES

Please answer the following questions:

1   What was the aim of Robbers Cave study conducted by Sherif *et al.* (1954/1961)?

2   What was the purpose of Stage 1, Stage 2, and Stage 3?

3   Give examples of in-group–out-group conflict in this study.

4   Why do you think conflict occurred?

5   How was conflict reduced?

Social categorisation

Social categorisation is another aspect of the intergroup approach. Social categorisation concerns *group membership*.

Henri Tajfel (1970) showed that group membership, even *in the absence of intergroup competition*, is sufficient for intergroup discrimination to happen.

Tajfel told 64 Bristol children aged between fourteen and fifteen who were acquainted with each other that they were to be in one of two groups. He allocated each individual to his or her group on the basis of a fictitious criterion. This was whether they were 'under-estimators' or 'over-estimators' of the number of dots that appeared on a screen.

Participants were then asked to give monetary rewards to *both* their in-group and the out-group. They were unaware of who else in their group, or the other.

Tajfel found in-group favouritism and out-group discrimination occurred.

His participants always allocated greater monetary reward to their in-group. But more importantly they did this in such a way so as to make the difference between their in-group and the out-group as great as possible! This occured even when it meant their group received less than they might have done.

For example, you are presented with the following two options:

➤ Giving £18 to your ingroup, and £12 to an outgroup (a difference of £6)

   or

➤ Giving £14 to your ingroup, and £6 to an outgroup (a difference of £8).

Tajfel tells us that even in a minimal group paradigm situation, where you are allocated to one group rather then another on the basis of a trivial criterion, you are more likely to choose option 2.

In 1974 Tajfel and Billig found that when participants clearly knew that their allocation to an in-group was entirely random, here being on the basis of liking very similar paintings by Bauhaus artists Klee or Kandinsky, intergroup discrimination still occurred. Their participants always went for the maximum difference in point allocation between their group and the out-group.

What is important about this research is that until Tajfel, it was thought intergroup competition was necessary and sufficient to produce prejudice and discrimination. This is not the case. Tajfel surmised that we are predisposed to discriminate because we like to categorise people. We do so on the basis of generic norms.

Generic norms

Tajfel says we all display a general tendency or **generic norm**, to categorise people in terms of in-groups and out groups. Generic norms are learned. This 'us and them' mentality has us act favourably in term of our own in-groups, and unfavourably towards out-groups. Hill (2001) tells us that this general tendency to discriminate happens in the absence of:

➤ Any individual interest or reason to discriminate.

➤ Any previously held negative attitude, hostility or dislike for an out-group.

➤ Any need for discrimination to occur, such as scarce resources.

We *automatically* discriminate without holding any prior prejudice merely on the basis of being a member of one group and not another (Tajfel, 1970).

So why does such in-group favouritism and out-group bias occur?

In-group favouritism and out-group bias

Turner (1981) offers two psychological explanations for in-group favouritism and out-group bias.

In-group favouritism and resultant out-group bias happens because individuals perceive greater similarities with members of their own in-group, and greater differences with members of out-groups than actually exist.

'Within category homogeneity' has us over-estimate similarities within groups. 'Accentuation of inter-category difference' has us exaggerate differences between groups.

'Us and them' in-group favouritism also occurs because we have a need to compare and evaluate ourselves against others in our search for a positive social identity.

Social identity

Our social identity is a set of beliefs about ourselves based upon our membership of different groups.

Tajfel and Wilkes (1963) discovered just how influential categorisation and grouping was on perception.

Categorisation and grouping

Tajfel and Wilkes (1963) conducted a laboratory experiment where they showed a series of eight lines of differing lengths to three groups of people. The independent variable concerned how the lines were categorised.

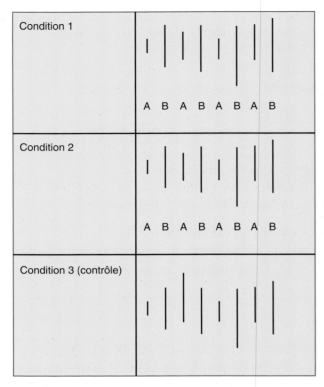

Figure 8.14 Tajfel and Wilkes (1963)

Group 1 were presented with the four shorter lines labelled 'A' and the four longer lines labelled 'B'.

Group 2 were presented with the eight lines labelled 'A' and 'B' but randomly i.e. their labelling was not associated with length.

Group 3 were shown the eight lines without any of the lines being categorised.

Groups 2 and 3 were the control condition. This was in order to compare the effects of categorisation by Group 1.

Participants in each group were then asked to estimate the length of each of the eight lines. It was found that the longest line in each category of shorter lines (A) was perceived by Group 1 participants to be much shorter than it actually was, and much shorter than that estimated by the control Groups 2 and 3.

In contrast, the shortest line in the category of longer lines (B) was perceived to be much longer by Group 1 participants than it actually was, and much longer than that estimated by the control Groups 2 and 3.

Tajfel and Wilkes (1963) helps us infer that if objective stimuli such as lines can be seen to differ in length on the basis of how they are initially categorised, then our perception of social stimuli

that can be grouped or categorised, such as personality traits, attitudes etc., will be even more marked and exaggerated.

In Tajfel and Wilkes (1963), once lines were categorised as (A) short or (B) long, similarity and difference was overstated thereafter. In short, social categorisation overemphasizes differences between groups of people and similarities within groups of people.

Turner's social identity theory

Turner (1981) tells us that our tendency to favour social categorisation results in social discrimination. This is because it forces us to make social comparisons between in-groups and out-groups.

Turner's theory further states that people make *social comparisons* because of their need for positive **social identity**. Positive social identity is important as it raises our self-esteem, self-respect and self-worth and a sense of 'belonging' in our social world.

Individuals make comparisons between groups on the basis of each groups status and value. This leads to social competition.

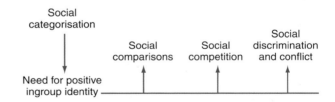

Figure 8.15 The social identity model

In their search for positive social identity people want to be categorised as members of highly valued, high status 'good' groups. They consequently indulge in social comparison and put their in-group in such a light as to be seen as 'better' than the out-group. In order to promote their in-group, false stereotypes and negative values may also be attributed to the out group. Social competition becomes evident. This exacerbates social discrimination and conflict.

The final point about social identity theory is that it is concerned with social competition, not realistic competition.

Realistic competition sees competition for real resources at the expense of another group. With social competition no real or tangible resources are being competed for. The benefit to the individual is psychological. They feel better about themselves.

The intergroup approach: Conclusion

The intergroup approach concerns social competition. Social competition helps fulfil our psychological need for a good self-image. This comes from being a member of an in-group. In-groups promote positive social identity. Overvaluing in-groups, and undervaluing, or being socially discriminative towards out-groups is the main means by which this is achieved. Even the smallest degree of such social categorisation, as illustrated in a minimal group paradigm is enough to produce social discrimination.

Social categorisation causes us to see greater similarities with in-groups, and greater differences in comparison to out-groups. We compare ourselves within- and between-groups because of our fundamental need for positive social identity.

Cultural, institutional and economic considerations

As stated earlier we look to sociology for the social context within which to operate as social psychologists. The social context is the backdrop to the study of prejudice. It includes our culture and subcultures, government, education, the law, and general economic considerations such as unemployment.

Without such factors supporting and perpetuating racism, sexism etc. the extent and depth of the problem would be much less.

It is thus important to consider the social context within which prejudice and conflict occurs in any attempt to reduce it.

Reducing prejudice and conflict

It may seem that psychology has been over-occupied in developing theories about prejudice and conflict, without paying too much attention to ways of reducing it!

This is not so, in that using such theory psychology proposes four strategies to lessen prejudice. These strategies include education, equal status contact, superordinate goals and social policy.

Education

Psychology thinks that educating people about the causes and effects of prejudice can help reduce its occurrence.

This is because education can help prevent society developing what Bem and Bem (1970) call a 'non-conscious ideology' about others. This is where prejudice becomes so entrenched that it becomes the accepted social norm.

Consequently education has the greatest effect on the young. As reported in Hill (2001), if adults 'are compelled to listen to information uncongenial to their deep-seated attitudes, they will reject it, distort it, or ignore it' (Aronson, 1992).

Jane Elliott (1968) was one of the first to promote education as a tool in the classroom to reduce prejudice. She demonstrated that it can be used to teach us to be more tolerant and respectful of others, and that this can have a positive influence on us thereafter.

The Assassination of Martin Luther King Jr
American civil rights leader and Nobel Peace Prize winner Martin Luther King Jr. was assassinated in Memphis, Tennessee, on 4 April 1968. He was to lead a protest march in solidarity with striking refuse collectors the next day.

His murder rocked the United States at a time when prejudice and discrimination against black and coloured people was particularly prevalent in the Southern states of America.

Following this terrible event, Jane Elliott a primary school teacher in Riceville, Iowa set out to teach her eight and nine years olds about prejudice. She did so in a very novel way, and in so doing become world famous.

Elliott (1968) supports aspects of the interpersonal and intergroup approaches to prejudice, as what follows should confirm.

'Brown eyes, blue eyes'

Just before Martin Luther King's murder Elliott had tried to introduce her young pupils to the idea of racial equality. She had for example made Martin Luther King her class 'Hero of the Month', but had struggled to explain what racism was really like. This was because her class was all white, and had never seen a black person in real life.

Using an **action research** strategy she first told her Primary 4 class a falsehood.

> Eye colour has nothing to do with being 'smarter, nicer, neater and better' than someone else. Eye colour is determined by the amount of melanin in the iris.

Elliott made up a story that people with blue eyes were cleverer, quicker, and more likely to succeed than others. They were superior to people with brown eyes whom she described as untrustworthy, lazy and stupid. Elliott then divided her class into two groups on the basis of whether they had brown eyes or blue eyes.

On the first day of the study she told the blue-eyed children they were 'smarter, nicer, neater and better' than those with brown eyes. Thereafter for the first day she praised the blue-eyed children, and gave them extra treats.

Her brown-eyed children were made to wear ribbons identifying them as 'different'. Elliott criticised and downplayed their classroom performance. The brown-eyed children were not allowed to drink from the same water fonts.

The blue-eyed children were allowed to ridicule them. This was met without comment or sanction from their teacher.

On day two Elliott reversed roles. She made the brown-eyed children feel superior by praising them and giving them treats. Alternatively the blue-eyed children were made to wear the ribbons, and their behaviours and class performance was criticised and ridiculed by her and the brown-eyed children.

Elliott noticed that whatever group had been made to feel inferior, they adopted the behaviours of genuinely inferior pupils. Their body language became defensive; their former friends teased them, and their academic performance dropped.

She noted that those pupils who had been kind and tolerant of others before the study, when assigned to the superior group became nasty and discriminatory towards those in the inferior group.

At the end of her brief study Elliott asked her pupils what it felt like to be thought of as inferior. The children reported feeling angry and confused. They talked of their frustration, pain and loneliness particularly when those in the superior group were treated as being better and rewarded with extra treats.

ONLINE INTERACTIVES

Go to 'A Class Divided' at: www.pbs.org/wgbh/pages/frontline/shows/divided/etc/view.html to watch a series of videos about Jane Elliott's historic study.

A direct link is available in the Chapter 8 section of the Higher Psychology Learning Suite at www.gerardkeegan.co.uk

Fifty years later many of the pupils who took part in the original study are still influenced by it. They learned that judging people as superior or inferior on the basis of the colour of their skin was and is an especially virulent form of evil and ignorance.

Martin Luther King's untimely death, used by Elliott in an educational context had fulfilled his vision.

I have a dream that my four little children will one day live in a nation where they will not be judged by the colour of their skin but by the content of their character"

(King, 1963)

While this study can be criticised in that it caused distress to its participants Jane Elliott has never claimed to be a psychologist. She is a teacher and a diversity trainer. Since the study took place she has spent her time promoting tolerance and kindness, and teaching people that everyone has value regardless of their colour.

1   What prompted Jane Elliott's famous study in 1968?

2   What did she then set out to do?

3   What research strategy did she adopt?

4   What was her procedure?

5   What were her results?

6   What conclusions can be drawn from her research?

7   What impact did the study have on her participants?

8   What aspects of the interpersonal and intergroup approaches to prejudice does Elliott's work support?

9   What does the Elliott discrimination inventory assess?

10 What has Jane Elliott discovered about prejudice in Scotland?

The jigsaw classroom

The jigsaw classroom was developed by social psychologist Elliott Aronson in 1978 to help improve racial integration in schools and colleges in Austin, Texas. An extension of the intergroup approach, the Jigsaw Classroom involves giving a group of students a superordinate task that cannot be done by one individual alone.

The class is then broken up into smaller groups, each of which researches one aspect of the task. All come back together again to report their findings to the others. Each group has to rely on another group's research in order for *everyone* to complete the original task successfully. The principle behind the jigsaw classroom is that 'children treat each other as resources' (Aronson *et al.*, 1997).

In an evaluation of the effectiveness of the jigsaw classroom Aronson *et al.* (1997) writes:

Children in the jigsaw classrooms grew to like their group mates even more than they liked others in their classrooms.

Children in the jigsaw classrooms liked school better (or, at least, hated school less) than their counterparts in competitive classrooms.

The self-esteem of the children in the jigsaw classrooms increased to a greater extent than that of children in competitive classrooms.

In terms of the mastery of classroom material, children in the jigsaw classrooms outperformed children in competitive classrooms. This difference was primarily due to improvement in the performance of underprivileged minority students; specifically, although white children performed as well in either type of classroom, African-American and Latino children performed significantly better in jigsaw classrooms than in competitive classrooms.

As a result of their experience in jigsaw groups, children learned to empathize with one another; that is, compared to children in traditional classrooms they found it easier to put themselves in another person's shoes and experience the world as if they were that other person."

Show Racism the Red Card

Margaret Nicol of the Educational Institute for Scotland tells us in the *Scottish Educational Journal* that:

> *All forms of discrimination – no matter if they are based on race, religion, gender, disability, age or sexual orientation – have absolutely no place in a civilised society. It is through young people that society's can most readily be changed"*

(SEJ. 2/2006. Vol. 90, 1)

In using education in the fight against inequality the EIS in conjunction with the charity Show Racism the Red Card (SRTRC) has since 2002 run a national competition in Scottish primary and secondary schools.

Backed by the Scottish Government the EIS-SRTRC initiative asks Scottish pupils and their teachers to consider racial discrimination and how to combat it using art and poetry. Their prestigious competition has different categories for pupils of different ages, and awards major prizes to the winning pupils and their schools. The Awards Ceremony is held annually at the National Stadium, Hampden Park, where it is given extensive media and press coverage.

Nil By Mouth

Similarly the charity Nil by Mouth uses education in its campaign to rid Scotland of sectarianism. Sectarianism in Scotland is prejudice based on being seen as either a Catholic or a Protestant. It has long been associated with Glasgow Celtic and Glasgow Rangers football clubs, and also the Troubles in Northern Ireland.

Sectarianism runs deep in Scottish society. Bigoted comments and jokes perpetuate a culture of prejudice that often results in violence. Nil By Mouth, and many others in Scottish society think that sectarianism has been tolerated for far too long.

Nil By Mouth tries to raise awareness and promote greater understanding of sectarianism through its workshops and training sessions in Scotland. It endeavours to raise the profile of just how evil sectarianism is through the media, publicity campaigns and presentations at key events. It encourages the Scottish government in their own efforts against sectarianism and works to persuade them to devote more resources to tackle the problem. Nil By Mouth also works with all sectors of Scottish society to promote a greater united effort amongst us all to challenge religious hatred.

INTERACTIVES

Please answer the following question:

How has education been used in Scotland to help reduce prejudice and discrimination?

Prejudice, education and psychological theory

From a theoretical perspective psychology has found education to be very important in battling prejudice and discrimination. Take the authoritarian personality for example. You may remember that Hyman and Sheatsley found an authoritarian personality more likely to exist among people who were and are less well educated than others. Hyman and Sheatsley (1954) also discovered that the higher level of educational attainment an individual has, the less likely they are to be authoritarian and prejudiced in outlook. Education counters the authoritarian personality, and all that comes with it.

Campbell (1971) discovered that attempts to get different races and ethnic groupings working successfully together are more likely when the participants have a high level of education.

This allows us to now turn to equal status contact as a strategy used in the reduction of prejudice.

The contact hypothesis

The best way to reduce tension and hostility between groups is to bring them into systematic contact with each other (Allport, 1954). Such social interaction can help reduce prejudice between different groups by challenging their stereotypes.

> *Prejudice... may be reduced by equal-status contact between majority and minority groups in the pursuit of common goals. The effect is greatly enhanced if this contact is sanctioned by institutional supports... and provided it is of a sort that leads to the perception of common interests and common humanity between members of the two groups.*

Allport (1954)

The contact hypothesis and acquaintance potential

Allport (1954) tells us that increased contact should foster and encourage 'acquaintance potential', or friendships between people of differing backgrounds. From an interpersonal point of view this should result in the dilution of in group-out group belief similarity and dissimilarity, and resultant prejudice and discrimination. As a consequence of coming together people of one social group should begin to see greater similarities with people of another social group. The shared belief hypothesis as proposed by Rokeach (1968) should be weakened.

The contact hypothesis and cognitive dissonance

As well as challenging the shared belief hypothesis, increased contact should also arouse **cognitive dissonance** in prejudiced individuals. This is because having a negative stereotypical attitude about someone, and then being friends with him or her is psychologically inconsistent.

The brilliant American psychologist Leon Festinger (1959) tells us that we strive to be to *cognitively consonant*. What this means is that we like our thoughts to be consistent, or in harmony with our feelings and behaviours.

Consequently a prejudiced individual in the above scenario would have to terminate their friendship, or change their negative thoughts or attitude about the other person. What option the person chooses depends on what one is more important to them (Festinger and Carlsmith, 1959).

When increased contact is used to reduce prejudice and discrimination, it has been found to work only when conflicting groups have *equal* status with each other. According to Allport, and later Sherif, contact alone is not a sufficient condition for reducing prejudice.

In contact situations four additional elements are needed. These are:

➤ Equal status contact

➤ Acquaintance potential

➤ Co-operation and the achievement of superordinate goals

➤ Social and institutional support.

(Allport, 1954; Sherif, 1966)

Equal status contact

 From the point of view of reducing prejudice and of creating harmonious intergroup relations, the net gain resulting from the integrated project is considerable; from the same point of view, the gain created from the biracial projects is slight."

(Deutsch and Collins, 1951)

Deutsch and Collins (1951) investigated prejudice among black and white housewives living in integrated and segregated housing estates in America. They found that prejudiced attitudes were less evident in women who lived in integrated housing projects, than in those who were segregated from each other.

Living in the same type of houses in integrated areas had created an equal status among residents *regardless* of their ethnic background. This had reduced previously held stereotypes, and had created greater cognitive consonance. As one white woman who lived in the integrated complex

remarked 'I started to cry when my husband told me we were coming to live here. I cried for three weeks… Well all that's changed… I see they're just as human as we are… I've come to like them a great deal' (Hill, 2001).

Equal status contact in the reduction of prejudice is also apparent in war situations. This is because soldiers get killed regardless of their colour, creed or background. In order to survive they have to rely on one another much more. In such situations they are less concerned about others' colour, creed or background.

During World War Two (1939–45) and the later Vietnam War (1965–73), Stouffer (1949) and Amir (1969) found that inter-racial attitudes improved markedly between American black and white soldiers and sailors when they served together in battle. Relationships were not so good in non-conflict situations.

As one white Second World War soldier put it 'they fought and I think more of them for it, but I still don't want to soldier with them in garrison'. One reason found for this animosity was that away from the combat zone personnel from different ethnic backgrounds did not mix with each other (Schofield, 1982). Contact between black and white soldiers and sailors were unequal. Prejudice was less likely to be reduced.

Some dispute the success of contact in the reduction of prejudice. Stephan (1978) in a review of desegregation studies found there was no significant reduction in prejudice towards black people, nor did desegregation of schools and housing in the USA increase black children's self-esteem. Stouffer (1949) confirmed Star *et al.* that a lack of prejudice between black and white soldiers in combat was not generalised to other situations.

It is also interesting to note Crosby who found as late as 1980 that white people in the USA were less likely to help black stranded motorists, less likely to make an emergency phone call for a black person in difficulty, and more likely to report black shoplifters than white.

US prison gangs

➤ Aryan Brotherhood

➤ Nazi Low Riders

➤ Dirty White Boys

➤ Black Gangster Family

➤ Mandingo Warriors

➤ Mexican Mafia (La Eme)

➤ La Nuestra Familia

➤ Los Hermanos de Pistoleros Latinos

It is clear that in institutional environments such as prisons inmates often group themselves on the basis of their race. This is particularly so in the United States of America today.

ONLINE INTERACTIVES

Why do race gangs such as the Aryan Brotherhood thrive in American jails? To find out go to: **news.bbc.co.uk/1/low/world/americas/ 4789537.stm**

A direct link is available in the Chapter 8 section of the Higher Psychology Learning Suite at **www.gerardkeegan.co.uk**

In order to reduce prejudice and discrimination other strategies as well as equal status contact need to be employed.

Acquaintance potential and the similarity–attraction hypothesis

Frequent systematic meetings between rival individuals or groups are vital to encouraging acquaintance potential and the reduction of prejudice.

This is because such *regular* contact exposes participants to new information about each other. It leads to what Byrne (1971) calls the similarity–attraction hypothesis. This is the realisation that you have much more in common with a rival than you initially thought. Stereotypes diminish. The more often such contact occurs the more positive we become about the other person, group, or situational outcome (Zajonc, 1968).

The similarity-attraction hypothesis and acquaintance potential helps explain the amazing relationship that has developed recently in Northern Ireland between its former First Minister, the Reverend Ian Paisley, and his then Deputy Martin McGuinness.

Dr Paisley who is of course famous for his cry of 'No Surrender to the IRA' now appears to be the best of friends with alleged former IRA commander Mr McGuinness. Their relationship developed as a result of meeting many times during the Northern Ireland peace process.

Figure 8.16 Martin McGuinness and the Reverend Ian Paisley

In a psychological sense such regular contact fostered their acquaintance potential and resulted in friendship. Similarity–attraction was also forged by their mutual desire to bring peace and prosperity to Ulster.

ONLINE INTERACTIVES

Read an excellent summary of 'A Meta-Analytic Test and Reformulation of Intergroup Contact Theory' by Pettigrew and Tropp available at: **www.bc.edu/schools/cas/ meta-elements/html/troppsummary.htm**

A direct link is available in the Chapter 8 section of the Higher Psychology Learning Suite at **www.gerardkeegan.co.uk**

Sawa Efroni: The choir for peace

Sawa Efroni, or the Choir for Peace, is a project that brings together 52 Israeli and Palestinian girls in order to promote social harmony and cultural diversity.

The Choir is a joint venture made up of the Sawa choir of girls from the town of Shafríam in the Lower Galilee, and the Efroni choir of Emek Hefer. They tour worldwide and perform songs from both the Jewish and Arab traditions singing in both Hebrew and Arabic.

Co-operation in the achievement of superordinate goals

As we read earlier, Sherif (1966) carried out extensive research that supports this third element to the reduction of prejudice. We found from Sherif (1966) that group conflict happens when two groups are competing for the same resources. They perceive each other in terms of an in-group and outgroup. Competition ensues.

Sherif (1966) confirmed that intergroup co-operation in the pursuit of superordinate goals helps reduce resultant in-group-out-group prejudice and conflict.

Working together also enhances social identity. What previously defined an in-group from an out-group becomes blurred as they merge together. At least during the period of inter-group cooperation.

Britain in Bloom

The annual Britain in Bloom competition sponsored by the Royal Horticultural Society has, somewhat remarkably, helped reduce prejudice. This is because intergroup co-operation is necessary to win one of their prestigious gardening awards.

Such intergroup co-operation came about in Derry/Londonderry in Northern Ireland, when in 2005 they put themselves forward in the City category of the RHS Britain in Bloom contest.

To be considered for a medal in the Britain in Bloom City category a great deal of cooperation is needed between all sorts of people. This is because of the very high gardening standards laid down by the RHS.

What made this problematic was that the City of Derry/Londonderry had until then been torn apart by decades of conflict between Nationalist and Loyalist forces. The bomb and the bullet were everyday occurrences.

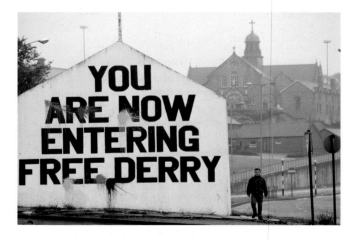

Figure 8.17

Undaunted, and led by Derry City Council, organisations like the North West Development Office, the City Centre Initiative, Derry Healthy Cities, the Roads Service, and the Northern Ireland Housing Executive, all worked together with community groups to prepare their City for entry to the competition.

To strive for such a superordinate goal in itself did much to help reduce conflict, sectarianism and prejudice in this previously torn community. Everyone's efforts were doubly rewarded when Derry/Londonderry won the 2005 Silver Medal.

In giving the City its Silver Medal the RHS recognised the efforts of community groups coming together – for the first time in many years - to shape, change and enjoy their local environment.

INTERACTIVES

With reference to Sherif (1966) describe a modern day example where intergroup co-operation helped reduce prejudice and conflict.

As with contact situations, the pursuit and achievement of superordinate goals by *representatives* of conflicting groups is often not generalised to the broader social group to which they belong.

Just because gardeners in Derry get together and win a prize doesn't mean to say that the Troubles between the Catholic and Protestant communities in Northern Ireland will be resolved as a consequence. Much more of the same is needed.

As we leave this element regarding the reduction of prejudice, an interesting question arises. What would happen if the superordinate goal were impossible to achieve? Would greater conflict, and worse prejudice emerge?

What do *you* think?

Social policy

Over and above equal status contact; the creation of acquaintance potential, and intergroup co-operation in the achievement of superordinate goals, psychologists have recommended that social policy be used to reduce prejudice, discrimination and conflict. Social policy helps address the social context within which such prejudice, discrimination and conflict festers. Social policy comes from a variety of bodies that includes the United Nations, the European Union, and the UK and Scottish governments.

Social policy helps address social inequalities. This sees politicians pass equal opportunities legislation, which influences how public authorities and other bodies deal with their employees, potential employees and those who use their services. This filters through to the private sector of the economy. Social policy also affects the media who often perpetuate discriminatory stereotypes.

Social policy tries to create a 'one-nation' social identity. It tries to dilute what defines particular in-groups and has us all merge together as one.

ONLINE INTERACTIVES

Read about Leeds University students banning *The Sun* newspaper from their Union Shop in protest against its portrayal of asylum seekers. Go to:
education.guardian.co.uk/higher/news/story/0,9830,895673,00.html

A direct link is available in the Chapter 8 section of the Higher Psychology Learning Suite at **www.gerardkeegan.co.uk**

Britishness
An example of one nation social policy would be current Prime Minister Gordon Brown's 'Britishness' initiative.

Britishness is the term used to refer to the common culture and national identity of the British people. It is associated with what it means to be British, as opposed to being French, German, or even Scottish!

Britishness has political undertones in that Mr Brown hopes it becomes associated with patriotism, 'one-nation' nationalism and British unionism.

What attributes, attitudes and values go to make up this common culture and national identity we call 'Britishness' are impossible to identify. This is because of such things as devolution with the establishment of separate national parliaments in Scotland, Wales and Northern Ireland, and the diverse multi-culturalism found within the United Kingdom.

Another problem for 'Britishness' is that a person's social identity is established from the bottom up, not the top down.

This author sees himself first as a Glaswegian. Glasgow is part of Scotland, which is part of the United Kingdom. He is also a particular type of Glaswegian, who has developed attributes, attitudes and values on the basis of his upbringing and the subcultures to which he belonged and belongs.

Scots and people from the rest of the UK share the purpose – that Britain has something to say to the rest of the world about the values of freedom, democracy and the dignity of the people that you stand up for. So at a time when people can talk about football and devolution and money, it is important that we also remember the values that we share in common".

Gordon Brown 'Veteran's Day Speech' 27.06.06

ONLINE INTERACTIVES

Would you be able to pass a Britishness test to get a British passport? Go to:
news.bbc.co.uk/1/hi/magazine/3077964.stm

and find out!

A direct link is available in the Chapter 8 section of the Higher Psychology Learning Suite at **www.gerardkeegan.co.uk**

Equalities legislation

A great deal of social policy exists to counter prejudice and discrimination. Take for example British legislation concerning race, sex and disability discrimination.

The Race Relations Act 1976 as amended by the Race Relations (Amendment) Act 2000
The RRA (1976) makes it unlawful to discriminate against anyone on the grounds of his or her race, colour, nationality or citizenship, ethnic or national origin. The RRA Amendment Act (2000) imposes general duties on public authorities and bodies, such as local councils and colleges, to promote racial equality. British race relations' legislation applies to jobs, training, housing, education, and the provision of goods, facilities and services. It makes it unlawful for public bodies to discriminate in carrying out any of their functions. The amended Act also imposes a general duty on public sector bodies to promote equality of opportunity, and good race relations as a matter of course.

Equality and Human Rights Commission

The Equality and Human Rights Commission overseas the workings of race relations legislation. Its predecessor, the Commission for Racial Equality issued a code of practice on the implementation of the various Acts. The code applies to all of those areas outlined above, and came into effect on 31 May 2002.

ONLINE INTERACTIVES

Read 'A Lot Done, A Lot Still to Do' the legacy of the Commission for Racial Equality at:

www.equalityhumanrights.com/en/publicatio nsandresources/Pages/legacypublications.asp x#SectionsTop

A direct link is available in the Chapter 8 section of the Higher Psychology Learning Suite at www.gerardkeegan.co.uk.

Sex Discrimination Act 1975, as amended in 1986 and 2003.

Sex Discrimination legislation makes it unlawful in the UK to discriminate against someone on the grounds of sex or marriage, and applies equally to men and women.

The SDA (1975) makes it unlawful to discriminate against, or in favour of, people on the on the grounds of their sex. More specifically, sex discrimination is not allowed in employment, education, and advertising or in the provision of housing, goods, services or facilities. It is unlawful to discriminate in job advertisements, or because someone is married, or in employment. There are very few exceptions to the rule.

The SDA identifies two kinds of discrimination:

Direct discrimination, which means treating someone unfairly because of his or her sex. An example would be an employer, who is not exempt from the Act, only employing an all male workforce.

Indirect discrimination, which means setting unjustifiable conditions that appear to apply to everyone, but in fact discriminate against one particular sex. An example would be in a job advertisement that states only people more than six feet tall will be considered. This condition would indirectly exclude far more women than men, and would thus be considered unlawful.

Disability Discrimination Act 1995

The DDA (1995) deals with discrimination against disabled people. It is unlawful without legal justification to treat a disabled person less favourably than someone else because of his or her disability. Such discrimination occurs if, without justification, a 'reasonable adjustment' is not made.

The Act applies to all those who provide goods, facilities and services to the public. The employment provisions of the Act regards recruitment apply to employers with fifteen or more employees.

Reasonable adjustments concern many things. An obvious one would be providing ramps or lifts for people with mobility issues etc.

As with race, sex and disability issues are now also overseen by the Equality and Human Rights Commission (EHRC).

ONLINE INTERACTIVES

Go to drc.uat.rroom.net/DisabilityDebate/ recommendations.aspx

and click 'Disability Agenda. Creating an Alternative Future'

A direct link is available in the Chapter 8 section of the Higher Psychology Learning Suite at www.gerardkeegan.co.uk

In conclusion social policy has a part to play in the in the reduction of prejudice. Social policy alone cannot solve prejudice. Intergroup co-operation in pursuing superordinate goals, regular and systematic equal status contact, *and* education should be used together to reduce prejudice in society.

Chapter summary

Conformity, obedience, and prejudice are all topics studied within social psychology. Any conformity, obedience, or prejudice that we display is influenced by the social situation in which we find ourselves. Conformity is a consequence of social influence, the pressure from which is often so strong we conform when others are not present. The study of conformity has us look at informational social influence and normative social influence. The former is related to internalisation, and the latter compliance. Conformity is a normal everyday behaviour but we should appreciate the importance of non-conformity and minority influence. Obedience sees us submit to an explicit demand from an acknowledged authority figure. The study of obedience allows us to understand why. We obey due to socialisation and what we believe to be legitimate authority. Studies of obedience are fraught with methodological and ethical problems. Prejudice is 'an attitude that predisposes a person to feel, perceive and act in favourable or unfavourable ways towards a group or its individual members'. Theories of prejudice concern the influence of personality, our environment and group membership. The goal of psychology in its study of prejudice is to reduce it. This is achieved by education, equal status contact, superordinate goals and social policy. Each approach should be seen as complementary to another.

ONLINE INTERACTIVES

1   Go to the Higher Psychology Learning Suite at **www.gerardkeegan.co.uk**. Click Chapter 8 'Social Psychology: Conformity, Obedience and Prejudice' to access direct links to all websites mentioned in this chapter.

2   Go to the Higher Psychology Learning Suite at **www.gerardkeegan.co.uk**. Click Chapter 8 'Social Psychology: Conformity, Obedience and Prejudice' and do the online interactive crossword. But don't cheat!

3   Go to the Higher Psychology Learning Suite at **www.gerardkeegan.co.uk**. Click Chapter 8 'Social Psychology: Conformity, Obedience and Prejudice' and do the online interactive hangman game. Try and beat the executioner!

4   Go to the Higher Psychology Learning Suite at **www.gerardkeegan.co.uk**. Click Chapter 8 'Social Psychology: Conformity, Obedience and Prejudice' and print off the hard copy crossword. When finished you might like to hand it into your teacher as homework.

5   Go to the Higher Psychology Learning Suite at **www.gerardkeegan.co.uk**. Click Chapter 8 'Social Psychology: Conformity, Obedience and Prejudice' and do the online interactive quiz. Try and win the prize!

STRUCTURED QUESTIONS WITH ANSWER GUIDELINES

1   What is conformity, how is it influenced and how is it reduced?

With reference to the preceding pages, structure your answer as follows:

● define conformity as a change our behaviour or opinions because of real or imagined pressure from a person or a group of people. Say we are influenced to conform due to compliance, internalisation, or identification. Say that compliance can be reduced however because of majority size, cultural differences and gender.

Then elaborate on the following remembering to refer to research studies where appropriate:

➤ compliance

➤ internalisation

➤ identification

➤ majority size

➤ cultural differences

➤ gender

STRUCTURED QUESTIONS WITH ANSWER GUIDELINES CONTINUED

2 What is prejudice and how can it be reduced?

With reference to the preceding pages structure your answer as follows:

● define prejudice as 'an attitude that predisposes a person to feel, perceive and act in favourable or unfavourable ways towards a group or its individual members' (Secord and Backman, 1974). Indicate that prejudice predisposes a person to behave in a particular way, and that it demonstrates itself in two ways. Firstly as preferential treatment for oneself or one's own ingroup. Secondly as disadvantaging or discriminating against another person or persons' outgroup. Suggest that prejudice can be reduced in a number of ways. For example, education, equal status contact, acquaintance potential and social policy.

Then elaborate on these features remembering to refer to research studies where appropriate:

➤ ingroups and outgroups

➤ discrimination and stereotypes

➤ the complementary approaches to prejudice: individual, interpersonal and intergroup

➤ reducing prejudice: education

➤ reducing prejudice: equal status contact

➤ reducing prejudice: acquaintance potential

➤ reducing prejudice: social policy

GLOSSARY

Action research: Action research is classroom-based research conducted by teachers often concurrent with their teaching.
Affective: Our feelings or how we feel.
Associationism: A theory developed by the philosopher John Stewart Mill and others about how ideas combine in the mind to form greater ideas.
Behaviourism: Behaviourism is an approach in psychology that analyses us from the point of view of learning in response to our environment.
Cognitive: Generally, the term

'cognitive' refers to our thoughts or mental processes. More specifically means the information processes of the human mind, which are perception, attention, language, memory and thinking or problem-solving.
Cognitive dissonance: Cognitive dissonance is a psychological term that describes the uncomfortable mental tension that comes from holding two conflicting thoughts at the same time. We strive for cognitive consonance. We thus change one of the thoughts to be more commensurate with the other.

What one we change depends on what is the more important to us.
Compliance: Compliance is a particular type of social pressure where we are seen to publicly agree with others' attitudes or opinions but privately disagree. Compliance describes the behaviour of someone who is wants to gain a reward or avoid punishment.
Conative: Our behaviours or how we act.

Confounding variable: A confounding variable is a variable, that if anticipated could be controlled in an experimental situation. If they are not controlled they can give rise to an alternative explanation of results.

Deindividuation: In a group situation the loss of one's personal identity.

DK filter: A DK filter is a 'Don't Know' response often used in surveys. It allows respondents who have no opinion, or genuinely don't know the answer to a question to say so.

Field experiment: A field experiment is an experiment that takes place outside a laboratory. They can occur in schools, playgrounds, shopping centres etc. As with a laboratory experiment the researcher changes or manipulates an independent variable, and measures the dependent variable as a consequence.

Gender roles: Gender specific behaviours associated with being male or female.

Ideal self: Ideal self is the personality we would like to be. It consists of our goals and ambitions, and is dynamic in nature. Our ideal self is forever changing. The ideal self of our childhood is not the same as the ideal self of our late teens etc.

Identification: Identification is a type of conformity where we adopt a particular behaviour to put us in a favourable relationship with the person or persons with whom we are identifying. We want to be like that particular person, or group of people. We may not wholeheartedly agree with the behaviour.

Informational social influence: Informational social influence is a type of conformity where we use the judgements of others to base our own actions or behaviours. It is particularly prevalent in situations where there is no obvious answer. Informational social influence assumes others know best.

In-group: A group to which we belong.

Internalisation: Internalisation is a type of conformity where we think feel and behave in a manner consistent with the social pressure to which we have become exposed. Internalisation sees us adopt the values of others. If the source of the influence is perceived by us to be trustworthy and of good judgement, we accept the belief he or she put forward, and integrate it into our belief system. Internalisation is the most enduring type of conformity to social pressure.

Internal validity: Internal validity questions whether surveys and questionnaires measure what they claim to measure. *Do* personality inventories (questionnaires) *actually* measure personality etc. What is personality after all?

Longitudinal: Refers to a study lasting a year or more.

Meta-analysis: A term used in research that means 'a study of all the studies'.

Norm: A norm, or social norm, is a rule that is socially enforced.

Normative social influence: A situation where we behave in a way in order to gain approval from others, even if we do not necessarily believe in what we are doing.

Out-group: A group to which we do not belong.

Peer group: A group of people who are equal in age, education, interests etc. and who come together socially with one another.

Placebo: A harmless treatment.

Pogrom: An organized, often officially encouraged massacre or persecution of a minority group, especially against Jews.

Positivism: Positivism is a philosophy developed by Auguste Comte that states that the only authentic knowledge is scientific knowledge, and that such knowledge can only come from finding positive support for theories using the scientific, or experimental, method.

Psyche: The Freudian Mind, in terms off its conscious, preconscious, and unconscious.

Similarity–attraction hypothesis: As a consequence of meeting others, Byrne's similarity–attraction hypothesis is the proposal that such contact creates in us a growing belief that we have more in common with other people than we initially thought.

Social facilitation: Social facilitation is the tendency for individuals to be motivated towards better performance on simple tasks, or tasks at which they are expert, when under the eye of others.

Standardised: Standardised/standardisation refers to the research situation where all participants undergo the same procedure. If for example one participant is given the instruction 'Please continue', all participants will be given the same *standardised* instruction in the same circumstance.

Unconditional positive regard: Unconditional positive regard is the love we get from other people for who we are as a person, warts and all. Most usually unconditional positive regard comes from our parents.

CHAPTER NINE

Atypical Behaviour

BY THE END OF THIS CHAPTER YOU SHOULD BE ABLE TO:

TOPICS

● Demonstrate a knowledge and understanding of atypical behaviour: its theories, concepts, research evidence and therapeutic applications

● Analyse and evaluate atypical behaviour: its theories, concepts, research evidence and therapeutic applications

What is the psychology of individual differences?

In this, our final Chapter, we examine the fascinating subject of **atypical behaviour**, or abnormal psychology. A topic studied within a domain called the psychology of individual differences.

Individual differences have us investigate issues of similarity and distinction between us, not only regards any atypical behaviour we may have, but also in terms of **personality** and **intelligence**.

A recognition of *individual differences* as being why we think, feel and behave similarly but differently from one another stretches back 2,500 years to Plato in Ancient Greece. In 'The Republic' Plato considers not only the different physical attributes necessary to become a soldier, but also the ideal personality he thought was required. He suggests people vary in personality, and because of this some are more suited to some occupations than others.

This becomes clear in his consideration of the variety of personality traits he found in Athenian women at the time. He identifies some as great healers, some as great musicians, and yet others are

great gymnasts. As Plato says, 'No two persons are born exactly alike; but each differs from the other in natural endowments, one being suited for one occupation and the other for another.'

The psychology of *individual differences* is then the study of those psychological attributes we share, but differ around.

A biological basis to individual differences

Individual differences are influenced by our genetic inheritance. Or put another way, abnormal behaviour, personality, and intelligence are to some degree a consequence of our biology. Consequently any individual difference between us has some kind of *biological* basis to it.

We came across this in our chapter on Early Socialisation. In Chapter 3 we discovered that *temperament*, the building block to personality, is influenced by our genetic inheritance.

Genetic inheritance is also thought important in determining our intelligence, and also in accounting for any biological predisposition we might have that affect the development atypical behaviours such as **schizophrenia** and **depression**.

As we discovered in Chapter 1 a biological understanding as to why we think, feel and behave as we do is considered from two perspectives, our physiology and our genetics. We saw the influence of physiological psychology on our thoughts, feelings and behaviours in our study of stress.

The influence of *genetics* on human behaviour, and thus on individual differences, is considered in the broader area of *evolutionary psychology*.

Evolutionary psychology

Evolution, genetics, individual differences and human behaviour

Evolution, genetics, individual differences and related behaviours have been of interest to the biological approach in psychology since Darwin wrote his theory of evolution by natural selection in 1859. The genetic, or evolutionary, perspective is particularly interested in inherited genetic characteristics, and how they influence our thoughts, feelings and behaviours. This is significant to the psychology of individual differences in general and atypical behaviour in particular.

These inherited genetic characteristics can either be common to us all, or pertinent to the individual. What this means is that a particular genetic inheritance can account for differences between individuals. This genetic inheritance can then help or hinder consequent physical and psychological development.

What is evolution?

Evolution is the lengthy biological process through which new species emerge as a consequence of gradual alterations to the genetics of *existing* species. The environment a species finds itself in strongly influences its evolution over time.

What are genetics?

As a subject, genetics is the study of inherited biological characteristics. Inherited biological characteristics account for the colour of our eyes, our hair, and our height and body shape. Genetics have been found to also influence our intelligence, personality and physical and mental health.

Our genetics further determine our physical development during the course of our life, affecting our body's anatomy (physical structure), and physiology, as already discussed. You may have realised in our look at Early Socialisation that in developmental psychology genetics are crucial to biological maturation (physical/bodily aging) that helps or hinders our cognitive, social and emotional development as we grow. As we read in Chapter 3, a common biological ancestry is the reason why we all physically develop, or biologically mature, at approximately the same age the world over, though the onset of physical change may vary slightly from one person to another.

Genotype

Our genetic inheritance is a mixture of both our biological parents' genes and is called our **genotype**. Our genotype is a sort of blueprint or plan of what we will be like as we develop and grow. Our genotype is thus our inherited genetic *potential*. It accounts for the colour of our eyes, hair, and height and body shape. Genetic inheritance is also an important factor to our physical and mental health, intelligence, and to some extent our personality.

Phenotype

Whether you fulfil your genotype or genetic blueprint depends upon your experiences in your environment. What we become as a result of interaction with our environment is called our **phenotype**. We may be, as a result of genotype, biologically predisposed with an extraordinary talent to play a sport or an instrument. Whether we go on to potentialise this genotype depends on the support and encouragement we get from our environment in infancy, childhood and adolescence. Our phenotype is the outcome of our genetics and our life story, or phenomenology. As we should now realise the degree to which genetic inheritance and/or environment affect intelligence, mental health, and personality is studied in the domain of psychology called individual differences.

To think that we *might* be *all* genetics as regards our intelligence, mental health and personality is quite a frightening thought. This could mean that we need not feel responsible, or be held accountable, for our actions. Our biology in general, and genetics in particular *could* be said to be to blame.

This is why the nature–nurture debate is of such great interest in psychology. The nature–nurture, or genetics–environment debate, tries to answer a question that has intrigued philosophers and psychologists for many years.

How much do our genetics, and how much does our environment contribute to our thoughts, feelings and behaviours?

Biological determinism

Environment can affect genotype and the development of phenotype. We need not necessarily become what we are biologically thought predestined to become. The biological approach, and its underlying assumption that our thoughts, emotions and behaviours are driven solely by genetics and physiology, is called **biological determinism**, and is a limitation to taking a purely biological approach to the study of psychology in general, and atypical behaviour in particular. Other factors as found in our environment must also be considered.

Darwin's theory of evolution by natural selection (1859)

Environment and genetics is related to the *theory of evolution by natural selection* proposed by the famous scientist Charles Darwin in the mid-nineteenth century. Before we look at this it would be useful to remind ourselves about the biological approach itself.

The biological approach suggests that all our cognitions, emotions and behaviours occur as a direct result of the physiological activity of our brain and nervous system. It also posits that we are genetically capable of these brain and neural activities because of our evolutionary history. Our prehistoric ancestors *Homo sapiens*, who thought, felt, and behaved as we do, were better able to survive than similar hominids called *Homo erectus*, who thought, felt and behaved in a less successful manner. *Homo sapiens* reproduced, passed on their successful brain, neural, and nervous system hard-wiring and evolved into the human beings of today. *Homo erectus* became extinct. How this transpired is called natural selection.

Natural selection

Charles Darwin's theory of evolution by natural selection is an attempt to explain why this happened. How does *natural selection* occur, a process that sees the survival of some species but not of others? To discover the answer we must to turn to Darwin's The Origin of Species by Natural Selection (1859).

The principles of natural selection

Darwin laid down that nature or the environment change over time. It is the environment that decides whether an organism survives or not.

➤ Successful organisms survive because they have a genetic/physical **trait** (characteristic, ability or behaviour) that allows them to adapt better to their changed environment. Having a successful **adaptation** is largely down to luck, as species can neither control their genetics nor their environment.

➤ Those individuals within a species that have the necessary adaptation, called a genetic **variation**, have a better ability in a changed environment to *reproduce* offspring that can themselves survive. Variations come about either as a consequence of genetic inheritance from the biological parents, or because of minor, random, genetic changes in an organism. These are called **mutations**.

Figure 9.1 The evolution of man

➤ Species are made up/not made up of individuals who, by chance, have this genetic variation. These individuals survive, while others don't. Variations and adaptations are therefore genetically inherited and passed from generation to generation. After a certain period of time the adapted species will appear so different from the original species that ultimately a new species has evolved.

➤ *Natural selection* best describes the process by which those species whose physical characteristics and behaviours are adapted to fit its changing/changed environment. These are the ones that survive. Hence Darwin's idea of *natural selection and the survival of the fittest*. Those who survive are those who have genetically adapted a physical characteristic or behaviour to fit their changed environment. It is environment that selects who survives, and who does not.

ONLINE INTERACTIVES

Watch Darwin's Dangerous Idea on BBC iPlayer at http://www.bbc.co.uk/iplayer/episode/b00j0c54/Darwins_Dangerous_Idea_Body_and_Soul/

A direct link is available in the Chapter 9 section of Higher Psychology Learning Suite at www.gerardkeegan.co.uk

---

Empirical evidence for Darwin's theory of evolution

A famous example of natural selection was brought to our attention by Kettlewell (1955), and his observations of the peppered moth in the UK. Kettlewell looked at two variants of the peppered moth. One variation is dark, the other light, and their colour being genetically inherited. Dark-peppered moths thus breed dark-coloured offspring, while light-peppered moths breed light-coloured offspring. Birds such as robins eat both types of moth – if they can see them!

Before the nineteenth century, it is thought that the light-peppered moth greatly outnumbered the dark-peppered moth. This was because birds found the light-peppered moth harder to see against the lighter-coloured trees (of the time), as opposed to the darker variety, which were easier to pick out. During the nineteenth century industrial revolution in Britain, factory pollution covered our trees in soot, making them naturally darker in colour. This became a problem for the light-coloured peppered moth, as birds could now see them much better than their darker cousins.

Kettlewell figured that if Darwin was correct, the environmental change to darker trees would favour the dark-coloured variation of peppered moth, but not be good news for the lighter coloured one. This he found to be just the case. Kettlewell (1955) reported that the number of dark-peppered moths went from being almost nil in the UK, to being over half the resident population of both types of moth in around fifty years. With concerns over industrial pollution, regulations were introduced in Britain to control factory pollution – and the amount of soot on Britain's trees declined. The number of light-coloured peppered moths has consequentially increased again.

Kettlewell (1955) is an excellent research example of natural selection.

Charles Darwin

Figure 9.2 Charles Darwin

Born in Shrewsbury in 1809, Charles Darwin developed the theory that all forms of life came about through a process of natural selection. Of a wealthy family, he went to school in Shrewsbury, and, after a brief spell at the University of Edinburgh, attended the University of Cambridge. His initial interest in medicine and the Church became overshadowed by his growing passion for life and earth sciences. After graduating from Cambridge, the 22-year-old was taken aboard the British survey ship, the *HMS Beagle*, as a volunteer naturalist. This scientific expedition around the world was to have a major effect on both the natural and social sciences. In his observations, the young naturalist was most impressed with the effect that natural forces had on shaping the earth's surface. He observed that fossils of supposedly extinct species closely resembled living species in the same area. In the Galapagos Islands he noticed, for example, that each island supported its own form of tortoise. The various forms were closely related, but differed in structure and eating habits from island to island. He began to wonder why this had come about, and formed a theory known as the origin of species by natural selection. This was published in *The Origin of the Species in 1859*.

The essence of the theory of evolution by natural selection is that genetic variations or traits are transmitted to offspring of species. Some of these genetic variations will have survival value for the organism. They increase the probability of these species surviving long enough to reproduce and ensure future offspring. The trait is genetically inherited generation after generation. As a result the organism becomes better suited, or adapted to its environment. Eventually the (successful) genetic variation becomes so numerous a new species is born. Darwin also introduced the concept that all related organisms are descended from common ancestors. The reaction to the *Origin* was immediate. Some biologists argued that Darwin could not prove his hypothesis. Others criticised Darwin's concept of variation, arguing that he could explain neither the origin of variations, nor how they were passed to succeeding generations. This particular criticism was not answered until the discovery of DNA in the middle of the twentieth century. The church was most vigorous in its attack. Bishop Wilberforce, in a famous debate at Oxford University denounced the theory as atheistic, and famously mocked the whole idea by asking Thomas Henry Huxley, a supporter of Darwin, whether he was descended from a monkey on his grandfather or grandmother's side. It was however the church that had to develop an adaptive ability!

Darwin was elected to the Royal Society in 1839 and the French Academy of Sciences in 1878. He was also honoured by burial in Westminster Abbey after he died in Downe, Kent, on 19 April 1882.

> **Darwin's publications include:**
> *The Variation of Animals and Plants Under Domestication (1868)*, *The Descent of Man (1871)*, and *The Expression of Emotions in Man and Animals (1872)*.

(With thanks to Richard Wilson of Shortlees.)

Darwin, James and Emotions

In his later book *The Expression of the Emotions in Man and Animals* (1872), Charles Darwin said that humans have evolved physically and psychologically. On the basis of his observations of different peoples on the voyage of the Beagle, Darwin thought that we have evolved, and therefore share and recognise the same emotions, such as happiness, sadness, anger, disgust, etc. He said these emotions were innate, unlearned responses, comprising a complex set of facial movements and expressions. The *expression* of emotion is as a result of our genetics, which construct our physiology.

In the biological sense our emotions are understood from the point of view of physical structures and processes in our cerebral cortex and nervous system.

The American psychologist William James in his work *Principles of Psychology* (1890) was later to agree with Darwin. James, who is considered by many to be the father of American psychology, said, *'we feel sorry because we cry, angry because we strike, afraid because we tremble'*.

What he meant by this is that a stimulus from our environment, i.e. a snarling dog will automatically trigger an innate bodily response in us, i.e. sweating, faster heart rate, trembling etc. It is these bodily responses that give us our *feelings* of fear. This is called the *peripheric* theory of emotion, better known as the *James–Lange theory*. James–Lange suggests we feel fear, etc. because of feedback got from internal bodily changes that have been triggered automatically by a stimulus in our environment. Their idea, then, rather counter-intuitively, is that we feel sad because we cry, rather than we cry because we feel sad.

It should be noted that the James–Lange theory has since been overcome by other theories about our emotions, such as those of Canon (1929), Schacter & Singer (1962), and Pinel (1993).

However James–Lange *is* important because the theory gave impetus to investigation into the biological basis to our emotions and behaviours. Such a biological approach explains us, physically and psychologically, as a result of genetically inherited biological characteristics.

Emotions are subjective feelings accompanied by physiological arousal that moves us to action. In the tradition of Darwin, Robert Plutchik (1994) categorised eight emotions, common to us all. They are called our primary emotions and are grouped in four pairs of opposites: expectation and surprise; anger and fear; acceptance and disgust; and joy and sadness.

Identify these individual emotions in the photos below. Compare your answer with others. You should find that you mostly agree on most. You confirm Darwin's theory that we have evolved common emotions.

Figure 9.3 Plutchik's Eight Primary Emotions

We are as we are because of our physiology and genetics. It is nature, largely, that gives rise to why we think, feel and behave as we do.

A biological cause to a number of atypical behaviours as a result of a particular genetic inheritance finds great favour in psychology.

Before turning to atypical behaviour it is worthwhile looking at two areas in psychology where our biology and principally our genetics are, or were, thought to play an important role: personality and intelligence.

Personality

'*Where does our personality come from?*' This is a question often asked by students of psychology. The answer was once thought to be nature – our biology.

As you may have read earlier in Chapter 3, Galen thought we behaved the way we do because of an excess of one of four bodily fluids in our body blood, phlegm, black bile and yellow bile. He thought an excess of one of these fluids or *humours* gave rise to a particular **temperament** or general personality. Thus, excess blood would lead to a sanguine personality according to Galen; excess phlegm – a phlegmatic personality; excess black bile – a melancholic personality, or excess yellow bile – a choleric personality.

As you may also remember, Galen's personality temperaments live on today in Eysenck's Personality Inventory (EPI). The EPI has four personality types into which we all fit.

Eysenck's stable extrovert reflects the traits of Galen's sanguine personality; his unstable–extrovert, Galen's choleric traits; his unstable–introvert, Galen's melancholic traits and his stable–introvert, Galen's phlegmatic personality traits.

We may well inherit such temperaments or general personality traits, not, of course, on the basis of excess bodily fluids, but because of our genetics. As has been emphasised temperament is the building block of our personality, which is thereafter greatly influenced by our experiences in our environment. Nature plays some part in the formation of our personality, but nurture has its influence as well. Otherwise, as a result of similar genetic inheritance we could have the same personality as a brother or sister, or worse – a parent!

Nomothetic and Idiographic Approaches to Personality

Psychologists have two distinct views on personality: nomothetic and idiographic.

> Those who take a *nomothetic* approach to personality all agree that personality can be categorised on the basis of those common traits that we share. Hence nomothetic personality theorists such as Hans Eysenck talk about extravert, introvert, stable, and unstable (neurotic) personality types.
>
> Alternatively those like Carl Rogers who take an idiographic approach to personality believe personality is unique and personal to the individual. Broad categorisations cannot be made.
>
> Eysenck would emphasise the nativist position to the origins of personality. He would say that genetic inheritance is important in shaping who we become.
>
> Alternatively, Rogers would emphasise the empiricist position to the origins of personality. He would say that experiences in environment are important in shaping who we become.

Intelligence

Intelligence, as with personality is another big area of study within the psychology of individual differences. Along with atypical behaviour what binds these three subject areas together is the contribution our biology in terms of our genetics makes to their understanding. Intelligence allows us to also empathise the use of measurement within the psychology of individual differences.

As with the study of personality and atypical behaviour a tradition has emerged in this area of psychology for **psychometric testing**. Psychometric essentially means measurable.

A psychometric test is a standardised written procedure that assesses our knowledge, abilities, attitudes, aptitudes, behaviours, traits etc. Eysenck's Personality Inventory that we read about earlier is an example of a psychometric test of personality.

The origins of psychometric testing particularly regards the study of intelligence was greatly influenced by family genetics themselves.

This was because Darwin had a cousin Francis Galton who became intrigued with his work, and consequently developed the idea that intelligence could be genetically inherited.

Galton is best known for his studies of heredity and intelligence published in *Hereditary Genius* (1869), which led to the founding of the controversial eugenics movement. Eugenics became particularly popular with the Nazis around seventy years later in their drive for racial purity and an Aryan master race: this was because eugenics advocated that in order to preserve desired genetic characteristics, selective breeding must occur within a population. Put simply, to create a very intelligent child, it is a good idea that a very intelligent male and female be its biological parents. This ultimately influenced the deaths of millions of Germans and non-Germans alike whose genetic characteristics did not fit the Nazi profile of a member of their abhorrent master race.

Does eugenics still exist today?

In the USA, men can donate their sperm to clinics, which then sell the sperm to women wanting babies by Artificial Insemination by Donor (AID). AID is very popular. Male sperm sells on the basis of the characteristics of the male donor. The sperm of a concert pianist is far more valuable than that of a refuse collector. What does this suggest?

Galton's is important to the study of intelligence both as a historical figure and in suggesting that intelligence could be measured. His work precipitated interest in the development of psychometric tests of intelligence.

Psychometric tests of intelligence

Psychometric tests of intelligence all see some kind of biological inheritance/maturation as their base. Thought because we share a common biology, intelligence tests have established that there is an average or mean IQ (intelligence quotient) in a normal population of people. This mean has been set at 100, so that if general intelligence were measured in a community, most would get an IQ score of around 100, with a few scoring much higher, and a similar amount much lower. This is illustrated in Figure 9.4.

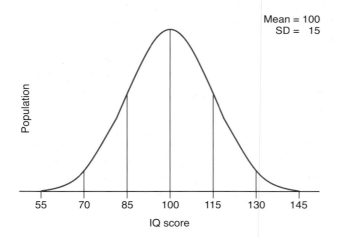

Figure 9.4 IQ scores

Those whose score is far from the mean of 100, whether higher or lower, are reflecting individual differences in intelligence in comparison to the bulk of the population. Such individual differences in intelligence are greatly influenced by our biology and our environment.

It is not intended here to debate intelligence. By way of introduction however, it may be useful to try to get a general idea of what intelligence might be, and more importantly, what influences the maximisation of whatever intellectual potential we have.

This sees us once again refer to the nature–nurture debate, or the influence our genetics and environment play in the unfolding of intellectual ability and potential. The nature-nurture debate continually arises within the psychology of individual differences.

Intelligence: the genetics–environment debate

The nature of intelligence has perplexed psychology since its early days. In a general sense, '*Intelligent activity consists of grasping the essentials in a situation and responding appropriately to them*' (Heim, 1970). The ability to do this is a result of our genetic inheritance from our biological parents and our own learning experiences in our environment.

Debate has raged as to how much genetics, and how much environment each contribute to our overall intelligence. Psychologists like Eysenck and Jensen have argued that genetics contributes over 90 per cent to our intelligence, while others like Kamin would argue the opposite – that environment makes a 90 per cent plus contribution towards intellectual ability. What influence is more correct still intrigues psychology.

Nowadays, there is a strong belief that biological/genetic inheritance does play a part in overall intellectual growth, contributing towards 60–70 per cent of our IQ. Therefore environment contributes 30–40 per cent (Bouchard & Segal, 1988).

As most of us share the same IQ of around 100, the genetics–environment debate about intelligence is a bit pointless. Psychology is maybe better occupied concerning itself with the outcome of the interaction of genetics and environment, and discovering more about how it can help maximise all peoples' intelligence(s), whatever these may be.

Interactionism

This is because environment is the factor that makes the difference between one person developing whatever intellect they have to the maximum, and another not being able to do so. As regards genotype, phenotype and intelligence, the *social setting*, or environment, in which we find ourselves and interact, is of immense importance to the maximisation of whatever abilities we have in the first place (Plomin & DeFries, 1998).

Let us now move on to more specific matters: atypical behaviour.

What is *atypical* behaviour?

It is extremely difficult to define normal let alone 'abnormal' behaviour. The definition of abnormality is a contentious issue. This is because abnormality is a *subjectively* defined characteristic, and is based on opinion. It is attributed to individuals with rare or dysfunctional conditions.

To date there have been three approaches to this tricky problem.

- the statistical approach
- the valuative approach, and
- the practical approach

The statistical approach to defining atypical behaviour

The statistical approach to defining atypical behaviour takes a numerical view. The statistical approach assesses abnormal behaviours in terms of **deviation from the statistical norm**. Put simply, what a lot of people do is deemed normal. What increasingly smaller numbers of people do is deemed abnormal. The more rare a behaviour the more likely the statistical approach would label it abnormal. A statistical approach to abnormality seems straightforward enough, but it has flaws.

Criticisms of the statistical approach to abnormality

In the UK most adult women take between a size 4 and a size 7 in shoes. If you fall outside this range and the statistical approach were to be applied to you, you would be seen as abnormal. This is because as far as shoe size is concerned you *deviate from the statistical norm.*

Take the study of intelligence and geniuses with an IQ of 130+. In Figure 9.4 they are the small number under the normal distribution curve +3 SD away from society's mean IQ. They are a statistically abnormal number when compared with those who cluster around the statistical norm of 100. But they aren't labelled abnormal or atypical.

Compare this with those who have an IQ of –70. In Figure 9.4 they are the small number under the normal distribution curve -3 SD away from society's mean IQ. They are a statistically abnormal number when compared with those who cluster around the statistical norm of 100. This group *are* labelled abnormal or atypical.

The statistical approach is inconsistent in classifying abnormal behaviour on the basis of deviation from a statistical norm. In our example above the numbers with an IQ of <70, and the numbers with an IQ of >130 were both equally rare. Yet one group is diagnosed and treated as abnormal, while the other group are not. This should not be the case.

The statistical approach does not say *why* a statistically infrequent behaviour is abnormal. Its purely numerical view would subsequently categorise a genius like Einstein as abnormal! Clearly the statistical approach to abnormality is unsatisfactory.

The valuative approach to defining atypical behaviour

The valuative approach to defining atypical behaviour assesses abnormal behaviours in terms of **deviation from social norms**.

The valuative approach to abnormal behaviour is flawed. Social norms differ between cultures. Social norms differ within cultures. Social norms also change with time.

The valuative approach imposes a *sociocultural* definition on what is thought abnormal. Abnormal behaviours are defined on the basis of prevailing cultural standards or social norms. The valuative approach can however be criticised.

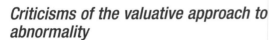

Criticisms of the valuative approach to abnormality

This is because social norms differ from one culture to another, and also within cultures. Social norms also change, sometimes quite dramatically. Take the following.

Between 1855 and 1860 in Scotland only 8.7% of babies born were to unmarried parents. In 1976 only 6,025 of newborn babies, or 9.3% had unmarried parents. For at least 125 years most couples that had babies were married. This was the sociocultural norm. There was a stigma attached to unmarried couples having children.

However by 2008 the situation had changed markedly in that of the 60,041 babies born in Scotland, 30,055 or 50.1% were to unmarried couples. Sociocultural standards of behaviour have radically changed.

'The proportion of births to unmarried parents has been rising steadily for several years and in 2008 topped 50% for the first time'.

Duncan Macniven
Registrar General for Scotland (2008)

The valuative approach is thus as inconsistent in its assessment of abnormal behaviours as the statistical approach. The valuative approach to abnormal behaviours as deviation from social norms is unreliable.

ONLINE INTERACTIVES

To appreciate just how much social norms have changed watch a BBC video of the Sir Elton John and David Furnish civil partnership.

In so doing please consider the main weakness of a valuative approach to abnormality. Sociocultural attitudes change.

Go to **http://news.bbc.co.uk/1/hi/ entertainment/4546670.stm**

A direct Link is available in the Chapter 9 section of Higher Psychology Learning Suite at **www.gerardkeegan.co.uk**

The practical approach to defining atypical behaviour

Nowadays the practical approach to defining abnormality is prevalent. It assumes that neither the statistical nor valuative approaches are satisfactory. The practical approach combines each view, and judges what is abnormal on the basis of the *content*, the *context* and the *consequences* of the behaviour.

The content of the behaviour

In taking a practical approach to a definition of abnormality, the *content* of a person's behaviour is taken into account. This concerns what they do, and how this affects others. Rosenhan and Seligman (1989) say behaviour is abnormal when maladaptive, disabling, bizarre, irrational or uncontrolled.

While such indices are useful they involve subjective judgement or *valuations* as to what are normal or abnormal behaviours. It is difficult to decide whether a person's behaviour *is* maladaptive, disabling, bizarre, irrational or uncontrolled.

The practical approach to a definition of abnormality then also looks at the *context* of the behaviour.

The context of the behaviour

The *context* of the behaviour concerns where the behaviour takes place. Behaviour in one situation, such as shouting at a football match, is entirely normal, while the same behaviour of shouting at a funeral is not! This would be abnormal.

In accounting for the context within which behaviours occur the practical approach is allowing for numerically rare behaviours such as eccentricities to be adjudged as normal. The practical approach has a place for people whose behaviours may be a bit odd, as long as that oddness is tempered, or confined to private places.

 Neither deviant behaviour, e.g. political, religious or sexual, nor conflicts that are primarily between the individual and society are mental disorders unless the deviance or condition is a symptom of a dysfunction (i.e. impairment of function) in the person".

Diagnostic and Statistical Manual of Mental Disorders DSM-IV (1994)

Rosenhan and Seligman (1989) 'Criteria of Abnormality'

Personal distress: Where a person permanently experiences uncomfortable emotions such as guilt, anxiety and depression

Maladaptiveness: Where a person exhibits a behaviour that interferes with their ability to cope with everyday life

Irrationality: Where a person exhibits thoughts and behaviour at odds with reality, e.g. thinking that Beatles John Lennon and Paul McCartney have stolen your songs, despite the fact you were born after the songs were written and released

Unpredictability: Where a person exhibits impulsive uncontrolled behaviour that disrupts the lives of others

Unconventionality and statistical rarity: Where abnormal behaviour is statistically rare. Such rare behaviour is only thought abnormal if it is undesirable. On this basis genius is not abnormal.

Observer discomfort: Where a person goes against the norms by which most live, and this leads to the majorities discomfort. An example might be where an individual is seen in a bus station going through bins looking for food, cigarette butts etc. Such violation of social norms is then considered abnormal.

Much more important to the practical approach are the *consequences* of the behaviour.

The consequences of the behaviour

The practical approach also assesses abnormal behaviour in terms of the *consequences* it has, both for the individual and for others. Consequences concern the distress an individual suffers because of their (ab)normal behaviour. Distress and suffering is assessed on the basis of intensity and duration.

Assessing consequences can be problematic as some mental health problems such as Obsessive Compulsive Disorder (OCD), are not distressful to the individual but to others! Further, many symptoms associated with the low mood state we call depression are entirely normal within other situations.

ONLINE INTERACTIVES: OCD

Obsessive Compulsive Disorder (OCD) is an anxiety disorder that affects 1–2 % of the Scottish population. People with OCD experience repetitive and disconcerting thoughts that prompt them to engage in repetitive and disconcerting behaviours. Consequently OCD has two main features: obsessions and compulsions.

To find out more about this intriguing condition go to **http://www.seemescotland.org.uk/aboutmental healthproblemsandstigma/ocd**

A direct Link is available in the Chapter 9 section of Higher Psychology Learning Suite at **www.gerardkeegan.co.uk**

According to the Depression Alliance Scotland at www.lookgoodfeelcrap.org the symptoms of a low mood state include:

- crying a lot and feeling sad a lot of the time
- feeling hopeless or inadequate
- not liking yourself
- lacking energy and the oomph to do anything
- being angry and irritable
- feeling lonely
- having trouble sleeping
- not wanting sex

Take each symptom and give an *everyday* situation where it occurs.

A related approach to abnormality is the *deviation from ideal mental health* model proposed by Marie Jahoda.

Jahoda's deviation from ideal mental health

Jahoda (1958) incorporates humanistic psychologist Abraham Maslow's work into her notion of what is ideal mental health. We came across the humanistic approach to psychology in Chapter 1, and will examine it further regards atypical behaviour shortly. Suffice to say here that Jahoda's six criteria for a 'mentally healthy individual' are:

➤ Someone who is self-reliant, self-confident and self-accepting

➤ Someone who promotes his or her individual growth needs and tries to be self-actualising

➤ Someone who can cope with stress

➤ Someone who is independent in outlook, is not reliant on others for their well being and accepts responsibility for their own actions

➤ Someone who has a realistic outlook or perception on their world

➤ Someone who is adaptable to changes in their world

Deviation from Jahoda's six criteria suggests an individual who is not in ideal mental health.

Criticisms of the practical approach to abnormality

The practical approach defines abnormality as maladaptive, disabling, bizarre, irrational or uncontrolled behaviour that disrupts daily functioning. Such behaviour is statistically infrequent in comparison to the norm, and harms the values of others.

Figure 9.5 Marilyn Manson

Using the statistical, valuative and practical approaches to abnormality how atypical is rock star Marilyn Manson? Give reasons for your answer.

The practical approach to abnormality, while useful, can be criticised. Whether behaviours *are* maladaptive, bizarre, irrational, unpredictable or uncontrolled depends on someone else *opinion*. A doctor or psychiatrist can only make a *subjective* assessment of behaviours. As we shall discover agreement as to whether any such behaviour is abnormal is problematic.

The practical approach also fails to adequately discriminate between abnormal behaviours that are mentally, physically and/or behaviourally disabling, and abnormal behaviours that are unconventional, eccentric etc.

Explaining atypical behaviour

History gives us three explanations of atypical behaviour.

The earliest explanation is the **demonological model**, which claims abnormal behaviour to be result of supernatural forces.

A second explanation first put forward in ancient times and dominant today is the **medical model**. A medical explanation of atypical behaviour looks to some kind of physical or biological cause behind it.

The third explanation is the **psychological model**, advocated in the late 19th Century. The psychological model holds that most abnormal behaviour is the result of psychological problems like personality conflicts, learned maladaptive habits, or distortion of perception in how some individuals view their world.

The demonological model

Our ancestors believed that supernatural forces caused odd behaviours. Good or evil spirits made people feel poorly, act differently, see things, talk unnaturally, walk differently etc.

Trepanning

Archaeologists tell us that 4000 years before the birth of Christ, people thought possessed by evil spirits underwent trepanning.

Trepanning is an ancient surgical technique where sharp stones and sticks were used to bore holes into a person's skull. This was thought to give release to the evil spirit inside the skull thought to be causing the sufferer's abnormal symptoms. It is remarkable to discover that trepanning is still practiced as an alternative medicine in the UK today!

ONLINE INTERACTIVES

Read 'Woman carries out DIY surgery' at **http://news.bbc.co.uk/1/hi/health/651892.stm**

A direct Link is available in the Chapter 9 section of the Higher Psychology Learning Suite at **www.gerardkeegan.co.uk**.

Self flagellation and exorcism

The demonological view of atypical behaviour was also very evident during the Middle Ages. From the 5th to the 15th Century abnormal behaviours were thought to be sinful and almost exclusively seen as being caused by demons. To drive such demons away and thus be free of sin many practiced self-flagellation (Kroll, 1973). People whose behaviours were so odd and were thought possessed by the devil often underwent Exorcism.

Exorcism

Exorcisms involved a lot of noise, beatings, and prayers. The priest would make their parishioner drink potions such as sheep-dung and wine as an emetic. An emetic is something that makes you sick. In so doing the victim would hope to expel the devil from their body. Similarly people would flog themselves with whips tipped with iron spikes (Meyer and Salmon, 1988). Comparable rituals are still practiced in some cultures today, as was the case in the blockbuster book and film 'The Da Vinci Code' by Dan Brown.

Witchcraft

The Middle Ages was also the time of the '*Malleus Maleficarum* or Witches Hammer. The *Malleus Maleficarum* was a church document that listed symptoms allegedly displayed by witches. These included sudden loss of reason, hearing voices, seeing visions etc.

Any woman unfortunate enough to display eccentric behaviours and came to the attention of the church faced further investigation. Following horrific torture mostly all 'admitted' being witches.

Unfortunately for them witches were thought to be creatures of the Devil. Witches practiced heresy. Anyone found to be a heretic was burnt alive at the stake. It is thought that between 40,000 and 100,000 women met this fate during the Middle Ages, all for acting a bit differently than others.

Asylums

As the Middle Ages drew to a close specialised hospitals or '**asylums**' began being built to accommodate people who thought, felt and acted differently from others. The word asylum literally means 'safe house'. The Lunacy Act of 1845 established a national asylum programme in the UK. By 1850 almost every state in America, and country in Western Europe had similar asylum facilities.

While initially meant to be places of quiet retreat, they soon became places of awful *bedlam*, as evidenced in 1792 by the famous French physician Philippe Pinel when he was put in charge of the Paris Asylum. On discovering his patients shackled to damp walls in cold, dark cells Pinel started to champion the medical approach to abnormality. He felt this was a much more humane way to treat people. The medical or biological model of abnormality came to the fore.

The medical model of abnormality

Pinel thought his *'lunatic'* patients to have an underlying medical or *physical* reason to their bizarre behaviours. The medical explanation of abnormality believes all problems are *biological* in origin. There is an internal physiological or genetic reason as to why someone is thinking, feeling and behaving abnormally.

The medical model of abnormality quickly established itself in psychiatry, the branch of medicine that specialises in mental health. Mental hospitals began to replace asylums, where psychiatrists began to diagnose and treat people from mainly a medical perspective. In so doing, psychiatrists emphasised the physical or medical reason(s) behind why their patients acted as they did. They reasoned if they could find the biological cause to a mental health issue, this might be able to be treated using a physical or biological remedy. Pharmacy might be able to provide a 'a pill for every ill.' It is here that the medical model falters in its diagnosis of atypical behaviours. As we will discover, only *some* kinds of mental health problems are *exclusively* physical or organic in origin.

Classification of atypical behaviours

The World Health Organisation (WHO) classifies all medical problems, physical and mental, in a manual called ICD-10. ICD 10 stands for International Statistical Classification of Diseases and Related Health Problems 10th Revision. ICD 10 is used in all branches of medicine in the UK, including psychiatry. ICD 10 is used to identify symptoms, diagnose and treat people with all manner of medical problem.

Of interest to psychology are ICD 10's mental and behavioural disorders, classified in Chapter V under 11 categories. The Americal equivalent of Chapter V of ICD 10 is DSM IV. DSM IV is the Diagnostic and Statistical Manual of Mental Disorders 4th Edition published by the American Psychiatric Association in 1994. A DSM-V is planned for publication in 2012.

Classification of mental and behavioural disorders in Chapter V of ICD 10

F00-F99

F00-F09 Organic, including symptomatic, mental disorders

F10-F19 Mental and behavioural disorders due to psychoactive substance use

F20-F29 Schizophrenia, schizotypal and delusional disorders

F30-F39 Mood (affective) disorders

F40-F49 Neurotic, stress-related and somatoform disorders

F50-F59 Behavioural syndromes associated with physiological disturbances and physical factors

F60-F69 Disorders of adult personality and behaviour

F70-F79 Mental retardation

F80-F89 Disorders of psychological development

F90-F98 Behavioural and emotional disorders with onset usually occurring in childhood and adolescence

F99 Unspecified mental disorder

Organic, including symptomatic, mental disorders

An organic mental disorder is caused by brain infection, tumour, brain damage or degeneration of the central nervous system. An excellent example of an organic mental disorder is dementia.

Dementia is a chronic and progressive disease that is characterised by a decline in the sufferer's memory and intellectual functioning. This decline is thought caused by changes to the person's brain chemistry and brain structure. This causes brain cells to die. There are over 100 kinds of dementia, the most common being Alzheimer's disease.

ONLINE INTERACTIVES

Find out more about dementia.

Go to:
http://www.alzheimers.org.uk/site/scripts/documents.php?categoryID=200171&gclid=CMussZC9wpYCFRpUEAodaGtoxg

A direct Link is available in the Chapter 9 section of the Higher Psychology Learning Suite at **www.gerardkeegan.co.uk**.

Alzheimer's disease

In the Alzheimer brain the cortex shrivels up. This affects thinking, planning and remembering. Such shrinkage is especially severe in the hippocampus, the area of the brain that helps us form new memories. Additionally with Alzheimer's disease the ventricles, which are fluid-filled spaces within the brain grow larger. Sufferers become unable to recognise family members, and sometimes even forget their own name.

Clearly such physical deterioration indicates Alzheimer's disease as a major organic mental disorder. Its specific cause is unknown at the moment. This makes treatment difficult.

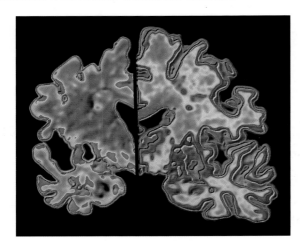

Figure 9.6 The brain on the right has been damaged by Alzheimers

ONLINE INTERACTIVES

Watch Terry Pratchett: Living with Alzheimer's at
http://www.bbc.co.uk/headroom/newsandevents/programmes/alzheimers.shtml

A direct Link is available in the Chapter 9 section of the Higher Psychology Learning Suite at **www.gerardkeegan.co.uk.**

Mental and behavioural disorders due to psychoactive substance use

This category covers mental and behavioural disorders caused by substance misuse such as alcohol, drugs and **toxins**. Psychoactive substance misuse often sees people develop a dependence syndrome.

A person has a dependence syndrome when drugs, alcohol, or toxins takes on a much higher priority than other things in their life. The individual becomes physically and psychologically dependent on the substance. There is a pattern in the person's repeated use of alcohol or drugs that results in increasing tolerance, withdrawal symptoms and habitual and increased substance-taking behaviour.

ONLINE INTERACTIVES

Want to find out more about psychoactive substance misuse? Go to Breathing Space Scotland at
http://www.breathingspacescotland.co.uk/bspace/181.51.79.html.

A direct Link is available in the Chapter 9 section of the Higher Psychology Learning Suite at **www.gerardkeegan.co.uk**. Just as well!

Schizophrenia, schizotypal and delusional disorders

According to the Rethink, 1:100 people will experience schizophrenia at some point in their lives, with early onset usually being in a person's late teens or early twenties. It should be noted that schizophrenia can be treated, and that the majority of people with schizophrenia lead ordinary lives.

Schizotypal personality disorder

Someone who has a schizotypal personality disorder will exhibit peculiar thoughts, feelings and behaviours. These are often viewed as eccentric, erratic, and bizarre. They have brief periods of mental illness. Their speech, while coherent, concentrates on trivia. A schizotypal's thinking sees an abnormal interest in magic. They are suspicious of others, and are often delusional. Psychiatrists believe this is the schizotypal's unconscious way of coping with social anxiety. To some extent, their behaviours stem from being socially isolated. Having a distorted view of appropriate interpersonal relations with others exacerbates this.

Symptoms of schizophrenia are twofold; *positive* and *negative*. Positive symptoms of schizophrenia develop gradually and include exaggeration or distortion of normal thoughts, emotions and behaviour. Negative symptoms of schizophrenia refer to the loss of social characteristics normally associated with our everyday interactions with one another. Both positive and negative symptoms can occur together.

A person affected by schizophrenia may also experience secondary symptoms such as depression. Secondary symptoms result from the difficulties they may be having in learning to cope with the onset of their disorder.

Positive symptoms: hallucinations and delusions

While visual, olfactory and tactile hallucinations are reported, most commonly, a person with schizophrenia hears thoughts spoken aloud in their head. These auditory hallucinations may take the form of an uncontrollable running commentary about what they are doing, and appear to come from an external source. MRI (magnetic resonance imagery) techniques have shown neurotransmitters firing off in speech areas of the brain when someone is reporting voice hearing. Voice hearing is a real neurological experience for the individual, and is not imaginary.

Rethink sees delusions as logical for the schizophrenic. The schizophrenic realises these voices are abnormal, and tries to find a reason for them. They come to believe they are coming from the television, the Martians, the government, God, the devil, and so on. Two types of delusion deserve mention. Delusions of grandeur occur where the sufferer comes to believe they are a very important person such as Jesus Christ or Napoleon. The other is delusion of persecution, where the sufferer believes they are being persecuted by an external source such as the government. These convictions can become overwhelming and all consuming for the person, and account for the person's strange behaviours.

Negative symptoms: loss of motivation

Negative symptoms emerge over time and eventually become everyday social (anti-social) or behaviours. A schizophrenic person gradually becomes slow to think, talk and move. They withdraw from their former social world and become socially isolated.

ONLINE INTERACTIVES: DELUSIONAL DISORDERS

According to the American Psychiatric Association the criteria for a delusional disorder are

Non-bizarre delusions which have been present for at least one month

Absence of obviously odd or bizarre behaviour

Absence of hallucinations, or hallucinations that only occur infrequently in comparison to other psychotic disorders

No memory loss, medical illness or drug or alcohol-related effects are associated with the development of delusions

For further details see **http://www.mind disorders.com/Br-Del/Delusional-disorder.html**

A direct Link is available in the Chapter 9 section of the Higher Psychology Learning Suite at **www.gerardkeegan.co.uk.**

Their sleeping pattern can change and they may stay up all night, and sleep all day. From a psychological point of view, motivation becomes seriously affected. They show a lack of *volition*, where they become indecisive, give up easily on things, and seem unaffected by concern shown by friends and family. These they can eventually lose.

ONLINE INTERACTIVES

Visit **http://www.mentalhealth. com/icd/p22-ps01.html** and outline the symptoms of:

1   Simple schizophrenia

2   Hebephrenic schizophrenia

3   Catatonic schizophrenia

4   Paranoid schizophrenia.

A direct Link is available in the Chapter 9 section of the Higher Psychology Learning Suite at **www.gerardkeegan.co.uk**.

R.D. Laing

Figure 9.7 R.D. Laing

This textbook would be lacking without mention of Ronnie Laing. Born in 1927 in Govan, Glasgow, he went on to become hugely important to 1960s psychiatry. After studying medicine at Glasgow University he was called up in 1951 to work as an Army psychiatrist. On his demobilisation in 1953 he returned to Glasgow University to teach. He later moved to the Tavistock Clinic and Institute for Human Relations in London, where he remained until his death in 1989. His particular contribution to psychiatry was in his use of phenomenology to the understanding of schizophrenia. He thought schizophrenia was exacerbated by how the schizophrenic perceived their 'self', and how others perceived the schizophrenic. Very much against traditional psychiatric treatments such as drugs, electro-convulsive therapy and psychosurgery he set up asylums (safe houses). Here the schizophrenic client could explore their perception of self in art, drama and music therapy. Sympathetic psychiatrists, psychologists and social workers used paintings, for example, to focus in on how the schizophrenic saw or perceived their condition. This helped them understand the way their clients saw their condition. If you are ever in Glasgow why don't you visit the amazing Kelvingrove Art Gallery? Here you will find the museum's unique collection of Mary Barnes artworks spotlighting R. D. Laing's work.

Mood (affective) disorders

Mood or affective disorders concern a variety of abnormal *feelings* people experience. These feelings influence their thinking and their behaviour. This category of ICD 10 includes mania, bipolar disorder, depression, and persistent mood states such as dysthemia.

A *mania* is a severe medical condition evident in an individual's mood state. They demonstrate an abundance of energy, have unusual thoughts and are sometimes psychotic.

A *psychosis* is a serious mental disorder involving a loss of contact with reality, as when hallucinations or delusions are present.

Bipolar disorder occurs when periods of mania cyclically alternate with episodes of depression. Bipolar disorder was once known as *manic-depression.*

Depression is a specific mood or affective disorder characterised by lack of appetite, chronic fatigue, lethargy, sleep disturbances and thoughts of suicide. We will examine depression in greater detail shortly.

Dysthemia is a *persistent* mood state, and is a permanent low-level depression that affects around 3% of the population. According to the American

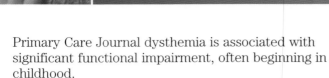

Primary Care Journal dysthemia is associated with significant functional impairment, often beginning in childhood.

Neurotic, stress-related and somatoform disorders

A neurosis is a mental disorder that does not have a medical or physical cause. We investigate neuroses further when look at the psychodynamic approach to atypical behaviour.

Neurotic disorders include phobias like agoraphobia, and other anxiety disorders such as OCD, which we came across earlier. Agoraphobia is an anxiety state arising due to fear of a panic attack in an open space.

A good example of a *stress-related disorder* is Post Traumatic Stress Disorder. PTSD is a severe and ongoing emotional reaction to traumatic events that has threatened or caused an individual grave physical harm. PTSD is often evident in soldiers exposed to the horrors of war. "A study of the first 100,000 [Iraq and Afghanistan] veterans seen at VA facilities showed that 25 % of them received mental health diagnoses. Of these, 56 % had 2 or more mental health diagnoses. The most common were PTSD, substance abuse, and depression. The younger the veterans are, the more likely they are to have mental health conditions" Kantor (2007).

A *somatoform disorder* is hysteria. Hysterias are obvious medical conditions that have no physical or medical cause. Their cause is psychological. The psychodynamic approach to atypical behaviour will shortly elaborate as to why this is.

Behavioural syndromes associated with physiological disturbances and physical factors

ICD 10 categorises eating disorders as *behavioural syndromes associated with physiological disturbances and physical factors*. An eating disorder is a pattern of eating behaviour harmful to the body and mind. We examine eating disorders in some detail shortly.

Also included in the ICD 10 category of behavioural syndromes associated with physiological disturbances and physical factors are sleep disorders and sexual dysfunction.

One such *sleep disorder* is somnambulism, or sleepwalking. A range of activities have been reported in those who sleepwalk including eating, bathing, urinating, talking, dressing, driving cars, painting, whistling, dancing, having sexual intercourse, and even committing murder (Broughton *et al.*, 1994).

Disorders of adult personality and behaviour

Disorders of adult personality and behaviour are manifold. They include specific personality disorders, habit and impulse disorders, gender identity disorders, Munchausen syndrome etc.

An example of a *specific personality disorder* is paranoid personality disorder.

A paranoid personality disorder should not be confused with paranoid schizophrenia. They are not the same thing. A paranoid personality is one that is pervasively distrustful and suspicious of others. Such hypersensitivity causes difficulties in interpersonal relationships, employment etc. People with a paranoid personality disorder hold grudges against others. Not unsurprisingly this further exacerbates interpersonal relationships, employment etc.

Pathological fires setting or pyromania is a *habit and impulse disorder*, as is kleptomania or pathological stealing.

Gender identity disorders include Transsexualism. Transsexualism occurs where an individual identifies with a physical sex different to the one they were born. Though more apparent in the modern age, it is fascinating to learn that some American Indian tribes have long accepted transsexuals as 'two-spirit' people (Lang, 1997).

Munchausen syndrome is another disorder of adult personality and behaviour. Munchausen syndrome is where someone affected fake disease, illness, or psychological trauma in order to draw attention or sympathy to him or herself. Munchausen syndrome is related to another disorder called Munchausen syndrome by proxy (MSBP). Munchausen syndrome by proxy occurs when someone abuses another, usually a child, because of a psychological problem they themselves have. Those who suffer from Munchausen syndrome by proxy are thought to be jealous of the attention their victim is receiving.

ONLINE INTERACTIVES

Read Troubled Love: Child Abuse and Munchausen Syndrome by Proxy at **http://www.happinessonline.org/LoveAndHelpChildren/p5.htm**

A direct Link is available in the Chapter 9 section of the Higher Psychology Learning Suite at **www.gerardkeegan.co.uk**.

Mental retardation

Mental retardation is a rather negative general term used to classify people with an intellectual disability. They have significantly below-average cognitive ability as measured in terms of their IQ being <70. Intellectual disability encompasses those with congenital disorders such as Down's syndrome evident from birth, as well as those who later suffer brain injury or dementias.

Class of intellectual disability	IQ
Profound mental retardation	Below 20
Severe mental retardation	20–34
Moderate mental retardation	35–49
Mild mental retardation	50–69
Borderline intellectual functioning	70–79

Disorders of psychological development

Disorders of psychological development include disorders of speech, language, and scholastic skills. Disorders of psychological development also encompass pervasive developmental disorders such as autism and Asperger's Syndrome.

Speech disorders refer to the problems people have when producing the sounds associated with speech or with the quality of voice used when talking. According to the self-help charity Asfasic over 1 million children and young adults are affected by the hidden disability of speech, language and communication impairments in the UK.

Stuttering and stammering are examples of a *speech disorder*. Their specific cause is unknown. Those with a speech disorder can be prone to bullying because of their speech impediment. This can have a devastating psychological effect on their self-esteem. In later life, when bullying is not as common, those with a speech disorder may experience social isolation because of the discomfort experienced by others when listening to them.

Speech impediments are treatable with speech therapy.

Readers should be familiar with at least one *scholastic skill* disorder. This is because this category includes dyslexia. The word *'dyslexia'* is Greek in origin and means 'difficulty with words'. Dyslexia was first diagnosed by Berlin in 1887 and presents itself as a problem with written language. Dyslexia concerns difficulties with reading, and thought to arise due to the different ways dyslexic and non-dyslexic people process spoken and written language. Dyslexia is not an intellectual disability in that it affects people of different intelligence. This includes entrepreneur Richard Branson the founder of the Virgin empire, the American singer Cher, actor Orlando Bloom of Lord of the Rings fame, and Noel Gallagher of the Manchester band Oasis.

Acalculia is another scholastic skill disorder. Acalculia is acquired in later life after a stroke. When evident patients have difficulty performing simple mathematical tasks, such as adding, subtracting, multiplying and even simply stating which of two numbers is the larger. Acalculia is different to the specific developmental disorder of dyscalculia. Dyscalculia sees an individual have difficulties in the acquisition of mathematical knowledge but is neurological in origin. Those with dyscalculia have had this since birth.

ONLINE INTERACTIVES

nterested in promoting a dyslexia-friendly society? Then visit the British Dyslexic Society at **http://www.bdadyslexia. org.uk/ extra10.html**

A direct Link is available in the Chapter 9 section of the Higher Psychology Learning Suite at **www.gerardkeegan.co.uk**.

Read more on autism and Asperger Syndrome from the Royal College of Psychiatrists. Visit **http://www.rcpsych.ac. uk/mentalhealthinfoforall/mentalhealthandg rowingup/12autismandaspergers.aspx**

A direct Link is available in the Chapter 9 section of the Higher Psychology Learning Suite at **www.gerardkeegan.co.uk**.

ONLINE INTERACTIVES

Discover more about speech and language difficulties. Visit **http://www.afasic. org.uk/**

A direct Link is available in the Chapter 9 section of the Higher Psychology Learning Suite at **www.gerardkeegan.co.uk**.

Behavioural and emotional disorders with onset usually occurring in childhood and adolescence

This penultimate category within ICD 10 identifies hyperkinetic, behavioural and emotional disorders found in children and teenagers. One such hyperkinetic disorder is ADHD. Attention Deficit Hyperactivity Disorder is a neurobehavioural disorder found in around 5 % of children worldwide (Polanczyk et al, 2007). Symptoms include impulsiveness and inattention.

Behavioural disorders are also found in this category. A conduct problem may be diagnosed when a certain pattern of behaviour emerges in young people. Symptoms of a conduct disorder are verbal and physical aggression, cruel behaviour toward people and pets, destructive behaviour, lying, truancy, vandalism and stealing (Loeber *et al.*, 1998). If a conduct disorder is not treated it can result in an individual developing an anti-social personality disorder in adulthood (Santrock, 2008).

We touched on *emotional disorders* in childhood and adolescence when we investigated early socialisation in Chapter 3. ICD 10 identifies *adult* separation anxiety. In America it has been found that adult separation anxiety disorder is more common than childhood separation anxiety disorder, the prevalence of which is 7% and 4% respectively (Shear *et al.*, 2006). Symptoms include extreme anxiety when apart from a significant other in life such as a father or mother. Such symptoms often accompany other psychiatric problems such as ADHD, bipolar disorder, panic attacks etc., all of which we came across earlier in our overview of ICD 10. This is known as **co-morbidity**.

Unspecified mental disorder

The 11th and final grouping found in ICD 10 concerns unspecified mental disorders. This category encapsulates any mental disorders not covered elsewhere in ICD 10 specifications. This would be used to diagnose unknown, unusual or unique psychological problems, or behavioural patterns presented by an individual that is causing them distress or disability not part of normal development or expected within their culture.

ONLINE INTERACTIVES

Why don't you have a look at the 2007 version of ICD available online at **http://www.who.int/classifications/apps/icd/icd10online/?**

A direct Link is available in the Chapter 9 section of the Higher Psychology Learning Suite at **www.gerardkeegan.co.uk**.

The Medical Model of Abnormality

Strengths	Weaknesses
Medicine is based on strong biological research.	There is no proof of an exclusive physical cause to most mental illnesses.
This has provided evidence of a link between genetic and biochemical abnormalities and *some* mental health problems e. g. schizophrenia.	If there are any physical symptoms medicine is unsure whether this is the cause or the effect of the mental illness.
Medicine provides a logical and structured approach to the diagnosis and treatment of medical problems.	The medical model does not take much account of environmental factors behind mental illness.
If there is a biological reason for an atypical behaviour the individual is not to blame. They are perceived, diagnosed and treated as a patient who is ill. The cause of their mental illness is outwith their control.	The medical model cannot explain the success of psychological treatments in addressing abnormal behaviours.

Problems with classification systems

The main problem associated with classification systems such as ICD 10 and DSM IV is *misdiagnosis* of abnormal behaviour. This is vividly demonstrated in a classic two-part study conducted by David Rosenhan and others in 1973.

On being sane in insane places

In the first study known as 'On Being Sane in Insane Places' Rosenhan got eight associates to turn up at twelve different hospitals in five different states in the USA. The group comprised of three women and five men.

His *'pseudopatients'* were told to report the same vague symptoms and thereafter act normally. After telephoning the hospital for an appointment they arrived complaining of hearing the words 'hollow', 'empty' and 'thud' in their heads. All eight were admitted. On the basis of DSM criterion seven were diagnosed as having schizophrenia, and one as having manic-depression, as it was called at the time. Once diagnosed, Rosenhan's pseudopatients were unable to get discharged until they agreed with their psychiatrists that they *were* mentally ill and would take appropriate medication!

Interestingly 35 out of 118 'real' patients in the various hospitals realised the eight individuals were not what they seemed! They accused them of being journalists or researchers. Notwithstanding, all but one of the pseudopatients was later discharged with schizophrenia "in remission." Their hospitalisation periods had ranged from 7 to 52 days, with the average being 19 days.

The mental health professionals in each hospital only looked at the pseudopatients presenting behaviours. The pseudopatients became a **self-fulfilling prophecy**. DSM criterion can result in labelling, which then creates part of the symptoms indicating a particular condition (Scheff, 1966).

The non-existent impostor

The second part of the experiment had Rosenhan tell a well-known and respected teaching hospital in America that during the next three months one or more pseudopatients would attempt to gain admission. The hospital had earlier read his work 'On being sane in insane places' and was adamant that they themselves could never be duped like other psychiatric hospitals had been.

Rosenhan therefore arranged with the hospital that for twelve weeks they use a 10-point scale to rate every incoming patient as to whether they were impostors. Of the 193 patients that sought admittance over the next three months, psychiatrists' thought 41 fakes, and considered a further 42 suspect. But as you may have guessed Rosenhan did not send anyone to the hospital! All 193 had been genuine patients seeking psychiatric help.

This led Rosenhan (1973) to conclude of DSM, and by implication ICD, that "any diagnostic process that lends itself too readily to massive errors of this sort cannot be a very reliable one".

ONLINE INTERACTIVES

Watch the excellent if disturbing BBC documentary 'Being Sane In Insane Places'.

Visit http://www.yoism.org/?q=node/234#laing

A direct Link is available in the Chapter 9 section of the Higher Psychology Learning Suite at www.gerardkeegan.co.uk.

Such criticism has found support from others. Using an independent group experimental design Termelin (1970) randomly split 25 mental health professionals and non-professionals into two groups. He then had each group listen to an actor of normal mental health.

The experimental group was told by a psychiatrist that the actor "was a very interesting man because he looked neurotic, but actually was quite psychotic". The control group was told nothing. Sixty percent of the experimental group diagnosed the actor suffering from a psychosis, most probably schizophrenia, while none of the control group did so.

ONLINE INTERACTIVES

Read an excellent synopsis of 'On Being Sane in Insane Places at http://www.holah.co.uk/ study/rosenhan/

Then do my friend Mark Holah's interactive online quiz at http://www.holah.co.uk/ quiz/rosenhanmulti.htm

A direct Link is available in the Chapter 9 section of the Higher Psychology Learning Suite at www.gerardkeegan.co.uk.

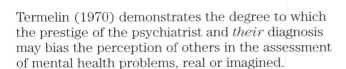

Termelin (1970) demonstrates the degree to which the prestige of the psychiatrist and *their* diagnosis may bias the perception of others in the assessment of mental health problems, real or imagined.

Diathesis-stress model

The medical model to abnormality nowadays emphasises a *diathesis-stress* approach to abnormality. What this means is that it looks to both medical *and* psychological causes behind atypical behaviours. The diathesis-stress model believes we are all born with a biological or medical predisposition towards particular problems. Whether we develop a problem depends upon the environments we find ourselves in. You may be born with a biological tendency to depression, but whether it develops turns on the environmental stressors we encounter. Our environment triggers the hormones that put us into the mood state we call depression. This is now an appropriate opportunity to turn to the *psychological* model of abnormality.

The psychological model

A number of mental disorders are determined by biological *and* psychological factors. These include depression, phobias and schizophrenia. Three psychological models address the psychological causes of such atypical behaviours. These represent the psychodynamic, behaviourist, and humanistic approaches found in psychology.

The psychodynamic approach to atypical behaviour

In the late 1800s, Sigmund Freud began to challenge the strictly physical interpretation of abnormality by the medical model. He created the first *psychological* model of mental disorder with his psychoanalytic approach. This was the first psychological perspective on abnormality contained within the broader psychodynamic approach.

The psychoanalytic perspective on abnormality

The psychoanalytic approach understands abnormalities in terms of neuroses. The psychoanalytic approach believes these develop from childhood trauma and inner psychic conflict.

Instincts

'An instinct differs from a stimulus in that it arises from sources of stimulation within the body, operates as a constant force and is such that the subject cannot escape from it by flight as he can from an external stimulus. An instinct may be described as having a source, an object and an aim. The source is a state of excitation within the body and its aim is to remove that excitation.' (Freud, 1938)

Neuroses are influenced by the struggle between **Eros** and **Thanatos**, our life and death instincts. Neuroses are further exacerbated by experiences during the oral, anal, phallic and genital stages of psychosexual development in childhood.

Examples of neuroses

➤ Anxiety neurosis or anxiety/panic attack

➤ Depressive neurosis or depression

➤ Somatisation (formerly called a **hysteria** or hysterical neurosis)

➤ Post-traumatic stress disorder (**PTSD**)

➤ Obsessive-compulsive disorder (OCD)

Of further significance is the stability of our personality, and the relationships between its component parts of id, ego and super-ego. Personality also contributes to any anxieties or neuroses we may develop. The psychodynamic approach believes the origins of neuroses to stem from life-shaping events in our environment, which we then internalise in our unconscious.

Eros

Eros is our life drive/instinct, or *libido*. Eros is driven to keep us protected, and to preserve our species. It drives us to fulfil our basic needs for health, safety, sustenance, and the survival of our species. Eros is crucial to our sex drive. Eros both preserves and creates life. Eros associated with positive emotions such as love. Eros drives us to be pro-social beings.

Thanatos

In 'Beyond the Pleasure Principle' (1920) Freud writes that Thanatos is "an urge inherent in all organic life to restore an earlier state of things". Thanatos is in opposition to Eros. Eros pushes us towards extinction. Thanatos drives negative emotions such as fear, hate and anger. Thanatos makes us anti-social beings.

There are various schools of thought within the psychodynamic approach all of which respect Freud's work. All recognize his importance but deviate from him. This is due to his lack of emphasis concerning the social world on the onset of neurotic behaviours. Freud viewed abnormal behaviours largely in *psychosexual* terms.

Carl Gustav Jung, Alfred Adler and Erik Erikson believe this to be too narrow a focus. Their broader psychodynamic approach thus sees atypical behaviours arising as a result of unconscious clashes between instinctual drives and the demands of our environment. This produces conflicts for the individual. If these conflicts go unresolved neuroses can develop.

Three psychodynamic perspectives on atypical behaviour	
Psychoanalytic Psychology	Sigmund Freud
Analytical Psychology	Carl Gustav Jung
Individual Psychology	Alfred Adler

Carl Gustav Jung (1875–1961)

Figure 9.8 Carl Gustav Jung

Jung left Freud's inner circle in Vienna in 1913. Jung was opposed to the emphasis Freud gave to sex. He disagreed about the nature of libido, ego and the unconscious. The libido, for Jung, was a biologically driven motivating force within us – but was non-sexual in origin. Jung said that the role of the ego is to provide us with information from the past that will help us to deal with our present reality. The ego is part of our process of consciousness. The unconscious consists of two parts: the personal unconscious and the collective unconscious. Jung agreed with Freud that the personal unconscious contains our repressed memories. Some material in the personal unconscious is not however necessarily forbidden or censored. It has merely fallen into decay through lack of use by our awareness or consciousness.

Personal unconscious

The personal unconscious is considered to be the 'opposite' of our conscious mind. This means for Jung that an extrovert with an outgoing passionate temperament is unconsciously an introvert with a thoughtful reserved temperament. The personal unconscious compensates for weaknesses in our personal conscious.

Universal archetypes

The collective unconscious contains information that we hold in common with others in our evolution and is genetically transmitted. Our collective unconscious contains many concepts which Jung calls *universal archetypes*, such as a God, demons, fear of the dark, fire, snakes and spiders. We react to the dark, fire, snakes and spiders in the same way as our ancestors did because of our connected evolutionary biology.

Collective unconscious

Our collective unconscious has survival value for us. Its ability to make us wary of snakes or spiders would have been especially important in our prehistoric past when spiders were the size of plates! Avoiding them increased your life expectancy.

Jung had three stages of personality development, the pre-sexual period (age 3–6), characterised by growth and nutrition, and the pre-pubertal stage, which is similar to Freud's latent stage. The last phase is the stage of maturity comparable to Freud's genital stage.

Jungian psychotherapy

Psychotherapy is the application of psychological theory in clinical practice. In Jungian psychotherapy, Jung was more concerned with a patient's future goals than their past history. He saw the cause of neuroses as being rooted in the present, unlike Freud who looked to the past. Jung's school of analytical psychology and its associated psychotherapy is still of great interest in the psychodynamic approach today.

Alfred Adler (1870–1937)

Figure 9.9 Alfred Adler

Alfred Adler left Freud's 'Vienna circle' in 1911. His initial interest in Freud's psychoanalytic theory of personality stemmed from a shared belief in the biological foundations of human behaviour. Both Freud and Adler thought the biological and the psychological were interlinked. Adler went on to develop his own theory known as individual psychology.

Individual psychology

Individual psychology sees us as striving for perfection in our personality. Further, we are motivated to confirm our personality – or who we think we are. We have a biological drive towards self-preservation and a '*will to power*'.

Will to power

Will to power is a striving for superiority over others. Our drive to superiority over others is influenced by any feelings of inferiority acquired during childhood. For individual psychology our goal is to be socially significant.

Adler disagreed with Freud's view of the importance of sexuality to the development of personality. Instead, Adler concentrated on how we come to terms with feelings of inferiority originating in childhood. Feelings of insecurity or inferiority in childhood can be the consequence of congenital or environmental physical deformity, our gender and perceived gender role.

Gender role and inferiority

Gender role is learnt, in part by the internalisation of stereotypes of what is masculine and feminine in our society. Simply put, boys are encouraged to be strong and superior, girls (in his day anyway) were/are encouraged to be weak and inferior.

Birth order and inferiority

Birth order or where you come in the family also affects feelings of inferiority. The second eldest in a large family can feel 'left out' or less loved than say the eldest (first born) and the youngest (last born or 'baby'). Further feelings of inadequacy arise due to negative learning experiences with adults such as being neglected, spoilt or unloved as a child.

The inferiority complex

All these factors can lead to feelings of inferiority or an 'inferiority complex' in adulthood. As we have an instinctive urge to be powerful, or at least to demonstrate that we have power, Adler thought that people showed their 'will to power' in ways that reflected their inferiority complex. They compensate for their unconscious feelings of inadequacy.

An example is the little man who makes a great show of smoking large cigars or driving a big car. The next time you see a Volvo, look at the size of the person driving it! Adler explained the development of our personality as arising from whatever *compensations* we make for our feelings of inferiority and related low self-esteem.

Successful compensation

For Adler, inferiority is almost natural. As individuals we deal with it in one of three ways. The particular strategy we each adopt to feel less inferior to others will affect our personality. The first strategy Adler calls *successful compensation*. This is where we compensate in a positive and constructive way for whatever handicap we have. Successful compensation is all about making the best of whatever we have as individuals. It is our successful adjustment to Adler's three challenges in life – society, work and sex.

An excellent example of successful compensation is the career of the Scottish classical percussionist Evelyn Glennie who became profoundly deaf in childhood. She turned a calamity to her advantage.

Overcompensation

Another technique is *overcompensation* for your feelings of inferiority, by trying too hard to achieve things in life. Often our goals are beyond us or exist only in our imagination. The person above with the Volvo or big cigar could be said by Adler to be overcompensating for their feelings of height inferiority, for example.

Escape from combat

Finally, there is '*escape from combat*'. Someone who reduces failure to a minimum by never trying to succeed in the first place shows escape from combat. Often they place impossibly high demands on themselves and tackle things that they are not yet ready to do.

Individuals who escape from combat might feign illness as an excuse for doing poorly in an internal assessment, for instance. The use of illness or running away from things can become a way of life. It becomes a cover for personal failure. Never having tried at all is their way of expressing power over others. What these individuals don't understand is that they are only damaging themselves at the end of the day. Everyone else moves on.

Many physicians, social workers and public in Europe and America accepted Adler's views. His popular, simpler view of the role of inferiority in the development of personality was welcomed.

The Scottish connection

Adler was an impassioned advocate of the relatively new subject of psychology; he died in Aberdeen while on a lecture tour of Scotland in 1937. His influence remains today in the work of other psychodynamic psychoanalysts such as Karen Horney.

Erik Erikson (1902–94)

Figure 9.10 Erik Erikson

More recently, American psychologist Erik Erikson disagreed with Freud with his over-emphasis on psychosexual stages of development during childhood, though he accepted the idea that children are sexual beings. Instead, he saw a link between our social experiences and personality development. Unlike Freud who saw the first five years of life alone as crucial to personality, Erikson saw experiences throughout the whole of our lifetime as being important influences on personality. Erikson's main contribution is his psychosocial theory of personality development.

Erikson's psychosocial theory of personality development

Erikson's psychosocial theory of personality development is an age-stage related theory of adult personality development. It shows that it is the interaction of the person and his or her social environment, which gives rise to personality characteristics. Unsuccessful resolution of key age-stages can lead to an individual experiencing a psychosocial crisis that can affect their mental health, and thus their personality. Erikson's theory is still used today, especially in teaching, nursing, social care and social work training. His emphasis on the social aspects of life as influences on what we become should not be underemphasised.

Recent advances in neuropsychology may suggest a biological basis to psychosocial development particularly during adolescence. Erikson's Identity v Role Confusion stage coincides with biological changes in a teenager's brain (Yurgelun-Todd, 2007). Such may account for Identity v Role Confusion thoughts, feelings and behaviours (Durston et al., 2006).

We shall return to the psychodynamic approach when we look at its clinical application in practice. In summary the psychodynamic model of abnormality has given us useful insights into the causes and treatment of mental disorder. Critics argue however that much of what the psychodynamic approach says is difficult to test scientifically. Such concern about a lack of support for its hypothetical constructs like id, ego superego etc. prompted the development of two other psychological models of abnormal behaviour: the behavioural model and the phenomenological model.

The behavioural model

According to the behavioural model abnormal behaviours are *learned*. They are not caused by unconscious conflicts from our past (Skinner, 1953).

Behavioural theorists argue that we learn abnormal or *maladaptive* behaviours similar to how we learn adaptive or normal ways to behave. This is in response to our environment.

The behaviourist approach suggests that while biochemical or other physical factors might see us predisposed towards particular behaviours, the degree to which we display such behaviours depends on how we have learned to behave. An obvious example here would be aggression. We are all biologically predisposed towards aggression. Being aggressive has survival value for us. For a behaviourist the *circumstances* when we display or do not display such emotion are learned. Learning normal and abnormal behaviours is as a consequence of classical conditioning, operant conditioning or social learning.

Classical conditioning

You may remember that 'conditioning' in psychology means learning. *Classical* conditioning means learning by *association*, and was first brought to our attention in the early 20th Century by the Russian animal physiologist Ivan Pavlov. Classical conditioning occurs when a stimulus, which does not normally produce a response in an organism, does so when paired with a stimulus that does produce a response. Thus Pavlov's dogs ultimately learned to salivate to the sound of a bell when it had been previously paired with food.

Figure 9.11

Operant conditioning

Operant conditioning concerns the idea that behaviours, when reinforced are likely to be repeated. For example, giving someone who suffers from depression attention may positively reinforce the repetition of his or her depressed behaviours. Depression is an atypical behaviour that we discuss in more detail shortly.

Social learning: observation, imitation and modelling

As we read earlier, the social learning approach believes individuals learn particular abnormal behaviours by observing others, and then imitating and modelling their own subsequent behaviour on what they see (Bandura, Ross and Ross, 1961). This may explain how eating disorders such as anorexia or bulimia develop. With the emergence of a social learning view of abnormality it becomes clear that advocates of a behavioural approach differ over the degree to which they see learned behaviours exclusively in S-R, or stimulus-response terms.

The cognitive-behavioural model challenges the traditional behaviourist view of abnormality as dysfunctional learning arising *exclusively* from classical and/or operant continuing.

The cognitive-behavioural model

The cognitive-behavioural model believes that atypical behaviours occur not only in response to environmental stimuli or factors. They *also* come about because of faulty cognitive processes. According to the cognitive-behavioural model a person's depression might first arise because of an environmental event such as losing their job. Such a calamity is then exacerbated by associated negative thoughts such as low self-worth, low self-esteem and low self-respect. The person enters a vicious spiral of psychological decay.

One weakness in the cognitive behavioural explanation of atypical behaviour centres on the cause and effect problem. It has yet to answer if such distorted and negative thinking *causes* depression, or is distorted and negative thinking the *result* of depression.

The behavioural and cognitive-behavioural approaches both help focus attention on an individual's strengths as well as their problems. Both psychological approaches avoid putting 'abnormal' labels on people. This is because both understand all behaviours as learned. If someone is behaving in an atypical manner, they are not 'sick'. They have *learned* such maladaptive behaviours and ways of thinking. The behavioural and cognitive behavioural perspectives think such individuals can address their behavioural disorders by learning new, more adaptive behaviours, and ways of thinking.

We will look at behavioural and cognitive-behavioural psychotherapies later on in this Chapter.

The humanistic model

The third major perspective on atypical behaviour is the humanistic model.

The humanistic model believes that human behaviour is guided by the way we *perceive* ourselves in our world. This is in terms of the **self**, or our inner personality.

The self

The humanistic approach concerns the study of personality formed by an individual's personal view of themselves in their world. Our personality – called the self – is influenced by the experiences, and interpretation of the experiences, we as individuals have in life. Our self-concept is our inner being, or who it is we come to perceive we are as individuals. The humanistic approach says the self is composed of concepts we view as unique, particular, and peculiar to ourselves. These include self-image, self-esteem and ideal self.

Self-image

The self is our inner personality and is influenced by our interpretation of the experiences we have in life. Self consists of self-image, self-esteem and ideal self. Self-image is how we see ourselves, which is important to our good psychological health. Self-image includes the influence of our body image on our inner personality. At a simple level, we might perceive ourselves as a good or a bad person, or as beautiful or ugly. Self-image, and how it comes about, has an effect on how we as individuals think, feel and behave in relation to our world. Self-image can make us feel psychologically healthy or otherwise.

Self-esteem

Self-esteem, which will be looked at in more detail when we examine Maslow's hierarchy of needs, concerns how much an individual comes to regard, or value, him- or herself as a person. Self-esteem is influenced by the reaction of others to us, and the comparisons made of us by other people (Argyle, 1983).

Ideal self

Ideal self is the personality we would like to be. It consists of our goals and ambitions and is, according to Maslow, dynamic in nature. What he means by this is that ideal self is forever changing. The ideal self of our childhood is not the same as the ideal self of our late teens or our late twenties, etc. Humanistic psychotherapy helps many people uncover their ideal self. Knowing who you would ideally like to be sees the humanistic psychotherapist move the client from a poor perception of self to a more psychologically healthy ideal self.

How the self is formed comes about as a result of phenomenology, personal agency, existentialism and gestalten. All interlinked, the humanistic approach says these influence self for good or ill. The humanistic approach emphasises that a healthy self should be seen particularly in terms of personal growth and self-actualisation.

Phenomenology and the self

Phenomenology concerns our personal, subjective interpretation of the experiences we have in life that mould us as an individual personality. These experiences come to us from our outside world, which is called our *phenomenological field*. Phenomenology is an element of personality that contributes towards why we think, feel and behave the way we do. Put simply, if a person's experiences in life have been negative, their interpretation of these experiences, their phenomenology, may result in that person thinking, feeling and behaving in a negative and often destructive way.

The humanistic approach consequently sees the self as fashioned by our phenomenology, or personal interpretation of experiences. Our phenomenology helps to form our inner personality of self and our personal perception of who we are, or think we are. Try the following.

INTERACTIVES: PHENOMENOLOGY

Phenomenology is your personal subjective view of the world.

Not surprisingly, as it is based upon your own life experiences. Read the following scenario. Two friends go to see an Old Firm Cup Final at Hampden Park. They each go to their designated parts of the ground. The Celtic fan to the Celtic end, the Rangers' fan to the Rangers' end. Both at an objective sensory level 'see' the exact same 90 minutes of football. At the end of the game they meet up and discuss the game. One reports it as the best game he has ever seen. The other claims it the worst!

Despite seeing the same game, why are their views different? Write a 500-word report using your knowledge of their phenomenology to help you. You can be as imaginative as you like!

Personal agency and existentialism

Also important to the formation of self, is the exercise of individual free will. The importance of free will, and how it can affect you, came to the humanistic approach from the writings of philosophers and writers such as Albert Camus (1913–60), Søren Kierkegaard (1813–55) and Jean-Paul Sartre (1905–80).

These existentialist writers emphasised that people make choices in life, and that with choice comes the *personal responsibility* for what follows. They wrote about people's individual destinies as a result of their exercise of free will and how this influenced their existence for good or bad at the end of the day. The impact our existence, or everyday environments, can have on the formation of our personality is called **existentialism**. Existentialism, the environment we find ourselves in, is affected by the choices we make in life.

Personal agency

The humanistic approach says that when we make choices in life and exercise free will we are using **personal agency**. Personal agency can be destructive if we make negative choices, or constructive if we make positive choices. Personal agency, which is the exercise of free will, affects your self, your phenomenology and your existentialism. One need only consider the very slippery slope a person may be embarking upon if they decide by the use of personal agency that the drug heroin is for them.

A criticism of the humanistic approach is that we are never entirely free to exercise complete personal agency and choose our own paths in life – but the degree to which we are able to exercise personal agency to influence our own destiny is important to how we feel about ourselves. Free will is related to self. The good and bad choices we make in life influence our phenomenology, which affects self – for good or ill. Another important strand to self comes from *Gestalt* psychology with its influence on the humanistic concept of the whole person.

Gestalt *psychology and the whole person*

Gestalt psychology contributed to the humanistic approach with their idea that we respond holistically – from the experiences of our whole person – to our world. Because the humanistic approach is interested in promoting the psychological good health of the whole person, a clear total perception of all the elements that go to make up our self is thought useful.

individuals. A greater awareness of all the issues that frustrate personal growth, and thus a psychologically healthier self, is helped by good *gestalt*.

Self-actualisation and personal growth

Humanistic psychology did not begin to achieve world prominence until the 1960s when, as we read, Abraham Maslow began to criticise behaviourism and psychoanalysis as promoting the idea that we are inevitably psychologically ill or average. He put forward an alternative view, which is that we are naturally motivated towards psychological good health because we are born with an innate need to be psychologically healthy. This is called personal growth, the peak of which Maslow called self-actualisation.

Self-actualisation is our natural predisposition to develop and grow as human beings. Often, however, personal growth towards self-actualisation is hampered by other factors. When self-actualisation is frustrated, the humanistic approach would say the individual is inevitably psychologically unwell. This is because before we can achieve self-actualisation, we have to first satisfy certain other innate needs. These are identified in Maslow's hierarchy of needs as physiological needs; safety needs; love and belongingness needs; esteem; knowledge and understanding – or cognitive – needs; and, ultimately, self-actualisation needs. The achievement of each of these by us is seen in terms of personal growth. Personal growth makes us feel good about ourselves, within ourselves and towards others.

Maslow's hierarchy of needs

Maslow says we need to first satisfy lower-order deficiency needs to experience personal growth and thus move towards self-actualisation. When deficiency needs are frustrated we behave in ways to safeguard ourselves. Essential to personal survival, the satisfaction of deficiency needs might see us lie, cheat, steal and be prone to violence in order to get them satisfied. Deficiency needs, as we shall see, are physiological, safety, love and esteem-orientated. Deficiency needs are, as a consequence, *prepotent*.

Prepotent needs

Prepotent means that the satisfaction of one or more of these lower order needs can occupy an individual's mind all the time. An unemployed homeless person's life is wholly preoccupied with meeting physiological and safety needs such as finding food, warmth and secure shelter. They have

---

INTERACTIVES: TRAINSPOTTING

Watch the DVD Trainspotting, or read the book by the same name written by Irvine Welsh, and consider the following questions.

1   Whose phenomenology does this film concern?

2   How does the idea of personal agency apply in this film?

3   Outline the phenomenological field of the central characters.

4   How does the central character's self, or inner personality, become influenced by his existentialism? Give reasons for your answer.

5   What exercise of personal agency does the central character employ to change his existentialism?

Our self – our inner personality that influences how we think, feel and behave in our world – is as it is, because of our phenomenology and use of personal agency. Being aware of these personality-shaping life events, and the significance of some of our choices, helps us achieve what is called 'good *gestalt*'. For the humanistic approach good gestalt means that you are aware, or helped to become aware, of all the elements that go to make up self or personality. As a result you understand your whole person better, why you are as you are, and why you respond and behave as you do.

If you are unhappy about aspects of your thoughts, feelings and behaviours, good gestalt can see you deliberately decide to make positive changes, which gives rise to a psychologically healthier personality. The humanistic approach says good *gestalt* makes us psychologically better able to respond to our world from the point of view of being a healthier whole person. You are aware of all the elements of your personality. The humanistic approach measures the psychologically healthy whole person in terms of personal growth.

Personal growth

Personal growth is a concept the humanistic approach believes we are all driven to achieve as

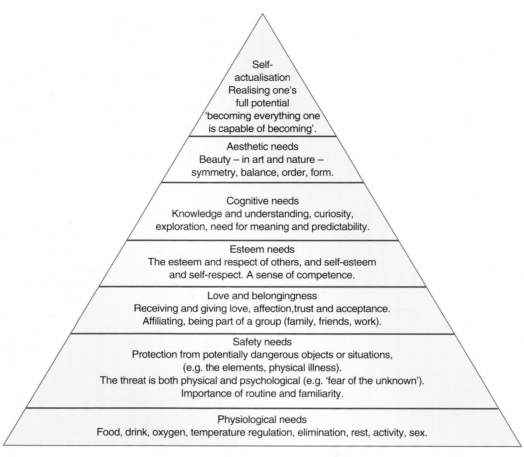

Figure 9.12 Maslow's hierarchy of needs: deficiency and growth needs

little time for anything else. They may, as alluded to earlier, be necessarily criminal in their behaviours in order to get their prepotent needs met. This is because if they don't satisfy them, they could die.

Prepotent needs are natural, and often very obvious in the behaviours of the person trying to get them satisfied. We all need to have enough to eat and drink in order to stay alive. We all need to feel comfortable and safe in our homes. We all need to be loved. We all need to be accepted for who we are by our peer group. If one, or more, of these needs are hampered, humanistic psychology thinks a psychologically unhealthy person, or self, will emerge.

Abraham Maslow

Best known for his theory of self-actualisation, Maslow was born in New York on 1 April 1908 and died in 1970. He initially studied psychology at the University of Wisconsin and later returned to New York where he studied *Gestalt* psychology at the New School for Social Research. This experience

was to have a profound effect on his thinking. A lifetime of teaching and research began when he joined the faculty of psychology at Brooklyn University in 1937. He left Brooklyn in 1951 to become head of the psychology department at Brandeis University in Massachusetts where he stayed until retirement in 1969.

He believed that we all have within our being a hierarchy of needs concerning our bodies, our need to love and be loved by others, the way we feel about ourselves, and the fulfilment of all the potentials we may have. These deficiency and growth needs have to be met in that we are biologically motivated to satisfy them. The more we achieve the satisfaction of physiological, safety, esteem, cognitive and self-actualisation needs, the more psychologically healthier and happier Maslow believed we would be. Maslow's major works include Motivation and Personality (1954), Towards A Psychology of Being (1962) and The Further Reaches of Human Nature (1971).

Deficiency needs

Within Maslow's hierarchy of needs, physiological, safety, love and belongingness and esteem needs are called deficiency needs.

Physiological needs

Physiological, or bodily, needs are essential to individual survival and include air, water, food and sleep. If these are not satisfied, we die. In the developing world, the major physiological need of getting enough to eat preoccupies the majority of the population most of the time.

Safety needs

Safety needs concern our need to feel secure. They are best met when we find ourselves brought up in a safe and stable family-type environment. Safety needs are about how safe we feel in relation to our world. If you feel safe and secure in your home environment, this helps you feel safe and secure in relation to your world and the people in it. As a result you feel more confident in your self, and in your world.

'The tragic case of Baby P in 2009 made us all very aware that not everyone has a safe and secure home environment.'

In our society tragic cases of child neglect make us very aware that not everyone has a safe and secure home environment. If safety needs are not met, this affects phenomenology, the self-concept and personal growth. If you had the type of background that unfortunately saw you hit or abused in childhood, this would very likely make you wary of your home environment. In the broader world your experiences would make you very unsure, and insecure, in relation to other people. You would tend to have difficulty trusting others. As a consequence, you could find personal growth and the journey to self-actualisation difficult. According to Maslow, this is because we need to have lower-order needs satisfied before we can address subsequent needs in the hierarchy.

Love and belongingness needs

Our love need is our inborn need for belongingness. We have all been, or are, members of a family, peer group, gang, club, organisation, work group, social group or religious group. Membership of such groups gives us a sense of being needed, wanted and loved. Membership of groups fulfils a need within us to feel that we are valued. We have a need to know that we belong and when an ability to 'belong' eludes us, we feel less of a person. Essentially we value our self less. Very often people with whom we want to be friends exclude us from belonging – as is often evident in childhood and adolescence. Those who are in groups often marginalize other children and teenagers who are seen as different. All they however want to do is belong. Rejecting others is very hurtful to them. It can be psychologically damaging in that when love and belongingness needs are met, we value ourselves more. If they are not – and this is very often in other people's hands – we value our self less.

Esteem needs

Esteem needs involve our self-esteem and self-respect. Self-esteem comes to us when we master a particular skill or task and feel good about ourselves as a result. Your self-esteem will inevitably soar when you pass an exam, or your driving test, etc. Self-esteem, an important aspect of self, concerns how much an individual values himself or herself as a person. It is influenced by the reaction of others to us and others' comparison of us with others.

If an individual goes through life being told by others that they are not very good at something, this can produce a person with low self-esteem. If, on the other hand, others encourage an individual in a positive fashion in the things they do, this can result in them having a self-concept that is high in self-esteem.

Comparison with others can also have an effect on self-esteem. Whether we like it or not, we need others around us to measure ourselves against to establish our own self-esteem. Put simply, if you see others around you getting on and you are not, your self-esteem will diminish. This can be exacerbated if parents constantly compare how their child is doing with the performance of another person. If they let their child know that they view the other person's performance as better, the child can view their parents as valuing them less in this comparison to others. Comparison with others is related to conditional regard in the humanistic approach and is as we shall explore later another important factor to the humanistic understanding of personality.

Self-respect is different. Self-respect comes from the relationship given to you by others because of the things they value in you. Respect is earned. Respect cannot be bullied or bought from people. Examples of respect might be the classroom relationship between you, and your psychology

teacher or lecturer. Another example of respect is the relationship between the older and younger generations in China. In China, and other cultures like Japan, the older generation is respected as a consequence of the wisdom that the younger generation perceive old age brings. The older person, because of the respect given them, has a greater self-esteem. They feel better about themselves. The respect you get from others allows you to value yourself more. Your self-respect is high, and as a consequence you experience personal growth in terms of esteem needs.

Growth needs

Within Maslow's hierarchy our quest for knowledge and understanding, and self-actualisation are called growth needs.

Knowledge and understanding needs

When our prepotent or lower-order deficiency needs (physiological, safety, love and esteem) are satisfied, we then have the time and motivation to turn our attention to understanding our lives better. Knowledge and understanding of our lives gives us a better idea of what it means to be human. According to Maslow, once lower-order deficiency needs are met, pursuing our knowledge and understanding need is the first important growth need we must satisfy. This is because knowledge and understanding lead to better psychological health for the individual. Their pursuit allows you to understand yourself, your world, and yourself in relation to your world that much better.

We satisfy our cognitive, or knowledge and understanding, needs in all sorts of ways – depending upon what we see as important knowledge and understanding for us at the time. This might be by taking up a series of night classes in psychology, art or literature just because we want to understand aspects of our world better. The pursuit of personally relevant knowledge and understanding needs might equally result in someone learning Spanish because they go to Spain every year for a holiday. Learning Spanish makes an important aspect of their life more meaningful. The person feels the better for it. We experience personal growth as our knowledge and understanding of our world grows. We have a clearer picture of what our life is all about.

Fulfilling knowledge and understanding needs can be an almost endless quest because our existence is so complex. It is rightly called a growth need.

Self-actualisation

Self-actualisation is:

 the desire to become more and more what one is, to become everything that one is capable of becoming".

(Maslow, 1955)

Self-actualisation is the epitome of personal growth. Originally, Maslow said that only the most eminent of people, such as Abraham Lincoln and Albert Einstein, had self-actualised. This he later revised in Towards a Psychology of Being (1968), and today it is accepted that self-actualisation is available to all who strive for it. Self-actualisation is embodied by what Maslow calls episodic peak experiences. An episodic peak experience is sometimes referred to as transcendence.

Episodic peak experiences

An episodic peak experience occurs when we get an insight into what it means to be human. Episodic peak experiences are mystical, and varied in substance. It can be that feeling we get when you put down our pen in our final exam and gain a momentary insight into what has been, and what might be in the future; it can be the experience of one day looking at our baby in that one-off way and realising what being human is really all about. An episodic peak experience might also be the personal triumph and insight gained into ourselves by coming through something when all the odds seemed against us. Self-actualisation and episodic peak experiences are available to us all. When achieved, our perception of our world and ourselves is never quite the same again. We understand more fully what it means to be human. A person who has achieved knowledge and understanding and self-actualisation, and thus fulfilled their growth needs would be said to have achieved the optimum in personal growth. They are a fully functioning person according to the humanistic approach.

A syndrome of decay

Someone who has fulfilled their lower-order deficiency needs (physiological, safety, love and esteem) and then does not go on to achieve their growth needs (knowledge and understanding and self-actualisation) would, for Maslow, fall into a syndrome of decay. Symptoms include despair, despondency, boredom and apathy. On the other hand, Maslow thinks a person who successfully fulfils their growth needs and achieves episodic peak experiences and self-actualisation would exhibit certain characteristics of personality.

The self-actualising person:

➤ holds high values

➤ is self-sufficient

➤ gives an objective factual account of what they see as truth

➤ is uniquely individual and at ease with who they are

➤ has a notion of beauty and form

➤ is spontaneous in action

➤ enjoys simplicity in life

➤ has a richness and complexity of character

➤ has a keen sense of fairness and justice

➤ shows a balance and unity of spirit while realising there is an inevitable ending to life

These personality characteristics of the self-actualising person are known as meta-characteristics. Do you recognise the personality of anyone you know?

Carl Rogers' contribution to a humanistic theory of personality

While Rogers' main contribution to the humanistic approach is considered later in the application of humanistic theory to humanistic psychotherapy and counselling, Rogers did make a number of valuable contributions to the theory of the formation of the self, or personality.

Carl Rogers

Figure 9.13 Carl Rogers

Important for his non-directive person-centred therapy, Rogers was born on 8 January 1902 in Illinois, USA. Like Maslow he went to the University of Wisconsin. His interest in psychology was sparked when he later studied for the ministry at the Union Theological College in New York. His growing passion for psychology saw him leave UTC and go to Columbia University to complete an MA in 1928. This was followed by a doctorate, PhD, in 1931. His first job was as Director of the Society for the Prevention of Cruelty to Children in Rochester, New York. From 1935–40 he lectured at the University of Rochester. He was elected professor of clinical psychology at Ohio State in 1940 where he first proposed non-directive counselling as a means of facilitating the client towards psychological good health. He then moved as professor of psychology to the University of Chicago in 1945 where he remained until 1957. It was here he pioneered a Counselling Centre where he was able to conduct investigations into the usefulness and effectiveness of his methods. His conditions for growth in the counselling situation, he extended, refined and promoted from 1957–63 at the University of Wisconsin, Madison, and at the Centre for the Study of the Person in La Jolla California. Rogers died on 4 February 1987. His major works include The Clinical Treatment of the Problem Child (1939): Counselling and Psychotherapy (1942); Client-Centred Therapy (1951); Psychotherapy and Personality Change (1954); On Becoming A Person (1961); Carl Rogers on Personal Power (1977) and Freedom to Learn for the 80s (1983).

Rogers' theory of personality: on becoming a fully functioning person

Rogers and Maslow agreed that we are all born with a biological predisposition towards self-actualisation. Self-actualisation, becoming all that you can become, can be either frustrated or nurtured by environmental forces.

The actualising tendency

Rogers (1959) maintains that we have a natural and innate actualising tendency that urges us to develop all our capacities. This fulfilment, or otherwise, of our actualising tendency helps make us feel the way we do about ourselves. If it becomes frustrated, we can become psychologically unwell.

It is interesting to discover that the actualising tendency is thought to be a '*biological pressure to fulfil the genetic blueprint*' (Maddi, 1996).

Rogers then believes us to be biologically predisposed to self-actualisation, in much in same

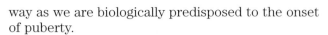

way as we are biologically predisposed to the onset of puberty.

The role of this actualising tendency is 'to confirm who we think we are'. Our actualising tendency is for Rogers *'the most profound truth about man'*. If, for example you believe yourself to be a seeker after knowledge, you will involve yourself in knowledge-driven pursuits. You will inadvertently push yourself towards experiencing yourself in ways that are consistent with your self, and consequentially confirm who you think you are.

Rogers and the self

Self is

 the organised set of characteristics that the individual perceives as peculiar to her/himself".

(Ryckman, 1993)

Self is your awareness of who you are based upon your conscious and unconscious experiences. As mentioned earlier, self develops as a consequence of an individual's interpretation of their experiences as they interact with their environment. Self is our unique personal evaluation of past experience as it has influenced us to think, feel and behave in our world.

Important to an understanding of atypical behaviour Rogers suggests that self ultimately shapes each individual's particular behavioural and psychological response to whatever life throws at them. An unhealthy self will think, feel and behave in a dysfunctional manner. For Rogers, a person being made aware of self is important.

Humanistic psychotherapy would try to make the client aware of why their unhealthy self has come about, and, consequently why they think, feel, and behave as they do. Rogers considers that a major step towards such self-awareness is self-acceptance.

Self-acceptance

Rogers' theory of personality in *Towards Being a Fully Functioning Person* initially attracted criticism because it suggested that only the very few were able to become fully functioning persons. By 1961 Rogers' position had become more open. Complementing Maslow's revision of self-actualisation, Rogers' theory now also advocates that becoming a fully functioning person is available to us all, especially if we show self-acceptance of whatever we have become.

Self-acceptance means that past experiences, good and bad, are accepted as just that. We examine and use past experiences in a constructive way to help us move forward (and upwards through Maslow's hierarchy of needs). This restores us to Rogers' natural (biological) state of psychological balance, and well-being.

Self-actualisation is impossible without self-acceptance, or acceptance of (your) self. We can decide to be self-accepting ourselves, or seek help to understand why we are as we are through humanistic psychotherapy, or humanistic counselling.

Conditions of worth

Central to Rogers' theory of personality, conditions of worth concern how we go about valuing, or 'seeing' ourselves. Conditions of worth, or the degree to which we value ourselves, come to us from birth. These conditions are twofold, unconditional positive regard and conditional positive regard, which either help or hinder us in the attainment of esteem needs.

Unconditional positive regard

Unconditional positive regard is given when parents or primary caregivers offer their unreserved support, love and acceptance for the things we do. We can see this in those adults who would say 'Well done' to a child who had come a valiant last in a primary school race. Unconditional positive regard is full acceptance by others of who we are as a person.

Conditional positive regard

Conditional positive regard is when parents or primary caregivers place conditions on the value, or worth, of something we do. An example might be when others, whom we love and/or hold in very high regard, criticise our performance by comparing it to those whose performance they see as better. As a consequence we feel our performance, and our self, to be less valued by them. Our self is shaped by the perceptions of others – whether these perceptions are right or wrong. Conditional positive regard can result in an individual being unable to know their true self (who they actually are), which can lead to confusion, tension and maladaptive behaviour (Rogers, 1959).

Rogers, the fully functioning person, and the self

A fully functioning person is the ultimate and natural state of being for Rogers and the humanistic approach. A fully functioning person displays personal growth as illustrated by the meta-characteristics of the self-actualising person (see page 383).

According to Maslow, a fully functioning person is one who is open to experience, past and present, and who uses what they have learned to live as free a life as possible. They would also be trusting in themselves, be able to express feelings freely, be able to act independently, and be creative in thought and action. For many who want to be fully functioning, self-application of humanistic theory is rewarding. Some however may want help.

This is where humanistic person-centred psychotherapy and counselling is useful, and is the area where Rogers has been most influential.

We will return to specific applications of our three psychological psychotherapies after having discussed depression and eating disorders.

Aetiology

Aetiology is the study of the cause or origin of a disease. Let us look at the aetiology of common mental disorders e.g. depression and eating disorders.

Aetiology of depression

As we discovered in our overview of ICD 10 depression is a mood or affective disorder. Until recently medicine believed a person suffered depression because of negative thoughts and emotions. Now depression is better understood as a result of biological, genetic and environmental factors.

Before diagnosing depression doctors will ask their patient's about their symptoms, and how long they have experienced them. They will also find out the degree to which such symptoms have interfered with their patient's everyday life. They will then turn to what they think is the root cause, an alteration in their patient's brain chemistry.

Pawlik-Kienlen (2007) tells us that depression is indicative in a person's thoughts, feelings and behaviours. Depression has cognitive, affective and behavioural dimensions all of which are inter-linked. Depression is truly a vicious spiral of despair.

Cognitive signs of depression include

➤ inability to make decisions

➤ lack of concentration or focus

➤ loss of interest in activities, people, and life

➤ self-criticism, self-blame, self-loathing

➤ pessimism

➤ preoccupation with problems and failures

➤ thoughts of self-harm or suicide

Affective signs of depression comprise

➤ sadness and/or misery

➤ overwhelmed by everyday tasks

➤ numbness or apathy

➤ anxiety, tension, irritability

➤ helplessness

➤ low confidence and poor self-esteem

➤ disappointment, discouragement, hopelessness

➤ feelings of unattractiveness or ugliness

➤ loss of pleasure and enjoyment

Behavioural signs of depression encompass

➤ withdrawal from people, work, pleasures and social activities is one of the first signs

➤ spurts of restlessness

➤ sighing, crying, moaning

➤ difficulty getting out of bed

➤ lower activity and energy levels

➤ lack of motivation, everything feels like an effort

Did You Know?

➤ 1 in 4 people will experience some kind of mental health problem in Britain in any one year

➤ Mixed anxiety and depression is the most common mental disorder suffered in Britain

➤ Women are more likely to have been treated for a mental health problem than men

➤ About 10% of children have a mental health problem at any one time

➤ Depression affects 1 in 5 older people living in the community, and 2 in 5 living in care homes

➤ British men are three times as likely as British women to die by suicide

➤ The UK has one of the highest rates of self harm in Europe, at 400 per 100,000 of the population

➤ 9 out of 10 prisoners in British jails suffer from some kind of mental disorder

Source: Mental Health Foundation (2008)

ONLINE INTERACTIVES

Read more about the cognitive, affective and behavioural signs of depression Go to **http://psychology.suite101.com/ article.cfm/signs_of_depression#ixzzOCjIqUrF 9&A**

A direct Link is available in the Chapter 9 section of Higher Psychology Learning Suite at **www.gerardkeegan.co.uk**.

Biological factors and depression

Depression is one of the most common of mental illnesses. It is thought that at some point during their lives between 8–17 % of adults in the United States experience serious depression. In the United Kingdom 7–12 % of men suffer from diagnosable depression, and 20 to 25 per cent of women. The reason for the uncertain figures is that many who suffer depression go undiagnosed. There are also many theories as to why the figure is higher for women than for men (Barry *et al*, 2008). The incidence of postnatal depression, which is anywhere between 4.4 and 13 % in the United Kingdom certainly contributes to the higher figure (Huang & Mathers, 2001).

Depression and the credit crunch

The gender imbalance may be closing because of the credit crunch. Men generally see themselves as the 'breadwinner' for their families. Research is showing that in the current uncertain economic climate many men are anxious about losing their jobs and being unable to fulfil their traditional role. Their concern is not unfounded. ITV's '*This Morning*' reported in March 2009 that many in the UK are only two pay cheques away from homelessness.

Job insecurity causes a greater long-term drop in mental well being than being made redundant. At a seminar at Cambridge University in 2009 sociologist Dr. Brendan Burchell reported that "Given that most economic forecasts predict that the recession will be long with a slow recovery, the results mean that many people – and men in particular – could be entering into a period of prolonged and growing misery. People seem not to be able to develop coping mechanisms for job insecurity as they do for unemployment. This means that people who have been in an insecure job for over a year continue to show a decline in their mental health."

Depression and brain chemistry

The biological causes of depression occur because of changes in our brain chemistry triggered by such stressful life events. This causes fluctuations in the levels of important hormones that influence mood state. The normal production of two neurotransmitters, Serotonin and Norepinephrine are disrupted in depressed persons. As we will read shortly antidepressant drugs have been developed to rectify such hormonal imbalance. Depression is also associated with an imbalance of Cortisol, the main hormone secreted by our adrenal glands.

Genetic factors and depression

There are other physiological or bodily factors associated with depression. Some are genetic in origin. For example, a connection has been found between depression and those with low thyroid levels. Some depressed individuals have also been found to have irregular biological rhythms.

Depression is a major symptom of premenstrual tension (PMT). PMT or *premenstrual syndrome* exhibits symptoms of "sufficient severity to interfere with some aspects of life" (Dickerson, Mazyck, and Hunter, 2003).

Types of depression

Mild depression

Mild depression is where everything seems harder to do, and life seems less worthwhile.

Moderate depression

Moderate depression has a significant impact on daily life.

Severe depression

Severe depression is where an individual feels so depressed they cannot function. They are uninterested in doing anything, and find daily activities almost impossible. Physical symptoms will be evident and include tiredness, loss of appetite etc.

Dysthymia

Dysthymia is a specific and chronic mild depression that lasts at least 2 years.

Bipolar affective disorder

This is a specific type of depression where a person's mood swings between high and low extremes. Bipolar affective disorder is also sometimes called manic depression.

Seasonal affective disorder (SAD)

This is a specific condition where extreme mood swings occur at different times of the year. Sufferers feel good in the summer, and bad in the winter.

Postnatal depression

Postnatal depression is associated with some women who become depressed after childbirth.

Source: BUPA (2008)

Environmental factors and depression

As we read earlier in this Chapter and in our Chapter on stress, significant life events can trigger symptoms that are recognised as depression. *Stressors* include physical illness, problems in intimate relationships, loss of a loved one, loss of a job etc. The effects of such stressors can be analysed from a number of psychological perspectives, or points of view.

The psychodynamic approach to depression

Within the psychodynamic approach classic psychoanalytic theory tells us that depression is the result of losing someone or something close to you. This may be because of death, separation, divorce, employment etc. Such abandonment sees individuals turn their feelings of anger and resentment inward. From a psychoanalytic point of view this grossly influences a depressed person's sense of self-worth and results in feelings of helplessness, shame, and humiliation. The physical and psychological effects of this comprise the symptoms of what we call depression.

The behaviourist approach to depression

Behaviourists understand depression in terms of learning. Negative life events such as the death of a loved one, the end of a relationship, or the loss of a job are associated with the removal of a source of reward.

The cognitive-behavioural approach to depression

Cognitive-behavioural theorists say that depression arises because of faulty or negative thinking. This leads to faulty and negative feelings, and faulty and negative behaviours. Depressed individuals are prone to destructive ways of thinking. This includes blaming themselves when things go wrong, concentrating on the negative side of life, and persistently coming to excessively pessimistic conclusions.

Learned helplessness

In Chapter 4 we read that one reason people experience stress is because of their inability to control their environment. A related behavioural and cognitive-behavioural explanation for depression is learned helplessness. Learned helplessness is the view that depression results from a perceived absence of control over the outcome of a situation (Seligman, 1975).

Learned helplessness was first observed in animals in a laboratory that had no control over their situation. They showed signs of depression. Lack of control over our own lives is also associated with powerlessness. We can't change things in our life, so we come to accept depression as inevitable. This may be especially relevant to depression in women, whose incidence of depression is twice that of men (Miller & Seligman, 1975).

Another factor that may be linked to depression in women is a tendency to dwell on negative events (Safford *et al.*, 2007). This cognitive style or negative way of thinking is more common among women than among men. Men are more likely to distract themselves from negative feelings by engaging in other forms of activity.

The humanistic approach to depression

The depressed individual is not 'a fully functioning person' according to the humanistic approach. To assist someone with depression it may be that the practical application of Maslow's theory of self-actualisation within Rogerian person-centred psychotherapy and counselling is appropriate. Humanistic psychotherapy, the combination of humanistic theory in clinical practice, may go some way towards helping such a client become a more fully functioning person.

The people involved in the application of humanistic psychological theory are not necessarily psychologists. What Rogers emphasises is applicable to other counselling situations as well as humanistic psychotherapy. Psychologists, psychiatrists, counsellors and others would apply humanistic theory to practice, if, in their work situation they show genuineness, unconditional positive regard and empathy towards people. Such elements in a counselling situation are known as 'conditions of growth'.

Conditions of growth

The use of genuineness, unconditional positive regard, and empathy by a *facilitator* (a person-centred humanistic psychologist, psychiatrist or counsellor) helps create essential *conditions of growth* within therapy to unlock difficulties for a client trying to become a more fully functioning person.

Genuineness, empathy and unconditional positive regard become fused to create a focused, non-judgemental, open and honest counselling environment in which the client can examine **self**. Genuineness, empathy and unconditional positive regard when used by a facilitator help the client towards self-acceptance and personal growth. The summit of the client's journey is self-actualisation, episodic peak experiences and psychological good health. This is for Maslow and Rogers a natural, biological state available to us all.

Genuineness, empathy and unconditional positive regard

Genuineness

Genuineness sees the counsellor, or facilitator, attempt to create the best conditions in therapy to nurture their client's journey towards self-actualisation. The facilitator should try to be relaxed, open and at ease about themselves. This genuineness is picked upon by the client hopefully making them think, 'If he or she can be honest, open and genuine, so can I'. The humanistic psychotherapy or counselling session is enriched and is more beneficial to the client as they seek to become more fully functioning. Genuineness encourages someone who is depressed to open up about their thoughts and feelings themselves.

Empathy

Empathy is where the facilitator tries to enter, and gain insight into, the client's world. They try to see the client's understanding of their situation from the client's point of view. They respond to the client using the 'reference points' their client uses.

Empathy is an appreciation of where the client is coming from in humanistic psychotherapy and counselling. Empathy allows the counsellor to better understand how a client is feeling regards the stressors in life that trigger depressive symptoms. Empathy is an appreciation of the cognitive, affective and behavioural symptoms of depression that a client might express. These include self-criticism, self-blame, self-loathing, sadness, apathy, low self-esteem etc.

Unconditional positive regard

Here, unconditional positive regard is the facilitator accepting the client unreservedly. A humanistic practitioner avoids making any value judgements about their clients in case they perceive the value judgement as a 'condition of worth' – conditional positive regard. This is avoided by the use of unconditional positive regard, which is acceptance of the client as a person and gives the client confidence to better, and more honestly, express thoughts, feelings and behaviours. They reveal more of themselves and self. Such as what in particular they find difficult to cope with in life.

Unconditional positive regard helps the client achieve a greater personal insight into their self and why they are as they are. Understanding their depression contributes towards personal growth and a more fully functioning person. The facilitator must be neutral, showing neither approval nor disapproval of anything revealed by the client, even though it may be illegal, unethical or immoral.

A decision to change

The purpose of genuineness, empathy and unconditional positive regard is to allow the client room to explore who they believe they are. The use of these three conditions for growth nurtures a developing awareness of self and helps lead the client to self-acceptance and a decision to change, as a result of which the client begins personal growth. Clients are, for the humanistic approach, satisfying their biological predisposition to be in a state of psychological good health. The decision to change will vary from client to client depending on why their self is as it is. For an alcoholic this might be 'to stop drinking'; for an abused woman this might be 'to leave the violent relationship' and so on. For a depressed person it is to accept that the negative messages they have perceived from others, which have harmed their self-esteem etc. are subjective. They are not factually correct, but another's *opinion*.

Counselling

'Counselling' is often quoted as a reason why many students are attracted to psychology in the first place. Many know of people who have been 'counselled', have been 'counselled' themselves, or think they want to be 'counsellors'. The desire to counsel is maybe indicative of something within us all. This, the humanistic approach would recognise, is the desire to give to others something of ourselves – from which we both benefit from the perspective of self.

However, psychology is not all about counselling and counselling need not involve psychology. An understanding of psychology is desirable for those who would like to offer counselling services but is also very relevant to those who don't! If you are one of the two million people the Department of Trade and Industry say are involved in 'counselling services' in the UK today and use empathy, unconditional positive regard and genuineness within your work situation, you would be said to be using the humanistic person-centred approach. You are not however a 'counsellor' – you are a facilitator. There are 'counselling psychologists' in the UK who have a psychology degree, have undergone post-graduate training as clinical psychologists and are members of the British Psychological Society.

It must be emphasised that accessing psychotherapy, counselling or any type of psychiatric help under our National Health Service is difficult. If suffering from an eating disorder, depression, etc. a patient will always have to be referred to one of these specialist services by their GP. There are very often long waiting lists, which is disadvantageous to the patient concerned.

Treating depression

Any humanistic counsellor or psychoanalytic, behaviourist or cognitive-behavioural psychotherapist would emphasise that depression is not just sadness, a sign of personal weakness, or grief. It is more than this, and a most debilitating condition that can last anything between three months and a lifetime. Even when stressful life events no longer happen, a depressed person's changed brain chemistry continues to alter. The stress of life becomes even more intolerable. Their symptoms get worse.

It is thus vital that depressed individual's consult their General Practitioner. The World Health Organisation predict that by 2020 depression will be the second most prevalent health problem in the Western world. In 2004, the estimated number of people in Scotland with depression seen by their Doctor was 321, 000. This is an increase of around 20% from 2003. Significantly and most worrying of all 70 % of recorded suicides in Scotland are by people who have experienced some form of depression (Faulkner, 1997). Depression can be addressed using *both* biological and psychological remedies.

As suggested above it is thought that an inability to produce the neurotransmitter Serotonin is related to depression (Gelder *at al.*, 1999). Serotonin is one of the key mood regulators in the human brain. Too little Serotonin production leads to depression.

Tebartz *et al.* (2000) indicates the amygdala as also having something to do with depression. They found that depressed patients have enlarged amygdala, and that the amygdala in their female patients was significantly larger than those of males. Depression is then a genetically influenced condition. Some aspect of our physiology is affected. More often than not a Doctor will rely on the biological approach in his or her treatment of depression.

Are you a SAD person?

SAD (Seasonal Affective Disorder) is a type of winter depression that affects an estimated half a million people in the UK every year, particularly during December, January and February. Symptoms include lethargy, overeating, depression, social problems, anxiety, mood swings and loss of sex drive. For many sufferers SAD is a serious condition, preventing them from functioning normally without medical treatment.

The root cause of SAD is unknown. Scientists believe it is caused by a biochemical imbalance in the hypothalamus triggered by the shortening of daylight hours and the lack of sunlight in winter. During the summer, bright light at dawn suppresses the body's production of melatonin, which makes us drowsy. Lack of bright light during the winter months could mean that the brain is not stimulated into waking up. This, and other chemical reactions in the brain, can trigger SAD.

The most popular treatment uses a special, highly fluorescent light bulb plugged in to a socket at home and turned on when it is dark. This appears to alleviate the symptoms, presumably by artificially suppressing the production of melatonin.

The UK Seasonal Affective Disorder Association suggests that this is much more useful than a prescription for anti-depressants. Interestingly, SADA highly recommend psychotherapy for SAD sufferers.

ONLINE INTERACTIVES

Read http://www.guardian.co.uk /Archive/Article/0,4273,4341235,00.html and the site's related articles.

Summarise those side effects associated with anti-depressants such as Prozac.

The biological approach and depression

Applying the biological approach is relatively easy, if only because we know that the approach looks for a physical or medical cause behind our thoughts, feelings and behaviour. Physical cause concerns a bodily process or function that has suffered damage, disease, accident or been genetically influenced in some way. If something has a physical cause, it is treated with a physical therapy, from a physical point of view. How then does this apply to depression?

Depression and antidepressants

The biological cause of depression is thought to be due to changes in neural receptors, sensitive to the 5–HT hydroxytryptamine neurotransmitter, serotonin and others like noradrenaline and dopamine. Serotonin helps control appetite, sleep and sexual activity. Noradrenaline regulates mood and motivation, while dopamine is thought to be involved in our ability to experience pleasure. Depression is treated mainly through the prescription of antidepressants. According to the Depression Alliance Scotland there are about 30 different types of anti-depressant. These act on the sensitivity of the dulled neuron receptor cells to Serotonin, noradrenaline and dopamine. As a consequence the depressed person's mood state is altered.

The main difference for the patient regarding the different varieties of antidepressants is their side effects (Gelder *et al.*, 1999). Most antidepressants take between 10–14 days to begin to have any effect. The safest nowadays are *specific serotonin reuptake inhibitors* (SSRIs), such as paroxetine and fluoxetine, better known as Prozac. Prozac is by far the most popular chemotherapy for those with depression. Since its introduction in 1988, more than 38 million people worldwide have been prescribed it (Costello *et al.*, 1995; Bosley, 1999). SSRI's block the re-uptake of Serotonin into the nerve cell that released it thereby prolonging its action. Other types of SSRI include Paroxetine (Seroxat), Citalopram (Cipramil), and Sertraline (Lustral).

The biological approach controls the symptoms...

The biological approach believes the cause of depression to be physical in origin. Depression occurs due to physical changes to neural receptors, which frustrate the normal workings of Serotonin, noradrenaline and dopamine. To solve the problem, or more precisely, alleviate the symptoms, the biological approach recommends chemotherapy, or the use of drugs, like Prozac. These help to control the symptoms for the sufferer...

... but maybe not the cause?

This is because of the impact nurture, or environment, has on depression. There is, as we have read, some evidence to suggest that environment plays its part in its onset. In the case of depression, something has influenced changes to our physiology that affects Serotonin. That something is environmental. Simply put, depression can be caused by the overwhelming pressures, stresses and strains of everyday living that will ultimately affect one in five of us.

A purely biological approach to depression takes an over-simplistic view of such a complex psychological issue. Consequently the medical profession should also consider psychological interventions in the treatment of depression.

Thus a doctor may suggest to a depressed patient that they consider counselling to identify and address the environmental triggers to their condition. This is because a purely medical approach to depression is often not enough. A patient's physical symptoms may well be controlled with an anti-depressant but the environmental causes of their symptoms will still remain.

Psychodynamic psychotherapy and depression

To recap, psychotherapy is the application of psychological theory in clinical practice. We have identified psychodynamic, behavioural, cognitive-behavioural and humanistic psychotherapies, some of which are appropriate in the treatment of depression. To *some* extent psychodynamic psychotherapy can be used to treat mood state such as depression. In psychoanalytical psychotherapy the psychoanalyst equates depression with the loss we experience in childhood when separated from our parent(s). The patient has never got over this. They have been unable to come to terms with this early separation, and this is linked to their depression later on in life.

Psychoanalytic psychotherapy would attempt to get the patient to recall this early experience and to untangle the *fixations* or neurotic behaviours that have stemmed from it. The aim is for clients to become less dependent and to develop a more functional way of understanding and accepting loss/rejection/change in their lives.

Shapiro *et al.* (1991) report psychodynamic therapies to have minimal success. This may be because depressed people are too inactive, passive or unmotivated to participate in psychoanalytic psychotherapy. A more directive, challenging psychotherapy is probably more appropriate. Another reason might be that patients may expect a 'quick fix', and lengthy psychoanalysis does not offer this.

A more common psychotherapy used in the treatment of depression is CBT or Cognitive Behavioural Therapy.

Cognitive Behavioural Therapy

Cognitive behavioural therapy is an umbrella term for a variety of psychotherapies emanating from the behavioural and cognitive-behavioural approaches to atypical behaviour. These include Cognitive Therapy developed by Aaron Beck. Cognitive therapy is extremely popular in the United Kingdom in the treatment of depression.

Aaron Beck

Aaron Beck, born in 1921, is Emeritus Professor of Psychiatry at the University of Pennsylvania. He is famous for a number of measures of mental health including the Beck's Depression Inventory, Beck Hopelessness Scale, and Beck's Anxiety Inventory etc.

Beck believes that depressed people develop unrealistic pessimistic views of themselves, their world and their future. Such negative thinking is known as a *negative triad*. The foundations of negative thinking lie in faulty relationships in childhood with parents, teachers, siblings, friends etc. This leads to low self-esteem.

A negative triad consists of negative schema and cognitive bias. Types of cognitive bias or *distortion* include arbitrary inference, selective abstraction, overgeneralisation, magnification and minimisation. Each influences the depressed person's negative perception of themselves in their world.

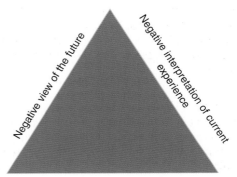

Figure 9.14 Beck's Cognitive Triad

Cognitive distortions

Arbitrary inference is 'the process of forming an interpretation of a situation, event or experience when there is no factual evidence to support the conclusion or when the conclusion is contrary to evidence' (Beck, 1975). An example of arbitrary inference as cognitive bias would be when a depressed person sees a friend in school or college. The friend fails to acknowledge them. The depressed person concludes that the person no longer wants to be their friend.

Selective abstraction is 'the process of focussing on a detail taken out of context, ignoring other more salient features of the situation, and conceptualising the whole experience on the basis of this element' (Beck, 1975). An example of selective abstraction would be when a depressed person is out with friends and one ignores him or her. The depressed individual takes this single event to indicate that they are boring, worthless etc.

Overgeneralisation is defined as 'drawing a general conclusion about ability, performance or worth on the basis of a single incident' (Beck, 1975). A good example here is the mature student who goes to pieces when giving a psychology presentation at University to their peer group. It is worth 10% of their overall grade. They are doing wonderfully well on other aspects of their course but conclude on the basis of this tiny element that they are not cut out to do a degree and should leave University.

Magnification is exaggerating the outcome of anything negative in life. An example would be a depressed person making a mistake in their psychology homework and thinking the teacher is going to recommend that they give up the subject.

Minimisation is where the depressed person discounts or downplays their accomplishments.

Evidence for negative schemas

In 1978 Weissman and Beck set out to investigate whether depressed people thought about themselves and their world in terms of negative schema. Using the Depression Attitude Scale (DAS), they asked a sample of American College students to indicate their strength of agreement/disagreement to statements that included 'It is difficult to be happy unless one is intelligent, good-looking, rich and creative', 'People will think less of me if I make a mistake', 'If someone disagrees with me it probably indicates he or she does not like me' etc.

They found that depressed participants made more negative assessments than non-depressed people. When given cognitive therapy to challenge and change their negative schemas, there was an improvement in their self-ratings. Later studies have also confirmed this (Keller, 1983; Silverman, Silverman and Eardley, 1984). Weissman and Beck (1978) allow us to conclude that depressed people utilise negative schemas. While criticism can be made of the DAS, Beck's Cognitive Therapy has been applied on its basis. CT has been shown to be effective in the treatment of some mood and anxiety disorders including depression.

Beck's Cognitive Therapy

This is because Beck's Cognitive Therapy (CT) engages clients about these negative *schemas*. They are persuaded that they are unrealistic, and encouraged to develop more realistic ways of thinking about themselves. Their view of themselves, their world and their future subsequently change. More positive thoughts influence their feelings and their behaviours to the good (Beck, 1967; 1976).

Various techniques are used in CT to address negative schema. Generally they involve activity schedules, identifying depressive thoughts, answering negative thoughts and problem solving.

Activity schedules

Activity schedules are arranged in conjunction with the cognitive-behavioural therapist. Such helps address the apathy experienced by many depressed individuals. Activity schedules have the client gradually re-engage in everyday activities that require little effort on their part. Activity schedules involve household tasks like doing the dishes, outside activities such as gardening, and simple social pleasures like walking the dog etc.

Identifying depressive thoughts

The second stage of CT usually concerns identifying depressive thoughts. The depressed individual is encouraged to keep a diary of recurring negative thoughts. These are later discussed with their therapist. Sometimes role-play is used to identify and re-visit negative mood states that occur in between cognitive therapy sessions.

Answering negative thoughts

It is important in Cognitive Therapy that the client address their negative thoughts and recurring mood states. This helps change how they think, feel and behave. A client is encouraged to examine their cognitive distortions or ways of thinking such as arbitrary inference, selective abstraction, overgeneralisation, magnification and minimisation.

The therapist challenges such cognitive 'errors' when they occur. The client is asked to justify why they think the way they do. The client is given homework or behavioural tasks to do between sessions. This is to help them examine the illogical way they think about themselves in their world. Once done, it becomes easier to work out more positive ways of thinking.

Problem solving

Sometimes the therapist may have to suggest strategies to help the client problem solve the persistent issues that get them down. An obvious example could be their job. The therapist may help them change job, and consequently remove a major stressor in the client's life.

The effectiveness of cognitive therapy

There have been innumerable studies done on the effectiveness of cognitive therapy (Keller, 1983; Silverman, Silverman and Eardley, 1984). Lam *et al.* (2005) conducted a 30-month study to compare the cost-effectiveness of cognitive therapy with standard care. They randomly allocated 103 individuals with bipolar disorder to receive either standard pharmaceutical treatment, or cognitive therapy and standard pharmaceutical treatment. Service use and costs were measured at 3-monthly intervals, as was cost-effectiveness in terms of patient net-benefit.

Lam *et al.* found that the group receiving cognitive therapy had significantly better clinical outcomes. Further, the combination of cognitive therapy and pharmaceutical mood stabilisers was found to be superior to mood stabilisers alone in terms of clinical outcome and cost-effectiveness for those with frequent relapses of bipolar disorder.

> ***When people are in distress, they often do not think clearly and their thoughts are distorted in some way. Cognitive therapy helps people to identify their distressing thoughts and to evaluate how realistic the thoughts are. Then they learn to change their distorted thinking. When they think more realistically, they feel better.***"

ONLINE INTERACTIVES

Visit the Beck Institute Blog at
http://www.beckinstituteblog.org/

A direct Link is available in the Chapter 9 section of Higher Psychology Learning Suite at **www.gerardkeegan.co.uk**.

Cognitive Therapy or CT has been found to be effective in the treatment of a variety of mood and anxiety disorders that include depression, phobias, panic attacks and eating disorders. It is to eating disorders that we now turn.

Eating disorders

ICD 10 categorise an eating disorder as a behavioural syndrome associated with physiological disturbances and physical factors, and is a pattern of eating behaviour harmful to the body and mind. Eating disorders have become extremely prevalent in the last 30 years and are estimated to effect 1.1 million people in the UK. To put this awesome figure in context 85 000 people in the UK have multiple sclerosis.

Currently 90 % of those with symptoms of an eating disorder are women (Hoek and van Hoeken, 2003). Eating disorders are almost exclusive to advanced capitalist societies as found in Western Europe and the United States of America.

'Heroin chic': the sociocultural hypothesis

While there is some evidence to indicate a biological basis to eating disorders, such as a dysfunctional hypothalamus, most would agree that eating disorders are influenced by societal norms regarding the pressure to be thin (APA, 1994). This is known as the sociocultural hypothesis. Such societal pressure to be thin was evident in the mid-1990s with the 'heroin chic' fashion look. British models such as Kate Moss personified a fashion for girls to be pale and skinny, and have dark sunken eyes with fine, blow-away hair.

Figure 9.15 The 'heroin chic' fashion look

The University of Maryland does however caution that there is no *single* cause for eating disorders. Although the sociocultural hypothesis concerning societal norms regards body shape and body image play a role in the onset of eating disorders their actual cause appear to result from many factors. These include family background, family pressures and emotional and personality disorders.

Eating disorders in Scotland

The number of people with an eating disorder in Scotland is difficult to calculate. This is because as in other parts of the UK many sufferers do not seek medical help. In 2006 NHS Quality Improvement Scotland estimated that the incidence of anorexia nervosa was 8.1% per 100,000 per annum and bulimia nervosa 11.4% per 100,000 per annum.

Onset of eating disorders

Depending upon type an eating disorder usually become evident during the teenage years initially as a 'psychological problem of adolescence' (ICD 10). In a number of cases an eating disorder will persist into adulthood, or emerge in these later years. Eating disorders have both a physical and psychological dimension. We will examine these in a little more depth shortly. Two well-known types of eating disorder are anorexia nervosa and bulimia nervosa.

ONLINE INTERACTIVES

Discover more about anorexia nervosa. Watch the YouTube video presentation by Professor Janet Treasure at **http://www.b-eat.co.uk/AboutEating Disorders/WhatisanEatingdisorder/WhatisAno rexiaNervosa**

A direct Link is available in the Chapter 9 section of Higher Psychology Learning Suite at **www.gerardkeegan.co.uk**.

Anorexia Nervosa

Around 10 % of those presenting with an eating disorder in the UK have anorexia nervosa. Anorexia Nervosa (AN) is a 'nervous loss of appetite' most common in the teenage years. Anorexia is most prevalent in girls, though increasingly boys have become susceptible (Seligman, 1994).

Anorectics are people with anorexia who become obsessed with being thin. They become terrified of gaining weight. As a result, they starve themselves, especially avoiding high-calorie foods, and exercise compulsively. Consequently they fall well below the normal weight or body mass index (BMI) for their age and height.

There are two subtypes of anorexia nervosa: the restricting subtype and binge-eating/purging type.

The restricting anorectic

The **restricting anorectic** maintains their low body weight by limiting their food intake, and sometimes by exercising frenetically. The **restricting subtype anorectic** also often masquerades as a vegetarian (Lipsedge, 1997b).

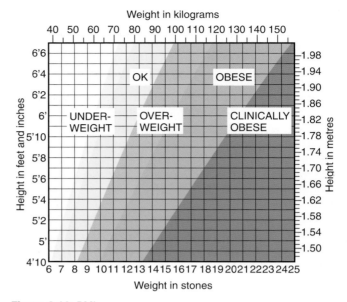

Figure 9.16 BMI

The binge-eating/purging anorectic

The **binge-eating/purging anorectic** also limit their food intake, but then engage in binge eating and purging behaviours involving being sick, and the misuse of laxatives, diuretics or enemas.

Many anorectics move back and forth between these two subtypes during the course of their illness. According to Beat, formerly the Eating Disorders Association, anorectics have the highest mortality rate of any mental disorder. Waterhouse and Mayes (2000) suggest an anorexic mortality rate of between 13-20%. This is due to the side effects of the disorder or because of suicide.

Bulimia Nervosa

Bulimia Nervosa (BN) more often occurs in adulthood and effects 40% of eating disorder sufferers in the UK. BN almost exclusively affects women, and becomes apparent in the early to mid-twenties. Like anorectics, people with bulimia are also terrified of gaining weight, but they can usually keep within normal weight. This is because bulimics indulge in binge eating, which is then followed by purging or strict dieting. This involves making oneself sick and/or taking excessive amounts of laxative. As with anorexia, there are two subtypes of bulimia nervosa: the purging type bulimic and the non-purging type bulimic.

The purging type bulimic

The purging type bulimic includes those who make themselves sick, use laxatives, diuretics, or enemas.

The non-purging type bulimic

The non-purging type bulimic refers to individuals who follow their excessive eating by excessive exercising or dietary fasting.

Until recently it was thought anorexia and bulimia were two different types of eating disorder. Each was thought to have a different cause, and thus was afforded different treatment. Nowadays they are considered to be different sides of the same coin (Milos *et al.*, 2005). This is because at least 33% of anorectics will go on to develop bulimia (Mitchell and McCarthy, 2000).

Binge Eating Disorder

A third kind of eating disorder that has become evident since 1992 is Binge Eating Disorder. Unlike bulimia those with BED do not purge themselves. It is thought that many more people suffer from binge eating disorder than either anorexia or bulimia nervosa. Because of the amount of food eaten, many people with BED become obese. This leads to problems with blood pressure, heart disease and a general lack of fitness. Controversy exists as to whether BED is a type of bulimia or an eating disorder in its own right. More research is needed in this area.

Other less well-known kinds of eating disorder include compulsive eating disorder, orthorexia nervosa or compulsive dieting and Prader Willi Syndrome, an eating disorder that is genetic in origin.

ONLINE INTERACTIVES

Read about former Deputy Prime Minister John Prescott and his battle with bulimia. Go to **http://www.timesonline.co.uk/tol/news/politics/article3780550.ece**

A direct Link is available in the Chapter 9 section of Higher Psychology Learning Suite at **www.gerardkeegan.co.uk**.

Biological signs of anorexia

The effects of anorexia on the body are manifold. These include extreme weight loss in adults, and poor or inadequate weight gain or substantial weight loss in children and teenagers. Extreme weight loss or inadequate weight gain is assessed at <85% of body mass in comparison to others of similar age and growth stage. This adversely affects bone mass, which results in osteoporosis or brittle bones. Another important biological indicator of anorexia, although exclusive to girls is amenorrea, which often occurs in the early stages of AN.

Amenorrea

Amenorrea is the absence of at least three consecutive menstrual cycles. Gross (2001) tells us that in around 20% of cases amenorrea precedes any obvious weight loss.

Other biological indicators of anorexia nervosa include constipation and abdominal pains; dizzy spells and feeling faint; bloated stomach, puffy face and ankles; lanugo or downy hair on the body; occasional loss of hair on the head when in recovery; poor blood circulation and feeling cold, and dry, rough, or discoloured skin.

Psychological signs of anorexia

The anorectic has an intense fear of gaining weight and develops an obsessive interest in what others are eating. They have a distorted perception of body shape or weight, which is exacerbated by a denial of the existence of a problem. They are prone to changes in personality and subsequent mood. This has them challenge other people's views on eating and exercise.

Behavioural signs of anorexia

The behavioural signs of anorexia see rigid and obsessive behaviour attached to eating. This more often than not involves cutting food into tiny pieces. The anorectic will be restless and hyperactive. They will wear big baggy clothes. They will also engage in self-induced purging by vomiting and taking laxatives.

Biological signs of bulimia

The main biological sign of bulimia is frequent changes in weight. This is due to the cycle of binge eating followed by purging. Related to purging are sore throats, tooth decay and bad breath caused by excessive vomiting. A bulimics face becomes rounder due to swollen salivary glands. Their skin gets into poor condition. They may experience hair loss. Girls

get irregular periods, and there is a general loss of interest in sex. They become lethargic and tired, with an increased susceptibility to heart disease and problems with other internal organs.

Psychological signs of bulimia

Figure 9.17 John Prescott

As bravely admitted by Labour politician John Prescott, someone who suffers from BN has an uncontrollable urge to eat vast amounts of food in a short space of time. They develop an obsession with food, and often feel out of control around it. This results in a distorted perception of their body weight and shape with ensuing emotional behaviour and mood swings. As a consequence the bulimic suffers secondary psychological symptoms of anxiety and depression; low self-esteem, shame and guilt. This is exacerbated by feelings of isolation and loneliness.

Behavioural signs of bulimia

DSM IV (American Psychological Association, 1994) believe a BN sufferer will binge eat and then purge themselves a minimum average of twice per week for three months. Purging involves going to the toilet after meals to vomit food just eaten. Bulimics will use an excessive amount of laxatives. They may also use diuretics to increase urination and enemas to increase defecation. Other behavioural indications of bulimia are periods of fasting, excessive exercise, and secrecy and an unwillingness to socialise. There are reports of bulimics shoplifting for food or spending an abnormal amount of money on things to

eat. Partners of bulimics report food in their fridge and larder disappearing unexpectedly, or discovering food being secretly hoarded.

Treating eating disorders

Our brain continues to mature until age 20. Prolonged starvation can have drastic consequences for brain development if an eating disorder is not addressed. The early detection of an eating disorder such as anorexia increases the likelihood of recovery.

If treated, as measured in a ten-year period, 50 % of anorectics recover satisfactorily (Herpertz-Dahlmann, 2001). Of those that don't a small number continue with the condition, while others go on to develop other kinds of eating disorder.

However, the eating disorder charity *Beat* indicates that 'even among those individuals who recover from an eating disorder, it is common for them to continue to maintain a low body weight and experience depression'. *Beat* report the treatment outcome for bulimia to be more successful with over 50% making a full recovery.

The complex nature of eating disorders consequently demands treatment at a number of levels. As with depression eating disorders are first addressed from a medical or biological point of view. This is because many sufferers- in particular anorectics – are dangerously ill because of their very low body weight and associated problems. More often than not they would be hospitalised. Once their body weight is stabilised the individual becomes more amenable to psychological treatment in the form of some kind of psychotherapy.

Treatment goals hope to:

➤ restore normal weight for sufferers of anorexia nervosa

➤ reduce, and hopefully stop, binge eating and purging for sufferers of bulimia nervosa

➤ treat physical/medical complications, and any associated psychiatric disorders

➤ teach sufferers proper nutritional habits and how to eat healthily and plan meals

➤ change sufferers faulty thinking about their eating disorder

➤ improve the sufferers self-control, self-esteem, and behaviour

General treatment approaches

There are three general approaches to treatment. These include

Medication

In the case of severe anorexia sufferers are more often than not hospitalised. Various medications may be administered to patients depending on the type of eating disorder, psychiatric state, and severity of the condition. Calcium and vitamin D supplements are prescribed. Zinc supplements may be used to help an anorectic gain weight.

Psychotherapies

Eating disorders are nearly always treated with some form of psychological treatment. Depending on the problem, certain psychological approaches may work better than others. Behavioural therapy may be used to break faulty S-R learning regards food. Motivational psychotherapy that links biological aspects of the condition with mental health is also often used to create a supportive and empathic environment to help those with AN or BN progress. The use of operant conditioning or reward to help the client achieve a more healthy body (and thus mind) is commonplace. Cognitive-behavioural therapy may also be used to change the negative way sufferers think about themselves. Humanistic psychotherapy may be used to address issues of low self-esteem.

INTERACTIVES

In what ways might operant conditioning be used to help treat an anorectic?

Nutritional Rehabilitation

Nutritional counselling can help patients regain weight and learn normal expectations concerning hunger and eating patterns. This may be delivered by a dietician or as part of psychotherapy. In whatever case, the anorectic is strongly encouraged to strive for a weight-gain goal of 2–3 pounds a week if an in-patient, and 0.5–1 pound a week if an outpatient.

ONLINE INTERACTIVES

For further information, support and help with eating disorders in the UK please visit Beat at http://www.b-eat.co.uk/HelpandSupport

A direct Link is available in the Chapter 9 section of Higher Psychology Learning Suite at www.gerardkeegan.co.uk.

Conclusion

Atypical behaviours such as Eating disorders should never be underestimated. For women aged 15–24, eating disorders are among the top four leading causes of disease in terms of years of life lost through death or disability. Anorexia nervosa has one of the highest overall mortality rates and the highest suicide rate of any psychiatric disorder. The probability of someone dying from an eating disorder is 3 times higher than the mortality rate for depression, schizophrenia or alcoholism. Someone with an eating disorder is 12 times more likely to die than those the general population as a whole. To avoid this and other serious complications those with an eating disorder must seek medical help.

Chapter summary

This chapter emphasised atypical behaviour as an individual difference. It defined and explained atypical behaviour from a statistical, valuative and practical perspective. It examined the medical, cognitive, behaviourist, psychodynamic and humanistic approaches to atypical behaviour. It further investigated the aetiology and treatment of depression and eating disorders.

It also brings this book to a close!

STRUCTURED QUESTIONS WITH ANSWER GUIDELINES

1 Describe and explain the treatment of depression.

With reference to the preceding pages, structure your answer as follows:

● define depression as an atypical behaviour. Define 'atypical behaviour'. Outline depression in terms of its aetiology (cognitive, affective and behavioural symptoms). Mention types of depression. Advise that psychology treats atypical behaviours like depression from five points of view. Say what these are.

Then elaborate on the following remembering to refer to research studies where appropriate:

➤ the medical/biological view of atypical behaviour

➤ the psychodynamic view of atypical behaviour

➤ the behaviourist view of atypical behaviour

➤ the cognitive-behaviourist view of atypical behaviour

➤ the humanistic view of atypical behaviour

➤ medical/biological treatment of depression

➤ psychodynamic psychotherapy and the treatment of depression

➤ behaviourist psychotherapy and the treatment of depression

➤ cognitive-behaviourist psychotherapy and the treatment of depression

➤ humanistic psychotherapy and the treatment of depression

2 How useful are classification systems in their diagnosis of atypical behaviour?

With reference to the preceding pages structure your answer as follows:

● say what classification systems are (ICD 10 and DSM IV). Indicate what one is used where, and why (dominance of the medical/biological model of abnormality). Suggest that the main problem associated with the use of classification systems is misdiagnosis of atypical behaviours. This can have dramatic consequences.

Then elaborate on the following remembering to refer to research studies where appropriate:

➤ give details of ICD 10

➤ give strengths and weaknesses of the medical model of abnormality

➤ give aim, method, results and conclusions of 'Rosenhan's 'On being sane in insane places' and 'The Non-existent imposter'

➤ refer to supporting studies of misdiagnosis such as Termelin (1970)

ONLINE INTERACTIVES

1   Go to the Higher Psychology Learning Suite at **www.gerardkeegan.co.uk**. Click Chapter 9 'Atypical Behaviour' to access direct links to all websites mentioned in this chapter.

2   Go to the Higher Psychology Learning Suite at **www.gerardkeegan.co.uk**. Click Chapter 9 'Atypical Behaviour' and do the online interactive crossword. But don't cheat!

3   Go to the Higher Psychology Learning Suite at **www.gerardkeegan.co.uk**. Click Chapter 9 'Atypical Behaviour' and do the online interactive hangman game. Try and beat the executioner!

4   Go to the Higher Psychology Learning Suite at **www.gerardkeegan.co.uk**. Click Chapter 9 'Atypical Behaviour' and print off the hard copy crossword. When finished you might like to hand it into your teacher as homework.

5   Go to the Higher Psychology Learning Suite at **www.gerardkeegan.co.uk**. Click Chapter 9 'Atypical Behaviour' and do the online interactive quiz. Try and win the prize!

GLOSSARY

Anorectic(s)
A person or persons who suffer from anorexia, an eating disorder.

Asylum(s)
A place of refuge.

Atypical behaviour
Behaviour that is deemed abnormal, such as schizophrenia. How *abnormal* is itself defined is controversial in psychology. (Ab)normal behaviour can be identified in terms of its statistical frequency, how much the behaviour deviates from social norms, or how mentally unwell an individual appears to be.

Biological determinism
The idea that certain characteristics and differences are determined by genetic factors, and are thus unchangeable.

Co-morbidity
Co-morbidity is the presence of two or more disorders at one time.

Hysteria
A hysteria or hysterical neurosis is a medical condition with a psychological rather than a biological or physical cause. Examples would include hysterical mutism where a person suddenly loses the capacity to speak. On examination it is discovered that there is nothing wrong with their vocalisation apparatus or ability to talk. There is no physical explanation for their problem. The cause of their hysteria is psychological. Something has happened in their environment to trigger their mutism.

Eros
Eros is a term attributed to Sigmund Freud. Eros is an instinct within us that drives our creativity and passion. It is in constant conflict with another instinct innate in us all called Thanatos.

Existentialism
Existentialism concerns the psychological impact the environment has on an individual. They can become confused and disorientated in an absurd world.

Genotype
Your genetic make-up and potential when born.

Individual differences
An area of study in psychology that looks at personality, atypical behaviour and intelligence.

Individual differences are thus those things we share, but differ around. Individual differences are thought influenced by our genetic inheritance. Or put another way, personality, abnormal behaviour, and intelligence are to a degree a consequence of our biology.

Intelligence
Intelligence is almost impossible to define! This is because 'What *is* intelligence' is an ongoing and controversial debate in the psychology of individual differences. Simply put *intelligence* is the demonstration of our ability to problem-solve. Intelligence is influenced by our genetics inherited from our birth parents, and learning experiences in our environment. Intelligence is also culturally influenced. What is deemed intelligent behaviour in one part of the world would not be recognised as such in another. An 'A' band pass in Higher or A level psychology is about as useful as a chocolate teapot in the middle of the Amazon rain forest!

Nature–nurture (debate)

The nature-nurture debate in psychology concerns the degree to which our genetics or environment plays in shaping who we are, and what we become. Also known as the nativist-empiricist, or genetics-heredity debate, it is an especially hot topic in the study of intelligence.

Personal agency

Our ability to make choices as a result of having free will.

Personality

Who you are as an individual. Personality can be seen in terms of our psyche or self. Our personality is influenced to some degree by heredity, but much more so by experience in our environment, and the situations we find ourselves in. There are two ways of looking at personality in psychology, the nomothetic view, and the idiographic view. If you take a *nomothetic* approach you believe peoples personality can be fitted into general, named categories, such as *extrovert* and *introvert*. The late Professor Hans Eysenck (1916-1997) took a nomothetic approach to personality. If alternatively you take an *idiographic* approach, you believe an individual's personality is *unique*. So unique that slotting us all into general categories is impossible. Carl Rogers took an idiographic view of personality, as does George Kelly with his Personal Construct Theory.

Personality disorder

A personality disorder is 'a severe disturbance in the character logical condition and behavioural tendencies of the individual, usually involving several areas of the personality, and nearly always associated with considerable personal and social disruption' (ICD 10).

Phenotype

What genotype becomes as a consequence of experiences in environment.

PTSD

Post Traumatic Stress Disorder is an anxiety disorder that can develop after exposure to a terrifying event or ordeal where grave physical harm occurred or was threatened. PTSD is common among soldiers and others exposed to combat and war.

Schizophrenia

About 1 in every 100 people are affected by schizophrenia Its onset may start in a person's late teens or early twenties, Schizophrenia is a condition where an individual suffers disturbances to their thinking, perception, affect (mood, or how one feels) and behaviour.

Self

Humanistic term for who we really are as a person. The self is our inner personality, and can be likened to the soul, or Freud's psyche.

Self-fulfilling prophecy

A self-fulfilling prophecy is a prediction that directly or indirectly causes itself to become true.

Toxins

A toxin is a poison that can damage cells in our body. Some toxins are thought harmless if ingested by us in small amounts. One of these is fluoride in toothpaste.

Thanatos

Freud tells us Thanatos is our death wish. Thanatos is in constant conflict with another instinctual drive called Eros. Thanatos is our inner drive towards death, destruction and non-existence.

References

Internet References

The Memory Exhibition
http://www.exploratorium.edu/memory/ *last accessed 28/2/09*

Bartlett & War of the Ghosts.
http://www.bbc.co.uk/radio4/science/mindchangers1.shtml *last accessed 28/2/09.*

The Lucifer Effect: Understanding How Good People Turn Evil
http://www.lucifereffect.com/ *last accessed 28/2/09.*

The US Constitution Online
http://www.usconstitution.net/dream.html last accessed 11/03/09.

The Psychology of Prejudice: An Overview
http://www.understandingprejudice.org/apa/english/page2.htm *last accessed 12/03/09.*

The Day His World Stood Still by Joanna Schaffhausen. Brain Connection
http://www.brainconnection.com/topics/?main=fa/hm-memory *last accessed 28/2/09.*

The Internet Classics Archive: Theaetetus by Plato
http://classics.mit.edu/Plato/theatu.html *last accessed 28/2/09.*

Chandler, D. (1995) **Texts and the Construction of Meaning**
http://www.aber.ac.uk/media/Documents/act/act.html *last accessed 28/2/09.*

BBC 4 **"All in the Mind" Flashbulb Memory**
http://www.bbc.co.uk/radio4/science/allinthemind_20030212.shtml *last accessed 1/3/09.*

Sir Richard F. **Burton on the Web** http://www.isidore-of-seville.com/burton/ *last accessed 1/3/09.*

Buzan World: Mind Maps
http://www.buzanworld.com/Mind_Maps.htm *last accessed 3/3/09.*

Gerard Keegan's Psychology Site http://www.gerardkeegan.co.uk/ *last accessed 30/4/09.*

Bureau of Labor Statistics http://www.bls.gov/ *last accessed 4/3/09.*

UK Statistics Authority http://www.statistics.gov.uk/ *last accessed 4/3/09.*

Understanding Eating Disorders, BEAT http://www.b-eat.co.uk/Home *last accessed 29/04/09.*

Eating Disorders in Scotland, NHS Quality Improvement Scotland
http://www.nhshealthquality.org/nhsqis/qis_display_findings.jsp?pContentID=3255&p_applic=CCC&p_service=Content.show *last accessed 29/04/09.*

Eating Disorders, University of Maryland
http://www.health.umd.edu/services/eatingdisorders.html *last accessed 29/04/09.*

Depression Alliance Scotland, **Annual Report**
http://www.dascot.org/about/aboutDAS.htm *last accessed 29/04/09.*

Depression, BUPA
http://hcd2.bupa.co.uk/fact_sheets/html/depression.html *last accessed 29/04/09.*

Men hit harder by credit crunch stress, University of Cambridge
http://www.admin.cam.ac.uk/news/press/dpp/2009040106 *last accessed 29/04/09.*

Depression, See Me Scotland
http://www.seemescotland.org.uk/aboutmentalhealthproblemsandstigma/depression last accessed 29/04/09.

Psychological Disorders: Symptoms, Treatments, & Statistics of Psychological Problems Laurie Pawlik-Kienlen
http://psychology.suite101.com/article.cfm/psychological_disorders#ixzz0E3YW6s8X&A *last accessed 29/04/09.*

The Herald More than half babies born in Scotland to unmarried parents
http://www.theherald.co.uk/news/news/display.var.2495078.0.more_than_half_babies_born_in_scotland_to_unmarried_parents.php *last accessed 25 April 2009.*

Text References

Abernathy, E.M. (1940). The effect of changed environmental conditions upon the results of college examinations. *Journal of Psychology*, 10: 293–301.

Adams, H. F. (1912). Autokinetic sensations. *Psychological Monographs, 14,* 1–45.

These are Primary Control, and Secondary Control. Adler, A. (1927). The Practice and Theory of Individual Psychology. New York: Harcourt Brace Jovanovich.

Adorno, T., Frenkel-Brunswick, E., Levinson, D. J. & Sanford, R. N. (1950). *The Authoritarian Personality.* New York: Harper.

Adorno, T.W., Frenkel-Brunswick, E., Levinson, J.D. & Sanford, R.N. (1950). New York: Harper & Row.

Ainsworth, M.D.S. & Wittig, B.A. (1969). Attachment and exploratory behaviour of one-year-olds in a strange situation. In B.M. Foss (Ed.) Determinants of Infant Behaviour, Volume 4. London: Methuen.

Ainsworth, M.D.S. (1969). Object Relations, Dependency, and Attachment: A Theoretical Review of the Infant-Mother Relationship. *Child Development*, 40, 969–1025.

Ainsworth, M.D.S. (1979). Attachment as related to mother-infant interaction. *Advances in the Study of Behaviour*, 9, 2–52.

Ainsworth, M.D.S. (1985). Attachments across the life span. *Bulletin of the New York Academy of Medicine*, 61, 792–812.

Ainsworth, M.D.S. (1989). Attachment beyond infancy. *American Psychologist*, 44, 709–716.

Ainsworth, M.D.S. & Bell, S.M. (1970). Attachment, Exploration, and Separation: Illustrated by the Behaviour of One-Year-Olds in a Strange Situation. *Child Development*, 41, 49–67.

Ainsworth, M.D.S., Bell, S.M., Blehar, M.C. & Main, M. (1971). *Physical contact: A study of infant responsiveness and its relation to maternal handling.* Paper presented at the biennial meeting of the Society for Research in Child Development, Minneapolis, MN.

Ainsworth, M.D.S., Blehar, M.C., Walters, E. & Wall, S. (1978). Patterns of Attachment: A Psychological Study of the Strange Situation. Hillsdale, New Jersey: Lawrence Erlbaum Associates Inc.

Allport, G.W. (1954). *The Nature of Prejudice*. Reading, Mass: Addison-Wesley.

Allport, G.W. (1935). Attitudes. In C.M. Murchison (ed.), Handbook of Social Psychology. Winchester, MA.

American Psychiatric Association (1994). Diagnostic and Statistical Manual of Mental Disorders DSM-IV.

Amir, Y. (1969). Contact hypothesis in ethnic relations. Psychological Bulletin, 71, 319–342.

Anderson, L.P. (1991). Acculturative stress: A theory of relevance to black Americans. Clinical Psychology Review 11: 685–702.

Argyle, M. (1983). The Psychology of Interpersonal Behaviour (4th edition). Harmondsworth: Penguin.

Aronson, E. & Patnoe, S. (1997). The jigsaw classroom: Building cooperation in the classroom (2nd ed.). New York: Addison Wesley Longman.

Aronson, E. & Thibodeau, R. (1992). The jigsaw classroom: A cooperative strategy for reducing prejudice. In J. Lynch, C. Modgil, and S. Modgil (Eds.),. Cultural diversity in the schools. London: Falmer Press

Asch, S. E. (1951). Effects of group pressure upon the modification and distortion of judgment. In H. Guetzkow (ed.) Groups, leadership and men. Pittsburgh, PA: Carnegie Press.

Asch, S. E. (1955). Opinions and social pressure. Scientific American, 193, 31–35.

Aspinwall, L. G., & Taylor, S. E. (1993). Effects of social comparison direction, threat, and self-esteem on affect, self-evaluation, and expected success. Journal of Personality and Social Psychology. 64, 708–722.

Atkinson, R.C. & Shiffrin, R.M. (1968). Human memory: A proposed system and its control processes. In K.W. Spence & J.T. Spence (Eds.) The Psychology of Learning and Motivation, Volume 2. London: Academic Press.

Atkinson, R.C. & Shiffrin, R.M. (1971). The control of short-term memory. Scientific American, 224, 82–90.

Axline, V.M. (1964). Dibs: In Search of Self. New York: Ballantine.

Ayllon, T. & Azrin, N.H. (1965). The measurement and reinforcement of behaviour of psychotics. Journal of the Experimental Analysis of Behaviour, 8, 357–83.

Ayllon, T. & Azrin, N.H. (1968). The Token Economy: A Motivational System for Therapy and Rehabilitation. New York: Appleton-Century-Crofts.

Baddeley, A., Chincotta, D., Stafford, L. & Turk, D. (2002). Is the word length effect in STM entirely attributable to output delay? Evidence from serial recognition. The Quarterly Journal of Experimental Psychology 55A (2), 353–369.

Baddeley, A.D. (1976). The Psychology of Memory. New York: Basic Books.

Baddeley, A.D. (1990). Human Memory. Hove: Lawrence Erlbaum Associates.

Baddeley, A.D., & Hitch, G. (1974). Working memory. In G.H. Bower (Ed.), The psychology of learning and motivation: Advances in research and theory (Vol. 8, pp. 47–89). New York: Academic Press.

Baltes, P.B., Baltes, M.M., Reinert, G. (1970). Relationship between time of measurement and age in cognitive development of children – application of cross-sectional sequences. Human Development;13:258.

Bandura, A., Ross, D. & Ross, S.A. (1961). Transmission of aggression through imitation of aggressive models. Journal of Abnormal and Social Psychology, 63, 575–82.

Barlow, D.H. & Durand, V.M. (2000). Abnormal Psychology: An Introduction (2nd edition). Media Edition, Pacific Grove, CA: Wadsworth Publishing Co.

Baron R. A. & Byrne D. (1984). Social Psychology: Understanding Human Interaction. Boston: Allyn & Bacon.

Baron, R. A., Byrne, D., & Suls, J. (1989). Exploring social psychology (3rd Ed.). Boston: Allyn and Bacon

Barrie J. M. (1951). The Admirable Crichton. Hodder and Stoughton, London

Barry, L.C., Allore, H.G., Guo, Z., Bruce, M.L. & Gill, T.M. (2008). Higher Burden of Depression Among Older Women: The Effect of Onset, Persistence, and Mortality Over Time Archives of General Psychiatry; 65:172–178.

Bartlett, F. (1932). Remembering. Cambridge, Cambridge University Press.

Bateson, P. (1986). When to experiment on animals. New Scientist, 109 (14960), 30–2.

Bateson, P. P. G. (1966). The characteristics and context of imprinting. Biol. Rev., 41, 177.

Baumrind, D. (1967). Child care practices anteceding three patterns of preschool behaviour. Genetic Psychology Monographs, 75(1), 43–88.

BBC TV Tomorrow's World, 13 March 2002.

Beck, A.T. (1967). Depression: Causes and Treatment. Philadelphia: University of Philadelphia Press.

Beck, A.T. (1972). Depression: Causes and Treatment. University of Pennsylvania Press.

Beck, A.T. (1975). Cognitive Therapy and the Emotional Disorders. Intl Universities Press.

Beck, A.T. (1974). The development of depression: A cognitive model. In R.J. Friedman and M.M. Katz (Eds.) The Psychology of Depression: Contemporary Theory and Research. New York: Wiley.

Bell, S.M. & Ainsworth, M.D.S. (1972). Infant crying and maternal responsiveness. Child Development, 43, 1171–1190.

Belsky, J. & Rovine, M.J. (1988). Nonmaternal care in the first year of life and the security of infant-parent attachment. Child Development, 59(1), 157–167.

Bem, S. L., & Bem, D. J. (1970). Training the women to know her place. Psychology Today.

Berlin, R. (1887). Eine besondere art der wortblindheit: dyslexia [A special type of wordblindness: Dyslexia]. Wiesbaden.

Berkowitz, L. (1969). The frustration-aggression hypothesis revisited. In L. ? check please Gerry

Berkowitz, L. (Ed.), Roots of aggression. New York: Atherton.

Berkowitz, L. (1989). The frustration-aggression hypothesis: Examination and reformulation. Psychological Bulletin, 106, 59–73.

Berry, J.W. (1966). Temne and Eskimo perceptual skills. International Journal of Psychology, 1, 207–199.

Bickman, L. (1974). The social power of a uniform. Journal of Applied Social Psychology, 1, 47–61.

Blakemore, C. & Cooper, G.F. (1970). Development of the brain depends on the visual environment. Nature, 228, 477–8.

Blakemore, C. (1988) The Mind Machine. London: BBC Publications.

Blehar, M.C., Lieberman, A.F., & Ainsworth, M.D.S. (1977). Early face-to-face interaction and its relation to later infant-mother attachment. Child Development, 48, 182–194.

Bleuler, E. (1911) Dementia Praecox or the Group of Schizophrenias, J. Avikin (Trans.). New York: International University Press.

Bond, R. & Smith, P. B. (1996). Culture and conformity: A meta-analysis of studies using Asch's (1952b, 1956) line judgment task. Psychological Bulletin. Vol 119(1), 111–137.

Bouchard, T.J., Lykken, D.T., McGue, M.M., Segal, N. & Tellegen, A. (1990). The sources of human psychological differences: The Minnesota study of twins reared apart. Science, 250, 223–8.

Bower, G. H., Clark, M. C., Lesgold, A. M., & Winzenz, D. (1969). Hierarchical retrieval schemes in recall of categorized word lists. Journal of Verbal Learning and Verbal Behaviour, 8: 323–343.

Bower, G. H. & Springston, F. (1970). Pauses as recording points in letter series Journal of Experimental Psychology 83 421–430.

Bowlby, J. (1976). Fry M (abridged & ed.). ed (Report, World Health Organisation, 1953. Child Care and the Growth of Love. Pelican books. Ainsworth MD (2 add. ch.) (2nd edn. ed.). London: Penguin Books.

Bowlby, J. (1995). Maternal Care and Mental Health. *The master work series (2nd edition ed.). Northvale, NJ; London: Jason Aronson. [Geneva, World Health Organization, Monograph series no. 3].*

Bowlby, J. (1988). *A Secure Base: Clinical Applications of Attachment Theory* (London Tavistock/Routledge).

Bowlby, J. (1944). *Forty-Four Juvenile Thieves:. Their Character and Home-Life.* International Journal of Psychoanalysis, 25, 19–52.

Bowlby, J. (1979). *The making and breaking of affectional bonds.* London: Tavistock.

Brandimonte, M. A., Hitch, G. J., & Bishop, D. V. M. (1992). Influence of short-term memory codes on visual image processing: Evidence from image transformation tasks. *Journal of Experimental Psychology: Learning, Memory, And Cognition, 18,* 157–165.

Brantlinger, P. A (2002). Companion to the Victorian Novel *Blackwell Pub.*

Breakwell, G. M. (1978). *Some effects on marginal social identity.* In H. Tajfel (Ed) Differentiation Between Social Groups. London: Academic Press.

Brehm, J. W. (1966). *A theory of psychological reactance,* New York: Academic Press.

Breuer, J. & Freud, S. (1895). *Studies on hysteria.* In J. Strachey (Ed. and trans.) Standard Edition of the Complete Psychological Works of Sigmund Freud Volume 2. London: Hogarth.

Briggs, R. (1973). *Urban cognitive distances.* In Downs, R.M. & Stea, D. (Eds.) Image and Environment: Cognitive Mapping and Spatial Behavior. Chicago: Aldine.

British Psychological Society & The Committee of the Experimental Psychological Society (1985). Guidelines for the Use of Animals in Research. Leicester: BPS.

British Psychological Society (1993). Ethical principles for conducting research with human participants (revised). *The Psychologist,* 6 (1), 33–5.

Bronfenbrenner U. (1973). *Two Worlds of Childhood: US and USSR.* Penguin.

Brown, R. (1995). *Prejudice: Its social psychology.* Oxford: Basil Blackwell.

Brown, R. (2000). Social Identity Theory: past achievements, current problems and future challenges. *European Journal of Social Psychology,* 30, 745–778.

Brown, R. (Ed) *New Directions in Psychology.* New York: Holt, Rinehart & Winston.

Brown, R. & Hernstein, R.J. (1975). *Psychology.* Boston, MA.

Brown, R., & Kulik, J. (1977). Flashbulb memories. *Cognition,* 5, 73–99.

Brown, R.J. (2000). *Group Processes: dynamics within and between groups,* 2nd Edition. Oxford: Blackwell.

Brown, T.A., Di Nardo, P.A. & Barlow, D.H. (1994). *Anxiety Disorders Interview Schedule for DSM-IV (ADIS-IV).* San Antonio, TX: The Psychological Corporation.

Bruner, J.S., Goodnow, J.J. & Austin G.A. (1956). *A Study of Thinking.* New York: Wiley.

Buri, J.R. (1991). Parental Authority Questionnaire. *Journal of Personality Assessment,* 57 (1), 110–9, Lawrence Erlbaum Associates.

Burn, S.M. (1991). Social Psychology and the Stimulation of Recycling Behaviours: The Block Leader Approach. *Journal of Applied Social Psychology* 21(8): 611–629.

Burne, J. (1999). Type D Personality and Heart Attacks *J. Amer. Med. Assoc.* 281: 1304,1328.

Buss, A.H. & Plomin, R. (1984). *Temperament: Early Developing Personality Traits.* Hillsdale: Lawrence Erlbaum Assoc Inc.

Bustamente, J. A., Jordan, A., Vila, M., Gonzalez, A., & Insua, A. (1970). State-dependent learning in humans. *Physiology and Behaviour, 5,* 793–796.

Butler, D. & Kavanagh, D. (Eds.) *The British General Election of 1997.* Macmillan.

Butterworth, G. & Harris, M. (1994). Principles of Developmental Psychology. Lawrence Erlbaum Assoc.: UK.

Byrne, D. (1971). *The attraction paradigm.* New York: Academic Press.

Campbell, A. (1971). *White attitudes toward black people.* Oxford, England: Institute for Social Research, University of Michigan.

Campbell, D.T. (1967). Stereotypes and the perception of group differences. *American Psychologist,* 22, 817–829.

Cann, A., Sherman, S. J., & Elkes, R. (1975). Effects of initial request size and timing of a second request on compliance: The foot in the door and the door in the face. *Journal of Personality and Social Psychology,* 32, 774–782.

Cannon, W. (1939). *The Wisdom of the Body,* 2nd ed., NY: Norton Pubs.

Cannon, W.B., Averido, A., Britton, S. W. & Bright, E. M. (1927). *American Journal of Physiology* 79. 466.

Cannon, W.B. (1929). *Bodily Changes in Pain, Hunger, Fear and Rage: An Account of Recent Research Into the Function of Emotional Excitement,* (2nd ed.) New York, Appleton-Century-Crofts.

Cardwell M., Clark E., & Meldrum C., (2003). *Psychology for AS-Level* Collins.

Cardwell, M. (2000). *The Complete A–Z Psychology Handbook* (2nd edition). London: Hodder & Stoughton.

Carlsmith, J.M. & Anderson, C.A. (1979) 'Ambient temperature and the occurrence of collective violence: New analysis.' *Journal of Personality and Social Psychology* 37: 337–44.

Challis, B.H. & Brodbeck, D.R. (1992). Level of processing affects priming in word-fragment completion. *Journal of Experimental Psychology: Learning, Memory, and Cognition,* 18, 595–607.

Chomsky, N. (1959). Review of Skinner's verbal behaviour. *Language,* 35, 26–58.

Chomsky, N. (1968). *Language and Mind.* New York: Harcourt Brace Jovanovich.

Christensen, L. (1988). Deception in psychological research: When is its use justified? Personality and Social Psychology, 14, 665–75.

Cialdini, R. B. (2003). Crafting normative messages to protect the environment. *Current Directions in Psychological Science,* 12, 105–109.

Clamp, A.G. (2001). Evolutionary Psychology. London: Hodder & Stoughton.

Clark, K.B., & Clark, M.P. (1947). *Racial identification and preference in Negro children.* In T.M. Newcomb & E.L. Hartley (Eds.), Reading in social psychology. New York: Holt, Rinehart & Winston.

Cohen, D. (1979) *J.B. Watson: The Founder of Behaviourism.* Boston: Routledge & Kegan Paul.

Cohen, F., & Lazarus, R. S. (1979). Coping with the stresses of illness. In G. C. Stone, F. Cohen, & N. E. Adler (Eds.), *Health psychology, a handbook.* San Francisco: Jossey Bass,

Cohen, S., & Rabin, B.S. (1998). Stress, immunity and cancer. *Journal of the National Cancer Institute,* 90, 3–4.

Conrad, R. (1964). Acoustic confusion and immediate memory. *British. Journal of Psychology* 55, 75–84.

Conway, M.A., Anderson, S.J., Larsen, S.F. *et al.* (1994). The formation of flashbulb memories. *Memory and Cognition;* 22:326–343 39.

Coolican, H. (1999). *Research Methods and Statistics in Psychology* (3rd edition). London: Hodder & Stoughton.

Coopersmith, S. (1967). *The Antecedents of Self-Esteem.* San Francisco: Freeman.

Coplan, J.D., Smith, E.L., Altemus, M., Scharf, B.A., Owens, M.J., Nemeroff, C.B. *et al.* (2000). Stress in women after sexual and physical abuse in childhood. *JAMA* 284:592–597.

Corneille, O., Klein, O., Lambert, S., & Judd, C. M. (2002). On the role of familiarity with units of measurement in categorical accentuation: Tajfel and Wilkes (1963) revisited and replicated. *Psychological Science,* 13, 4, 380–383.

Cottingham, J. (1992). The Cambridge Companion to Descartes. Cambridge University Press.

Craik, F. I. M., & Lockhart, R. S. (1972). Levels of processing: A framework for memory research. *Journal of Verbal Learning and Verbal Behavior, 11,* 671–684.

Craik, F.I.M. and Tulving, E. (1975). Depth of processing and the retention of words in episodic memory. *Journal of Experimental Psychology: General, 104,* 268–294.

Crandall, C. S. (1988). Social contagion of binge eating. *Journal of Personality and Social Psychology, 55,* 588–598.

Crooks, R., & Stein, J. (1991). *Psychology: Science, behaviour, and life (2nd, ed.).* Fort Worth, TX: Holt, Rinehart.

Crosby, F., Bromley, S. & Saxe, L. (1980). Recent Unobtrusive Studies of Black and White discrimination and prejudice: a literature review. *Psychological Bulletin,* 87, 546–63.

Crutchfield, R.S. (1955). Conformity and character. *American Psychologist, 10,* 191–198.

Curtiss, S. (1977). *Genie: A linguistic study of a modern-day 'wild child'.* New York: Academic Press.

Czeisler, C.A. *et al.* (1981). Chronotherapy: resetting the circadian clocks of patients with delayed sleep phase insomnia. *Sleep,* Vol 4: pp 1–2.

Darwin, C. (1859) The Origin of Species by Means of Natural Selection. London: John Murray.

Darwin, C. (1871) The Descent of Man and Selection in Relation to Sex. London: John Murray.

Darwin, C. (1871) The Expression of Emotion in Man and Animals. London: John Murray.

Davey, A. (1983). *Learning to be Prejudiced: Growing up in Multi-Ethnic Britain* London: Edward Arnold Publishers.

Davison, G. C. & Neale, J.N. (1994). *Abnormal Psychology* (6th. ed.), New York: John Wiley & Sons, Inc.

Delfabbro, P.H. & Winefield, A.H. (1999). Poker-machine gambling: An analysis of within session characteristics. British Journal of Psychology, 90, 425–39.

Delgado, J.M.R. (1969). *Physical Control of the Mind.* New York: Harper & Row.

Denmark, F., Paludi, M.A. & Lott, B. (2008). *Psychology of Women: A Handbook of Issues and Theories* Greenwood Publishing Group.

Dennerstein L., (1995). Mental health, work, and gender. *Int J Health Serv.* 25(3): 503–9.

Dennis, W. (1960). Causes of retardation among institutional children*: Iran. Journal of Genetic Psychology.* 96, 47–59.

Derrida, J. (1987). *The Post Card: From Socrates to Freud and Beyond* 2nd edition. Chicago University Press.

Deutsch M & Gerard H B. (1955). A study of normative and informational social influences upon individual judgment. *Journal of Abnormal Social Psychology* 51:629–36.

Deutsch, M. & Collins, M. E. (1951). *Interracial Housing: A Psychological Evaluation of a Social Experiment.* University of Minnesota Press, Minneapolis.

DiCara, L. V., & Miller, N. E. (1968). Changes in heart rate instrumentally learned by curarized rats: shaping, and specificity to discriminative stimulus as avoidance responses. *Journal of Comparative Physiological Psychology* 65(1): 8–12.

Dickerson, L.M., Mazyck, P.J. & Hunter, M.H. (2003*).* Premenstrual syndrome. American Family Physician; 67:1743–52.

Diener, E. (1980). *Deindividuation: The absence of self-awareness and self-regulation in group members.* In P. B. Paulus *(*Ed.), The psychology of group influence (2nd Ed) Hillsdale, NJ: Erlbaum.

Disability Discrimination Act 1995.

Dollard J., Doob L. W., Miller N. E., Mowrer O. H., and Sears R. R. (1939). *Frustration and aggression.* New Haven: Yale University Freer.

Dollard, J. and Miller, N. E. (1950). *Personality and psychotherapy.* New York: McGraw-Hill.

Dostoyevsky, F. (1880). *The Brothers Karamazov.* Oxford University Press.

DSM IV (1994). *American Psychological Association.*

Dunckner, K. (1939). The influence of past experience upon perceptual properties. *American Journal of Psychology,* 52, 255–265.

Durkin, K. (1995). *Developmental Social Psychology: From Infancy to Old Age* (Cambridge Mass: Blackwell).

Dworkin, B.R. (1993). *Learning and Physiological Regulation.* Chicago: University of Chicago Press.

Eagly, A.H. & Carli, L.L. (1981). Sex of researchers and sex-typed communications as determinants of sex differences in influenceability: A meta-analysis of social influence studies. Psychological Bulletin, 90, 1–20.

Ebbinghaus, H. (1885). *Über das Gedächtnis.* Leipzig: Duncker & Humbolt.

Ebbinghaus, H. (1885). *On Memory.* Leipzig: Duncker.

Ebbinghaus, H. (1913). *Memory. A Contribution to Experimental Psychology.* New York: Teachers College, Columbia University (Reprinted Bristol: Thoemmes Press, 1999).

Effective Health Care (1999). Drug treatments of schizophrenia. *Effective Health Care,* 5, 6.

Eich, J.E., Weingartner, H., Stillman, R.C. & Gillin, J.C. (1975). State-dependent accessability of retrieval cues in the retention of a categorized list *Journal of Verbal Learning and Verbal Behaviour* 14: 408–417.

Eisler, R. M., & Blalock, J. A. (1991). Masculine gender role stress: Implications for the assessment of men. *Clinical Psychology Review,* 11, 45–60.

Elkind, D. (1980). Erik Erikson's eight ages of man. New York Times Magazine, 5 April.

Elliott, J. (1968). A Class Divided Yale University Films, Frontline, WGBH, Boston.

Ellis, A. (1973). Humanistic Psychotherapy. New York: Julian Press.

Ellis, W.D. (1938). A Source Book of Gestalt Psychology. New York: Harcourt, Brace & World.

Erikson, E.H. (1963). *Childhood and Society* (2nd edition). New York: Norton.

Erikson, E.H. (1968). *Identity: Youth and Crisis.* New York: Norton.

Erikson, E.H. (1980). *Identity and the Life Cycle.* New York: Norton.

Estes, W. K. (1972). *An associative basis for coding and organization in memory.* In A. W. Melton & E. Martin (Eds.), *Coding processes in human memory* (pp161–190). Washington, D. C.: Winston.

Eysenck, M.W. & Keane, M.T. (2005). *Cognitive Psychology: A Student's Handbook.* Psychology Press.

Eysenck, M.W. (2001). *Principles of Cognitive Psychology.* Psychology Press.

Eysenck, H. J. (1954). *The Psychology of Politics.* London, Routledge and Kagan Paul.

Eysenck, H. J. (1961). Personality and social attitudes. *Journal of Social Psychology,* 53, 243–248.

Eysenck, H.J. (1947). *Dimensions of Personality.* London: RKP.

Eysenck, H.J. (1952). The effects of psychotherapy: An evaluation. *Journal of Consulting Psychology,* 16, 319–324.

Eysenck, H.J. (1985). *Decline and Fall of the Freudian Empire.* Harmondsworth: Penguin.

Fantz, R. L. (*1961*). The origin of form perception. *Scientific American,* 204, 66–72.

Faulkner, A. (1997). *Suicide and deliberate self-harm* Mental Health Foundation.

Fechner, G.T. (1860). Elemente der Psychophysik. Leipzig: Bretkopf and Hartnel.

Feshbach, S. & Singer, R.D. (1972). Television and aggression: A reply to Liebert, Sobol and Davidson, and Sobol review and response. Television and Social Behaviour, Vol. V.

Festinger, L. & Carlsmith, J. M. (1959). Cognitive consequences of forced compliance. *Journal of Abnormal and Social Psychology,* 58, 203–210.

Festinger, L. (1957). *A theory of cognitive dissonance.* Evanston, Ill: Row Peterson.

Feuk, L., Carson, A.R., & Scherer, S.W. (2006). Structural variation in the human genome *Nature Reviews Gen*etics 7, 85–97.

Fisher S. & Greenberg R. (1977). The Scientific Credibility of Freud's Theories and Therapy. Harvester.

Fisher, R.P. & Geiselman, R.E. (1988). Enhancing eyewitness memory with the cognitive interview. In M.M. Gruneberg, P.E. Morris & R.N. Sykes (Eds) Practical Aspects of Memory: Current Research and Issues. Vol 1. Memory in Everyday Life. Chichester: Wiley.

Fisher, R.P., Geiselman, R.E. & Amador, M. (1989). Field test of the cognitive interview: enhancing the recollection of actual victims and witnesses of crime. Journal of Applied Psychology, 74, 722–727.

Flanagan, C. (2000) Early Socialisation: Routledge Modular Psychology Series.

Flanagan, C. (1999). Early Socialisation: Sociability and Attachment. Routledge Modular Psychology.

Folkman, S., Lazarus, R.S., Dunkel-Schetter, C., DeLongis, A. & Gruen, R.J. (1986). Dynamics of a stressful encounter, Cognitive appraisal, coping and encounter outcomes. Journal of Personality and Social Psychology, 50: 992–1003.

Fontana, A. M., Hyra, D., Godfrey, L. & Cermak, L. (1999). Impact of a peer-led stress inoculation training intervention on state anxiety and heart rate. Journal of Stress Medicine. 15:69–77. 31.

Fouts, R.S., Fouts, D.H. & Van Cantfort, T.E. (1989). The infant Loulis learns signs from cross-fostered chimpanzees. In Gardner, R.A., Gardner, B.T. & Van Cantfort, T.E. (Eds.), Teaching Sign Language to Chimpanzees. Albany, NY: SUNY Press.

Frankenhauser, M. (1983). Stress in Professionals and Non-Professionals, Men and Women. Innovation Abstracts; 5: 9.

Frankenhauser M. et al. (1991).Women, Work and Health. Stress and Opportunities. Plenum Press, New York.

Freedman, J. L., & Fraser, S. C., (1966). Compliance Without Pressure: The foot-in-the-door technique, Journal of Personality and Social Psychology, 4, 196–202.

Freeman, D. (1983). Margaret Mead and Samoa. The Making and Unmaking of an Anthropological Myth. Cambridge: Harvard University Press.

French, C.C., & Richards, A. (1993). Clock this! An everyday example of a schema-driven error in memory. British Journal of Psychology, 84, pp. 249–53.

Freud, A. (1936) The Ego and Mechanisms of Defence. London: Chatto and Windus.

Freud, S. (1924) 'The passing of the Oedipus complex.' In E. Jones (Ed.) Collected Papers of Sigmund Freud, Volume 5, New York: Basic Books.

Freud, S. (1933) New Introductory Lectures on Psychoanalysis. New York: Norton.

Freud, S. (1949) An Outline of Psychoanalysis. London: Hogarth Press.

Freud, S. Standard Edition of the Complete Psychological Works of Sigmund Freud. (Trans.) Strachey, J. Vol. IV, The Interpretation of Dreams (I) (1900).

Freud, S. Standard Edition of the Complete Psychological Works of Sigmund Freud. (Trans.) Strachey, J. Vol. V, The Interpretation of Dreams (II) and On Dreams (1900–1901).

Freud, S. Standard Edition of the Complete Psychological Works of Sigmund Freud. (Trans.) Strachey, J. Vol. VI, The Psychopathology of Everyday Life (1901).

Freud, S. Standard Edition of the Complete Psychological Works of Sigmund Freud. (Trans.) Strachey, J. Vol. VII, A Case of Hysteria, Three Essays on Sexuality and Other Works (1901–1905).

Freud, S. Standard Edition of the Complete Psychological Works of Sigmund Freud. (Trans.) Strachey, J. Vol. X, The Cases of 'Little Hans' and 'The Rat Man' (1909).

Freud, S. Standard Edition of the Complete Psychological Works of Sigmund Freud. (Trans.) Strachey, J. Vol. XV, Introductory Lectures on Psychoanalysis (Parts I and II) (1915–1916).

Freud, S. Standard Edition of the Complete Psychological Works of Sigmund Freud. (Trans.) Strachey, J. Vol. XVI, Introductory Lectures on Psychoanalysis (Part III) (1916–1917).

Freud, S. Standard Edition of the Complete Psychological Works of Sigmund Freud. (Trans.) Strachey, J. Vol. XVIII, Beyond the Pleasure Principle, Group Psychology and Other Works (1920–1922).

Freud, S. Standard Edition of the Complete Psychological Works of Sigmund Freud. (Trans.) Strachey, J. Vol. XIX, The Ego and the Id and Other Works (1923–1925).

Friedmand, M., Rosenmann, R.H. (1974). Type A Behaviour and Your Heart. London, Wildwood House.

Funk, SC (1992). Hardiness: A review of theory and research. Health Psychology, 11,–345

Galton, F. (1869). Hereditary Genius: An Inquiry onto its Laws and Consequences. London: Macmillan.

Gamson, W., Fireman, B. & Rytina, S. (1982). Encounters with Unjust Authority. Homewood, Illinois: Dorsey Press.

Garcia, J. & Koelling, R.A. (1966). Relation of the cue to consequence in avoidance learning. Psychonomic Science, 4, 123–124.

Gardner, B.T. & Gardner, R.A. (1969). Teaching sign language to a chimpanzee. Science, 165 (3894), 664–672.

Gardner, B.T. & Gardner, R.A. (1998). Development of phrases in the early utterances of children and cross-fostered chimpanzees. Human Evolution, 13, 161–188.

Gardner, R.A. & Gardner, B.T. (1998). Ethological study of early language. Human Evolution, 13, 189–207.

Geiselman, R.E., Fisher, R., Mackinnon, D. & Holland, H. (1986). Enhancement of eyewitness memory with the cognitive interview. American Journal of Psychology, 99, 385–401.

Gelder, M.G., Lopez-Ibor, J.J. & Andreasen, N.C. (2000). The New Oxford Textbook of Psychiatry (2nd edition), Oxford: Oxford University Press.

Gershon, E.S. & Rieder R.O. (1992). Major disorders of mind and brain. Scientific American; September 88.

Giddens, A. (2006). Sociology (5th edition), Polity, Cambridge.

Glanzer, M. and Cunitz, A.R. (1966). Two storage mechanisms in free recall. Journal of Verbal Learning and Verbal Behaviour, 5, 351–60.

Glasgow University Social and Public Health Unit 1999 survey.

Glassman, W.E. (1995). Approaches to Psychology (2nd edition). Buckingham: Open University.

Godden, D.R. & Baddeley, A.D. (1975). Context-dependent memory in two natural environments: on land and underwater. British Journal of Psychology, 66 (3): 325–31.

Goffman, E. (1971). The Presentation of Self in Everyday Life. Harmondsworth: Penguin.

Goldfarb, W. (1943). The effects of early institutional care on adolescent personality Journal of Experimental Education, 12, 106–129.

Goldfarb, W. (1943). Infant rearing and Problem Behaviour, American Journal of Orthopsychiatry 13: 249–65.

Goldstein, N. J., Cialdini, R. B., & Griskevicius, V. (2008). A room with a viewpoint: Using normative appeals to motivate environmental conservation in a hotel setting. Journal of Consumer Research, 35, 472–482.

Goodwin, D., Powell, B., Bremer, D., Hoine, H., and Stern, J. (1969). Alcohol and recall: state-dependent effects in man, Science, 163, 1358–1360.

Goossens, F. A., & Melhuish, E. C. (1996). On the ecological validity of measuring the sensitivity of professional caregivers: The laboratory versus the nursery. European Journal of Psychology of Education, 11, 169–176.

Gottesman, I.I. & Shields, J. (1976). A critical review of recent adoption, twin and family studies of schizophrenia: Behavioural genetics perspectives. Schizophrenia Bulletin, 2, 360–398.

Gottesman, I.I. (1991). Schizophrenia Genesis. New York: W.H. Freeman.

Gough,H.G. & Bradley, P. (1996). *CPI Manual*. Ed.3. Palo Alto, CA: Consulting Psychologists Press.

Gregory, R.L. & Coleman, A. (Eds.) Sensation and Perception. London: Longman.

Gregory, R.L. & Wallace, J. (1963). Recovery from Early Blindness. Cambridge: Heffer.

Gregory, R.L. (1972). *'Visual illusions.'* In B.M. Foss (Ed) New Horizons in Psychology, 1. Harmondsworth: Penguin.

Gregory, R.L. (1973). *Eye and Brain* (2nd edition). New York: World Universities Library.

Gregory, R.L. (1980). Perceptions as hypotheses. *Philosophical Transactions of the Royal Society of London*, Series B, 290, 181–197.

Griffiths, M. (1990). The cognitive psychology of gambling. Journal of Gambling Studies, 6, 401–407.

Griffiths, M. (1997b). Selling hope: the psychology of the National Lottery. Psychology Review, 4 (1), 26–30.

Gross, R. (1995). *Themes, Issues, and Debates in Psychology*. London: Hodder & Stoughton.

Gross, R. (1996). *Psychology: The Science of Mind and Behaviour* (3rd edition). London: Hodder & Stoughton.

Gross, R. (1999). *Key Studies in Psychology*. London: Hodder & Stoughton.

Gross, R. (2001). *Psychology: The Science of Mind and Behaviour* (4th edition). London: Hodder & Stoughton.

Gross, R., McIlveen, R., Coolican, H., Clamp, A. & Russell, J. (2000). *Psychology: A New Introduction*. London: Hodder & Stoughton.

Guiton, P. (1959). Socialization and imprinting in brown leghorn chicks. *Journal of Animal Behaviour*, 7, 26.

Gunter, B., Berry, C. & Clifford, B. R. (1981). Proactive interference effects with television news items: Further evidence. *Journal Experimental Psychology of Learning Memory and Cognition*. 7: 480–487.

Haber, R.N. (1979). Twenty years of haunting eidetic imagery: Where's the ghost? *Behavioural and Brain Sciences*, 2, 583–629.

Haney, C., Banks, W.C. & Zimbardo, P.G. (1973) A study of prisoners and guards in a simulated prison. *Naval Research Review*, 30, 4–17.

Harlow, H., (1958). The Nature of Love. *American Psychologist* 13: 673–85.

Harlow, H., (1959). *The Development of Affectional Patterns in Infant Monkeys*. In B. M. Foss ed., Determinants of Infant Behaviour. London: Methuen.

Harlow, H.F., and Harlow, M.K. (1966). *Social Deprivation in Monkeys*. In M. L. Haimowitz and N. R. Haimowitz eds. *Human Development*. New York: Thomas Y. Crowell.

Hayes, N. & Lemon, N. (1990). Stimulating positive cultures in growing companies. Leadership & Organisational Change Management, 11(7), 17–21.

Hayes, N. (1998). *Foundations of Psychology* (2nd edition). Surrey: Nelson.

Hazan, C., & Shaver, P. R. (1987). Romantic love conceptualised as an attachment process. *Journal of Personality and Social Psychology, 52*, 511–524.

Head, H., Rivers, W.H.R., Holmes, G.M., Sherren, J., Thompson, H.T. & Riddoch, G., Studies in Neurology. *2 volumes. London, H. Frowde, Hodder & Stoughton, 1920.*

Heather, N. (1976). *Radical Perspectives in Psychology*. London: Methuen.

Hebb D. *(1949).* The organization of behaviour, *New York: Wiley.*

Heim, A. (1970). *Intelligence and Personality – Their Assessment and Relationship.* Harmondsworth: Penguin.

Herpertz-Dahlmann, B., Hebebrand, J., Müller, B., Herpertz, S., Heussen, N. & Remschmidt, H. (2001). Prospective 10-year Follow-up in Adolescent Anorexia Nervosa—Course, Outcome, Psychiatric Comorbidity, and Psychosocial Adaptation. *The Journal of Child Psychology and Psychiatry and Allied Disciplines*, 42, pp 603–612.

Higher Still Development Unit (2000). Higher Still Support Materials HSDU: Edinburgh, Scotland.

Higley, J.D., Suomi, S.J. & Linnoila M. (1992). A longitudinal assessment of CSF monoamine metabolite and plasma cortisol concentrations in young rhesus monkeys. *Biological Psychiatry*. 32:127–145.

Hilgard, E.R., Atkinson, R.L. & Atkinson, R.C. (1979). *Introduction to Psychology* (7th edition). New York: Harcourt Brace Jovanovich.

Hill, G., (2001) *AS Level Psychology through diagrams* Oxford Revision Guides.

Hiroto, D. S., & Seligman, M. E. P. (1975). Generality of learned helplessness in man. *Journal of Personality and Social Psychology*, 31, 311–327.

Hobbes, T. (1651) *Leviathan*. London: Dent, 1914.

Hoek, H. & van Hoeken, D. (2003). Review of the prevalence and incidence of eating disorders. *International Journal of Eating Disorders* 34: 383–96.

Hofling, C.K. *et al.* (1966). An Experimental Study of Nurse-Physician Relationships. *Journal of Nervous and Mental Disease* 141:171–180.

Holmes, T.H. & Rahé, R.H. (1967). The social readjustment rating scale. *Journal of Psychosomatic Research*, 11, 213.

Homicide in Scotland 2000, Scottish Executive 2001.

Honzik, M.P., MacFarlane, H.W. & Allen, L. (1948). The stability of mental test performance between two and eighteen years. *Journal of Experimental Education*, 17, 309–324.

Howie, D. (1952). Perceptual defence. *Psychological Review*, 59, 308–315.

Hraba, J., & Grant, J. (1970). Black is beautiful: A re-examination of racial preference and identification. *Journal of Personality and Social Psychology*, 16:398–402.

Huang, Y.C. & Mathers, N.J. (2007). An investigation of Postnatal depression and the experience of South Asian marriage migrant women in Taiwan using the Edinburgh Postnatal Depression Scale and semi-structured interviews. *International Journal of Nursing Studies.*

Hull, C.L. *Principles of Behaviour.* New York: Appleton-Century-Crofts.

Hume, D. (1757). *Four Dissertations, IV, Of The Standard of Taste.* London: Millar.

Hunt. R.R., & Worthen, J.B. (2006). *Distinctiveness and Memory* Oxford University Press.

Hyde, T. S., & Jenkins, J. J. (1973*)*. Recall for words as a function of semantic, graphic, and syntactic orienting tasks. *Journal of Verbal Learning and Verbal Behaviour, 12,* 489–498.

Hyman, H. H., & Sheatsley, P. B. (1954). *The Authoritarian Personality: A methodological critique.* In R. Christie & M. Jahoda (Eds.), Studies in the scope and method of "The Authoritarian Personality" Glencoe, IL: Free Press.

Iversen, L.L. (1979). The chemistry of the brain. *Scientific American*, 241, 134–149.

Izard, C. (1977). Human Emotions. New York: Plenum Press.

Jacobs, M. (1992). *Freud*. London: Sage Publications.

Jahoda, M. (1958). Current Concepts of Positive Mental Health. New York: Basic Books.

James, W. (1884). What is an emotion? *Mind*, 9, 188–205.

James, W. (1890). *The Principles of Psychology*. New York: Henry Holt & Company.

Javornisky, G. (1979). Task content and sex differences in conformity. *Journal of Social Psychology, 108*, 213–220.

Jenkins, J. and Dallenbach, K. (1924). Obliviscence during sleep and waking. *American Journal of Psychology* . 35, 605–612.

Jenness, A. (1932). The Role of Discussion of Changing Opinion regarding a Matter of Fact, *Journal of Abnormal and Social Psychology*, Vol. 27 pp.279–96.

Jensen, A.R. (1969). How much can we boost IQ and scholastic achievement? *Harvard Educational Review* 39: 1–123 8.

Johnson, J.H. & Sarason, I.G. (1978). Life stress, depression and anxiety: internal-external control as a moderator variable, *Journal of Psychosomatic Research*, 22: 205–8.

Johnstone, E.C., Owens, D.G.C., Crow, T.J. et al. (1989). Temporal lobe structure as determined by nuclear magnetic resonance in schizophrenics and bipolar affective disorder. *Journal of Neurological and Neurosurgical Psychiatry*; 52:736–741.

Jones, J.M. (1972). *Prejudice and Racism* Reading, Mass: Addison-Wesley Publishing Company.

Jung, C.G. (1963). *Memories, Dreams, Reflections*. London: Collins/RKP.

Jung, C.G. (1964). (Ed) *Man and His Symbols*. London: Aldus–Jupiter Books.

Kagan, J. (1984). *The nature of the child.* New York: Basic Books.

Kagan, J. (1989). Temperamental contributions to social behaviour. *American Psychologist*, Vol. 44, no. 4, 668–674.

Kagitçibasi. Ç. (1996). *Family and Human Development across Cultures: A View from the Other Side.* Mahwah: Lawrence Erlbaum.

Kamin, L.J. (1974). *The Science and Politics of IQ.* Potomac, N.J.: Lawrence Erlbaum Associates.

Kanner, A.D., Coyne, J.C., Schaefer, C. & Lazarus, R.S. (1981). Comparison of two modes of stress measurement: daily hassles and uplifts versus major life events. *Journal of Behavioural Medicine* 4: 1–39.

Karlins, M., Coffman, T.L. & Walters, G. (1969). On the fading of social stereotypes: Studies in three generations of college students. *Journal of Personality and Social Psychology*. 13:1–16.

Kaye, K. (Ed.) (1982). *The Mental and Social Life of Babies: How Parents Create Persons.* Chicago: University of Chicago Press.

Keegan, G. (2002). Delirium on helium. *Psychology Review*, Vol 9 Phillip Allen Updates.

Keegan, G. (2002). Developmental Psychology Staff Resource Pack Advanced Higher. Dundee: Learning and Teaching Scotland.

Keegan, G. (2003). Cognitive Psychology Staff Resource Pack Advanced Higher. Dundee: Learning and Teaching Scotland.

Keirsey, D. (1978). Please Understand Me II: Temperament, Character, Intelligence (1st Ed. ed.). Prometheus Nemesis Book Co.

Keller, M.B., Lavori, P.W., Rice, J., Coryell, W. & Hirschfeld, R.M. (1986). The persistent risk of chronicity in recurrent episodes of nonbipolar major depressive disorder: a prospective follow-up. *American Journal of Psychiatry.* Jan;143(1):24–28.

Kellogg, W.N. & Kellogg, L.A. (1933) *The Ape and the Child.* New York: McGraw Hill.

Kelman, H. (1958). Compliance, identification, and internalisation: Three processes of attitude change. *Journal of Conflict Resolution*, 1, 51–60.

Kempermann, G. & Gage, F.H. (1999). New nerve cells for the adult brain. *Scientific American*, 280 (5), 38–43.

Kettlewell, H.B.D. (1955). Selection experiments on industrial melanism in the Lepidoptera. *Heredity*, 9:323–42.

Keverne, E.B., Kendrick, K. (1994). Oxytocin facilitation of maternal behaviour: adolescent perceptions of attachment to mother and father. *Infant Behav. Dev.* 7: 405–412. 679.

Kilpatrick, D.G., Acierno, R., Saunders, B., Resnick, H.S., Best, C.L. & Schnurr, P.P. (2000). Risk factors for adolescent substance abuse and dependence: Data from a national sample. *Journal of Consulting and Clinical Psychology* 68(1):19–30.

Kobasa, S.C. (1979). Stressful life events, personality and health: An inquiry into hardiness. *Journal of Personality and Social Psychology*, 37: 1–11.

Koffka, K. (1935). *Principles of Gestalt Psychology*. London: Lund Humphries.

Kohler, W. (1947). *Gestalt Psychology*. New York: Liveright.

Kohn M. (1977). *Class and Conformity* (2nd Ed.). Chicago: University of Chicago Press.

Koluchová, J. (1972). Severe deprivation in twins: A case study. *Journal of Child Psychology and Psychiatry*, 13, 107–114.

Koluchová, J. (1991). Severely deprived twins after 22 years observation. *Studia Psychologica*, 33, 23–28.

Krech, D., Crutchfield, R.S. & Ballachey, E.L. (1962). *Individual in society*. New York: McGraw-Hill

Kreger, D.W. (1995). Self-esteem, stress, and depression among graduate students. *Psychol Rep.* 76(1): 345–6.

Kreuz, L. & Rose, R. (1972). 'Assessment of aggressive behaviour and plasma testosterone in a young criminal population.' *Psychosomatic Medicine*, 34, 321–2.

Kroll, J. A. (1973). A reappraisal of psychiatry in the Middle Ages. *Archives of General Psychiatry*, 29, 276–283.

Kuhn, T.S. (1970). *The Structure of Scientific Revolutions* (2nd edition). Chicago: Chicago University Press.

Laing, R.D. & Esterton, A. (1964). *Sanity, Madness and the Family*. London: Tavistock.

Laing, R.D. (1959). *The Divided Self: An Existential Study of Sanity and Madness*. London: Tavistock.

Laing, R.D. (1961). *Self and Others*. London: Tavistock.

Laing, R.D. (1967). *The Politics of Experience and the Bird of Paradise*. Harmondsworth: Penguin.

Laird, J.D. Self-attribution of emotion. The effects of facial expression on the quality of emotional experience. *Journal of Personality and Social Psychology*, 29, 475–486.

Lam, D.H., Hayward, P., Watkins, E. *et al.* (2005). Relapse prevention in patients with bipolar disorder: cognitive therapy outcome after 2 years. *American Journal of Psychiatry*; 162:324–329.

Lamb, M.E., Thompson, R.M., Gardner, W., Charnov, E.L. & Estes, D. (1984). Security of Infantile attachment as assessed in the 'Strange Situation'; its study and biological interpretations. *Behavioural and Brain Sciences*, 7, 127–147.

Lang, S. (1998). *Men as women, women as men: Changing gender in Native American cultures*, Austin, TX: University of Texas Press.

Lange, C. (1885). *Om Sindsbevaegelser. Et psychko. Fisiolog. Studie.* English translation in Dunlap, K. (Ed) The Emotions. London: Haffner, 1967.

Langer, E.J. and Rodin, J. (1976). The effects of choice and enhanced personal responsibility for the aged: a field experiment in an institutional setting. *Journal of Personality and Social Psychology* 34, 30–40.

Larsen R. J. and Diener E. (1987). Emotional response intensity as an individual difference characteristic. *Journal of Research in Personality* 21: 1–39.

Latané, B. & Rodin, J. (1969). A lady in distress. Inhibiting effects of friends and strangers on bystander intervention. *Journal of Experimental Social Psychology*, 5, 189–202.

Latane, B., & Wolf, S. (*1981*). The social impact of majorities and minorities. *Psychological Review*, 88, 438–453.

Lazarus, R.S., & Folkman, S. (1984). *Stress, Appraisal and Coping*. New York: Springer.

Le Bon, G. (1995). *The Crowd: A study of the popular mind*. London: Transaction Publishers. (Original work published in 1895).

Lennenberg, E.H. (1967). Biological Foundations of Language. New York: Wiley.

Levine, J.M. (1989). *Reaction to Opinion Deviance in Small Groups.* In P. Paulus (ed.): Psychology of Group Influence. Hillsdale, NJ: Lawrence Erlbaum.

Levinger, G. & Clark, J. (1961). Emotional factors in the forgetting of word associations. *Journal of Abnormal and Social Psychology*, 62, 99–105.

Lewin, K. (1935). *A Dynamic Theory of Personality.* New York: McGraw-Hill.

Lewin, K. (1951). Field theory in social Science. New York: Harper & Row.

Lewin, K., Lippitt, R., & White, RK. (1939). Patterns of Aggressive Behavior in Experimentally Created social climates." *Journal of Social Psychology*. 10, 271–299.

Lieberman, S. (1956). The effects of changes in roles on the attitudes of role occupants. *Human Relations*, 9, 385–402.

Liebert R.M. & Sprafkin J. (1988). *The Early Window: Effects of Television on Children and Youth.* New York: Pergamon Press.

Likert, R. (1932). 'A technique for the measurement of attitudes.' *Archives of Psychology*, 22, 140.

Lindsay, P. H., & Norman, D. A. (1977). *Human information processing: An introduction to psychology* (2d ed.). New York: Academic Press.

Lindzey, G. & Aronson, E. (Eds.), (1985). *Handbook of social psychology* (3rd Ed., Vol. 1, pp. 509–566). New York: Random House.

Locke, J. (1690). *An Essay Concerning Human Understanding.* New York: Mendon (reprinted, 1964).

Loeber, R., Farrington, D.P., Stouthamer-Loeber, M., & Van Kammen, W.B. (1998). *Antisocial behaviour and mental health problems: Explanatory factors in childhood and adolescence.* Mahwah, NJ: Lawrence Erlbaum Associates.

Loftus, E.F. & Burns, T.E. (1982). Mental shock can produce retrograde amnesia. *Memory and Cognition*, 10, 318–323.

Loftus, E.F. & Palmer, J.C. (1974). Reconstruction of automobile destruction. An example of the interaction between language and memory. *Journal of Verbal Learning and Verbal Behaviour*, 13, 585–589.

Loftus, E.F. & Zanni, G. (1975). Eyewitness testimony. The influence of wording on a question. *Bulletin of the Psychonomic Society*, 5, 86–88.

Lorenz, K. (1961). *King Solomon's Ring* Translated by Marjorie Kerr Wilson. Methuen, London.

Lowe, G. (1995). *Alcohol and drug addiction*. In A.A. Lazarus & A.M. Coleman (Eds.) Abnormal Psychology. London: Longman.

Maccoby, E. E. (1990). Gender and Relationships: A Developmental Account. *American Psychologist* 45:513–520.

Maddi, S.R. (1996). Personality Theories: A Comparative Analysis (6th edition). Pacific Grove, CA: Brooks/Cole.

Maddi, S.R., & Kobasa, S.C. (1984). *The hardy executive: Health under stress.* Homewood, IL: Dow Jones-Irwin.

Main, M. & Solomon, J. (1986). *Discovery of an insecure-disorganized*/disoriented *attachment pattern*. In T. B. Brazelton & M. W. Yogman (Eds.), Affective *development in infancy*. (95–124)

Malinowski, B. (1929) The Sexual Life of Savages. New York: Harcourt Brace Jovanovich.

Manic Street Preachers, 'I'm Not Working.' Lyrics, Nick Jones.

Markle, S. (1969) *Good Frames and Bad* (2nd edition). New York: Wiley.

Marr, D. (1982). *Vision: A Computational Investigation into the Human Representation and Processing of Visual Information.* San Francisco, CA: W.H. Freeman.

Martin S.M., Manning J.T. & Dowrick C.F. (1999). Fluctuating asymmetry, relative digit length and depression in men. *Evolution and Human Behaviour,* 20: 203–14.

Martin, P. & Bateson, P. (1996). *Measuring Behaviour* (2nd edition). Cambridge, UK: Cambridge University Press.

Martinch, A. P. (1999). Hobbes: A Biography, *Cambridge: Cambridge University Press.*

Maslow, A. (1968). *Towards a Psychology of Being* (2nd edition). New York: Van Nostrand Reinhold.

Maslow, A. (1970). *Motivation and Personality.* (2nd edition). New York: Van Nostrand Reinhold.

Matteson, M. T., & Ivancevich, J. N. (1982). *Managing job stress and worker health.* New York: Free Press.

Mayall, B. & Petrie, P. (1983). *Childminding and Day Nurseries: what kind of care?* London: Heinemann.

McCloskey, M., Wible, C. G. & Cohen, N. J. (1988). Is there a special flashbulb-memory mechanism? *Journal of Experimental Psychology: General.* Vol. 117 (2) 171–181.

McDougall, W. (1908) An Introduction to Social Psychology. London: Methuen.

McGeoch JA and McDonald WT (1931). Meaningful relation and retroactive inhibition. *American Journal of Psychology, 43:*579–588.

Mead M., (1928) *Coming of Age in Samoa.* New York: Morrow.

Meichenbaum, D. (1993). *Stress inoculation training: A twenty year update.* In R. L. Woolfolk and P. M. Lehrer (Eds.), Principles and practices of stress management. New York: Guilford Press.

Memon, A. & Stevenage, S.V. (1996a). Interviewing witnesses: What works and what doesn't? *Psycoloquy,* 7(6).

Memon, A. & Stevenage, S.V. (1996b). A clarification of the importance of comparison groups and accuracy rates with the CI. *Psycoloquy,* 7(41).

Meyer, R. G., & Salmon, P. (1988). *Abnormal psychology* (2nd ed.) Boston: Allyn & Bacon.

Milgram, S. (1961). Nationality and Conformity; with a biographical Sketch. *Scientific American,* 205: 34; 45–51.

Milgram, S. (1963). Behavioural study of obedience. *Journal of Abnormal and Social Psychology*, 67, 371–8.

Milgram, S. (1974). *Obedience to Authority*, Harper and Row.

Milgram, Stanley. (1974), *Obedience to Authority; An Experimental View*. Harper Collins.

Miller, G.A. (1956). The magical number seven, plus or minus two. Some limits on our capacity for information processing. *Psychological Review*, 63, 81–97.

Miller, G.A. (1978). The acquisition of word meaning. *Child Development*, 49, 999–1004.

Miller, N. E. (1941). The frustration-aggression hypothesis. *Psychological Review*, 48, 337–342.

Miller, N. E., & Bugelski, R. (1948). Minor studies in aggression: The influence of frustrations imposed by the ingroup on attitudes toward outgroups. *Journal of Psychology,* 25, 437–442.

Miller, W. R., & Seligman, M. E. P. (1975). Learned helplessness, depression, and anxiety. *Journal of Nervous and Mental Disease;*161, 347–357.

Milner, B. (1971). Interhemispheric differences in the localization of psychological processes in man. *British Medical Bulletin*, 27, 272–7.

Milos, G., Spindler A., Schnyder, U. and Fairburn, C.G. (2005) Instability of eating disorder diagnoses: prospective study. *British Journal of Psychiatry*, 187, 573–578.

Morris, C.C., Bransford, J.D. & Franks, J.J. (1977). Levels of processing versus transfer appropriate processing. *Journal of Verbal Learning and Verbal Behaviour.* 16, 519–533.

Morris, T., Greer, H.S. & White, P. (1979). Psychological and social adjustment to mastectomy: a study into psychiatric problems in the first year after mastectomy. *British Medical Journal* 1(6161):456–456.

Moscovici, S. (1985). *Social Influence and Conformity.* In G. Lindzey & E. Aronson (Eds.), Handbook of social psychology (3rd ed.). New York: Random House.

Moscovici, S., & Zavalloni, M. (1969). The group as a polarizer of attitudes. *Journal of Personality and Social Psychology* 12, 125–135.

Mowrer, O.H. (1960) *Learning Theory and Behaviour.* New York: John Wiley.

Mudrack, P.E. & Farrell, G.M. (1995). An Examination of Functional Role Behaviour and its Consequences for Individuals in Group Settings. *Small Group Research*, November 1, 26(4): 542–571.

Neisser, U. (1982), *Memory Observed: Remembering in Natural Contexts*. San Francisco. W. H. Freeman.

Neisser, U. (1976) *Cognition and Reality*. San Francisco CA: W.H. Freeman.

Neisser, U. (1982). *Snapshots or benchmarks*? In U. Neisser & I.E. Hyman (Eds.), Memory observed: Remembering in natural contexts: 68–74. San Francisco: Worth Publishers.

Nelson, T. O. (1977). Repetition and depth of processing. *Journal of Verbal Learning and Verbal Behaviour,* 16, 151–172.

NICHD Early Child Care Research Network. (1977). The effects of infant child care on infant-mother attachment security: Results of the NICHD Study of Early Care. *Child Development*, 68(5), 860–879.

Nickerson, R. S. (1965). Short-term memory for complex meaningful visual configurations: A demonstration of, capacity. *Canadian Journal of Psychology*, 19, 155–160.

Nisbet, Robert A. (1967). The Sociological Tradition, Heinemann, London.

Norman, D. A. and Shallice, T. (1986). *Attention to action: Willed and automatic control of behaviour.* In Davidson, R. J., Schwartz, G. E., and Shapiro, D., editors, Consciousness and Self-Regulation: Advances in Research and Theory. Plenum Press.

Novak, M. A., & Harlow, H. F. (1975). Social recovery of monkeys isolated for the first years of life. *Developmental Psychology*, 11, 453–465.

Olds, J. & Milner, P. (1954). Positive reinforcement produced by electrical stimulation of the septal area and other regions of a rat brain. *Journal of Comparative and Physiological Psychology*, 47, 419–427.

Olds, J. (1956). Pleasure centres in the brain. *Scientific American*. October. 105–6.

Olds, J. (1958). Self-stimulation of the brain. *Science*. 127, 315–23.

Orne, M.T. & Holland, C.C. (1968). On the ecological validity of laboratory deceptions. *International Journal of Psychiatry*, 6, 282–93.

Orne, M.T. (1962). On the social psychology of the psychological experiment with particular reference to demand characteristics and their implications. *American Psychologist*, 17, 776–83.

Ornstein, R. (1986). *The Psychology of Consciousness* (2nd edition). Harmondsworth: Penguin.

O'Sullivan, C. & Yeager, C.P. (1989). *Communicative context and linguistic competence*. In R.A. Gardner, B.T. Gardner & T.E. Van Cantfort (Eds.), Teaching Sign Language to Chimpanzees. Albany, NY: SUNY Press.

Parten, M.B. (1950). *Surveys, Polls and Samples*. New York: Harper.

Paivio, A. (1971). *Imagery and verbal processes*. New York: Holt, Rinehart, and Winston.

Papagno, C., Valentine, T. & Baddeley, A. D. (1991). Phonological short-term memory and foreign–language learning. *Journal of Memory and Language*, 30, 331–347.

Parke, R. D. (1979). *Perspectives of father-infant interaction*. In J. D. Osofsky, J. D. (Ed.) Handbook of Infant Development. New York: Wiley, 549–590.

Parkes, K.R. (1990). Coping, negative affectivity, and the work environment: Addictive and interactive predictors of mental health. *Journal of Applied Psychology*, 75, 399–409.

Parkes, K.R. (1991). Locus of control as moderator: An explanation for additive versus interactive findings in the demand-discretion model of work stress. *British Journal of Psychology*, 82, 291–312.

Parkin, A.J. (1984). Amnesiac syndrome: A lesion-specific disorder, *Cortex*, 20, 479–508.

Paul, G. & Lentz, R. (1977). Psychosocial Treatment of Chronic Mental Patients. Cambridge, Mass.: Harvard University Press.

Pavlov, I.P. (1927). *Conditioned Reflexes*. Oxford: OUP.

Pechacek, T. F., Murray, D. M., Luepker, R. V., Mittelmark, M. B., Johnson, C. A. & Schultz, J. M. (1984). Measurement of adolescent smoking behaviour: Rationale and method. *Journal of Behavioural Medicine.* 7(1): 123–140.

Penfield, W. & Roberts, L. (1959). *Speech and Brain Mechanisms*. Princeton: Princeton University Press.

Pennington, D.C., Gillen, K. & Hill, P. (1999). *Social Psychology*. London, UK: Arnold.

Perrin, S. & Spencer, C. (1980). 'The Asch effect – a child of its time'. *Bulletin of the BPS,* 33, 405–406.

Peterson, L.R. & Peterson, M.J. (1959). Short-term retention of individual verbal items. *Journal of Experimental Psychology* 58, 193–8.

Peterson, L.R. & Seligman, M.E.P. (1984). Causal explanations as a risk factor for depression: Theory and evidence. *Psychological Review*, 91, 347–74.

Pettigrew, T. *et al.*, (1982). *Prejudice*. Cambridge, MA: Belknap Press.

Pettigrew, T. F. (1959). Regional differences in anti-Negro prejudice. *Journal of Abnormal and Social Psychology*, 49, *28–36*.

Pettigrew, T.F. (1958). Personality and sociocultural factors in intergroup attitudes: a cross-national comparison. *Journal of Conflict Resolution*, 2, 29–42.

Piaget, J. & Inhelder, B. (1956). *The Child's Conception of Space*. London: RKP.

Piaget, J. & Inhelder, B. (1969). *The Psychology of the Child*. London: RKP.

Piaget, J. (1950). *The Psychology of Intelligence*. London: Routledge & Kegan Paul.

Piaget, J. (1952). *The Child's Conception of Number*. London: Routledge & Kegan Paul.

Piaget, J. (1963). *The Origin's of Intelligence in Children*. New York: Norton.

Piaget, J. (1973). *The Child's Conception of the World*. London: Paladin.

Piliavin, I.M., Rodin, J. & Piliavin, J.A. (1969). 'Good Samaritanism: An underground phenomenon?' *Journal of Personality and Social Psychology*, 13, 289–99.

Pinel, J.P.J. (1993) *Biopsychology* (2nd edition). Boston: Allyn & Bacon.

Pinker, S. (1997) *How The Mind Works*. New York: Norton.

Plato. *Republic*. Translated by Benjamin Jowett. New York: P. F. Collier & Son.

Plomin, R. & Rowe, D. C. (1978). *Genes, environment, and development of temperament in young twins*. In G. M. Burghardt & M. Bekoff (Eds.), *The development of behaviour* (279-296). New York: Garland.

Plomin, R. & DeFries, J. C. (1998, May). The genetics of cognitive abilities and disabilities. *Scientific American*, 278 (5), 62–9.

Plutchik, R. (1994). *The Psychology and Biology of Emotion*. Harper Collins.

Polanczyk, G, de Lima, M.S., Horta, B.L., Biederman, J. & Rohde, L.A. (2007). The worldwide prevalence of ADHD: a systematic review and metaregression analysis. *American Journal of Psychiatry* 164 (6): 942–48.

Popper, K. (1968) *Conjecture and Refutations: The Growth of Scientific Knowledge*. New York: Harper & Row.

Postman, L., Bruner, J.S. & McGinnies, E. (1948). Personal values as selective factors in perception. *Journal of Abnormal and Social Psychology*, 43, 142–54.

Power, M. J., Ash, P. M., Schoenberg, E., & Sorey, E. C. (1974). Delinquency and the family. *British Journal of Social Work*, 4, 17–38.

Pringle, M. L. K. & Bossio, Z. (1960). Early prolonged separation and emotional *maladjustment. Child. Psych Psychiatry.* 1:37–48.

Psychiatric Morbidity Among Prisoners (1997). ONS (Office of National Statistics) survey.

Race Relations (Amendment) Act 2000.

Reitman, J. S. (1974). Without surreptitious rehearsal, information in short-term memory decays. *Journal of Verbal Learning and Verbal Behaviour. 13*, 365–377.

Wheeler, M.E., Petersen, S.E. & Buckner, R.L. Memory's echo: vivid remembering reactivates sensory-specific cortex. *Proc. Natl. Acad. Sci.* Vol. 97, No. 20.

Richardson, J.T.E., Engle, R.W., Hasher, L., Logie, R.H., Stoltzfus, E.R. & Zacks, R.T. (1996). *Working Memory and Human Cognition* Oxford University Press US.

Robertson, J. & Robertson J. (1989). *Separation and the Very Young.* Free Association Books.

Robinson P.W. (1996) *Social groups and identities*. London: Routledge.

Roethlisberger, F.J. & Dickson, W.J. (1939) *Management and the Worker*, Cambridge, Mass.: Harvard University Press.

Rogers, C.R. & Dymond, R. (1954) *Psychotherapy and Personality Change*. University of Chicago Press.

Rogers, C.R. (1942). *Counselling and Psychotherapy: Newer Concepts in Practice.* Boston: Houghton Mifflin.

Rogers, C.R. (1951). *Client-centered Therapy – Its Current Practices, Implications and Theory.* Boston: Houghton Mifflin.

Rogers, C.R. (1961). *On Becoming A Person*. Boston: Houghton Mifflin.

Rokeach, M. (1956). Political and religious dogmatism: An alternative to the authoritarian personality. *Psychological Monographs*, 70, Whole no. 425.

Rokeach, M. (1960). *The open and closed mind*, New York: Basic Books.

Rokeach, M. (1968). *Beliefs, attitudes, and values*. San Francisco: Jossey-Bass.

Rokeach, M., Smith, P. Evans, R. (1960), *Two kinds of prejudice or one?* In M. Rokeach (Ed.) *The open and closed mind*. New York: Basic Books, 132–168

Rosenhan, D.L. (1973) 'On being sane in insane places.' *Science*, 179, 250–8.

Rosenhan, D.L. and Seligman, M.E.P. (1984). *Abnormal Psychology*. New York: W.W. Norton.

Rosenthal R. & Rosnow, R.L. (1975) *The Volunteer Subject*. New York: John Wiley.

Rosenthal, R. & Fode, K.L. (1963) 'The effects of experimenter bias on the performance of the albino rat.' *Behavioural Science*, 8, 183–89.

Rosenthal, R. (1966) *Experimenter Effects in Behavioural Research*. New York: Appleton-Century-Crofts.

Rotter, J. (1966). Generalized expectancies for internal versus external control of reinforcements, *Psychological Monographs*, *80*, Whole No. 609.

Rubin, E. (1915) Synsoplevede Figurer. Kobenhaun: Gyldendalske.

Rubin, Z. & McNeil, E.B. (1983) *The Psychology of Being Human* (3rd edition). London: Harper & Row.

Rutter, M, (1972), '*Maternal deprivation realised*' in Rutter M. and Madge N, (1976), Cycles of disadvantage: a review of research. Heinmann Educational Books.

Rutter, M. (1981). *Maternal Deprivation Reassessed* (2nd Ed.) (Harmondsworth: Penguin).

Rutter, M. (1986). *The developmental psychopathology of depression: Issues and perspectives*. In M. Rutter, CE Izard, & PB Read (Eds.), Depression in young people: Developmental and *clinical* perspectives 71–134.

Ryckman, R.M. (2000) *Theories of Personality* (7th edition). Pacific Grove, CA: Brooks/Cole Publishing Co.

Safford, S., Alloy L., Abramson L., Crossfield A. (2007) Negative cognitive style as a predictor of negative life events in depression-prone individuals: A test of the stress generation hypothesis *Journal of Affective Disorders*, Volume 99, Issue 1, Pages 147–154.

Santrock, J. W. (2008). A Topical Approach to Life-Span Development. *Moral Development, Values, and Religion: Antisocial Behaviour*. Boston, Massachusetts: McGraw-Hill.

Saarinen, T.F. (1973). *Student views of the world*. In Downs, R.M. & Stea, D. (Eds.) Image and Environment: Cognitive Mapping and Spatial Behavior. Chicago: Aldine.

Scarr, S. (1998). American childcare today. *American Psychologist*, 53, 95–108.

Schacter, S. & Singer, J.E. (1962) 'Cognitive, social, and physiological determinants of emotional states.' *Psychological Review*, 69, 379–99.

Schaffer R. (1977) *Mothering* (Glasgow: Fontana/Open Books)

Schaffer, H.R. (1989). *Early social development*. In A.Slater & G.Bremner (eds), Infant Development. Hillsdale, NJ: Erlbaum.

Schaffer, H.R. (1995). *Early Socialisation*. Leicester: British Psychological Society

Schaffer, H.R. and Emerson, P.E., The Development of Social Attachments in Infancy, *Monographs of Social Research in Child Development*, 29, Serial No. 94

Schank, R.C. and Abelson, R.P. (1977). *Scripts, Plans, Goals and Understanding: an Inquiry into Human Knowledge Structures*. L. Erlbaum, Hillsdale, NJ.

Scheff, T. J. (1966). Being mentally ill: A sociological theory. Chicago: Aldine Publishing Co.

Scheier, M., Matthews, K., & Owens, J. (2003). *Dispositional optimism and recovery from coronary artery bypass surgery: The beneficial effects on physical and psychological well-being*. In P. Salovey & A. J. Rothman (Eds.), Social psychology of health. (pp. 342–361). New York: Psychology Press.

Scottish Educational Journal February 2006. Vol. 90. No. 01

Scottish Qualifications Agency (1997) *Arrangements for Psychology* (1st edition). Glasgow, Scotland.

Scottish Qualifications Agency (2000) *Arrangements for Psychology* (4th edition). Glasgow, Scotland.

Scottish Qualifications Authority (2001) Arrangements for Psychology (5th edition). Glasgow, Scotland.

Scottish Qualifications Authority (2004) *Arrangements for Psychology* (1st edition). Glasgow, Scotland.

Scottish Qualifications Authority (2008) *Arrangements for Psychology* (Draft). Glasgow, Scotland.

Scoville, W.B. and Milner, B. *(1957). Loss of recent memory after bilateral hippocampal lesions*. Journal of Neurology, Neurosurgery and Psychiatry *20: 11–21.*

Sebrechts, M.M., Marsh, R.L., & Seamon, J.G. (1989). Secondary memory and very rapid forgetting. *Memory & Cognition, 17*, 693–700.

Secord, P.F, Backman, C.W (1974), *Social Psychology*, 2nd ed, McGraw-Hill, New York.

Segall, M.H., Dasen, P.R., Berry, J.W. & Poortinga, Y.H. (1999) *Human Behaviour in Global Perspective* (2nd edition). Boston: Allyn & Bacon.

Seligman, M.E.P. & Hager, J. (Eds) (1972) *Biological Boundaries of Learning.* New York: Appleton-Century-Crofts.

Seligman, M.E.P. (1994). *What you can change and what you can't.* New York: Knopf.

Selltiz, C. et al. (1976) *Research Methods in Social Relations*. (3rd edition). New York: Holt, Rinehart & Winston.

Selye, H. (1950). Stress and the general adaptation syndrome. British Medical Journal *4667: 1383–92.*

Selye, H. (1956). *The Stress of Life*. New York: McGraw-Hill.

Sex Discrimination (Amendment) Act 1986

Sex Discrimination (Amendment) Act 2003

Sex Discrimination Act 1975

Shallice, T. (1982). Specific impairments of planning. *Royal Society of London Philosophical Transactions Series B, 298*:199–209.

Shapiro, D.A., Rees A. & Barkham M, *et al.* (1995) Effects of treatment duration and severity of depression on the maintenance of gains after cognitive-behavioural and psychodynamic-interpersonal psychotherapy. *J Consult Clin Psychol.*; 63: 378–387.

Shear, K., Jin, R., Ruscio, A. M., Walters, E. E., and Kessler, R. C. (2006). Prevalence and Correlates of Estimated DSM-IV Child and Adult Separation Anxiety Disorder in the National Comorbidity Survey Replication *American Journal of Psychiatry* 163:1074–1083.

Sherif, M. & Sherif, C. W. (1969). *Social Psychology.* New York: Harper & Row.

Sherif, M. (1935). A study of some social factors in perception. *Archives of Psychology, 27* (187).

Sherif, M. (1966). *In common predicament: Social psychology of intergroup conflict and cooperation,* Boston: Houghton-Mifflin.

Sherif, M., Harvey, O. J., White, B. J., Hood, W. R., & Sherif, C. W. (1961). *Intergroup conflict and co-operation: The Robbers Cave experiment.* Norman, OK: University of Oklahoma Book Exchange.

Sigman, A. (2007) Visual Voodoo: The biological impact of watching television, *Biologist,* 54:1, 14–19.

Silverman, J.S., Silverman, J.A. & Eardley, D.A. (1984). Do maladaptive attitudes cause depression? Archive of General Psychiatry. Jan; 41(1):28–30.

Silverman, S., (2004) *Totems and Teachers: Key Figures in the History of Anthropology.* New York: AltaMira Press.

Simon, H.A. (1974). How big is a chunk? *Science,* 183, 482–488.

Skeels, H.M. (1939): Mental Development of Children in Foster Homes, *Journal of Consulting Psychology.* 2 33–43.

Skeels HM., and Dye HB. (1939). A Study of the Effects of Differential Stimulation on Mentally Retarded Children, *Proceedings and Addresses of the American Association on Mental Deficiency* 44:114–136.

Skinner, B.F. (1948). Superstition in the pigeon. *Journal of Experimental Psychology,* 38, 168–72.

Skinner, B.F. (1950). Are theories of learning necessary? *Psychological Review,* 57(4), 193–216.

Skinner, B.F. (1953) *Science and Human Behaviour.* New York: Macmillan.

Skinner, B.F. (1954). The science of learning and the art of teaching. *Harvard Educational Review,* 24(2), 86–97.

Skinner, B.F. (1957). *Verbal Learning.* New York: Appleton-Century-Crofts.

Skinner, B.F. (1968). *The Technology of Teaching.* New York: Appleton-Century-Crofts.

Skinner, B.F. (1971). *Beyond Freedom and Dignity.* New York: Knopf.

Skodak, M. (1939). Children in Foster Homes: A Study of Mental Development, *Studies in Child Welfare* 16, 1–156.

Sluckin, W. (1964). *Imprinting and Early Learning* (Methuen, London).

Sluckin, W., and Salzen, E. A., (1961) *Quart. J. Exp. Psychol.,* 13, 65.

Smith, M., Zhan, G. Q., Huntington, N., & Wethington, E. (1992). *Is Clarity of Self-Concept Related to Coping Styles?* Poster presented at American Psychological Association Annual Convention, August, Washington, D. C.

Smith, P. B., & Bond, M. H. (1998). *Social psychology across cultures* (2nd ed.). Hemel Hempstead, UK: Prentice Hall.

Spitz, R,A. & Wolf, K.M. (1946). Anaclitic depression: An inquiry into the genesis of psychiatric conditions in early childhood, II. *Psychoanalytic Studies* 2:313–42.

Stephan, W.G. and Feagin, J.R. (Eds.) (1980). *School desegregation,* Plenum, New York.

Stephenson, W. (1953). The Study of Behaviour: Q-technique and its Methodology. University of Chicago Press, Chicago.

Stern, D. N., Beebe, B., Jaffe, J. and Bennett, S. L. (1977) *The infant's stimulus world during social interaction: a study of caregiver behaviours with particular reference to repetition and timing.* In: H. R. Schaffer (ed.) Studies in Mother-Infant Interaction. New York: Academic Press, 177–202.

Stone, R., Cafferata, G. L., & Sangl, J. (1987). Caregivers of the frail elderly: A national profile. *The Gerontologist,* 27(5), 616–626.

Stouffer, S.A. (1949). *Studies in Social Psychology in World War II: The American Soldier. Vol. 3, Experiments in Mass Communication.* Princeton: Princeton University Press.

Stouffer, S.A. (1949). *Studies in Social Psychology in World War II: The American Soldier. Vol. 4, Measurement and Prediction.* Princeton: Princeton University Press.

Stroebe, W., & Inkso, C. A. (1989). *Stereotype, prejudice, and discrimination.* In D. Bar-Tal, C. F. Graumann, A. W. Kruglanski, & W. Strobe (Eds.), Stereotyping and prejudice: changing conceptions New York: Springer-Verlag.

Tajfel, H. (1970). Experiments in intergroup discrimination. *Scientific American, 223,* 96–102.

Tajfel, H. (1974). Social identity and intergroup behaviour. *Social Science Information, 13,* 65–93.

Tajfel, H. (Ed.). (1978). Differentiation between social groups: Studies in the social psychology of intergroup relations. London: Academic Press.

Tajfel, H. and Turner, J. C. (1986). *The social identity theory of inter-group behaviour.* In S. Worchel and L. W. Austin (eds), Psychology of Intergroup Relations. Chigago: Nelson-Hall.

Tajfel, H., & Turner, J. C. (1979). *An integrative theory of intergroup conflict.* In W. G. Austin & S. Worchel (Eds.), The social psychology of intergroup relations Pacific Grove, CA: Brooks/Cole.

Tajfel, H., & Wilkes, A. L. (1963). Classification and quantitative judgment. *British Journal of Psychology,* 54, 101–114.

Tajfel, H., Billig, M., Bundy, R. P. & Flament, C. (1971). Social categorization and intergroup behaviour. *European Journal of Social Psychology, 2,* 149–178.

Takahashi, K. (1986). Examining the strange situation procedure with Japanese mothers and 12-month-old infants. *Developmental Psychology, 22,* 265–270.

Tebartz, E. *et al.,* (2000). *The amygdala.* New York, Oxford.

Temoshok, L. (1987). Personality, coping style, emotion and cancer: towards an integrative model. *Cancer Surveys,* 6, 545–567.

The Lunacy Act 1845 (8 & 9 Vict., c. 100).

The Race Relations Act 1976.

The Scottish Executive Central Research Unit 2002. Scottish Crime Survey 2000.

Thomas, E. L, & Robinson, H. A. (1982). *Improving reading in every class.* Boston: Allyn and Bacon.

Thorndike, E.L. (1898) 'Animal intelligence: An experimental study of the associative processes in animals.' *Psychological Review, Monograph Supplements,* No. 8). New York: Macmillan.

Thorndike, E.L. (1911) *Animal Intelligence.* New York: Macmillan (Reprinted Bristol: Thoemmes, 1999).

Tolman E.C. & Honzik C.H. (1930) *Introduction and removal of reward and maze-learning in rats.* University of California Publications in Psychology, 4, 257–75.

Triandis HC, Davis EE, Takezawa SI, (1965) Some determinants of social distance among American, German, and Japanese students. *Journal of Personality and Social Psychology.* 2(4):540–51

Triandis, H. C., & Triandis, L. M. (1960). Race, social class, religion, *and* nationality as determinants of social distance. *Journal of Abnormal and Social Psychology* 61: 110–118.

Triplett, N. (1898). The Dynamogenic Factors in Pacemaking and Competittion. American Journal of Psychology, 9, 507–533.

Tulving, E. and Z. Pearlstone. (1966). Availability versus accessibility of information in memory for words. *Journal of Verbal Learning and Verbal Behaviour.* 5: 381–391.

Tulving, E. In E. Tulving and W. Donaldson (Eds.), *Organization of Memory.* New York: Academic Press. pp. 381–403. 1972.

Tulving, E., & Psotka, J. (1971). *Journal of Experimental Psychology.* 87, 1–8.

Tulving, E., & Thomson, D.M. (1971). *Journal of Experimental Psychology*, 87, 116–124.

Turner, J. C. (1982). *Towards a cognitive redefinition of the social group.* In H. Tajfel (Ed). Social Identity and Intergroup Relations. Cambridge: Cambridge University Press.

Turner, J.C. (1981), *The experimental social psychology of intergroup* behaviour, in Turner, J.C., Giles, H. (Eds), Intergroup Behaviour, Blackwell, Oxford.

Underwood, B.J. (1957). Interference and forgetting. *Psychological Review* 64:49–60.

Van Ijzendoorn, M.H., & Kroonenberg, P.M. (1988). Cross-cultural patterns of attachment: A meta-analysis of the Strange Situation. *Child Development*, *59*, 147–156.

Vaughn, B., Waters, E., Egeland, B., & Sroufe, L.A. (1979). Individual differences in infant-mother attachment at 12 *and* 18 months: Stability and change in families under stress. *Child Development*, 50 (4); 971–975.

Wade, C. and Tavris, C. (2005) *Psychology* (8th Edition) Prentice Hall

Watson, J.B. & Rayner, R. (1920) 'Conditioned emotional reactions.' *Journal of Experimental Psychology*, 3(1), 1–14.

Watson, J.B. (1913) 'Psychology as the behaviourist views it.' *Psychological Review*, 20, 158–77.

Watson, J.B. (1913) 'Psychology as the behaviourist views it.' *Psychological Review*, 20, 158–77.

Watson, J.B. (1919) *Psychology from the Standpoint of a Behaviourist* (1st edition). Philadelphia, PA: Lippincott.

Waugh, N. C. and Norman, D. A. (1965). Primary Memory. *Psychological Review* 72 (2), 89–104.

Weatherly, D. (1961) Anti-Semitism and the expression of fantasy aggression, *Journal of Abnormal and Social Psychology*, 62, 454–457.

Weins, A.N. & Menustik, C.E. (1983) 'Treatment outcome and patient characteristics in an aversion therapy program for alcoholism.' *American Psychologist*, 38, 1089–96.

Weissman, A. N., & Beck, A. T. (1978, November). *Development and validation of the Dysfunctional Attitudes Scale.* Paper presented at the annual meeting of the American Educational Research Association, Toronto, Ontario, Canada.

Wheeler, M.E., Petersen, S.E., Buckner, R.L., (2000). Memory's echo: vivid recollection activates modality specific cortex. *Proceedings of the National Academy of Sciences USA*, 97, 11125–1129.

Whyte, W.F. (1943) *Street Corner Society. The Social Structure of an Italian Slum.* Chicago: University of Chicago.

Wickens, D.D., Born, D.G., Allen, C.K. (1963). Proactive inhibition and item similarity in short-term memory. *Journal of Verbal Learning & Verbal Behaviour* 2:440–445.

Wolpe, J. 'Psychotherapy by reciprocal inhabitation.' In C.H. Patterson (Ed.), Theories of Counselling and Psychotherapy. New York: Harper & Row, 1973.

World Health Organization International Statistical Classification of Diseases and Related Health Problems, 10th Revision (ICD-10), Geneva.

Wren, K., (1999) *Social Influences* Routledge.

Wright, D.B. (1993). Recall of the Hillsborough Disaster over Time: systematic biases of flashbulb' memories. *Journal of Applied Cognitive Psychology* 7:22, 129–138.

Wundt, W. (1897) *Outlines of Psychology.* Wilhelm Engelmann.

Zajonc, R.B. (1968), Attitudinal effects of mere exposure, *Journal of Personality and Social Psychology Monographs*, Vol. 9 No.2, 1–27.

Zimbardo, P. G., & Leippe, M. (1991). *The psychology of attitude change and social influence* (3rd ed.). New York: McGraw-Hill.

Zuzne, L. (Ed.) (1957). *Names in the history of psychology.* New York: John Wiley & Sons.

Index

Page numbers in italics show illustrations, figures and tables. Page numbers in bold show glossary entries.